Other Planets

The Music of Karlheinz Stockhausen

Robin Maconie

The Scarecrow Press, Inc.
Lanham, Maryland • Toronto • Oxford
2005

SCARECROW PRESS, INC.

Published in the United States of America
by Scarecrow Press, Inc.
A wholly owned subsidary of
The Rowman & Littlefield Publishing Group, Inc.
4501 Forbes Boulevard, Suite 200, Lanham, Maryland 20706
www.scarecrowpress.com

PO Box 317
Oxford
OX2 9RU, UK

British Library Cataloguing in Publication Information Available

Library of Congress Cataloging-in-Publication Data

Maconie, Robin.
    Other planets : the music of Karlheinz Stockhausen / Robin J. Maconie.
       p. cm.
    Includes bibliographical references (p.) and index.
    ISBN 0-8108-5356-6 (pbk. : alk paper)
     1. Stockhausen, Karlheinz, 1928—Criticism and interpretation. I. Title

ML410.S858M29 2005
780'.92—dc22

2004062109

♾™ The paper used in this publication meets the minimum requirements of
American National Standard for Information Sciences—Permanence of
Paper for Printed Library Materials, ANSI/NISO Z39.48-1992.
Manufactured in the United States of America.

CONTENTS

In Place of a Foreword   v

Preface   ix

Acknowledgments   xi

Introduction: On Telling the Truth   1

1   Formation   13

2   Early Works   31

3   Polarities   49

4   Rhythmic Cells   69

5   Music on Tape   93

6   Watching Time   109

7   Meyer-Eppler   125

8   Temperaments   139

9   Aleatory   157

10   Revolution   173

11   Contacts   193

12   Theater   211

13   Uncertainty   227

14   Process   249

15   Anthems   271

16   Figures   289

17   White Space   307

CONTENTS

18	Findings	327
19	Rites	347
20	Stagecraft	365
21	Allegories	387
22	Mysterium	403
23	Donnerstag	421
24	Samstag	439
25	Montag	459
26	Dienstag	477
27	Freitag	491
28	Mittwoch	507
29	Sonntag	527
	Bibliography	545
	Index	557
	About the Author	579

ABBREVIATIONS

SoM	*Stockhausen on Music*
Texte	*Texte zur Musik, Bände 1–10* (1963–1998)

In Place of a Foreword

R. M.: Would you care to enlarge on the tendency of commentators to look for external reasons for what you do?

Kh. S.: It is apparent to me that a number of different authors have attempted to explain ideas, choices of subject, and forms of my music as the outcome of events in my life. I am totally opposed to the widespread belief, which one might call the Pavlov attitude to human behavior, affecting the whole of Western education and philosophy, whereby everything, even the arts, is interpreted as a result of something that has happened before. It is totally contrary to my own concept of history and of the evolution, not only of mankind, but of all things. From my own work I know that everything is fundamentally the result of inspiration, of inner visions, of the desire to *make* something of these visions, and of subsequently living them out, in daily life as well as in my work.

If there are events in my earlier life, or factors in the environment, which you can later on relate to aspects or elements of my work, then I think it is rather that the same spirit is manifested in both. Or even, since the relationship is perceived through me, through my work, that it is not the environment that informed me, but that I have given form to the environment.

My parents did not choose to make me what I am, nor did the country in which I was born. Rather, they are chosen,—identified,—in me: in that "me" which is known in my works. And the same is true for what I am able to do as a composer as for who I happen to be at a particular time. My skills as a composer are the fruit of many lives' training in musicianship. How else can it be that we are so different?—that my little son Simon for example can compose much better than other children? Certainly not "because of his parents": he might have been born with many talents, but that doesn't account for his unquestionable technique, which allows him to write music without thinking twice about it. There is a very profound antecedence in each one of us, which has led to this present life.

R. M.: You are saying that the approach that I and perhaps others represent is too deterministic?

Kh. S.: Yes: it starts on the surface and remains on the surface; it does not really reach the more profound sources of art and music, which are not based on psychology, and can never be the object of psychological analysis, because they have nothing to do with the psyche. You see, the psyche of a human being and the soul of a human being are two entirely different things: the psyche will die with the body, is limited to a single life, though it may be tuned in like a crystal to wavebands of a higher intelligence that beam constantly into our human atmosphere. But the real reason for important events in the life and work of an artist is to be found in realms far beyond the psyche, and of a different quality: from the awakening of a higher kind of mentality, and from an existence that transcends the individual psyche. The spiritual in man is something very concrete, and not identified with the psyche. It follows that psychology can only help us a little: only the surface can be explained, you see.

R. M.: I won't justify what I agree is an inadequate approach. However, as an intermediary between yourself and your music, and a public who thinks in terms of making connections, I have to ask myself, if such and such an aspect of your music is strange to me, is it really utterly strange or could I not recognize it in some other context? Which is not to claim that there is a causal connection between the two, but to show that what may seem strange is capable of being understood.

Kh. S.: Yes, but what I am saying is that in my experience it is by emphasizing the strangeness, and not trying to do away with it or diminish it, that you are more likely to reach the truth. For the moment you try to explain things that appear to be strange, and you think you have explained them, then you have completely missed their message and their importance. I think it is more important than anything else to draw attention to the strange and inexplicable, for only that is truly original.

R. M.: It is also beyond words.

Kh. S.: Certainly: as the Chinese say, like understanding the hole in the middle of the wheel, which you reach by discarding everything which is explainable and deducible. I mean, I could have made any number of analyses of Bartók: the point was afterward, *because* of the analyses, to do something really different, so that I myself should have as little in common with what I knew. I think every experience I have gone through has been a means of elimination, a systematic shedding of influences in order to arrive at the original kernel of my being,—however little it may be,—which has come down through the centuries along with my identity, and which I now want to formulate in a very personal way. You would help my music much more, I think, if you would give equal attention to that, as to those surface features which can be explained in terms of prior influences and experiences.

From an interview with the composer recorded in 1981.

PREFACE

The present commentary continues a conversation that began in 1964–1965, in the composer's composition class in Cologne, and continued with the publication in 1976, and in revised and enlarged form in 1990, of my *Works of Karlheinz Stockhausen*. The issue in 1976 was whether contemporary music could be discussed intelligently, and more generally, whether it was music at all. At that time it seemed to me inevitable that future generations would eventually be able to talk much more easily, and in a common language, about composers as different in their outlooks as Stockhausen, Boulez, and Cage. The problem was to discover appropriate terms of reference and a new approach. If that could be shown to work for the music of the most difficult and controversial composer now living, it might also change our perception of the history and development of Western music in general. To a certain extent that has since happened. The digital revolution has made the conceptual bases of post-1950 avant-garde music much more transparent and intelligible, as well as greatly improving conditions for information sharing.

In the meantime, however, the philosophical debate has shifted ground. The composer continues to maintain, with emphasis, that no third party explanations of his work could possibly be meaningful, and that even he himself cannot explain why he does what he does. In my introduction I have tried to represent his position, which is argued with great force and sophistication, with the respect and sympathy it deserves. My own feelings are more complicated. As the aesthetic and technical consistencies of Stockhausen's musical evolution become clearer, a latent philosophical agenda has also begun to emerge. This subtext of meaning cannot be described as inadvertent. Among other issues, it addresses the status of the artist in modern society, the historic aspirations of German nationalism, and more specifically a defense of the role of post-Enlightenment European culture in the wider world. That such an agenda may be a necessary ingredient of genius is open to consideration, and certainly deserving of further inquiry. That it entails maintaining attitudes and beliefs that are not always easy to deal with in today's world, is also true.

For an English-language readership, however, by far the greatest obstacle to understanding the composer and his music in context has been the lack of essential documentation in reliable English translation. Much of the evidence on which the present text and its conclusions are based has come from sources such as the ten volumes of Stockhausen's collected *Texte*, not to mention essential writings of such key players as Herbert Eimert, Pierre Boulez, Pierre Schaeffer, Olivier Messiaen, and Werner Meyer-Eppler, materials that even after forty years either remain unobtainable in English, or worse, have been rendered in an English incomprehensible to most readers. Given the absence of relevant material to discuss, a lack of vigorous debate is hardly surprising. I have done my bit, I trust, to draw the reader's attention to a fascinatingly rich and under-appreciated resource.

Serialism, its companion issues of directed and negotiable form, and the competing aesthetic claims surrounding live, electronic, and concrete music, can now be seen as elements of a grander aesthetic and intellectual enterprise, beginning in the late eighteenth century, concerning the nature and evolution of language, and its implications for post-revolutionary democracy. Music is implicated in this enterprise because the art of music has to do with how inflected sound is able to express refinements of objective meaning in everyday speech, as well as revealing inner subjective emotions. For both language and music the critical task began with the decoding of the Rosetta Stone nearly two hundred years ago. It gained momentum throughout the nineteenth and twentieth centuries, aided by the invention of ever more sophisticated machines for recording and reproducing the dynamics of human behavior. The renaissance we celebrate in Stockhausen's electronic and instrumental music is a culmination of that process, building on the reduction of musical expression to pure essentials by Webern and others, and advancing the corresponding task of formal renewal that such an achievement entails.

ACKNOWLEDGMENTS

I am, as always, deeply obliged to Karlheinz Stockhausen for his continued support and encouragement, and to Kathinka Pasveer for her always punctilious and prompt responses on behalf of the Stockhausen-Verlag. Preparation of this volume was aided by a generous grant from the Deutscher Akademischer Austauschdienst, and I express my sincere thanks to His Excellency Ambassador Erich Riedler of the German Embassy in Wellington, New Zealand, and to Wolfgang Gairing of the DAAD in Bonn, for their helpful intervention. My thanks are also due to James Stonebraker, web master of the Stockhausen website www.stockhausen.org for his continuing support.

I am grateful to Universal Edition A. G., Vienna, for kind permission to reproduce excerpts from Stockhausen's *Choral* and *Prozession*, and from the *Trio* Op. 20 by Anton Webern. The excerpt from Hermann Schroeder's *Der römische Brunnen* is reproduced courtesy of the publisher Schott & Co. Limited, London, and of the three divisions of Olivier Messiaen's *Mode de valeurs et d'intensités* by courtesy of the publisher Editions Durand.

Catalogue numbers of Stockhausen's compositions and compact discs incorporated in the text may be quoted to order music or recordings from the publishers *Universal Edition A. G., Bösendorferstrasse 12, A-1010 Vienna, Austria* www.universaledition.com, the *Stockhausen-Verlag, 51515 Kürten, Germany* (fax: 02268-1813), or online via www.stockhausen.org, from whom a complete list of Stockhausen's works and compact discs is available free of charge.

Unless otherwise indicated, citations from French and German publications have been translated into English by the author.

The cover photograph by Alex Agor is reproduced by kind permission of Robert Slotover of Allied Artists.

INTRODUCTION

On Telling the Truth

Was hilft die Wahrheit?
Es ist nicht bequem.
Nur wer im Wohlklang lebt
Lebt angenehm.

(after Brecht)

In 1932 Schoenberg's son-in-law, the violinist Rudolf Kolisch, figured out the note-row to the composer's Third String Quartet, and wrote to tell him. Schoenberg responded:

> You have rightly worked out the series in my string quartet (apart from one detail: the 2nd consequent goes: 6th note, C sharp, 7th, G sharp). You must have gone to a great deal of trouble, and I don't think I'd have had the patience to do it. But do you think one's any better off for knowing it? . . . This isn't where the aesthetic qualities reveal themselves, or, if they do, only incidentally. I can't utter too many warnings against over-rating these analyses, since after all they only lead to what I have always been dead against: seeing how it is *done*; whereas I have always helped people to see: what it *is*! I have repeatedly tried to make Wiesengrund [Adorno] understand this, and also Berg and Webern. But they won't believe me. I can't say it often enough: my works are twelve-note *compositions*, not *twelve-note* compositions. In this respect people go on confusing me with Hauer, to whom composition is only of secondary importance.[1]

When I first spoke to Stockhausen in London, in 1972, about embarking on the original *Works of Karlheinz Stockhausen*, he promised his cooperation and said to me, "You must tell the truth." I am a composer, not a musicologist. I think Schoenberg is right, even though it is convenient for me to say so, since I have no aptitude for row-counting and am lost in admiration for the latter-day Talmudists who do (even if they do grumble a lot). Of psychology all that I know is that it has manifestly failed to discover any common ground between music and people who like music; and of philosophy, a dedication to the proposition that music is essentially meaningless. So: no Neo! And no "-ologies" either. So, what then? The music continues to exist, making statements, affecting listeners, in need of explanation—if only for the sake of giving the willing executant a sense of direction.

In 1978, with the composer's fiftieth birthday approaching, I went to the BBC with an idea for a television documentary based on Stockhausen's lectures filmed by Robert Slotover during the composer's successful tour of Great Britain in 1971. It was to be a concise account of Stockhausen and his music, given *entirely in his own words*: nobody else saying anything, no interpretation, no possibility of bias or recrimination. After two years' preparation, the late birthday offering, directed by Barrie Gavin and titled "Tuning In," was finally transmitted in 1981 to friendly notices even from the London tabloid press.

All of the 1971 lectures are exciting events, and the composer is in excellent form. Toward the end of the documentary, in a clip from the lecture "Questions and Answers on 'Four Criteria of Electronic Music,'" it seems as though an idea suddenly comes to him to say: "Liking is remembering." This is the actual transcript of what he said:

> You are always referring to *my* music, *my* music. What does it mean, *my* music? It's just something that has come into my mind and I am working all the time and that's it. So: I am a *myth*, I am a name, and if I go away then they just attach on something that vibrates within yourself, where you are confronted with this so-called music. It has a name so in order to identify it. That's all. Like "Beethoven:"—who was he? He was a very miserable person, I must say, as a human being. And he is a myth for something that we are, that is within ourselves. We are echoing: Beethoven is part of us or he doesn't exist. And in that sense I think it [music] is only a means, it's like a spiritual food, and it will be used by certain people who discover a certain identity of what they are and what there is vibrating. They choose more of it, they like it—*liking means*, as I always say, *remembering*: when I like something, then I discover something that I have been before, that is profoundly already within me. It resonates, like a piano that you hit.[2]

It is in every sense an "inspired" remark, the sort of remark that reminds a listener that Stockhausen is not only an imaginative thinker, but that he also has a philosophy (the thought actually derives from Plato).[3]

Stockhausen's thought is predicated on language: the notion that words are not just labels that we attach to ideas for the purpose of talking, but that words actually embody ideas, so that when we use words we are actually committing to the ideas they embody in preference to any ideas we might think we have. (This transfer of meaning is implicit in the statement itself, in that by liking one is necessarily identifying with a meaning more fundamental than one might have thought.) To an English reader, his remark is a play on the meaning of the terms *like, liking,* and *likeness,* which is intriguing coming from Stockhausen because while there may be something in the notion of seeing oneself in the things one likes, it puts the listener rather too readily in mind of Freud, perhaps, for a view coming from an avowed antipsychologist. The word *likelihood* also suggests antici-pation, implying a Janus-like opposition of forward- and backward-looking.

> The artist has long been regarded as an individual who reflected the spirit of his time. I think there have always been different kinds of artists: those who were mainly mirrors of their time, and then a very few who had a visionary power, whom the Greeks called augurs: those who were able to announce the next stage in the development of mankind, really listen into the future, and prepare the people for what was to come.[4]

In German we encounter the same parallelisms: the word *ähnlich* means "like" in the sense of a resemblance to something; *es gefällt mir*: "I take pleasure in it;" whereas *erinnern* and *bedenken* are words for remembering. *Bedenken* not only means "remembering," but also "doubting" or "hesita-ting;" the word *er-innern* is a construct signifying "to internalize," while the verb *fallen* in the phrase *es gefällt mir* is used of sensory impressions: "it struck me" or "it fell to me," in addition to "I like it"—the German passive voice is interesting here, implying an absence of conscious intention. As with *likelihood* in English, the word *Ahnung* in German implies a presenti-ment of the future, as when he says that certain visionary artists are *augurs*; but *ahnlich machen* means "to assimilate" while *Ahnenprobe* signi-fies "proof of noble ancestry," something once sought after as a requirement for entrance to the élite schools. All of this makes sense in terms of who Stockhausen is and what he finds meaningful: the conjunction of opposites; the dualism of subject–object, anticipating–remembering, same–different; finally, that same urge to possess that Stravinsky identified in himself as "probably a rare form of kleptomania."[5]

Philosophical wordplay has a long history, especially in Germany where they are adept at finding meanings even where they don't exist. In England, Shakespeare's puns are witty and done for comic effect: nobody for an instant believes they are literally true. In Europe, however, the accidental conjunction of meanings in a pun may be interpreted with great seriousness as a spiritual revelation, even when in reality it is merely a distortion of meaning for the sake of reinforcing a particular point of view. The very idea that a basic misinterpretation of words can be justified by appealing to some notion of a deeper truth might appear ridiculous, if it were not so widespread. A case in point is the 1962 indictment, by physicist John Backus in the new American journal *Perspectives of New Music,* of the music periodical *die Reihe,* edited by Stockhausen and Herbert Eimert, in which Backus draws attention to a systemic misuse by contributors of term-inology having precise mathematical and scientific meaning. This unusually vituperative piece was reprinted in the English periodical *Composer,* which later published a rejoinder by Hugh Davies, at the time an assistant to Stockhausen in Cologne. An Oxford graduate in philosophy, Davies argued in effect that "it had yet to be shown that an incorrect use of language could not all the same communicate correct information," a logic almost as baffling as Backus's in his original article. That the American author had misquoted *die Reihe* in the first place was not noticed by either side of the debate.

Wordplay is not just a recreation for philosophers: it is also deeply embedded in continental European culture, including educational theory. Stockhausen is the son of a schoolmaster and studied to become a teacher both under the Nazi regime and again after the end of the 1939–1945 war. Teaching plays as vital a role in the composer's mission as it did for Gropius, Klee, and Schoenberg at the Bauhaus, and Messiaen at the Conservatoire. The following passage from an influential early treatise on the education of the child is representative of a prevailing aesthetic (it is hardly a philosophy) that colored the most fundamental precepts of German teaching and learning. The author yokes together words that have no meaningful connection in order to establish an absolute moral imperative:

> The inner being is organized, differentiated, and strives to make itself known (*Kund* thun), to announce itself (*verkündigen*) externally. The human being strives by his own self-active power to represent his inner being outwardly, in permanent form and with solid material; and this tendency is expressed fully in the word *Kind* (child) *K-in-d*, which designates this stage of development.[6]

Elsewhere in the same manifesto the author (Friedrich Froebel, the pioneer of kindergarten education, and of whom more later) would have his readers believe that the word *Sinn* (sense) is a combination of *S-* (meaning "self") and *-Inn* (meaning "inwardness" or "inner being"). This is not very different from me claiming that the word *Identity* is the same as saying "you are what you eat" (in German, presumably, "man ist was man isst"), since it divides into the syllables *I-* and *-dentity*—of which the first undoubtedly corresponds to the first person singular, and the second is clearly a reference to teeth.

That wordplay of this sort acquired a mystique among middle-class intellectuals in the nineteenth century is certainly true, though why is not altogether clear, considering the damage that can be caused by the manipulation of language for effect. We can still take pleasure at false relations in comedy, and admire the same in poetry where a reader is conditioned to, as they say, "rich text," and poetic meaning is enhanced. Modern advertising is the legitimate domain of wordplay, where secondary implications are often of vital commercial significance, as in the famous case a few years ago of a new model compact car with the name "Nova" that had to be renamed because in Latin America it means "it doesn't go." In dealing with language at this level the literal meaning of words in print is not the only consideration; how they actually sound when spoken on the radio or on television introduces an additional dimension of meaning that has to be taken seriously into account.

Nineteenth-century society was drawn to wordplay as a fashionable recreation that indicated that the speaker was literate as well as aware, and perhaps envious, of the special relationship of word- to knowledge-acquisition exemplified, for example, in Linnaeus's classification of living things, in Darwin's account of the origin of species, and the achievements of Champollion and others involved in the decryption of the mysterious Rosetta Stone. For language itself to be subjected to exacting Darwinian scrutiny and reveal a connected history of derivations and mutations, as it came to do for the generations following Champollion, must have seemed totally baffling to some members of literate society. To an educated bourgeoisie believing in Bishop Usher's acount of the Creation as a spontaneous act of divine will in the year 4004 BC, Darwin's evolutionary hypothesis represented a challenge not only to received religion but also to the holistic visions of nature associated with Goethe and Wordsworth. This disturbing new dynamic of biological interconnection caught the public imagination through a range of parlor games and entertainments, from charades to crossword puzzles, based on word-formation and perceived or intuited relationships.

Hence a fashionable eagerness among educated people to plunder everyday language in a vain quest for hidden pearls of meaning. Decoding the ancient pictograms of Egypt found a popular echo in the *rebus*, a puzzle message concealed in a fanciful montage of unrelated images. Making the leap from a harmless recreation of deciphering messages concealed in pictograms, to discovering meaning in the dreams of the emotionally disturbed as a profession, is the story of psychoanalysis in a nutshell; but in making a corresponding leap, from puzzle-games to surrealism, the object of analysis changes from isolated individuals in distress to society as a whole, as is seen in the response of art and poetry, in the years leading to the First World War, to the industrialization of international conflict that threatened the whole of Western civilization with collapse.

Musical codes have always been a recognized element of rebuses and spelling games, though their implications are normally relatively benign: themes based on BACH or DSCH, the ABEGG Variations of Schumann, Berg's *Lyric Suite,* Boulez's *Messagesquisse.* We can do this too. On the surface, the name "Karlheinz Stockhausen" is just that; but if we examine its spelling more closely, a secret message is suddenly revealed:

k a r l h E I N z   s t o c k h A U S e n

To the cabbalist, this is a profound and awe-inspiring mystery. What does it mean? In German, "ein" and "aus" are what you do when you breathe: you breathe *in* and *out*. That these two words are found in the composer's name is undeniable: that they pertain to the act of taking and releasing breath, for German speakers, is self-evident. That the presence of these words in his name is as a consequence of parental choice may be true, but is unlikely; that they signify divine pre-ordination, merely fanciful. For the hidden words to confer meaning on the composer's life and work is for the composer

himself to decide and of no concern to anybody else. All the same, they are
something to think about, a charming poetic discovery, to be recalled when
we listen to the ending of *Hymnen*, or read the opening page of *"Atmen gibt
das Leben . . ."*

The composer's name also translates, Schumann fashion, into a five-
term, quasi-serial grouping:

—which one is genuinely tempted to interpret as a Beethovenian *"Muss es
sein? Es muss sein!"*—a motto to which the composer is certainly entitled.
But is it "true?" The motif of a five-note permutatable set is very apt; the
connection with Tchaikovsky's *Slavonic March* is perhaps less flattering, or
some might think.

Just how much thought Stockhausen gives to words and their derivations can be gauged from a typically scrupulous footnote to the essay
"Erfindung und Entdeckung" (Invention and Discovery):

> In the first version of this text I employed the word *Formentwicklung*
> (form-development) in relation to "punctual form," "group-form" etc. This
> was not a reference at all to specific forms, but to processes that lead to
> an indefinite variety of similar forms, hence to the origin of form on the
> basis of a "punctual," "group-moderated," etc. preconception. Recently I
> read *La Genèse des Formes Vivantes* by Raymond Ruyer, in which I
> found the word *formation* to mean "origin of form," "achieving form,"
> "the process of forming" —as distinct from forms that are the result of
> the action of forming. The form-principles named in my text belong in
> the domain of *morphogenèse* rather than *morphologie*. The concept of
> formation in the sense that I use it, is different from the word as it is
> understood in German. Originally I wanted to write *Formung* or
> *Formentstehung* [coming-into-being-of-form] or *Formbildung* [growth-of-
> form]. However there were composite terms already in use, such as
> *Reihungs-Formbildung* [note-row formation], or *Moment-Formbildung*
> [moment-formation] that I found equally unsatisfactory. Finally, to
> encompass the cluster of terms *Formwerdung* [form-becoming], *Form-
> entstehung, Formung* (or *Formierung*) [formation], *Formbildung*, and
> *Formentwicklung* [development of form], I chose the word *Form-Genese*
> [form-genesis]. This should be understood as corresponding to what
> Ruyer means by *formation*, and to his description in the book of "the
> passage from an *absence* of structure to a *presence* of structure."[7]

So then, what does "the truth" mean? Since absolute truth is unknowable,
we are in the realm of *Wahrnehmung*, which in effect is "taking for
granted," or *Wirklichkeit*, which I prefer because it contains the notion of a
"working hypothesis." If asked to choose between truth and reality, I incline
to reality, meaning the music and how it sounds—and that means, faced

with the question *"Ist das wirklich wahr?"* that I would rather defend the reality of the question than the truth of any one answer. There is a further term in German, and that is *echt*, meaning "genuine" and a term of approbation. In 1960, anticipating public controversy arising from the 34th Festival of the International Society for Contemporary Music, about to take place in Cologne, the music periodical *Melos* circulated a request to a list of composers and writers on music, to ask where each stood in relation to the statement *Musikalische Avantgarde: echt oder gemacht?* which might be rendered as "The musical avant-garde: genuine or manufactured?" (or in today's parlance, "organic or synthetic?"). In reply the composer created a photo-montage depicting, in a mixture of Giotto and John Heartfield, a paradise of younger-generation composers presiding over a netherworld of elderly artists, conductors, and administrators, including Schoenberg, Berg, and Webern, a recumbent John Cage defining the frontier between the two realms. Framed prettily in lace, it looks just like a nineteenth-century Valentine's day card. Stockhausen's message in response to the question? *kein Wort.*

Soon after James Stonebraker opened his Stockhausen website he asked me to contribute, and I did and still do. In an effort to dispel public scepticism over remarks that had been widely misinterpreted in the press, and in a vain attempt (as it turned out) to stimulate discussion, I included a set of hypothetical FAQs, or frequently asked questions, the first being "Does Stockhausen really come from a planet of Sirius?" together with the answer "No, it's a German joke." Now I have to confess having made up the bit about the planet of Sirius. Sirius is a double star: it does not have planets as far as we know. It just seemed a tad more probable to have the composer located on solid ground in preference to the *Feuerofen* of an actual, even if minor, star. This time, the composer's response was swift. [8]

Dear Jim Stonebraker,

I just read the Maconie-text again. Please take it away from the "HOME PAGE". In a "home page" is no space for private opinion. It should be a source of objective information on the scores, discs, concerts, books. No gossip!

Yours Stockhausen

Something about the sentiment seemed vaguely familiar, but several years were to elapse before I discovered much the same form of words in an official decree promulgated some sixty years earlier.

"Decree concerning Art Criticism" issued November 11, 1934,
by the Ministry of Propaganda.

"From today, the art report will replace art criticism. . . . The art report will be less an evaluation than a description and appreciation. . . . The art report of the future presupposes reverence for artistic activity and creative achievement. It requires an informed sensibility, tact, purity of mind, and respect for the artist's intentions." This decree forbade art as a means of public discussion and communication; art was made instead into an aid to contemplation, empathy, and spiritual edification.[9]

In retrospect perhaps it was not surprising that the composer took umbrage, and that in consequence my contributions were banished into electronic limbo and I must bear the stigma of "nihilist" (unbeliever). Since Boulez labelled Cage a "nihilist" I ought to feel rather complimented by the appellation. (Well, yes, I suppose I do.) What grieves me is the misinterpretation of my original message. Surely *anybody* can see that I am not real, that my name is simply an anagram, and that what I actually said to the umpire was: "You can*not* be serious!"

$$\text{R\ \ JOHN} \qquad \text{M}^{\text{ac}}\text{O N I E}$$
$$\text{I\ \ JOHN} \qquad \text{M}^{\text{c}}\text{E N R O}^{\text{e}}$$

In his English lectures of 1971 Stockhausen refers to "the truth" only once, but powerfully and poetically; it would be unfair not to mention it. He is speaking of a moment in *Kontakte,*—I think it is Moment XIV, beginning at 31' 08", so toward the end,—where one seems to hear imaginary doors clanging shut, and has the impression of a silence descending. The world, the composer says, is visual in orientation; we believe in what is visible in preference to what we hear. The truth, he says, is in what we hear and not what we see. Art is revelatory. In the spirit of St. Paul, declaring "The substance of things hoped for, the evidence of things not seen, is faith," the artist declares the evidence of his music to be not an illusion, but true.

> Now I come to my point: when they hear the layers revealed, one behind the other, in this new music, most listeners cannot even perceive it because they say, well, the walls have not moved, so it is an illusion. I say to them, the fact that you say the walls have not moved is an illusion, because you have clearly heard that the sounds went away, very far, and that is the truth. Whether the walls have moved at all has nothing to do with this perception, but with believing in what we hear as absolutely as we formerly believed in what we see or saw. That's what we are struggling with, and that's what will change mankind as gradually more and more people perceive this music in its real terms.[10]

The fragment of conversation standing in for a foreword to this volume is from the tape-recorded question and answer sessions with the composer that came to form the second part of *Stockhausen on Music*. It was not printed then for the very good reason that the composer was referring to the first edition of my *Works of Karlheinz Stockhausen,* published in 1976, and his concerns over my obvious interest in discovering prior influences and alleged resemblances between his music and the music of others. His reaction placed me in a dilemma, because it seemed to me that the proper role of a student or researcher was to situate the object of study within a context that would make it more accessible to an observer. My own training in English literature, by articulate and eager disciples of F. R. Leavis, Raymond Williams, and William Empson, led me to believe in criticism as a dialogue or debate intended to honor the artist and his (or her) ideas by taking them seriously, and by examination to bring out those features of his (or her) work that deserved wider approbation. To encounter a habit of mind for whom the artist and the artwork are inviolate was quite a culture shock, particularly since I had made it my goal to prove that music of the twentieth century in general, and Stockhausen's music in particular, was both rational and coherent in meaning.

Books by their very nature are a form of colonization of the reader by the author; conversation books can also suggest a spiritual colonization, by

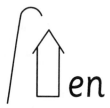

Stockhausen's signature in the form of a rebus: Stock–Haus–en. The choice of a walking-stick may allude to age, or to Chaplin. From a calligram by the composer on the text of "Engel-Prozessionen," 2004.

the interviewer, of the one being interviewed. In order the better to understand what Stockhausen might mean by "liking is remembering," and to fathom the composer's seemingly paradoxical perspective on history and the creative process, I made an attempt to tease out what he was saying, but in my own words. Twenty years on I am no longer sure how much of the following is the composer's voice, and how much my own imagination; but I read it today as if it were the voice of a third person explaining just how I got it wrong. What he seems to be saying is this:

—Ideas are not things which you have, exchange, and realize. They are not elements of a trade detached from the minds that trade in them. So the question of inferences, of borrowing ideas, which are then added to or incorporated in my art, like materials or decorations, or which serve to start me thinking, is not the way it is at all. I live in the world and I notice things. Some things I like, and I call what I like "*re*-cognition"—"re-knowing." And certain things are amazing to me. Now how do I *know* I like these things, or that they are "right?" Sometimes I am more amazed by certain things I see being done in the name of other people, than those who are doing it. And why is this? When you discover something it is always as though you were looking for it, sometimes knowingly, sometimes without knowing. But it hits you with such force that the discovery is an answer, and you know it is the answer, because *the question is in you*—it has been molded by your previous thoughts. You do not know what molding or thought process has gone on in anyone else for that discovery to have been

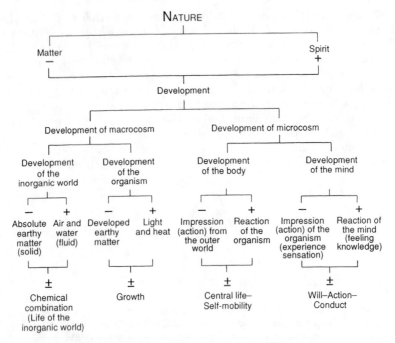

Friedrich Froebel: Law of the Connection of Contrasts
"*In his Hamburg lectures of 1849 he furnishes the following systematic presentation of all development, in which (−) designates fixed or constant, and (+) fluid or variable elements, and (±) the connection of the two.*"

---

made, or even if there has been any thought process behind it at all.

I am not interested in any case in exchanging reasons with anyone for arriving at a particular discovery. It is *my* discovery, and its quality and importance to me are that it fits *my* thought, and that my thought is the result of a lifetime of practice in thinking and hard work, which is more than most people do. And certainly nobody else can possibly know the importance to me of a discovery whose importance is only *in relation to* my thought, and not in itself.

If discoveries were objects then we would be reduced to a marketplace of ideas, and artists would become specialist manufacturers of only one thing and would demand a fee if somebody else wanted to do it, lay bricks, or write music for the bass flute. And those people who had the patent on such things would command high prices and become very successful. But this is not the case because we know that artists who work in this way are very boring people. And it is also not true, because we know from the Scriptures and for a fact that ideas and images do not coincide. You cannot make an image of the divine. So what I perceive, what I discover, what I recognize, is a divine gift:—of the divine that is *in me*, and it will live or die in what I make. And my music is not simply a means of patenting certain images, but it has a purpose of divine revelation. But I will not say what my music shall reveal, only that it was revealed to me and may reveal the divine to somebody else in ways I cannot imagine. So this notion of intellectual property arising from influences of certain images, which suggests I do not think for myself but only assemble bits of other people's thinking, is false when applied to the practice of thought, and certainly not true in my music.

And it follows that since what is revealed *to* me is part of the divine that is revealed *in* me, i.e. is not distinguishable from me, then I am changed by the recognition of part of me that always existed, but I didn't recognize it before. And it is inconceivable that I should not be changed in how I live.

So when you try to relate elements in my work to aspects of previous events, it is that the same *spirit* is perceived in the environment as in my work, and even that you are perceiving the environment in a way which is the result of your having been affected by my work. It becomes a case of projecting my work onto my environment, not the other way round. Extending this argument would mean that I am also responsible for my background, my cultural milieu, even my parents, insofar as what is known of them in my work is only known through what I have done. Because without me these relationships would not be meaningful, or even exist. What *am* I? If I *am* the result of many previous lives then I *am* those lives as well, since there is an unbroken genetic connection with the past, and since also the genes and the mind are altered by what I do and how I think. Even my own children are not what they are because of me: my son Simon is not a better composer because of his parents. He doesn't think about things that way. He simply writes music without question. And all of us are what we are "without question" and it is of no consequence to be told that you *are because* of something else. *You are* what you make, and it is *your* responsibility.

Notes

1. "To Rudolf Kolisch; Berlin, 27 July 1932." In Arnold Schoenberg, *Letters* ed. Erwin Stein, tr. Eithne Wilkins and Ernst Kaiser (London: Faber and Faber, 1964), 164–65.

2. BBC transcript from the lecture "Questions and Answers on 'Four Criteria of Electronic Music'" filmed by Allied Artists, 1971, incorporated in the documentary "Tuning In" directed by Barrie Gavin for the BBC-tv "Omnibus" series, 1981.

3. "Of Plato it may be said that the whole of his philosophical system is centered around this concept [of requiredness] . . . the notion of 'something which ought to be.' 'People feel moral obligations,' he would say, 'they recognize ideals, they speak about truth. Though they are not very clear about such "oughts," there must be some source even for imperfect convictions of this kind. . . . New insight about things as they "ought to be". . . may happen, although during their actual lives they have never had this particular knowledge before, and even though they are certainly not reading it directly from any facts of outer experience. All

this would be easily explained if the new insight were . . . a case of recall or remembrance—not of facts experienced in this life, to be sure, but of facts in a previous life and in a better, an imperishable world.'" Wolfgang Köhler, *The Place of Value in a World of Facts* (New York, Mentor, 1966), 40–41.

4.   "On the Musical Gift." In *Stockhausen on Music: Lectures and Interviews* compiled by Robin Maconie (London: Marion Boyars, 1989), 31–32.

5.   "I have very little gift for teaching, and no disposition for it. . . . When composers show me their music for criticism, all I can say is that I would have written it quite differently. Whatever interests me, whatever I love, I wish to make my own (I am probably describing a rare form of kleptomania)." Igor Stravinsky, in Igor Stravinsky and Robert Craft, *Memories and Commentaries* (London: Faber and Faber, 1960), 110.

6.   "A play on the word *Kind*, probably referring back to the words KUND and ver*KÜND*igen in the same paragraph." [Translator's note.] In Friedrich Froebel, *The Education of Man* tr. W. N. Hailmann (London: Appleton, 1906), 50. In German, *Die Menschenerziehung, die Erziehungsunterrichts und Lehrkunst. . .* (Keilhau: Froebel Institute, 1826).

7.   "Erfindung und Entdeckung: ein Beitrag zur Form-Genese" (Invention and Discovery: A Contribution to the Origin of Form). In *Texte 1*: 222–58.

8.   My FAQs and Stockhausen's fax responses are posted on www.jimstone braker.org/maconie.html

9.   Berthold Hinz, *Art in the Third Reich* rev. tr. Robert Kimber and Rita Kimber (Oxford: Basil Blackwell, 1979), 37.

10.   *SoM*: 107–8.

CHAPTER ONE

Formation

Karlheinz Stockhausen was born in Mödrath near Cologne on 22 August
1928, the year of Ravel's *Bolero*, Schoenberg's Orchestral Variations Op. 31,
Stravinsky's *Apollo* and *The Fairy's Kiss*, the Webern Op. 20 Trio, and Kurt
Weill's *Die Dreigroschenoper*. During the twenties, led by Max Ernst and
Hans Arp, Cologne was a focal point for Dada, reaching out to Berlin to the
northeast, Zürich to the southeast, and Paris to the West. Spiritually, the
composer is a child of the Great War: when he speaks of his "earlier lives on
this planet" it may be taken as a way of identifying with the spirit of Dada-
ism as manifested in the lives of artists like Ernst, also with André Breton,
leader of the Surrealists, whose experiences as a medical orderly in the
trenches of 1914–1918 were as life-transforming as Stockhausen's as a
young stretcher-bearer in the war of 1939–1945.

His father, a schoolteacher, was Simon Stockhausen; his mother's name
Gertrud, her family name Stupp. Karlheinz was their only child. The father
was descended (or so he believed) from noble forebears, the Stockhausens of
Asbach in the Westerwald; he was proud to be the first of his family in
many generations to gain an education and rise on the social ladder. The
Stupps, for their part, were an old and well-respected Neurath farming
family, and quite well off. A handsome woman, Gertrud was sensitive and
evidently musical; the family piano had been purchased for her to play, and
to protect her hands she was given household duties instead of having to
work in the fields. These were notable sacrifices for music at a time of great
national hardship. Simon Stockhausen had some natural musical ability
himself, the composer recalls: his duties as a teacher obliged him to play
violin, which he did passably well, and piano, on which he was able to pick
out a tune on the black keys. As a small child, the young Stockhausen had a
toy wooden mallet with which he liked to hit objects and listen to their

different sounds; long before he learned to play the piano, he was already tapping at it with his little wooden hammer like a doctor testing a patient for soundness of heart, wind, and limb. The household was hardworking and religious, of the Catholic faith, from which the boy acquired a lifelong sense of the sublime, matched by an equally developed sense of the theater of ritual.

Early life was unsettled. The pay of a newly-qualified teacher was meager and life was grim. The father was obliged to move from one temporary post to another, on average twice a year, so it was a peripatetic existence, moving from village to village. In 1932 Stockhausen's mother began to show signs of a severe depression, talking to the voice on the radio and being frustrated that the voice did not answer back, and imagining that down in the cellar of the house was hell and up in the attic, heaven: vivid memories that return like film clips in Act I of *Donnerstag aus LICHT*. His mother was first committed to a sanatorium when the boy was only four years old, but her belief in the radio as a medium of enlightenment and dialogue made a powerful impression on her son.

Radio was a new medium for most people, and in the Germany of the thirties it was fast developing as an instrument of social control.

> On 22 August 1930 Berlin Radio, Germany's seventh radio station, was officially opened by Nobel prizewinner Albert Einstein. "Ladies and Gentlemen, present and absent: . . . (laughter) . . . When I listen to the radio, I consider how mankind has come into possession of this wonderful apparatus. . . . Let us remember to give thanks to the army of anonymous technicians that has simplified the equipment for radio communication, and adapted it for mass production, so that it may be accessible to everyone. Those people should be ashamed who thoughtlessly employ the wonders of science and technology without bothering to consider how wonderful they really are, like cattle who graze in comfort without any conception of botany."
>
> Scarcely a year had passed before "Black Friday" in New York precipitated the world stock market collapse. An extraordinarily large number were fearful and isolated from world events. The "golden" twenties were gone: only radio, theater, and the movies were left to provide a semblance of reality.[1]

In a strange way the radio affected, and even came to define, the destinies of father, mother, and child. To the father, radio came to represent the voice of authority, and to the mother, a source of deep frustration; to the child, however, the radio was a perpetual window into a world of music that he could learn from and imitate. When visitors came to the house, the boy would be put on show. Stockhausen does not say what music he acquired from the radio. Before the Nazi clampdown in 1933, however, the new medium was already shaping up as a vehicle for "the people's music," and not just art music. Many popular songs of the Weimar era survive today, and it is not unthinkable for the young boy to have memorized songs of this kind issuing from the family VE 301.[2]

On the 30th January [1933], Herr Hitler became Chancellor, and the microphone was at his disposal. Herr Eugen Hadamovsky . . . was appointed its General-Director, a new plenipotentiary position responsible only to the Ministry of Propaganda. Herr Hadamovsky's aims may be given in his own words: . . . "German broadcasting should be made the chief instrument of political propaganda. I have always ridiculed the old idea that there is such a thing as objectivity and neutrality *per se*." And at the opening of the Berlin Wireless Exhibition on 18th August: "All that happens in and through broadcasting to-day happens in order . . . that one day the entire nation will be drenched through and through with our philosophy, that one day it will be a thing taken for granted and an intimate need felt by every German to confess National Socialism."

Instructions were given to the industry to produce "the people's set," a two-valve receiver now on sale at about 76 Marks; this set will be the greatest concrete weapon in the Unit's propaganda campaigns . . . under Dr. Goebbels; the explicit intention is to "put a set into every house." Urban and rural district advisory centres will set out to gain new listeners, through placards posted in every town and village, and illustrated pamphlets distributed from house to house.[3]

A great deal of German popular music of the thirties was social protest music, among which "negro" jazz, or its blackface equivalent (Al Jolson in *The Jazz Singer* and *The Singing Fool*) was the image of urban decadence. The sardonic tones of Kurt Gerron as Mack the Knife gave voice to *Die neue Sachlichkeit*—the bitter reality of a culture and an economy spinning out of control, laid bare in the art of Georg Grosz and the musical moralities of Brecht and Weill. This music survives and can be experienced in its original sound, so it is possible to imagine its impact on the young son of highly moral parents living in a state of great social anxiety. In the jazz "breakouts" of Stockhausen's *Drei Lieder* of 1950, one can hear echoes of the frantically bizarre "German jazz" of the era: for instance, the middle-eight by Peter Kreuder and orchestra (with Marlene Dietrich, vocalist) of the risqué Friedrich Hollaender song "Jonny, wenn du Geburtstag hast."[4] The irony of the lyrics of such songs would naturally be lost on a young child eager to identify with the divine Marlene:

> *Ich bin von Kopf bis Fuss*
> *Aus Liebe eingestellt;*
> *Und das ist meiner Welt*
> *Sonst gar nichts.*

In 1935 Stockhausen's father was promoted to the position of head teacher at the village school in Altenberg, a position of some influence in the local community and one exploited by the Nazi party for propaganda purposes. Sincerely believing in their promises to restore a strong Germany, Simon Stockhausen took on his duties as local organizer for the movement with responsibility for fundraising for the numerous charities (the "Winterhilfe," VDA etc.) set up as fronts to finance the party bureaucracy.

Karlheinz entered primary school in Easter 1935 and began to take piano lessons with Franz-Josef Kloth, Protestant organist of the village church. He practised diligently, and made rapid progress, picking up tunes that he heard on the radio. Stockhausen does not allude to hearing his mother play, only to discovering his own gift of being able to hear music on the radio and being able to play it back straight away, as a source of family pride. (He makes a fine distinction between *hearing* music on the radio and *listening* to the news, which is a text medium. It is easy to understand a perceived difference between a radio voice issuing instructions and delivering information that adds to a family's sense of foreboding, and tuning in to a music that gives pleasure and comfort, and is delivered in a mysterious language that always tells the truth. Hence: "My father *listened* to the news and that was it.")[5]

That the son also acquired a repertoire of pieces by ear as a child is not in dispute, indeed, it is an achievement of which he is still very proud: "Being musical is something very special, which is recognized even among families who have no special training, when the father and mother can say a child is very musical, because he can immediately pick up a tune and sing it, whereas other children can't."[6] In *Kurzwellen, Spiral*, and *Opus 1970* he revisits the experience of listening to a radio and imitating the music that just happens to be playing at the time, taking possession of, and transforming it. It is worth pointing out that these pieces employ or evoke *short-wave* radio transmissions, which during the thirties and forties would carry the implication of a dispassionate "voice of freedom" bringing hope to the oppressed. In 1935 the community of European and international broadcasting services was still trying to formulate an agreed policy for transmissions that might be received in countries abroad, whether radio should be politicized and used to criticize the internal policies of other nations. At first this was seen as primarily a diplomatic, and only secondarily a moral issue. "The essential essence," according to a spokesman for the BBC at the time, "is the thing said, and the spirit in which it is said."[7]

When the boy's right ear became infected the district nurse was sent for, since his father could not afford to pay the doctor. The infection was treated by repeated applications of hydrogen peroxide; unfortunately the treatment caused cartilaginous adhesions to form in the middle ear, leaving him with permanent high frequency hearing loss in his right ear.

Stockhausen recalls having to deliver leaflets and collect dues as a schoolboy for the various funds administered by the Party, while his father worked after hours as a farm laborer in order to make ends meet. Many years later, speaking of the "runner" who carries musical messages from group to group in the composition *Sternklang*, he was to say of the composer's role "I am the postman who is bringing the mail without knowing what is in the letters" (unwittingly echoing Pushkin, to whom the saying "I am the mailman" is also attributed). In 1936 he attended confession for the first time. "It made an enormously deep impression on me. Confession is like practicing music. You have to practice confession, again and again."

At home the politicization of village life became daily more oppressive.

School prayers were forbidden, and his father was obliged publicly to renounce devotions he continued to practice privately at home. One day, in honor of a visit by the bishop to Altenberg cathedral, the boy recited an idealistic poem of his own composition that included the words "Though the storms of unbelief and destruction rage still more strongly than they do now, yet we will hold up our faith."[8] That evening the Gestapo arrived at the Stockhausen home and took the father away for questioning, accusing him of having coached his son in the poem's anti-Party sentiments. Simon Stockhausen returned home badly shaken, and made him swear never to say anything that might implicate him ever again. After that, the boy kept his thoughts and hopes to himself. Unable to cope on his own, the father married a second time; Luzia Nell, from the Westerwald, the most recent of a succession of all too transient housekeepers, was to bear him a daughter, Waltraud, and a son, Gerd. At the first opportunity Simon Stockhausen volunteered for active military service.

In 1939, despite research into his family history that suggested a favorable bloodline, Karlheinz was refused admission, on account of his mother's ill-health, to the élite "political" high school that his father would have preferred. Instead, he was enrolled at the Pastor-Löhr-Gymnasium, a "humanistische Oberschule" in nearby Burscheid, where he studied Latin, mathematics, and English. By now the ruling propaganda machine had given up any pretense of concern for the people's welfare. One BBC writer monitoring a German children's hour programme, noted an announcement to young listeners that "It doesn't matter whether food is good or bad, all that matters is the spirit in which it is eaten."[9]

Preferring to live away from home, in January 1942 the young Stockhausen became a boarder at the LBA or *Lehrerbildungsanstalt* at Xanten on the lower Rhine, a teacher training college established in a converted monastery and run on strict disciplinarian lines. The war was at its height, and the school, like everyone else, was daily subjected to radio exhortation and propaganda on behalf of the war effort. These broadcasts included highly-charged "Front-line news reports" or *Frontberichte*, and the occasional "Special operations despatch" or *Sondermeldung*, a highly ritualized affair bringing the latest news of combat success on all fronts.

> In fact they were montages, sound pictures put together in the studio. Although the correspondents' reports came from the front, and some of the sound effects were recorded on the same occasion, the programme was produced—concocted—with an eye to the maximum dramatic effect. . . . The high spot of Nazi radio propaganda—and the one technique that no radio has rivalled ever since—was the *Sondermeldung*. A perverted atmosphere of revivalist religion pervaded much of Nazi broadcasting, but this was its apotheosis. News from each front was often prefaced by its own fanfares, drum-rolls and songs; the *Sondermeldung* itself was a pre-packaged montage of bombastic classical tunes and warrior songs interspersed with dramatic silences. . . . On 29 June 1941, no less than twelve *Sondermeldungen* announced the success of the first days of the Russian campaign.[10]

Metal tape had been developed in Germany in the twenties and was adopted by the BBC as a storage medium for international newscasts; by 1935,
the German firm BASF (Badische Anilin- und Soda-Fabrik) had developed
paperbacked magnetic tape that could be easily cut and pasted. Paper tape
remained exclusive to the German propaganda effort, and early in the war
its sound quality was greatly improved by a chance discovery arising from a
wrongly soldered wire that caused an ultrahigh frequency tone to be superimposed on the recorded signal. The "bias tone," as it came to be known,
had the effect of clarifying the recorded sound quality to a level indistinguishable from a live relay, making it possible for a taped special effect to
be edited, stored, and inserted into a news broadcast for dramatic purposes,—an illusion perpetuated after the war, rather less convincingly, in
spy movies such as the early Michael Caine thriller *The Ipcress File*.

   Asked about his experiences of the *Frontberichte*, Stockhausen recalled
music and sound effects: "mainly marching music at the beginning and end,
a Wagner motif to announce the most important news items from the front,
which were broadcast every once in a while, and then we used to hear just
the voice. . . . Aha! Sometimes there were sound effects of airplanes. But, I
mean, the reality was much more interesting: every night I heard such
sound effects for real."[11]

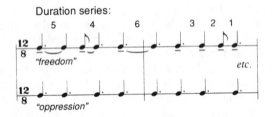

Syncopation of the "Swing" era: in the wartime Glenn Miller/Jerry Gray hit
"A String of Pearls," an expressive rhythm, symbolic of freedom, based on
a recurrent serial pattern, is set in opposition to a marching back beat,
symbolic of militarism.

   Stockhausen was the youngest student of his year. Student life was a
totally regimented existence, he later recalled: everything was organized,
down to the last fingernail; one had no privacy, and one was never alone.
There was nevertheless a considerable emphasis on music. In addition to
regular Sunday parades and outdoor concerts, in which he played oboe and
came to loathe the regular beat of a marching band, the college of 190
students boasted a 36-piece symphony orchestra, a dance orchestra, and a
jazz band, in all of which he took part, playing piano and violin. On rare
occasions he and a few friends used to listen in secret to late-night broadcasts of American jazz from the BBC. For the oppressed, American jazz was
symbolic of freedom, and the freedom was musical as well as political and
moral. The amiable syncopations of "swing" held a particular fascination for

the young musician. In hits such as the Glenn Miller/Jerry Gray classic "A String of Pearls" he seemed to discern not only a music that symbolized opposition to the regulation beat of militarism, but also a coded intimation of the higher discipline of serialism that he was to carry through into his role after the war as a jazz pianist, and his early attempts at serial syncopation in *Formel* and *Kreuzspiel*. (Even the name "A String of Pearls" hints at a mysterious connection with the *Glasperlenspiel* of Herman Hesse and its tale of an esoteric game of musical intelligence that was to have so profound an influence on his musical idealism.)

During his first year at Xanten he was called home to Altenberg to see his father on special leave, and told that his mother had officially been put to death. "There was a law during the war that these people could be killed because they were just useless, and because their food was needed. My mother was said to have died of leukaemia; we were told we could have the ashes, which was quite unusual as we were a Catholic family. But everybody who died at that hospital was supposed to have died from the same illness. The authorities just didn't want to leave any trace."[12]

Stockhausen remained at college until October 1944 when, too young for active service, he transferred to a teacher training college at Bedburg on the Erft, soon afterward converted into a military hospital. The war was in its last stages; he became a stretcher-bearer, and being fluent in English, was called upon to attend wounded and dying English and American soldiers, and translate for them. There was a piano on which he would play requests. "When everything else was gone, music seemed to them still to have value." Some would ask for Beethoven, others for ballads or music hall songs. Shortly before the end of the war he saw his father for the last time. Fearful of the consequences of a return to civilian life, and determined to seek a hero's death, Simon Stockhausen returned to the front line somewhere in Hungary. He did not return. A comrade later told Karlheinz of seeing his father wounded in action.

In the final desperate months of World War II, when the life of a young musically gifted hospital orderly came to consist in dodging phosphor bombs by day and playing American jazz on the piano to console the dying by night, the Propaganda Ministry launched a major new movie in a last-ditch effort to distract the minds of an exhausted and disillusioned population away from the grim realities of moral and technological defeat into a world of technicolor fantasy and amazing special effects. The movie centered on the life and times of the fictional Baron Münchausen, teller of outrageous and endlessly inventive tales of fabulous exploits, extravagant machines of war, romantic conquests, miraculous escapes, and ultimate survival.[13]

Although he mentions few movies by name, images from the movies are scattered through Stockhausen's oeuvre. Stylized attitudes of the era of F. W. Murnau's *Nosferatu* are recalled in the *estarrt* (transfixed) poses demanded in *Trans, Musik im Bauch, Der Jahreslauf,* and elsewhere; and Fritz Lang's vision of Moloch in *Metropolis* is sardonically evoked in the orchestrated face of Lucifer that fills an entire wall in *Samstag aus LICHT*. He

speaks of being deeply impressed as a student by movie themes of a
"fantastically idealized, fictional love;" and while he enjoyed Charlie Chaplin's *The Gold Rush* as much as anyone, he found the earlier slapstick
movies "terribly primitive" and the later Chaplin "exaggerated:" "the more
successful he became, the more his films emphasized the sentimental side,
and the formal side became weaker and weaker."[14] Later, in the sixties and
seventies, he is aware of Italian neorealism, in particular the movies of
Antonioni, but seems to be more impressed by technical issues: the feeling
for empty spaces in *L'Avventura*, the stillness in *La Notte*, and the theme of
image-enlargement in *Blow-Up*, a conception that resonates with the composer's newly-discovered attraction to musical forms in which motives are
simultaneously presented in varying timescales.

In his own works of music theater, Stockhausen tends to avoid conventional narrative, creating instead a synthesis, of expressionist formality of a
kind that he recognizes not only in German silent movies of the Weimar era
but also in classical Japanese theater, together with the "objective" reality
of the documentary form that also began to assert itself during the thirties
as a viable art. What many find hard to take in the opera cycle *LICHT*:
apparent absence of plot, dispassionate presentation of events; indifference
to character development; and,—in a paradoxical inversion of the alienation principle of Brecht (and Greek drama)—the undisguised appropriation not only of past events from the composer's life as dramatic material,
but also their reenactment by a *dramatis personae* of current family members,—all of which speaks of a perception of dramatic function in terms of
the formal presentation of events that are real in being incomprehensible to
everyone other than those involved, or to the gods. The choreographed pram
scene in *Montag aus LICHT,* for example, would be merely surreal if it were
not taken straight out of a forties newsreel staged to encourage Aryan wom-
en to produce more children for the war effort.

For some eight months after the war ended Stockhausen took work on a
farm in Blecher, to support his stepmother, half-sister, and half-brother. He
practiced piano, and took night classes in Latin to take the entrance examination to the Bergisch-Gladbach Gymnasium, which he entered as a sixth-
form student in February 1946. His former piano teacher Franz-Josef Kloth
took charge of an operetta production for the Blecher Theater Society, and
asked Stockhausen to assist with the chorus; he ended by staying on, first
as repetiteur, then as a performer and music director, for three years.
Between times there were stints afternoon and evening as accompanist for
dancing classes.

In Easter 1947, after matriculating, he moved to the old walled town of
Cologne, dominated by the imposing and relatively undamaged Dom cathedral, but otherwise brutally devastated by Allied bombing. There he
enrolled as a part-time student at the Staatliche Hochschule für Musik, in
the Dagobertstrasse just north of the Dom, as a member of the piano class
of Hans-Otto Schmidt-Neuhaus. The following year he became a full-time
student in the music education (school music) course, majoring in piano.
Among his fellow students in piano was Doris Andreae, the daughter of a

prosperous Hamburg shipbuilder, later to become his first wife. In addition to his music studies, Stockhausen also took classes in musicology, philosophy, and German studies at Cologne University, supporting himself by taking a variety of student jobs, among them car-park attendant, night-club pianist, and night watchman.

At the Musikhochschule Stockhausen began studies in harmony and counterpoint with Hermann Schroeder, the first real composer with whom he had contact. A composer of organ music in what he himself described as "an atonal dissonant style influenced by Hindemith,"[15] Schroeder had been a tutor at the Musikhochschule until 1938, and had resumed composition teaching there in 1948. His *Der römische Brunnen* (Roman Spring) of 1951 exhibits stylistic traits one can also detect, for example, in Stockhausen's *Choral* of the same year—in the movement of individual voices, parallelisms, exposed fifths, tritone harmonies, and a tendency to interpret the rise and fall of a melody in terms of a rise and fall of heroic tension:

Hermann Schroeder: Der römische Brunnen

Stockhausen: Choral

Life in the Hochschule music education department had become more lively since the appointment in 1947 of a new director, Hans Mersmann. Co-publisher of *Melos*, an important periodical of modern music that had been banned by the Nazis and only recently revived, Mersmann was something of an expert on Schoenberg at a time when the latter was still highly unpopular among conservative musicians.[16] (Stockhausen recalls one tutor asking him what score he was carrying under his arm, and who on being told it was Schoenberg's Op. 20 *Herzgewächse* exclaimed in broad dialect "That Schoenberg an' Hitler ought to 've bin drowned at birth: would ha' saved all of us a load of trouble.") Mersmann introduced his analysis students to composers who had been suppressed for many years, in particular Hindemith, Stravinsky,—and Bartók, whose synthesis of structural and folk elements moved him to raptures: "Perhaps the opposite pole from Schönberg and his school. . . . One has the impression, from the changing play of motives within a movement, of a natural growth, putting out forms, not like crystals, more like flowers. . . ."[17] Mersmann's enthusiasm for Bartók may have helped to provoke the skepticism that rises to the surface in the unexpectedly sharp (and for the era, daring) criticisms of the older composer's method expressed in Stockhausen's final-year analysis.

Stockhausen's discovery in 1948 of Hermann Hesse's novel *Das Glasperlenspiel* (in English *The Glass Bead Game*), first published under the title *Magister Ludi* (Master of the Game) had been a spiritual revelation. On the one hand the book evokes a timeless culture of music based on an esoteric code of order-relationships (the glass beads of the title); on the other hand the story was bound to impress him as a magical prophecy of his own destiny as a composer. Hesse imagines a future civilization in which music has become the most refined and universal expression of human thought. The Game itself appears to be an elusive amalgam of plainchant, rosary, abacus, staff notation, medieval disputation, astronomy, chess, and a vague premonition of computer machine code. The author not only evokes an intellectual climate with which the young composer could identify, but also envisions a future age of digital information technology that even by 1947 was beginning to become a reality. In terms suggesting more than a passing acquaintance with Alan Turing's 1936 paper "On Computable Numbers,"[18] the author describes a game played in England and Germany, invented at the Musical Academy of Cologne, representing the quintessence of intellectuality and art, and also known as "Magic Theater." The book's hero Joseph Knecht "either lost his parents early in childhood, or the Board of Educators removed him from unfavorable home conditions and took charge of him. . . . As Magister Ludi he became the leader and prototype of all those who strive toward and cultivate the things of the mind." There are further allusions to "games of memory and improvisation," to Hegel, to a Swiss musicologist who modifies the Game, to "Life," an exercise in the form of "a fictitious autobiography set in any period of the past the writer chose," and to his study of the *I Ching* with a character named "Elder Brother,"—a premonition of Cage, perhaps. There is even a scene of Knecht ruminating on the character of Lucifer:

> Laugh at me if you like, but in spite of everything there's something impressive about these apostates, just as there is a grandeur about the fallen angel Lucifer. Perhaps they did the wrong thing, or rather, undoubtedly they did the wrong thing, but all the same they did something, accomplished something; they ventured a leap, and that took courage. . . . I wouldn't want to leap back to my former home and my former life; it doesn't attract me and I've almost forgotten it. But I do wish that if ever the time comes and it proves to be necessary, that I too will be able to free myself and leap, not only backwards into something inferior, but forward and into something higher.[19]

Stockhausen has named Joseph Knecht as one of his two literary heroes (the other being Novalis' Heinrich von Ofterdingen). While the coincidences between the real and the fictional life are astonishing, what is perhaps more significant is the extent to which Stockhausen seems to have determined, early in his career, to model himself on the character as well as embrace the underlying philosophy and musical symbolism of Hesse's imaginary game. With *Kreuzspiel* the persona of "player" is taken on board; later in *LICHT* the duality of Knecht/Stockhausen is effectively mythologized.

Two events at the Musikhochschule brought Stockhausen into contact with twelve-tone composition. The first, in December 1949, was a listening experience: the pianist Else C. Krauss gave a recital of Schoenberg's solo piano music, organized by Hans Mersmann in response to a request by a group of students. There is visually little in common between Schoenberg's and Stockhausen's piano music, just from looking at the scores; but when instead of looking one listens, it is possible to hear an impulsive quality in the musical action, proceeding in short bursts characterized by sharp changes in tempo and mood, in the Schoenberg Op. 11 No. 1, the Op. 19 "Little Pieces" No. 1, and the Op. 33a,—an improvisatory feeling for movement, in short, that a performer also brings to Stockhausen's first piano pieces. (In Stockhausen's violin *Sonatine* the influence of Schoenberg is more direct, but also, shall we say, more "literary.") In 1950, again at the request of students, a formal presentation on the twelve-note method was given at the Musikhochschule by the Darmstadt composer Hermann Heiss, a former student not of Schoenberg, but of Josef Matthias Hauer, who in 1919 had developed a very different method of composing with twelve tones, called *Zwölftonspiel* (twelve-tone game). Schoenberg's method is thematic in origin and classically linear in procedure, whereas Hauer's is an essentially distributive method in which the twelve pitch-classes are divided into freely rearrangeable hexachordal sets, interestingly called *Bausteine* (building blocks).

> The atonal melody is the result of the working of the *Bausteine*: Their logical, strictly lawful and impersonal development results in a composition. All possible combinations of the twelve sounds of our scale can be divided into groups (*Tropen*). The latent forces of an interval lie within each *Tropus* and cause the further development of the latter as regards sound and rhythm.[20]

Claiming to be based on Goethe's theory of color, Hauer's method was formulated and expounded in two treatises, *Über die Klangfarbe*, and *Vom Wesen des Musikalischen*, published in Vienna in 1920. "His conscious desire to avoid any trace of thematicism, his efforts to achieve a music 'free of nature,' his hatred of the dynamic and the emotional, and his flight into a world of abstract, oriental mysticism lend his work a coolness, as his adherents would have it, or a monotony to the uninitiated."[21] Hauer did not attract much of a following outside Austria. Herbert Eimert, however, was favorably impressed. In his booklet *Atonale Musiklehre*, published in 1924, Eimert compares Hauer's method sympathetically with Schoenberg's, in addition, drawing attention to the little-known Russian painter, composer and dada sympathizer Jefim Golyscheff, whose *Zwölftondauerkomplexen*, a procedure for generating constellations of pitches by assigning each note of the chromatic scale a different duration, directly anticipates Messiaen's *Mode de valeurs et d'intensités*. Eimert's interest in Hauer is of more than passing significance given his close association with the young Stockhausen and the numerous points of resemblance between Hauer's contemplative philosophy of twelve-tone composition and Hesse's fictional game. Certainly it helps to explain why, after the Schoenbergian twelve-tone thematicism of the 1951 *Sonatine* for violin and piano, Stockhausen's serial style changes so drastically; something of Hauer's aesthetic, as well as his approach to twelve-tone composition, chimes with what we now know of Stockhausen's musical aspirations, extending to the point-fields and note-showers of some of the early piano and electronic compositions. Another correspondence can be found in Hauer's preference for tempered keyboards over conventional strings and wind instruments, a "chamber orchestra" typically consisting of piano and harmoniums, in line with Stockhausen's more recent gravitation toward a "modern orchestra" of keyboard synthesizers.

Another piece of the jigsaw seemed to fall into place in 1950 with the arrival of the Swiss composer Frank Martin at the Hochschule as visiting professor in composition. By this time Stockhausen was composing in earnest, completing the *Chöre für Doris*, and the *Choral*, writing exercises in the styles of various composers, and the *Drei Lieder* for alto voice and orchestra, settings of his own poems, a tremendous effort. He played the *Drei Lieder* for Martin and was accepted into the composition class. Although there seems to have been little to interest him in the older man's music, Stockhausen has described their relationship as friendly. In an essay "The Responsibility of the Composer," published a year or so before his arrival in Cologne, Martin expresses sentiments that chime rather well with Stockhausen's own feelings:

> Is [the composer] fully responsible for his work, or, if not, what is it in his work that escapes his authority? He is searching, then, for something. If he finds it, it is all down to his work, in the full exercising of his technique, in the full *joy* of his technique, because what he has found is in perfect accord with the work he anticipated. The right solution, the elegant solution comes to him as it would to a mathematician. The process is the same; but for the artist, the solution has to meet a requirement of sensitivity and beauty. So if the artist is reponsible for what he seeks, it is only in the merest degree; that confers on him a sort of innocence in success, as in chess, and that innocence can set him free and give him the right to meditate on his work and even, in all humility, to bring the fruits of that meditation to the attention of others.[22]

The year 1951 saw an end to Stockhausen's years of formal apprenticeship and a dramatic change in his personal fortunes. His final year at the Hochschule was devoted largely to composition, and analysis of the works of advanced composers, notably the *Sonata for Two Pianos and Percussion* of Béla Bartók, of which he made a characteristically thorough analysis, running to 186 pages, as his final examination thesis. During this time he was still working as a pianist at nights, as a jazz pianist in local bars, and in his final year as piano-playing accomplice to a touring magician named Adrion: "I improvised on the piano, and distracted the audience at crucial moments."[23]

Late in 1950 a group of music education students had organized a pantomime, *Burleska*, to be performed at the end of an off-campus study week. Stockhausen composed the music (none of which has survived) and directed the orchestra of string quartet and drums from the piano. It was quite a local success, and a repeat performance took place at the Musik-hochschule in January 1951. A mission to request press coverage for yet another performance in May 1951 brought the young composer into contact with Herbert Eimert, music critic for the newspaper *Kölnische Rundschau* and a veteran of the new music scene. In addition to his press duties, Eimert was also in charge of a late-night series of programmes on contemporary music, broadcast by the NWDR (North-West German, later WDR, West German Radio). After only a few words of conversation he recognized a kindred spirit and a friendly association began that was to lead to Stockhausen becoming involved in electronic music composition and research. Eimert gave Stockhausen a copy of his *Atonale Musiklehre* and invited the young composer to condense his Bartók analysis into a script suitable for broadcasting. (Sharp-eyed readers will note that the talk as given is on Bartók's *Concerto* for two pianos, percussion and orchestra, not the Sonata in its original form; a change no doubt arising because music examples on tape or disc were only of the 1940 orchestrated version of the score.)

Stockhausen's shortened text, reproduced in *Texte 2*, speaks of the remarkable development of a new rhythmic language in contemporary music. From listening to a work of Schoenberg, Stravinsky, or Bartók, he begins, an impression arises that the pursuit of ever more refined rhythmic principles involves changing the way melody and harmony are handled. People say there are few melodies and little opera written in this new musical language, perhaps for the reason that rhythm, melody, and harmony are actually interrelated. We can express the relationship in simple terms: a strongly rhythmic musical language is incompatible with the development of a flowing melodic line, and a strongly melodic musical language requires rhythm to play a simpler and subordinate role. In Bartók's Concerto, for example, each theme is either totally rhythmic or totally melodic in construction. This can be heard perfectly clearly in the first movement, where after a slowly building introduction, the first theme is revealed, consisting of a stamping, syncopated succession of chords, monotonous and obsessively repetitious (measures 33–40). A second theme, a free-flowing melody, makes its first appearance in measures 105–15: its rhythm is very simple. The melody develops in mirror-imitation, then in canon, elaborations of a kind that require a simple underlying rhythm.

Stockhausen goes on to distinguish Bartók's canonic and fugal writing, which are harmonically impoverished, from traditional fugue, where melody and harmony are strongly integrated. Here his criticisms indicate a comparison with Schoenberg's use of canon and counterpoint to create expressive tensions that work in both the horizontal and the vertical. In Bartók, by contrast, excessive parallelism reduces the function of harmony to merely melodic coloration. Summing up, Stockhausen sees the work as a deliberate polarization of forces: "homophony versus polyphony; rhythm

Modern music:

Concerts and broadcast talks from
Cologne Radio in the Eimert era
1949–1957

10 14 1949 Bartók *Hans Mersmann*
01 03 1950 Aphoristic music *Mersmann, Hans*
            Schulze-Ritter
03 28 1950 Schonberg *Josef Rufer*
09 05 1950 Aphoristic Music (repeat)
11 14 1950 Tradition and renewal in church music
            Messiaen. "3 Petites Liturgies" *Eimert*
11 20 1950 Sonderkonzert· Berg Violin concerto
12 04.1950 Milhaud Symphony No 3
05 12 1950 Hindemith's criticism of Schonberg *Eimert*
01 22 1951 Hindemith Horn concerto
03 05 1951 Mahler Symphony No 3
05 24 1951 Is music at an end? *Wolfgang Steinecke*
08 17 1951 In the beginning was rhythm *Eimert,*
            Blacher, Heiss, Werner Meyer-Eppler
10 08.1951 Musik der Zeit: Stravinsky Apollo.
            Symphonies, Oedipus Rex
10 18.1951 The sound-world of electronic music
            Eimert, Friedrich Trautwein, Robert
            Beyer, Meyer-Eppler

10 22 1951 Berg: Five Pieces from "Lulu," Mahler.
            Symphony No 5
11 08 1951 New synthesis in 12-tone music *Eimert*
11 22 1951 Arnold Schönberg's Violin concerto
            Op 36 *Ernst Krenek*
12 20 1951 The younger generation of German
            composers *Eimert, Steinecke*
01 24 1952 Bartók's Concerto for 2 pianos,
            percussion, and orchestra *Stockhausen*
02 21 1952 New music heating up *Eimert*
05 29 1952 Young composers 1952 Stockhausen,
            Karel Goeyvaerts, Luigi Nono *Eimert*
11 12 1953 Young composers Boulez, Goeyvaerts,
            Nono, Stockhausen, honor Webern
11 27 1952 Cage works for prepared piano,
            Maderna Concerto for two pianos *Eimert*
12 11 1952 Tone-color as a dimension of new
            music *Eimert*
04 30 1953 Acoustic research in relation to new
            music *Eimert, Meyer-Eppler*
06 11 1953 From the 1953 Cologne New Music
            Festival 1 *Stockhausen*
06 25.1953 Musique concrète and electronic music
            From the 1953 New Music Festival 2
            Stockhausen

versus melody; vertical integration versus mixture-harmony:" all united in the form of a thematic conjunction of opposites.

> In all three movements, each manifesting it in a different way, the conflict between rhythm and melody is resolved in favor of rhythm; he [Bartók] doesn't seek a synthesis of the two elements, just places them in an opposition that continues throughout the entire work, and allows the composer the possibility of highlighting the one particular rhythm that is in a subordinate relationship to melody.[24]

This is a fascinating conception of music as an interaction of forces in dynamic opposition: melody (the horizontal, the voice); rhythm (time, the dynamic impulse); and harmony (vertical, collective integration). What this short text does not disclose is any inkling at this stage of the influence on Bartók's melody and structure of the proportional series derived from Fibonacci: 1, 2, 3, 5, 8, 13, 21, 34, etc. First published in 1953, Ernò Lendvai's celebrated treatise "Einführung in die Formen- und Harmonien-welt Bartóks" (Introduction into the formal and harmonic world of Bartók) would reveal startling evidence of hidden proportioning of entire movements and, in the pitch domain, of melodic themes and harmonies.[25] As editor of *Melos*, Mersmann may well have had advance notice of Lendvai's theory, which also has elements in common with Swiss architect Le Corbusier's treatise *Le Modulor*, a theory of human proportion in architectural form based on the "Golden Mean" [a : b = (a + b) : a], a refinement of the Fibonacci series known to ancient Egyptian and Greek civilizations.

07.09.1953 From the 1953 New Music Festival 3
            Stockhausen
04.29.1954 Musik der Zeit: Boulez, Webern
06.10.1954 Electronic music: a status report *Eimert*
06.24.1954 Electronic music: works by Stockhausen,
            Paul Gredinger, Henri Pousseur *Eimert*
09.16.1954 Acoustic research in relation to new music
            Eimert, Meyer-Eppler (repeat)
10.14.1954 Bartók's Concerto for 2 pianos and
            percussion *Stockhausen* (repeat)
10.19.1954 New piano music from America:
     Part 1 *John Cage, David Tudor (pianos)*:
            Feldman Intersection 3; Christian Wolff
            For prepared piano; Earle Brown Per-
            spectives; Cage 23' 56.176" for 2 pianists
     Part 2 Electronic music: Stockhausen Studie II;
            Eimert Glockenspiel; Goeyvaerts Kompo-
            sition Nr. 5; Pousseur Seismogramme;
            Gredinger Formanten I, II; Stockhausen
            Studie I; Eimert Etüde über Tongemische
11.07.1954 Considerations on the history of elec-
            tronic music *Meyer-Eppler*
12.09.1954 First compositions from the Electronic
            Studio *Eimert*
12.23.1954 From Anton Webern to Claude Debussy
            Stockhausen

12.23.1954 From Anton Webern to Claude Debussy
            Stockhausen
04.18.1955 Hans Rosbaud conducts Schönberg:
            Kammersinfonie
07.21.1955 On statistical and psychologic problems of
            sound *Eimert, Meyer-Eppler*
10.28.1955 Hermann Scherchen conducts Schönberg:
            Five Orchestral Pieces; Webern: Kantate II
01.04.1956 Musik der Zeit: Commentary *Stockhausen,
            Hans Metzger*
05.30.1956 Concert of electronic music: Bengt Ham-
            braeus Doppelrohr 2; Gottfried Michael
            Koenig Klangfiguren II; Hermann Heiss
            Elektronische Komposition I; Giselher
            Klebe Interferenzen; Stockhausen Gesang
            der Jünglinge 1 Teil; Eimert 5 Stücke; Ernst
            Krenek Spiritus Intelligentiae Sanctus
11.07.1956 Music by Stockhausen
12.19.1956 Synthesis of Webern and Debussy in
            French 12-tone works *Antoine Goléa*
01.16.1957 David Tudor plays new piano works by Bo
            Nilsson, Stockhausen, and Cage
01.31.1957 Stockhausen: Zeitmasse
07.31.1957 Information theory and musical acoustics
            Eimert, Meyer-Eppler

In his radio talk, Stockhausen mentions only that Bartók "avoids tonal relationships by restricting his melody to interval progressions that are especially appropriate to his purposes: whole tones, tritones, minor thirds, and sixths," a choice of intervals that suggests he might well have worked out Bartók's system of melodic and harmonic proportion for himself. Other features of the Sonata, not mentioned in the shortened talk but reflected in Stockhausen's own music, include the symmetrical ensemble of two pianos, with percussion in between providing an "alternate domain" of physical action-sounds of more or less indefinite pitch. Such a perception underlies the relationship of timpani and piano in the *Schlagquartett* (revised *Schlagtrio*) of 1952, between shortwave radio and instruments in *Kurzwellen*, and even the relationship of ring-modulated and unmodulated sounds in *Mantra*, a work also for two pianos. Superficially, Bartók's daring use of percussion in 1937 evokes the decadent world of jazz, but this is more than offset by the strong, military beat of the opening first movement theme. Another clearly interesting feature, for a composer drawn to Webern's suggestion of multiple tempi in the Concerto Op. 24, is Bartók's overlapping five-note "morse" signal in the final measures of the Sonata slow second movement.

The culture and mindset that shaped Stockhausen's early life was not specifically German, nor was it created by National Socialism; it was however adapted and greatly intensified by the party in Germany for political ends made all the more devastating by the sophisticated use of radio as a

medium of mass influence. One has only to read the Einstein speech of 1930
to appreciate the depth and intensity of unconscious prejudice among even
the most enlightened of leading intellectuals of the day toward the less educated and the less fortunate. Here was a great humanist referring to those
ignorant of science and technology as *cattle*: such a remark would be unthinkable now.

Fibonacci intervals in Bartók's Sonata for two pianos and percussion *(1937),
third movement (counted in semitones).*

Educational reforms inspired by the French philosopher Jean-Jacques
Rousseau, implemented in the nineteenth century by the Swiss Johann-
Heinrich Pestalozzi and the German Friedrich Froebel, and thereafter by
Maria Montessori and others, form a continuum linking enlightened
educational practices today with the prerevolutionary world of eighteenth-
century European culture. For these visionaries the function of education
was to civilize as much as to teach; their methods were designed and intended, in the sense parodied by Bernard Shaw in *Pygmalion*, not only to
elevate the condition of lower-class individuals within society, but also
thereby to consolidate the numbers of cultivated people in societies at risk
of being overwhelmed in the revolutionary climate of the late eighteenth
century and thereafter. A mission to develop inquiring minds among the
young was therefore offset, to some extent, by a concern to foster social
harmony: a moral duty to enlighten held in check, as it were, by a more
fundamental spiritual obligation to emphasize community values and the
duties and responsibilities of citizenship. By subjecting the individual will
to the will of society, such educational philosophies implicitly defined acts of
creativity as intrinsically antisocial; thus nurturing a climate of artistic
rebellion that would erupt during the Romantic era and attain its zenith in
the Modern era. What is remarkable in Stockhausen's music and texts is
the as yet unresolved (but fruitful) coexistence of contrasting elements: the
one a willful individualism, the other an equally implacable patrician conservatism of the classic-romantic tradition. One can describe Stockhausen
as an educator in principle who works through music to change our
perception of the world, rather than in the conventional terms of an artist
inspired but essentially alone.

The law of the connection of contrasts Froebel designates variously as
the law of development and as the law of unification. To Fichte and
Hegel it is a law of mere thought; to Froebel it is more a law of life: "The
pantheistic view of life belongs to the past: we see no longer an
inseparable One, but a Three. *Trinity* has become a cornerstone which
eyes that can see, the trinity of God is manifest in all his works. Do we

not everywhere see the Three in *contrasts and their connection?* And where do we find *absolute* contrasts, contrasts (opposites) that have not somewhere or somehow a connection? In action and reaction the contrasts that we see everywhere give rise to the motions of the universe as they do in the smallest organism. This implies for all development a *struggle*, which, however, sooner or later will find its adjustment; and this adjustment is the connection of contrasts resulting in harmony among all the parts of the whole."[26]

Froebel's chart of Nature and the Human Mind is an apt illustration of that mindset into which he was born. While only an illustration, it is all the same descriptive of an organized totality of artistic and aesthetic purpose that clearly resonates with Stockhausen's published views concerning the composer and music's role in the world. One has only to acknowledge the polarities, the triune relationships and interactions, the imperative toward connection, and the underlying concept of personal development as a *struggle*, to recognize an affinity with this tradition, elective or otherwise, in the composer's music, as in his life.

Notes

1. Walter Bruch, *Erinnerungen an Funkausstellungen* (Berlin: Presse- und Informationsamt, 1979), 36. Note: Einstein's play on the word *absent* is revealing of a perception of unseen radio audiences as virtual rather than real, as distinct from the "anonymous technicians" whose reality is conferred by the actuality of the box itself.

2. VE 301: Model name of Germany's "People's Radio," chosen to honor the date in January 1933, on which the Nazi Party took control of German Radio.

3. "The Re-Organisation of German Broadcasting." Unsigned article in the *BBC Year-Book 1934* (London: British Broadcasting Corporation, 1934), 296–98. The VE 301 "People's Radio" was designed to receive only broadcasts issuing from within Germany.

4. Preserved in *Die Dreigroschenoper; Berlin 1930: Songs & Chansons.* Teldec Cedar: 9031-72025-2, track 19.

5. *SoM*, 136.

6. *SoM*, 24.

7. "The vital and fundamental criteria of proper broadcasting practice, in the international sphere, are internal and subjective. The essential essence is the thing said, *and the spirit in which it is said*, [ensuring] that the content, intention, and tendencies of internal broadcasts are devoid of any idea of offence to other countries." Ernest Barker, in the *BBC Annual, 1935*. London: British Broadcasting Corporation, 1935, 153.

8. *SoM*, 18.

9. E. A. Harding, "Listening Post 1939." *BBC Hand-Book 1940* (London: British Broadcasting Corporation, 1940), 87.

10. Julian Hale: *Radio Power: Propaganda and International Broadcasting* (London: Elek, 1975), 11–12.

11. *SoM*, 137.

12. *SoM*, 20–21.

13. *Münchausen*: movie directed by Josef von Báky, script by Gottfried August Buerger and Berthold Bürger (Erich Kästner); stories by Rudolph Erich Raspe. 1943. Filmed in Agfacolor.

14. *SoM*: 142–43.

15. *Dictionary of Twentieth-Century Music* ed. John Vinton (London: Thames and Hudson, 1974), 662–63.

16. Mersmann had good Schoenberg credentials: when Schoenberg wrote to Theodor Adorno in December 1934 with the proposal that the latter compile a dictionary of music aesthetics or music theory, he suggested Mersmann as a contributor, along with Heinrich Schenker and his own pupils Egon Wellesz and Erwin Stein. Mersmann was presenter at an early postwar revival of Schoenberg's First Chamber Symphony by the Munich Philharmonic Orchestra under Hans Rosbaud in 1947. See H. H. Stuckenschmidt, *Schoenberg: His Life, World, and Work* tr. Humphrey Searle (London: John Calder, 1977), 339, 484.

17. Hans Mersmann, "Der Spätstil Bartóks." In Heinrich Lindlar ed., *Musik in der Zeit*, Heft 3 (Bonn: Boosey and Hawkes, 1953).

18. A. M. Turing, "On Computable Numbers, with an Application to the Entscheidungsproblem." *Proc. London Mathematical Society* 42 (1937: 230–65. Turing visualized a universal computing machine as an endless tape on which calculations were expressed as a sequence of filled or vacant spaces, not unlike beads on a string.

19. Hermann Hesse, *Glass Bead Game* tr. Richard Winston and Clara Winston (Harmondsworth: Penguin Books, 1972), 73–74.

20. Paul Stefan, entry in A. Eaglefield-Hull ed., *A Dictionary of Modern Music and Musicians* (London: J. M. Dent, 1924).

21. R. T. Beck, "Austrian Serialism." In F. W. Sternfeld ed., *Music in the Modern Age* (London: Weidenfeld and Nicholson, 1973), 188–89.

22. Frank Martin, "La Responsabilité du compositeur." *Polyphonie* (Paris: 1948), 85–88.

23. Stockhausen interviewed in "About the House:" *New Yorker*, 18 January 1964.

24. *Texte 2*, 136–39.

25. Ernö Lendvai, "Einführung in die Formen- und Harmonienwelt Bartóks" (1953). 105–49 in *Béla Bartók: Weg und Werk* ed. Bence Szabolcsi (Kassel: Bärenreiter, 1972).

26. W. N. Hailmann, in Friedrich Froebel, *Education of Man*, 42.

CHAPTER TWO

Early Works

Stockhausen had originally intended to put himself through college and university and, like his father, become a teacher. He had already gained more practical experience in music than the average entrance-level student. His musical ear and professional experience as a jazz pianist and repetiteur were substantial assets toward a teaching qualification; but original composition was neither a requirement for certification, nor, in the first instance, a priority for the candidate himself. Stockhausen's passions were writing poetry, reading plays, and debating the philosophy of modern art with other students. What interested him was the morality of art, and the relationship of modern art to the state. To find modern musical culture as riven by challenge and controversy as the world of the fine arts may have come as a surprise. The infamous 1938 exhibition of *entartete Kunst* (degenerate art) had not been confined to paintings and sculpture, but had also targeted the music of Schoenberg, Stravinsky and others. Even now that the war was over, and modern art was being rehabilitated, he was discovering that among musical conservatives in a music college the name of Schoenberg was continuing to excite the kind of extreme animus one might have expected before the war. To a young student that intensity of reaction was both an indication of the power of music in society, and also cause for reflection about the social and philosophical implications of such a reaction. For anybody intending to become a teacher, those implications could also be disturbing. Teaching after all is a conservative profession, founded on principles of social harmony. The question was whether modern music, representing individual freedom of conscience, would ever be compatible with the objectives and requirements of being a teacher within the state system. As a child Stockhausen had seen his own father's religious convictions and sense of social responsibility compromised by the government of the day.

It was not any particular artist or artwork that fired Stockhausen's imagination so much as the evident power of modern art and music to inspire awe; a power, by extension, to confront evil with good. In Hesse's *Glass Bead Game*, the quest for absolute knowledge is expressed as a mind game rather than a physical conflict. In *Humayun*, a novella he wrote at this time, based on the life of a sixteenth-century Moghul emperor, Stockhausen also chooses a setting remote in space and time in which to deliberate on the meaning of life, birth and death: "the whole mystery whereby beings come into existence in time and space, and then return once more into the realm beyond space and time."

It was in 1950, his third year, when he first took classes in free composition in various classical styles, that Stockhausen discovered a gift for inventing music, and for creating and solving problems in musical terms. Music became a means of expressing himself in a way beyond words, and perhaps in that sense, in a way beyond logical reproach. Music was nevertheless capable of provoking a response. He tells of showing Hermann Schroeder a manuscript sketch of a couple of bars seething with notes, perhaps an early attempt at composing the effect of a "swarm of bees." His teacher was nonplussed. "Who can hear all these notes?" To which Stockhausen replied, "I don't want you to count them." "You don't control what you are writing," came the aggrieved response. "Just put one note, be precise."

Chöre für Doris (Choruses for Doris)

1950: No. ¹⁄₁₁ (UE 15135; cd Stockhausen Verlag SV-1)
Three movements after Verlaine for unaccompanied mixed choir.
(Original title: *Chöre nach Verlaine*)
1. "Die Nachtigall" (The Nightingale) SATB (3/8/50)
2. "Armer Junger Hirt" (A Poor Young Shepherd) SSAATTBB (n.d.)
3. "Agnus Dei" SATB (1/8/50)
Duration: 9' 30.

Stockhausen's themes are faith, hope, and love: faith in an uncertain future, hope after suffering, and the anxieties of youthful love. Other than that, there is not much to connect these three poems. They are provocative exercises in a genre, four-part choir music, that has its roots in educational and social discipline. For a nature poem, "Die Nachtigall" in the translation of Georg von der Vring, is a strongly-textured, very physical lyric, combining a declamatory freedom of rhythmic expression with a use of assonance and alliteration that hearken back to medieval style.

> Wie ein *Schwarm* *sch*reiender Vögel
> *St*ür*tz*en *s*ich die Erinnerungen
> Unter das *gelb*er *Laub* meines *Leb*ensbaumes, . . .

Appropriately, this is a poem about a lone musical bird pitting its voice against a flock of noisy and frightened birds. Although the word-setting is relatively plain and syllabic, the rhythm is more volatile. Stockhausen employs the Schoenbergian device of a neutral "Moderato" tempo within which the musical flow can vary in an impulsive manner as the emotion of the lyric seems to dictate. The character of the nightingale is expressed in a solo soprano part that asserts its independence from the accompanying chorus, to a point where it almost loses touch—an interesting foretaste of future rhythmic complexities. The word-setting for the choir is generally syllabic, and for the solo voice, more melismatic; indeed, the relationship between solo and choir appears to be worked out quite systematically:

Solo	Choir
melody	harmony
dynamic	static
impulsive	controlled
more variable	more consistent
horizontal	vertical
individual	group
etc.	

At least, there is evidence here of a principled "constructive harmonization of opposing forces" to validate Stockhausen's later adoption of serialized structural criteria.

There is a hint of Billie Holliday in the solo (the composer has a soft spot for African American female singers), and of barbershop in the choir. If that seems strange, one has to remember that until the seventies, musicians of many central European nationalities had difficulty coping with the fluid vocal and instrumental styles of imported American jazz and popular music. The Germans, it was said, could not "swing," and the French did not understand syncopation (which may still be true). That would explain the absence of a guiding tempo or mood indication, combined with a welter of peripheral instructions to performers on how to make the music flow.

"Armer junger Hirt" is another pastoral lyric, this time about a boy shepherd in love who has a fear of being kissed, as of being stung by a bee:

> *Angst hab' ich vor Küssen,*
> *Als wären sie Bienen.*
> *Wozu sie nur dienen!*
> *Ach, wird man es müssen?*
> *Angst hab' ich vor Küssen!*

Stockhausen sets the lyric as a mini-cantata, in the form of a dialogue between high female and low male voices who simultaneously interpret the lyric as characters and comment as a chorus. (He returns to the same idiom in *"Atmen gibt das Leben . . .",* which also began life as a piece for unaccompanied school choir.) As with "Die Nachtigall," the poem of "Armer junger Hirt" articulates a range of interesting contrasts: asymmetrical stanzas, variable rhyming structure and childlike metrical structure. There are five stanzas of five lines in the poem; the fifth line repeats the first line of each stanza, and the fifth stanza is a repeat of the first stanza, a symmetry of macrocosm and microcosm of a kind that would come to assume formal significance in later years. Although the simple meter suggests a simplicity of treatment, this is not what the composer has in mind. For this "young shepherd" love, too, is presumably a confrontation of opposites, and the kiss, the predestined outcome (the kiss recurs literally as a musical resolution, interestingly enough, in the duet "Ave" from *Montag aus LICHT*).

Whereas the impulsive character of "Die Nachtigall" is in a sense consistent with the rhythmical freedom of the verse itself, what Stockhausen is doing in "Armer junger Hirt" seems more deliberately subversive and "difficult"—not just in his expressionist distortion of rhythm, but in the tonal domain as well. In conventional tonal music a cadence is a point of rest and resolution; in this piece however Stockhausen uses tonal cadences both to break the lyrical flow, and to interrupt the dramatic mood. They seem to function almost as windows into a different world. This same cadential idiom returns in "Düfte-Zeichen" of *Sonntag aus LICHT*.

A listener is reminded of William Holman Hunt's *The Scapegoat* in the image of Verlaine's "Agnus Dei," a lamb who "goes in search of the bitter heather, . . . his footsteps the sound of rain on the dust." This is a dark and complex image far removed from the innocent sacrificial lamb of popular convention; in Rilke's translation, Verlaine's iambic pentameters give an impression of stumbling erratically. The poem is a prayer tied like a ribbon to a sacrificial animal sent into the wilderness, a prayer in the hope that the sacrifice will have the desired effect of alleviating human suffering: "Grant us peace, bestow on us no war." Stockhausen's setting alternates two-part counterpoint for high and low female and male voices, with a chorale-like harmonized melody in four parts. Countering the closed three-line verse form of the poem, he creates a freely-expressive episodic structure responsive to the slightest nuance of feeling.

Drei Lieder (Three Lieder)

1950: No.¹⁄₁₀ (UE 15154; cd Stockhausen Verlag SV-1)
For alto voice and chamber orchestra: flute, e flat clarinet, clarinet in a; bassoon; trumpet in c (also d); trombone; percussion, xylophone, piano, harpsichord (amplified), strings 8.0.6.4.4.
1. "Der Rebell" (The Rebel) (Baudelaire)
2. "Frei" (Free) (Stockhausen)
3. "Der Saitenmann" (The String Man) (Stockhausen)
Duration: 19' 30.

Stockhausen's writing for instruments, in his first attempt at an extended work, reveals a very different character. Surprisingly for an aspiring poet, it almost seems as though words intimidate him by virtue of the limitations they impose on what music can express (a sentiment echoed by the poet Paul Valéry). In writing for instruments by contrast the composer appears more lucid and direct, less emotionally wrought, and more open to grotesque and humorous effects. The emotional setting of the *Drei Lieder* is an ironic, mordant world in the spirit of Georg Grosz, a Germany in post-war

moral decline. Instead of the high tone of conventional lieder, Stockhausen
turns to the rebel spirit, the jester, and the down and out street musician.
Michael Kurtz notes that there may have been as many as five songs in the
original set; however only these three survive, all originally settings of his
own poems. Stockhausen sent off the score to be considered for performance
at the 1951 Darmstadt International Summer Courses, in a concert set
aside for promising young composers. Eimert was on the selection jury,
whose opinion was that the lyrics were too bleak and the music "too old-
fashioned." Stockhausen substituted "The Rebel" by Baudelaire for his own
lyric for the first song, leaving the other verses in place. The jury's view of

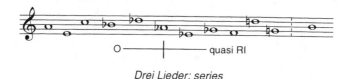

Drei Lieder: series

the music as "old-fashioned" is a little harder to understand, unless the
revised score has also been modified, and this the composer does not say. In
revising the lyric, it would not be out of the question, given what he has
said about his manner of composing, for him to have seized the opportunity
to renovate the songs and introduce some light relief. An "insert" for Stockhausen is an arbitrary break in the flow, like a gap in a wall, through which
it is possible to hear something very different, or even nothing at all. The
jazz "breaks" in *Drei Lieder* actually give the impression of an unseen hand
"tuning out" from a broadcast of solemn singing to an adjacent channel
where big band jazz is playing. In any event, the music as we know it is
subject to sudden changes of mood and instrumentation that call to mind
the stop-and-start behavior of a Scott Bradley music track for a Tex Avery
cartoon. Stockhausen has a weakness for treating instruments as characters in an animated movie, and the cartoon idiom (especially the surreal
expressionism of a Tex Avery) is one to encourage spontaneity in a composer, not to mention a reckless disregard for musical propriety. His delicacy of scoring for an ensemble including a harpsichord is another clue: a
feature of cartoon "action music" that allows for sudden changes of pace and
character. By all accounts the *fons et origo* of musical animation is the
ballet *Petrushka* by Stravinsky, one of the few scores by other composers
that Stockhausen admires, not least for the flatulent noises made by the
contrabassoon.

To achieve all this expressive flexibility and compose with a series as
well is no mean achievement. Stockhausen asked around at the Musikhochschule for help in composing with a series. Schroeder declined, but Fritz
Schieri, a tutor in harmony, had devised a method of constructing a row
with tonal properties, and in Eimert's book *Atonale Musiklehre* Stockhausen found examples of rhythmic variations of a row that bear a passing
resemblance to the opening measures of "Der Rebell" as well as to those of
the *Sonatine*.

"Der Rebell" takes the form of a dialogue between the solo voice and the trumpet, whose toy-soldier image, with side-drum flourishes, sets an ironic tone at the beginning of each song. (Schoenberg makes a similar, though more painful, allusion to life under the military in his *A Survivor from Warsaw.*) Baudelaire's poem is about refusing to submit to authority; what Stockhausen's original verse was about is unknown; however the image of rebellion that comes more readily to mind is the fallen, rather than the avenging angel, an interesting twist. Harlequin in "Frei" exceeds his royal dispensation to play jokes at the expense of authority. The king gives the jester a knotted rope, symbolizing a "string of knots" or perhaps even a "knot-row" (in German *Knoten* and *Noten* sound the same). Instead of untying the knots and revealing the line in all its majesty, Harlequin seizes the royal axe and cuts the knots in front of the court of royal (i.e., academic) prerogative, a gesture of defiance toward the meaningless authority of his conservative teachers, described as "the dead lying in state," an act received in stunned silence. In contrast to the gallows humour of the poem, the music is light and volatile, and the vocal line spacious and eloquent, for example the melisma on the words "am süssen Ort." No less impressive are the orchestral glissandi at number 13 and again at the climax near 24, where Harlequin's mocking reference to *la dolce vita* triggers a burst of luxuriant big band harmony, an allusion to human weakness to be revisited in *Der Jahreslauf.* Stockhausen is said to have been especially proud of the lyric of "Der Saitenmann," though for some the image of a derelict musician, as in Picasso's "Blue Guitar," may seem to teeter on the brink of sentimentality. The music, on the other hand, is highly accomplished, still ironic in tone, but at times ravishing in sound.

These three songs form a personal credo, offered to the person with whom he was in love, declaring who he is. Behind the serious mask is a rebel, a jester, a visionary and a suffering human being, a street musician plucking at his violin and straining to hear "das Ungespielte" —a music beyond the realm of the performable.

Choral (Chorale)
1950: No.⅑ (UE 15169; cd Stockhausen-Verlag SV-1)
For four-part unaccompanied mixed choir.
(Poem by Stockhausen)
Duration: 4'.

Two five-line stanzas of which the fifth is a repeat of the first: the structure imitates "Armer junger Hirt" and the scansion "Agnus Dei." The first stanza is a prayer to the Mother of mothers, "who has borne us in pain into this life;" the second stanza alludes to the birth of "a child of light" whose destiny is to take the terror out of death and prepare humanity for a life of service. The soprano melody is a tone-row with key of d implications; the general style however is closer to Schroeder than Schoenberg. The return to d bends the row in a circle, like the row of *Mantra* twenty years later. The series appears in original, inverted, and retrograde forms, in the soprano voice only.

Stockhausen's rhythmic composition is interesting. While the pace varies from line to line in a natural *parlando*, there are nevertheless precise formal symmetries within the lyric, of a clearly intentional design, and on a separate plane from the verse structure. So while the melody rhythm follows an ABABA pattern, in a written time-scale of four beats per measure,

"Schmerzen"   "Schmerz"

Choral: *the series. The key of d tonality is reinforced by dissonances coinciding with the word "pain"*

the pulse is constantly changing: the first line in quarter-notes, the second line in eighth-notes, the third compressing the line 1 rhythm into eighth-notes, the fourth permutating line 2, and the fifth line an expansion of the line 1 rhythm to half-note values. The effect, as one might expect, is of a controlled rhythmic expression within a uniform beat. It is unusual for Stockhausen to repeat himself, as he does with these two verses; the build-up to the fifth-line cadence creates an impression that in reversing the order of the note-row, the composer is actually reversing time.

Sonatine (Sonatina)
1951: No. ⅛ (UE 15174; cd Stockhausen Verlag SV-1)
For violin and piano (originally "for piano and violin")
1. "Lento espressivo—vivacetto irato—tempo 1"
2. "Molto moderato e cantabile"
3. "Allegro scherzando"
Duration: 10' 30.

These are three disparate "stylistic studies" related by a common note-row in which thirds and fifths predominate. Although later in order of composition than the *Drei Lieder*, the *Sonatine* does not sound quite so radical; it is quite charming and a lot more fun than the youthful Hindemith violin sonata of 1918. Kurtz lists a 1951 *Präludium* for piano solo among the unpublished works, identical to the piano part of this first movement. Just over a couple of minutes in duration, it amounts to a three-part invention in which rhythmic formulae play a structural role along with transpositions of the row. After a slow espressivo introduction, it becomes a little irascible, with rhythmic gestures not unlike trumpet calls; the general mood however is quite lyrical and contained, the violin only once soaring to a three-line e flat. The second movement Stockhausen describes as "a greatly slowed down woogie-woogie" [*sic*], in which the muted violin (a nice touch) detaches itself and floats away while the piano part, enriched by parallel harmonies, gets increasingly bogged down, the movement ending with the violin in sixes against the piano in four. Stockhausen describes the slowing-down process as "incredibly meditative, like *Stimmung*," an interesting if unexpected observation; unusually, the movement is through-composed and free of the composer's trademark interruptions. The third movement, also the liveliest, could be described as a dramatic altercation without words in which the violin takes on a feminine, emotional, reflective character, while the masculine piano part is more assertive and brusque in manner. The

Sonatine: note-row

piano writing contains some interesting inventions. Eimert was sufficiently impressed by the score to arrange a broadcast performance, the first of Stockhausen's works to be publicly performed, by Wolfgang Marschner, concert-master of the Cologne Radio Symphony Orchestra, with the composer at the piano.

It was also at Eimert's instigation that Stockhausen made his way to the 1951 Darmstadt New Music Courses. Schoenberg had been booked to take the composition class. Eimert himself was taking part in a seminar "Musik und Technik" (Music and technology) along with Robert Beyer and Werner Meyer-Eppler of Bonn University, with whom plans were already under way to create an experimental studio for electronic music at Cologne Radio. Pierre Schaeffer was also due to give a lecture-presentation at Darmstadt on the musique concrète activities of the *Club d'Essai* at Paris Radio.

The Darmstadt Summer Courses in New Music had been founded in 1946 on the joint initiative of Wolfgang Steinecke, cultural affairs adviser to the township, and Everett Helm, a Harvard-trained musicologist and composer on assignment to the US military government in post-war Germany.[1] Steinecke hoped that a new Bauhaus for music would eventuate; a library of new music was set up, and summer courses and concerts established. Among early course leaders were René Leibowitz, who had carried the banner for Schoenberg and his school in Paris, Hermann Heiss, the J. M. Hauer-schooled "twelve-tonist," Wolfgang Fortner, and from New York Edgar Varèse, whose own compositional activities had been curtailed by the war, though not by combat. Darmstadt as a center, and new music as its medium of communication, rapidly came to manifest a cultural and spiritual renewal as real and significant as the rise of a new and modern European industrial and urban infrastructure out of the ruins of war.

For the transitional US government it made good sense to revive musical activity at the local level. Making music was a good morale-booster to aid recovery. Music is also a cooperative enterprise, so the benefits are social as well as individual. For young people like Stockhausen who had in a sense been formed by a culture of censorship and denial of freedom of individual expression and fantasy, the festival had added significance on a number of levels. First, the new music symbolized a new freedom, a sense that anything was possible; second, the new spirit was international, and aimed to do away with narrow nationalist dogmas that had contributed to the disasters of two world wars; third, a new language of music would also arise: objective, scientific, reflecting the universality of human experience and not the inherited prejudices of history. The symbolism of modern art was cultivated by those involved in its administration: any regime that promoted abstract art, music, drama, or poetry, was by definition a government that valued freedom of expression for all its citizens. Nicolas Nabokov, a Russian-born American composer and friend of Stravinsky, was attached to the US occupying forces based in a divided Berlin in 1945–1946. His view of the duties of a music adviser were rather more sanguine:

> Officially we were supposed to be concerned only with the following:
> 1.   To eject the Nazis from German musical life and license those German musicians (giving them the right to exercise their profession) whom we believed to be "clean" Germans.
> 2.   To control the programs of German concerts and see to it that they would not turn into nationalist manifestations.
> 3.   To guard and protect the "monuments" and "treasures" of Germany's culture which had by virtue of conquest fallen into our hands. . . .
> Most of us were, in civilian life, professional musicians or intense music lovers who were trying to help the Germans re-establish a semblance, a modicum of culture on the ruins of twelve years of the Nazi Reich. . . . Questions raised at staff meetings included such ticklish problems as whether a trombonist is justified in getting more calories than a string player. . . . The bombed-out orchestra libraries needed parts and scores; composers needed music paper and ink; opera houses needed performers and costumes; and everybody needed shelter, food, and fuel.[2]

Stockhausen came to Darmstadt in the hope of meeting Schoenberg, but the ailing composer could not face the journey from Los Angeles and had to cancel. In his place, perhaps to speak for Schoenberg in his absence, came Theodor Weisengrund Adorno, a former composition pupil of Berg and disciple of philosopher Walter Benjamin. Adorno was no more a composer than Otto Klemperer, however his claim to lead a composition class was founded on a mission to pass judgement on the ethics and aesthetics of twentieth-century music, an issue encapsulated in a manufactured opposition between the expressionist and thematicist Schoenberg and his "method of composing with twelve notes related only to one another," and the antiexpressionist rhythmician Stravinsky, emblematic of an ironic neoclassicism. Adorno was a product of the German tradition of philosophy that included Hegel and Schopenhauer and represented a nineteenth-century outgrowth of the eighteenth-century Enlightenment. He had a mission to educate others rather than to inform himself, and like a stereotype evangelist, wrapped his patronizing attitudes in dense and impenetrable prose. Schoenberg disliked him intensely: for his moralizing, for his lack of basic musicianship, for the confusion he was creating around a music for which clarity of exposition was essential, and for his having brought about a painful rift with his old friend Thomas Mann, to whom Adorno furnished sketchy information about the twelve-tone method as background material for the fictional composer Adrian Leverkuhn in Mann's novel *Doktor Faustus*. Adorno was a busybody, but as author of the *Philosophy of Modern Music* he was also an authority on a music Europeans of Stockhausen's generation knew little about.[3]

A charming snapshot survives from that Darmstadt summer of 1951, of Stockhausen in conversation with two new acquaintances in the grounds of the Marienhöhe estate. Stockhausen, in shorts, totally relaxed, leans up on his elbow in the long grass and seems to be looking down at a musical score to his right; beside him a pensive Karel Goeyvaerts, in casual dress, hand on head, gazes downward, perhaps at the same music. Both are being lectured by a tense Luigi Nono sitting bolt upright in front of them, his right fist resting in his left hand like a gavel. He is wearing a suit.[4]

Webern String Trio Op. 20, first movement, measures 4–7.

The young Belgian composer Karel Goeyvaerts had been a student of Messiaen at a time when Messiaen was interested in Webern. Stockhausen knew a little of Webern's music, but he was also interested in Goeyvaerts' perception of Webern as the musical embodiment of the transcendental, for instance the concentration of material into single notes and the perfect symmetry of Webern's Op. 27 Piano Variations, second movement, where left and right hands pick off notes to opposite points of a compass pivoting on the one note, like a child picking petals off a daisy. Much as he approved of Webern's use of register and time as coordinates of a uniform musical space, Goeyvaerts was worried by what he saw as inconsistencies in Webern's serialization of pitch, dynamics and expression. Based on readings of the Op. 27 Piano Variations and the Symphony Op. 21, two of the few works of Webern in circulation at the time, his view was that the time domain (meter, rhythm, tempo) was not as fully realized as the other serial dimensions (pitch, register, attack, dynamic).

That is one view. In works such as the Trio of 1928,—for Webern, a "neoclassical" work in the strict sense,—it is clear to see that cellular rhythmic combinations also play a significant role. The Trio is a work the Messiaen of *Technique de mon langage musical* would certainly recognize. What Webern's music and phrasing appear to be discussing is precisely the "transition from becoming into being" that so fascinated the young Stockhausen, a dialectic predicated on a conception of music as a consequence of activity, not just as data points on paper in the abstract. If, for the sake of argument, an arco tone is taken to signify "being in time," since what one hears is the expression of a continuous bow *action*, then how such a sound makes the transition into being and how it departs into the void become poetic elements in a musical drama of beginnings and endings. Grace notes for the sake of argument are thus "hors tempo;" harmonics signify a realm of pure disembodied tone; a staccato, a lifting or departure; a pizzicato, a tone that is swallowed up, leaving only reverberation. Webern's dynamic indications interact both with the notated gestures and with the pattern of strong and weak pulses, tension and release, implicit in every measure. This is a music whose density and subtlety of discourse are belied by an outward transparency and lightness of touch. It is not the work of a cerebral mathematician or a musical Wittgenstein; rather it is the product of a refined and tactile artisan working with the substance of sound.

Goeyvaerts had brought along to the composition course a *Sonata Nr. 1* for two pianos, composed in 1950, in which he proposed a total serialism in which time is incorporated in the serial matrix.[5] To organize musical time in such a way requires a conceptual leap whereby chronometric time and keyboard pitch are equally abstract and independent of the human performer and listener. Goeyvaerts was certainly influenced by Le Corbusier's theory of "beautiful" and "functional" form, both natural (discovered) and man-made (invented), as equal manifestations of a scale of relationships inherent in the branching pattern of a twig, or the spiral growth of a seashell or sunflower, and applicable to every dimension of a habitable space.[6]

Goeyvaerts called his early works "static music" and it seems that he, too, regarded them as projections in sound of an ideal formal perfection. Richard Toop recalls that Stockhausen was attracted to the monastic austerity of Goeyvaerts's ideas, and though their musical expression did not greatly appeal to him, certain of the Belgian composer's formal stratagems did, notably his conception of register-form. In the second movement of the two-piano sonata each repeated pitch is transposed up an octave, reappearing in the lowest available octave when it "goes over the top." In this way Goeyvaerts compensates for an intrinsic lack of forward momentum by rotating the pitch series like a cylinder about a horizontal pitch-axis. At the same time, he narrows the available pitch range during the movement gradually from just over five to two and a half octaves. In the third movement of the sonata the process is reversed, the pitch range gradually opening out from two and a half octaves to just over five octaves, the recurring pitches transposing downward and reappearing at the top. Stockhausen would also be impressed by Goeyvaerts's *Nr. 2* for thirteen instruments, his *Nr. 3* for bowed and struck sounds, and *Nr. 5*, an early sine-tone piece "for dead sounds." But it was above all the idea of register-form embodied in the Belgian's *Nr. 1* that influenced his own compositions up to the first version of *Punkte*, and most clearly *Kreuzspiel* and the *Schlagquartett* (later *Schlagtrio*).

Goeyvaerts was a little taken aback by Stockhausen's immediate grasp of the two-piano score and its transcendental implications, but was grateful for his assistance when the time came to present the piece in Adorno's composition seminar. Adorno did not know what to say, and attempted to make fun of the work. Goeyvaerts was dismayed that a person in his position should attempt to belittle a pupil, asking "so why have you written it for two pianos?" in the same patronising spirit as Stockhausen had received from Schroeder in Cologne, to "use one note, be precise." Since Goeyvaerts spoke little German, Stockhausen defended his friend, saying that this was abstract music, one shouldn't look for recognizable objects in it. At which point Adorno again tried to make light of his own inadequacy, and mocked the two young men as "Leverkuhn and his apprentice," a reference to the Thomas Mann novel (which both Goeyvaerts and Stockhausen had read) as much as to his own rather discreditable role in the affair (of which both were most likely unaware).

Another memorable event of Darmstadt 1951 was hearing Messiaen's *Mode de valeurs et d'intensités* for the first time. The French author and music critic Antoine Goléa, visiting Darmstadt informally, brought along a small collection of the latest French compositions in manuscript and on disc.

> This selection included *Le Soleil des Eaux* by Boulez, recorded by French Radio from a 1950 concert performance conducted by Désormière, and, significantly, the *Quatre Études de Rythme* of Messiaen, in the Columbia recording, with the composer himself at the piano. One of these studies in particular, the profoundly radical *Mode de Valeurs et d'Intensités*, had a decisive effect on the young Karlheinz Stockhausen, then an unknown student at Darmstadt. . . . I will never forget with what passion he listened over and over again to this study; the outcome of this revelation of a sound world of which he had no doubt had an obscure presentiment, was his move to Paris for the scholastic year 1952–1953, and his assiduous attendance at Messiaen's classes.[7]

Messiaen had composed the *Quatre Études* in 1949 and 1950, that is, after Goeyvaerts had left his class. A citation of Webern is concealed in *Île de Feu 1* (measure 10, 'Modéré', page 2), composed in 1950: Stockhausen liked its pounding rhythms and one can hear a certain echo of this work in the hammering left hand repetitions of Piano Piece XIII. The epiphany however was *Mode de valeurs*, composed in 1949, a work from which even the slightest motivic remnant is eliminated. To Stockhausen it sounded like "star music:" a reference perhaps to the note-constellations of Hermann Heiss (or indeed, to the serial "constellations" of Thomas Mann's Adrian Leverkuhn). What is clear is that this music was "point music" in the sense implied by the beads of Hesse's *Glass Bead Game* as Stockhausen understood it. Each note was entire in itself: serially fixed in pitch, attack quality, duration, loudness, and totally unconnected with every other note. Even the Webern Op. 27 second movement did not get that far, because every note for one hand is grouped with its reflection in the other hand. Eimert claims to have coined the term "punktuelle musik" in a concert review of 1953, whereas Stockhausen recalls having invented it in preference to "star music" as early as 1951; however "pointillist music," the equivalent term in French and English, had already entered the lexicon some years earlier.[8]

An admiring Stravinsky remarked: "The ordinary musician's trouble in judging composers like Boulez and the young German, Stockhausen, is that he doesn't see their roots. These composers have sprung full-grown. With Webern, for example, we trace his origins back to the musical traditions of the nineteenth and earlier centuries. But the ordinary musician is not aware of Webern. He asks questions like: 'What sort of music would Boulez and Stockhausen write if they were asked to write tonal music?'"[9] To discover "the roots" of Boulez or Stockhausen,—or indeed, to discover a common thread underlying the whole of twentieth-century music, tonal, atonal, serial, and indeterminate,—is the challenge that at one level, excites listeners, while at another, practical level, creates difficulties for performers and instructors, and at the theoretical level has eluded most specialist commentators. It arises in part from what one might call an aesthetic of impenetrability whereby the justification of a work of art is that while it may be contemplated or listened to easily enough, and in the case of music, is written in a notation designed in principle to aid and not inhibit performance, its reason for existing is bound to remain a secret. We recognize an analogous aesthetic in the puzzling juxtapositions of surrealist art, and at a deeper level, in abstract art that is uncontaminated even by symbolism; it is quite right in these cases to conclude that to inquire after a particular meaning or explanation of a work of inspiration is a futile exercise, since its "roots," if there are any, are inaccessible.

A more helpful approach, indeed the only approach remaining, considers the new work of art or music as a contribution to art or music as a whole, or as we know it, which for most observers amounts to the same thing. Accordingly, what the work means "in itself" is no longer the issue; reasonable people understand that what matters is the intensity of the response it evokes. "It speaks of you" as the poet observed, meaning that the work in the strict sense is *informative* (or in Stockhausen's sense, "revelatory"). That being the case, one can only talk about the work in terms of what it is, and how it acts: what it is, a collection of signs that can be evaluated in the context of signs and their relations; how it acts, in the case of music, in terms of what a particular set of resources is capable of expressing, and whether the work in question enlarges a listener's understanding of those resources. The work of art is thus both a statement and a configuration: it defines a potential for meaning through what it is, and a mode of representation, in how it unfolds in time. The striking impression Stockhausen's music makes on a listener can perhaps be more meaningfully discussed, therefore, in terms of the density, complexity, and workmanship of the information delivered, than in terms of the incidental meanings the composer chooses to attach to it. If, as T. S. Eliot said, the poet's duty is "to purify the dialect of the tribe" then the value of Stockhausen's music to his musician listeners lies principally in its ability to extend our collective understanding of what music in general is capable of expressing.

Another part of the fascination music holds, for both musicians and non-musicians, and in particular philosophers of music, is what is assumed to be its inherent mystery: that music is "abstract" by nature, meaning that it "does not represent anything directly knowable or tangible." But if that were indeed true, the music of a song would not add anything of value or significance to the lyric, which we all know is not the case. Were it not for music, the dancers of a ballet (or even a fox-trot) would not be able to move gracefully and synchronously, or in such a way as to tell a story, which surely is anything but abstract. If it were not for music, the flimsy plots and stereotyped acting of a great many movies would be only too obvious. The myth of "abstract music" maintained by philosophers is simply the perception of a nineteenth-century bourgeoisie whose residual conception of classical music is as a transient and élitist entertainment for a discredited aristocracy. Today the argument from transience is no longer valid. We now have digital recordings, documents of actual human behavior, often in multiple editions, endlessly repeatable and therefore as profoundly "knowable" as poetry; in addition we can make comparisons of performances, and draw inferences of absolute meaning from what they have in common, as well as from what they do not.

Stockhausen was drawn to Goeyvaert's idealism, which chimed with his own Mondrian-like quest for ultimate perfection. Not only religion played a part; in the interwar years science, philosophy, art, and design were united in a quest for the fundamental data of existence:

> We could speak of the strong influence on musicians during the early fifties, of certain books for the general reader by Einstein, or Heisenberg, of biologists like Weizsäcker, or Norbert Wiener. There was similar thinking everywhere: reduction of the process of forming to the smallest possible element. When I use the word "forming," I mean it in the sense of the crystallized result of the creative act, the form being just an instant in a process, and that what was happening among scientists as well as artists was that attention was increasingly focusing on the process. . . . According to Viktor von Weizsäcker, a German medical specialist and biologist, things are not in time, but time is in things. That is very important, in leading away from objective astronomical time to a consideration for organic, biologic time.[10]

Von Weizsäcker belonged to a group of intellectuals attracted to *holism*, in German *Ganzheitslehre*, a mixture of rational and esoteric belief that took hold in Germany in the aftermath of the 1914–1918 war. Responding to a perception, formulated among others by the sociologist Max Weber, that modern science was undermining spirituality, adherents of holism, who came from a wide range of occupations and beliefs and included prominent Jewish scientists, sought to reintegrate a belief in rational determinism with a consciousness of a supervening system of moral and spiritual values.[11] Under the Nazi regime the principle of submission to a higher authority was coopted by the state and intellectual ability became racially stereotyped to a point where certain areas of intellectual skill, in particular those involving the most fundamental propositions of nature, came to be characterized as mechanistic, contrary to common sense, and evidence of a conspiracy to undermine public well-being. Science's reduction of reality to fundamental particles and their interactions was considered a perversion of reason and a Jewish trait, whereas a capacity to think simply, organically, and creatively indicated a wholesome mind "born out of creation." A biologist, Viktor von Weizsäcker trained in medicine; after the 1939–1945 war, during which he was alleged to have conducted research on the brains of victims of the Nazi euthanasia programme, he defended holism as the antidote to a mechanistic ideology attributed to National Socialism itself. Viktor von Weizsäcker is the author of *Gestalt und Zeit*,[12] from which Stockhausen draws his citation of 1971; however there is another scientist of the same family name who shared the same publisher and holistic persuasion, and whose influence on Stockhausen's thinking is also clearly demonstrable.

In a letter to the British art historian Herbert Read, the sculptor Naum Gabo defended his aesthetic of constructivism in terms harmonious with Stockhausen's observations:

> I believe art to be the most immediate and most effective of all means of communication between human beings. Art as a mental action is unambiguous—it does not deceive—it cannot deceive, since it is not concerned with truths. We never ask a tree whether it says the truth, being green, being fragrant. We should never search in a world of art for truth —it is verity itself.
>
> The way in which *art perceives the world* is sensuous (you may call it intuitive); the way it acts in response to this perception is spontaneous, irrational, and factual, and this is the way of life itself. . . . I have chosen the absoluteness and exactitude of my lines, shapes and forms in the conviction that they are the most immediate medium for my communication to others *of the rhythms and the state of mind I would wish the world to be in.* This not only in the material world surrounding us but also in the mental and spiritual world we carry within us. I think that the image they invoke is the image of good—not of evil; the image of order—not of chaos; the image of life—not of death. And that is all the content of my constructions amounts to.

Read adds: "Gabo rejects entirely the idea of a constant reality. In his view reality is continuously being created anew, it has no fixed or absolute identity (a view that seems to be in accordance with the latest theories of cosmology—cf. C. F. von Weizsäcker, *The History of Nature*)."[13] Freiherr Carl Friedrich von Weizsäcker, another distinguished representative of the German *Ganzheitslehre* movement, author of *Die Atomekerne* (1937), *Zum Weltbild der Physik* (1943), *Die Geschichte der Natur* (1948) and many other titles, was a former assistant of Werner Heisenberg; later in life as director of the Max Planck-Institute for Research on Preconditions of Human Life in the Modern World he became known as a notable advocate of esoteric philosophy. His writings, which include an introduction to a collection of meditations by the Indian mystic Gopi Krishna entitled *Biological Basis of Religion and Genius*, incorporate key definitions of time and eternity for

Stockhausen's compositions of the sixties.[14]

In a recent study Anne Harrington defines German holism as a largely twentieth-century response to the increasing mechanisation of society and culture. It can be traced much further back, however, to the late eighteenth, early nineteenth-century utopian mission of philosophers of education such as Friedrich Froebel, aiming to elevate unenlightened humankind to a state of "one-ness with Nature,"—an attitude naturally entailing a belief in the intellectual and moral superiority of the enlightened few.[15]

Stockhausen's 1971 allusion to the intellectual climate of the fifties is necessarily impressionistic: he is careful to express it in terms of books written for the general reader, implying a perception more aesthetic than philosophical in nature: "atomic music for an atomic age," perhaps. In his 1975 study *Austerity/Binge* the art historian Bevis Hillier draws attention to the appearance, post-1945, in fabrics, dinnerware, domestic furniture, and sculpture, as well as among artists such as Picasso and Miró, of a decorative imagery based on the "ball and stick" of molecular modeling, an aesthetic culminating in the signature stainless steel "Atomium" of the 1958 Brussels World Fair, based on a cubic salt molecule.[16] The ball and stick image serves to highlight a wider perception of organic beings or processes reduced to a skeleton of structural components and connections expressing locations and relationships in a state of dynamic tension (of which perhaps the best-known application today is movement capture of athletes for computer games).

No discussion of the sources of pointillism would be sufficient without reference to Ludwig Wittgenstein, whose *Tractatus Logico-Philosophicus*, published in 1922, famously represented the world as a set of facts, or "atoms of signification" (*Sachverhalten*) that themselves have no meaning, but may be constructed into sentences expressing either a true, or a false elementary proposition, or the truth value assignable to an elementary proposition. Wittgenstein makes the mysterious but musically prophetic assertion that "in a state of affairs objects fit into one another like the links of a chain" (*Tractatus* 2.03). He subsequently abandoned this "atomistic" conception of meaning in favour of a more user-friendly thesis according to which "meaning" is decided by common usage and consent. Whether or not Stockhausen read any Wittgenstein as a student, the "language game," as the philosopher called it, had entered the vocabulary of contemporary thought and would be certain to invite comparison with the play of abstract ideas of which Hesse writes in the *Glass Bead Game*. There is an echo of the positive-negative dialectic of Wittgenstein in Stockhausen's remark "Everything that is determined once and forever is like an order: you either submit to it or go against it, in which case you make a mistake."[17]

Stockhausen returned to Cologne after Darmstadt to prepare for his State examinations in secondary school music education. His Bartók thesis was submitted on 1 August and the examination results, announced in mid-October, confirmed a pass with distinction. He returned to composing with renewed energy. A new piece, *Kreuzspiel*, embodying Goeyvaerts's notion of register form, and dedicated to Doris Andreae to whom he was now formally engaged, was completed on 4 November. With a commission pending from the Donaueschingen Festival, Stockhausen began work on *Formel*, a movement for orchestra continuing to develop the idea, already formulated in *Kreuzspiel*, of a melodic sequence that mysteriously condenses into existence out of a chaos of "points;" the work was completed in a heat of inspiration by the following month. On 29 December he and Doris were married, and in January 1952 he left for Paris to take up another year of study that would bring him to Messiaen's class at the Conservatoire, to Boulez's attention, and ultimately to Pierre Schaeffer's studio for musique concrète.

Stockhausen's music is difficult to characterize as a totality for two main reasons: one, because its terms of reference tend to be momentary, changing from work to work; and two, because the composer himself does not consistently follow his own rules. But that is also a way of saying that each work of music corresponds to one statement in a logical sequence in the development of a theory; in other words, the content of each composition is both the examination of the implications of a particular set of conditions and the set of conditions itself—a definition that allows for the nonsuccess of a work aesthetically, as a legitimate consequence. With *Kreuzspiel* and *Formel* we embark on a journey into what might once have been called "a new reality," but that today can be more comfortably described as a progression of realized determinations of the musically possible, to be understood in terms of the totality of the musically possible as far as we know it. What is noteworthy at this stage is that neither *Kreuzspiel* nor *Formel* resembles "point music" in the sense Stockhausen recognized in the works of Goeyvaerts, Webern, or Messiaen.

Notes

1. Everett Helm studied composition with Walter Piston at Harvard, and with Malipiero and Vaughan Williams in Europe 1937–1938, and knew Milhaud in 1941 at Mills College. From 1948–1950 he was responsible for Theater and Music for the state of Hesse under US military rule, and for many years his "Current Chronicle" reports from Europe for the *Musical Quarterly* provided insightful information about significant new musical developments to readers in the English-speaking world.

2. Nicolas Nabokov: *Old Friends and New Music* (Boston: Little, Brown, 1951), 263–64.

3. Theodor W. Adorno: *The Philosophy of Modern Music* tr. Anne G. Mitchell and Wesley V. Blomster (New York: Continuum, 1973).

4. *Texte 1*, facing 33.

5. The title "Sonata Nr. 1" does not signify Goeyvaerts' Op. 1, but the first piece in this new idealist mode of composition.

6. Stockhausen's interest in Goeyvaerts's music is elaborated and samples of both composers' scores along with relevant correspondence from this time are reproduced and discussed in Hermann Sabbe, *Karlheinz Stockhausen:... wie die Zeit verging...* (Munich: texte + kritik, 1981).

7. A. Goléa, *Rencontres avec Pierre Boulez* (Paris: 1958), 77–78.

8. For example, the following: "As for Webern, in his orchestrations are to be found some curious combinations. For example, one of his *Five Pieces*

for Orchestra (Op. 10, 1911–13) is for clarinet, trumpet, trombone, mandolin, celesta, harp, drum, violin, and viola; instruments, be it understood, treated as solo voices. This pointillist technique is illustrated by measures from the *Six Bagatelles for String Quartet*, Op. 9." Adolfo Salazar, *Music in our Time: Trends in Music since the Romantic Era* tr. Isabel Pope (London: Bodley Head, 1948), 241–42.

9.   Igor Stravinsky and Robert Craft, *Conversations with Igor Stravinsky* (London: Faber and Faber, 1959), 127.

10.   *SoM*, 37. Stockhausen makes an identical citation in the lecture "Four Criteria of Electronic Music" (*SoM*, 96).

11.   Holism has been embraced by a plurality of intellectuals and artists, including Aldous Huxley and John Cage. Its defining characteristic is an insistence on the dual nature of belief in Western rationalism and esoteric mysticism. In some cases it provides adherents with an excuse for retaining a belief in the doctrine of the *Übermensch* by appealing to non-European traditions of racial supremacy, for example Sri Aurobindo's contention that evolution is moving the human race toward god-like status.

12.   Viktor von Weizsäcker, *Gestalt und Zeit* (Göttingen: Vandenhoeck und Ruprecht, 1960).

13.   Herbert Read, *The Philosophy of Modern Art* (Reprint. New York: Meridian, 1955), 272. Emphasis added.

14.   Gopi Krishna, *Die biologische Basis der religiöse Erfahrung* (Biological basis of religious experience). Introduction by C. F. von Weizsäcker (Munich: Wilhelm Heyne, 1968).

15.   Anne Harrington, *Reenchanted Science: Holism in German Culture from Wilhelm II to Hitler* (Princeton, NJ: Princeton University Press, 1996).

16.   Bevis Hillier: *Austerity/Binge: The Decorative Arts of the Forties and Fifties* (London: Studio Vista, 1975).

17.   *SoM*, 29.

CHAPTER THREE

Polarities

Paris in 1952 was busy rediscovering, reevaluating, and redefining modern music. Among all of Europe the city in greatest intellectual ferment was Paris; not even Cologne could boast so many partisan aesthetics clamoring simultaneously for attention. Messiaen's analysis class at the Conservatoire attracted young radicals and introduced them to new ideas of harmony, phraseology, and musical time, while across town at the École Normale, Nadia Boulanger, a figure representing clarity and neoclassical values, continued to attract a steady stream of young American composers as she had done since the roaring twenties. The Viennese Max Deutsch, a composer of salon music and former student of Schoenberg, was also teaching at the École Normale, while from his Quai Voltaire apartment the Polish expatriate René Leibowitz, teacher, conductor, and author of the ground-breaking *Introduction à la musique de douze sons* (Introduction to twelve-tone music), who at some risk to himself had carried the banner for Schoenberg, Berg, and Webern through the war, continued to advocate the cause to all who would listen.

Among survivors and sympathisers of *La Jeune France,* a group of composers formed in the thirties by Messiaen and others to advocate a post-Debussy tradition of French music purged of Germanic traits (a group from which Messiaen had subsequently distanced himself), an older generation of figures such as André Jolivet, the Swiss-born Arthur Honegger, and Henri Dutilleux, stood for a conservative modernism that in any other center than Paris,—London, for example, or Boston,—would pass for dangerously radical. The older guard did not share Leibowitz's, Boulez's, or Messiaen's passion for doctrinaire musical systems, were no longer controversial, and had only their convictions to defend. The majority were still wrestling with the issue of tonality versus atonality, whereas the younger generation were already talking of abandoning atonality and twelve-tone music in favor of a comprehensive systematization of music. A sense of the older generation's inability to grasp, let alone deal with the issue of serialism, emerges from a reading of a survey of leading composers published by the International Society for Contemporary Music in 1949 under the rubric "Music's Future: Tonal or a-Tonal?"[1] Schoenberg's contribution, among the handful still worth reading today, is profoundly touching. He was old and frail; his method had not brought him material success, and he had reason to be angry with those in the musical establishment who had, as he saw it, conspired against him.

> Their objections . . . reached from the pre-Wagnerian horror of dissonances to the more romantic and sentimental reproach of cerebrality, that is to the pretention that such compositions were the result of uninspired, dry construction, of a kind of engineering. One could ignore this criticism because of its sterility. But now opponents to this my manner of organization have attained the succour of a considerable number of young composers. This offers now a different aspect. This is no longer a mere aesthetic fight. By manifesting itself in undeniable *vitality* productive musical compositions resulting from theories based on these objections bear witness that a change of direction is in the making. Among the avantgards [*sic*] one meets some real talents, some full-blooded musicianship.
>
> It is not the first time to proclaim "ars nova;" history repeats itself. The tendency to start on new ways is attractive to the mind of the young. Small causes have thus produced great changes, and it was not for the first time that the Telemans [*sic*] and Keysers have paved the way for a Mozart, a Beethoven, a Wagner. . . . This might be considered a statement of an old man who no longer understands his time. This is not quite true. I know that history repeats itself, and I understand that works produced at a turn of time—that is, when a new period is in the process of development—have always been viciously attacked. I expect history to repeat itself also this time: real merits, if they are present, will not be forgotten.[2]

To an older generation, the debate was essentially about aesthetics and marketing (composing music that the public would buy). For this older generation the idea of advocating a new music that was even more strictly organized than Schoenberg, Berg, or Webern seemed incomprehensible. The reality, for what it was worth, was that in Paris the younger generation *wanted* a more doctrinaire position, one moreover that would establish both an aesthetic ascendancy and accord them the political authority needed to prevail against the same kind of diehard conservatism that under the Nazis had sought to demonize modern art and music. Boulez was the young firebrand of the day. A brilliant intellectual but also a street fighter, his searching polemics in the musical press could not be equaled, and he took no prisoners.

By a doctrinaire position is simply meant a new musical language, appropriate to the age, structurally coherent, abstract, objective, uncontaminated by nationalism, and offering unbounded creative potential. The young composers had rejected neoclassicism as the music of tyranny. To Boulez, Schoenberg was "Kokoschkasierte Brahms:" Brahms in expressionist guise, with added dissonance; to Goeyvaerts and Stockhausen, who had heard the "Dance around the Golden Calf" from *Moses und Aron* in a concert performance at Darmstadt, "c'était du Verdi sériel:" it was twelve-tone Verdi. In the long run Boulez made amends as a conductor and advocate of music of the Second Viennese School, but his rejection of any return of music to neoclassical tradition was as fiercely polemical as it was total (and political, as well: neoclassicism discriminated against the working class). Boulez was not alone: repudiation of the past, fuelled by Sartreian pessimism, affected attitudes to the arts in general:

> These painters and writers had no new constitution in their pockets: they did not know where they were going or what they might discover. They were quite sure about the sterility and rottenness of the academic standards which then prevailed everywhere, but they had no pre-conceived ideas about new standards. They were explorers, but they had no compass bearing. . . . A revolutionary philosophy, Sartre has said, must be a philosophy of transcendence. . . . The revolutionary artist is born into a world of clichés, of stale images and signs which no longer pierce the consciousness to express reality. He therefore invents new symbols, perhaps a whole new symbolic system. Then the academicians come along and try to generalize his symbols. . . . Many artists, once revolutionary, fall into the same contented frame of mind. We might not call them reactionaries, but in the ceaseless unfolding of existence, it is reactionary to stand still. Or, as Sartre puts it, the slightest human act must be construed as emanating from the future; therefore even the reactionary is oriented toward the future, since he is concerned with making a future that is identical with the past.[3]

This was an intellectual debate about finding a style, an *écriture*, for the arts in a nuclear age. Western music had historically evolved as an international language of notational symbols: today it was necessary to reinvent it as an international language of brotherhood. All the same, it is disconcerting to reflect that the Nazis and the advocates of Soviet realism had used (and in the case of the Soviet Union, were continuing to impose) precisely the same kind of arguments, of cleansing and renewing art, and of breaking with history, in justification of their own brands of *volkisch* representationalism:

> The "cultural speech" Hitler gave at the opening of this exhibition [the Great German Art Exhibition of 1937] began by calling attention to the obvious break that had occurred in the history of German art. "When we celebrated the laying of the cornerstone for this building, we were all aware that we had to lay not only the cornerstone for a new home but also the foundations for a new and genuine German art. We had to bring about a turning point in the evaluation of all our German cultural activity."[4]

Serialism is defended historically as an extension of the method of twelve-tone row composition introduced by Schoenberg and employed in different ways by himself, Berg, and Webern. Logically, any new rationalization of musical language would have to begin with the twelve tones (pitch classes) of the chromatic scale, so in that sense would have to take into account what Schoenberg and his disciples had already achieved. The sticking point was Schoenberg's thematicism which, despite being imperfectly understood in its own terms, was already totally at odds philosophically with the new aesthetic of a music of "sound atoms." While Boulez found much to admire in his free atonal compositions of the period up to 1924, Schoenberg's invention of a system to direct his intuition in a formally sustainable manner, and his compulsion to prove the system through adapting it to classical models, seemed to Boulez like a failure of nerve, a Freudian exercise in the psychology of dreams.

In hindsight, even after all the polemics have been digested, the case for serialism still seems inconclusive and unpersuasive. How do you invent a language? Why would anyone want to *invent* a musical language? What is the attraction of creating a language that makes the argument for serialism so convincing that it will sideline serious consideration not only of the coherent theories of Schoenberg and his school, but also those of Varèse, Hindemith, and even Messiaen himself? How could these young intellectuals, with their limited knowledge and scant practical experience of composing, be so sure of themselves? To find the answer one has to look beyond music in isolation, to music as a subset of information and linguistic science, and its development in relation to prevailing technologies of information transmission.

Music as a branch of semiotics is not a subject taught in music colleges or universities, but since the late nineteeth century French-speaking scholars had been at the forefront of research into language as a connected system of signs. This new area of expertise had not only changed how the structures and organization of language were perceived; it was also widely interpreted as sanctioning post-1792 revolutionary attitudes concerning the place of the individual in society (society being considered as a structure held together by language), and also concerning human growth and development (including the acquisition of language in infancy, and of the language of law and order by native oral cultures under European colonization). The study also created its own paradoxes: of how it could be possible for language, a stable system, to be modified over time; on the critical question of values (of interpretation, including emotions) in relation to facts (words as data); and ultimately concerning the philosophy of language itself (what words mean, what limits there are to what can be said, and how we can ever be sure). This intellectual movement, combining a late Classical fascination with ancient history and the origins of language, a Romantic preoccupation with nature and human emotions, and a middle-class rejection of individualism, propelled by the invention of radical mechanisms for capturing and revealing the natural world and the dynamics of human behaviors (phonograph, daguerrotype, moving pictures), was aimed at elucidating what the existence of a language signifies, in terms both of how words are able to convey meaning, and how meaning may be conferred by society. It generated a raft of influential theories and philosophies concerning the nature of thought, the relationship of the individual to the state, and the limits of representation. These theories were colored by a revolutionary conscious-ness opposed to any return to eighteenth-century élitist values, and had the effect of reinforcing the authority of a politicized middle class, and alien-ating the artist as an outcast or social rebel. Music was implicated in the meaning of language because music is an art of intonation and inflection, and how a sentence is spoken or sung influences what meaning it may be perceived as conveying. That is one reason why music in the Romantic era is dominated by art song, popular song, opera, and music for choir—in short, by the orchestrated and artistic interpretation of a text.

To understand a historical trend that embedded the idea of music as a language in Western consciousness, and gave rise during the early twen-tieth century to so many competing theories of music: tonality, atonality, bi-tonality, twelve-tone, Schoenberg, Varèse, Hindemith, Messiaen, Partch, Boulez:—not forgetting Deryck Cooke's *The Language of Music*, Donald Mit-chell's *The Language of Modern Music*, and a steady stream of more recent titles by noncomposers, it is necessary to begin by examining the musical implications of theories of language. Composers at heart are practical people rather than theorists: what they see in a representation of language is what it means in musical terms. When a language is "artificial" the task is made easier, since understanding is necessarily more basic.

Messiaen compared Stockhausen as a student in his analysis class to the young French genius Jean-François Champollion who successfully de-crypted the ancient Egyptian inscription of the Rosetta Stone. That remark tells the reader two things: one, that Messiaen was familiar with Champoll-ion and the implications of his discovery, and two, that he was at ease comparing Stockhausen's contribution to the development of music as a lan-guage, with Champollion's contribution to the advancement of knowledge of the evolution of language in general. The comparison is not surprising for a composer who at the age of 35 had already published a study text entitled *Technique de mon langage musical* drawing on his own research into music of remote times and cultures.

The Rosetta Stone was unearthed by French archaeologists following in the wake of Napoleon's invasion of Egypt in the last years of the eighteenth century. Handed over to the British after the defeat of Alexandria in 1801, it was transported to the British Museum, where it became an object of excited speculation. The stone was inscribed with the same text in three different languages, one of them ancient Egyptian hieroglyphics, which had never been successfully deciphered. The sticking point lay in deciding whether individual Egyptian pictograms corresponded to letters of the alphabet, or to ideas. A young English medical scientist and linguist, Thomas Young, discovered the answer by an inspired guess that the symbols represented sounds. By 1819, when he abandoned the project, Young had succeeded in deciphering most of the inscription. The task was completed soon after by an equally gifted French scholar, Jean-François Champollion, who was able to show that the cuneiform script was not a consistent system, but a mixture of phonetic and alphabetic writing.

Both Young and Champollion were qualified and had done significant research in anatomy in addition to their work in linguistics, an unusual combination of skills that surfaces again in this connection later in the nineteenth century. Particular importance attaches to their joint discovery of the acoustic dimension of written language, saying in effect that in order to understand what a language means (and how to read it) one has to know how it sounds.

The nineteenth century also saw the development of a number of artificial languages, the earliest of which also have musical implications. Morse code was an audible communication code devised in 1832 by the American Samuel Morse, a Yale-educated portrait painter and pioneer photographer, as an aid to long-distance signaling, employing the new principle of electromagnetism, and offering a number of advantages over semaphore, a visual system invented in France in 1816. Morse telegraphy made use of the principle that information, encoded by a simple key or switch turning the current on or off, could be transmitted along a wire connection between a sender and a receiver. Messages could be sent letter by letter in a simple digital code with very few states: a signal could be *on* or *off*, and either state *short* or *long* in duration—two lengths for "on" states (dots and dashes), and three for "off" (dot length within a letter group, dash length separating letter groups, two dashes for word breaks).

Morse code lends itself to being incorporated in music, for British readers perhaps most famously in the theme music by Barrington Pheloung for the television series *Inspector Morse*. Imitation morse code is specified in Stockhausen's *Mantra*. Stravinsky's 1964 *Symphonic Variations* opens with what sounds like a rhythmic statement of morse code:

$$\bullet - \bullet \quad - \bullet \quad - - - \quad - \bullet \quad \bullet -$$

"In these *Variations*," Stravinsky remarked, "tempo is a variable, pulsation a constant."[5] The implications of morse code are especially interesting in relation to Messiaen's musical language. First, it is *monotone*, a feature of Gregorian chant, in which Messiaen was well-versed; second, it relies on a perception of *time as a constant, and rhythm as a variable*; this is also a feature of plainchant, in which each rhythmic unit is self-referential and situated in a neutral nonrhythmic temporal sequence governed by breath and articulation. Third, morse is a code of *constant loudness* and therefore lacking in expression, a property that is also a value, to ensure constant audibility of the signal. Fourth, morse is *a code of rhythm units* designed with the potential to be compiled into larger units. Finally, it has the interesting characteristic of being rhythmic, but of never falling into a regular pattern, the exceptions (S O S, for example) being deliberately chosen as alarm signals. The ability to sustain rhythmic invention without falling into repetition is of considerable appeal to serial music.

Louis Braille (1809–1852) became blind as a child. Books for the blind were available in the Napoleonic era but embossed letters were difficult to read by touch. While still in his teens, Braille encountered and modified a system of "night writing" invented by Charles Barbier, a French army officer, for passing messages in the dark without making any sound, using a code of raised dots in a matrix of 2 × 3 locations designed to sit easily under the fingertip. Barbier's original code used configurations of points representing the *sounds* of individual syllables, was complicated to master, and difficult to interpret. Braille realized that having the code stand for letters rather than sounds would simplify matters. The unit 2 × 3 matrix allows for 64 dot combinations, more than enough to include a full alphabet, numerals, case indications, accents and punctuation marks.[6] A "higher-order" version of Braille, employing contractions representing commonly-used words by single letters, evolved in the late nineteenth century and is still widely employed today. The same process by which a language code is enriched by contractions and additional symbols has been repeated in recent times by internet users (inventors of the smiley face :) and other punctuation based symbols), and today by cell-phone users for text messaging.

From a musical point of view, Braille is a distributive system that builds up a statement through the repetition of unit cells of the same basic configuration, differentiated in terms of the number and location of active data points within each cell. Braille can also be compared to dominoes, and to card games, though the rules for creating meaningful sequences are different in each case. Such systems have time implications: instead of time flowing continuously, a sequence unfolds (is read) as a succession of states, like letters, each state a moment frozen in time, and each change of state essentially instantaneous, just as a moving picture is a sequence of still images linked by instantaneous transitions, making up a meaningful statement in terms of variations in the distribution of information within the frame. Both Messiaen and Boulez sought to spell out the syncopations of Stravinsky's notorious repeated-chord dance of the "Augures Printaniers," in *Le Sacre du Printemps*, in this way: interpreting it as a kind of morse code of "rhythmic cells" following a secret logic:

The rhythmic theme is formed by accents upon a regular succession of eighth-notes. The first appearance of these repeated chords lasts for eight measures and is developed in groups of two by two measures. To begin, a preparation of two measures without accent. Then, a two-measure cell A, which divides into two subdivisions, the first measure accented on the two weak beats (a_1) and a second of silence. Cell B, also of two measures, is accented on the strong off-beat of the first measure (b_1), and on the strong beat of the second measure (b_2). The second cell B^1 is the retrograde of the first: b_2b_1 with similar characteristics.[7]

Of special interest in the present case is that a distributive system of the Braille type corresponds to Stockhausen's version of serialism as we see it in

Kreuzspiel and *Formel.* In each case the music advances in unit sections within which a preordained set of pitches is repeatedly reconfigured. In *Kreuzspiel* structural time-units or modules are of fixed duration, and in *Formel* they are variable in duration by a process of serial addition. The composer's model for the distributive serial process corresponds to a development of the *Zwölftonspiel* of Josef Matthias Hauer.

Both Stockhausen's and Messiaen's cellular styles imply a sense of progression at odds with a classical sense of continuous musical flow, even one as syncopated as Stravinsky's *Le Sacre*, or as undelineated as Ligeti's *Atmosphères*. It amounts to a spatialization in visual terms of time relations conceived as discrete but perceived as continuous. A shift from the aural to the visual mode is characteristic of literate cultures, and consistent with a music modeled on written language—though for Stockhausen other models were available, such as Le Corbusier's tiling game, a tangram or mosaic in which a set of proportionally related rectangular panels generated from a rectangular module is rearranged in a variety of different ways, all of which are aesthetically satisfying. "The 'Panel Exercise' (Le Corbusier observes) has the satisfying effect of showing that in the very heart of this impeccable geometry—which some might think *implacable*—the personality has complete freedom of action."[8]

The essential difference between music and language is that music operates on a system of signs that correlate directly with individual experience and are not subject to socially imposed meanings. At the level of audible signals, music is a universal language. Western classical music, having evolved a system of writing, is conditioned by the possibilities of visual representation as well as by more fundamental tactile relations. Notation allows for greater complexity of organization, both aural and social. The Romantics, including composers, were interested in modeling human emotions, or "states of being." Instruments of scientific enquiry such as the stethoscope (invented around 1815) made it possible to establish previously unsuspected correlations between external states and internal rhythms and pulse-rates. In 1850, Léon Scott's phonautograph, an instrument invented for recording the vibration of a musical tone or voice, was developed as an aid to elucidating the fundamental sounds of language and their rules of association. Although such early recordings were only graphic traces and not reproducible as sound, as representations of the continuous pressure fluctuations of actual speech, they proposed an entirely different paradigm of language from the orthodox view based on letters or signs. A continuous curve traced on a page does not resemble words or letters, even though the action creating it is in effect writing of a kind. After 1850 we distinguish two schools of thought in relation to linguistic theory: one founded on *l'écriture*, the visual representation, the other founded on the dynamics of the speech act itself.

The American artist and designer of letters Ben Shahn tells a nice story that illustrates perfectly the difference between writing as an act of self-expression, and lettering as a code of communication. Visiting Singapore in 1959, he noticed banners of "stunning and immense calligraphs" waving outside a sign-writer's shop, and went inside to ask if the sign painter could make such a sign out of the syllables of his name in Chinese. The following day he returned to collect it, but was disappointed that the letters appeared "stilted, hard, and seemed to possess none of that rather violent and very fluid quality of the signs I had most admired." For that he needed an artist calligrapher, a person who could only work when he was in the right mood. Shahn said that he could take all the time he wanted. "No sign the second day. On the third I began to think I was being hoaxed, but I returned to the shop anyway. My friend was all smiles; the sign was ready. We looked at it and agreed that it was perfect. To me it was a revelation."[9]

The story is an illustration of the different priorities and values that attach to writing considered as letter forms and as a social act, and writing considered as physical gesture. The sign-writer was concerned with precision and accuracy of finish according to the standard forms of letters. A lettrist approach is analytical, divisive, and impersonal: its standards are legibility and freedom from error. A text consists of a sequence of such objects arranged to spell words and sentences. Each letter or ideogram is an object in itself: it has no other meaning. What Shahn as an artist was attracted to, by contrast, was the visible evidence of the energy and inspiration of the gesture revealed in calligraphic art. The letter forms may be rough and approximate, but the sign is the mark of a personality and contains a history of its creation. It is self-referential, a sign *of* the name "Ben Shahn," a gesture *of* the artist who made it, and a statement *about* the nature of the process: the paper, the ink, the brush, the hand, the mind. Music is just such a composite art. It involves notation, which is lettrist, and also performance, which is physical action driven by technique and inspiration. Language is the same. A text implies speech. A lettrist theory of music or language is likely to find meaning in those values that attach to visual forms: precision, clarity, legibility, impersonality, standardization. A gestural approach on the other hand acknowledges the individual artist, the organic unity of the process, also the possibility of distortion or error (of personality influencing clarity and precision), and communicates information on many levels, implicit as well as explicit. Ironically, despite the priority accorded to visual recognition of a text, Western print-based societies continue to acknowledge the value of the individual signature as a personal identifier and legal guarantee.

The critical distinction between *la langue* and *la parole* was formulated in the late nineteenth-century by the Swiss Ferdinand de Saussure, and published (in French) in 1915.

But what is language [*langue*]? it is not to be confused with human speech [*langage*], of which it is only a definite part, though certainly an essential one. It is both a social product of the faculty of speech and a collection of necessary conventions that have been adopted by a social body to permit individuals to exercise that faculty. Taken as a whole, speech is many-sided and heterogeneous; straddling several areas simultaneously—physical, physiological, and psychological—it belongs both to the individual and to society; we cannot put it into any category of

human facts, for we cannot discover its unity. . . . Language, on the contrary, is a self-contained whole and a principle of classification. As soon
as we give language first place among the facts of speech, we introduce a
natural order into a mass that lends itself to no other classification.[10]

The first edition of this text in English translation appeared only in 1959. By
then, the damage had long since been done, and all that was left for English
scholars to do was somehow to account for the demoralizing impact of a
brilliantly pernicious theory, one that in claiming to inquire into the nature
and meaning of language had the effect of legitimizing the authority of the
state over the freedom of expression of the individual.

> The study of speech is then twofold: its basic part—having as its object
> language, which is purely social and independent of the individual—is
> exclusively psychological; its secondary part—which has as its object the
> individual side of speech, i.e., speaking, including phonation—is
> psychophysical. Language exists in the form of a sum of impressions
> deposited in the brain of each member of a community, almost like a
> dictionary. . . . Speaking is not a collective instrument; its manifestations
> are individual and momentary. . . . Taken as a whole, speech cannot be
> studied, for it is not homogeneous.[11]

De Saussure was a talented linguist in the tradition of Young and Champollion, with a mission to discover the growth and evolution of language
from its Indo-European roots just as Darwin had discovered a hidden structure to the origin of species. From a scholarly perspective, his apocalyptic
claims for the superiority of text over speech are simply unnecessary, and
ultimately self-defeating, since they involve a definition of language aspiring
to the status of a theory of knowledge while at the same time denying the
origins of language in ordinary human speech. A theory claiming to determine that which is knowable, and all that can be said, has sinister implications, which is why reading Wittgenstein's dictum "Whereof one cannot
speak, thereof one must remain silent" can make a reader feel uneasy. But
these claims are founded on sheer convenience. De Saussure chooses to
ignore the audible component of language because it is inconvenient, difficult to record, and almost impossible to interpret. That is all. We might
simply say that such a theory was incomplete. However, in rejecting the
speech act as an essential component of meaning, his theory is also denying
music a place in the scheme of reality: music, an art of mass communication
as old as the Rosetta Stone and a vital component of all oral cultures. Not
surprisingly, the model of language de Saussure proposes is essentially
static, "like a game of chess:" it has rules that are agreed upon once and for
all, and transitions always instantaneous, like a movie, passing from one
state of equilibrium to the next. "Only states matter."[12]

Assigning priority to the printed word, and authority to the state to
decide what meanings it may have, clears the way for new disciplines to
arise: the sociology of an Émile Durkheim, an inquiry into the social consequences of determining that language is essentially a social construct (even
among peoples who can neither read nor write), and thereby an intellectual

endorsement of the position that linguistics has assigned to it; and the psychology of Sigmund Freud, a study of how language (or any symbolic representation of thought processes) can have meaning for the individual, logically entailed by the Saussurian position that language cannot be meaningful in any private sense.

Champollion's achievement in decrypting Egyptian hieroglyphics popularized the history of civilization as code; Braille introduced the concept of language as a letter-based code independent of speech and adapted to a single sense; Morse introduced letter-based language by wire as a secret code with military and political applications; philosophers such as Hegel developed the implications for knowledge and the ordered society of language considered as a social system; and de Saussure endorsed their position though unnecessary and spurious claims for the supremacy of *la langue* over *la parole*.

Among the consequences of signing on to such a view of reality are intellectual attitudes that to ordinary citizens are strikingly counter-intuitive and even disturbing. In the BBC Reith Lecture for 1950, a leading British zoologist specializing in the brain and its functions declared that human emotions, and even sensations of pleasure and pain *do not exist* for the reason that they cannot be adequately described in words by a person experiencing them.[13] Malcolm Budd, a philosopher of music, introduces his recent study of Schopenhauer with the remark that music "is essentially the art of uninterpreted sounds. It is not the art of sounds understood as signs with nonauditory meanings and composed in accordance with syntactic rules: it is not the art of speech."[14] To a practicing musician, the notion that music is uninterpreted is very odd indeed; a conclusion forced on the writer by extravagantly narrow definitions, of "art" as higher-order communication, and "interpretation" as a procedure that can only be applied to (as he says) "a system of signs with nonauditory meanings composed according to syntactic rules." By "the art of speech" Budd means not *la parole* but *la lecture*, which is not the same thing.

For a young student newly arrived in Paris in 1952, the message of Roland Barthes, semiotician and disciple of Marx, Freud, and de Saussure, was that "the work"—of art, of literature, of film, of music,—was henceforth "the Text:" a configuration of signs no longer understandable in its original meaning and only available to be read. To interpret Beethoven, he says, would oblige one to think like an orchestra (i.e., with collective knowledge): and since an individual cannot think collectively, all that the reader can do is invent a private and incommunicable meaning.

> The amateur is unable to master Beethoven's music, not so much by reason of the technical difficulties as by the very breakdown of the code of the former *musica practica*. *To want* to play Beethoven is to see oneself as the conductor of an orchestra. Beethoven's work forsakes the amateur and seems to call on the new Romantic deity, the interpreter. The operation by which we can grasp this Beethoven can no longer be either performance or hearing, but reading. One must put oneself in the position of an operator, who knows how to displace, assemble, combine,

fit together; reading this Beethoven is *to operate* his music, to draw it
into an unknown *praxis.*[15]

(The "Operator" makes a return appearance as a comedy act in "Michaelion"
from *Mittwoch aus LICHT*, an alien geek at the end of the universe, doomed
to listen to intelligence transmissions in every language from everywhere
else.) Haunted by epithets of violence and fetishism, Barthes evokes an
Orwellian culture of art reduced to a centerfold and its message to the
momentary *jouissance* of a sterile onanism. Reading Barthes is unbelievably
tedious, but a necessary chore if one is to understand Boulez, who employs a
similar vocabulary to rather more elevated purpose. For Stockhausen, whose
musical ideas were initially shaped by the Catholic faith, respect for authority, a determined resistance to all forms of categorization, and a sense of
fellowship with surrealism and its world of dreams and suspension of logic,
the first contact with Parisian intellectual life must have been quite a shock.
How much of this history he already knew is difficult to say, but as a child
he had endured the consequences of a social order predicated on the supremacy of language as a social construct, one that had sought to deprive him of
his religion, destroy his family, militarize his education, and eliminate every
last trace of modern art and music.

Theodor Adorno's *Philosophy of Modern Music* opens with a quotation from
Walter Benjamin's *Ursprung des deutschen Trauerspiels* (On the Origin of
German Tragedy): "The history of philosophy viewed as the science of origins
is that process which, from opposing extremes and from the apparent
excesses of development, permits the emergence of a configuration of an idea
as a totality characterized by the possibility of a meaningful juxtaposition of
such antitheses inherent in these opposite extremes."[16] In a letter dated 1
November 1952, addressed to Herbert Hübner, director of Hamburg Radio's
new music series "das neue Werk," Stockhausen outlines a proposal for a
new composition for piano and three pairs of timpani: "Two entities emerge
from beyond the physically describable and perceivable, into a region bound-
ed by space and time. They are diametrically opposed (*als Pole aufeinander
bezogen*)."[17] Now consider this definition of music from Hermann Hesse's
Glass Bead Game: "Music arises from Measure and is rooted in the great
Oneness. The great Oneness begets the two poles: the two poles beget the
power of Darkness and of Light. . . . Perfect music has its cause. It arises
from equilibrium. Equilibrium arises from righteousness, and righteousness
arises from the meaning of the cosmos."[18]
    Taken individually, each quotation seems needlessly obscure; collec-
tively, however, they grapple with the notion of explaining the birth of an
idea as arising from a conjunction or annihilation of opposites, like a burst of
energy created by the collision of an electron and positron, particle and anti-
particle, an appropriately radioactive image for the age. Nevertheless, it is
also a modern formulation of a dynamic view of creation that has come down
to us from the ancient Greeks, and is also acknowledged in Japan and the
far east, a belief according to which the natural world is not stable in the

sense of being static or inert, but dynamically stable in the sense of competing forces held in a balanced equilibrium. Drawing on the musical model of a string held in tension by forces pulling in opposite directions, the classic view also holds that the highest degree of self-expression (in its full sense of self-realization), as revealed by the quality and intensity of tone of a musical instrument, relates directly to the degree of tension to which the string or the performer is tuned; hence a person of the highest quality is one of high inner tension or temperament, since it follows that the clearest and most brilliant sound arises from a combination of critical internal stresses. When pressure is applied to an instrument under extreme tension, the resulting sound is heroic. That is the classic definition of genius, of musical virtuosity, or of successful leadership in the field of battle.

Kreuzspiel (Cross-play)

1951: No. ⅟₇ (UE 13117; cd Stockhausen Verlag SV-1)
For oboe, bass clarinet, piano (woodblock), percussion (6 tomtoms, 2 tumbas or congas, 4 suspended cymbals: 3 players).
Original title: *Mosaik.*[19]
Duration: 11' 30.

This image of creative tension, of the Idea born out of a juxtaposition of antitheses, is interpreted literally in this charming exercise in musical precision engineering designed to "come to life" in a magical scene reminiscent of the awakening of Maria, the female automaton in Fritz Lang's movie *Metropolis*. Stockhausen describes this music as an example of dramatic form, in the classical sense of a developmental process governed by the arrow of time: a movement of pitches from the extremes to the centre of the keyboard, where the brittle, "static" sounds of the piano come alive in the expressive, breathing tones of oboe and clarinet. One is reminded of early hit songs of the thirties that have long introductions, often an entire verse, for the band alone; just at the point when a listener has adjusted to the piece as an instrumental number, suddenly a voice appears, magically introducing a human dimension of living emotion. In assuming human form, however, the song also becomes a piece of history, a part of time.

Kreuzspiel began life as a sketch for a song for high soprano voice and piano, and was subsequently revised for high female voice, male voice, and piano, before Stockhausen finally settled on the present instrumentation, originally for four percussionists, later edited down to three.[20] Inherent in the oboe and clarinet parts is the notion of wordless vocalise; the composer's own voice timbre is actually quite similar to a bass clarinet (and even more similar to a basset-horn): here the instrument appears in the guise of "his master's voice" for the first time. The original song was to have been based on the sound elements or phonemes that make up the name "Doris," an idea that already seems to prefigure the condensation of language out of a cloud of vowels and consonants that drives *Gesang der Jünglinge*. That would explain Stockhausen's original choice of percussion, tambourines and snare drums, musical equivalents of the consonants [d] [rrr] [ss] (in "Doris") and [k] [tz] (in "Karlheinz"). (A preoccupation with consonantal textures and especially the trilled "rrr" are still recognizable in *LICHT* as signature elements of the composer's vocal writing.) After changing his mind and deciding not to include voices, Stockhausen altered his choice of percussion to sounds of "more resonance" in imitation of the natural percussiveness of the piano, —the audible thump, or for the higher notes more of a click, of the hammer hitting the strings, carefully matched and imitated at various pitch levels by accompanying tom-toms and congas. All the same, they still function perfectly well in the role of attack consonants to the vowels of the solo woodwinds, the tumbas imitating [d], drumrolls [rrr], and cymbal strokes [k] and [ts].

Goeyvaerts had introduced Stockhausen to register form, and also to "interversion:" Messiaen's method of varying a series by turning it inside out, like a sock. The Belgian objected to voices in principle, on account of their "imprecision." For the same reason he would also have disapproved of approximately-pitched percussion. Stockhausen by now was following an alternative agenda, interpreting their imprecision as necessary "human" and "fallible" antitheses to the austere and uncompromising pitch- and time-values of the keyboard. In addition to providing a parallel complementary sound-world, the percussions serve also as an image of chronometric time, like the whirring clockwork drive of a musical box or pianola. In time-honoured musical tradition, percussions also emphasize physical action, while the woodwind melodies convey emotion.

Kreuzspiel falls into three sections with introductions, link passages, and coda. In 4/8 time, MM 90, part I is preceded by a 13-measure introduction articulated by tumbas in triplets (twelve pulses per measure, coincidentally the same as Glenn Miller's "A String of Pearls"). In his commentary Stockhausen remarks "each time notes and noises occur at the same point in time,—which happens fairly frequently,—the note in some way or other drops out of the series, alters in intensity, transposes into a different octave-register or takes a different duration from the one preordained."[21] During the opening measures, tumbas beat out an identificatory duration series in sixteenth notes: 2–8–7–4–11–1–12–3–9–6–5–10, followed by the scale 1–2–3–4–5–6–7–8–9–10–11–12, a touch reminiscent of the Asian practice of identifying the mode at the beginning of a performance. At this point the tempo changes to MM 136 and the piano part to two widely-separated lines teetering toward each other as if on stepping-stones. Each statement of the series occupies a fundamental duration unit of thirteen quarter-note beats, or 6½ measures (in part III this unit changes to a duration of thirteen eighth-notes). At 28, after two statements of the duration-series on tumbas, the woodwind instruments appear, and after three further rotations a woodblock signal by the pianist triggers another serial accelerando, to the midpoint of measure 52 (13 × 4). From this point the form is retrograded and inverted, so that by 91 the piano parts have retreated to the extremes of the keyboard, but with the original pitches transposed, the six highest at the beginning now lowest, and vice versa.

Part II follows without a break, introduced by a new statement of the duration-series, played this time by suspended cymbals. Unlike I and III, where interest is created mainly by distributive interaction, in II the emphasis is on consolidation and coordination; here the woodwinds take a more active, leading role, an opportunity to make the two melody lines "speak" in a kind of wistful dialogue that nevertheless remains true to the dynamics of the score (such as the gently nudging style of Paul Desmond's alto sax in the Dave Brubeck Quartet). The movement of notated dynamics between *forte* and *pianissimo* is a little misleading for a music intended to be performed more in the intimate style of close-microphone song. Achieving the same degree of intimacy on piano can be done through a trade-off between dynamic levels and microphone positioning. In the detailed positioning of percussion around the piano, like violins around a harpsichord in a baroque orchestra, the composer makes it very clear that they are to be heard as "interior resonances" of the keyboard.

A change to compound time and return to MM 136 marks the transition to part III, announced again by an identifying statement of the duration-series. This time the accents describe a crescendo, to be matched by a corresponding diminuendo at the end: yet again the music displaying the scales on which it is composed. For a pointillistic work, the suggestion of dynamic continuity in a crescendo or diminuendo is also consistent with the development of a sense of melodic continuity through the emergence of the woodwind voices. This final section combines elements of I and II, a procedure suggesting limitless possibilities of extension (one thinks of Berg's *Kammerkonzert*, Bartók, or Berio).

Formel (Formula)

1951: No. ⅙ (UE 15157; cd Stockhausen Verlag SV-2)
Movement for orchestra: 3 oboes, 3 clarinets in a, 3 bassoons, 3 horns; 6 violins, 3 cellos, 3 double basses; vibraphone (glockenspiel), celesta, piano, harp.
Original title: *Studie für Orchester.*
Duration: 13'.

Originally intended as one movement of a projected three-movement work (the other two comprising *Spiel für Orchester*), *Formel* belongs to the same family group of compositions as *Kreuzspiel, Spiel, Schlagquartett, Punkte 1952* (the original version), and *Kontra-Punkte*. In all of these works an initial "gestalt," or pattern of notes describing fundamental interval and time relationships, is transmuted by degrees into something else. The evolutionary process characteristically depicted in these early instrumental works can be compared to a game of chess, in that an initially symmetrical, static arrangement of elements is systematically rearranged, move by move, until a self-governing dynamic situation is created, leading to the eventual dominance of one element or element combination. Two types of displacement are found: a note may be dislodged vertically from its octave register, or it may be pushed aside from its original position in the time frame. In *Formel*, complete melody or harmony units (the latter understood as "vertical melodies") are manipulated in the same way as individual "points" in other pieces.

In Debussy's *Prélude à l'Après-midi d'un faune*, a music is spun out of a flute melody of limited range that is always there and always the same, but at each recurrence is harmonized in a different way, leading the musical exposition outward in ever-changing directions. In *Bolero* by Ravel, a germinal melody of limited range is progressively amplified and expanded in harmony and range until it fills the entire envelope of a listener's hearing. Though their idioms are very different, Stockhausen's conception is strictly comparable. *Formel* describes a chevron-shaped unfolding from the center to the extremes of pitch, first broadening outward to fill the pitch space, then systematically withdrawing from the center (middle c, to be exact) to the outer extremes. The time-structure is based on an additive series. The expansion procedure is itself an "interversion" (or turning inside-out) of *Kreuzspiel*, in which the musical tendency as we recall is from the extremes to the center.

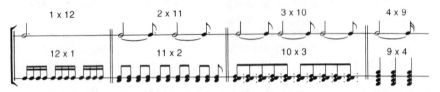

Superposition of time-divisions in Formel

The musical aim of this quirky but interesting piece is to reconcile the x and y coordinates of musical space-time in a manner perhaps suggested by analysis of the Webern Concerto Op. 24, a field in which melody expresses the horizontal, and harmony the vertical orientation of the series. Two reciprocal processes unfold simultaneously. They are defined instrumentally by bright metallic sonorities (vibraphone alternating with celesta and glockenspiel in the high register, representing white light), and the darker textures of the remaining instruments (6 + 6 high and low winds, 6 + 6 high and low strings, high piano, and low harp) representing tone colors, or simply colors. Out of a starting point in the center, a melody for the crystalline tones of the vibraphone (shared with glockenspiel and piano) opens up by graduated stages, moving from a middle c occupying a duration of 12 sixteenth-notes, to two notes oscillating within two durations of 11 sixteenth-notes, then three notes in three units of ten, and so on, ending with a statement of a full twelve-note melody adding up to twelve units, each one sixteenth-note in duration. Simultaneously, vertical collections of notes converge, starting from a single chord of 12 notes, followed by two of eleven notes, to three of ten notes, to culminate in a succession of twelve single notes, the same as a melody. A cumulative process or stretching of a single note into a melody in the horizontal dimension, is matched to a compression or flattening of a vertical twelve-note harmony into a one-dimensional melody. A visual impression of the two processes on the page is of an accented counterpoint of layered tempi, all reducible to a common pulsation: 11 in 2, 10 in 3, . . .

crossing at 7 in 6, 6 in 7, etc. (The nominal duration values are altered from time to time, to avoid too mechanical an effect.) It is as though the composer had tried to create a serial idiom that would "swing" spontaneously in the manner of big band jazz, and then, finding it didn't work quite as intended, set the piece aside. When the score was finally published in 1971, the precisely notated tempo-structure had been overlaid with a thick layer of expression marks: "moderate"—"slow down"—"not too fast"—"broaden out" —"much faster!"—"very slow," etc.

Despite a feeling of awkwardness, this is an intriguing piece, not only because it is Stockhausen's first "formula" composition before *Mantra*, but also because the relation of rigid structural durations and more fluid internal figurations makes it a significant precursor of *Gruppen*, and eventually the formula structures of *LICHT*. Apart from which, the test of an interesting work is whether it maintains its freshness. Like the music of Harry Partch, which still has something to say about the richness of natural timbres, *Formel* continues to engage the reader and surprise the listener, like an older vintage that is still surprisingly loaded with tannin.

That the work paradoxically lacks movement could be explained as a natural consequence of a sound-universe designed to be completely in balance. Goeyvaerts was aware of the possibility, and philosophically inclined toward the idea of a totally static perfection, a quest that was to lead inevitably to the tape piece *Nr. 5* "for dead sounds," literally, to a dead end. "In a perfectly defined universe," A. J. Ayer remarks, "all relations are internal. In its extreme form monism sees it as a matter of logic that everything is unified. It is in this spirit that metaphysicians since the time of Parmenides have denied the reality of change and evolution."[22] (This is the same paradox that de Saussure is forced to confront as a consequence of his definition of *la langue* as an ideally static system.) Stockhausen himself was not so committed to dead sounds; instrumentation was another matter of earnest debate between the two young idealists. Ever the purist, Goeyvaerts contended that the human voice and classical instruments were too contaminated by use, and too incoherent as a collective resource, to serve the purpose of absolute music. In choosing the vibraphone/glockenspiel/celesta combination to carry the symbolism of the generative melody, Stockhausen may well be attempting to create a bridge between the Goeyvaerts ideal of pure crystalline tone, and the human dimension of the rest of the orchestra, expressed in the physicality of breathing, bowing, and touch. That would be understandable, but the piece still doesn't quite come off: the light, as it were, not shining with enough searing intensity to dominate the rest of the orchestra.

Other options might have been available. Messiaen's ondes martenot from the *Turangalîla-Symphonie* comes to mind as a disembodied and powerful sonority, capable of great penetration ("as unpleasantly invasive as a colonic irrigation," Stravinsky judiciously observed). Donizetti chose the glass *armonica* devised by Benjamin Franklin, an authentically crystalline sound, to represent the tortured psyche of Lucia di Lammermoor, ethereal and also powerful. Other composers have employed wineglasses, rubbed or bowed, to similar effect. Alternatively, *Formel's* juxtaposition of thin melody and thicker, more abrasive collective harmonies can be interpreted as a traditional antiphon, the vibraphone leading in the role of cantor, the orchestra responding in the manner of a congregation. The formula's restricted compass and fluid, ululating manner evoke a liturgical chant.

Whether the composer's choice of conventional instruments is ideal for exploring the outer limits of pitch is another issue; other composers, Ligeti (*Atmosphères*) and Scelsi (*Konx-Om-Pax*) among them, have employed larger instrumental forces to the same purpose and perhaps achieved a more palpable impression of spatial height and depth. Both composers also adopt very much slower tempi, however, a reminder that *Formel* is also Stockhausen's first composition of multiple time-layers, and thus dynamic in conception.

Walter Friedländer, of the *Frankfurter Allgemeine Zeitung*, criticized the uncompromising serial rigidity of some "point" music auditioned at a 1952 Darmstadt concert of new music by young composers that included *Kreuzspiel*. In a follow-up article Stockhausen conceded that too uncompromising an application of preordained rules could lead to music lacking in human interest, adding "it cannot be denied that even we ourselves are tempted by such devils."[23] Despite issues that led to its being withdrawn for twenty years, *Formel* remains the prototype of a long line of melody-based compositions, notably *Mantra*, *Inori*, and the "Aries" and "Capricorn" melodies of *Tierkreis* and *Sirius*, and culminating in the triple formula of *LICHT*. *Formel's* group formations in layered tempi prefigure the more elaborate formations of *Gruppen*, and the conception of a central voice in dialogue with attendant groups is revisited successfully in *Momente*, where the liturgical implications of *Formel* are more fully acknowledged.

Notes

1. The first (and only) issue of *Music Today*, journal of the International Society for Contemporary Music, published a survey of prominent composers on the continued viability of tonality (i.e., "neoclassicism") with contributions from Schoenberg, Alban Berg (a reprint of his 1930 article "Was ist atonal?"), Darius Milhaud, Francis Poulenc, André Jolivet, René Leibowitz, Georges Migot, Humphrey Searle, Lennox Berkeley, Herbert Murrill, Wilfrid Mellers, Norman Demuth, and Rollo Myers. Charles Koechlin's essay "Quelques Réflexions au sujet de la musique atonale" appeared separately in the same volume. *Music Today*. First issue (in English and French) ed. Rollo H. Myers. (London: Dennis Dobson, 1949).

2. "Keysers:" possibly alluding to Reinhard Keiser (1674–1739), a leading German composer of baroque operas, Passions, and oratorios incorporating French and Italian traits, who influenced Handel. In Rollo Myers ed., *Music Today*, 132–34.

3. "The Situation of Art in Europe at the end of the Second World War." Herbert Read, *The Philosophy of Modern Art* (New York: Meridian Books, 1955), 38–40.

4. Berthold Hinz, *Art in the Third Reich* tr. Robert Kimber and Rita Kimber (Oxford: Basil Blackwell, 1979), 2.

5. Igor Stravinsky, *Themes and Conclusions* (London: Faber and Faber, 1972), 62–63.

6. Charles Petzold, *Code: The Hidden Language of Computer Hardware and Software* (Redmond, Wash: Microsoft Press, 2000), 3–31.

7. Pierre Boulez, "Strawinsky demeure." 151–224 in *Musique Russe I* ed. Pierre Souvtchinsky (Paris: Presses Universitaires de France, 1953).

8. Le Corbusier, *Le Modulor* tr. Peter de Francia and Anna Bostock (London: Faber and Faber, 1961), 93–96.

9. Ben Shahn, *Love and Joy about Letters* (London: Cory, Adams & Mackay, 1964), 19–27.

10. Ferdinand de Saussure, *Course in General Linguistics* ed. Charles Bally and Albert Sechehaye in collaboration with Albert Reidlinger; tr. Wade Baskin (Glasgow: Collins, 1974), 9.

11. Ferdinand de Saussure, *Course in General Linguistics*, 18–19.

12. Ferdinand de Saussure, *Course in General Linguistics*, 88–89.

13. J. Z. Young, *Doubt and Certainty in Science* (New York: Galaxy Books, 1960), 211.

14. Malcolm Budd, *Music and the Emotions: The Philosophical Theories* (London: Routledge, 1992), ix.

15. Roland Barthes, "Musica Practica." In *Image—Music—Text* tr. Stephen Heath (London: Fontana, 1977), 149–54.

16. Charles Rosen, "Should we Adore Adorno?" *New York Review of Books* (XLXI: 16): 59–66.

17. *Texte 2*, 13.

18. Hermann Hesse, *Glass Bead Game* tr. Richard Winston and Clara Winston (Harmondsworth: Penguin Books, 1972), 31, 41.

19. *Mosaik*: in *Atonale Musiklehre*, Herbert Eimert compares Josef Matthias Hauer's art of *Zwölftonspiel* with Muslim abstract tiling.

20. Michael Kurtz, *Stockhausen: A Biography* rev. tr. Richard Toop (London: Faber and Faber, 1992), 40–41.

21. Hermann Sabbe, *Karlheinz Stockhausen: . . . wie die Zeit verging . . .* , 18–19.

22. A. J. Ayer, *Philosophy in the Twentieth Century* (London: Unwin, 1984), 10.

23. Walter Friedländer, "Experiment oder Manier?" (Experiment or Mannerism?), *Frankfurter Allgemeine Zeitung*, (25 July 1952). In Karl H. Wörner, *Karlheinz Stockhausen: Werk + Wollen 1950–1962* (Rodenkirchen: P. J. Tonger, 1963), 126, but omitted from the English edition. Also cited by Seppo Heikinheimo in *The Electronic Music of Karlheinz Stockhausen: Studies on the Esthetical and Formal Problems of its First Phase* tr. Brad Absetz. *Acta Musicologia Fennica* 6 (Helsinki: Musicological Society of Finland, 1972): 18–19.

CHAPTER FOUR

Rhythmic Cells

It might easily be supposed, from the tone and temper of the previous chapter, that serialism in music, being founded on principles of reduction of knowledge to language, language to text, and text to letter code, is no more than an extreme example of the sterile and impersonal bureaucracy of the mind to which such systems inevitably tend. That is neither fair nor true. Semiology, sociology, and psychology captured public attention because, as constructs of language, they adhered easily to any discipline already relying on language (which among the humanities is virtually any subject one cares to name), and bestowed on literary professionals a gratuitous expertise in areas in which they were otherwise unqualified, on the shaky foundation of a real or imaginary competence in academic discourse. Monsieur Jourdain, the "bourgeois gentilhomme" of Molière's comedy, is astonished to be told that his everyday conversation is in fact prose, a discovery he understands as investing his every remark with intellectual gravitas. Pronouncements on music by nonmusicians sometimes bring to mind the exponent of swimming of *The Virtuoso* by Molière's English contemporary, the playwright Thomas Shadwell:

> When the curtain goes up, Sir Nicholas Gimcrack is seen making frog-like swimming movements on the table in his workroom. Does he intend to swim in the water? he is asked, and he replies: Never, sir: I hate the water. "I content myself with the speculative part of swimming and care not for the practical." And: "I seldom bring anything to use; it is not my way. Knowledge is my ultimate end."[1]

"Thus there was tension between 'pure' and 'applied' science then as there is now," Peter Medawar comments. The *scians* are those whose knowledge is tested in the real world of experience: physicians, opticians, electricians. Musicians are part of that group. Their knowledge is practical knowledge.

Practical knowledge is managed knowledge. Music is an information transaction; it involves data storage and retrieval encoded in an international language of signs and symbols standardized around 1600; it is about people management, those who employ notation, those who read and transform the printed page into audible patterns, and those who pay attention to the music they produce. Like science, music has the virtue of consistency based on repeated proof of successful performance involving executants and listeners who are to a greater or lesser extent innocent of philosophy.

> Science is never long in a turmoil of self-questioning about its fundamental premises and presumptions. Another property that sets the genuine sciences apart from those that arrogate to themselves the title without really earning it is their predictive capability: Newton and cosmology generally are tested by every entry in a nautical almanac and corroborated every time the tide rises or recedes according to the book.[2]

Music demonstrates a truly phenomenal degree of consistency from one performance to the next, a level of predictability extending to compositions of major length employing over a hundred players at a time.

When Hollywood gets around to making a movie of Stockhausen's life it will explain his move to Paris in a key scene in which the young composer and his fiancée celebrate their engagement by going to a movie. It is Jean Cocteau's *Orphée*, a recreation of the Greek myth in which a young but famous poet suffering from a crisis of creativity is singled out by a mysterious woman in black who becomes his muse. She takes him for a ride in her black Rolls Royce, from the radio of which cryptic messages can intermittently be heard. He incorporates some of these surreal phrases, sounding like coded messages from the Resistance, into his poems; his creativity is miraculously restored, and he becomes a celebrity once more. Fearing his source of inspiration will dry up, and desperate to discover the origin of these enigmatic messages, he abandons his wife, who is expecting their first child, and embarks on a quest that leads him through a landscape ravaged by war to an underworld inhabited by a humorless bureaucracy empowered to judge whether, as an artist revealing privileged information, he should live or die.

Music, not Messiaen alone, was Stockhausen's purpose. He had scoured the libraries of Cologne for everything he could find about new music. What he was looking for were features of music he was unable to find in Bartók, contrapuntal rhythm especially. He had heard and perhaps read about the French composer Darius Milhaud, whose music in the twenties was impregnated with popular and Brazilian rhythms and a spirit of cheerful fantasy. Behind the mask of traveler and raconteur in Milhaud's autobiography *Notes sans musique*, published in 1949, lurked a darker intelligence: of one who in 1917 had written six chamber symphonies, each of a few minutes' duration that could easily be fitted on to one side of a gramophone record.[3] In 1920 Milhaud composed the *Cinq Études* for piano and orchestra, miniatures of extraordinary density and concentration lasting just ten minutes in total. As compact as Webern, they are Webern's opposite in temperament.

There is a distinct foretaste of Stockhausen in Paul Claudel's mythic scenario for Milhaud's ballet *L'Homme et son désir*, composed in 1918, and the composer's ideas for the musical staging:

> "The principal character (said Claudel) is Man, over whom the primitive forces have resumed their sway, and who has been robbed by Night and Sleep, of Name and Countenance. He enters, led by two veiled shapes, who spin him around like a child that is caught in the game of Hide-and-seek, and make him lose his way. One is Image and the other Desire, one Memory and the other Illusion." . . . Already I could visualize several independent groups: on the tier, to one side a vocal quartet, and on the other an oboe, trumpet, harp and double-bass. On the second tier, on either side, the percussion. On one side of the first tier, the piccolo, the flute, the clarinet, and the bass clarinet; on the other a string quartet. I wanted to preserve absolute independence, melodic, tonal, and rhythmic, for each of these groups.[4]

Milhaud's experiments in polytonality have a technical dimension. Polytonality allows a greater density of information to be packed into the same duration. By focusing the mind on a particular key, a listener can extract each strand from the music at will, in a sophisticated musical equivalent of the "cocktail party effect" beloved of cognitive psychology, meaning the brain's ability to pay attention to one conversation in a crowded room and ignore the rest.

Polytonality is adapted from *multiplexing*, on which Thomas Edison had worked some fifty years earlier. Reasoning from the fact that morse code is monotone, he imagined that more than one message could be transmitted along the same telephone wire if each were transmitted on a different pitch; one needed only to tune a receiver to the desired frequency to extract the one message and discard the rest, exactly like tuning a radio. Milhaud's polytonality however was making the interesting biological point that the human ear and brain are capable of processing multiplexed information that is a lot more highly modulated than morse code, and doing so in real time.

Schoenberg was impressed. In a letter to Alexander Zemlinsky dated 26 October 1922 (thus, before the era of twelve-tone music), he rejected the prevailing view of Milhaud as a lightweight. "I don't agree. Milhaud strikes me as the most important representative of the contemporary movement in all Latin countries: polytonality."[5] At the time, Schoenberg himself was at work on the Op. 25 Suite for Piano, published in 1923, of which the second piece, "Gavotte," has distinctly polytonal tendencies.

Milhaud seemed like an attractive prospect as a composition teacher for Stockhausen, newly-arrived in Paris; but after only a few lessons, during which the older composer was pleased to recognize himself in the "twenties" style of the *Sonatine*, Stockhausen realized he was getting nowhere and decided his time would be better spent in attending Messiaen's classes in analysis, twice a week, at the Conservatoire at 14, rue de Madrid.

Messiaen was known as a rhythmician. A devout Catholic, as a teacher he was always open to new ideas. He did not impose, he demonstrated. To the general public and the wider musical community he seemed like an innocent, credulous child of nature, his music the product of an uncritical acceptance of all of creation. Sheltering behind the M. Hulot façade, however, lay a keen intelligence that refused to be drawn into the polemics of art. Denied a class in composition at the Conservatoire by an administration who thought his music too radical, Messiaen was content to lead a course in analysis and aesthetics free of any hint of authoritarianism. Stockhausen was fascinated by Messiaen's capacity to absorb and transform new information, and while claiming (as young composers do) that what he was grateful to have learned from Messiaen had been what to *avoid* in his own music, it is nevertheless clear that what particularly impressed him as a student was Messiaen's expertise in the field of rhythm and timing.

> He interpreted the neumes of Gregorian notation in such a way as to be able to make a piano piece, *Neumes rythmiques*, out of them. He turned the *podatus*, *clivis*, *porrectus* and *torculus* into elements of a new composition. He transformed Indian rhythms into elements of his own music. In the Tierra del Fuego he had noted down rhythms and a few melodic formulas, from which he made two piano pieces.[6]

Commentators on his music, Boulez and Stockhausen among them, tend to reinforce a general impression that Messiaen's interest in plainchant and exotic idioms was instinctive in nature and decorative in intention, like the art of Kurt Schwitters, whose *Merzbilder* made of discarded scraps of office stationery comment wryly on the nineteenth-century passion for compiling scrapbook images from glossy decals of cherubs and birds. Messiaen was a visionary in the ecstatic tradition of St Francis; his word-setting is sentimental, at times to an extreme, and much of his music is suffused with harmonies of an over-ripe sweetness that can appear very cloying to non-French ears—though this overrefinement, bordering on kitsch, is a trait Messiaen shares with Milhaud, Poulenc, and other French composers of his generation. Stockhausen could identify with the intense Catholic faith, the visionary imperative, the impulsiveness, the interlocking shapes, the quality of finish, the poet (Messiaen wrote his own verses), perhaps even the avowed synaesthesist (identifying harmonies with colors, after the manner of Scriabin).

More than the music itself it was Messiaen's theory that attracted Stockhausen to him. Building on a study of oral traditions, including medieval plainchant, Greek modes, and the deçî-tâlas of classical India, Messiaen had developed a distinctly personal aesthetic of modes, chosen for their intervallic symmetry or invertibility, and for their melodic and harmonic quality or "color." While his melodic and harmonic aesthetic can be related to the tradition of Debussy and Ravel, and also to the Russian chromaticism of Scriabin's *Prométhée* and Stravinsky's *Le Roi des Étoiles*, Messiaen's conception of rhythm is something entirely different, drawing on Greek scansion, Dom Moquereau's interpretation of Gregorian chant, and his own understanding of Sharngadeva's catalogue of 120 "rhythms," or as Messiaen understands them, units of rhythm called "cellules" or cells. What

Messiaen does with these units of rhythm is more like a code than any traditional Western conception of rhythm as an ongoing pattern, as for instance, in dance; indeed, completely removed from classical Indian music as well. Having discovered these rhythms in an encyclopedia, he seems to have interpreted them literally in the absence of available music on record. What is interesting to examine is the process by which, as a student, he arrived at an interpretation of rhythm that could be so productive in terms of his own musical aesthetic, and at the same time so oblivious of its own cultural tradition (an issue comparable with Stockhausen's assimilation of ethnic musics in *Telemusik*, for example, or of Japanese tradition in *Der Jahreslauf*). To object to such practices for their apparent lack of cultural sensitivity is to miss the point: their existence says something about the composer's message, and in Messiaen's case the message is very significant.

"The organ," Kandinsky observed, "is quite typically a 'linear' instrument as the piano is a 'point' instrument."[7] Messiaen's sense of timing is that of an organist. An organist in fact has no sense of time—or rather, a sense of time as arbitary motion. Play a note on the piano or guitar, and it will remain audible until the sound dies away of its own accord. A note sung or played on a wind instrument is sustainable only until the performer runs out of breath. Most instruments are like that, and in nature sound dies away, which is one reason (the other being an intuition or belief in the persistence of being) why music of every culture is normally structured on cyclical rhythms embodying continuity and renewal. Messiaen's music alternates between rhythms of singsong banality and an absence of rhythm that is totally fascinating. A sensation of timelessness, or of frozen time, is second nature for organists, for whom the duration of a note is governed entirely by the performer and can be prolonged undiminished for as long as the key remains depressed. For composers in that situation, a perception of time as inherent in music and not an external measure to which music conforms, is perfectly logical. In the absence of any natural momentum being generated by the normal cycle of decay and renewal, an organist has the freedom to develop an enriched but essentially static harmonic aesthetic as a way of showing that such music does not rely on classical harmonic tensions in order to move forward.

Such a perception of time as "within things, not external to things," corresponds to the definition by Viktor von Weizsäcker mentioned by Stockhausen, and is also inherent in Boulez's striking image of time as a conveyor-belt onto which objects can be placed and removed at will. The notion of time as a field, and events in time as movable objects within the field, conforms to that same lettristic conception of reality associated with the world of the printed text. Though Messiaen's interest in Indian rhythms might be interpreted as an expression of holistic thinking, it simply conforms to a worldview deeply conditioned by the medium of print, in which time appears as a blank sheet onto which actions are arbitrarily inserted, like birdsong jettisoned into the open air. In the piano piece *Île de Feu 1*, for example, a reader discovers neither time signature nor any indication of metronomic tempo, only qualities: "Vif," "Presque vif," "Très vif," "Modéré," etc. In the absence of a regulating pulsation, such indications do not amount to very much: "a bit more," "a bit less," that sort of thing. —And no rhythmic shaping of the phrase either: no rallentandi, no ritardandi, *no swing.* Instead, notes at the end of a segment momentarily lengthened by the addition of a dot, or a rest inserted to give the effect of a break between segments. If dense and energetic, the effect resembles an improvised cadenza, if slow and meditative, a baroque unmeasured prelude "in the French style." This strange, literary conception of time, which Messiaen evokes more transparently than any other composer, affected Stockhausen greatly.

Messiaen's achievement was to replace the linear, continuous, real-time narrative of the nineteenth century, epitomized by Wagnerian opera and Viennese waltz, with a new, fragmented narrative style that is not hostage to the tyranny of causality. The new style resembles improvisation but conforms actually to an arranging of facts, in retrospect and out of chronological sequence, to reveal a hidden pattern. In traditional narrative (the eighteenth-century novel, for example, or John Bunyan's *The Pilgrim's Progress*) events follow a temporal order and that order defines a life that expresses causality as a moral imperative: make a mistake, and you get caught; invest wisely, and you will prosper. Literary models for nonlinear narrative, on the other hand, are the newspaper (more particularly, the tabloid), and the detective novel. Laurence Sterne's comic novel *The Life and Opinions of Tristram Shandy, Gentleman* (1767) is an early example of a fictional narrative rendered totally nonsequential: the reader is referred to Book 6, Chapter 40, to see the story lines of the first five volumes graphically depicted as random walks. Marshall McLuhan draws attention to reverse induction in the pioneer detective fiction of Edgar Allan Poe:

> Poe set this method to work in many of his poems and stories. But it is most obvious in his invention of the detective story in which Dupin, his sleuth, is an artist-aesthete who solves crimes by a method of artistic perception. Not only is the detective story the great popular instance of working backward from effect to cause, it is also the form in which the reader is deeply involved as co-author. Such is also the case in symbolist poetry whose completion of effect from moment to moment requires the reader to participate in the poetic process itself.[8]

In the more elaborate detective fictions of Dorothy L. Sayers, a collection of facts, characters, and motives is repeatedly permutated and tested until a solution satisfying all the conditions is discovered. The story unfolds, not in time, but in the detective's mind (and by association, the reader's mind also). The essential timelessness of the process is established by the convention that the hero or principal character is in fact already dead.

We can therefore distinguish the polytonality of Milhaud and twelve-tone thematicism of Schoenberg and Berg (though perhaps not Webern), which corresponds to a multilayered narrative unfolding in linear time, from the fragmented expository narratives of newsprint, advertising, and detective fiction, in the reading of which a sense of real time is suspended, and it becomes the *reader's* task to organize material that is presented consecutively, but not in logical or causal sequence.—A definition, in fact, not only of serialism but of aleatory as well.

Stravinsky's ballet *Le Sacre du Printemps* is often perceived as the violent prototype of a fragmented twentieth-century musical narrative, but its message,—mythic, symbolic, and actual,—delivered in the continuous actions of dance, is rather more about the ritual death of conventional linear narrative than a model of the timeless hereafter envisioned, for instance, by Scriabin (though an acknowledgement of the gestural dimension, not to mention an element of wishful thinking, can be read into Messiaen and Boulez's interpretations of *Le Sacre*'s syncopations to fit their own rules of modular process planning). The narrative form most closely identified with Messiaen has to be the movie, however. As Boulez has commented, "Messiaen does not compose: he juxtaposes."[9] Messiaen is sure to have read Debussy's injunction, first published in 1913, "to apply to pure music the techniques of cinematography."[10] (Though Debussy was writing in the era of the silent movie, he had in mind the stream-of-consciousness aesthetic evoked by movies and emulated by poets and novelists, but rarely achieved by real-time cinema musicians.)

On the subject of montage, which in the movies is both elision of time, and juxtaposition of material related in time but separated in space, to create a dynamic continuum, the Russian filmmaker Sergei Eisenstein is another invaluable guide. Writing in 1933, Eisenstein draws attention to the property discovered by early filmmakers whereby "two film pieces of any kind, placed together, inevitably combine into a new concept, a new quality, arising out of that juxtaposition." Caught between those he calls the "leftists of montage," and the dogmatists of documentary, who defended chronological realism, Eisenstein argues for intelligent compromise, drawing on examples of expository writing from Pushkin, Tolstoy, Leonardo, Dante, and many others:

> Though the image enters the consciousness and perception *through aggregation*, every detail is preserved in the sensations and memory *as part of the whole*. This obtains whether it be a sound image—some rhythmic or melodic sequence of sounds, or whether it be a plastic, a visual image, embracing in pictorial form a remembered series of separate elements. . . . In one way or another, the series of ideas is built up in the perception and consciousness into a whole image, storing up the separate elements.[11]

What Stockhausen is likely to have recognized in the piano music of Messiaen is a formal process ideally suited to his concept of open serialism, conforming to a permutational aesthetic, and offering the possibilities of serially modular structure, dynamics, and time controls. Some of this emerges in his own *Klavierstücke I–IV* in which an impulsive quality reminiscent of Schoenberg is tempered by a clangorous and Messiaen-like objectivity. He may also have been impressed by the ecstatic timelessness of "Liturgie de Cristal" (and probably only that first movement) from Messiaen's aptly-named *Quartet for the End of Time*, composed when the

French composer, interned by occupying forces during the Second World War, feared for his life and the future of civilization. This haunting polyphony of melodic and harmonic processes repeating in cycles of different periodicities, like a planetary model, incorporates unearthly wailing cello harmonics in glissando that sound like the sweep frequency of a radio receiver. In 1951 Messiaen had also pushed the boundaries of organ technique in his *Livre d'Orgue*, experimenting with untried combinations of mixture stops to create a strange intermediate sound world between harmony and timbre that at the same time restored the instrument to its historic status as a programmable synthesizer.

Messiaen's paradoxical reputation as a rhythmician was based on the appropriation of a vocabulary of rhythmic types, called *personnages* (characters) that function as units of rhythmic code and are open to various forms of modification: expansion, contraction, elaboration by addition, and so on. This modular conception, so alien to classical practice, resembles montage in technique and morse code in texture; it can also be related back to the older but still lively conventions of Gregorian chant, a vocal music that unfolds in a timeless present and is free of any human measure of pulsation or rhythm. In his comment, Stockhausen mentions the names of several of the neumes of plainchant: *podatus, clivis, porrectus*, and *torculus*. There are of course others. What is interesting is that these are notations of inflection as well as pitch, reflecting a manner of singing sensitive to the syllabic articulation of normal everyday speech, but formalized into ritual. We recognize the property of movement within a syllable in the rising inflection of a question (*quilisma*), the melodic up-and-down greeting of "Ahoy there!" (*torculus*), the concessionary decline of "Oh, well. . ." (*climacus*), and so on. Both the punctuation marks and diacriticals of print derive from plainchant notation, and both reflect musical distinctions of inflection, tessitura, and timing, that affect *la parole* as well as *la lecture*—proving, contrary to de Saussure, that speech patterns do have their well-established written protocols.

Messiaen's daring innovation, openly declared in *Neumes rythmiques*, was to compose with unit rhythms in the manner of the neumata of plainchant. This allowed the composer to develop a *modular* idiom of precisely interlocking structures that at the same time avoided the repetitive beat that Debussy, Messiaen, and even Stockhausen himself, had come to feel was emblematic of an oppressive and outdated militaristic nationalism. At the same time, it provided a rationale for developing a music of points into a music of groups.

In his *Technique de mon langage musical* Messiaen defines a rhythm as a beginning, a middle, and an end: *anacrouse, accent, désinence* (anacrusis, accent, decline). These terms have their origin in plainchant, where they refer to the onset, the steady state, and the falling-away of a cadenced phrase. However, it is already very odd to describe a rhythm in such a way, since for most of us a rhythm is not a phrase but a cyclical phenomenon and therefore implicitly unbounded. Considered in the context of a theory of rhythm related via plainchant to morse code, however, such a description alludes directly to phonology, the study of speech and its meaning as sound. The rise of the semiotics of de Saussure, and of phonology, coincided with the development of sound recording, as has been noted. At the same time as the semioticians were loudly arrogating meaning to the printed text alone, and adopting a defensive posture against attributing significance to acoustic speech, scientists in Europe and the United States were already working with phonograph recorded material to confront the difficult issues of definition arising from the oscillatory trace evidence of the words and syllables of continuous speech, evidence that appeared to defy reduction to any known form of writing or ideogram.

The definition of a *sound* or wave-form as a compound of onset, steady state, and decay is fundamental to synthesizer music. What is not generally realized is that the formula derives from motor phonetics, the study of recorded speech. Research into the analysis of speech and practical applications of recording and telephone technology, to aid person to person communication and alleviate problems of the hearing impaired, began with Alexander Graham Bell in the late nineteenth century and continued under the Bell Laboratories name into the twentieth century. The Americans were unfazed by philosophy and dedicated from the outset to dealing with sound on its own terms. R. H. Stetson, the author of *Motor Phonetics* and a leading independent researcher in this new field, was part of this wider enterprise aimed at elucidating the basic elements of spoken language. Stetson was an interesting and multitalented individual; a capable musician, he studied zoology at Oberlin College before going on to Harvard, eventually to earn a doctorate in the new discipline of psychology. In 1897, while still at Oberlin, he wrote a paper "Piano Tone-Color from a Physical and Psychological Standpoint" in which he concluded that musical expression in terms of the keyboard was a meaningless concept, a finding of relevance to researches of the time that led to the development of the touch-sensitive reproducing piano. In his research into motor phonetics, Stetson worked with a cylinder recording device called a kymograph, a laboratory version of the Scott phonautograph, by means of which the sound of a voice speaking through a stethoscope-like tube caused a stylus to trace a line of vibration corresponding to the change of pressure on a moving paper surface. The kymograph was a very insensitive recorder, even by the modest standards of Bell's improved wax cylinder recorders; however it had the virtue of representing speech as a *visible* continuous trace, and not as a sequence of discrete syllables. The task of identifying separate syllables within the continuum of vibration was addressed in terms of the dynamics of the speech act. What Stetson was looking for were the basic *gestural* units of speech as they function in ordinary discourse to generate meaning. In a splendid aphorism he was to define speech as "rather a set of movements made audible than a set of sounds produced by movements." Such research also served as a reminder to the semioticians that Young and Champollion's breakthrough in decoding Egyptian cunieform had come about through recognizing that certain signs corresponded not to letters, but to sounds.

In 1905 a French scholar, François Thureau-Dangin, produced the first translation of Sumerian, a system of writing the symbols of which are not complete words or ideas, but constituent sounds of syllables. Furthermore, the division of the syllable is *tripartite*. As Stetson observed: "The structure of the Sumerian led to the recognition of the three factors in the syllable, each of which might on occasion be distinguished in notation: 1. Releasing factor, usually a consonant; 2. Vowel shape giving the syllable a definite quality; 3. Arresting factor, usually a consonant."[12] These three factors correspond exactly to Messiaen's *anacrouse, accent*, and *désinence*, expressed in terms of breath and muscular tension and release. This might just be a coincidence were it not for the fact that Stetson continued his studies in motor phonetics in Paris, in 1922–1923, when Messiaen, himself the son of a poetess and a professor of literature, was entering his mid-teens. Stetson's mentor in Paris was the Abbé Rousselot (a name deserving pride of place, one is tempted to think, in the composer's *Catalogue d'Oiseaux*). Here then is clear evidence of current research in Paris into the dynamics of motor phonetics, relating to the history of language, available to the composer at a time when Messiaen was eagerly inquiring into alternative theories of musical rhythm grounded in ancient and exotic cultures.

While still at Harvard, prior to his studies in Paris, Stetson had come under the influence of the philosopher William James, brother of the novelist Henry James; and it was at Harvard in 1906 that Stetson completed his Ph.D. dissertation entitled "A Motor Theory of Rhythm and Discrete Succession" under the supervision of Hugo Münsterberg. Another contemporary of Stetson who studied at Harvard, graduated in zoology and psychology, was influenced by William James, whose first appearance in print was a paper, supervised by Hugo Münsterberg, entitled "Normal Motor Automatism," published in the September 1896 edition of *The Psychological Review*, and who eventually became one of Paris's most celebrated American residents, was the poet Gertrude Stein. It is fascinating to reflect that at the very same time and place that Milhaud was creating polytonal works admired by Schoenberg, Stetson and the Abbé Rousselot were also collaborating in research that directly or indirectly impacted on Messiaen, while Gertrude Stein, taking her cue from the frame repetition of the movies, was developing a distinctively mantric poetic of speech destined to lead, forty years on, to the American minimalist movement of Philip Glass, John Adams, and others.

At absolute zero all movement ceases. When everything comes to a stop the question is not just where do we go from here, but how. For Boulez and Cage, degree zero was 1952, the year of *Structures* for two pianos by Boulez, and Cage's tribute to ultimate nothingness, the piano piece *4' 33"*, 273 seconds of silence corresponding to a temperature of –273 degrees Celsius. While the word does have philosophical (absence), apocalyptic (zero hour, ground zero) and mathematical associations (the boundary between negative and positive), a term signifying complete absence of movement can also be read as defining the ultimate in reductionism, the exclusion of change implicit in a lettrist conception of reality. Stillness is also an aesthetic convention; we recognize the message of a still life painting (which the French, interestingly, call *nature morte*) as a meditation on the transience of life and beauty, while in French classical theater the convention of the three unities (time, space, and action) declares a specifically cultural attachment to the idea of suspension of time as a necessary condition for drama (which is to say, for studying and resolving a problem arising from human actions). French moviemakers were always very aware of the possibilities of reversing time or stopping it altogether. René Clair's charming silent movie fantasy *Paris qui dort* of 1924 plays out on the observation deck of the Eiffel Tower during a moment suspended in time, suggesting that with absence of time comes freedom of action; for Jean Vigo, whose *Zéro de Conduite* (No marks for behavior) of 1933 relates to a more stressful era, zero-ness suggested youthful rebellion or anarchy.

Every year Messiaen's class in aesthetics and analysis would focus on a single topic. In 1952 the topic was rhythm. Stockhausen recalls "rhythmic analyses of all of Mozart's piano concerti, the rhythm of Gregorian chant, Indian rhythm; analyses of Debussy, Webern, and Stravinsky, and of Messiaen's own works (from the original sketches to the final score)."[13] In Gregorian chant he encountered a notation implying intuitive timing rather than a beat, and inflection groups functioning as syllabic units, both of which emerge in the graphics of *Zyklus* and *Kontakte* (having picked up a hint or two of Paul Klee along the way). Messiaen's "magic syllables" of *Harawi* foreshadow Stockhausen's "magic names" of *Stimmung*; the isorhythms and duration-scale canons of *Cantéyodjayâ* reappear in *Kontra-Punkte*. Goeyvaerts had introduced Stockhausen to the transformation of a row by interversion, and the latter had put it to use in *Kreuzspiel*, but Messiaen's analysis of "Reprises par Interversion," the first piece of the *Livre d'Orgue*, introduced a further twist. This work is built around three "personnages rythmiques," *pratâpacekhara, gajajhampa*, and *sârasa*, which are rotated in the first statement of "Reprises" in the order:

1 2 3	1 3 2	2 3 1	2 1 3	3 2 1	3 1 2
P G S	P S G	G S P	G P S	S G P	S P G

The number three is one of Messiaen's symbolic numbers (five and seven are also important to him, as they become to Stockhausen). Here the three characters imply a triplet of relationships, each element of which evolves in a different way. With every repetition, the note-values of *pratâpacekhara* increase in duration by a constant value, while those of *gajajhampa* decrease in duration by a constant value, and *sârasa* remains the same.

To Stockhausen, the three characters symbolized the family: father, mother, and child: —both the Holy family, and also an image, eventually to surface in *Donnerstag aus LICHT*, of himself and his parents, a human group transformed by circumstance into a bitter parody of what a family should be. The symbolism of an active element that increases, a passive element that diminishes, and a neutral element that remains unchanged, would also come to light in "Oben und Unten," a piece of intuitive theater from *Aus den Sieben Tagen* in which "The Man" is aggressive, "The Woman" passive, and "The Child" an innocent bystander (a symbolism equally applicable to the characters of Wozzeck, Marie, and their child in Berg's opera, though in the latter case it is the wife Marie who is the active, and Wozzeck the passive victim).

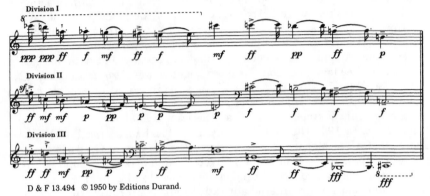

D & F 13.494 © 1950 by Editions Durand.

Messiaen's Mode de Valeurs et d'intensités*: the three modes*

Messiaen's method of augmentation and diminution by added or subtracted duration values changes the internal ratios of the unit rhythm and therefore its conventional rhythmic identity; in an expansion process differences of duration tend to level out, while in a contraction the tendency is for the differences to become more exaggerated, eventually to a point where the shortest are threatened with elimination. For example, in the sequence 7 : 3, 6 : 2, 5 : 1, the next step would be 4 : 0. *Plus-Minus*, Stockhausen's composition game of 1963 that allows for certain elements to be eliminated altogether, resembles the earlier aspect of Messiaen's concept of nonlinear growth. Messiaen's signal challenge to the younger generation of Boulez and Stockhausen (we may take it to be so as Messiaen never attempted anything quite like it afterward) is *Mode de valeurs et d'intensités* for piano. This was the leap into the future that inspired Boulez, after the crisis of *Polyphonie X*, to produce *Structures Ia*, the first piece, and by far the most visceral in impact, from that series.

> There was a very special moment at this time when Messiaen's students —Boulez, Barraqué, Michel Fano, Yvonne Loriod and Yvette Grimaux —persuaded him to synthesize the different influences that he had already incorporated in his own work; influences from the Viennese school, because they were more interested in them than in their own tradition of Debussy and Ravel, and the techniques of Indian *raga* and *tala* that Messiaen had learned from Indian music. . . . This was terribly exciting, to discover that there was music which I couldn't make sense of. Webern's two-note formulae were reduced even further, extending the idea of a melody of tone-colors, represented by different instruments, or vowels, to one of giving each note a different duration, a different dynamic, a different pitch, a different form of attack.[14]

In claiming this music for themselves as a point of departure, the younger generation (and their observers) diverted attention away from its radical significance in Messiaen's own terms. To describe *Mode de valeurs* as "not truly serial," for example, is to say in effect that Messiaen's theory is incomplete or insufficient, and that as an exposition of theory the piece is not fully worked out. Both criticisms may be true, but for them to make sense involves an assumption that what Messiaen was trying to achieve in the work was what his students wanted him to achieve. In reality *Mode de valeurs* is much more interesting as an extension or break with the composer's previous music, than as the precursor of a then still hypothetical serialism. To begin with, *Mode de valeurs*, this work of a master rhythmician, is the *antithesis* of rhythm, even in Messiaen's restricted sense of the term. That says something about the logic of reducing the language of music to single notes. It is also a music *without form*.

> In 1944, at the end of the year, I showed the students in my harmony classes *Pierrot Lunaire* by Schoenberg and the *Lyric Suite* by Berg (at that time, alas, the works of Webern were unobtainable). A propos these two works, of which only the second is serial, and then only for brief moments, I remember getting to my feet, and, raising my voice, denouncing the unilateral tendency that possessed these musicians to prospect only in the domain of pitch. Even then I used the terms "series of timbres," "series of intensities," and above all "series of durations" which as a rhythmician was closest to my heart. . . . At the time of *Mode de valeurs*, I had the idea of a series of attacks, to which Boulez added series of tempi and series of "complexes sonores," no doubt prompted by his contact with Pierre Schaeffer and musique concrète.[15]

"There is no trace of sectional form, which is so characteristic of Messiaen's other work," comments Robert Sherlaw Johnson.[16] But if there is neither any trace of form, nor any rhythm, to what then does the music compare? A Lisztian fantasy? A vastly accelerated unmeasured prelude by Couperin? The "form" of the work in this case is Messiaen's determination of the musical "language" itself: a music defined in accordance with de Saussure's conception of *la langue* but incorporating Messiaen's own values relating to the physical components of gesture and emphasis. Just as the semiotician's theory of language is of a catalogue of terms, ideograms, or letters comprising an alphabet, that can be arranged in an infinity of different orders to convey information, so Messiaen defines a catalogue of musical terms or ideograms that renders each note as a "syllabic unit" in the terms of Abbé Rousselot's and Stetson's motor phonetics; that is, as particles of a musical speech in which not only the triplet *anacrouse–accent–désinence* but *all other* components of the physical gesture are inseparably combined.

This is radical thinking beyond the comprehension of the younger generation. The distinctive and consistent texture of this new language is calculated, like morse code *and* twelve-tone music, to prevent alien meanings from being generated spontaneously (repetitive rhythms in the case of morse code, octaves in twelve-tone music). Since the original mode, in three registers, each consisting of twelve "phonemes," provides the entire content of the work, one to be read like an inscription in ancient Sumerian, and the few rests to be found are not part of the language, but gaps in the inscription, the only way of ensuring that unwanted harmonies or rhythms do not arise is by juggling the sequence, as the scribes of the cunieform inscription on the Rosetta Stone were wont to do, rearranging the ideograms for purely aesthetic effect.

By a strange coincidence, or effect of the *zeitgeist*, the musical language of *Mode de valeurs* also has elements in common with John Cage's prepared piano, which made its first appearance in Paris in 1949. Cage's point of departure was not notation but the piano itself. Whatever may have been Cage's practical motive for reinventing the piano as an exotic percussion orchestra, the effect of introducing foreign materials between the strings is to transform an instrument designed and regulated to represent pitch as a continuum, for uniformity of tone and touch, and for unrivaled ease of movement from one domain of pitch to another, into a different instrument that no longer exhibits any of these consistencies. The tone of a prepared piano varies from note to note, from pitched to unpitched, and from clangorous to clipped, dull, or muted. A performer has *less* control of touch than with a normal piano, and even less control of dynamics, since the vibration is damped to a greater or lesser degree by the foreign materials wedged between the strings. Lacking uniformity and consistency of timbre, pitch, and touch, the prepared piano is a keyboard rendered defiantly unsuitable for a Western music founded on those principles (not forgetting that these same values of uniformity and consistency, as McLuhan reminds us, underpin the whole of Western civilization as well). Following a completely different rationale, therefore, Cage has come up with a music in which every note *has the potential* to assume completely different characteristics from every other note. (In practice, not every set of strings in a Cage prepared piano is interfered with, so giving the instrument a mixed palette of timbres that includes regular tones.)

Stockhausen was already dealing with the prepared piano as a source vibration for musique concrète, and it appears heavily disguised as the source timbre of his *Konkrete Etüde* later in the year. He firmly rejects any suggestion of any influence of the prepared piano, for example on *Mantra*, but while Cage's procedure is clearly mechanical, and Stockhausen's electronic, as processes sharing the same goal of transforming piano tone from a uniform continuum into a disparate collection of metallic percussion sounds, it requires no leap of faith for the listener to conclude that Cage's idea did have an effect.

Spiel für Orchester (Game for Orchestra)

1952, revised 1973: No. ¼ (UE 15915; cd Stockhausen-Verlag SV-2)
1. "Paris 11. III. 52."
2. "Paris 4. V. 52."
Two movements for orchestra: 3 oboes, 3 clarinets in a, 3 bassoons, contrabassoon, 3

horns; glockenspiel, vibraphone, celesta, electric organ, piano; strings 6.6.0.3.3.
Two groups of percussion (1973 revision) (7 players):
Spiel I: ① small Indian bell, small triangle; ② 2 susp. cymbals (high and low), ③ 2 suspended cymbals; ④ hi-hat; ⑤ African pod rattle, small snare drum; ⑥ ratchet (e.g. washboard), 2 antique cymbals; ⑦ 2 tam-tams, pedal timpano.
Spiel II: ① 5 cinelli (tuned small cymbals); ② 2 suspended cymbals; ③ 2 suspended cymbals; ④ hi-hat; ⑤ large sizzle-cymbal, ⑥ 3 tom-toms, ⑦ pedal timpano.
Duration: 16'.

Spiel was originally planned as second and third movements of a three-movement work, with *Formel*, but having completed all three, Stockhausen became dissatisfied with what he felt to be the imbalance of a thematic orientated opening followed by two pieces of a more pointillistic tendency and on a larger scale. The three pieces form a set nevertheless, each being a formulation of a relationship of a central instrument embodying light and brilliance, and the orchestra which seems to circulate around it like a planetary system and draw energy from it. In *Formel* and *Spiel I* this radiant sonority is represented by the vibraphone and glockenspiel, timbres that glisten rather than glow hot; in *Spiel II* Stockhausen introduces a real crystal goblet with the idea of producing a stronger and more lasting ringing tone at the work's climax. It is interesting once again to recognize the composer's attachment to imagery of generated and reflected light at this early stage in his career.

Both pieces display a greater sense of physical energy and texture after the relative coolness of *Kreuzspiel*; even *Formel* is more lyrical, despite the extreme registers. In his layout of the orchestra Stockhausen follows *Kreuzspiel* in locating the bass instruments to the bass register side of the piano, and the higher instruments to the treble. The arrangement is once again reminiscent of baroque music, and Stockhausen's primary purpose seems to be for the orchestra to be perceived as fractionated timbres of an extended keyboard.

This is Stockhausen's first unambiguously pointillistic work. Like Messiaen's *Mode de valeurs*, it can be appreciated and studied as a test case for serial practice, with the difference that Messiaen's modes are designed for the piano, and the series of *Spiel* for a much larger and less homogeneous ensemble. A piano is a chamber instrument and also an acoustic environment defined as a uniform pitch-space, within which the performer at the keyboard can control a range of dynamic and other distinctions considerably greater than can be heard in a concert hall. An orchestra by contrast is a "broken consort:" a collection of timbres defining a nonuniform pitch domain, and occupying rather than defining a much larger acoustic enclosure. In writing for orchestra the composer may be faced with a challenge of creating the perception of a uniform pitch-space. For Webern (as for Kandinsky) line, color, and space were interrelated but to reveal that to an observer took enormous skill and sensitivity to timbre and dynamics. Prior to *Inori*, the most celebrated orchestral definition of a uniform dynamic space is probably Ravel's *Bolero*, an extraordinary feat of intuitive balance engineering with live instruments, dating from the first

years of radio broadcasting. Goeyvaerts, who was in constant communication with Stockhausen, warned him about the futility of trying to realize
purely formal relationships by such acoustically impure means. The young
Belgian was even more vehemently opposed to the use of unpitched percussion of any kind; despite the advocacy of Varèse and Messiaen (most
recently in *Turangalîla*), "noise instruments," as they were called, were still
regarded with suspicion in orthodox musical circles as late as 1952, and
with disfavor by other serialists, whose theories did not allow for sounds of
imprecise pitch. So *Spiel* is already interesting, not only as a statement of
serial principles, but as a statement of defiance.

1	2	3	4	5	6	7	8	9	10	11	12
									sf	sf	

Messiaen's Mode de valeurs: *the mode of attacks*

Messiaen's mode of attacks for *Mode de valeurs* is a rough and ready
affair, even in terms of the piano, though it is worth noting how carefully he
distributes dynamics and attacks through the three pitch and duration
registers in the layering of the three modes. Stockhausen expended an
enormous effort in selecting percussion instruments to improve on Messiaen's mode of attacks (so many revisions, in fact, that even today they are
not specified in the publisher's catalogue). His attention to attacks is
telling, given that Stockhausen makes no other change to *Formel's* textbook orchestra of 4 × 3 winds, 4 × 3 keyboard registers, and 4 × 3 strings
(—and with the same hole in the middle, too: no violas). In *Kreuzspiel* the
ultimate function of the "complementary zone" percussion is limited to
imitating the sound of the piano action and the hissed intake of breath of
the wind instruments; for *Spiel I* Stockhausen reverts to an earlier plan to
create a vocabulary of attack possibilities based on spoken consonants.
From the the 1952 manuscript of *Spiel I* the percussion listed consists of 6
unpitched metal resonators, one for each of the six octave registers
(triangle, 2 suspended cymbals, hi-hat, 1 cinelli, gong); and 4 × 3 ancillary
groups: pitched metal, wood "click," wood and drum "trill," and low drums,
each of the latter centered in a defined register. For *Spiel II* in 1952 this
formidable array of attack instruments is reduced to the glistening sounds
of eleven cymbals (the glass making twelve), and four low drums (with the
addition of an extra tom-tom).

Stockhausen was already at work on the *Konkrete Etüde*, a composition
in which the attack parameter is absent, and while his project to measure
attack and decay envelopes of recordings of ethnic percussion instruments
in the collection of the Musée de l'Homme did not officially begin until after
the premiere of *Spiel*, it is clear that percussion instruments were high on
the composer's agenda at this time. Meanwhile in Cologne, Herbert Eimert
and Werner Meyer-Eppler were in animated discussion about the vocoder
donated to Bonn University by Bell Labs for research, and its musical
possibilities. In addition to its intended functions of speech analysis and

synthesis, the vocoder was regarded by all involved as an instrument of exciting potential for electronic music.

The combination of a more pointillistic texture and added percussion puts *Spiel* already some distance ahead of *Formel*. Stockhausen has clearly taken on board some of Messiaen's ideas about "attack" and "resonance," and organization of register and dynamics, from *Mode de valeurs*. Sometimes the transference of ideas from piano to orchestra does not quite work out, for example, serial dynamics (which the composer has conceded), and also the serial organization of register. According equal status to every octave division of the keyboard has the effect of spreading the normal bell-curve of activity within a composition from the center to the margins. *Spiel* seems to spend a lot of time at the extremes of pitch; this is unobjectionable in itself, except that the human ear being what it is, pitch is not as clearly discernible at the outer edges of perception as in the mid-range; added to which, when instruments are asked to play at extremes of their range *and* at dynamic extremes, unwanted noise and distortion begin to have an effect on the purity of the sound.

Dynamics are another issue, both as a parameter for serial organization, and in particular compositions. Hiding behind an outwardly gentle disposition Messiaen was a ferocious pianist, and an echo of the strenuous quality of his pianism can be detected in *Spiel* as well. *Spiel* gives the impression of lacking a middle dimension of loudness between the random gunfire of fortissimo attacks and the almost inaudible ringing of pianissimo sustain. Messiaen himself used to distinguish between composers such as Berlioz, whose dynamics are relative to the overall balance, and others, like Debussy, whose dynamics are specific to the individual instrument. In cases where dynamics are subject to serial manipulation a further layer of complication arises, which has to do with maintaining the integrity of the series itself.

Where the issue is speech-related, as in the relationship of attack consonants to vowels, notated dynamics have very little to contribute, because of the ear's greater sensitivity in the frequency range of consonantal and percussive noises. One has only to listen to a choral work recorded in a cathedral to become aware that it is the vowels that carry the melody and generate a lingering reverberation, while the consonants sound just as loud as the vowels, but do not sustain at all. It is only because human ears are especially sensitive to higher frequencies that consonants appear to be on the same loudness level as the vowels, even though the latter require considerably more energy to make them audible. What that suggests in the instrumental domain is that dynamic indications for percussion are largely superfluous. Elsewhere, in writing for nonpercussion instruments, Stockhausen strives toward a *Gleichberechtigkeit* or equivalence of energy distribution relating to the duration of a note, an interesting idea in which the longest durations are the most pianissimo, and the shortest, the loudest.

There is not a single book that talks about the *relative* dynamics of

instruments, and this is the most important aspect of orchestration. I
have never yet seen a book which explains why, in a certain score, one
instrument can play *piano* and be in balance with another instrument
playing *forte* at the same time.[17]

Series IV of Spiel, *showing a mode-like relationship
of duration to dynamics and attack*

Spiel 1, of 100 measures, completed in March, depicts a gradual accretion of
melodic chains from atomistic "points." The tempo is a brisk 12/8 (again) at
MM 96, later altered to 120. It is a music of high contrasts between the
brilliant flashes of percussion and the muted glow of the sustaining instruments: a nocturne with exploding shells. Out of a hovering background of
sustained strings and ringing keyboards, one by one the wind instruments
appear as if picked out by the searchlight of the vibraphone. A rising inflection in the opening measure recalls a similar gesture in *Formel*, but here
the dynamic range *ppp–ff* is more extreme. In fact extreme dynamics prove
to be the rule, with the vibraphone struggling to reach *sfff* from the very
start. Periodic repeating sixths on d sharp/ b enter very quietly from measure 2 at both extremes of range (an interesting interval, close to the Golden
Mean ratio) and continue to the end. The middle ground is occupied by
percussion alternating sharp attacks and *ppp* ringing or tremolo resonances. High and low pairs predominate. A suggestion of a theme from the
oboe at 21, in unison with the vibraphone, is taken up by violins at 31;
gradually more links are added to the chain until at measure 42 the vibraphone articulates a complete series *minus* the b natural, which continues to
ring on celesta and piano. At 40 strings sustain high and low pitches, and at
49 the vibraphone begins a statement of the series in two-note groups,
provoking a full entry of percussion in their different periodicities. At 56 the
vibraphone theme is more "pointed" and sharp *fff* pitches on strings and
woodwinds begin a process that leads to gradually more sustained pitches
collecting in the mid-range, restoring an uneasy calm.

Completed two months later, *Spiel II* of 114 measures is visibly a leap
ahead technically. In 4/2, with a given tempo of MM 48 (altered in performance to MM 40), this movement begins quietly with sustained *ppp* pitched
and unpitched percussion in three parts at extremes of high and low
register, a resonant background out of which point and group formations
condense and are transferred to wind and strings. The distribution of
elements within the pitch space reaches a maximum at measure 56, the
midpoint in the original score, where the clear crystalline tone of the glass
was originally due to ring out, a moment of climax after which the music

would decline to a calm ending. For the premiere performance under Hans Rosbaud the valuable crystal goblet donated for the purpose was struck rather too vigorously with a metal beater, and shattered. That the premiere ended in confusion at this point is a story that has passed into myth; according to Stockhausen, he and Rosbaud had already decided to curtail the performance there, though it had not been their intention to mark the conditional ending in so unexpected a fashion.

In a perceptive if generally sceptical review betraying no hint of irony (bearing in mind the contemporary fashion for "jungle music" in Hollywood at the time) the Belgian critic R.-A. Mooser observed "Thirty or so traditional instruments . . . provide a resonant background, sometimes scarcely audible, upon which the percussive elements in turn project their particular vibrations, at irregular intervals and in very free rhythmic patterns. . . . One is forcibly reminded of the primitive orchestras dreamed up by the inhabitants of darkest Africa."[18] It is certainly interesting to find Stockhausen employing the sustained resonances associated with his much later work at this early stage. In this connection, some of his own comments of the period are relevant, among them "Pre-formed material cannot be organized, only arranged,"[19] and

> The inherent instantaneity of through-organized music, the fact that it does not "develop," can only induce a state of meditative listening. Attention becomes fixed in the music, having no need to consider what goes before or what follows, in order to perceive the actual, present event (the individual sound). Certainly it is assumed that the individual event is already complete in itself, satisfying at once all the order-criteria specific to the whole work—thus, absolute and incontrovertible.[20]

Debussy reportedly said of Liszt's *Mazeppa* "This symphonic poem is full of the worst faults, and yet the tumultuous passion which never ceases to agitate it ends by gripping you with such force that you find yourself liking it and make no effort to explain to yourself why."[21] There is a power and a strength to *Spiel* despite the imbalances, a serenity behind all the detonations, an emotion: part battleground, part fireworks display, of an eerie calm that surfaces again literally in *Dienstag aus LICHT* with its perpetual drone of waves of bombers passing overhead and the fearful uncertainty of where the next explosion will fall. With that image in mind the emptiness in the center begins to make its own sense, and one has to agree with the composer that a strongly musical conception will always work if it has integrity, even if how it works is not always as originally intended. *Spiel's* spiritual antecedents include Varèse, Bartók's *Music for strings, percussion and celesta* (the Adagio: the glissando on timpani a small souvenir), and Messiaen's *Turangalîla-Symphonie* (the battle-scene of VII). More recently, in 1993 Elliott Carter has composed a *Partita* for orchestra that uses a very similar gestural language to *Spiel* and even shares the same name (the word *partita* in Italian means "game"). Whether or not Carter intended his work as a compliment to a colleague younger by twenty years, it is interesting to compare the two, and the comparison reinforces a listener's admiration for both.

Schlagtrio (Percussive Trio)

1952, rescored 1973: No.⅓ (UE 15943; cd Stockhausen-Verlag SV-2)
For amplified piano (+ antique cymbal) and 2 × 3 timpani (1. + triangle; 2. + bongo).
"Paris, den 1. Juni 1952."
Original title: *Schlagquartett für Klavier und 3 × 2 Pauken.*
Duration: 16' at MM 90.

The stasis or absence of movement, meditative or otherwise, that affects pointillistic music at this time and, judging by his remarks above, both puzzles and bothers Stockhausen, is inherent in the conception of a musical language organized on the basis of a closed system or alphabet of signs. De Saussure is very clear about this: a formal system, he says, is unable to account for its own evolution over time.

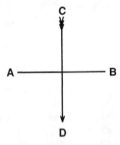

De Saussure's graph of axes of simultaneity (AB) and succession (CD)

Applied to speech, articulation designates either the subdivision of a spoken chain into syllables or the subdivision of the chain of meanings into significant units; *gegliederte Sprache* is used in the second sense in German. Using the second definition, we can say that what is natural to mankind is not oral speech but the faculty of constructing a language, i.e., a system of distinct signs corresponding to distinct ideas. . . . Everywhere distinctions should be made between (1) *the axis of simulta-neities* (AB), which stands for the relations of coexisting things and from which the intervention of time is excluded; and (2) *the axis of successions* (CD), on which only one thing can be considered at a time but upon which are located all the things on the first axis together with their changes. . . . The multiplicity of signs . . . makes it absolutely impossible to study simultaneously relations in time and relations within the system.[22]

Musicians understand simultaneity as the vertical axis and succession as the horizontal, but illustrating his lecture is a simple graph in which de Saussure paradoxically represents simultaneity as the horizontal axis and succession as the vertical (confirming, at the very least, his unfamiliarity with music notation). Issues of connectivity (syllables into words, words into sentences, sentences into a dynamic message) also operate at the smallest intervals where attack, steady state, and decay meet and combine. Stockhausen returns to these fundamental issues, and to his ongoing conception of music as a "third force" arising from the conjunction of positive and negative spaces, in terms of the much reduced instrumentation of piano and timpani, in the *Schlagquartett*, subsequently revised as *Schlagtrio,* a work in his own words, of "an unusually idealistic conception." Cocteau's image in *Orphée* of the mirror as Orpheus's gateway to the Underworld is an apt metaphor for this musical conception of reciprocal appearances. The significance of this outwardly austere study should not be underestimated. Time and again Stockhausen returns to the same opposition of real and virtual worlds, in *Kontakte* and *Mantra* most overtly, but in *Mixtur* and *Kurzwellen* too.

And not only Stockhausen: in *Différences* Berio juxtaposes live and not-live instruments, and Boulez, in *Répons, Anthèmes 2,* and other works for instruments and their digital transformations. Among the more recent is Boulez's *Sur Incises* (1998) for pianos, harps and keyboard percussion, a work in which, according to Wolfgang Fink, "the harps represent the piano's strings, the bells, vibraphone, and marimba its sound-board," while the role of "negative sound-space" is (somewhat incongruously) assigned to steel drums,—a role precisely analogous to that of the timpani in *Schlagtrio.* In his cd notes Boulez refers rather disingenuously to Stravinsky's *Les Noces* as a source of inspiration, but on the evidence of the music, this is a work that continues a conversation that had begun among Pierre Schaeffer and his coworkers in musique concrète, a conversation in which Stockhausen too would have had a say.

For the rest of us the issue of positive and negative, real and virtual acoustic spaces is less about aesthetics or philosophy than hard reality; it comes down to a perception of tone coloration (resonance, reverberation) as a variable distinct from the timbre of the instrument, a discovery underscored by studies in the early fifties of the effects of transmitting music from an anechoic (acoustically dead) studio. Three commonplace areas of tone coloration are:

1. Room response (also wood and air tones of piano, guitar etc.);
2. Microphone and speaker coloration; and
3. Added reverberation.

Passive reflection or reverberation is the shadowy reality that accompanies every sound processed in real space. Musicians understand and adjust their playing to a performance acoustic, and balance engineers are trained to manipulate local and ensemble timbre by their choice and positioning of microphones. The listener at home also influences the quality of reproduced sound both in the choice and positioning of hi-fi equipment and in the levels to which they are set. It is a fact of life that coloration, the invisible presence, requires music or sound as a precondition of being noticed; and for most people, —and particularly the blind, —a dynamic of constant involuntary adjustment to differences in acoustic space develops an awareness of reverberation as a distinct variable, an effect by definition controllable and thus potentially musical.

Schlagtrio is music for a piano, in the revised version an amplified piano, playing a role similar to the piano in *Kreuzspiel*. In attendance are a group of six tuned timpani, a uniform timbre substituting for the various

Piano	Timpani
V secco, staccatissimo, no pedal	V with 1 (felt) stick; simultaneously dampened with the other hand
. staccato + ½ pedal, ⌒ [sustaining]	. with 1 stick; at the edge
▼ as · but stressed: ‾	▼ with 1 stick; in the middle (mid-way between skin edge and center)
⁔ ℘₀ •Vₛ ⁕staccato + pedal: released almost at once	⁔ with 2 sticks: at the edge
— portato senza pedal	— 1 stick at edge, 1 at the center simultaneously
∩ attack senza pedal, release with pedal	∩ with 2 sticks; in the middle (mid-way between edge and center)
⌒•᙭— precede with pedal, staccatissimo attack, pedal resonance	⌒ with 2 sticks in the middle, then tremolo *pppp* until next note
ℙ "normal": "as far as possible, without sustaining pedal."	ℙ with wooden part of stick, or hard felt

Original attack series for Schlagquartett

unpitched percussion of the earlier work. The timpani are tuned to quarter-tone pitches in an attempt to locate them outside the pitch regime of the piano. They correspond to six "reverberant spaces" or virtual echo chambers selectively set in vibration by a variety of carefully defined piano attacks (a rationale looking ahead to the solo tam-tam of *Mikrophonie I*). The timpani here are clearly *passive* resonators of fixed tuning, so their behavior acoustically resembles six resonating chambers. That passivity also connects them with loudspeakers, which are also circular, vibrating surfaces.

Though couched in esoteric terms, Stockhausen's description of the work, reproduced *in extenso* in *Texte 2*, describes it as a process in which the two sound-worlds, one clear and precise, the other shadowy, approach from different directions, make contact, eventually overlap, then withdraw (one thinks of the truce meetings between the North Korean and US forces that began in the no-man's land of the demilitarized zone in 1951).[23] Like *Kreuzspiel*, the zone of contact generates a new musical entity (a twelve-tone melody). Unlike *Kreuzspiel*, the contact is between the piano and percussion (in the earlier work the "two approaching entities" were both represented in the piano part). What Stockhausen is clearly trying to achieve is a reconciliation of extreme and median values; also of interest is his modification of series durations to incorporate degrees of silence, or rests.

The work is a considerable challenge to the interpreter, but productive all the same. The revised score is less intimidating and beautiful to look at, but the real attraction lies under the surface: how to realize the interplay Stockhausen has in mind. Yet again the answer seems to lie in maximum discretion and "close-microphone" technique; timpani coperti for a quieter tone, and smaller "Mozart" sticks for sharper accentuation. The register and precise pitch of timpani raise a number of issues of principle: in their role as instruments "of the center" (imitating the role of the vibraphone in *Spiel*, but passive rather than active), they seem rather low in pitch, and perhaps too close in pitch to be perceived as alternates to the octave registers of the piano. The counter-objection might be that Stockhausen needed large and deep resonators to simulate actual spaces, in which case a set of "gong" drums might be the answer: wonderfully deep and ringing bass drums, a sound heard to great effect in Messiaen's *Turangalîla-Symphonie* and in Bartók's *Sonata for two pianos and percussion*.

Notes

1. Peter Medawar, "An Essay on Scians;" *The Limits of Science* (Oxford: Oxford University Press, 1984), 8.
2. Peter Medawar, *The Limits of Science*, 7.
3. Darius Milhaud, *Notes without Music* tr. Donald Evans (London: Calder and Boyars, 1952).
4. Darius Milhaud, *Notes without Music*, 68–69.
5. "To Alexander Zemlinsky. Mödling, 26 October 1922." Arnold Schoenberg, *Letters*, 79–80.
6. Referring to the *Îles de Feu 1* and *2*. Michael Kurtz, *Stockhausen, A Biography*, 47.
7. Wassily Kandinsky, *Point and Line to Plane* tr. Howard Dearstyle and Hilla Rebay (Reprint. New York: Dover Publications, 1979), 98.
8. (Herbert) Marshall McLuhan, *The Gutenberg Galaxy: The Making of Typographic Man* (London: Routledge & Kegan Paul, 1962), 277.
9. Pierre Boulez, *Rélévés d'Apprenti* (Paris: du Seuil, 1966), 68.
10. *Debussy on Music* ed. François Lesure, tr. Richard Langham Smith (London: Secker and Warburg, 1977), 297.
11. Sergei Eisenstein, *The Film Sense* tr. Jay Leyda (London: Faber and Faber, 1948), 23.
12. R. H. Stetson, *R.H.Stetson's Motor Phonetics: A Retrospective Edition* ed. J. A. S. Kelso and K. G. Munhall (Boston: College Hill Press, 1988), 155.
13. *Texte 2*, 144.
14. *SoM*, 34–35.
15. Antoine Goléa, *Rencontres avec Olivier Messiaen* (Paris: Julliard, 1961), 247–48.
16. Robert Sherlaw Johnson, *Messiaen* (Berkeley and Los Angeles: University of California Press, 1988), 105–108.
17. *SoM*, 167.
18. R.-A. Mooser, *Panorama de la Musique Contemporaine* (Geneva: René Kister, 1955).
19. "Situation des Handwerks," Paris, 1952. *Texte 1*, 19, 21.
20. *Texte 1*, 21.
21. Léon Vallas, *The Theories of Claude Debussy, musicien français* tr. Maire O'Brien (London: Oxford University Press, 1929), 144.
22. "On 'Static and Evolutionary Linguistics.'" Ferdinand de Saussure, *Course in General Linguistics*, 10, 80–81. The term *gegliederte Sprache* is interesting. Stockhausen also refers to the structural elements of his compositions as *Glieder* or "limbs."
23. *Texte 2*, 13–18.

CHAPTER FIVE

Music on Tape

Stockhausen is a child of radio, just as Debussy is a child of the cinema and Webern a child of the phonograph. Twentieth-century music is a confusion, though not (as some claim) a chaos, of competing media conventions; deciding which set of conventions applies to a particular composer or work, and how coherently, is the task of aesthetics. His studies with Messiaen brought Stockhausen face to face with the major issues and associated contradictions of analytical serialism, which are essentially issues of *l'écriture*: the idea that notation corresponds to a musical language, and that notational differences correspond to real differences in language function. To give serialism its due, it is a rational way of coming to terms with what notation actually stands for. Only by testing the system to breaking point is one able to discover its practical limits.

There was a wider, if clandestine, interest among the intelligence community in understanding the structure of music, which was considered a system of communication having language-like properties, if not a language in the ordinary sense. The outcome of such research is to be heard in the artificial voice of Professor Hawking, "intelligent" airline telephone booking, voicemail, and similar applications that take messages and answer back. In 1952, however, voice recognition matters had more to do with national security than domestic travel. This involvement of music in affairs of security was not a sudden or new development. The music industry had long been associated with innovation in defense technology, not all of which was for propaganda purposes. Alan Blumlein's pioneering researches into stereophonic recording for EMI in the thirties were intimately related to the development of radar, a vital line of British defense against air attack during the war. During the cold war of the fifties, an important part of national defense was related to intelligence gathering, the encryption and decryption of coded messages, and for that a comprehensive theory of language was essential (in fact it was never found). Part of the fascination of serial music has to do with the mysterious art of codes and ciphers, which are essentially alphanumeric systems, that played so powerful a role in two world wars and led to the development of the computers of today. On the technological side, in matters to do with the dynamics of signal transmission and detection, other musical factors came into play.

Radio was a new renaissance fusion of technology and culture. Nineteenth-century science had revealed the mysterious nature of electricity; in the late nineteenth and early twentieth centuries engineers developed new forms of communication by wire and, strangest of all, without wire. The arrival of radio as a public medium of communication during the twenties provoked poets and artists, in the spoken word, in music, and drama, to invent new forms of discourse that in the absence of any visual element or text, were bound to rely entirely on aural modalities, requiring both a new intensity of listening and a renewal of oral conventions of representing the processes of human thought. The medium attracted visionaries. A. R. Burrows's *Story of Broadcasting*, an introduction to radio for BBC listeners published in 1924, the Company's first year of operation as a public service, contains some wonderful lines:

> Man, with his limited number of senses, lives this present life somewhere between the infinitely great and the infinitely small. His senses reveal to him only certain things essential for his early wants and safety. They are blind to many things now proven to exist and probably to countless other things of which we are still completely ignorant. . . . The science of wireless—and broadcasting—deal with media, agencies, and intervals of space and time which are outside our powers of appreciation, yet have been proved to exist. . . . All matter, however dense and substantial, consists of charges of electricity in rapid motion. Motion, in one form or another, seems to be one of the governing factors of existence. The spinning of a world around its orbit, or its regular course around another large body, gives to that world its seasons and the periods of light and darkness. In the life of man there is a growth of mentality followed by decay.[1]

The modern science of musical communication could be said to have begun with Hermann Helmholtz, whose classic *On the Sensations of Tone*, first published in 1862, remains in print; the English edition, translated and heavily annotated with lists of exotic modes and scales by Alexander J. Ellis, provided a foundation for theories of composers as different as Hindemith and Harry Partch.[2] Helmholtz's own experiments in pitch relations, using sirens of various kinds, helped inspire Varèse's adoption of these instruments and indirectly provided a tone-generation methodology for Stockhausen's *Kontakte*. Typical of the science of the era is R. H. Stetson's Ph.D. paper "Piano Tone-Color from a Physical and Psychological Standpoint" dating from 1897, an inquiry into the fundamental elements of musical expression in terms of the piano, which came to the stark conclusion that everything a musician or listener might understand as a technique or mode of expression could be expressed as a relationship of just two measurable quantities: the force with which a key is struck, and the timing of the action of striking a key. Research of this kind led to the development after 1900 of the reproducing piano, an improved paper-roll technology able to capture every nuance of a virtuoso performance. The fact that the new technology *worked* amounted to compelling evidence that (for piano music at least) the infinite nuances and complexities of traditional notation were in reality, just *Augenmusik*: conventions of writing, with no acoustically perceptual basis.

Stetson comes to mind because in a key paper, ". . . wie die Zeit vergeht . . ." (How time flies), published some sixty years later, we discover Stockhausen still ruminating over the paradox that different notations may lead to the same results, signifying that the elaborate system of visual categories on which serialist thinking is based, may after all be meaningless. "In some recent scores (he writes) the notation of duration-relationships has become extremely differentiated. The result has been that as rhythmic-metric complexity has increased, the degree of precision in playing has correspondingly decreased. . . . One and the same value can be notated in quite different ways."[3] Stockhausen goes on to give alternative notations of a half-note followed by a quarter-note. So much is clear, but in raising the matter the composer is making two very interesting points: first, in admitting to an aesthetic of complexity, since as he says, a simpler notation may be possible, but not desired; second, the rather more critical point that notation is not necessarily made more efficient or more precise by adding extra expression marks, if we measure the test of an efficient notation in the properties of the actual performance. These issues of definition are self-evident to musicians, less so to cognitive scientists, and in this case it was probably the latter group, Werner Meyer-Eppler among them, who needed to know.

A relatively trivial example, taken out of chronological sequence, it does nevertheless illustrate the fundamental difference in approach to musical essentials that has already been aired in terms of the wider debate between semiotics and motor phonetics, a debate in which for the time being the followers of de Saussure were temporarily in the ascendancy. Serialism in the fifties conformed to the alphanumeric approach of semiotics, whereas Pierre Schaeffer's musique concrète defended the alternative, behaviorist approach of motor phonetics. What Schaeffer was looking for was a theory to account for sounds as they are heard and manipulated through recording and reproduction technology. Over the years Schaeffer has received rather a bad press, both musically and intellectually. His early pieces, many of which were collaborative efforts, and in some of which Pierre Boulez and Pierre Henry took part, sadly never reached a very high level of musical or technical quality, and Schaeffer's theoretical writings, despite technical assistance, tend to remain querulous in tone, as well as being difficult for the lay reader to follow. His approach is summed up in the term "l'objet musical" (musical object); a name that is also the title of a significant essay by Schaeffer published in 1952, in a special edition of *La Revue Musicale* dedicated to twentieth-century music.[4] It appears alongside the rather more celebrated polemic "...éventuellement..." (contingencies) by Pierre Boulez, its title a specimen of French wordplay hinting at the disclosure of secret information.[5]

The political context of this special edition, and the International Exposition of the Arts that provided for its publication, deserve closer scrutiny. An extraordinarily sumptuous affair, the Exposition included a series of concerts running from 30 April to 1 June 1952,—among which evenings of *Wozzeck* under Karl Böhm, a double bill of Schoenberg's *Erwartung* and Stravinsky's *Oedipus Rex* under Rosbaud, Virgil Thomson's *Four Saints in Three Acts* (to texts by Gertrude Stein), and two evenings of George Balanchine's New York City Ballet, were only some of the highlights. The Exposition and special edition of *La Revue Musicale* were underwritten by a mysterious organization styled the *Congrès pour la Liberté de la Culture*, funded by the CIA, whose spokesperson and guest editor were none other than Nicolas Nabokov.[6]

> If the music of this century is what it is, in sum, so extraordinarily lively, so unusually rich in success, so full of promise, much as that is due to the talent or genius of the musicians, as much is also due to the spirit of liberty which has in a number of different ways watched over its destinies. Freedom to experiment, freedom of expression, freedom to choose whom to follow and what harmonic practice (*liberté de choisir ses maîtres et ses accords*), to choose irony or naïveté, to be esoteric or popular. The scores to be heard during this forthcoming Exposition, almost without exception, draw their qualities, their very soul, from the fact of being the music and art of people who know the value of this freedom.[7]

The Statue of Liberty, one recalls, was France's tribute to the United States in a previous century. The light of Liberty's torch was certainly shining for young artists living in free Paris in 1952.

Pierre Schaeffer came to music from radio drama, for many years the most imaginative sector of broadcasting. Radio's inventive applications of technology were not limited to faking news reports from the front line; in Britain and the US from the early thirties the medium inspired a new dramatic art, and subsequently a new style of advertising, destined to have enormous impact on musical culture. The mixing techniques of musique concrète and electronic music in the radio era of the fifties, and of pop music in the television era, are descended from live techniques originally developed for radio drama between the wars. The very first mixing desk, the "Dramatic control panel" was designed and installed at the BBC in 1929 for the Head of Radio Drama, Val Gielgud; the echo or reverberation chamber was introduced in the same period, and the "grams" made their debut as precision disc turntables for adding background music and prerecorded sound effects (an art unexpectedly revived by disc jockeys in the digital era).

> The [BBC's] Drama Suite consisted of five Speech studios, an Effects studio, and a Gramophone studio. Of the Speech studios, two on each floor were of moderate size; one was 'dead,' giving the impression of a confined space; the other 'live,' with the properties of a normal acoustic.

In addition, there were two Echo rooms, by means of which 'artificial echo' could be added to the output from any individual studio. In the case of the radio play the producer remains directly involved and practically responsible until transmission is over. By the balance resulting from the the related movements of his control knobs, by the *tempo* achieved by the exact use of his key-switches, the radio producer controls his play during the actual time of performance.[8]

The superior sound quality of radio compared to disc and early optical (sound on film) recording meant that microphone techniques and the voice and music skills associated with them were a higher priority and therefore more rapidly acquired in radio broadcasting than in other media. Radio drama developed during the Depression years and reached a peak of popularity during the 1939–1945 war years. Stage actors new to radio drama had to acquire distinctive microphone skills that included a new and outwardly inexplicable choreography of movement and stillness in relation to the microphone, and above all a natural and unrhetorical tone and manner of speaking.

In dealing with recording devices limited to a single sense the artist is faced with the dilemma that realism *per se* is typically flawed, disorganized, and difficult to follow, and that to achieve the *effect* of realism a producer has to be selective, to edit, and to enhance. Such distinctions have corresponding aesthetic implications, as when one compares a photograph and a painting or sculpture based on the same photograph: the *Odalisque* of 1857 by Delacroix, for example.[9] For artists in musique concrète and electronic music, the same lesson had to be learned: that reality is a creation, and real life, in real time, just a rather messy rehearsal.

The French took radio drama to their heart as the perfect medium for a surrealist stream-of-consciousness poetic. Schaeffer came under the spell of Jacques Copeau, an innovative producer of radio plays whose wartime interpretation of André Breton's *Nadja Étoilée* pushed available techniques, including vari-speed, to the limits.[10] From the earliest days of the industry, gramophones were fitted with simple speed regulators to deal with the fact that record manufacturers were not agreed on a standard playback speed. In the mid-thirties, when the BBC began reluctantly to broadcast recorded material, the playwright George Bernard Shaw recorded a short speech on disc to remind the public of the virtues of listening to a recording at the correct speed. In it he tells of visiting a record shop where a speech by the British politician Ramsay MacDonald was being played, but at the wrong speed. It made MacDonald, whose voice was very widely recognized, sound sharp and irascible. Shaw "moved the screw that regulates the speed" until the familiar dulcet tone of his friend reappeared. The alteration in character of a voice or sound that arises from varying the playback speed became a valuable technique for radio drama, but the philosophical implications of "finding the right speed for the person" are quite profound. In effect, our perception of reality could be said to be conditioned by the speed at which we experience reality: a relativistic conceit recalled yet again in Viktor von Weizsäcker's observation that "things are not in time, but time is in things"

—and by extension, in the notion so central to Stockhausen of a music of variable timescales.

Bernard Shaw interpreted the change of speed of his friend's voice as a change of personality and identity; for the radio drama effects experts who operated the gramophones, the creation of realistic incidental noises also involved a great deal of experiment and intuition, in which vari-speeding, —altering the scale of a sound by making it sound higher or lower in pitch, and thus smaller or larger in size, —played a significant role. In the early days of electric recording many sounds from real life were impossible to capture on disc, and had to be simulated. For example, to recreate on radio the effect of W. B. Yeats's "lake waters lapping with low sounds by the shore" might call for the slow rotation of an inverted tambour de basque containing a quantity of lead shot: an instrument (the *géophone*) employed by Messiaen in the orchestra of *Des Canyons aux Étoiles*. The art of simulating natural sounds depended to a considerable degree on an understanding of differences of acoustic *scale*. When it proved impossible to record the churning of propellors of the liner *Queen Mary* leaving the quayside at Southampton on her record-breaking maiden voyage to New York, even after dangling microphones close to the surface of the water, effects artists after anxious trials in the studio contrived a realistic effect by recording on to disc the sound of a manual egg-beater whisking a bowl of water, and replaying the disc at a much slower speed. In art, for instance the surrealist art of Salvador Dalí, such distortions of scale are called anamorphism; for the artisans of sound, who do not enjoy such luxuries of terminology, the time-dilation of a musical object signifies a new art of audio perspective. Stockhausen learned from such effects, as much for their poetry as for their realism: we hear it in the gradual diminution of scale from boughs to sticks to twigs in the sound of breaking brushwood in *Herbstmusik*, and the transformation of clogs into hand-claps in *Der Jahreslauf*. The recording studio is a place of magical reality.

Schaeffer first conceived of an abstract art of sounds in 1948. His materials were disc recording equipment, recording on soft acetate, and a library of pre-recorded sounds. A French Radio broadcast of some early studies, including *Étude aux chemins de fer*, a rhythmic invention based on recorded steam train sounds, attracted the attention of Pierre Henry and other young composers, among them Boulez. The composition technique was essentially montage. Facilities for transforming sounds were primitive. With each new generation of copying a sound from one disc to another, the level of surface noise increased, so the montage process had to involve as few dubbings as possible. Using a disc-cutting lathe Schaeffer created the "sillon fermé" or closed groove on which a recorded sound could be heard as an endless loop; he also employed the vari-speed mechanism of the regular turntable to alter the character, pitch, and tempo of a prerecorded sound, and thus enlarge its musical resources.

Noises as material for music was not itself a new idea. As early as 1900 recordings of patriotic songs were being made to celebrate the departure of British troops to fight in the Boer War, with crowds cheering, train whistles, and ships' sirens in the background. During the 1914–1918 war, when many artists were on active service, the self-effacing Erik Satie provided music for *Parade*, an avant-garde entertainment devised by Jean Cocteau and decorated by Picasso. Inspired by cinema orchestras in the era of the silent movie, Satie's aimless, amiable music incorporated unexpected sound effects: a pistol, a ship's horn, a typewriter—sounds the artist Georges Braque aptly referred to as "facts."

Once subjected to relativistic alterations of speed, sounds tend to lose their natural identity, becoming indeed "musical objects" identical in their inner structure but more or less differentiated in timbre, tone, and gestural significance. The art of musique concrète was by definition an art of modulating sounds in time. A music based on such transformations of perception could be interpreted, in a reciprocal sense, as an experience of time travel, of moving through time at different speeds, sometimes slower than normal, sometimes faster, sometimes both at once. The "musical object" thus exchanged its commonplace existential reality to be reborn as a process whose identity is conditional on the timescale of the listener. The intellectual concept is fascinating, and one only wishes the musical results were more rewarding to listen to. In 1952 Schaeffer's studio had acquired new funds and better equipment, including tape recorders, specially-designed diffusion speakers, and a tape vari-speed device, the *phonogène*. Needless to say, both Schaeffer's entire philosophy of continuous transformation of sound objects, and Stockhausen's in electronic and instrumental music, are predicated on the experience of analogue disc and tape: these transformations are not generic to digital or alphanumeric media.

Toward the end of March 1952 Stockhausen visited the Club d'Essai studios for the first time at the invitation of Boulez, then engaged on the preparation of a tape étude. Some three years his senior, the firebrand from Montbrison was already a force to be reckoned with. To group sessions on a methodology for musique concrète he brought practical experience of music for the stage, acquired since 1946 as a composer, ondes martenot player, and musical director for the Théâtre Marigny of Jean-Louis Barrault and Madeleine Renaud. An actor-director equally at home with classical and avant-garde theater, Barrault's international reputation was made as the mime in the Marcel Carné movie *Les Enfants du Paradis*. His wide circle of artist friends extended from Paul Claudel and André Gide to André Breton, Antonin Artaud, and the composer Darius Milhaud (whose opera *Christoph Colombe* Barrault was to tour in 1953, with Boulez conducting). Barrault had been a passionate advocate of the theater of revolution, perhaps inspiring Boulez's similarly combative stance against academicism in music:

> To the Surrealists, the citadel had cracks in it: form and content must be blown up simultaneously. . . . This revolution struck me as an extraordinary cleaning operation, beginning with the brains. Automatic writing, waking dreams, hallucinations. To blow up the Others, lock, stock, and barrel is not enough. The real courage consists of blowing up one's own lock, stock, and barrel.[11]

It is Boulez to a T. Barrault had trained under Jacques Copeau at the Vieux Colombier and had absorbed some of the latter's sense of the transcendental. Boulez, an archetypal "angry young man" of the fifties, but a strict rationalist, also carried the banner for Artaud as a revolutionary; but Artaud had another side that appealed to Barrault and seemed destined to appeal to Stockhausen: a mystical devotion to the triple nature of everything, or "cabbalistic ternary" in its several identities: spatial (Movement,

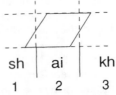

R. H. Stetson's tripartite division of a syllable.
"1. Releasing factor, usually a consonant; 2. Vowel shape giving the syllable a definite quality; 3. Arresting factor, usually a consonant." The diagonal shape shows that consonants and vowel influence one another (co-articulation).

Exchange, Rhythm); breathing (Inspiration, Expiration, Retention); gender (Masculine, Feminine, Neuter); and also color (Yellow being neuter, Blue masculine, Red feminine): hence a total theater of the senses of a kind eventually to be embraced by the composer of *LICHT*. In opposing war as a disastrous consequence of institutional rationalism, and aligning itself with the rich and unfathomable domain of the magical, the exotic, and the arcane, the surrealist movement of Artaud and Breton embraced a holism of the superconscious. Inspired by Artaud, Barrault's mystical conception of acting as an "art of breathing," is nevertheless in close alignment with the dynamic theories of Messiaen, Stetson, and Rousselot:

> Speech is originally a pantomime of the mouth. There is therefore no break of continuity between a gesture and a word: both of them, physically, are a part of the same creation, the result of a muscular contraction and a respiration. Magic of life; religion, that is, extreme physical sensation.[12]

To Schaeffer, a musical object was a *gestalt*. In contrast to semiotics, whose starting-point for a theory of knowledge is the letter or ideogram, Gestalt psychology's starting-point for a theory of perception was the primitive object of awareness. And in order to be identified as an object, it had to have objective qualities, including wholeness. A musical object is thus not a neutral datum like a letter of the alphabet, but a meaningful unit:

> Since the time of Goethe the noun *"Gestalt"* has two meanings: besides the connotation of shape or form as an attribute of things, it has the meaning of a concrete entity *per se*, which has, or may have, a shape as one of its characteristics. . . . According to the most functional general definition of the term, the processes of learning, of recall, of striving, of emotional attitude, of thinking, acting, and so forth, may have to be included.[13]

A recorded sound or musical object *has* a beginning, a middle, and an end, like a Messiaen rhythmic cell or a gesture of vocalization, but it does not *consist* of a beginning, a middle, and an end. There are important differences. While a disc or tape recorded audible event could be modified in a limited number of external ways: cropped, compressed, dilated, and transposed,—more often than not, in several ways simultaneously,—its internal structure or content of information, once recorded, could not be touched.

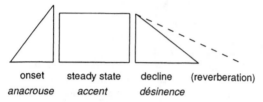

onset   steady state   decline   (reverberation)
anacrouse   *accent*   *désinence*

Tripartite description of a tone, as based on Stetson
and adapted to tape and synthesizer tone creation.

These techniques did not alter the object itself as much as they altered a listener's ability to hear it: editing the attack, for example, did not change the remainder of the sample, it merely allowed a listener to listen to a sound undistracted by the impact of its natural onset. Filtering likewise did not alter the original sound, but merely prevented parts of it from being heard. These manipulations or transformations operated on the observer and not the object itself. Schaeffer pursues his thesis to interesting conclusions:

> We can attempt to create a family of objects similar to the prototype, but with interventions in form: a progression of attacks in intensity, in concision, by enlargement of the internal rhythm, or by accentuating the beginning or end of a sound. This succession, by transformation of the object's intrinsic form, consitutes a series, a sort of anti-melody. . . . A series of the same sound-object, identical with one another, but at different intensities, could in fact be taken not as a series but as a *dynamic melody*. A precedent may be recognized in ordinary music: the repetition of a particular note in crescendo, diminuendo, or with sforzando accents.[14]

Conclusions of particular interest since they establish a rationale for Stockhausen's plus-minus compositions of the sixties, as well as prescribing the interpreter's role in *Prozession, Kurzwellen, Spiral* and other exercises in the transformation of musical "found objects."

Written in tenacious but labored prose, uncertain of direction, looking for coherence, Schaeffer's paper is a world away from Boulez's supreme self-confidence and agile, elegant, surgical wit. In "L'Objet musical" Schaeffer is at least writing of the studio's actual experiences of making and modifying sounds. Boulez's essay ". . . éventuellement . . ." (the dots are iconic) reads in illuminating contrast to Schaeffer's notes from the workbench, expressing the views of a patrician intellectual, concerned above all with *l'écriture*. Drawing on an intimidating familiarity with the music of Debussy, Webern, Schoenberg, Stravinsky, Messiaen, and Cage, Boulez's reflections on serial

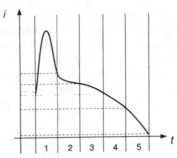

Tape recording allows one to play equally with the curve of a sound. Leaving aside considerations of tape reversal and filtering, we can describe the serial permutations to which a given sound can be submitted. Take a sound, drawn as a curve on axes of intensity [amplitude] and time. Divide it into five parts. . . . If we apply a given series to this sound divided thus, hence:

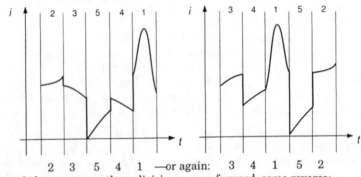

        2   3   5   4   1   —or again: 3   4   1   5   2
—and if we sequence these divisions, some forward, some reverse:
            2f   3r   5f   4r   1r   3r   4r   1f   5f   2f
—we obtain artificial curves that introduce a new dimension to the possibilities of variation.

The notation is done with reference to a scale of lengths of recorded tape; once the conventions are worked out for defining the material employed and a corresponding tablature, the printed layout should be just as readable as a normal musical score.

Boulez on the possibilities of dissecting a sound.[15]

---

organization as applied in the studio are conceived entirely in terms of manuscript transformations of musical objects as rhythmic cells. For Boulez the electronic medium is ideally an instrument for the realization of abstract formal concepts, a "print-out" for the imagination, so to speak, and not an investigative medium having its own rules and possibilities. Brushing aside Schaeffer's years of experience of working with recorded sounds, he credits Cage with the discovery of a new art of complex sounds, and the prepared piano as its staple instrument, just as, in an earlier polemic, "Propositions," he had attributed to Messiaen the discovery of principles of cellular organization in rhythms invented by Stravinsky for the "Danse Sacrale" of *Le Sacre du Printemps* (and the source, as a matter of record, of Messiaen's doctrine of cell modification by addition or subtraction of an irrational value).[16] Misrepresentation was not even an issue: Freudian analysis, as practiced by the surrealists, had made it perfectly legitimate for the analyst to project a meaning onto the imaginative work of others, whether or not the hapless artist had intended it in the first place. In a bravura assertion of the primacy of intellectual organization over practical experience, Boulez conceives a tape study on a single sound treated as a Messiaen-like "cellule rythmique." The entire exercise is a fascinating example of a lettrist mindset applied to a temporal and physical process. In breaking up the natural continuity of the sound-curve (effectively cutting the tape sample into arbitrary sections and reassembling them in different orders), Boulez introduces abrupt discontinuities of amplitude, that are heard in turn as noise that was not there before. Sounds recorded on tape do not respond to permutation of their components in the same way as notated rhythmic cells. (Instruments whose waveforms actually exhibit regular discontinuities of amplitude, incidentally, are the violin family, and the texture associated with the discontinuity is the scrape of the bow.)

At the very time these two essays by Schaeffer and Boulez were being prepared for publication, across the Atlantic, in the New Jersey studio of Louis and Bebe Barron, John Cage was experimenting with much the same tape procedure as Boulez describes above (though naturally without the serial component). Cage's *Williams Mix* of 1952, laboriously assembled out of tiny segments of tape to an elaborate, imaginative, and largely futile schema, is still available on disc, a perfect example of how noisy unrestricted tape montage can sound (though what is still interesting to note is that the clearer elements, as might be expected, are those higher in pitch).

In a strange kind of way, it was the relative failure of musique concrète to produce results that may have proved to be its greatest success. These experiments had to be done, and that they led to unexpected, often counter-intuitive discoveries, forced the more ambitious composers among the group to abandon some of their original preconceptions, and consider the possibility of alternative ways of thinking. A reader might be tempted to dismiss musique concrète exponents as dilettantes and their work as of no practical value; improbable as it sounds, however, the philosophical implications even of failure are still of lively interest. Schaeffer's musical object had its counterpart in Gestalt theory: its smallest possible units of meaning stood in the same relation to serialism as structuralism to semiotics. The musical experience was just another modality.

> As a first approximation (wrote Piaget) we may say that a structure is a system of transformations. Inasmuch as it is a system and not a mere collection of elements and their properties, these transformations involve laws: the structure is preserved or enriched by the interplay of its transformation laws, which never yield results external to the system nor employ elements that are external to it. In short, the notion of structure is comprised of three key ideas: the idea of wholeness, the idea

of transformation, and the idea of self-regulation. . . . All structuralists are at one in recognizing as fundamental the contrast between *structures* and *aggregates*, the former being wholes, the latter composites formed of elements that are independent of the complexes into which they enter.[17]

Eventually Boulez went on to compose *Structures I* and became reconciled to Messiaen. Stockhausen, meantime, decided to steer well clear of musical objects, and recorded the following credo in his notebook:

> No more repetition, no variation, no development, no contrast, all of which assumes *Gestalten*: themes, motives, objects, to be repeated, varied, developed, contrasted; dissected, worked over, expanded, contracted, modulated, transposed, inverted or turned back to front. All that has been given up since the first purely pointillistic works. Our world—our speech—our *Grammatik*. . . . No going back: no Neo . . . ! So what, then? Counter-Points: a series of infinite possibilities for change and renewal. Never the same thing twice, but always the sense of an unchanging and absolute underlying unity, expressed in related proportions: a structure. Not the same *Gestalten* in different lights. Rather: different *Gestalten* in the same light, that penetrates everything.[18]

Konkrete Etüde (Concrete Study)
1952: No.⅕ (Unpublished; cd Stockhausen-Verlag SV-3)
Concrete music.
Duration 3' 15.

In November 1952 Boulez's absence from the studio gave Stockhausen the opportunity to undertake some research and experimentation of his own. With *Spiel* in mind, he used the opportunity to discover more about attack instruments and their characteristics; in a separate initiative he attempted to synthesize timbres additively from pure tones (sine tones) using a standard sweep frequency generator. This latter exercise in Fourier synthesis was pure electronic music: it had nothing in common with Schaeffer, and everything to do with the proposals of Eimert and Meyer-Eppler.

> I made hundreds of analyses of sounds of European and exotic musical instruments (in the musique concrète studio; tapes of exotic sounds were recorded in the Musée de l'Homme, Paris). In a basement studio of the PTT there was a large sine-tone generator with which I generated the first sound spectra to be produced by the systematic superimposition of sine-tones. The work was infinitely arduous; as there was no tape recorder in the studio I had to copy each sine-tone on to disc and then recopy it from disc to disc!! Work on this first "Klangkomposition" was witnessed by the French scientist Abraham Moles, who thought me rather naïve.[19]

Later, given limited access to a studio equipped with tape recorders but lacking a sine-tone generator, he continued working with percussion sounds, isolating and splicing the onsets to hear if it might be possible to create continuous or impulsive noise-tones, perhaps in an effort to simulate consonants. Again, he would have discovered that editing tape is not like editing film; each edit creating a discontinuity that is audible as a sharp onset, hence a sequence of attacks would not sound as clean and distinct as (for instance) an alarm clock, a drumroll or a ratchet; rather every sound, of whatever source, would be overlaid with extraneous noise.

Stockhausen had always been accustomed to working to detailed plans containing many imponderables, but the tape medium is unforgiving, and he was constantly being surprised when things did not work out. In a letter to Goeyvaerts he complained that whenever he attempted to create a series of tone qualities, or durations, or dynamics, the audible result in practice was a hierarchy in which one sound overwhelmed all the others: the richest timbre, the loudest, or the longest.[20] Tape edited sounds produce an aural effect quite different from similar procedures notated for instruments (e.g., the piano, in *Klavierstück I*, or woodwinds, in *Zeitmasse*). Not only does the act of editing sounds on tape introduce a specific kind of attack quality, but in addition, in the absence of a resonating body, when a number of sounds are superimposed by repeated copying, the longer and louder components tend to overwhelm and eventually obliterate the rest. To ensure against such a result, the composer is faced with finding compromise solutions that include reducing or eliminating differences of amplitude, or of duration, or both. His experiences with the *Konkrete Etüde* gave Stockhausen the initial experience and confidence to adopt similar compromise procedures as the basis of tone generation techniques for *Studie I*, *Studie II*, *Gesang der Jünglinge*, and *Kontakte*.

Interviewed in 1985, Schaeffer recalled Stockhausen creating a "Study on one Sound" out of permutations of an original short segment of tape, spliced together in millimetre sections. Schaeffer cautioned him that the result would be a noise, and so it turned out—"Shuuutt!" Nevertheless, he says, Stockhausen was pleased with the result. This description (an episode uncannily similar to Stockhausen's earlier "swarm of bees" encounter with Hermann Schroeder, and perhaps exaggerated in the telling) does not exactly tally with the *Konkrete Etüde* now issued on cd, in which the sounds are relatively clean, if wheezy. The music, for many years presumed lost, but rediscovered by Rudolf Frisius on an archive disc transfer, offers a fascinating preview of techniques and sound qualities of the two electronic studies produced in the more congenial surroundings of Cologne Radio. It offers persuasive evidence, in fact, in support of Stockhausen's claim, to be disputed by Eimert, of having been the first to create purely synthetic timbres.

To create the *Etüde* Stockhausen recorded a clangorous tone of a prepared piano, of a lower string struck with a metal beater.[21] From this tone, prepared specially to sound at a clean and relatively stable pitch, a steady state portion was isolated, transposed and recopied at six pitch levels forming an ascending scale approximately of fourths: c – f sharp – b – f natural – b flat – e (almost amounting to a quotation from the Schoenberg *Kammersymphonie I*).

From his correspondence with Goeyvaerts it is clear that Stockhausen intended to create artificial tones whose inner structures were microcosms or scale models of the form of the entire work, for him a first attempt at a totally integrated serial music. In a letter to Goeyvaerts, Stockhausen confesses that his initial attempts to create a family of tone qualities from scaled versions of the larger form have been in vain. The visual and spatial transpositions of scale employed by a Le Corbusier in architecture and painting, did not work in the same way in the acoustical domain. Artificial waveforms edited together on tape to schemas reproducing in microcosm the

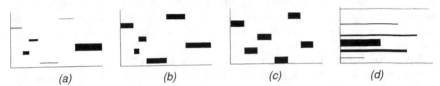

Waveforms in microcosm: in (a) serial durations and amplitudes mean only the loudest is heard; in (b) equal amplitudes; (c) equal amplitudes and durations; (d) when partials of serial amplitude are superimposed.

same proportions of durations and amplitudes as the macro form, in practice end up sounding relatively undifferentiated, because in every case the longer durations and higher-amplitude elements overwhelm the rest,—a result proving Boulez wrong for the very good reason that tape is not a vibrating body, and an edited sequence of fragments of tape does not constitute an organic vibration. That is why, paradoxically, in order to preserve a series of distinct tone qualities at the macro level, the composer is obliged to make sacrifices at the microstructural level, for instance make all the durations of an artificial waveform the same, or all amplitudes the same. These conclusions directly influenced the microsynthesis techniques of later electronic compositions. Judging by the tone characteristics of the *Konkrete Etüde*, Stockhausen's method of assembling sonorous complexes corresponds in a general sense to that of *Studie I*; a listener notices a surprising freedom from generational noise and a more or less well-defined harmonic character to each tone-complex.

One is also unexpectedly reminded of *Stimmung* in two ways, first, in the stammering but recognizably vocal quality of the tone materials, a product of amplitude differences in each partial mixture, and secondly, in the fact that the entire work sounds like a set of dynamic transformations on the constituent notes of a dominant seventh chord based on an approximate f fundamental (the very last sound cheekily resolving on an approximate c). Given the extraordinary technical difficulties Stockhausen had to endure, the *Konkrete Etüde* is a very impressive achievement.

Notes

1. A. R. Burrows, *The Story of Broadcasting* (London: Cassell, 1924), 2–3. Burrows was an Assistant Controller and Director of Programmes for the newly-formed British Broadcasting Company.

2. Hermann Helmholtz, *On the Sensations of Tone as a Physiological Basis for the Theory of Music*. Second rev. edn tr. Alexander J. Ellis. (Reprint. New York: Dover Publications), 1954.

3. ". . . wie die Zeit vergeht . . ." tr. Cornelius Cardew and Leo Black. 10–40 in *die Reihe 3: Musical Craftsmanship* (Bryn Mawr: Theodore Presser, 1959). Revised in German, with annotations by Georg Heike, in *Texte 1*: 99–139.

4. Pierre Schaeffer, "L'Objet musical." 65–76 in *L'Œuvre du XXe siècle*, numéro spécial 212, *La Revue Musicale*. Paris: April, 1952.

5. Pierre Boulez, ". . . éventuellement . . ." 117–48 in *L'Œuvre du XXe siècle*, numéro spécial 212, *La Revue Musicale*. Paris: April, 1952.

6. "The earnest young CIA historian . . . confirmed that the agency, through the CCF, had staged the Festival of Paris in 1952, which—aside from symphonies, operas, ballets, and the like—included an exhibition of about 150 modern paintings and sculptures." David Wise, "Spook Art: Was the CIA really behind the rise of Abstract Expressionism?" *ARTnews* Vol. 99 No 8 (September 2000), 160–64.

7. Nicolas Nabokov, "Introduction à L'Œuvre du XXe Siècle. 5–8 in *L'Œuvre du XXe siècle*, numéro spécial 212, *La Revue Musicale*. Paris: April, 1952.

8. Val Gielgud, *British Radio Drama 1922–1956: A Survey* (London: Harrap, 1957), 55–57. Elder brother of actor John Gielgud, Val Gielgud was responsible for directing Radio Drama at the BBC, from almost the inception of the Company, to the end of the Reith era.

9. Aaron Scharf, *Art and Photography* (Harmondsworth: Penguin Books, 1968).

10. John Rudlin, *Jacques Copeau* (Cambridge: Cambridge University Press, 1986).

11. Jean-Louis Barrault, *Memories for Tomorrow* tr. Jonathan Griffin (London: Thames and Hudson, 1974), 78.

12. Jean-Louis Barrault, *Memories for Tomorrow*, 84–87.

13. Wolfgang Köhler, *Gestalt Psychology: An Introduction to New Concepts in Modern Psychology* (New York: Mentor Books, 1959), 104–105.

14. Pierre Schaeffer, "L'Objet musical," 69–70.

15. Pierre Boulez, ". . éventuellement . . . ," 144–46.

16. Pierre Boulez, "Propositions." 65–72 in "Le Rythme Musical" *Polyphonie 2e cahier* (1948). Paris: Richard-Masse.

17. Jean Piaget, *Structuralism* tr. ed. Chaninah Maschler (London: Routledge and Kegan Paul, 1971), 5–7.

18. *Texte 1*, 37.

19. *Texte 3*, 342.

20. Richard Toop, "Stockhausen's 'Konkrete Etüde.'" 295–300 in *Music Review* (1976).

21. The bass piano string timbre returns with interest in the "Monsalvat bells" sonority that haunts the sound-world of *LICHT*.

CHAPTER SIX

Watching Time

Stockhausen was a rebel, but not a revolutionary by nature. In stark contrast to his fellow Parisians, he saw himself as a healer and disciplinarian. They were atheistic, he was religious; where they saw despair, he sensed optimism; while they talked, he worked; whereas they denounced the older generation, Stockhausen, even if he did not agree with his teachers, remembered that they shared a common goal and maintained a studiously *höflich* and courteous respect toward his elders. While his fellow students spoke of a new world order under Marxism, he dreamed of a new spiritual order. Where they found easy answers, he found difficult questions. Where they improvised, he planned.

To a majority of musicians the whole purpose of modern music is still, I suspect, a complete mystery. The idea of a music whose rationale is to inquire into the nature of music is difficult to grasp from the outset, and especially so among those whose musical education has led them to believe that the nature of music is to represent harmonious activity and to entertain. The conservative attitude is retrospective, superficial, and essentially static. Cleaning away the accumulated grime of centuries from the Sistine Chapel frescoes is one manifestation, Boulez's interpretations of Wagner and Varèse another: both have their virtues, both change our perception of the past, but neither activity creates an appetite for new art.

To understand why new music is necessary and interesting, and why it is different from previous music, imagine consulting a cookery book that gives the following recipe for a cake: *Take one plump wallet and a good supermarket; ask where the cakes are located, look for the sell-by date on the wrapper, and proceed to the check-out.* That is a perfectly comprehensible procedure, but it is not about baking a cake. A cake recipe starts with ingredients that look nothing like a cake and by detailed induction into the mysteries of ingredient interactions in proper quantities and sequence, and the effect of adding heat at the right temperature and for a prescribed length of time, indicates how a cake may be created from scratch. The difference between obtaining a cake from the supermarket and learning to bake it yourself is the same philosophical difference as between a conventional training in musical interpretation and training to be a composer.

In his *Science and the Modern World* the English philosopher Alfred North Whitehead said:

> The greatest invention of the nineteenth century was the method of invention. A new method entered into life. In order to understand our epoch, we can neglect all the details of change, such as railways, telegraphs, radios, spinning machines, synthetic dyes. We must concentrate on the method in itself; that is the real novelty, which has broken up the foundations of the old civilisation.[1]

McLuhan adds, "It is, quite simply, the technique of beginning at the end of any operation whatever, and of working backwards from that point. . . . It is the method inherent in the Gutenberg technique of homogeneous segmentation, but not until the nineteenth century was the method extended from production to consumption. Planned production means that the total process must be worked out in exact stages, backwards, like a detective story."

Serial music as originally *envisaged* by the composers of Stockhausen's generation had a double aim: first, to determine the basic ingredients, or fundamental particles, of music; second, to establish their principles of interaction and combination. In an ideal world the outcome of such a process of discovery would be music indistinguishable in essential respects from music of the past: a cake, after all, is a cake. That is what conventional music analysis aims to do: to validate a procedure (e.g., tonality, sonata form, etc.) and in doing so, to entrench it as a value. In reality, however, conventional analysis does not work. Academic analysis of a Bach fugue neither explains what a fugue is, nor does it provide the essential knowledge or inspiration to enable the student to compose a fugue; at best one acquires a method for simulating a fugue in a particular style. Such instruction was (and perhaps still is) part and parcel of an orthodox conservatoire education. But since conventional analysis can neither explain the past, nor provide the methods and inspiration for composing the music of the present, let alone the future, alternative methods are needed. The methods applied by Messiaen and younger composers draw on the same techniques of induction to which Whitehead refers.

Analysis of language, or of mental representations in general, begins by dissolving the connections that characterize statements or representations in normal behavior; then, in order to discover the principles of connection, it substitutes for the remainder a set of a priori unconnected elements. The inexplicable yoking together of unrelated images is a defining characteristic of human behavior in the worlds of surrealist art, symbolist poetry, visions, altered states of consciousness, and the mythology of every culture. Through juxtaposing unrelated images the artist unlocks a higher reality than that available to reason (which is what the term "surrealism" means). Only by working with disconnected materials can the researcher in turn hope to understand how connections are actually formed in the first place. In this sense science preceded music by half a century; the scientific method adopted by Hermann Ebbinghaus in his pioneer investigations into memory offers a startling foretaste of creative procedures associated twenty years later with Max Ernst in the world of art, forty years later with Tristan Tzara in the realm of poetry, and sixty years later with John Cage in music:

> In order to test practically, although only for a limited field, a way of penetrating more deeply into memory processes . . . I have hit upon the following method. . . . Out of the simple consonants of the alphabet and our eleven vowels and diphthongs all possible syllables of a certain sort were constructed, a vowel sound being placed between two consonants. These syllables, about 2,300 in number, were mixed together and then drawn out by chance and used to construct series of different lengths, several of which each time formed the material for a test.[2]

In the mid-twentieth century the linguist Noam Chomsky arrived at his generative grammar hypothesis by a similar route. Chomsky's goal was the same as Ebbinghaus's, but his conclusion, that rules of association were somehow structured into the brain, reflected a growing sense during the cold war era that the classic atomistic approach of linguistics had failed, and that the new fundamentals of mental life were not syllabic data but systems of relationship.

> For areas that are important to human life, knowledge claims must be grounded; for example, in science, in the laborious construction of systems of knowledge. . . . In the whole long and very rich history of what is now called linguistics, the object of investigation was essentially language; that is, people wanted to find what the elements were of particular languages, where the properties of those elements were, and so on. . . . As the shift of focus goes from language to grammar, a new domain of investigation opens, . . . [a] new discipline which really belongs to the natural sciences in principle. It is dealing with the current state, the mature state of a particular organism, . . . and it is trying to characterize that state.[3]

Stockhausen was beginning to have doubts about pointillism. Boulez also. Boulez had embraced Messiaen's cellules rythmiques with enthusiasm, applying the principle with equal panache to musique concrète and instrumental music. He had exchanged a lively correspondence with Cage on the subject, the latter having employed charts containing cell-like elements in his *Concerto for Prepared Piano and Chamber Orchestra* of 1950–1951, even more so in the *Music of Changes* for piano of 1951.[4] However, Messiaen's *Mode de valeurs et d'intensités* had shaken that confidence by demonstrating a further reduction of musical elements, from Webernian intervals in pitch and time, to single notes. And not just single notes: one could say a reduction to essentially *one note* in different transpositions of pitch, touch, dynamics, and duration.

Stockhausen had never been convinced by the idea of rhythmic cells, but he was persuaded by the Schaeffer principle of infinite transposition of a single datum on a multiplicity of scales. His first response, as we have seen, was to focus on the microstructure of a single tone. Messiaen's variables (pitch, attack, dynamics, duration) can all be regarded as characteristics *applied* to a note regarded as a datum or position on a stave; they are not inherent in the note. The characteristic omitted from Messiaen's variables, understandably since he is working with a single instrument, is timbre. With the arrival of Cage's prepared piano, timbre enters the list of controllable variables for the first time (that is, unless one includes Messiaen's grand organ, which most commentators fail to do). The degree of control of timbre for a prepared piano is limited at best, however, and the procedure varies from instrument to instrument. Perhaps in an ideal world one should be able to assign a fixed internal structure to every pitch element in a composition. Moreover, if that internal structure were designed as a microcosm or serial combination representative of the formal structure of the entire work, then every new composition would come fully equipped with an entirely new and distinctive set of musical terms.

Punkte (Points)

1952: withdrawn (recomposed 1962–1966)
For orchestra: flute, 2 oboes, 3 clarinets (e flat, b flat, bass), 3 saxophones (soprano/alto, baritone, bass or bass sarrusaphone), 2 bassoons, horn, cornet in b flat, trumpet in c, trombone; 12 tuned bongos b4 flat – a5 (3 players); 2 pianos (I. "soft," II. "hard"), 2 harps (II. muted); strings 2.2.2.1.1.
Duration: 8' 30.

The original *Punkte* was composed immediately prior to *Kontra-Punkte*, the first version of which dates from 1952. The similarity in their names is deliberate; when Stockhausen finished *Punkte* and decided he was not satisfied with it, he began again with the initial "points" of the earlier score and gradually transformed them into group-formations (the "counter-points" of the title).

Little apart from the underlying point structure relates *Punkte* to its revision of 1962, and further modifications of 1964 and 1966. *Punkte* 1952 is shorter in duration, written for an orchestra of smaller dimensions, and mapped out to a regular MM 112 grid, without tempo variations. All the same, the composition of the orchestra is fascinating in its own right, being made up entirely of instruments of tempered pitch, including a chromatic scale of bongos that the composer later decided to omit.

The music of *Punkte* differs from *Spiel* in having less to do with the juxtaposition of attack and resonance instruments, and more with the gradual transformation of pitch orders by semitonal and register displacement in the manner of *Kreuzspiel*, within a strict, seemingly logarithmic time structure. Unlike *Spiel I*, and also unlike *Kontra-Punkte*, this process leads neither to the generation of linked themes, molecular chains, nor to the unification of timbre depicted, for instance, in *Kontra-Punkte*'s progressive reduction of instrumental diversity into one highly-inflected sonority. The compositional process allows only compression or rarefaction of density.

Dissatisfied at his attempt to serialize orchestral timbres, Boulez had withdrawn the score of *Polyphonie X* after the first performance under Rosbaud, and reverted to the single tone colour of the piano for *Structures*. Stockhausen drily commented, "Just how much Pierre Boulez must have sensed the unresolvable inconsistency, after completing the 'Polyphonie X' for 17 instruments, of composing serially with a variety of instruments, can be judged by his latest composition, the 'Structures' for 2 pianos, a work dispensing with the search for a serial ordering of different instrumental timbres and restricting itself to a single instrument, the piano."[5]

What can be learned from *Punkte* as a score? The new work exhibits serial proportioning in both macro-time (time signatures) and micro-time (irrational values), a move up from *Formel* where the changes of time-signature are not quite so overtly proportioned (and neither is the music). A lot more can be read into the choice of instrumentation, however, even without the music. Stockhausen's orchestra has changed from a basic set of tone-colors in multiples of three, to a much more self-aware ensemble containing families of tone-colors, and complementary intensities within similar families. What this indicates is a conscious attempt by the composer to devise an orchestra exhibiting serial properties. Though he later said that it could not be done,—or certainly not to the degree that he would have wished, or to the accuracy he believed electronic music to be capable of providing,—it was a fascinating exercise and the first of many. In future years he would go on to compose more works for conventional instruments, and every time he has returned to an orchestra he has continued to refine his specification. A shift of attention both to the acoustic characteristics of instruments that make up an orchestra, and to the notations that have to be developed to guarantee production of the correct tone-colors, represent new subplots in the Stockhausen narrative that deserve attention.

The timbre or tone-color of an instrument is dependent on its structure and manner of performance; since some instruments are blown, others played with a bow, or struck with a beater, and all are made of different combinations of materials, it would seem a hopeless task to arrive at a comprehensive theory of tone-color corresponding, for example, to the classification of vowel positions in the study of speech. However, a steady tone emitted by any one instrument expresses those specifics in a distinctive waveform, or cycle of pressure fluctuation, that can be visualized in a sound laboratory as an oscilloscope trace. Such equipment was available in 1952, and electronic musical instruments based on the manipulation of simple waveforms had been in existence for twenty or more years: the trautonium of Friedrich Trautwein and Oskar Sala, the sphärophon of Jörg Mager, and many others. A knowledge of waveforms might be expected to assist in the classification of musical timbres at this time, but judging by the writings of Schaeffer, Stockhausen, and others with a vested interest, either the studios were unequipped with oscilloscopes, or the studio personnel were unable to interpret the information provided by them. A remark by Schaeffer provides an indication:

> A frequency analysis, an oscillogram or a sonogram are indeed the exact, analog records of the sonorous phenomenon itself. But although visualized, the sound is not further explained. We have its physical description, sometimes in a more *legible* form; but this is no description of what the *audible* is or a record of the perception criteria; i.e., the aptitudes of sound to carry specifically the marks of the musical or the linguistic.[6]

Stockhausen himself does not begin to discuss waveform manipulation until the seventies, at the time of composing *Sirius*, an exercise demonstrating the possibilities and limitations of the EMS Synthi 100. Prior to that time, and most notably in *Kontakte*, he creates his own vocabulary of sounds by a systematic process, and then chooses conventional instruments that most closely resemble the elements of that vocabulary. And because there is not always an exact correspondence between a synthesized sound and a musical instrument, occasionally he improvises, or substitutes from an unexpected source, as in *Kontakte* (the wooden tom-toms), *Momente* (the shot-rattles), and *Mikrophonie I*, all of whose sounds are derived from the tam-tam. So the instrumentation of *Punkte* represents a significant stage in the development of his thinking about tone-colors and their relationships. One notices a reciprocal pairing of "soft" and "hard" timbres: flute and oboe, clarinet and saxophone, the pairs of pianos and harps. "Soft" and "hard" are subjective distinctions. In addition, he opts for families in preference to multiples of instruments: the three clarinets, the three saxophones, the flute/cornet/horn combination, and also the strings (which now include violas I and II), for which there is some evidence of division into "hard" and "soft" roles (loud/soft, pizzicato/arco, unmuted/muted, etc.). Given his attention to exploring attack and resonance characteristics within each tone color group, it seems logical for him to have decided to dispense with the added percussion.

sine wave   square wave   ramp wave

Stockhausen may have been guided in his choice by information about early electronic instruments that were being considered for the Cologne electronic music studio. The trautonium, for instance, initially a mono device of programmable timbre, an instrument for which Hindemith had composed a neoclassical *Konzertstück* back in 1931, came with an operator's manual describing the various tone settings and how they could be used. These early electrical instruments employed simple circuits for generating essentially three waveforms: the sine wave, the square wave, and the sawtooth wave. In very simple terms, the sine-wave output resembles the sound of a flute, the square-wave output that of a clarinet, and the richer sawtooth-wave output an oboe or trumpet. If we look at Stockhausen's orchestra for *Punkte*, we see it includes instrumental families that correspond to these three types: sine wave (flute/cornet/horn); square wave (clarinet/saxophone); and sawtooth wave (oboe/bassoon; trumpet/trombone). (In years to come, the three wind instrument types will return as emblematic characters in the instrumentation of *LICHT*.) That leaves the strings as active resonating instruments, and harps/keyboards as passive resonators.

When the attack characteristic is removed from a piano or harp tone, or a tape recording of piano or harp music is played backwards, the timbre is markedly altered and the waveform appears very much simpler. These perceptions were familiar to Schaeffer and his associates. But Stockhausen was also guided by his experience with the *Konkrete Etüde*, in which synthetic sounds appear that resemble the saxophone and the sarrusophone, neither of which belong in the conventional orchestra (that a listener can recognise the sarrusophone at all is thanks to Stravinsky including the instrument in the orchestra of *Threni*).

By the time it came for him to write "The Origins of Electronic Music" for an evening radio broadcast, Stockhausen had changed his mind about serialization of an orchestra. "Any attempt to subordinate the different structures of the different instrumental tones to a general rational principle of proportions is bound to fail."[7] But that is not the whole story, as his subsequent music amply proves. The complementary statement is equally true, and more to his point: any general rational principle of proportions for instrumental tone color can only be successfully implemented in the electronic medium. Only through their (often imperfect) resemblances to standard electronic timbres can any such relationship between conventional instruments be rationally demonstrated.

Kontra-Punkte (Counter-Points)

1952–1953: No. 1 (UE 12207 rev. 12218; cd Stockhausen-Verlag SV-4)
For ten instruments: flute, clarinet, bass clarinet, bassoon; trumpet, trombone, piano, harp, violin, cello.
Duration: 12'.

Stravinsky was impressed by *Kontra-Punkte*; in *Movements* for piano and orchestra the piano acts as serial coordinator of the orchestra in a similar way (and both allude to baroque practice). The orchestra is slimmed down from *Punkte*, implying that each instrument now has to play a number of different roles (high *and* low, hard *and* soft, etc.)—which in itself is an indicator of a greater sense of malleability within the ensemble. "*Kontra-Punkte* for ten instruments (says the composer) originated from the idea of resolving the antitheses of a many-faceted world of individual notes and temporal relationships to the point where a situation is reached where only that which is homogeneous and unchanging can be heard." As always, Stockhausen's choice of terms is artful; the remark implies both a general and a specific statement. That in pointillist music contrasts act to cancel one another out and produce a neutralized result is generally true; but paradoxically the statement refers to *Kontra-Punkte* as solving the problem by actually eliminating the contrasts as a structural determinant of the work (which is really quite witty). In the context not only of his own *Punkte*, but of Boulez's *Polyphonie X* as well (sharp observers should also note the criticism implied by Stockhausen's choice of title, though Boulez seems to have forgiven him), *Kontra-Punkte* comes as a gesture of relief: "a plague on trying to serialize orchestras! I'm going back to the piano!" In Stockhausen's terms this is a work that for once is not determinedly symmetrical, in threes, meeting then retreating, but instead cheerfully one-directional, indicating a new dynamism (though a true pedant could say that *Kontra-Punkte* is going forwards and backwards at the same time, since while the resolution of diversity in unity for Stockhausen is a conceptual advance, in Boulezian terms going back to the piano amounts to a retreat).

In its own terms the new work comes across as exuberant, colorful, outgoing and impatient, in marked contrast to the cautious precision of earlier works. Here the theme of reconciliation of opposites, fusion, and generation of something new out of the process takes the form almost of a reverse explosion, a music that begins as floating particles that over the course of the work are drawn together and one by one merge with the piano. Comparisons with Haydn's "Farewell" Symphony spring to mind, but in this case the musicians are not blowing out their candles one by one and leaving the stage, rather their different identities are reincorporated in the central sonority of the keyboard.

> The work is in one movement. Six different timbres are employed: flute—bassoon, clarinet—bass clarinet, trumpet—trombone, piano, harp, violin—violoncello (three characteristically differing types of wind instrument, in pairs, and three types of stringed instrument with struck, plucked, and bowed strings respectively). These six timbres are resolved into one, that of the piano (struck strings). One by one the trumpet, trombone, bassoon, violin, bass clarinet, harp, cello, and flute drop out. Six different loudness levels (*ppp–sfz*) likewise reduce one by one to *pp*. Great differences between very short and long durations are gradually eliminated, leaving closely related middle values (sixteenth-note, triplet sixteenth-note, dotted sixteenth-note, quintolet sixteenth-note, etc.). Out of the opposition between vertical and horizontal tone-relationships emerges a two-voice, monochrome counterpoint.[8]

The musical texture, at times unusually dense, appears to derive from preordained blocks of pitches distributed and combined in a manner not dissimilar to the electronic studies shortly to follow. These collections of pitches are shared among groups of instruments, to be revealed in the interplay of time-point structures that "disturb" them into life, creating repetitions, *klangfarben* conjunctions, and echoes at pitch. In this respect *Kontra-Punkte* plays the scherzo to Boulez's *Polyphonie X*, whose pitches form similar constellations and are subject to the same echo-repetitions. Combinations of attack and sustaining instruments articulate lines and phrases of enormous length; here more clearly than ever the listener is made aware of the coexistence of time structures, the very large simultaneously with the very small.

In a 1962 "Muzik der Zeit" programme note Stockhausen admits that

the real "counter-action" of *Kontra-Punkte* lies in the process of transforming "points" into "groups," and thereby from a notional conceptual order that
is essentially static, to an audibly organized dynamic continuum. This is
Monteverdi's issue in the *Vespers*, of reconciling the timeless present of
plainchant with the dynamics of Renaissance dance rhythms and new perspectives of space and time. For Stockhausen it signifies a reconciliation of
Webernian *klangfarben* technique with a notional thematicism. The work
alternates sections of more or less dissociated "points" with sections of a
more assertive thematic counterpoint, the latter increasingly assigned to
the piano. These sections are also defined by variations in tempo, a unit

pulsation of MM 120 associated with the more cohesive sections, alternating
with six other tempi, together making up an incomplete tempo scale
corresponding to the frequency-relationships as shown. Missing chromatic
values may be accounted for by substitution of another duration unit (e.g.,
in the above scale, f sharp corresponds to a dotted sixteenth-note in the
tempo "eighth-note 120"). Stockhausen's unit measure of a dotted quarter-
note is particularly suited to serial combinations and complex rhythms,
allowing not only Boulez's and Messiaen's additive mode of durations from
one to twelve, but also the possibility of division of the unit measure from
one whole to one-twelfth. Stockhausen returns to the issue of a divisive

Additive and divisive duration scales compared.

series being preferable to an additive series in his essay ". . . how time
passes . . ." but here the music itself makes the point that in a French
duration scale of 1–12 sixteenth-notes the longer durations predominate,
whereas in music composed to a German scale of $\frac{1}{12}$ – 1 dotted quarter-
note the shorter durations predominate and produce a more textured result.

The general structure of *Kontra-Punkte* suggests that it was originally
planned in sections of twelve units of 22 measures (of which two are composed, with the possibility of more). The 22-measure subdivision is clearly
indicated in the first half of the piece, in which the basic tempo is alternated
with each of the other tempi in ascending order, after which the divisions
become subject to creative interference. The number 22 is itself significant
from a serial perspective, both as the sum of the series (1, 2, . . . 6) + 1, and
(in terms of 66 eighth-notes) as the sum of the series (1, 2, . . . 11)—that is, a
complete series 1–12 *minus* the maximum value.

Structural considerations aside, this is a wonderful work, very demanding to play but filled with an extraordinary elation. The writing is as close to Webern as Stockhausen ever attains, but this is a Webern in exuberant mood. The music sparkles with wit and invention like a Kandinsky improvisation; the line arches, the cadences resonate. With this work the composer gives the impression of moving with a new sense of freedom; its reach extends to the extremes of the keyboard with Mozartean ease, and there is no sense, as perhaps there is in *Formel*, of an Atlas straining to keep heaven and earth apart.

Rather optimistically, Stockhausen originally demanded an incandescent MM 60 *per measure* (i.e., twelve thirty-second notes per second) and was prevailed on by Hermann Scherchen, who conducted the première at the 1953 ISCM Festival in Cologne, to slow down to a more negotiable beat. Even so, the rehearsals were fraught with difficulty and in consequence of resistance and some despair on the part of musicians, the first performance had to be curtailed. After this experience the alternate tempi were written into the score.

Unusually, metrical combinations such as 5 : 3, 7 : 6, etc. are quite rare. Though some were introduced in revisions and corrections made after the premiere (leading to a second, revised edition of the score being published soon after), the composer's original plan seems to have been to treat each measure as a unit subject to "irrational value" subdivision as a whole, the chosen value applying to every orchestral part. Even after the revisions, the divisions of a measure into fives or sevens tend to apply one for all, which suggests that Stockhausen is treating divisions as changes of tempo or pulse, a trait that reappears notoriously in *Klavierstück I*. In that situation, to superimpose changes of metronomic tempo on top of notated tempi calls both into question; when taken together with the inconsistencies of verbal and notated tempi in *Formel* and later in *Klavierstück I*, it suggests that the way to achieve a dynamic control of tempo is an issue for him at this time.

Klavierstücke I–IV (Piano Pieces I–IV)

1952–1953: No. 2 (UE 12251; cd Stockhausen-Verlag SV-56)
Durations: I 2' 50; II 1' 30; III 0' 40; IV 2' 15.

The first set of *Klavierstücke* were composed at different times during the composer's stay in Paris, III soon after his arrival as a birthday present for his wife Doris. The collection marks a stage in Stockhausen's evolution from "point" to "group" composition, and in many ways may be regarded as a sketchbook for his later electronic studies. The deceptively simple Piece III has been analyzed almost to extinction in search of clues to Stockhausen's serial method. Most studies have focused only on the pitch relationships and ignored the piece's rhythmic and expressive qualities. An exception is Rudolf Stephan's early commentary, including the unexpected observation that the piece has some of the features of an old German *lied*:

It consists of 16 measures with 55 notes. The note sequence of the first measures: (1) a – b – d – a flat – b flat – a (2) g sharp – b etc. indicates straight away that this piece is no twelve-tone composition in the strict sense, since the last note of the first measure and first of the second are doubled. If one counts up the individual pitches we find the following: c and f sharp each appear twice, c sharp (d flat) three times, d and g four times each, e flat (d sharp), f and a five times each, e, b flat (a sharp) and b each six times, and a flat (g sharp) seven times.

This finding shows unequivocally how far this piece is from Schönberg's twelve-tone method, which has as one of its functions the equal representation of all the pitches. . . . The formal conception amounts to a continuous expansion, the last two notes marking low and high extremes of pitch. . . . Behind the serial disguise, the piece is closer in form and style to an old German lied.[9]

Most of the arguing over serial orders arises from trying to apply rules of analysis derived from twelve-tone theory, in particular the ideas, one, that the series is an intervallic sequence, and two, that the rules are consistent. Neither apply here. Stockhausen is using a different code. The piece is not based on a theme, rather on a distribution of elements, so to decode it involves an understanding of wartime code-breaking, or its equivalent in J. M. Hauer's *Zwölftonspiel*, itself a distributive system.

Here, for what it is worth, is my reading of the distribution: the pitch organization based on three abutting groups of four adjacent pitches: d – f, f – g sharp, and g sharp – b, an arrangement leaving c and c sharp as "free radicals"—they do not appear until measure 8, giving the sense of a change of key. As the piece progresses, the groups exchange notes and change their identities; the final sequence of seven pitches filling the interval of a perfect fifth g – d and, measuring from the c sharp of measure 13, forming the interval series 3 5 6 1 4 2. Just as important for a sense of phrasing are Stockhausen's dynamics, which are also grouped, and individual note durations, the dotted quarter-note tending to act as anchor for every phrase.

The ordering of durations, once recognized, looks like an early reaction to Messiaen's method of composition with rhythmic cells, which is a little unexpected. Essentially the piece is made up of variants and superimpositions of an initial sequence of six values expressed as two groups of three, the first group of three consisting of a longer note followed by two equal shorter values; the second group forming an unbroken succession of which the first is short, the second long, the third of medium duration:

4 5   6 3 2   1   4   5   6   3 2   1

In measure 2 the order is changed. Then follows a sequence of five combinations, here represented schematically, of the three unequal durations
leading to the midpoint of measure 8:

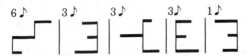

At measure 10 Stockhausen transposes the break from the first to the
second subgroup. The play of elements is not hard to follow: in measure 5
for example the dynamics are graded according to note-duration, whereas in
measures 3 and 4 the longest note of the group is softest, and the shortest
note the loudest. On one level the piece plays like a rather loopy waltz, and
at another level it sounds like the kind of wayward vocal line that is so
strong a feature of the *Gesang der Jünglinge*. Technically, the pianist is
obliged to pay particular attention to endings of notes as well as beginnings,
a useful mental discipline relatively neglected elsewhere, in Boulez for
example (honorably excepting the Third Sonata).

Piece II is a study in vertical note-groups treated as electronic tone
mixtures, for which an instrument of good natural resonance is desirable,
since control of individual durations within a complex has to be manually
effected and not just left to the sustaining pedal. Ampler in sound, it also
introduces "non-retrogradable rhythms" i.e., symmetrical patterns of division within a structural unit; the sustaining pedal is also employed to define
individual groups. Five dynamic levels are employed, a sixth, *ppp*, being
saved until the last chord. Four groups of three pitches are rotated, two of
them diatonic: d – e flat – f, and its retrograde inversion b – a – g sharp, and
two chromatic: c – c sharp – d, and its inversion g sharp – g – f sharp. The
notes d and g sharp link diatonic and chromatic pairs at a tritone distance.
At measures 8 and 9 the diatonic triplets become whole-tone; other interval
and order permutations appear as the piece continues. Piece II is mainly
restricted to the mid-range, with bass-notes functioning as large-scale punctuation (as in *Refrain*). It ends on a typically emphatic extreme, this time a
low b flat (compare the ending of *Kontra-Punkte*).

Forward and reverse note-groups of durations, and in particular non-
retrogradable formations, give Piece II an idiosyncratic charm (compare the
"reverse" formation of measure 3 with the "forward" group of measure 22).
Such formations are taken over from the *Konkrete Etüde*. Conventional
notation is very explicit about where notes begin, much less so about where
they end, an instance where space-time graphics after the style of Earle
Brown, by which the length of a note is shown by a line, makes a lot of
sense. In contrast, the strictly linear two-part counterpoint of Piece IV, and

Stockhausen's use of dynamics to distinguish the two lines, reads and sounds like an insider commentary on Boulez's *Structures Ia*. A lean, bouncy piece, with the kind of exuberant hocketing also found in *Kontra-Punkte*, its richness of rhythm is related to the progressive shortening of fundamental durations by serial fractions, each note in succession either followed by a rest, or alternatively preceded by a rest. The technique allows the composer to make the termination of a note the time-point reference, as an alternative to the attack point. The note itself is merely the sounding portion of a duration that may be larger in extent; the ratio of sound to silence then becomes a matter of serial proportioning within the duration (again, the same as in *Konkrete Etüde*). In Piece IV two wide-ranging lines interact in a lively counterpoint generally emphasized by well-contrasted dynamic labeling which, apart from occasional excursions, is either *pp* or *ff*. The surprise ending is a two-part diminuendo.

Boulez liked the piece and said so in a paper, "Vers une musique expérimentale" originally written for Schaeffer in 1953 but not published until 1967. Boulez summarized his article in a letter to Cage that included a manuscript copy of a few measures from the final page of the score (omitted in subsequent publications).[10] He brackets Piece IV along with Cage's *Music of Changes*, an interesting juxtaposition since by the time of Piano Pieces V–VIII, Stockhausen's *écriture* had undergone considerable revision and simplification, and adopted some features of Cage's space-time notation.

Piece I, the last to be composed, is also the most substantial. The group composition is explicit, down to the timescales of successive measures, which form order-permutations, with occasional slight variations, of a series of 1–6 quarter-notes:

①   ②   ③

5 2 3 1 4 6   3 6 5 4 1 2   2 6 4 1 3 5

④   ⑤   ⑥

4 1 6 2 5 3   6 5 1 4 3 2   3 5 (1) 1 4 2 (4+)

In the first group, 1 is actually 1½ (a 3/8 measure); in group 4, 2 is actually slightly less (two measures adding to a 7/16 measure); in group 6, a quarter-note rest has been transferred from the final value (nominally a 6) to come between 5 and 1, leaving the final measure as a 4 plus a rest of indeterminate duration. These rotations of six durations are "groups of groups," since each serial unit of duration is subdivided internally and occupied by a differently characterized collection of pitches. Unlike earlier pointillist compositions, there are calculated degrees of uniformity within each internal group: an average dynamic, or tempo, or a general upward or downward movement, specific to the collection. Each note group is distinguished by its number of attacks, number of notes (two or more notes played simultaneously count as one attack), their range, direction, and degrees of internal contrast (in duration, dynamic, or pitch, and evolution from vertical to horizontal). A succession of notes may be transformed into a chord by use of the sustaining pedal (or third pedal, if not all notes are to be sustained, as in measures 6, 7, and 8); contrariwise, the notes of an initial chord may be released one by one, making a sort of negative melody—an invention later adopted by Boulez in the *Troisième Sonate*. The choice and combination of tendencies within a group is also determined by serial rotation.

Piece I was composed at great speed in two days, and its energy is only too visible on the printed page. The notation with multiple irrational values quickly attracted criticism from composers and others who believed the piece *should* have been notated more simply; Gunther Schuller arguing in *Perspectives of New Music* for "more logical and practical" notations (measure 6, he thought, could just as easily be written in triplet sixteenths), while elsewhere in the same issue Leonard Stein complained that the irrational values could not be quantified.[11] Such criticisms may have taken effect, in that the published score carries a superfluous note to the effect that equivalent metronomic values should be calculated based on the fastest speed possible for the smallest note-values. In an essay "À la Limite du Pays Fertile," published in *die Reihe*, even Boulez enters wordily into the fray.

> Let us return to the first objection which may be raised against this new concrete way of dissecting time: namely that there is a danger that the unit will not be perceived by the listener; that it exceeds the lowest limit of differentiability. We have already referred to irrational values; their use does not represent only a written out *rubato* but a point of contact between the variation of a unit value and the variations of the particular duration itself. This meeting point gives rise to fractions of irrational values within a group of irrational values at another level! . . . In short, to realize these instrumentally and at the same time to retain the sense of pulse of the unit value, the player must be able to realize three mental operations, the one deduced from the other, almost simultaneously: supposing the initial pulse to be established, we have the metre, the irrational value of the first level, the further irrational value or the fraction of it, which depends upon it. . . . The process of simultaneous deduction is, however, for all practical purposes impossible.[12]

Boulez has his own reasons for playing on the difficulties of Stockhausen's notation of Piece I, namely, to reinforce his case for the virtues of tape as a medium for editing time. Personally, having played all four pieces as written, I think Boulez is mistaken, and that interpreting irrational values as metronomic indications is also a mistake. This is not splitting hairs. First, the piece is playable in its own terms: one only has to "feel" the phrasing in a special way. But pianists should be used to that already, if they play Chopin or Liszt, or even Beethoven. Second, to interpret irrational subdivisions as alterations of tempo changes the tension within the group, which is an expressive variable related to an underlying but unstated quarter-note pulse. That tension and release dynamic is surely part of the meaning of a group composition (it certainly is in *Gruppen*, for example, and arguably in Piano Piece VI), and if the performer behaves as though the underlying pulse were not there, that dynamic is lost. Analogies exist in compound speech patterns: my preferred example in English advertising being:

Fantastic acceleration from the | ninety-five brake horse-power |
Coventry Climax O. H. C. engine

—an antique specimen of advertising copy for a Jaguar car.[13] The natural
rhythm of this compound phrase, if notated as a rhythm, would be very
close to the Stockhausen measure in Piano Piece I. German speech is full of
such compound rhythms: the language is designed for it. Here is an example
taken at random:

Diese neuen Klangmöglichkeiten | sind an den | elektro-akustischen
Instrumenten | der letzten zwanzig Jahre | enwickelt worden.[14]

We observe a corresponding ambiguity in Stockhausen's attitude to the
written-out tempi of *Formel*, nevertheless, and his reluctance to interpret
them as in any way syncopated in relation to the stress pattern implied by
the written time signature. It is true that Stockhausen is comfortable with
changes of absolute tempo, providing that formal relations between tempi
are maintained. In the present case, none of the four pieces has a prescribed
tempo, other than "as fast as possible," leading one to suspect that what is
more important is the sense of nervous energy created, rather than the
actual tempo, in the style of Debussy, or Boulez himself, who often uses
emotional terms to signify tempi: "*animé*," "*nerveux*," and who in an
interview with the BBC *Listener* offered the following definition: "tempo is
only a quality of speed in the passage of time," a remarkable perception of
musical time as a moving conveyor-belt on which the notes pass by faster or
slower.[15] The pianist David Tudor has also described his experience of
performing pulseless works such as Cage's *Music of Changes* as "watching
time, rather than feeling time."

Notes

1. Marshall McLuhan, *Gutenberg Galaxy* (London: Routledge & Kegan Paul, 1962), 276.
2. Hermann Ebbinghaus, *Memory: A Contribution to Experimental Psychology* tr. Henry A. Ruger and Clara E. Bussenius (Reprint. New York: Dover Publications, 1964), 22.
3. Noam Chomsky, *Modular Approaches to the Study of the Mind* (San Diego: San Diego State University Press, 1984), 22, 26–27.
4. James Pritchett, *Music of John Cage* (Cambridge: Cambridge University Press, 1993), 63–81. See also Jean-Jacques Nattiez ed., *Boulez–Cage Correspondence* tr. ed. Robert Samuels (Cambridge: Cambridge University Press, 1993), 98–103.
5. *Texte 1*, 43.
6. Pierre Schaeffer, "Sound and Communication." *Cultures* I/1 ed. G. S. Métraux (Paris: Unesco et la Baconnière, 1973), 56.
7. *Texte 1*, 39.
8. *Texte 2*, 20–21.
9. Rudolf Stephan, *Neue Musik: Versuch einer Kritischen Einführung* (Göttingen: Vandenhoeck und Ruprecht, 1958), 60–67.
10. Letter 42: "Pierre Boulez on John Cage in 'Tendencies in recent music.'"

Jean-Jacques Nattiez ed., *Boulez-Cage Correspondence,* 140–41.

11. Leonard Stein, "The Performer's Point of View." *Perspectives of New Music* I:2 (1963), 68.

12. Pierre Boulez, "At the Ends of Fruitful Land . . ." tr. A. Goehr. *Die Reihe I: Electronic Music* (Bryn Mawr : Theodore Presser, 1958), 23–24.

13. Geoffrey N. Leech, *English in Advertising: A Linguistic Study of Advertising in Great Britain* (London: Longmans, 1966), 127.

14. Friedrich Herzfeld, *Musica Nova: Die Tonwelt unseres Jahrhunderts* (Berlin: Ullstein), 313.

15. Pierre Boulez, "Music and Invention." Interview with Misha Donat. *Listener* Vol. 83 No. 2125 (22 January 1970).

CHAPTER SEVEN

Meyer-Eppler

All musical instruments, including the voice, are synthesizers. The term "synthesizer" is misleading. When Stockhausen met the ninety-year-old Japanese sage Daisetsu Suzuki in 1966, he introduced himself as a person who made sounds "in a laboratory, in a very artificial way." Suzuki replied that to make sounds using electronic apparatus and equipment was perfectly natural. Stockhausen was talking about the sounds themselves, and interpreted Suzuki's response as an endorsement of the creation of sounds having an artificial inner life. Suzuki however, having no knowledge of artificial sounds, says only that the activity of making sounds by whatever means is perfectly natural to him.[1] The difference between natural and artificial sounds lies not in how they are made but how they strike the ear. A "natural" sound could be defined as the acoustic product of a physical action of one material upon another within a conducting medium, or alternatively, as a sound that is inherently unstable. An "artificial" sound by contrast is one that is not atmospheric in origin but generated within an electrical system as a noise or waveform and subsequently expressed as sound by means of an output device such as a loudspeaker. Such "artificial" sounds tend to remain invariant in pitch, amplitude, and timbre.

The desire to synthesize pure and complex tones is deeply rooted in Western culture. The baroque organ did not appear overnight, being designed to produce "pure, controllable timbres" across a wide range of pitches without the interference of human variables such as a wavering tone, poor tuning, or loss of breath. During the nineteenth century organ-builders tried to make the organ more natural-sounding by introducing onset noises, swells and tremulants to the plain uninflected tones of the classical instrument. In the twentieth century Messiaen, an organist himself, realized the instrument's potential to create a range of unorthodox timbres by unusual couplings of mixture stops, a feature of the *Messe de la Pentecôte*, the *Livre d'Orgue*, and other works. Since the organ was originally designed for such a purpose, experimenting with timbre is easy to do, and the result will tend to "work" acoustically. The fact that organ music in general, and Messiaen's organ music in particular, are not usually mentioned in connection with the origins of electronic music, speaks more of inherited musical prejudice than the physical reality.

Western music can in fact be defined in terms of a history of scientific and mechanical inventions designed to introduce rational consistency into the normally disorganized realm of natural sound. Inherent in the design of the keyboard, equal temperament, and music notation are artificial concepts of pitch and time that have little to do with how human beings manage and interpret sound in real life, a fact acknowledged by every melody line freely distorted by a soloist for expressive effect. Among mechanical acoustic instruments that belong to this history are the seventeeth-century musical box, the eighteenth-century glass *armonica*, and the nineteenth-century player piano. In every case the motivation for inventing such devices is to create "pure, controllable sounds that eliminate the performer." Mechanical performing automata and singing birds, ornaments of Mozart's and Beethoven's time, were designed as objects of scientific and engineering interest. When musicians joined with mechanical instruments, as Haydn became involved with the inventions of Pastor Niemecz, and Beethoven in arranging pieces including "Wellingtons Sieg" for Maelzel's panharmonicon, they too had to deal with the absence of the human dimension from mechanically reproduced music, a task requiring just as much imagination as the composer of the twenty-first century dealing with the commercial synthesizer of the present day.

Electronic music in the sense promoted by the studio at Cologne Radio arose from a meeting of two technologies, the vocoder and the tape recorder. The latter, of course, was invented in Germany and techniques of editing sounds together like a movie had been developed during the war. The vocoder, an instrument developed by Bell Laboratories in New Jersey, is a speech analyzer and synthesizer originally designed in the late thirties. A voice sample spoken into a microphone, and passed repeatedly through a filter, emerged as a graduated sequence of rhythmically modulated current fluctuations corresponding to successive cross-sections of the original signal descending from a high bandwidth of about 4–5 kilohertz to a low of about 50 hertz. This sequence could be used to drive a passive oscillator to reconstitute the original signal in an approximate but recognizable form; or alternatively, to modulate a sound from another source, preferably one of a rich and relatively dense spectrum, such as a locomotive or a jetliner, thus making the machine appear to be talking, that is, to be alive. During the fifties the vocoder figured briefly in a number of American popular children's recordings, such as "Jack Benny plays 'The Bee,'" in which the American comedian's violin talked back, and Henry Blair's "Sparky and the Talking Train," a story of a friendly train engine warning a young passenger of approaching disaster. The vocoder was only moderately accurate, could handle only a short sample of speech at a time, and did not resynthesize in real time; nevertheless the result was good enough to suggest an exciting potential for musical and radiophonic applications. The vocoder now bundled in with modern synthesizer packages operates in real time, and an analogue EMS vocoder from the seventies plays a starring role in the tapes of *Freitag aus LICHT* and "Orchester-Finalisten." The original vocoder is demonstrated in Herbert Eimert's recorded "Einführung in die Elektronische Musik" (Introduction to electronic music).[2]

Electronic music in the postwar era was not intended to sound natural, rather it was considered as a medium of sonic purity. In this respect the scientific goal approached the spiritual ideal of Goeyvaerts and others like him. Harry F. Olson, designer of the Mark I Princeton-Columbia Synthesizer, expressed it in this way:

> There is the possibility of entirely new tone complexes and combinations which cannot be achieved with conventional instruments . . . [where] the musician is limited to the use of lips, mouth, ten fingers, two hands and two feet to perform the different operations. This limitation does not exist in the electronic music synthesiser. Conventional instruments produce various noises such as the rushing of wind in wind instruments, bow scratch in the viol (sic) family, various clatters and rattles in plucked and struck-string instruments, and mechanism rattle in which keys, valves, levers, and shafts are used. These undesirable noises do not exist in the electronic music synthesiser.[3]

The aesthetic of clean lines and no extraneous decoration attaches to the architecture and design ideals of the Bauhaus of Mies van der Rohe and Walter Gropius, of Le Corbusier in Paris, and Philip Johnson in the United States, a machine aesthetic reborn after the war as the "International Style." The proponents of this style believed in social equality and the obligation of modern industrial design and mass production to provide not merely tolerable living conditions for the population, but an aesthetically and morally uplifting domestic and working environment. This could be achieved by a combination of quality materials, uncluttered surfaces, and perfect proportions, epitomized in the Barcelona Pavilion of Mies van der Rohe and gently satirized in Jacques Tati's movie *Mon Oncle*. In today's era of international tourism the high ideals of the International Style linger on in the impersonal "people processing" aesthetic of international airports, art gallery extensions, and shopping malls, but in 1953 good design was a moral as well as a social issue, a desire to rebuild on a basis of essential human values, adapted to modern materials and manufacturing processes. As Stockhausen said, you cannot make a suspension bridge out of adobe. "What does an architect do if he has to build a bridge without supports, a skyscraper or an aircraft hangar? Does he still use adobe, wood and bricks? New forms demand reinforced concrete, glass, aluminium—[and] aluminium, glass, reinforced concrete make new forms possible."[4] The moral and spiritual authority assumed by proponents of good design, the unstated message that it was an influence for good and that the unwitting user should be grateful for it, went beyond the brief of efficiency, ergonomics, and a respect for materials, and elevated the designer to the status of social philosopher, a position of direct influence the artist had last enjoyed in the eighteenth-century Europe of Goethe and Beethoven. That combination of moral authority, allied to good design, based on abstract philosophical principles, and executed to the highest standards of workmanship, is a formula by which Stockhausen's ongoing sense of the artist's role is maintained and can also be interpreted. It is all the same worth remembering that this sense of authority is not a peculiar personal trait but has its roots in a period of history between the wars from which modern design emerged as a force for good.

Werner Meyer-Eppler, who was to have a decisive influence on Stockhausen's conceptual development in the fifties, had been a professor of theoretical physics; after the war he switched to the study of phonetics, which despite its apparently benign nature had serious defense implications during the cold war era. The history of cooperation between defense interests, linguistics, and electronic music has yet to be written, but it is certainly true that electronic music had the potential to make a significant contribution to a theory of language developed with defense applications in mind, and the proliferation of radio and university electronic music studios in the West during the fifties, their common interest in language and communication theory, and their equally sudden decline in the mid-sixties, tell their own story.

As a newly-installed professor of phonetics at Bonn University, Meyer-Eppler was visited in 1948 by Homer Dudley of the Bell Laboratories, bearing the gift of a vocoder. The following year Meyer-Eppler published a book with the bland title *Elektrische Klangerzeugung*, in English "Electrical sound generation" but perhaps more accurately translated as "The generation of tone qualities by electrical means." For a specialist in phonetics he displayed an unusual interest in music, a subject in which he was hardly qualified, and initiated contacts with music colleges to try and interest them in the possibilities of music synthesis. At Detmold Music Academy, where there was a Tonmeister studio for training balance engineers, he caught the attention and interest of Robert Beyer, a lecturer in sound recording at Cologne Radio. Beyer had been interested in the possibilities of electronic music from the mid-twenties when, coinciding with the establishment of public radio in Europe, electric instruments starting with the sphärophon in 1924, followed by the theremin and ondes martenot in 1928, the Givelet organ in 1929, the trautonium in 1930, and the Hammond organ in 1931, began to appear on the scene.

Meyer-Eppler and Beyer joined forces in a presentation on "The Sound World of Electronic Music" at Darmstadt in 1950, an event that Stockhausen unfortunately did not attend. Schaeffer was there however, and even at this early stage aesthetic divisions between concrete and electronic music were already emerging, the Germans seeing no future in trying to work with the impure material of prerecorded concrete sounds. Herbert Eimert, in his capacity as a journalist, and also as an informal colleague of

Beyer at Cologne Radio, was happy to lend his musical authority to help promote the aim of establishing a research studio for electronic music. After a period of negotiation the project was approved, and work on installing equipment in the new studio continued while Stockhausen was in Paris. During the studio refurbishment an old tape of former Propaganda Minister Goebbels was discovered, and preserved as a grisly memento.

His own preference for a purist approach to synthesis is clear from a letter to Goeyvaerts in which Stockhausen declares "From day one I sensed that musique concrète is nothing more than wilful capitulation in the face of indeterminacy, a perversely amateurish game of chance and undisciplined improvisation." He also had an exchange of courtesies with Messiaen over the latter's concrete study *Timbres-Durées*, a piece designed as a modest endorsement of the Schaeffer initiative but one that Stockhausen convinced his teacher could be better served in every respect by conventional instruments.[5] Stockhausen returned to Cologne in March 1953, newly appointed as permanent collaborator in electronic music, joining studio director Eimert and engineer Heinz Schütz, who had earlier assisted Meyer-Eppler and Beyer in the creation of prototype electronic sequences. The studio was equipped with a variety of tone-generating and modifying devices, including a melochord (an electronic keyboard), a trautonium, two ring modulators, an octave-filter, two W49 filters developed in-house for radio drama, a ¼-inch full-track tape recorder, an elderly AEG (Allgemeine Elektrizitäts Gesellschaft, now Telefunken) variable-speed ¼-inch tape recorder, and a ½-inch, four-track tape recorder, all operating at a tape speed of 30 inches (76.2 cm) per second. Stockhausen spent some time getting acquainted with the various items of equipment, including the ring-modulators, which operated in real time and with which he may initially have hoped to produce vocoder-like intermodulations. He discovered the results of modulating a sine tone with a melochord were unexpectedly noisy, and the effect of changing the balance of the two signals, unpredictable: he also found inequalities and distortions in tape recorders and other precision studio equipment, problems excerbated by his decision (following on from his experiments in Paris) to work with sine tones alone. The ear is very forgiving of distortions where speech is concerned, and somewhat forgiving where music is concerned, but because of their purity and simplicity of form, sine tones are the least forgiving of sounds, and most revealing of operational defects: indeed, that is why sine-tone generators are found in a studio.

Elektronische Studie I (Electronic Study I)
1953: No. 3/I
Unpublished (cd Stockhausen-Verlag SV-3)
Duration: 9' 42.

By July 1953 Stockhausen was able to report, in a letter to Goeyvaerts, "I am putting sine tones together to make sounds for a new piece . . . and have just composed some examples of superimposed sine tones, which are totally still, but out of which individual partials emerge into the foreground one after another at predetermined times."[6] Superimposing sine tones is what he had attempted to do in the PTT basement studio in Paris, but this time Stockhausen had the advantage of recording to tape rather than disc. Many photographs remain in circulation from this inaugural period, showing Stockhausen's hands holding lengths of tape carefully assembled on white leader tape. The procedure is similar to that of *Konkrete Etüde*, but with the difference that, not trusting the fader controls to work smoothly, Stockhausen is also painstakingly shaping the onset and decay of each composite tone dynamically by hand, and mounting the result on white leader tape:

As in the *Konkrete Etüde*, Stockhausen is working with steady-state sound materials. When the recorded sound has no starting transient, a straight 90° cut creates an instantaneous onset that in audible terms, depending on frequency, adds a click or thump to the tone. To ensure a graduated transition from silence to sound and back to silence, either the sound has to be copied and shaped with a potentiometer (a fader), or it can be tapered mechanically with scissors, shaping the area of recorded tape and thus varying its amplitude. The problems with recopying and shaping individual tones electronically, using a fader, are twofold: first, copying causes a loss of quality of the copied sound (leading to inconsistencies within the family of sounds); second, manual fading has the potential to introduce inconsistencies into the shaping process, in both the timing and the angles of onset and decay curves. It is very much to Stockhausen's credit that he had the persistence to strive for the best result possible when others might have taken an easier route. In shaping the tape by hand he is adapting a technique known to optical sound in the film industry, by which the strength of the audible signal varies directly in proportion to the area of tape passing the playback head. Since this time Stockhausen has taken considerable pride in his mastery of fading sounds in and out, and in the perceptions of spatial perspective, of sounds approaching and receding, associated with fading. In his description of an ideal synthesizer, for example, he asks for faders of exceptional length, 30–40 cm,[7] and in performances and recordings of works such as *Kontakte* he is constantly having to monitor the result to ensure that the final fadeout is not prematurely terminated. (The inherent drama of the fadeout acquires dramatic significance in the slow-motion, meditative context of the *LICHT* cycle, where it can sometimes be easier to follow the arrival and departure of the music than to keep track of the action on stage.)

The tone complexes of *Studie I* are superimposed sine tones, derived from a symmetrical series of intervals related to the tuning of a 5 : 4 ratio or nontempered major third, which when added cumulatively to a reference frequency produces a nontempered interval set chiming pleasantly on the ear. Remarkably for a first attempt Stockhausen has produced an electronic timbre clearly analogous to the crystal goblet of *Spiel* and the vibraphone/

glockenspiel combination of *Formel*. In the electronic domain, the timbre is also amplified, and thus more powerful, to a point that the composer might have considered revising the two earlier scores and substituting a tape for these focal instruments.[8]

$$\frac{12}{5} \qquad \frac{4}{5} \qquad \frac{8}{5} \qquad \frac{5}{12} \qquad \frac{5}{4}$$

Tone proportions and collections of Studie I

Like the later *Refrain*, *Studie I* appears to inhabit the treble register, an effect of the ear's greater efficiency in processing pure tones at higher frequencies. A gentle, transparent piece, its slightly tremulous quality is enhanced by frequent small echoes. The range of tones, deliberately restricted to approximately five octaves (in round numbers, 66–2000 hertz) extends from low drum-like reverberations at close range (at times resembling decompression effects), to small chimes in the middle distance, creating an impression of a dynamic plane that slopes up and away from the listener, like a di Chirico perspective. On the night of 24 September, Doris Stockhausen was admitted to a maternity clinic, and gave birth to Suja, their first daughter, early the following morning. The happy event is commemorated in *Studie I*, in Richard Toop's phrase, by the insertion of a serially unauthorized 108–hertz "one-gun salute."

Elektronische Studie II (Electronic Study II)
1954: No. 3/II (formerly UE 12466, now Stockhausen-Verlag; cd SV-3)
Duration: 3' 20.

Studie II is complementary to *Studie I*. Where the earlier work consists of stationary sounds, the new work is dynamic: its provisional title was *Bewegungen* (Movements), and where the earlier study is harmonious, the new study is more textured, choric, and even noisy.

Even before his first hands-on experiences in Paris, Stockhausen was aware of alternative techniques to additive synthesis for the production and manipulation of complex electronic sounds. To Goeyvaerts he writes, "With electronic sound material most of the time you are not dealing with tones any more, but with more complex sounds, and the production of different sounds already implies the creation of inherent differences in density, over which we are still a long way from having any control. I'm going to talk it over thoroughly with Dr. Meyer-Eppler again next week."[9] This advice seems to be part theory, from reading Meyer-Eppler's *Elektrische Klangerzeugung*, and part personal experience of the problems for a composer of musique concrète of deriving a vocabulary of differentiable sounds from prerecorded source material. That Stockhausen's conception of music, both electronic and non-electronic, extended beyond Goeyvaerts' ideal purity to include imperfect sounds and noises we already know, both from the opposition of percussion and tone instruments in *Kreuzspiel* and *Spiel*, and from his allusions to noise and tone as complementary components of speech. A sine-tone generator is a device producing a pure tone of continuously variable frequency, so to create a complex sound with such a generator implies many cumulative iterations of the synthesis process and consequent overcopying of material, which is both unsatisfactory from the viewpoint of quality, and impossibly long-winded in practice. On the other hand, a white-noise generator, which is also standard studio equipment, generates a wideband signal containing every frequency within a selected bandwidth, and all at the same amplitude. Using a sufficiently precise band-pass filter, therefore, it is possible in theory to derive a sine tone of any desired frequency from the output of a white-noise generator. The additional advantage of doing so would be that by varying the width of the band, a graduated scale of values from pure tone to noise could also be generated. Such a scale would have very interesting applications musically, would facilitate the synthesis of speech sounds, and could also be serially justified. A major incentive to pursue this line of possibility was the publication in 1947 of Potter, Kopp and Kopp's pioneering study *Visible Speech*, a publication with which both Eimert and Stockhausen were clearly familiar.[10]

Electronic organ designers were also aware of the commercial potential of filtered noise as a means of adding realism, whatever objections might be raised to such a procedure by composers. In reality all naturally generated musical sounds incorporate some noise: on the one hand action noise, such as breathing, or bowing, or mechanical clatter; on the other hand natural uncertainties of intonation and timing. The use of filtered noise could lead to the production of sounds with an apparent "inner life." In an essay "Statistic and Psychologic Problems of Sound" written in 1954, the year Stockhausen began attending his classes at the Institute of Phonetics and Communications Research at Bonn University, Meyer-Eppler addresses the issue of liveliness in the tone quality of commercial organs, and regrets the lack of imagination of manufacturers who limit themselves to a mechanical tremulant effect, produced by summing the outputs of just two oscillating circuits, when by adding just one more circuit, an "aleatoric," i.e., unpredictable, and much more natural, choric effect could be simply produced. This aleatoric component is created by filtering the output of a noise generator in a narrow bandwidth in the subaudio range of 5–15 hertz, resulting in an unstable vibrato. "The composer who takes advantage of the possibilities of aleatoric modulation will be surprised to discover that this kind of modulation leads him directly into a world of phenomena, previously described as 'noises.'"[11] Meyer-Eppler goes on to discuss the perceptual implications of statistical processes in terms that indicate an awareness of Stockhausen's pointillist music, and the composer's urgent need to find a method for producing complex sounds in the studio. Apropos pointillism, Meyer-Eppler observes that sounds "are only differentiable when they follow one another in close sequence. Where the stimuli are presented in isolation their valency locations can only be approximately differentiated,"—saying in effect that too much separation in frequency and time leads to a sense of unrelatedness. Stockhausen is quick to seize on this observation to account for the listener's loss of temporal orientation in a composition where the durations exceed a certain threshold, such as Messiaen's "Soixante-Quatre Durées" from the *Livre d'Orgue*. There is a corollary however; since there are limits to the ear's powers of resolution in a given region of frequency, and these limits are subject to the frequency, amplitude, and density of events within that region, it follows that a configuration of sounds that exceeds the ear's powers of resolution (for example, a greatly accelerated sequence of sounds on tape) will be perceived only qualitatively. In turn, that means a composer is at liberty to simplify the microstructure of an artificial waveform so that no element is needlessly suppressed, remembering how he agonized over the microsounds of *Konkrete Etüde*. So it is now possible for him to create the microstructure of a waveform without exactly reproducing the proportional disparities of amplitude and duration of the macrostructure of the work itself. Meyer-Eppler's involuntary benediction freed Stockhausen from the theoretical constraint under which he had been suffering, and authorized him to produce *Studie II* and future compositions using a variety of simplified microsequences. He talks enthusiastically about this new freedom in his conversations with Jonathan Cott.[12]

The sound-world of *Studie II* is of interest in a number of ways. In order to create a coherent tone structure the composer has first to devise a system of tuning or temperament. *Studie I* is based on an interval succession in simple harmonic ratios of 5 : 4 (major third transpositions, alternately up and down); these are realised as sine tones and superimposed in varying numbers as virtual partial tones of bell-like timbres, which are then manually shaped to provide different degrees and combinations of onset and decay. *Studie II* is more "scientific," but also more compromised musically. The musical material is developed from five pentatonic interval clusters calculated to a nonstandard tempered frequency scale ascending from a reference 100 hertz by constant degrees of 1/25 root of 5, rounded to the nearest whole number for frequencies below 1,000 hertz, and to ten above 1,000 hertz, a temperament possibly related to Le Corbusier's *Modulor*.

The resulting inharmonic scale is only slightly out of tune compared to equal tempered tuning, and both the calculation and the rounding-off of values suggest a form of compromise suggested by Meyer-Eppler or studio technical advisors. In the first place, the concept is purely mathematical; second, the starting point of 100 hertz is just twice the standard 50 hertz of an electrical system; third, it is also a standard test frequency for a studio tape recorder; and fourth, the compromises in rounded tuning arise from the limited resolution of a studio sweep frequency oscillator. That the calculation of pitch involves powers of five does however connect the procedure with the 5 : 4 tuning of *Studie I* (and beyond it, conceivably, to the serial

Group I tone mixtures of Studie II

fives of Boulez's concrete study).

The diagram shows the five tone-groups, in "five degrees of separation," derived from numbers 1–25 of Stockhausen's frequency table. There is surprisingly good agreement with regular (imperfect) tuning: an indication of how difficult it is to create a system of tuning that the ear will not accept. A similar interval sequence to Group 5, starting from the same 100 hertz g sharp and leading upward in gurgling arpeggiated form, introduces the seventy-fifth birthday piece "Zu Ehren von Igor Stravinsky" presented to Stravinsky on the occasion of his visit to the studio in 1957.[13] Stravinsky's visit followed an interview with Hans Heinz Stuckenschmidt in which the venerable composer expressed particular enthusiasm and admiration for Stockhausen and the work of the Cologne electronic music studio. "What are these sounds?" he asked. "On what system of tuning are they based? I would like to study everything that Ernst Krenek and the young Karlheinz Stockhausen have worked on. Krenek is a bright spirit; [Giselher] Klebe and Stockhausen are musicians I hold in the highest esteem. One must take an interest in such matters. These things, and *only* these things, bring us further."[14]

The *Studie II* tone-groups are produced by a radically different method from *Studie I*. The production of five-layer tone-groups on a four-track tape recorder would normally imply copying back and forth until all five tones are superimposed, a procedure that as we have said is both time-consuming and leads to degradation of the signal. The underlying theory of the *Studie I* can be inferred from the discovery attributed to Jean-Baptiste Fourier (1768–1830) that any complex waveform may be expressed as a superimposition of sine tones in harmonic relation. That suggests that waveforms corresponding to new sounds or timbres may also be synthesized by the superimposition of sine waves, and for that reason may be made in conformity with a serial order-principle that is not found in nature. (The Fourier Theorem dates from the early Romantic era of Faraday and Mary Shelley, so there is a historical, albeit tenuous connection between the idea of creating new sounds by electronic means and the electrical resuscitation of life dreamed by the author of *Frankenstein.*)

Sine-tone material is also employed in *Studie II*, but in a way that might suggest Stockhausen was abandoning his purist ideals. Instead of layering sound upon sound to create aggregates, he employs an acceleration technique that recalls Helmholtz's use of the siren in the pursuit of analogous inquiries into the properties of harmony and timbre, including partials, difference tones, frequency ratios and phase relationships. Phase relationship has to do with the temporal alignment of partial tones, meaning whether they vibrate in synchronization (or march in step). Ideally, for sine-tone partials to be perceived as a unified tone-colour they should oscillate in step. Such fine-tuning was not feasible under the studio conditions of that time, and since the component partials of *Studie I* tone-groups do not vibrate perfectly in phase, a listener hears the resulting combinations sometimes as bell-like tones, at other times as liquid harmonies.

In the much more primitive conditions of the mid-nineteenth century Helmholtz had struggled with the same issue of how partial tones combine when they are in and out of phase. His test equipment was a laboratory siren with two adjustable discs; a concentrated air stream passing through perforations in the rotating discs emerging as a tone of constant pitch and distinctive tone colour. Whether by chance or design, Stockhausen follows an analogous process in the tape domain. The tone collections to be combined are sampled at constant length and amplitude, and edited together into a sequence in descending arpeggio formation:

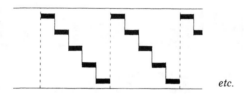

etc.

This procedure is employed for each group of tone mixtures, the sequence being repeated several times to create a short burst of sound. One by one the resulting soundbursts were transmitted at high speed into a reverberation chamber and the resulting burst and a long reverberation re-recorded. By speeding up the original sound-burst samples the arpeggiated material is compressed; increasing the playback speed also transposes the complex to a higher pitch level and shortens its duration, helping to compress the edited sequence into a single attack and create a uniform reverberation. Since a reverberation chamber has a maximum reverberation time (the length of time during which the sound decays), it follows that the greater the acceleration, the shorter the onset burst and thus the greater tape length in proportion of usable steady-state reverberated sound is produced. As with the *Konkrete Etüde*, it is the steady-state reverberation in which Stockhausen is interested, the onset burst being edited out to leave a usable tape length of steady-state tone mixture, which can then be cut to shape.

Such a method of creating sound might seem to resemble, at the most rudimentary level, the effect of dragging a stick along a corrugated iron fence. Many musical instruments however could be said to operate in a similar way, a violin by friction against a reverberating string, a trumpet by the forced reverberation of an air column, and so on. The physical process is arguably similar to tone production in the human voice, the onset burst corresponding to excitation of vibrations in the larynx, and the reverberation chamber acting like the resonant chambers of the throat, mouth, and nasal passages. This is a process and a sound material of justified scientific interest. In an echo-chamber, a relatively large open space, the forced vibration results in a mixture of airborne reflections, uncolored by wood or metal resonances, and sounding relatively diffuse. Closer-knit groups, where the arpeggiated intervals are a minor third or less, resemble organ clusters, whereas the wider-interval groups sound more like choric syllables. Though denser to the ear than the constellations of *Studie I*, the groups and their constituent tones are not at all difficult for a musical ear to distinguish. One can also detect a slight tremor that is the faint residue of the tape arpeggiation process.

The steady-state materials are then assembled into serial formations that express different degrees of spatial and temporal distribution, from simultaneously to sequentially, just like the note complexes of *Klavierstück I*. As with *Studie I*, the serially determined amplitudes of block sonorities are again individually shaped, very simply, and in one direction as shown:

—an ascending triangle corresponding to an onset crescendo, a rectangle to a steady state (constant dynamic), and a descending triangle to a more or less rapid fade.

Although only three minutes in duration, *Studie II* is rich in implication and (in graphic terms) seductively beautiful. It explores the area of aural response between consciousness of the external shape and awareness of the inner structure of sounds, corresponding for example to a listener simultaneously being aware of the "tone of voice" of a speaker, which is a *constant* acoustic feature, subject to spectrum analysis,—and the "sense" of what the speaker is saying, which arises from a complementary *dynamic* process of "content" evaluation involving pattern recognition. In assessing the block frequencies in their macroconfigurations, the key ingredient is duration: the longer the time interval between successive changes, the more the ear focuses on the internal structure, and complexes tend to sound harmonic, whereas when changes are more rapid, the more the ear pays attention to the outer contour or group inflection, and the more noisy the effect. Hence the second group of five "blocks" (pages 1–2 of the score) resembles a parallel harmonic progression (for example, the woodwinds introduction to Debussy's *Le Martyre de Saint-Sébastien*), whereas by contrast the complex central group on page 12 of the score has a more pronounced syllabic character.

Complexes of rising intensity seem to create energy and momentum, though the effect is dependent on duration and complexity as well. It is also easier for the ear to distinguish the partial inner structure of groups of rising intensity than those that die away: this reflects on the importance of the starting transient in regular instruments, and the masking effect of an instantaneous onset (compare the rising complex in the score on page 11, with the falling complex on page 9). Superimposed groups with overlap tend to sound "choric." A rare example of the opposite effect occurs on page 16 of the score, where the final complex consists of superimposed narrow-band blocks with no overlap: this complex is both more "noisy" and, paradoxically, more realistic as a timbre. When groups are well separated in time as well as in frequency space, the effect is rhythmic and energetic, the short percussive sounds of pages 13–15 being among the most spontaneously allusive of the entire work. The terminal "drum-roll," a characteristic Stockhausen surprise ending, is also very impressive.

These two electronic studies, building on the composer's Paris experiences, provide coherent and perfect images of the passive and active modes of musical audition, *Studie I* expressing the contemplative mode, and *Studie II* the gestural or participational mode. In later years Stockhausen returns to this same pair relationship, albeit in instrumental terms, contrasting the still tone-mixtures of *Refrain* for three keyboards, and the dynamic scatter of *Zyklus* for solo percussionist. *Studie II* can also be seen as a prototype of later musical forms, influenced by his studies with Meyer-Eppler, in which the external features are determined but the inner composition is aleatoric.

Notes

1. Jonathan Cott, *Stockhausen: Conversations with the Composer* (London: Robson Books, 1974), 29–30.

2. Herbert Eimert, "Einführung in die Elektronische Musik." lp. Wergo 60006.

3. H. F. Olson, *Music, Physics, and Engineering*. 2nd edn. (New York: Dover Publications, 1967), 415.

4. "Elektronische und Instrumentale Musik." *Texte 1*, 140. Cited in Seppo Heikenheimo, "Electronic Music of Karlheinz Stockhausen" tr. Brad Absetz. *Acta Musicologica Fennica* 6 (1972), 14.

5. Hermann Sabbe, *Karlheinz Stockhausen: . . . wie die Zeit verging . . .* (Munich: texte + kritik, 1981), 42–44.

6. Hermann Sabbe, *Karlheinz Stockhausen: . . . wie die Zeit verging . . .* , 44.

7. *SoM*, 133–34.

8. These two musical illustrations, in Boulez's manuscript, are taken from the French edition of Stockhausen's essay "Une Expérience Électronique" published in *Musique et ses Problèmes Contemporains 1953–1963* (Paris: Julliard, 1964), 91–105. They do not appear in the German edition, *Texte 2*, 22–36.

9. Hermann Sabbe, *Karlheinz Stockhausen: . . . wie die Zeit verging . . .* , 40.

10. Ralph K. Potter, George A. Kopp, and Harriet Green Kopp, *Visible Speech*. Revised edition (New York: Dover Publications, 1966).

11. Werner Meyer-Eppler, "Statistic and Psychological Problems of Sound" tr. A. Goehr. 55–61 in *die Reihe I* (Bryn Mawr: Theodore Presser, 1958).

12. Jonathan Cott, *Stockhausen: Conversations with the Composer* (London:

Robson Books, 1974), 85–89.

13.   "Zu Ehren von Igor Stravinsky:" an electronic "round" for vocoder and tone mixtures included in Eimert, "Einführung in die Elektronische Musik," Wergo lp WER 60006.

14.   "Was sind das für Klänge, welches Tonsystem dient als Grunglage? Ich möchte alles studieren, was Ernst Krenek und der junge Karlheinz Stockhausen gearbeitet haben. Krenek ist ein klarer geist, Klebe und Stockhausen sind Musiker, die ich hochschätze. Man muss sich dafür interessieren. Diese Dinge, und nur diese Dinge, bringen uns weiter." Stravinsky as reported in H. H. Stuckenshmidt, "Strawinsky und Sankt Markus" in *Der Tagesspiegel* (Berlin: 18 September 1956). Reprinted in Helmut Kirchmeyer, *Zur Entstehungs- und Problemgeschichte der 'Kontakte' von Karlheinz Stockhausen*. Essay enclosed with Wergo lp recording Wergo WER 60009.

CHAPTER EIGHT

Temperaments

Stockhausen's persistence and self-discipline through the difficult years of 1951–1953, during which he overcame daunting technical problems of notation, instrumentation, and studio practice, paid dividends in an extended period of extraordinary invention between 1954 and 1961, and composition of a succession of small and large masterpieces, every one different, and all brilliantly realized in visual terms. This was a period of serious professional rivalry among the radio stations of Europe and their orchestras. Under the stewardship of radio new music regained the prestige it had previously enjoyed under the aristocratic leaders and patrons of the principalities of continental Europe in the late eighteenth century. Public and media interest in new music were high. An articulate and productive young composer of Stockhausen's caliber was clearly destined for greatness; that he also enjoyed the direct patronage of Cologne Radio was an added advantage as well as a very useful discipline. Stockhausen's meticulously planned and executed scores of the period reflect the methodical procedures and detailed documentation of a state radio administrative culture. In addition, his role as an associate of the electronic music studio involved him in writing and presenting broadcast programmes on contemporary music, much of which can only have been of marginal interest to him, and do so in a dignified and objective manner. There were other, more attractive duties: in December 1954 he acted as tape operator for a first performance in Hamburg of *Déserts* for orchestra and tape by Edgar Varèse, under the baton of Bruno Maderna. Far from being isolated from his contemporaries, at a time when his own music was rapidly gaining in confidence Stockhausen was actively involved in directing and helping to promote performances and discussion of the avant-garde.

In October 1954 he met and sensed an instant rapport with John Cage and David Tudor, who were visiting Cologne as part of a tour of Germany. Cage and Tudor performed new American piano music in the first half of an historic concert given in the Large Broadcasting Hall of Cologne Radio, the second half being given over to first performances of electronic music by Eimert, the Swiss Paul Gredinger, Belgian composers Goeyvaerts and Henri Pousseur, and including the two electronic studies of Stockhausen himself. The electronic part of the concert created a strange impression on the public, similar to musique concrète concerts in Paris, in providing nothing for the audience to look at apart from two large loudspeaker cabinets, one on either side of the stage. The absence of visual stimulation, coupled with new advances in stereophony, was ultimately to provoke Stockhausen to consider new ideas for the distribution and movement of sounds in three dimensions, and their imitation in visual reality.

Stockhausen's liking for Cage is reminiscent of his fascination with Messiaen's music, as for any music he could not immediately understand. "Cage is the craziest spirit of combination I have ever come across; . . . he has that indifference towards everything known and experienced that is necessary for an explorer" he wrote.[1] To the piano music of Cage, Morton Feldman, and Christian Wolff, David Tudor brought the same sublime quality of no-mindedness, allied to fabulous technical gifts. Hermann Hesse's *Glass Bead Game* tells of an encounter between the youthful Knecht and an "older brother" who initiates him into the mystery of the *I Ching*, the ancient Chinese system of divination by the casting of yarrow sticks.[2] To Stockhausen, hearing Cage's *Music of Changes* performed by Tudor in the same concert as his electronic studies was more than a revelation: it was as good as the fulfillment of a prophecy, since Cage was known to use the *I Ching* as a randomizing procedure, and the *Music of Changes* books had been composed using a combination of serial charts for permutation and the *I Ching* for selection. Having deconstructed the philosophy of tempered tuning and tonal consistency by means of the prepared piano, the New York composer had since applied himself to redefining the systems of notation and interpretation that had evolved in conformity with that same Western tradition.

Cage's "indifference" had a serious purpose, and his method of randomization, however esoteric it might appear, was essentially objective in intention, neither religious, nor an aesthetic pose. The purpose of indeterminacy in music is to reveal underlying natural processes: in this case, the underlying processes of music, on what assumptions it is based, and how it caters to those (social, perceptual) assumptions, for which the word "aesthetics" is a term of convenience. A composition organizes the environment just as a laboratory technician prepares a glass slide, and the actions of the performer are directed by the stimulus of a form of notation, just as the specimen is conditioned by exposure to a chemical or biological agent. The listener and composer observe the result, repeat the procedure a number of times, and learn from it. Audiences are taken aback by such a procedure, because it puts them in the spotlight. Instead of giving pleasure by confirming their conventional terms of reference, the new music demands conscious and active engagement, on the one hand, in monitoring the musical performance for information, and on the other hand, in monitoring the reaction such a performance may provoke. In today's world of audience polling and voter sampling, such self-aware participation in issues of perception has become quite normal; ever since the time of Cézanne the public has been coopted by artists into a process of dialogue or debate concerning the nature of art and established conventions of beauty. That such an approach was (and is) still controversial in relation to music tells us something about the culture's relative unsophistication in the aural as distinct from the visual domain.

Klavierstücke V–VIII (Piano Pieces V–VIII)
1954–1955, VI rev. 1961; No. 4 (UE 13675a–d; cd Stockhausen-Verlag SV-56)
Durations: V 5' 00; VI 16' 20; VII 6' 50; VIII 1' 40.

Like the first set of piano pieces, numbers V to VIII are studies, but unlike the former set, which are essays in formal organization, these are focused on sonority, timing, and gesture: the dynamics of performance, one might say. The difference in emphasis reflects not a change of direction but a shift of attention to new ways of perceiving and articulating sounds arising from Stockhausen's experiences with taped sounds in the studio, and his studies of acoustics and communication theory under Meyer-Eppler.

> If after eighteen months of work devoted exclusively to electronic compo-
> sitions, I now find myself working at piano pieces, it is because in the
> most strongly structured compositions I have come across important
> musical phenomena that are non-quantifiable. They are no less real,
> recognizable, conceivable, or palpable for that. These phenomena I am
> better able,—at the moment, anyway,—to clarify with the help of an
> instrument and interpreter, than in the field of electronic composition.
> Above all it has to do with the provision of a new sense of time in music,
> whereby the infinitely subtle "irrational" nuances, and stresses, and
> delays made by a good interpreter are often truer to the piece's intended
> effect than measurement by centimeters. Such statistical form criteria
> will give us a completely new, hitherto unthought-of style of relationship
> between sound that is "of the instrument" and sound that is "of *playing*
> the instrument."[3]

After completing the Piano Pieces I–IV, Stockhausen had the idea of adding five more sets to create an extended cycle of twenty-one pieces forming a super-set: 4 6 1 5 3 2, the number 21 (as we recall from *Kontra-Punkte*) being the sum of the series 1 through 6. (The principle of a serial set also looks ahead to the serial segmentation of *LICHT*.) The second set was intended to consist of six pieces, V–X, and the third, of the single Piano Piece XI. Pieces V–VIII of the second set were realized in 1954–1955, XI in 1956; but completion of the second set had to wait until 1961 when IX and X were composed, by which time Stockhausen's thinking had considerably evolved.

Richard Toop has written at some length about the original sketches.[4] In common with Pieces I–IV, all were fairly short: V a study in "far-flung constellations of grace-notes," set in opposition to a foreground of long, measured pitches; VI a tiny one-minute Webernian structure of fixed intervals within a two-octave space; VII a study in metrical invariance, possibly inspired by the second movement of Webern's String Quartet, which he had analyzed and which is composed entirely in quarter-notes.[5] All except VIII were substantially revised after his encounter with Cage and Tudor.

Piece V is in six sections, identified by tempo: MM 80; 90; 71; 113.5; 101; and 63.5, tempi representing whole-tone divisions of a chromatic "tempo-octave" MM 60–120. Since the music lacks an articulate pulse, alterations of tempo are more psychological than real. These tempi are also a way of avoiding a continuous regular beat while at the same time allowing complex interior divisions as in Piano Piece I to be notated more simply. In Piece V the underlying structure is also very sparse. When the grace note material is taken into account, however, each section is seen to be characterized by a density of events in inverse proportion to its chronometric duration (though not its tempo). The question at issue is whether average density is perceived for relatively long durations, as it is for the relatively short durations, say, of Piece I (the point Meyer-Eppler had made about group perception). Stockhausen's use of half-pedal and full sustain is designed to help the listener hear particular constellations of grace-notes and main notes as structural entities. The grace-note anacruses appear to connect with their longer notes in much the same way as the arpeggio note-bursts of *Studie II* act as "attacks" to their reverberated complexes. An attractive and newly time-sensitive layout of the printed score, without barlines, encourages the performer to scan the page continuously instead of measure by measure. These revised scores look a lot more like Cage's *Music of Changes* and certainly conform to Tudor's style of "watching time rather than feeling time." A comparable fluidity of timing may be found in music of nocturnal character, for example the Night Music of Bartók's "Out of Doors" Suite, in which a similar balance of structural and ornamental figures can be found. And though aesthetically their musical content stands at the opposite pole from Stockhausen, a similar attention to visual presentation of primary and subordinate complexes can also be found, strangely enough, in the piano scores of Percy Grainger.

Piece VII is in five tempo-defined sections (MM 40; 63.5; 57; 71; 50.5) —a third slower than the standard MM 60–120 tempo scale. Its most interesting feature is the definition of favored resonances by silently-depressed keys (the lozenge-shaped notes in the score), regions set in reverberation by accented single notes. The aim is to turn the piano into a flexible, selective resonator, and the resonant character of the piece evolves organically and with the same deliberation as the active notes and groups. A listener is thus able to "hear" the work on two different levels: in terms both of the primary action, and of the secondary reverberation, the latter acting like formant shaping in human speech. The combination of manual and pedal sustain options creates a rich resource of resonance possibilities, from secco through to indefinite sustain. Here the left *una corda* pedal is employed not to dampen the tone, but to provide a further tone-color (thus the paradox, *sforzato una corda*). Stockhausen also employs a scale of pauses, differentiated by the duration of rests over which the pause sign is placed.

By far the most intriguing section of Piece VII is the fourth episode, MM 71, where a fast, articulate beginning progressively disperses into shifting resonances in the bass, which in turn become more and more attenuated, as if the music were being slowed down on a vari-speed tape recorder. Suddenly, when time and motion have almost ceased, rapid grace-notes reappear in the extreme high register, a dramatic effect experienced in studio real life when a prerecorded reel to reel tape is slowed down to a point where the ultrasonic bias tone suddenly descends into audibility. (Similar dramatic effects are incorporated in *Kontakte*, at 19' 31,5", and *Telemusik*, at 16.)

The brief Piece VIII, in two sections (MM 90; 80), is also the most complex of the set, working on

at least a dozen simultaneously operative serial levels: two for pitches (grace notes and 'main notes'), and the others for such things as number of subordinate groups (groups of groups) per section, number of groups per subordinate group, number of attacks per grace-note group, number of notes in each grace-note attack, dynamic level of the grace-note groups, and an even larger number of specifications for the main notes.[6]

Each of the major formal units selects six adjacent values from a basic scale of ten dynamics. Different dynamics within the chosen selection articulate the internal structure, with the average dynamic value serving to distinguish one group from the next. Major structural divisions are indicated by long durations; internal subdivisions, as in Piece V, by grace-note anacruses. Whereas the anacruses in Piece V are strings of one to six single notes, those of Piece VIII are composed of successions of chords of one to six notes' density, and varying in attack as well. This complexity in material of ostensibly incidental character puts the composer's regular tempo indication "as fast as possible" under a certain amount of strain, since somewhat complicated shifts of hand position are required. Here more than ever the boundary is blurred between chronometic regularly-notated groups and "time out" incidental groups, a dramatic opposition to be further revisited and graphically depicted with great elegance and sophistication in *Zyklus* some years later.

Piece VI, in revised form now the longest of the set, draws upon all of the modes of coordination employed in V, VII and VIII, and anticipates the extraordinary temporal flux of Piece X. Here for the first time, tempo-changes corresponding to the verbal indications of Piece V, are rendered as linear shifts on a 13-line stave, a line moving upward for an accelerando, downward for a ritardando, and vanishing completely where there is a pause. This compares to Cage's introductory advice to the performer of *Music of Changes* that "accelerandos and ritards are to be associated with the rhythmic structure, rather than with the sounds that happen in it." The connotation of tempo as a gradient to be controlled like a player-piano perhaps envisages a future synthesizer keyboard with swell control. In a

1958 article Christian Wolff speaks of Stockhausen's interest in "a new instrument of electronic means, with the attending range of possibilities, but also subjected to the actions of a performer."[7] Like so many of Stockhausen's good ideas, use of the linear notation of tempo has since lapsed, though a similar graphic reappears as a dynamic control, and also as a microtonal pitch indication, in later pieces.

Grace-note groups take on a new function in Piece VI, partly as a consequence of the graphic transformation of tempo into an external and (to all appearances) mechanical modulation. They appear in this context less as attack formations than to blur the structural timings. "Passive" sympathetic resonances provide a further level of phrasing. The vocabulary of articulation is extensive, and it is interesting to compare Stockhausen's functional notation with Boulez's in the latter's Third Sonata. In turn, Cage's pieces derive much of their stage presence from the example of Boulez, in particular his Second Sonata, which Cage had got to know from his first Paris visit. So in a convoluted way *Music of Changes* in effect is the catalyst causing a reaction between Stockhausen and the French tradition, which in turn may explain why Boulez took such a proprietorial interest in Stockhausen's piano pieces, in particular Piano Piece XI. The advantage to Stockhausen of reviewing the French pianistic temperament through Cage could well be related to the American composer's more detached interpretation of Boulez's rather fiery rhetoric. In Pieces IV and VIII, Stockhausen appears to draw on his knowledge of Boulez's scores, reproducing the wide leaps and contrasts and contrapuntal complexities of his Second Sonata and *Structures*, but ignoring their relationship to Boulez's tempi, which in characteristically Gallic fashion are notated as modes of performance rather than metronomic tempi ("Vif," "Modéré," "Assez Large," etc.). The virtue of *Music of Changes* is that the notated material is so obviously incidental to the dynamic of performance that one cannot help noticing how dependent the piece is on the quality of performer action.

Zeitmasse (Time Measures)
1955–1956: No. 5 (UE 12607; cd Stockhausen-Verlag SV-4)
For woodwind quintet: oboe, flute, cor anglais, clarinet, bassoon.
Duration: 14' 15.

The relationship of pitch and time is a recurrent theme in Stockhausen's thinking between 1952 and 1959. His efforts at reconciling the two principal dimensions of serial form are set out in the celebrated essay ". . . how time passes . . ." published in *die Reihe 3*. As a sequence of speculations on the nature of time the essay is difficult to follow or digest. As an exposition of textbook acoustics it has been criticized. But Stockhausen's essay is concerned less with the wider implications of his theorizing (though he was sensitive to them) than with solving practical questions of compositional efficiency, and these are less difficult to understand.

Stockhausen had two reasons for integrating pitch and time: one aesthetic, the other rational. Aesthetically he inclined to the principle of one set of proportions for all musical parameters, whatever Goeyvaerts might say about their essential incompatibility, pitch being perceived logarithmically, duration arithmetically. Rationally, however, pitch and time *had* to be related, since Stockhausen had experienced for himself in the studio the auditory effect of speeding up an impulse stream or arpeggiated note-burst: beyond a density of fifteen to twenty impulses per second the rhythm is spontaneously transformed into a rasping pitch. It followed that the difference between hearing a rhythm and hearing a tone is not inherent in the stimulus itself but in the way the body is designed to process periodic phenomena occupying different regions in the frequency scale, sounds above 4 kilohertz being perceived as "tone-color," statistically, sounds in the region of 20 hertz to 4 kilohertz as pitch, and below 20 hertz as pulse and rhythm. This information would have come from Meyer-Eppler if Stockhausen had not already discovered it for himself. It reinforces a radio person's intuitive belief in an integrated frequency scale extending, as the man said, from the vibrations of the atoms to the primal oscillation of the entire universe.

From that basic principle of vibratory connectedness flows a host of consequential pronouncements and attitudes, of which the most critical for a listener to Stockhausen's music is the notion, also common to ancient civilizations, of the coexistence in nature of organic processes at different time-scales, and its corollary, that human perceptions of natural processes are geared to only a small segment of the universal spectrum of frequencies. Our perception of color and light, for instance, is limited to the visible spectrum and not sensitive to X-rays, radio waves, the ultraviolet or the infrared. Conveying that awareness of a broader spectrum in a musical sense, and as it applies in his own compositions, leads the composer from time to time to express himself in statements of a deliberately Ptolemaic or Keplerian symbolism that can be readily misconstrued or misunderstood: "If you are able to compress an entire Beethoven symphony into half a second, then you have a new sound. . . . Naturally it has a very particular quality compared to the sound resulting from the compression of a Schoenberg symphony, because there are many more aperiodicities in Schoenberg."[8]

In Piano Pieces V–VIII Stockhausen examined the relationship between musical events perceived as grouped and those perceived as discrete. Just as Cage had invented the prepared piano, Stockhausen, with David Tudor's help, was busy inventing the "prepared pianist," conditioning the articulation of groups through a changing combination of psychological and notational variables. With *Zeitmasse* for wind quintet, and *Gruppen* for three orchestras, these techniques of performer preparation are extended to instrumentalists for whom additional physical limitations apply: the length of a breath for a wind player, a bow action for a string player, or speed of articulation for a keyed instrument. "Zeitmasse" is the German word for "tempi" but in the sense of *measures of time*, which is more precise (chronometric) in implication than the English use of the word as a synonym for speed, or pace. Here we are dealing with a treatment of tempo relationships that goes beyond synchronization to address individual perceptions and articulations of groups and extended phrases.

Stockhausen's inspiration for *Zeitmasse* came in the form of an interruption while he was in seclusion working on the sketches for a commissioned work for orchestra that eventually became *Gruppen*. Asked to contribute to a collection of musical tributes to Heinrich Strobel in honour of the tenth anniversary of the Donaueschingen Festival, he quickly dreamed up a very beautiful setting, for alto voice, accompanied by flute, clarinet in a, and bassoon, of an epigrammatic verse penned in idiomatic lowercase by Strobel himself and rendered into French by Antoine Goléa:

on cherche	trying
pour trouver	to find
quelque chose	something
mais au fond	but really
on ne sait pas	not knowing
ce qu'on cherche	what to look for
au juste	exactly
et cela est vrai.	and that's the truth.[9]

The humorous spirit of this caprice persists in the recomposition for wind quintet, the voice replaced by cor anglais and an oboe added. The work was first premiered as a wind quintet in December 1955, with the addition of a pre-coda at measure 290 characterized by more elaborate subdivisions of 5, 7, 9, and 11. It was almost doubled in length again the following year by the insertion of what Stravinsky calls "the free but coordinated cadenzas . . . a rhythmic innovation of great value."[10] Stravinsky was also intrigued by the group dynamics at 187, where in imitation of the electronic partial tones of *Studie I* Stockhausen varies the level of each voice independently. It is probably fair to say that *Zeitmasse* provided a major stimulus to Stravinsky's serial and rhythmic language in the late fifties, and especially *Movements*: the woodwind trio at measure 39 of the concerto, for instance, or the flute cadenza at measures 13–17, which comes at a similar point in the score as Stockhausen's flute outburst at measure 16 of *Zeitmasse*.

In his introduction to *Perspectives of New Music*'s Stockhausen seventieth birthday Festschrift, Jerome Kohl identifies the added insertions, —measures 29–39, 73–104, 153–206, 229–266 [flute–oboe–cor anglais], –269 [clarinet–bassoon], and 275–89,—without mentioning that these constitute the defining moments of the entire work. They represent a new form of time control based on Stockhausen's invention of a procedure for creating impulse showers in *Gesang der Jünglinge*.[11] In fact, with this information in mind one can visually trace the history of the score from its roots in Webern (measures 271, 281) and *Kontra-Punkte* (1–27, 298–307) via the Piano Pieces V–VIII (the grace-note formations, e.g., at 189, 275) to *Gesang der Jünglinge* (the cadenzas) and *Gruppen* (the tuplet combinations of the cadenzas, though not their independent time control). The rhythmic vocabulary is abundantly rich, for performers even unnervingly so, and to be executed at speeds ranging from fixed and collective tempi via subjective (with variable ornamentation) to independently variable: (1) metronomic tempi from the scale MM 60–120; (2) "as fast as possible;" (3) a subjective ritardando, slowing from "very fast" to "about a quarter" of very fast; (4) a subjective accelerando, rising from "a quarter of as fast as possible" to "as fast as possible;" and (5) "as slow as possible." The five instrumental parts may be likened to five tracks of taped music which in the mixing process may be independently varied in speed (or, remembering Stockhausen's early experiences in the studio, vary in speed because the tape has stretched or the tape machines refuse to synchronize exactly), sometimes aligned to a common ad hoc pulsation, at other times individually fading into, out of, or across an imaginary tempo of reference. To convey such an effect in a recording or live performance is desirable but not easy to do without amplification; ideally the work should also be performed unconducted (or with the conductor hidden from view) to give an impression of spontaneity, independence when it is necessary, and tight control where all five parts are meshed together like clockwork. Acoustically a dry articulation is best, like cool jazz, very sparing of vibrato. The cadenzas should create the effect of an impulse shower in *Gesang der Jünglinge*, and are probably best performed with the players' eyes tightly shut.

Stockhausen has challenged the reader to devise a more appropriate ensemble to achieve the effects he has in mind. In a certain sense such effects suggest a more uniform sonority, in the spirit (though not the manner) of a recorder consort or, better still, a family of shawms: that way one can expect a tighter corporate sound when they all come together, and the more fragmented passages can be heard for what they are. Among modern instrumental sets one can think of a saxophone quintet: very breathy, textured, physical, articulate, and apt to convey shifts of tempo by degrees of noise content. Saxophonists are also used to the kinds of gesture-related performance effects required. (Stockhausen has since expanded his range of clarinets, so a future optional version for clarinets in e flat, b flat, a, basset-horn and bass clarinet may not be quite out of the question.) Separate microphones are probably part of the ideal solution. Lurking under the surface of *Zeitmasse*, as in Piano Piece VI, is a feel for jazz: not so much big band jazz (which comes later, in *Trans*) as the exuberant choruses of dixie-land jazz from the acoustic era. Through his American contacts, Cage and Earle Brown in particular, Stockhausen would certainly have heard of the compositional procedures of Joseph Schillinger, author of the influential two-volume *Schillinger System of Musical Composition*, a rhythm-based method in which the Russian-American author describes in Stockhausenian language the sense of exaltation that can be aroused by contemplating a music of varying speeds:

> The rhythm of variable velocities presents a fascinating field for study and exploration. The very thought that various rhythmic groups may speed up and slow down at various rates, appearing and disappearing, is overwhelming. . . . The idea stimulates one's imagination towards the complex harmony of the universe, where different celestial bodies (comets, stars, planets, satellites) coexist in a harmony of variable velocities.[12]

Gruppen (Groups)

1955–1957: No. 6 (UE 13673: cd Stockhausen-Verlag SV-5)

For three orchestras:

I: flute (piccolo), alto flute, oboe, cor anglais, clarinet, bassoon, 2 horns (high, low); 2 trumpets, 2 trombones, tuba; percussion (4 players: marimbaphone, glockenspiel, 5 cowbells, tam-tam, 3 suspended cymbals, 2 wood drums, 4 tom-toms, snare drum, tambourine); keyboard glockenspiel (or celesta), harp; strings 10.0.2.4.2.

II: 2 flutes (piccolo), oboe, e flat clarinet, alto saxophone (clarinet), baritone saxophone, bassoon, 3 horns (high-low-high); 2 trumpets, trombone, bass trombone; percussion (4 players: vibraphone, tubular bells, 4 cowbells, tam-tam, 3 suspended cymbals, 2 wood drums, 4 tom-toms, snare drum, tambourine, ratchet, 2 (high, low) triangles); piano (uncovered); amplified guitar; strings 8.0.4.2.2.

III: flute (piccolo), oboe, cor anglais, clarinet, bass clarinet, bassoon, 3 horns (high-low-high); 2 trumpets, 2 trombones, contrabass trombone (or tuba); percussion (4 players: (xylorimba, 4 cowbells, tam-tam, 3 suspended cymbals, 2 wood drums, 4 tom-toms, snare drum, tambourine); celesta, harp; strings 8.0.4.2.2.

Note: cowbells, cymbals, tam-tams, wood drums, and tom-toms are of specified pitch.

Duration: 24' 25.

Zeitmasse is a sketchbook for rhythm, a collage with many different layers; its absence of coherent overall structure is part of its humor and charm. It asks for a performing style that dramatizes its sudden shifts of style, tension, and ensemble. Cage tells an amusing story of passing by a mechanized shop window display set up to demonstrate the smooth writing and continuous flow of a fountain pen. The demonstration had gone horribly wrong, bending the nib and scattering ink in every direction. Like everybody else who has worked with German-style open reel tape Stockhausen had known the disastrous consequences of a tape spontaneously de-spooling all over the floor. Part of me thinks of the cadenzas in *Zeitmasse* as little disasters inserted into the structural tightness of the work, where the music springs apart and has to be reassembled in order to continue.

Gruppen introduces a new grandeur of scale to the serial music of the fifties. Here emphasis returns to theoretical integrity and coherence. It is Stockhausen's longest and most ambitious music to date, its size an assertion that he is no longer to be considered a "post-Webern" miniaturist, but also a consequence of its major premise, which is the unification of structures of pitch, rhythm, and tone color. The work is in one continuous movement split among three separate orchestras, each under its own conductor. The music is Stockhausen's most elaborate translation of pitch relationships into time- and pulse-ratios, and brings to a peak a period of concentrated research into the unity of musical time in the instrumental domain. Although it benefits from the technical and notational experience of Piano Pieces V–VIII and *Zeitmasse*, conceptually *Gruppen* derives from *Formel* and Piano Piece I, in both of which the interior structure is articulated by changes of metre, and procedurally from the two electronic studies. To arrive at a precise formulation of a fully integrated serial structure involved an enormous effort of will.

From a distance of fifty years it is easy to be dismissive of a Grand Unified Theory of music relying on the commensurablity of so many perceptual and physical incompatibles. What needs to be remembered is that the science of complex sounds, and their organization as connected and meaningful sequences of speech or music, was still very much in its infancy in the fifties. Werner Meyer-Eppler was a second-generation scientist in a discipline that had only just advanced from the cylinder recording technology of the Abbé Rousselot and Stetson, to the technology of tape and the vocoder, instruments several orders of magnitude more revealing of the inner structures of speech sounds and their manipulation. If Stockhausen had waited for science to come up with a coherent theory of music and speech before acting on his imaginative visions, we would not have *Gruppen*, *Gesang der*

Gruppen: *the series*

Jünglinge, *Momente* and a host of other extraordinary works of music. Those who criticize Stockhausen's theory, just as much as those who zealously defend the theory to the exclusion of everything else, need to be reminded of Schoenberg's dictum, echoed by Stockhausen himself, that the music is what matters, and for musicians that means the quality of writing, the inventive orchestration, the power and pleasure of being caught up in so exciting and turbulent an experience. Again, Stravinsky recognized the quality of the notation, the novel uses and combinations of instruments, the organizational genius. He did not inquire into the rationale, but he did give the music that resulted from it his personal endorsement with a quotation from the score copied in his own hand on the title page of *Memories and Commentaries*.

Stockhausen's formal logic is laid out in great detail in the essay ". . . how time passes . . . ," and sketch diagrams representing a rationalization of the temporal (metronomic tempo, unit pulse, and phrase duration) implications of the intervallic relations, octave-transposed, of *Gruppen*'s twelve-tone *Grundgestalt*. The notated pitches correspond to the series, and the octave transposition of each note is part of its definition. Transposed within an octave, the series divides into two hexachords, the second a retrograde of the first at the tritone. From the untransposed series Stockhausen has generated a chain of linked interval ratios, in a manner similar to the derivation of intervals for *Studie I*. Following Schoenberg's dictum that a series is "twelve tones related one to another," each note in the series is treated as forming an interval relationship with the preceding note and the following note, but not with the collection as a whole, we can see that, consistent with *Studie I* but contrary to classical tonality, this is a system where each note defines itself as a tonal centre, an arrangement not only ideal for atonal music, but also in agreement with Stockhausen's aesthetic of variable tempi. Accordingly, each pitch class in the octave corresponds to a frequency that can be expressed as a metronomic value between MM 60 and its higher octave, MM 120. This we know from *Kontra-Punkte.* For every octave higher a note is transposed, its frequency doubles, e.g., 100–200–400–800 etc.; to every octave lower it is transposed, its frequency reduces by half, e.g., 200–100–50–25 etc. Stockhausen simplifies matters by maintaining the tempo assigned to each pitch class in the series, and increasing or decreasing the unit pulse according to its octave transposition, from a whole note upward to a half- or quarter-note, or downward to a breve or double-breve.

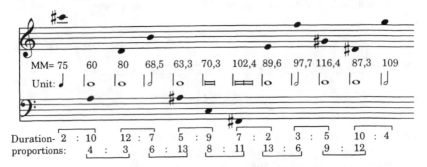

Gruppen: *tempo and duration proportions*

The metronomic values assigned to each note differ in small degrees from Stockhausen's standard tempo-scale, since these tempi are also subject to the ratios corresponding to adjacent intervals, whereas the standard tempo-scale is the equivalent of an equal-tempered scale. Now we are getting into a new version of the Galileian controversy over just and mean-tone temperament. Stockhausen is looking for the best small-number ratios possible between successive intervals in his series, ideally those that can be expressed in the temporal domain as simple tuplet relationships: 3 : 2, 5 : 4, 7 : 5, and so on. To achieve the goal of continuously harmonious interval relationships from tempo to tempo, and within a tempo, the same order of compromise is needed as the generation of Galilei and Zarlino found necessary to achieve a workable closed system of equal temperament in the domain of pitch. In the course of an extended discussion of Greek temperament, Helmholtz considers the possibilities of alternative harmonic proportions within the tetrachord, and employs ratio illustrations very similar to Stockhausen in a similar context, specifically to show how the Greeks avoided what they called "irrational" subdivisions.[13]

Frequency and tempo are analogous in the sense that both are periodicities: the one expressed as a number of pressure oscillations in a second, the other as a number of pulses in a minute. Neither term has anything to say about duration, that is, how long a note lasts, or a pulsation continues. The fact that a single cycle of a middle c is 3.83 thousandths of a second in duration, or that a single beat at MM 71.4 is 0.84 second in duration, is really neither here nor there; they are simply units of measurement, not

perceptions of time. To get over the problem of deducing structural durations from frequency relationships Stockhausen finesses from the octave
transpositions of his original series, to arrive at a form-scheme of overlapping and intercalated moments. The corresponding rationale would be a
deduction from the relative pitch of a tone sounded on the monochord, to the
length at which the string is stopped. Stockhausen's willingness to make the
imaginative leap from frequency ratios to structural dimensions distinguishes his interest in temperament from Harry Partch, whose exhaustive
treatise on tuning, in many ways complementary to Schillinger's on rhythm,
was published at about the same time, in 1947.[14]

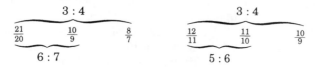

Alternative temperaments (after Helmholtz)

Stockhausen's growing interest in American new music puzzled Boulez,
whose patience with Cage was wearing thin. Still focused on *l'écriture*,
Boulez could not see the intellectual point of procedures that led to inele-
gant results, which is perfectly reasonable in its own way. Stockhausen
however had other reasons for finding out more about where the Americans
were going, and it had less to do with personal friendship than with a sense
that they were on to something relevant to his studies of communication
theory under Meyer-Eppler, and what he wanted to do musically. It is an
odd trait among composers of the postwar generation that they tend to be
extremely protective of their personal claims to ideas as intellectual property, even when (and in a number of cases, perhaps especially because) the
music ostensibly embodying these ideas all too often fails to deliver a clear
representation of what it is really about. Scientists are no less proprietorial,
one imagines, but at least they acknowledge collective goals and the influence of others, and of course they abide by exacting standards of formulation
and presentation.

That Stockhausen had the motivation to learn as much as he could
about American initiatives is certainly unarguable. He had had unsatisfactory experiences with his first two major orchestral compositions, *Spiel*
and *Punkte 1952*, and did not want this new commission to go the same
way. In addition he was competitive, and knew that with his knowledge of
speech and acoustics allied to his energy for work, he could outdo any competition. The other side, of course, is his discovery that a diverse group of
American composers, unacknowledged by an American musical establishment that had been taken over by expatriate European interests, had been
quietly and persistently working toward musical goals of alarming relevance to his own objectives. Symptomatic of the trend is Elliott Carter's
article "The Rhythmic Basis of American Music," published in *The Score* in
1955, a time when Stockhausen was working on preliminary drafts of the

score. A former student of Nadia Boulanger whose own interest in composing with layered tempi had begun in 1944–1945, Carter's international breakthrough had come about in 1951 with his String Quartet No. 1, a work in which each instrument follows an independent tempo, but to a meticulously coordinated notation. His article, modestly illustrated with music examples from Charles Ives and Conlon Nancarrow but not from his own music, is revealing proof of a serious and protracted interest among the Americans in a music of multiple timescales.[15]

Other names that Carter might have mentioned, apart from his own, are Henry Cowell, Charles Ruggles, and Henry Brant; the trend was to continue, in more repetitive mode, with the minimalists Terry Riley, Alvin Lucier, Steve Reich, Philip Glass, and their successors. A musical fascination with the exact depiction of multilayered real-time temporal processes is philosophically aligned with the "actions speak better than words" mindset of William James, Gertrude Stein, and R. H. Stetson at the turn of the twentieth century, and reflected clearly today in the intuitive acting traditions of Hollywood and Broadway. American composers in the fifties were not interested in producing "art music" in the sense understood by the European post-romantic industrial culture. With few exceptions (Carter among them) this new music is not "finished" or "literary" and is therefore inexplicable to European minds; but it does signify a developing body of knowledge of *how to track* complex acoustic processes in real life, whether that real life is the multiple marching bands of Ives's youth, or the unpredictable modulation of vocal harmony and noise that constitutes a spoken language. Historically, the interest of Stockhausen's essay ". . . how time passes . . ." resides less in its factual content (which is arguable) than in the recognition by a European composer of the importance for musical expression of dynamic processes (which is certainly true).

Initially *Gruppen* was intended to be a composition for orchestra and electronic music. In Varèse's *Déserts* the tape episodes are independent of the orchestra, and alternate with it; for a younger composer with access to a studio, the self-evident challenge is to create a music where live musicians and tape are heard simultaneously, and ideally appear to interact. This initial plan was discarded fairly quickly, most probably because of practical difficulties of coordination. An alternative solution in such a situation would be to recast the original work-plan for multiple orchestras, and leave the overall coordination of the various tempo structures to their conductors who would be able to adjust their beat to one another in real time, as in the case of the Ives Fourth Symphony. In opting for three orchestras, Stockhausen is certainly creating new and dramatic possibilities of musical dialogue, and it is reasonable to imagine that his layout of the three orchestras may also allude to the innovative three-sided stage productions (with simultaneous film projections) pioneered by Erwin Piscator in the twenties.

Content for Stockhausen, as for Cage, is a separate issue from structure. If the composer's purpose is to invent, define, simulate, or synthesize a new musical language, the task says nothing about what information the language is destined to say (though, as the scholarly inventors of Klingon appreciate, the linguistically possible is conditioned by the range of vocal distinctions physically available). The detailed inner structure of *Gruppen* arises from the structural distinctions of speech as revealed by sonagram recordings of visible speech. Suppose, for the sake of argument, a computer program is programmed to understand speech in real time; such a program has first to break the flow of speech into syllables, and second to characterize each unit of speech by its content. That is, a first process of *segmentation* of the speech flow, involving a recognition and tracking of the natural pulsation and tempo of individual speech (aided by envelope following of melodic inflection), followed by a second process, of *word recognition*, relying on qualitative distinctions within the syllable, between noise (consonants, aperiodic, varying by bandwidth), vowels (harmonic, periodic, varying by intensity), and diphthongs (dynamic tendencies within a syllable, usually harmonic). The work-scheme outlined by Stockhausen in ". . . how time passes . . ." has to do with generating a segmentation structure in tempo and pulse relationships, after which the "syllabic content" of the structure, as long as it relates consistently to the serial programme, can be disposed of relatively freely. In this sense, like Cage, content is incidental to form; the religious content of *Gesang der Jünglinge* by the same token could also be interpreted as the highest expression of no content at all. In *Gruppen* Stockhausen uses that freedom within serial constraints to let his imagination wander. Hence the portions of the score where the notation is modeled on the contour of the mountain range seen from the window of his mountain retreat, not to mention the "abstracted jazz" episodes Boulez is reported (by Joan Peyser) to have objected to,[16]—as he had earlier fulminated against Alban Berg's citations of Bach, military bands, and folk music in the *Lyric Suite*, *Wozzeck*, and the Violin Concerto.[17] Perhaps Stockhausen is just winding Boulez up. Perhaps he is also acknowledging a debt to Berg, whose Op. 6 Three Pieces for Orchestra ("Marsch" for example) marks his own European point of departure.

A further compromise relates to Stockhausen's expression of the inner structure of each group. His theory of "formants," by which he simply means the representation of a partial structure as a superposition of pulse-divisions, involves an assumption that these note-structures are analogous to the sine-tone partials of a synthesized tone, as for instance in *Studie I*. In other words, that the *frequency* of a partial tone (for example, the seventh or eleventh partial of a fundamental beat) can be expressed by impulses of the same periodicity (a 7- or 11-tuplet). Once again, Stockhausen uses a form of mental sleight of hand, though after the experience of *Studie II*, in which pulsed sine-tones substitute for continuous sine-tones in the composition of a mixture, he might be excused for treating his orchestral groups in the same way. Since according to Meyer-Eppler in electronic tone-synthesis such pulsed material can be freely ordered within the cycle without affecting the resulting tone quality, so Stockhausen allows himself to order the displacement of pulses within a group with perfect freedom without compromising the status of the group-spectrum.

There is evidence in the score, in any event, that the flow of points within each group has been composed to correspond to the characteristic vibration structure of a particular type of musical sound. "Points" of short duration (staccati, pizzicati, quickly dampened percussion notes, etc.) belong to one category. Generally of rapid onset, they start complex, building rapidly to a peak in which the upper partials (the high tuplets), which define the attack and to a great extent distinguish the timbre, are strongly audible. The complexity thereafter rapidly attenuates into a slower pulsation representing the fundamental. A group pattern based on the structure of such a short sound would consist initially as a dense complex of higher tuplets with the fundamental (pulsation) audible, if at all, as a regular dynamic fluctuation. An example of this type of group is found in Orchestra I, group 1.

A tone of abrupt onset that is allowed to reverberate settles into a more or less coherent periodic vibration, gradually losing intensity as its energy is used up. Such a group could be initially "statistical" in density, and gradually resolve into coherent and relatively simple pulsations corresponding to the lower partials. An example of this second type is the Orchestra II ritardando from measures 113 to 115 (though the ritardando itself is strictly a solecism, since a reverberation in nature does not slow down).

A third type of evolution is a tone that builds gradually to a peak, like a clarinet or a string harmonic, or an organ tone played with a swell (or indeed, a recorded piano tone played in reverse). Rhythmic passages corresponding to this type resemble ostinato figures that accumulate complexity over a regular underlying pulse, as in Stravinsky's *Le Sacre du Printemps* at score numbers [7] and [10]. Patterns of this type are rare in *Gruppen*, understandably in view of the composer's aversion to a periodic beat; however the synchronized buildup of brass "points" in all three orchestras at 118, culminating in the remarkable stereo exchanges of harmonies at 119, could be construed as an image of an accelerating tremolo on tam-tam that ends with the instrument swinging alone, back and forth, casting its resonances first one way, then another.

A fourth type of evolution is the kind produced when a tone is generated by friction or rapid repeated action, such as a drum roll. Sounds of this type maintain their complexity: if harmonious, like a string tone, a coherent complexity; if percussive, like a cymbal, a more or less random complexity. Many groups in *Gruppen* correspond to this fourth type.

These observations arise as a logical extrapolation of Stockhausen's pointillistic earlier scores, and their combinations of attack and resonance characteristics, into the microdomain of *Gruppen*; they are not identified in this way by the composer. It is all the same curious that nearly all of the groups in *Gruppen* relate in inner structure to short sounds abruptly suppressed, or long sounds prolonged by continuous agitation, i.e., to the accented "points" and sustaining wind or string tones that are the hallmark of both *Spiel* and *Punkte 1952*. It is also notable that the sound patterns of *Gruppen* do not so much define the form as occupy and animate it. Are these groups comparable with the ornamental flourishes of classical music? Yes and no: that they are "incidental" to the formal structure makes them the same in kind, and they relate to an expressively inflected overall tempo in much the same way as ornamental figurations to the compliant pulse of a classical slow movement.

Out of the impersonal system arises a personal imagery: impressions and reflections of natural movement, leaves disturbed by the wind, patterns of rainfall, sunlight dancing on the waves—audible manifestations of invisible forces, composed with a deep understanding of their inner movement, and not random or disordered events. "It is always a question of functionally directed form," says the composer, and the function—the motivation—is musical as well as representational. Out of a personal mixture of formal and visionary motivations emerged a masterpiece, and out of the system a new delicacy of imagery, plasticity of movement, and musical perspective. By any standard *Gruppen* counts as a formidable accomplishment. That it was done by a composer in his twenty-eighth year is truly astonishing.

Notes

1. *Texte 2*, 249.
2. James Pritchett, *Music of John Cage* (Cambridge: Cambridge University Press, 1993), 78–88. The I Ching employs a system of counting similar to binary code in computing and analogous to the binary notation of classical music. See Alfred Douglas, *The Oracle of Change: How to Consult the I Ching* (Harmondsworth: Penguin Books, 1972).
3. *Texte 2*, 43.
4. Richard Toop, "On Writing about Stockhausen." *Contact* 20 (1979): 25.
5. "Struktur und Erlebniszeit" (Structure and Experiential Time). *Texte 1*, 86–98.
6. Richard Toop, "On Writing About Stockhausen," 27.
7. Christian Wolff, "New and Electronic Music." *Audience* V:3 (1958), 122–31.
8. *SoM*, 47.
9. Stockhausen omits the last line of Strobel's verse, ". . . non seulement pour l'Allemagne musicale" (not only for music in Germany). Michael Kurtz, *Stockhausen: A Biography* rev. tr. Richard Toop (London: Faber and Faber, 1992), 85. The complete song in Stockhausen's manuscript is reproduced in Ingeborg Schatz ed., *Heinrich Strobel: "Verehrter Meister, lieber Freund:" Begegnungen mit Komponisten unserer Zeit* (Stuttgart, Belser, 1977).
10. Igor Stravinsky and Robert Craft, *Conversations with Igor Stravinsky* (London: Faber and Faber, 1959), 110, 130.
11. Jerome Kohl, "Guest Editor's Introduction." 59–64 in "A Seventieth-Birthday Festschrift for Karlheinz Stockhausen (Part One)." *Perspectives of New Music* 36: 1 (1998).
12. Joseph Schillinger, *The Schillinger System of Musical Composition.* 2v. (New York: Carl Fischer, 1946). Vol. I, 95.
13. Hermann Helmholtz, *On the Sensations of Tone* tr. Alexander J. Ellis. (Reprint, New York: Dover Publications, 1954), 264.
14. Harry Partch, "The One-Footed Bride." *Genesis of a Music* 2nd edn. (New York: Da Capo, 1975), 138–89.
15. Elliott Carter, "The Rhythmic Basis of American Music." First published

in *The Score* 12 (June 1955). Reprinted in *The Writings of Elliott Carter* comp. ed. Else Stone and Kurt Stone (Bloomington: University of Indiana Press, 1977), 160–66.

16. Joan Peyser, *Boulez: Composer, Conductor, Enigma* (London: Cassell, 1977), 132–36.

17. According to Boulez, writing in 1948, quotation is montage in the manner of musique concrète: hence the *trio estatico* in the Berg *Lyric Suite* is "vulgar," the military march and polka in *Wozzeck* are "stupid jokes," and the quotation of the Bach chorale "Es ist genug" in the Violin Concerto "a grave error." "Incidences actuelles de Berg." *Polyphonie* (1948: 2), 104–8.

CHAPTER NINE

Aleatory

At a crucial moment in the Buster Keaton movie *The General* the dauntless hero and heroine entrust their lives to the strength and endurance of the eponymous steam engine (and the integrity of the interstate rail system) in a bid to escape a vengeful Southern cavalry in hot pursuit. Keaton asks for help in stoking the wood-burning boiler; the heroine, clearly a lady of class, hesitates over which log to choose for the fire and, finding one that is not straight, casts it away. In some situations it does not help to be picky. Boulez's criticisms of Stockhausen, which came to a head over the inde-terminacy of *Klavierstück XI*, are reminiscent of the fastidiousness of the lady in question. Composed of a number of segments the order of which can be varied at random, Piece XI both challenged and offered itself as vindi-cation of a freedom of choice ethic endlessly debated in Europe (in the context of American music by Cage, Feldman, Wolff and others) but never seriously tested. The response to Piano Piece XI was remarkable. Everybody criticized it: Boulez, Stravinsky, even Cage. When that happens, something interesting is clearly going on.

Boulez was not averse to the idea of a serial music composed of modules that could be shuffled and rearranged in performance, but he was concerned that such a composition be designed so that the pieces would always fit, and the final result invariably make musical sense. This was quite a challenge. Boulez took inspiration from Messiaen's 1944 theory of rhythm, by which a composition is more or less freely put together from a repertoire of rhythmic cells that in turn allow for expansion, contraction, and other modifications. He was also strongly drawn to the poetry of Stéphane Mallarmé, and espec-ially the structural challenge of Mallarmé's poem "Un coup de dés" (A throw of the dice), an imaginative exercise in statement and parenthetical comm-entary that can be read in different ways and outwardly resembles the kind of learned analysis of a haiku in a literary magazine that smothers the original text in editorial overgrowth.[1] By 1950 Boulez, in correspondence with Cage, declared himself committed to a major setting for choir and orchestra of "Un coup de dés."[2] It did not happen. Perhaps Boulez felt pre-empted by Cage's 1951 *Concerto for Prepared Piano and Orchestra*, in the composition of which a collection of musical syllables or phrases is organized by "a throw of the dice," an effort apt in the circumstances but not very diplomatic, and leading furthermore to musical results both inconclusive in themselves and insupportive of an aesthetic principle that Cage in his inno-cence had taken to represent no more than a stimulus to action.

Boulez was also powerfully drawn to the conception of open form advanced in Mallarmé's *Livre*, a notional literature capable of being con-strued in an infinite variety of ways. With "Un coup de dés" the essential meaning of the poem does not change in whatever order a reader chooses to read the text, parentheses, and commentaries; in the *Livre* on the other hand, the poet appears to be envisioning a literary resource whose meaning is subject to change from one reading to the next. That is a very different challenge. It is perhaps a little deflating to realize that what the French symbolist poet had vaguely in mind is probably the equivalent of a present-day computer game. However the possibility of alternative readings of the same information had already surfaced in the late nineteenth century in the form of the detective novel, a literary form in which a number of different possible outcomes are tested before one that fits all the conditions is finally chosen. As a poet, Mallarmé would also have been sensitive to the narrative implications of the new medium of cinema, an invention claimed for France by the Pathé brothers, and one defining, through montage, new possibilities of editorial intervention in the ordering of materials to create alternative readings (a technique perfected in the documentaries of Robert Flaherty).

At an even deeper level however a concern for variable form is a concern for language and grammar. If, following de Saussure, language is founded on vocabulary, then not only conversation but also literature involves the selection and arrangement of words according to rules that guarantee meaning and sanction the communication of new ideas. Semiotics insists on the primacy of *la langue*, intelligence manifested in words that can be precisely codified, but is terrified at the implications of *la parole*, which raise the awful possibilities that meanings evolve and change, are subject to the individual will of the poet, and are open to error. In that sense, in proposing the concept of open form Mallarmé is simultaneously defending the liberty of the poet to say what he chooses.

Klavierstück XI (Piano Piece XI)
1956: No. 7 (UE 12654a/b, cd Stockhausen-Verlag SV-56)
Duration: 7– 9' 30.

Piece XI is certainly more closely related to *Gruppen* than to Pieces V–VIII. The gap in numbering arises because the piece is based on the serial orders originally calculated for the eleventh piece in a cycle of twenty-one pieces, and because the position of XI in the cycle is also serial in implication. Its affinity with *Gruppen* is twofold. First, its latent time-structure is based on a magnification of the vibration characteristics of a pitch series. Second, the relationship between fixed and variable time-structures in Piece XI inverts the order of priorities of the orchestral work. Each "group" in *Gruppen* translates the underlying pitch of a tone into a pulsation, and the partial frequencies of the same tone, representing its timbre, into metrical subdivisions of that fundamental periodicity. The same relationship of partials to frequency connects the tempi and inner subdivisions of segments of Piece XI to the mean tempo chosen by the performer for the performance as a whole.

> Piano Piece XI is nothing but a sound in which certain partials—components—are behaving statistically. There are nineteen components, and their order can be changed at random, except that once you choose a connection from one element to the next, the following element is always influenced by the previous one. . . . As soon as I compose a noise,—for example, a single sound which is nonperiodic, within certain limits —then the wave structure of this sound is aleatoric. If I make a whole piece similar to the ways in which this sound is organised, then naturally the individual components of this piece could also be exchanged, permutated, without changing its basic quality.[3]

Stockhausen's argument is a little disingenuous, since it does not take into account the variation in tempo from component to component. In *Gruppen* the composition of each group (i.e., its allocation of materials) is strictly preordained, but the evolution of partial frequencies within a group (how they play out) is relatively free. In terms of the impulse sequences that create the tone mixtures of *Studie II*, the actual order of the arpeggiated tone-pulses is immaterial to the result. By analogy with formant resonances in music and speech, the vibratory characteristics (but not the frequencies) of a vowel or clarinet aperture remain constant whatever the tone of voice or note of the scale (or even noise) is sounding at the time.

Stephen Truelove's detailed and thorough analysis of the pitch and rhythm content shows that the pitch content is derived from duration-ratios and not from permutations of a twelve-tone series.[4] The rhythmic content in turn is based on elaborations of a rhythmic cell matrix, a procedure ultimately derived from Messiaen. In Piece XI the sequence and "frequency ratios" (relative tempi) of sections is left free. This freedom is theoretically permissible if the piece is supposed to be modeled on the evolution of a complex waveform of unspecified pitch, such as a magnified tam-tam tone. By comparison, *Gruppen*'s more orderly note-groups correspond to fixed pitches and timbres. The range of six tempi chosen by the performer of Piano Piece XI thus constitutes a formant structure or "timbre" for the entire performance; the fact that these tempi are associated with passages of variable density can therefore mean that at times certain formants are more pronounced than others. Just as in *Gruppen* an octave transposition of a defining pitch class can be rendered as a change of unit pulsation from whole- to half- to quarter-note, so in Piece XI alterations of tempo from section to section and performance to performance can be said to correspond to transpositions of frequency within the tempo-octave in accordance with a nontempered but consistent system of tuning. That is not quite what Stockhausen is saying, however.

Objections to the work expressed by Stravinsky, Boulez, and Cage are all variations of the lettrist fallacy. Stravinsky did not like the idea of the performer being permitted to determine the piece's "final shape," as if the final shape were a priority (one asks what is the "final shape" of a Calder mobile, for instance).[5] His response is consistent with Stavinsky's own dictum about the role of the performer being to play as the composer requires, and not to interpret, and suggests that the pianist's freedom of choice is an embarrassment. Cage, on the other hand, repeatedly objected to what he perceived as the philosophical inconsistency of determining the piece in every respect save the order of segments; not that the piece was indeterminate, but that it was not indeterminate enough.[6] He ignores the fact that random ordering also changes the way successive segments are interpreted. Indeed, Stockhausen is doing no less than emulating explicitly Cage's covert method of assembling material for his own *Music of Changes*. Piece XI can be construed in this sense as a real tribute to *Music of Changes*, in light of which it seems a little curmudgeonly of Cage not to acknowledge the gesture. Despite being deeply impressed (a contemporary photograph from André Hodeir's book *La Musique Depuis Debussy* depicts him gazing intently at the score),[7] Boulez nevertheless concludes that Piece XI is inherently unstable, because segments do not remain identifiably the same (in duration, tempo, dynamic, and touch) from version to version, unlike his own "Constellation–Miroir," Boulez's corresponding essay in pianistic peregrination from the Third Sonata, a piece in which the mobility principle is reduced to a choice of pathways (like a map of the Paris Métro), and is perhaps a more appropriate candidate for Cage's criticism.[8]

Boulez of all people should have recognized the brilliance and logic of Stockhausen's formal invention. The term "aleatoric" that many ascribe to Boulez, was actually used by Meyer-Eppler in the context of processes investigated in seminars on information theory that Stockhausen attended and that profoundly influenced his musical thinking:

> He would give us exercises demonstrating the principles of Markoff series; in one we were given cut-outs of individual letters from newspaper articles, and we had to put them in sequence by a chance operation, and see what sort of a text came out. Then we would repeat the operation with individual syllables, then with combinations of two syllables, and so forth, each time trying to discover the degree of redundancy, as we called it, of the resulting texts.[9]

Research into the effect of randomization of word, syllable, and letter content of a text flourished in the early era of information theory during the fifties. It was serious, it was scholarly, and it was interested in discovering aspects of language that are embedded not in the sense content of a message but in the texture of the verbal material, qualities for instance that allow a listener to perceive that German is being spoken, or Chinese, while at the same time not understanding a word of what is actually being said. These qualities being investigated are essentially musical, and their research would clearly benefit from the input of a musical sensibility. A relevant starting point for such inquiries is wartime code- and cipher-breaking, the rapid advance of which during the war had led to the development of early computing devices and analytical methods of pattern recognition for text and speech intercepts. Cryptic messages addressed to agents in hiding were broadcast into Europe during the 1939–1945 war and the secret significance of such messages is transformed into poetry by Cocteau in the movie *Orphée*. Text encryption, for messages delivered in typescript, involved highly sophisticated randomization procedures and equally ingenious methods of decryption including matching the statistical incidence of individual letters and letter sequences to the language in which it is written.

These procedures both suggested a new and objective rationale for semiology, and also inspired a number of poets and novelists to explore the literary possibilities of deliberately fractured or denatured prose. The movement took hold in France, with Raymond Queneau's amusing *Exercices de Style* (e.g., "Permutations by groups of two, three, four and five letters").

> *Jo un ve ur mi rs su di ap rl te. . . . Dai sou int nil ell erp nvo aso nen isi. . . . Ando ilab aill nnad rapi eurs ntla dema ussi disc. . . . Ueshe quelq lustra uresp erevi rdjel ntlag sdeva intla aresa . . .* etc.[10]

There is even a musique concrète connection: Abraham Moles, the mysterious scientific observer to Pierre Schaeffer who peered over Stockhausen's shoulder as he worked on the sine-tone generator in the basement studio of the PTT, incorporates a related sequence of French language texts in a discussion of Markoff processes in his *Informationstheorie und ästhetische Wahrnehmung*, published in France in 1958 and in German translation by the Cologne firm of DuMont, publisher of Stockhausen's *Texte 1–4*.[11]

```
          Quatrième texte : 35%
AINSI   E   I   U TR ELS O    D NS    UR C BINE DE   CA T S
E LA PR   USTION MO   IALE DES VUES D   LEURS   TE I RS A
DIFFE EN E EPOQ ES DES   HOT G AP S    NE   UI
```

In the United States, randomization procedures involving Cage and his associates were matched, in the literary sphere, by William Burroughs and his "cut-outs," and in the scholarly domain by the investigations of Lejaren A. Hiller and Leonard Isaacson into the probabilistic structure of musical sequences, research that led to publication of the *Illiac Suite*, some of the first music composed by computer and a significant contribution intellectually (if less so aesthetically) toward a theory of artificial intelligence.[12]

So talk about randomization processes was not only current and not only in Meyer-Eppler's classes, it was a topic of recognized musical relevance in Europe and America and had also been discussed in the context of

Boulez's and Stockhausen's work under Schaeffer. For Boulez, Cage, and Stockhausen not to have been aware of these current developments, when their music was coincidentally so richly influenced by them, is clearly unthinkable. A more plausible scenario comes to mind, of Stockhausen telling Boulez, in great excitement, of his classes with Meyer-Eppler in analyzing texts cut up into syllables and words, and Boulez dismissively responding that yes, he knew all about that from Barrault's stories of Tristan Tzara drawing words from a hat, and that Stockhausen should read Mallarmé, who saw it all coming, and whose poetry is of greatly superior quality—and, by the way, I too am already working on a masterly setting of "Un coup de dès."

The point, surely,—and Mallarmé's point too,—is that Piece XI is about *how a text is read*. After all, the typographic layout of "Un coup de dés" is part of the poem as well: the different typefaces both guide the reader and identify the different parts, the main text, the parenthetical asides, the commentaries. Naturally, you don't *hear* the typefaces when the poem is interpreted. But the equivalent to variant typefaces,—some large, some small—could be enlargement and diminution of tempo, or dynamic indications, which is how one makes distinctions in music between principal and subordinate themes. Again, the fact that the Mallarmé poem can be read in alternative ways does not mean that the reader is *responsible* for the final form of the poem. That would only be the case if the poem were read a single time; but the poem, and Piece XI, like any poem or piece of music, are designed to be read an indefinite number of times, and potentially in an indefinite number of ways, some more satisfactory than others. The only difference is that in order for the full number of possible meanings to be grasped, an indefinite number of permutations would have to be comprehended. They are works, therefore, that are not to be disposed of at a single sitting. If that is a matter for objection, it is surely a novel one.

Far more fruitful is the transformational argument of Piece XI, which connects Stockhausen's conception of formation with Piaget's exposition of group transformation, and in literally more concrete terms with Pierre Schaeffer's formal theories of musique concrète. For Boulez, the composer of *Structures*, not to have grasped the structuralist message of Piano Piece XI, is almost as surprising as Cage's refusal to recognize its significance in relation to his own *Music of Changes*. In the following extract Piaget is writing about transformations in geometry, but the musical implications are clear:

> The group concept or property is obtained by a mode of thought characteristic of modern mathematics and logic—"reflective abstraction"— which does not derive properties from *things* but from our ways of *acting on things*, the various fundamental ways of *coordinating* such acts or operations, [in accordance with] the following very general conditions:
>   1. the condition that a "return to the starting point" always be possible (via the "inverse operation");
>   2. the condition that the same "goal" or "terminus" be attainable by alternate routes and without the itinerary's affecting the point of arrival ("associativity").

Group structure and transformation go together. Groups are systems of transformations; but more important, groups are so defined that transformation can, so to say, be administered in small doses. Thus we can go on to the next "higher" group by letting the dimensions vary while preserving the other properties [angles, parallels, straight lines, etc.]. The various kinds of geometry—once taken to be static, purely representational, and disconnected one from another—are thus reduced to one vast construction whose transformations under a graded series of conditions of invariance yield a "nest" of subgroups within subgroups.[13]

The language of Piaget's general description, and his employment of a terminology already familiar in Stockhausen's own commentaries and analyses, invite the reader to consider Piece XI as a structuralist essay, a music both allowing for alternate routes and subject to transformations of varying degrees applied to different structural properties while preserving others. The abstract conceptual basis of structuralism connects, in the practical domain of sounds and their transformational possibilities, with Schaeffer's theory of transformation of the internal structure of a "complex note" and generation of "a sort of anti-melody" by successive modifications, either of the intrinsic form, or of its relationship to the listener.

Piaget's definition even implicates Messiaen's *Mode de valeurs*, now revealed as an ultimate statement of transformational principles applied to music, one in which every single note is defined as a combination of scalable properties, infinitely modifiable and infinitely connectable. Stockhausen's system of liaison in Piece XI could even have been inspired by Messiaen's organ music: not just in the convention of notating changes of registration, which is well-established, but the formal and transformational functions of change of registration in the context of a music of free association. The piece "Chants d'Oiseaux" is an interlude in Messiaen's *Livre d'Orgue*, an ostensible escape from the serial rigors of the other six pieces into the composer's private world of birdsong. In it, however, we discover six identifiable structures (bird songs, link material) are rotated; each has its own subjective tempo; the structures vary in length, and repetitions of the same structure may also vary. Furthermore, at the end of each structure there is a pause, while the performer reads and changes the registration of the instrument. The performer pauses to read these instructions, e.g.:

> *R: flûte 4, octavin 2, bourdon 16;*
> *Pos: flûte 4, nazard 2 $^2/_3$, tierce 1 $^3/_5$;*
> *G: plein jeu, clairon 4;*
> *Péd: violoncelle 8*

—and then to make the necessary alterations, that have the effect of changing the timbre, the dynamic, and (on occasion) even the transposition of the music to a higher or lower octave. Though composed to a fixed order, the sequence of events in "Chants d'Oiseaux" is intended to give the impression of a random walk,—in this case, a walk through the woods, listening to the birds. In the performance of such a work, time is not felt as measure, but as place: each event a self-contained moment of awareness, and the duration of each corresponding to an intensity of awareness.

Group transformation as a structuralist concept founded in geometry refers in the first instance to movement capture in the general sense of Eadweard Muybridge and the early movies, and more specifically in the temporal structures of flight and motion captured in the multiple images of Louis Marey that form the basis for computer animations today. The aim of such a geometry is to formulate the image as a system of joints and weights conforming to a network of relationships that is capable of being modulated to emulate natural motion while at the same time retaining its integrity.

In Piece XI Stockhausen addresses the twin issues of identity and transformability with great skill, building on his experience of the Piano Pieces V–VIII and *Zeitmasse*. The score is an object lesson in notational distinctions, clearly differentiating global (so to speak "register") changes in value of tempo, duration, dynamic, and timbre (touch) represented by the symbols terminating each segment and influencing the next,—from local deviations of accelerando, ritardando, pausation, grace notes, and accentuation, which are "added on" as it were to whatever global values obtain in any given reading. Since the grace notes are always played "as fast as possible" they are a constant foil to the arbitrarily changing tempi of the main structures (and incidentally, act as aides-mémoire to the listener to help keep track of the segments as they occur). Grace notes, accents and other expressive variables define a domain of performer freedom of action within the larger-note structural contrasts. In this way a certain balance and reciprocity is obtained between the rigid demands of abstract form on the one hand, and performer freedom of expression on the other.

It has been suggested that the modulations of time, dynamic, and touch that transform each reading of Piece XI into a different experience deprive the work of a proper identity. It is certainly true that recorded performances to date are difficult to "hear" as alternative versions of the same piece. For the piece to work as intended, a performer has to create very clear distinctions separating the six levels of global tempo, touch, and dynamic, to be executed perhaps in imitation of mechanical transformations effected in a studio, for instance, by varying the playback speed, level, and equalization of a tape recording. These global changes influence the relatively sparse larger notations in the score, but leave the grace notes and local accents unaffected. Logically, these latter components in small notation should be played as far as possible with a lighter touch and in a consistent fashion throughout: they correspond to the "real" or internal performer variables that hold the performance together no matter how the external dimensions may vary.

It is worth remembering that art and music have been addressing the principles of transformational theory since the Renaissance. The art of caricature founded in the sixteenth century is an art of manipulating the geometry of an ideal face to express (and in some measure, explain) physical and underlying character distortions in human nature. The art of perspective involves size transformations in the pictorial plane to simulate depth in the visual field. Equivalent processes in music include the sequence, the movement of a phrase-group within the pitch plane, all other characteristics remaining intact; modulation from key to key; and augmentation and diminution, for instance in a fugue. The identity relationship of a fugue subject and its tonal answer is an early example of the identity question embodied in Piece XI, and raised to a higher power in the plus-minus works of the sixties. After reading the biologist Wolfgang Wieser, Stockhausen was moved to compare his scale transformations to the visually analogous biomorphic transformations of animal species, observing "nature creates divergent species by expanding certain parameters. . . . Parametric transformations, that's what serial music is all about," an observation lending new meaning to the term "species counterpoint."[14]

Piece XI is an interesting challenge to interpret, and I am not at all sure that any of the interpretations issued on record to date do justice to the composer's dramatic conception, which involves a sense of humor. Stockhausen's "species" remark offers a clue. In essence, each segment of music on the page is a statement; the interpretation of each statement is governed by applied tempo, touch, and dynamic indications. Each combination of indications amounts to a dramatic character or personality: a placid temperament, a fiery temperament, a soulful personality. In the days of silent movies, the appearance of the hero, heroine, villain, or mother-in-law was reflected in music expressing the character, not always by a specific theme or motif (though this could occur) but rather as a composition of stylistic traits that could be applied to any ongoing music. In the same way we see the normally blank-faced hero of a Chaplin or Keaton movie transformed into different characters, as a consequence of the vagaries of circumstance, through adopting particular combinations of mannerisms and modes of behavior. The interpretative task facing the pianist of Piano Piece XI may therefore reside not so much in the notated segments themselves, mastery of which is a matter of technique,—in dramatic terms simply the dialogue,—as in the performance indications, which define the characters.

Since it was composed as a rejoinder to Piece XI, a comparison with Boulez's Third Piano Sonata "Constellation-Miroir" may be useful. This striking score is composed of a large number of unequal segments printed in red and green, and distributed seemingly at random over a single large sheet of paper, with arrow traffic signs to guide the performer along a number of optional but predetermined routes. (I recall once departing by train from the Paris Gare St.-Lazare and noticing through the carriage window that the signals at intersections in the marshaling yard were exactly like Boulez's arrows in "Constellation-Miroir.") The two-color score distinguishes "Points" (green) and "Blocks" (red) in alternation; unlike Piece XI, however, the music is all projected onto the same temporal plane and segments are subject only to minor internal tempo inflections (one rather wishes the red and green segments were performed in concert by two pianists on pianos of different timbre). In its own way, Boulez's simpler formal structure is closer to the Mallarmé ideal, its plain literalism remote from Stockhausen's authentically relativistic conception, despite the structural resemblances they share.

Gesang der Jünglinge (Song of the Youths)
1955–1956: No. 8 (unpublished; cd Stockhausen-Verlag SV-3)
Electronic music.
Duration 13' 14.

Gesang der Jünglinge is Stockhausen's first work since the early vocal pieces to carry an explicit extramusical message. With his talent for choosing personally appropriate texts, the story of the three young men cast into the fiery furnace by Nebuchadnezzar (Daniel 3) lends itself to be interpreted as a parable of three young composers (Boulez, Nono, and himself) surviving the fires of public incomprehension. Cynics have pointed out that there is only one boy's voice to be heard, but Boulez (*Le marteau sans maître*), Nono (*Il Canto Sospeso*), and himself (*Gesang der Jünglinge*) are the chosen subjects of Stockhausen's "Music und Sprache I, II, III," analytical studies of music and speech developed by Stockhausen for the 1956 Darmstadt courses and later broadcast by Cologne Radio. If not a meeting of minds, an affinity of interest is certainly indicated. Boulez and Nono were among the few avant-garde composers of Stockhausen's generation to compose for the voice, a very difficult instrument to work into an integrated serial matrix. A recent study of the composer's sketches and work notes by Pascal Decroupet and Elena Ungeheuer exposes Stockhausen's serial generative procedures to view, and it is clear that these differ only in emphasis, not in kind, from the instrumental works. Though interesting in themselves, the serial matrices do not explain why the piece is so good, or where it came from, and these are the questions a listener to the music is more likely to ask. Because the work incorporates the sound of a treble singing voice, it was immediately pounced on by the supporters of musique concrète as a climb-down by the Cologne purists and an admission that they got it wrong. As late as 1999, even after having considered the entire documentation, Decroupet and Ungeheuer still persist in describing *Gesang* implicitly as a compromise.

> In spite of certain bitter opposition due to the use of the child's voice, at the time of its premiere this work gave the feeling that the phase of etudes was over . . . a real turning-point in musical thought, precipitating certain beginnings of a broadening and reassessment of serial thought as it had been formulated in the first half of the decade.[15]

The idea that the work could be construed as a concession to musique concrète opinion betrays a misunderstanding of the role played by information theory in the determination of this composition and its serial objectives. The very title "Musik und Sprache" (Music and Speech) provides a clue. Why, one asks, since the title of the work is "Song of the Youths," is Stockhausen's radio series entitled "Music and Speech?" Why not "song?" Stockhausen was studying the fundamentals of language and speech under Meyer-Eppler; the general purpose of such research was to disassemble speech into its basic components, the phonemic equivalent of the syllabic breakdown of a text to which Stockhausen refers in his activities with the cutout newspaper articles. Stockhausen's private reason for taking an interest in speech may have been to gain insight into the microstructure of communicable sounds, but the *institutional* interest in his studying at Bonn University under Meyer-Eppler as a representative of Cologne Radio, resided in the possibility of creating a music of "reconstituted speech" that would contribute to scientific understanding of the defining parameters of speech and enable speech recognition technologies to be developed. Stockhausen has borne a heavy burden of criticism for having incorporated a prerecorded element in *Gesang der Jünglinge*; in an ideal world perhaps the perfect solution would have been one in which the boy's voice (or at least, a voice) is recreated as a consequence of serial analysis and resynthesis. For that to happen, however, electronic music has to extract a vocabulary of fundamental particles of speech from a careful dissection of tape-recorded spoken material.

> The core of the difficulty is the complex and variable way linguistic messages are encoded in speech. . . . For a computer to "know" a natural language, it must be provided with an explicit and precise characterization of the language. . . . Although a capacity for understanding language may be the ultimate goal, the enterprise of speech recognition is founded on the identification of words.[16]

As Stockhausen, the Meyer-Eppler group, and all subsequent research has discovered, the audible continuum of speech is not so easily anatomized. Even in today's world of talking computers the analytical task remains impossible. Normal continuous speech cannot be reduced to intact syllables, vowels, or consonantal components. In acoustic terms, they do not exist as discrete entities, only as transitional events within a continuum of action.

The Bell vocoder slices a sample of speech into amplitude modulations of frequency bands, and the latter can be applied to other dense sound material to resynthesize the voice pattern so the new sound, such as a jet airliner, appears to be speaking. But this is mechanical sectioning and not true analysis, since it does not lead to the isolation and definition of speech particles. Once again the lettrist conception of language fails to translate into speech gesture in the sense of motor phonetics. If Stockhausen set out to create an electronic work in which the sounds of a human voice mysteriously condense out of a plasma of electronically-realized phonemic particles, then it was a beautiful idea but a doomed enterprise. That he did in fact set out with this objective can be inferred from the composer's lengthy writings on the work and its difficulties:

> The desired blending of discrete sound elements into a continuum (in hindsight especially in the case of timbres) was unrealizable, as it would be for instruments, for example; simply because in order to manipulate the extremely complex phonetic structures of speech (German in this case) in the terms of serial composition, it is necessary to allow for an indefinite number of transitional stages between (say) one vowel and another vowel, or between a vowel and a half-consonant or consonant. In principle that can only be achieved by electronic means. However, one can formulate the process the other way round, and say that in a particular scale of electronically generated tones certain positions in the

continuum are occupied by [i.e., resemble] sung speech sounds. Only in such a way is it possible to experience a unified family of sounds, where at certain points sung sounds meet electronic, and electronic sounds meet those that are sung. In order for the best possible unification of sung speech sounds (in the sense of individual articulation and formant character) a twelve-year-old boy sang all the required sounds, syllables, words, and occasional word groups on tape.[17]

This is from a technical report, remember, to be read by studio administrators and technical experts like Meyer-Eppler. It is not an aesthetic description of a musical work. Its message is that for the time being, in terms of an assembly process from the smallest units, the synthesis of realistic speech is impossible. The project of creating a music in which a voice magically emerges out of a phonemic flux in that sense cannot succeed. But in a masterly example of lateral thinking Stockhausen goes on to say that all is not lost. Instead of defining the human voice as a set of discrete sound elements that can be synthesized and recombined, the realistic alternative is to generate a scale, or series of scales, electronically, by continuous transformation of serially-derived sound elements (i.e., in the manner of *Studie II*). One then finds certain points in the continuum of electronic transformation where the synthetic sound resembles a singing voice. Since it is impossible to recreate the infinitely subtle gradations of real speech, the more feasible solution is to produce a repertoire of electronic phonemes based on the chosen few that appear voice-like. The piece then becomes an artificial blend, or montage, of sung speech sounds, together with electronic sounds that have been chosen for their resemblance to speech sounds.

There were voice-like sounds already appearing spontaneously in the *Konkrete Etüde*, and more emerged from the serial manipulations of impulse phenomena in *Studie II*. So the issue for Stockhausen is not the simple one of tabulating methods that produce speech-like sounds by chance, as a by-product of serial synthesis, but rather of finding a unified serial rationale for the generation of a comprehensive range of voice-like sounds. When this objective turns out to be inachievable Stockhausen deftly changes the terms of reference while at the same time defining the task in suitably professional terms. Stockhausen's classification of the sound-elements of German speech, for instance, is methodical but necessarily incomplete, dictated by the practical limitations of the studio equipment he had to work with:

SK = pulsed sine-tone complexes (*Studie II*: quasi-vowels)
IK = pulsed complexes of filtered noise (equivalent consonants)
LS = tones and syllables (boy's voice)
R = noises filtered to a 2% (hertz) bandwidth ([f] [ts] [sh])
I = single impulses ([t] [b] [k] [d])
SV = synthesized vowels (*Studie I*-type sine-tone spectra)
RO = broadband filtered noise 1–6 octaves ([ha] [ho] hi [hu])
IO = pulse showers of fixed bandwidth 1–6 octaves ([rr] [zz])
IA = single-impulse chords

RA = chords of 2% (hertz) bandwidths, middle-range (*Studie II*)
S (A) = sine-tone chords (inharmonic or borderline) (*Studie I*)
GA = sung chords (aggregations of sung speech sounds)

Stockhausen adds, "In order to systematize the sound element scale (assimi-late the electronic sounds into the family of synthesized sounds) criteria from analytic phonetics were applied (vowels–sine tones; consonants–noise bandwidths; plosives–impulses; various mixture forms)." The vocalized speech sounds so incorporated are extracted from the sung text as follows:

vowels		voiced cons.		unvoiced cons.		termination	
ju-	[u]	tuj	[j:]	-wig	[ç]	jep	[p]
belt	[e]	ult	[l:]	Preis	[s]	Lob	[b]
dem	[ə]	-ren, dem	[n, m:]	Reif	[f]	Werk	[k]
Herrn	[ɛ]	Her-	[r:]	-belt	[t¹] long	Tag	[g]
all	[a]	Wer-	[v:]	-ze	[ts]	preist	[t²] short
ihr	[i]	-set	[z:]	Scha-	[ʃ]	Wind	[d]

It is an incomplete series, that is perfectly clear.[18] These are speech sounds that relate to electronic impulse and sine-tone complexes. Had they been produced synthetically, it would be possible to hear them in relation to a scale of comprehensibility from pure tones to filtered noise. But since they are articulated by a boy's singing voice, their relation to the electronic ma-terial is virtual rather than real, no different from that of a voice to a piano, or voice to violin. (In the sense of exploiting the transformational relation-ship of speech sounds to instrumental sounds, Boulez's *Le marteau* arguably offers a more serially congruent scheme of timbres, one that also separates the vowel components (melody) from the consonantal components (percus-sion). As an example of transformational poetics within the alto range *Le marteau* is surprisingly well-conceived, the singing voice timbre mutating by degrees via flute, viola, guitar, xylorimba, and vibraphone back to the voice. Nothing else in Boulez's oeuvre is quite as sophisticated in the instru-mental sense, even including his recent dialogue pieces of live instruments and computer, which leads one to wonder whether Boulez talked about this issue with Stockhausen at this time and received any helpful advice.

So formidable a technical description of a composition is hard for a lay reader to resist. At no point does Stockhausen claim to have synthesized human speech, but an impression is created of an electronic music of speech-like qualities systematically produced, which is not really the case. When the theory is set aside and a listener focuses on the musical experi-ence it is obvious that this is a work of exceptional invention and dazzling effects, a work of magic. Like magic, it is produced by richness of invention rather than exact science. There is no doubt that from calculated and heavily worked material, seductive effects can be produced; but with *Gruppen* and *Gesang der Jünglinge* the technical brilliance of Stockhausen's end-product reaches a level where the listener is persuaded that the musical result and the composer's formal specification (as suggested by the work notes) actually coincide. *Gruppen* is a wonderful feat of musical imagination, but the idea that the music corresponds in the formal domain to a magnification of the microstructure of a *klangfarbenmelodie*,—so that if the whole work were to be speeded up its structure would be audible as a sequence of tones,—is clearly fanciful, since the groups are each only a few cycles in duration and would be heard in speeded-up form as no more than a series of blips. Though presented as science (and certainly informed by a knowledge of speech processes) *Gesang der Jünglinge* succeeds as pure theater. The boy's voice, always praising God, is a compelling dramatic focus, and by whatever means the electronic fires are ignited, the presentation of dramatic and complex effects in an early form of surround sound could not fail to impress any audience, even one familiar with *Déserts* by Varèse, the only comparable work for tape of such grand design. Musically it may not matter that the composer's dream of a grand unified theory of synthesized speech sounds and the acoustical result do not quite match up; but with these two great works an ongoing inconsistency or creative tension between the stated objective and the musical result, an inconsistency that has always been a feature of Stockhausen's works,—is elevated to an aesthetic principle. In a well-deserved twist on convention, the programme note becomes a means of distracting the audience's attention and allowing the music to create maximum impact. In later years, the period of the plus-minus and the intuitive scores, the creative gap between intention and realization becomes even more visible.

Electronic music is fixed, instrumental music is interpreted, and in the case of Piece XI, subject to the the same general kinds of transformation that electronic music explores. *Gesang der Jünglinge* organizes and distributes objects in an acoustic perspective that enlarges and compresses images as well as positioning them in time and space. But because it comes to the listener ready-made, the procedural relationships embodied in the electronic work are easy to overlook. Piano Piece XI represents essentially the same process, but applied in real time to the materials on the printed page. Through observing the transformation processes in action in the piano work the listener ideally learns to recognize, or at least appreciate, the same processes effected in the electronic domain: there is a clear didactic connection between the two.

Stockhausen's treatment of the voice should be distinguished from the relatively naïve dissection process employed by Berio for *Thema: Omaggio a Joyce* (though there is an added correspondence between Berio's tape editing process and James Joyce's multilevel textual wordplay that Stockhausen's biblical text does not allow for). In the Berio work, as for musique concrète in general, prerecorded material is progressively degraded at every stage of technical intervention: editing, copying, filtering etc. In Herbert Eimert's *Epitaph für Aikichi Kuboyama*, the progressive degrading of the narrator's speaking voice by ring-modulation and vocoder is dramatically justified as a representation of the effects of radiation on the fishermen who innocently strayed into the radioactive cloud of a nuclear test. *Gesang der Jünglinge* is unique among works of this period in seeking to preserve the original quality of the recorded voice by a policy of minimal intervention. The young vocalist was recorded singing as closely as possible to the required pitches, syllables and sequences. Those corrections of pitch that had to be made were within the acceptable range of speed change laid down for radio; likewise the number of recopying stages was kept to a minimum in accordance with good recording practice.

Whereas *Studie I* gives an impression of sounds radiating outwards, and *Studie II* introduces a keyboard-like freedom of movement, with *Gesang der Jünglinge*, in many respects Stockhausen's most perfectly contained electronic work, musically and dramatically, the music is clearly focused on the middle range occupied by the boy's voice, just as in *Kreuzspiel* the piano music comes to a focus in the oboe and clarinet melodies. The conception of the work as a sacred ritual, and of its meaning being concentrated in a specific timbre, whether a pure voice, a crystalline or metallic resonance, or a coruscating electronic tone mixture, are confirmed in this extraordinary sacred cantata as defining traits of Stockhausen's music.

Notes

1. "Un coup de dés." With English translation, in Anthony Hartley ed., *Mallarmé* (Harmondsworth: Penguin Books, 1965), 214–31.

2. Jean-Jacques Nattiez ed., *Boulez-Cage Correspondence* tr. ed. Robert Samuels (Cambridge: Cambridge University Press, 1993), 62, 64. See also Joan Peyser, *Boulez: Composer, Conductor, Enigma* (London: Cassell, 1977), 117–19.

3. Jonathan Cott, *Stockhausen: Conversations with the Composer* (London: Robson Books, 1974), 70.

4. Stephen Truelove, "The Translation of Rhythm into Pitch in Stockhausen's *Klavierstück XI.*" *Perspectives of New Music* 36/1 (1998), 190–220.

5. Igor Stravinsky and Robert Craft, *Conversations with Igor Stravinsky* (London: Faber and Faber, 1959), 112.

6. John Cage, "Indeterminacy," in *Silence* (Cambridge, Mass.: MIT Press, 1966), 35–36.

7. André Hodeir, *La Musique Depuis Debussy* (Paris: Presses Universitaires de France, 1961), facing 128.

8. See Joan Peyser, *Boulez: Composer, Conductor, Enigma*, 124–29.

9. *SoM*: 50.

10. Raymond Queneau, *Exercices de Style* (Paris: Gallimard, 1947), 100–103.

11. Abraham A. Moles, *Informationstheorie und ästhetische Wahrnehmung* tr. Hans Ronge mit Barbara und Peter Ronge (Köln: M. DuMont Schauberg, 1971), 67–70.

12. Lejaren A. Hiller and Leonard M. Isaacson, *Experimental Music* (New York: Wiley, 1959).

13. Jean Piaget, *Structuralism* tr. ed. Chaninah Maschler (London: Routledge and Kegan Paul, 1971), 18–22.

14. Wolfgang Wieser, *Organismen, Strukturen, Maschinen* (Berlin: Fischer, 1959). See also Michael Kurtz, *Stockhausen: A Biography* rev. tr. Richard Toop (London: Faber and Faber, 1992), 124, and Jonathan Cott, *Stockhausen: Conversations with the Composer*, 102.

15. Pascal Decroupet and Elena Ungeheuer, "Through the Sensory Looking-

Glass: the Aesthetic and Serial Foundations of *Gesang der Jünglinge*," tr. Jerome Kohl. In *Perspectives of New Music* 36/1 (1998): 97–142.

16. Stephen E. Levinson and Mark Y. Liberman, "Speech Recognition by Computer." *Scientific American* 244/4 (1981).

17. "Musik und Sprache III." *Texte 2*, 60–68.

18. *Texte 2*, 66.

CHAPTER TEN

Revolution

Although his wider reputation rested on a combination of inventive daring and formidable technical knowledge, Stockhausen felt ambivalent about science. Hans Gunther Tillmann, a young composition student, came for lessons during the time Stockhausen was taking part in Meyer-Eppler's seminars. After matriculating, Tillmann wanted to become a composer and asked what he should do next. Stockhausen's reply is interesting: either he should study the scientific and acoustic fundamentals with Meyer-Eppler, or continue studying compositional craftsmanship with Stockhausen. Tillman's decision is also interesting. He opted to study with Meyer-Eppler.[1]

Georg Heike, a composer and violinist, later to become Director of the Phonetics Institute at the University of Cologne, was also a participant in the Meyer-Eppler seminars. "Stockhausen was always listening out for anything that he believed he might be able to incorporate in his music: he followed the proceedings from the position of a composer. Meyer-Eppler was very proud of him, and would mention his name to others as his student."[2] There can be no doubt that Meyer-Eppler's Institute for Communications Research provided a congenial environment, that Meyer-Eppler himself was knowledgeable and interested in areas well beyond the expertise of any music department, and that his teaching and endorsement of Stockhausen's musical modeling of statistical, aleatoric, and phonetics-related processes was immensely helpful both in a musical and in a professional sense. But there was another agenda also at work. The new sciences of communication and information theory that flourished during the height of the cold war attracted scientific minds who were genuinely interested in decoding modern art, in particular surrealism in art, literature, and also music—not just for their own sakes, as for their insight into the artist's mind, perception, and decision-making, essentially those arts based on intuitions not reducible to conventional logic. Understanding the operation of higher forms of artistic communication might aid the development of thinking machines.

In 1958 Stockhausen embarked on a lecture tour of the United States, where he encountered considerable interest in the scientific implications of European new music, accompanied by a certain amount of envious apprehension among musicians. In addition to promoting the work of the Cologne studio, his visit was also destined to generate support for American initiatives such as the new computer-controlled synthesizer, designed by Harry Olson, to be installed at a facility jointly administered by Princeton and Columbia Universities. For a tour of this kind speeches are prepared, and Stockhausen's presentations are especially revealing. Stockhausen the visionary has yet to be revealed, but in plain language free of any special pleading the composer asserts the primacy of a new and self-sufficient musical art, owing allegiance to a principle higher than science, and reflecting the spiritual values of holism.

Even in Stockhausen's own terms, the text "Electronic and Instrumental Music" is a utopian declaration, very much of its time. Though he does not say in so many words, as did Boulez, that Schoenberg is dead, what he does declare is that everything about European music had been brought into question by composers like Schoenberg, who at the turn of the twentieth century had wanted to express themselves in new ways, but had found historical instruments, that had evolved in close relationship with harmonic ("tonal") music, to be unsuited to the purpose.[3] There is a chill to Stockhausen's rejection of the past, echoing the political environment to which he was born, and the doctrinaire musical environment in which he was raised, both of which had rejected the music of Schoenberg and his school. Surprisingly for so radical a figure, Stockhausen's arguments from historical necessity are essentially populist, more in tune with Adorno's reactionary psychology that one might expect. To allege a contradiction between the new formal conceptions and the physical nature of traditional instruments —probably an allusion to their dependence on the tempered scale, though this is only true for keyboards—acknowledges the very prejudices a reader would have expected a young composer in his position to transcend, or at least confront with reasoned argument, since Schoenberg's method was the first to carry through the logic of equal temperament to its ultimate conclusion. Reason however is not the point at issue. It was twelve-tone music, Stockhausen says, that finally put an end to the harmonious relationship that had previously existed between musical materials and musical form: a fairly comprehensive denial of any possibility of new relationships that Webern and Messiaen may have brought to light, that at the same time ignores the contribution of radio (i.e., Schaeffer) and electrical instruments (e.g., Jörg Mager) to the formation of a knowledge base, let alone a methodology, for electronic music. Radical twelve-tone music of the first half of the twentieth century, says Stockhausen, was effectively "impure," since it used existing materials in a nonfunctional way: this is an argument from design, but with overtones of distaste not far removed from the conventional attitude that dissonance in modern music expresses a society in decay. In twelve-tone composition, harmonic and melodic relationships that obtain for fundamental tones (i.e., the notated pitches) are not in agreement with the relationships that obtain within the microstructure of individual timbres: here Stockhausen combines a not too subtle rejection of conservative twelve-tone doctrine as it had taken hold in American universities, with a restatement of the idealist position originally promulgated by Goeyvaerts, an aesthetic of uncompromising purity that Stockhausen himself had never hesitated to overrule when it suited him, and that so far had not been shown to work in practice.

How these arguments were received is impossible to know, though not difficult to imagine. Scientists, who in general had not suffered professionally or personally from the war to the same degree as had artists, were fascinated by the musician and his music, impressed by his professional delivery and technical competence, and did not know enough or care to dispute his thesis of historical necessity. Older musicians, on the other hand, were easily intimidated by his confident manner and fluency in areas they had neither the competence nor the experience either to concede, or to refute. That of course was partly the point.

It was not all bad. Stockhausen took pains to promote interest in home-grown American composers who were outside the mainstream or had been sidelined by the musical academic community. We cannot afford to be too hard on him given the historical necessities of 1958. All the same, Stockhausen is rather too hard on Schoenberg.

> Schoenberg wrote a *Harmonielehre*, that deals only with the relationship of fixed frequencies; it lay not yet in the perspective of his times to consider the properties of "consonantal" sounds, and bring them into an inseparable continuity with the harmonic, as it applies to meter, rhythm, and dynamics, and as he had done for tone-color. During their lifetime he and his school dealt with the problems of a new pitch composition, for which new laws of equal justification were devised, while at the same time they remained slaves of classical meter, rhythm, dynamics, and instrumental color (*Koloristik*), hierarchies in crass contradiction to dodecaphonic harmony and melody. Schoenberg's irritation at the term "atonal music" can thus be understood; it is a term that introduces a basic change in the conception of musical material.[4]

This, by the way, is the same Schoenberg who composed *Pierrot Lunaire* for a speaking voice and chamber ensemble. the composer whose *Herzgewächse* is a miracle of timbral balance and miniaturization, the composer whose *Moses und Aron* perfectly integrates the textures of speaking and singing soloists and choruses with orchestra, and whose unfinished cantata *Die Jakobsleiter* imagines an apotheosis in which the soul of the blessed, spiraling upwards in a wordless vocalise, is heard from multiple loudspeakers high above the audience. In 1958 neither Stockhausen nor anybody else would have heard much of Schoenberg's music apart from the piano pieces and a few songs, and most of that only once. And while that is no excuse, it at least allows a reader today to recognize the rhetorical, indeed, defensive purpose, of these observations. In later years Stockhausen would quietly adopt Schoenberg's ritualistic *sprechgesang* and be discreetly inspired by one or two of his scenic conceptions: *Die Glückliche Hand*, for example. His emphatic denial of Schoenberg is of a piece with Boulez's 1952 polemic "Schoenberg is dead" and that generation's willful obliteration of historical consciousness, denials resting on the vain expectation that no composer or musician of earlier times had ever thought about music in similar terms.[5]

More engaging is the long essay "Musical Impressions of an American Journey."[6] An invitation by Leonard Stein and Lawrence Morton, organizer of the Los Angeles Monday Evening Concerts, to visit Los Angeles, direct a concert and give seminars at two universities, grew into a six-week flying tour of the United States and Canada, coast to coast, encompassing thirty lectures and a dozen media interviews in addition to the public concert. The English editions of *die Reihe* were beginning to appear, and there was a great deal of interest in European musical developments throughout the academic community. At Columbia University Stockhausen was pleasantly surprised at the quality of American tape equipment and loudspeakers, the efficiency and hospitality of his hosts, and the first of innumerable cocktail parties, which took some getting used to "but we got to know some interesting people." At Columbia and again at Juilliard, the lecture room was packed with attentive listeners. "I thought how conservative, compared to Juilliard, the situation was in German music colleges, where nobody was interested in finding out about new music." At Harvard and MIT he was astonished at the attendance and interest shown in the work being done in Cologne, by professors in other disciplines: acousticians, psychologists, mathematicians, physicists, architects—an interest shown overall by non-musicians, scientists of all faculties, throughout his tour; "their openness and understanding of electronic and new instrumental music was quite overwhelming."

During a break at Buffalo State he listened to recordings of contemporary American music, among them an unnamed work for orchestra by Varèse's collaborator Chou Wen-Chung, *Four Strict Songs for Eight Baritones* by Lou Harrison, and *Signs and Alarms* and *Galaxy 2* by Henry Brant. "Brant lives in New York, where he envisions a music theater in which the performers are the actors. His most recent premiere in New York, according to reports, was a musical circus. It was called 'A World Circus' and in all four corners of the hall, in the balconies, and out of windows here and there were groups of musicians singing or playing; some also moving about while they were singing and playing. I was unable to obtain a recording for myself, since it was only available on subscription, but I did get a recording of his *Galaxy 2* for ten instruments, dating from 1954."[7]

But there was also a measure of hostility toward him, especially among expatriate Austrian and German musicians, many of whom were in positions of leadership in American music colleges and music departments, —in some institutions actually outnumbering their American colleagues. To Stockhausen it seemed they represented a conservative influence, one moreover in opposition to everything new that had taken place in Germany since their departure.

> They talk and talk of their musical upbringing at the turn of the century, and are totally set in their opinions; from the day they crossed over they have stopped in their tracks and become Apostles of European music in the land of the Heathen. Some of them display a scrupulous hauteur in remarking on the lack of culture among American musicians.
>
> I met one of these in Madison, a German professor who came up to the podium where I was talking with a group of students and said reprovingly in German, "It is unacceptable that you should come here with these ideas of yours and poison the minds of these materialistic young people, already obsessed with technology. Each one of them has lost contact with the spiritual and eternal values. What have you got to say?" His wife, who was standing nearby, piped up "He has got to answer. What was it he said about the European bourgeoisie? That concerts and operas are a product of a middle-class era? The man's a Communist, I am sure of it."[8]

On his final evening in New York, evidently at his own request (since his guide, John Lewis of the Modern Jazz Quartet, had not been there for some years), Stockhausen visited Birdland to see and hear Count Basie. He had been a jazz pianist himself, imitating the music he heard on the radio openly as a boy, and in secret as a teenager. In his role as accompanist to the magician Adrion, improvised jazz had been his means of captivating and distracting an audience. The music of Cage and Tudor, and his 1958 encounters with American academic musicians, appealed to his sense of adventure, and of risk—indeed, a comment from LaMonte Young: "I am not interested in good; I am interested in new—even if this includes the possibility of its being evil"—applies with some emphasis to Stockhausen himself.[9]

White American musicians fascinated him intellectually, to some extent also philosophically, often more than their music, which by comparison could appear desultory, unfinished. Jazz was different: it carried no intellectual baggage, rather, it was an art of movement and interaction of a naturalness and fluency he dearly wished could be reproduced by European musicians, even though the idiom, the musical material (yet again) seemed to him so banal, worn out, and empty. That he identified so strongly with authentic jazz performance and style, with its sense of directed freedom, the ability of black musicians to pick up and go with an idea, and above all the sense of a theater created on the spur of the moment and in real time, throws some light on what his music would be destined to expect of performers in the years to come, and the spirit in which his own music theater should be interpreted and perceived.

> On my last night in New York, John Lewis, the pianist of the Modern Jazz Quartet, took me to Birdland, a basement where Count Basie plays from ten every night to around five in the morning. John introduced me to a string of famous jazz musicians: Basie, Gillespie (who just happened to be there), and many others. . . . For two hours I listened intently to music being played with incomparable skill. It taught me a lot, both about instrumentation and about playing technique. What

impressed me most of all was when suddenly and totally unexpectedly a
well-known black female vocalist got up from her table right in front of
the orchestra, took the microphone, started to sing, and wouldn't stop.
Basie, at the piano, signaled his musicians to play along; one of them
prompting her, in her ear, line by line, with the words. By the next verse
it was apparent that she didn't know any of the words, since she repeated the same phrase over and over, or just sang syllables. She sang
herself into a stupor, suddenly dropping the microphone on the floor
with a bang, after which I could hear no more of her voice, even though
she was only five meters away. Everybody went very quiet, and from
afar off I could finally make out her small, husky voice.

One of the musicians picked up the microphone, but it didn't work
any more. A Lilliputian, who had been acting as Interlocutor for the
evening, scowled in her direction, but the singer, oblivious, descended
the podium and began weaving her way around the tables, still singing.
At a nod from Basie, the orchestra started up again with a loud number,
and I heard no more of her.

During the next break a female friend brought her back to her
table. She was terribly ashamed and sat with her eyes downcast for the
rest of the evening. I don't remember her name.[10]

Carré (Square)

1959–1960: No. 10 (UE 14815 I–IV (four scores); cd Stockhausen-Verlag SV-5)
For four orchestras and four choirs.
Orchestra I: flute (alto flute), oboe, tenor saxophone, bass clarinet; d trumpet, high horn,
bass trumpet, bass trombone; choir 2.2.2.2; percussion (2 players): 2 tom-toms, bongo, 3
cowbells, snare drum, bass drum, Indian bells, suspended cymbal, hi-hat, gong, tam-
tam; strings 4.0.2.2.0.
Orchestra II: flute, cor anglais, clarinet, bassoon; c trumpet, high horn, low horn, tenor
trombone; choir 2.2.2.2; vibraphone; percussion (2 players): 2 tom-toms, bongo, 3 cowbells, snare drum, Indian bells, suspended cymbal, hi-hat, gong, tam-tam; strings
4.0.2.2.0.
Orchestra III: oboe, clarinet, baritone saxophone, bassoon; c trumpet, low horn, alto
trombone, bass tuba; choir 2.2.2.2; amplified cimbalom; percussion (2 players): 2 tom-
toms, bongo, 3 cowbells, snare drum, bass drum, Indian bells, suspended cymbal, hi-hat,
gong, tam-tam; strings 4.0.2.2.0.
Orchestra IV: flute, clarinet in a, alto saxophone, bassoon; c trumpet, high horn, low
horn, tenor trombone; choir 2.2.2.2; harp; percussion (2 players): 2 tom-toms, bongo,
snare drum, Indian bells, suspended cymbal, hi-hat, gong, tam-tam; strings 4.0.2.2.0.
Duration 30' 50.

In view of their juxtaposition on disc and outward similarity of design
(multiple orchestras, sounds moving in space, etc.), the listener is easily
drawn to the conclusion that Carré continues a line of development initiated
by Gruppen. This is not so: Carré is no "son of. . .," it is something else.
Gruppen represents the climax of a synthetic phase in Stockhausen's music,
marked by intense activity, high speeds, and strict hierarchies of space and
time. If there is an audible link between these two major works, it is
perhaps the moment at figure 119 in the earlier score that, as the composer
observed,

. . . led to something I hadn't expected myself—a chord is moving from orchestra to orchestra with almost exactly the same instruments (horns and trombones) and what changes isn't the pitches but rather [the location of] the sounds in space. Each orchestra, one after another, makes a crescendo and a decrescendo; at the moment when one starts fading out, the next orchestra begins to fade in, producing these very strong waves of revolving timbres.[11]

An accidental discovery, arising unexpectedly out of a methodical working-through of a research procedure, and taking on a life and momentum of its own, is the kind of outcome one normally associates with a scientific break-through, like the discovery of penicillin; that music can be discovered in a similar way is not something listeners are used to thinking about, even though trial and error is just as natural to the composer and sculptor as to the research biologist. The conventional audience perception of the artwork or musical composition as a complete and finished object reflects an essentially nineteenth-century consumerist attitude, one that ignores the process of making, and the implications of the underlying skills and techniques involved. Stockhausen's music has the merit of confronting an audience with the reality of a work in progress—a "work experience," perhaps,—that cannot be grasped spontaneously as a totality, but has to be lived through in real time, savored, and digested. Traditional and folk musics of every culture incorporate memory aids of various kinds: symmetries, repetitions, regularities of pace and phraseology, that allow a listener to accommodate, remember, and eventually anticipate; but a music lacking these traditional cues, as twelve-tone music eliminates conventional melody and harmony, and serial music conventional timing, is an experience for which even a knowledgeable listener is likely to be totally unprepared, like the subjects of Ebbinghaus's memory studies. All the same, the psychological consequences of comprehensive unfamiliarity are invariably illuminating: the listener is laid open to suggestion, so that the concert event, like a séance, becomes an experience impossible to remember, even though it may be preserved in a recording and the experience repeated indefinitely.

If *Gruppen* is "about" the (expanded) point, then *Carré* is "about" the line: length, duration. Not for the first time is one reminded of Paul Klee's definition of the dimensions of art as "dot, line, plane, and space." In contrast to the shimmering busy-ness of the earlier work, *Carré* opens into a world of meditative listening, a music of being rather than of doing. In part this is a transference into real time of the detached sound- and temporal world of electronic music, with its instantaneous transitions and vibrant inner life. It is also a change of role for the conductors, who are entrusted with a clearly more interpretative function than in *Gruppen*, where their attention is necessarily largely devoted to keeping time.

Carré takes the interior fluctuations of a sound gesture or continuous reverberation as its line of departure; no longer the dynamics of onset or attack, rather the dynamics of response and decay. Gone is the desire to model patterns of impulses after the frequency ratios of complex timbres; in its place a simpler attention to individual sounds or combinations that have

organized interior rhythms. Many of these sounds are typical of an environment of machines and vehicles in motion, so the sounds themselves move,
and are heard to change in pitch, loudness, and timbre as a consequence of
that movement: in this respect the heavily disguised city sounds of Varèse's
Déserts and *Poème électronique* can be construed as distant precursors of
Stockhausen's instrumental tone mixtures (Varèse's timing in these works
is equally monumental and introspective, perhaps for the same reason).

> I was flying every day for two or three hours over America from one city
> to the next over a period of six weeks, and my whole time feeling was
> reversed after about two weeks. I had the feeling that I was visiting the
> earth and living in the plane. There were just very tiny changes of bluish
> colour and always this harmonic spectrum of the engine noise.
> At that time, in 1958, most of the planes were propellor planes, and
> I was always leaning my ear—I *love* to fly, I must say—against the win-
> dow, like listening with earphones directly to the inner vibrations. And
> though a physicist would have said that the engine sound doesn't
> change, it changed all the time because I was listening to all the partials
> within the spectrum. . . . I made sketches for *Carré* during that time,
> and thought I was already very brave in going far beyond the time of
> memory, which is the crucial time between eight- and sixteen-second
> long events. When you go beyond them you lose orientation.[12]

Carré's poetic of expressive nuance and change within the sound,—effects
he had found impossible to achieve in electronic music,—relates the work by
default to the electronic speech world of *Gesang der Jünglinge*, in the
making of which Stockhausen had come face to face with the impossibility of
realizing the infinite gradations of natural speech depicted so clearly in
Potter, Kopp, and Kopp's voiceprint images of visible speech: transitional
effects that prior to the era of *Montag aus LICHT* could only be produced
vocally and instrumentally by human performers.

Once again the orchestras of *Carré* consist of mixed foursomes: four
woodwinds, brass, high and low voices, percussion, high and low strings,
along with a different "keyboard" for each orchestra: piano, vibraphone,
cimbalom, and harp (prefiguring their similar roles twenty years later in
Boulez's *Répons*). Whereas the triple forces in *Gruppen* add up to a traditional Mahler or Berg orchestra, in *Carré* by adding voices and reducing the
string numbers Stockhausen has lightened the texture and emphasized
instrumental color as opposed to weight. That a spatial distribution of forces
also contributes to greater transparency of sound, and clarity of complex
textures, are factors also brought to light in Henry Brant's original study of
sounds in space. However, similar changes in orchestral balance, in particular the lightening of string sections, also deprive the composer of a subtle
means of controlling and shifting the center of reverberation, an effect first
exploited in the era of Vivaldi. Massed strings, the foundation of the symphony orchestra, were introduced initially to add substance and reverberation to ensemble music performed in secular environments that lacked the
natural reverberation of a cathedral or basilica; discovering that the diffuse
sound of massed violins could influence the acoustic environment in a

controllable manner independent of the room structure quickly led to the development of a music that modulates from key to key, and effectively changes the acoustic characteristic of the performance space. Stockhausen had discovered in *Gruppen* that directional effects similar to pan-potting in a studio could be simulated with brass instruments, and that effects of such a kind had been exploited by Gabrieli and others in the late sixteenth and early seventeenth centuries. He may have been aware of similar spatial effects being achieved by voices, for instance in the *Spem in Alium* motet for forty real parts by Thomas Tallis. That massed strings, especially violins, could also be employed for spatial effect was not so widely appreciated.

By his own admission a well-disposed critic, Stravinsky remarked that *Carré* appeared timeless in the wrong sense when instead of following the score, he merely listened.[13] "In the wrong sense" may be a way of expressing the nonappearance of an effect the listener has been led to expect, like a car that refuses to start. Stravinsky continues, "Stockhausen is most interesting when he is busiest (as in the section after [82X])," a reference to the cascading inserts added at a later stage in the composition (and at 82X, track 78 in the SV cd, marvelously if inadvertently enhanced by the sound of a passing jetliner).

Just as *Gesang*'s austere antiphony is energized by impulse showers that burble like soda filling or poured from a tumbler, so the austere soundscape of *Carré* is invaded from time to time by avalanches of "colored noise" sweeping and spiraling among the four orchestras. These statistical effects in both compositions represent the same radical distraction designed to conceal essentially the same problem, which is that sounds originally designed to express some inner life, and move in space, tend in practice to refuse to budge. The dramatic success of the inserts in *Carré*, which consist largely of textured orchestral noise that has boundaries but no strongly-defined harmonic properties, is a significant achievement in itself, but can also be construed as reflecting on the comparative nonsuccess (in performance terms, at least) of the static non-insert material, which I think is what Stravinsky is saying. Of course to make such a judgement presupposes an intention by Stockhausen to simulate spatial transitions by varying the relative dynamics among the four orchestras, as distinct from plain antiphonal oppositions. The evidence of the written score is in fact consistent with such an intention, and of a piece with *Carré*'s highly-inflected musical language.

The detailed working-out of the four part-works from the composer's sketches (each conductor has a separate score, like a sixteenth-century madrigal) was assigned to an assistant, the English composer Cornelius Cardew. By his own account Cardew worked for most of the time with only the haziest notion of what Stockhausen intended.[14] The instrumental score is visualized in an apt space-time notation that acknowledges a debt to Earle Brown and Cage; for the vocal parts Stockhausen adapts the extended alphabet and intonation graphics devised by Daniel Jones and adopted by the London-based International Phonetics Association, a source likely to have been recommended by Meyer-Eppler, and typical of Stockhausen's

scrupulousness in researching the best and most apt graphics for his
musical needs. Devised by phoneticians for the approximate transcription of
prerecorded speech (so not for performance purposes, hence unspecific as to
pitch and time), it employs a scaled-down vocabulary of symbols within the
limits of a two-line stave. Visually it resembles a primitive form of plainchant; though lacking the priorities required for exact musical reproduction,

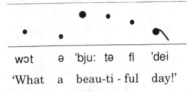

it does distinguished stressed and unstressed syllables by larger and smaller dots, and upward and downward inflections by curving extensions (the
"nuclear tail").[15] Stockhausen uses phonetic notation in *Carré* as an extension of grace-note notation, and only one size of dot for the time being, until
Zyklus and *Refrain*.

Although the choir voices occasionally emit recognizable names, among
them "E-va!" in an early premonition of *LICHT*, they are employed chiefly
as an instrumental resource, just as the speech sounds are treated as a
timbre and texture resource. The ambiguous nature of Stockhausen's text
materials, not to mention his fondness for childlike alliterative refrains and
counting games, has its origin in the composer's encounter with information
theory and the wider intuition that such childhood speech play, in addition
to its musical interest, is evidence of an ancient culture engraved, like
Mayan or Egyptian hieroglyphs, on the mind of humankind—a view unexpectedly reinforced by Noam Chomsky's well-publicized theory of the period
that generative grammar is mysteriously programmed deep into the human
genetic code.

Stockhausen was simultaneously working on *Kontakte* during the composition of *Carré*, and there is a considerable cross-fertilization of ideas
between the two works. *Kontakte* was also originally conceived as a four-
channel work in which movement in space of the tape-recorded electronic
sounds was to be controlled by four soloists operating potentiometers; this
idea was abandoned and subsequently transformed by the introduction of a
mechanism (the famous turntable) for rotating the sounds in space. In both
Carré and *Kontakte* an initial conception of sounds floating and orbiting in
the center of the auditorium had to be set aside in favor of a mechanical
system of rotating sounds around the periphery. The rotation of orchestral
sounds in space around the audience had previously been successfully
achieved by RCA-Bell Labs in 1940 for the original Disney movie *Fantasia*,
and for electronic and concrete music by an analogous Philips process for
the Brussels World Fair premiere of Varèse's *Poème électronique* in 1958.
For a composer in the employ of a radio station, in daily contact with audio
engineering colleagues, and engaged in research into the projection of
sounds in space, it is unlikely that Stockhausen would not have heard of

"Fantasound;" something of the kind seems to have provoked him to discuss with studio officials whether it would be possible to suspend musicians in chairs and spin them round the hall. The orchestra players objected to the idea, surprisingly not because it would make them dizzy, but because they thought it unprofessional to be asked to play music from a position that was moving in relation to the hall acoustic. It seemed too that the German Musicians' Union would also not allow it.[16] In 1990 Disney issued a remastered original music track of *Fantasia* (1940), marking the movie's fiftieth anniversary. Reports at the time in the audio engineering press reflect an admiring consensus on the technical brilliance of this achievement in surround sound in the era of the 78 rpm shellac platter and low-fidelity AM radio. Most of the *Fantasia* music was optically (sound-on-film) recorded under Stokowski's direction in the spacious acoustic of the Philadelphia Academy of Music, home of the Philadelphia Orchestra, and from 1931 the location of many previous test stereo recordings by the same conductor and orchestra for RCA. A Disney colleague recalled:

> Stokowski was fascinated by the mixing board—the sound control panel. He said this was the ultimate in conducting: he could dial up the strings, or turn down the others, getting exact mixtures of sounds. With the panel he could control the entire orchestra. . . . Stokowski recorded each section of the orchestra individually: strings, winds, horns, etc., then mixed the nine separate optical tracks that resulted on four master tracks. These tracks were heard by the audience from three sound horns behind the picture screen instead of the usual one, plus sixty-five small house-speakers placed strategically throughout the auditorium.[17]

Stokowski's fascination with the recording process was legendary, and in his memoir he took care to include a reliable description of the technical and scientific principles behind Fantasound:

> When the sound waves of all the instruments are combined in a single channel, they often interfere with each other and cause cross-modulation, which makes the music sound distorted. With three separate channels, it is possible to send out the music on each channel from relatively few instruments. This reduces cross-modulation and gives greater purity to the sound of the instruments. Another great advantage of three sound channels is that the tone of the various instruments can be blended in the air after the sound has left the speakers. This corresponds somewhat to the blending of colors in *pointillisme*, the method of painting in which the colors are not mixed on the canvas, but are blended in the space between the canvas and our eyes as we look at the picture.[18]

Especially fascinating is Stokowski's division of the orchestra by tone color, into woodwinds, brass, strings, and percussion, the reduction of instrumental numbers this allows, the importance he attaches to (and the feeling of power he derives from) controlling the balance himself from the mixing desk, and his ultimate goal,—to all intents and purposes, achieved,—that the sounds be perceived as moving within the auditorium space, and not just skirting its edges. In a number of significant respects *Fantasia* reads like a blueprint for *Carré*: it also suggests the intriguing possibility that to record *Carré* in Fantasound,—a technology which after all is not dependent on Tchaikovsky,—could give rise to startling results.

Ligeti and Penderecki were both deeply influenced by the dense orchestral textures of *Carré*, and it is interesting to observe that their employment of related effects is associated with meditative or ritualistic subjects (*Atmosphères, Threnody*, etc.) that tend to reflect, in the absence of any underlying serial or structural imperative, a nineteenth-century aesthetic of the beautiful and mysterious in nature (it is a feature of Stockhausen too, but Stockhausen is a lot more than just a pretty surface). Judging by *Pli selon pli*, Boulez seems also to have been impressed by *Carré*'s monumentality, and also its orchestration, in particular the insert material; there are passages in "Don" and "Tombeau" where staccato chords are set against a sustained resonance in contexts reminiscent of *Carré* at 32X and 63X. There are, all the same, intriguing differences. Stockhausen's tenuti, of single notes or chords, are always clearly defined in pitch, whereas Boulez's sustained sounds tend to be indeterminate in pitch, often gong or cymbal tremolandi. Stockhausen superimposes percussion attacks on his staccato chords; Boulez leaves his woodwind chords exposed. The combination implies a different attitude to aural perspective, and perhaps a difference of intellectual focus as well. Whereas Boulez invites the listener to pay attention to the staccato foreground, leaving the background a continuous hazy blur, Stockhausen's balance of staccato and sustain seems designed to draw the listener's attention away from the foreground, which the percussion highlights render too bright and dazzling to grasp, out to a more distant horizon.

Zyklus (Cycle)

1959: No. 9 (UE 13186; cd Stockhausen-Verlag SV-6)
For solo percussionist.
Snare drum, 4 tom-toms, 2 African log drums, guero, triangle, Indian bells, 4 cowbells, 2 suspended cymbals, hi-hat, gong with dome, vibraphone, marimbaphone.
Duration: 10'–16'.

Composed as the official test piece for percussionists for the 1959 Kranichstein Music Competition, an event won by Christoph Caskel (who remains the work's leading interpreter on disc), *Zyklus* is one of three works of this period of an unequivocal genius and perfection: formally, musically, and philosophically; the other two works being *Refrain* and *Kontakte*. One could classify the three as "the Meyer-Eppler set," given that they reconcile so elegantly and explicitly those critical polarities of freedom and determinism, of open and closed form, and of objective and subjective experience, that define serialism in the fifties and its relationship with the sciences of communication. What makes *Zyklus* all the more remarkable is that so audacious a reconciliation of antitheses is achieved in a music for percussion at a time when so-called "noise" instruments were still regarded with disdain by the generality of classical musicians, and with suspicion by orthodox serialist composers. It is also wonderfully apt for a musical conception of such intellectual sophistication to be realized in a work calculated to give the impression in performance of an uninhibited jazz break. (As it should: in Birdland Stockhausen witnessed for himself an art of mediating between strict and free interpretation, playing with or against the model, raised to a higher power in jazz than in orthodox classical music.)

In an introductory note Stockhausen describes *Zyklus* as "a dynamic, closed form" in contrast to the open form of Piano Piece XI. In retrospect the two works are very different: Piece XI is a study in depth perspective where objects are constantly shifting in virtual space, and the performer's freedoms correspond to changes in focus or orientation, some objects approaching, others receding, and expanding and contracting in time as well. Temporal sequencing is much more consciously directed in *Zyklus*, however, and the freedoms of choice are now strictly controlled within a notional tempo of reference that remains constant throughout the piece (and is indicated in the score by regular if unspoken barlines).

Stockhausen compared the indeterminate structure of Piece XI to a statistical process or "noise" expanded from the micro- to the macro domain. In that respect a comparison with *Zyklus* is also illuminating. The basic "skeleton" cycle of the latter work is modeled on a tape-loop structure of the kind originally synthesized as source material for *Kontakte*, dated 4 June 1958 in the realization score, and reproduced on page 204. In this structure, five monotone layers of edited sine-tones, serially differentiated in frequency (60, 84, 105, 160, and 200 hertz respectively), are superimposed "out of phase"—each layer reaching its maximum density at a different point in the cycle,—to comprise a single tape loop or "cycle" to be endlessly copied and speeded up until it became audible as a modulated tone. *Zyklus* is a further example of a siren-based generative process, and a step forward from the simple arpeggio structures of *Studie II*. The tape procedure of editing loops from fragments had proved hugely time-consuming, and Stockhausen may well have taken advantage of the commission to consider speedier procedures for creating and modifying a range of artificial waveforms. Since a synthetic waveform is also impulsive in character, it makes sense at least to have a single percussionist imitate the studio process in real time, performing a variety of textures and patterns employing different combinations of instrument and degrees of randomness. At the same time, of course, the exercise could also lead to the creation of a vocabulary of real-time sounds corresponding to speeded-up electronic timbres in the micro domain, a very beguiling objective for *Kontakte*.

At this point one notices a curious, distant affinity, in texture and acoustic character if not aesthetically, with the opening "avant l'Artisanat furieux" of Boulez's *Le marteau sans maître*, another toccata-like movement based on a cycle of timbres and coordinated to a rapid pulsation. Discussing the structure of *Livre* for string quartet, Boulez uses language very apt for *Zyklus*:

This oscillation between the austerity of some passages that are deliberately stripped to their essentials, rigid even, and the flexibility of
other movements or passages based on very profuse melismata and
supple rhythmic structures that give permanent flexibility and a quasi-
improvisatory style, makes a contrast that is fundamental to me. . . .
Sometimes the music reveals its bare bones while at other times the
whole structure is concealed beneath a much more flexible, much more
fragile covering.[19]

Zyklus is a structure of nine layers of instrumental impulses. Each
layer is assigned to a different instrument, and each contains a different
number of pulses (so in principle corresponding to a different partial tone).
The overlapping cycles of acceleration and deceleration are contained in a
fundamental duration divided into seventeen equal periods, drawn to scale
and marked to facilitate reading in units of constant duration, 30 per period.
The score is sixteen pages, spirally bound, and invertible, so a performer
may start at any point and read straight through to end back at the same
point, in either direction. Performed in one direction the notation becomes
progressively more aleatoric; in the other direction, the perfomer's freedom
of choice is progressively limited (though the music never arrives at total
periodicity). Fifteen of the seventeen periods are printed one to a page;
periods 17 and 1, the point where free association and determinism meet
and merge imperceptibly, occupy the remaining page, which is divided in
two by a double black line. That meeting and merging of determinate and
indeterminate structures is an act of genius.

A skeletal impulse structure is fixed for the entire work, each layer a
symmetry comprising a logarithmically measured accelerando over eight
periods, a one-period climax of maximum activity, during which the number
and distribution of attacks is free, followed by a further eight periods of
measured ritardando. These fixed structures are recognizable as heavy, fortissimo accents. Successive maxima occur in odd-numbered periods: the
snare drum during period 1, the hi-hat during period 3, the triangle in
period 5, and so on.

Over this skeletal structure Stockhausen has composed a second cycle
of points and groups that also oscillates between complete determinism (this
time, conformity with the underlying point structure) and various degrees of
indeterminacy (freedom of timing, choice, or sequence within defined limits).
This secondary flexible tissue overlaid on the more rigid bones of the work,
to borrow Boulez's analogy, is lighter in touch and more supple in articulation, and introduces cycles of increasing and decreasing clarity. The alternate blurring and focusing relationship of secondary and primary structures
is beautifully controlled, and oscillates at twice the fundamental period,
peaking at the fifth and thirteenth periods, with corresponding nodes of "no
interference" in the first, ninth, and seventeenth periods.

It is important for the performer to think of each instrument in the
ensemble as related to every other, as a location or absorption line in a
continuous spectrum between noise and pitch, defined by its degree of

resonance, and richness of timbre. By analogy with tape impulses, the drier the tone and and higher the pitch, the "faster" the sound. It is another of the hidden beauties of the score that while the entire work is structured as an immensely slowed-down impulse waveform, in performance the "fastest" elements, i.e., guero, vibraphone, and marimbaphone glissandi, are also the most melodic or musical in character, hinting that beyond the speed limit of articulation lies another realm of pure music waiting to be discovered.

Compared with Piano Piece XI, the degrees of freedom available to the performer of *Zyklus*, as distinct from the progression from fixed to statistical notation laid down by the composer, are limited to choices and orders of subsidiary points or groups within invariant divisions of the principal time-structure. The compositional rules regulating the size and relationship of subsidiary to primary elements, for instance the influence of the Fibonacci series on subsidiary orders, are comparable to those regulating the grace-note constellations of Piano Pieces V–IX, or of the "Nebennoten" (auxiliary notes) to the "Zentralklänge" (central sounds) of *Plus-Minus*.

> This is what I do in music. I go into the deepest possible layer of the individual sound. . . . In *Kontakte*, I composed every sound from individual pulses which I spliced on tape. I made loops of one rhythm with individual electric pulses that I recorded on tape with a duration of one second, for example, and sped the rhythms up a thousand times, . . . so that in the evening I had [a tone of] about 1,000 cycles per second. And one cycle of the 1,000 cycles per second is my original rhythm.[20]

For its era, a time of graphic impoverishment tending to anarchy, Stockhausen's notation for *Zyklus* is a model of exemplary design: clear, functional, and perfectly adapted to a music of "attack" structures. Since a piece for sticks is a piece where only the onset needs to be indicated, Stockhausen is able to employ a scale of note-sizes corresponding to loudness levels, a simplification that would not be possible if the size of a note were to indicate its duration as well. Such a notation has features in common with Paul Klee (the music-inspired graphics, for instance, illustrating "The natural organism of movement") further allowing the various degrees of indeterminacy of timing and internal configuration to be displayed with masterly elegance and economy.[21] (Pianists struggling to grasp the difference between metronome time and "action-time" in Piano Pieces V–XI would do well to study Caskel's recording of *Zyklus* with the score, paying particular attention to the tom-toms. Functional clarity and precision distinguish Stockhausen's graphics from the many derivative and desultory imitations of the time, for instance Roman Haubenstock-Ramati (*Liaisons, Mobile for Shakespeare*), François Bayle (*Points Critiques*) and other fashionable exponents of "musikalische Grafik." For a composer with an established reputation for hard-to-read scores, *Zyklus* marks a significant turning point.

Zyklus is the first of three pieces dating from this period,—the others being *Carré* and *Kontakte*,—manifesting a conception of rotation and enclosure proposed in Stockhausen's *die Reihe V* essay "Music in Space." In *Zyklus* of course only the performer is enclosed in a circle of instruments, whereas in the other two works it is the audience around whom the sounds rotate. Such a concept of in-centeredness leads to meditation, for all the intensity of *Zyklus'* activity; there may yet come a time when, thanks to surround sound, when we may yet experience its cyclic evolutions and revolutions from the still point of the center.

Refrain

1959: No. 11 (UE 13187; cds Stockhausen-Verlag SV-6, SV-62)
For three players: piano (woodblocks); vibraphone (cowbells); amplified celesta (antique cymbals).
Duration 11'–13'.

The title refers to recurrent disturbances that ruffle the ringing tranquility of the music. These disturbances are notated on a transparent strip that is overlaid on the music, in effect to distort perception of those parts of the music that lie beneath. Although her name is not usually acknowledged in this context, such distortion effects in the visual domain are a feature of the art of Mary Bauermeister, a young student of Max Bill, and daughter of a professor of anthropology and genetics, who in 1959 had moved into a rented studio in the older part of Cologne that quickly became a stopover, concert venue, and meeting-point for local and visiting avant-garde artists. The introduction of transparencies to music rests with John Cage, who while on a visit to Europe in 1958 composed *Music Walk* for one or more pianists, *TV Köln*, and *Fontana Mix*, in all of which transparent sheets marked with reference staves or grids are laid over pages containing dots or lines in seemingly random configurations, allowing the latter in theory to be interpreted musically. At this point, any further comparison comes to grief. The difference between Cage's interesting thought experiment and Stockhausen's adaptation of it is, as we have come to expect, that Stockhausen has fully appreciated the limitations and possibilities of the concept, and produced an intelligent solution that is both beautifully designed and also a perfectly imagined work of music.

Visually arresting, *Refrain* nevertheless makes good design sense and is not difficult to read. The curvature of staves allows the "refrain" strip to be rotated across the page to introduce shimmering disturbances to the placid calm of the music below. The musical conception and audience perception are not affected in any way by changes in location and timing of the refrain itself; indeed one could claim that a listener's sense of a natural event is enhanced by the uncertainty built into the design. As the refrain strip is turned from left to right, symbols change orientation: so a cluster may turn into a glissando, and a slow glissando into a vertical cluster, since the convention of reading vertical alignments as simultaneous still applies. The beautiful graphics, different from *Zyklus* but just as completely appropriate for a music of suspended motion as the notation of *Zyklus* is suited for a music of action, corresponds to a modern interpretation of the familiar "unmeasured prelude" notation of French composers Jean-Henri d'Anglebert and Louis Couperin: a music where the timing of events is dependent on the sound being produced, and its interaction with a room acoustic. Such passages of music tend to be notated in whole notes of indeterminate length, interrupted at times by grace notes or quarter-note figurations played rapidly, features that have already been seen in Stockhausen's Piano Pieces V–VIII, and are destined to reappear in the instrumental score of *Kontakte*, where the timing of events is also controlled by external factors (i.e., by the events on tape).

Refrain is scored for superimposed keyboard timbres: piano, celesta, and vibraphone, and occupies the mid-range, with occasional excursions into the bass. The "steady state" score, as it were, (without the refrain element), alternates chiming chords,—in which all three keyboards play as one, producing subtle interior oscillations that seem to chase one another into the distance,—and grace-note sequences in which the same note material is circulated independently, producing kaleidoscopic cut-glass textures that rustle and sparkle, and to which auxiliary percussion and occasional voiced attacks add a discreet flavor of ritual.

Introducing Cage's *Music of Changes* to a radio audience in 1957, Stockhausen remarked how pianist David Tudor would sit "almost motionless, letting the last sound before a pause die away very gently," before making his mext move "with unbelievable rapidity," a description of how *Refrain* should be approached.[22] Its clangorous mix of sonorities also bears comparison with Boulez's *Improvisation II sur Mallarmé* ("Une dentelle s'abolit") of 1958, of which Boulez has written in very similar terms "the work is scored for voice and instruments. I place the instruments on the platform in such a way that the three different kinds of sound—fixed pitch, partially pitched, and unpitched 'noise')—blend with one another."[23] Boulez's chamber ensemble is larger, including tubular bells and harp as well as piano, vibraphone, and celesta; it also incorporates a female voice, which tends to take the limelight and distract attention from the accompanying mixed sonorities, which tell their own story. Half a century on, the glossy opulence of Boulez's sonority is beginning to sound just a little tarnished, its aesthetic somewhat dated; by comparison Stockhausen's drier, denser, and sharper imagery seems to have lost none of its freshness and immediacy.

The phonetic content of *Refrain*, comprising not only the voices attacks but also the woodblocks, cowbells, and crotala (corresponding to "k," "g," and "t" consonants respectively), introduce a tactile element absent from the keyboard attacks, which need to sound precise, like musical boxes. While the glottal "clicks" work well in practice, the voiced diphthongs do not liaise as easily with their accompanying instrumental tones, and are now to be articulated in a higher-pitched head-tone, with a trailing intonation, after the manner of Noh percussionists.

In 2000 Stockhausen produced a new cd recording, "3 × *Refrain* 2000" for teaching purposes. Three versions of the score are introduced and discussed by the composer, and performed in full. Although the performances are musically very clear, something very strange has happened to the mix, which sounds incomprehensible in stereo, as if the three performer spaces have somehow been superimposed. (The recording of "Mittwochs-Abschied" from *Mittwoch aus LICHT* dates from this time and is also perplexing in the same way.) The third and final version of *Refrain* in the new recording terminates with a newly-composed, unnecessary and grotesque flourish, completely out of character, intended it seems as a gesture of rejection of the piece itself, and of all keyboard instruments.

Notes

1. Michael Kurtz, *Stockhausen: A Biography* rev. tr. Richard Toop (London: Faber and Faber, 1992), 68.
2. Michael Kurtz, *Stockhausen: A Biography*, 72.
3. "Electronic and Instrumental Music" tr. Ruth Koenig. In *die Reihe V: Reports – Analyses* (Bryn Mawr: Theodore Presser, 1961), 50–59.
4. *Texte 1*, 144–45.
5. Boulez has persistently denied that it was ever Schoenberg's intention that *Pierrot Lunaire* should be half-spoken, half-sung; but the voice in *A Survivor from Warsaw* speaks to the listener in Schoenberg's own inflection, just as the bass voice in *Sirius* and Luzifer in *Jahreslauf* (*Dienstag aus LICHT*) are exact transcriptions of Stockhausen's voice.
6. "Musikalische Eindrücke einer Amerikareise." *Texte 2*, 219–32.
7. Stockhausen is reported to have consulted Brant's paper "Uses of Antiphonal Distribution and Polyphony of Tempi in Composing" (*American Composers' Alliance Bulletin* IV/3, 1955: 13–15) while working on the orchestration of *Gruppen*. (See Joan Peyser, *Boulez: Composer, Conductor, Enigma* (London: Cassell, 1977), 132.) Here Stockhausen appears to be referring to Brant's *Grand Universal Circus*, "a spatial theater piece for 8 singing and speaking voices, 32 choristers, and 16 instruments," composed in 1956.
8. *Texte 2*, 224.
9. LaMonte Young: "Lecture 1960." *Tulane Drama Review* 10/2 (1965): 73–83.
10. *Texte 2*, 232.
11. Jonathan Cott, *Stockhausen: Conversations with the Composer* (London: Robson Books, 1974), 200–201.
12. Jonathan Cott, *Stockhausen: Conversations with the Composer*, 31.
13. "Contingencies." Igor Stravinsky and Robert Craft, *Themes and Episodes* (New York: Knopf, 1966), 11–12.
14. Cornelius Cardew, "Report on Stockhausen's *Carré*." In two parts. *Musical Times* 102 (1961), 619–22; 698–700.
15. Daniel Jones, *The Pronunciation of English*. 4th edn. (Cambridge: Cambridge University Press), 1956.
16. *SoM*: 101–102.
17. John Culhane, *Walt Disney's* Fantasia (Reprint. New York: Abrams, 1999), 19–20.
18. Leopold Stokowski, *Music for All of Us* (New York: Simon & Schuster, 1943). Cited in John Culhane, *Walt Disney's* Fantasia, 19.
19. Pierre Boulez, *Conversations with Célestin Deliège* tr. Robert Wangermée (London: Eulenberg, 1976), 53–54.
20. Jonathan Cott, *Stockhausen: Conversations with the Composer*, 76.
21. Paul Klee, *Notebooks Volume 1: The Thinking Eye* ed. Jürg Spiller, tr.

Ralph Manheim (London: Lund Humphries, 1961), 325–29.

22. *Texte 2*, 148.

23. "Constructing an Improvisation." In *Orientations: Collected Writings* tr. Martin Cooper (London: Faber and Faber, 1986), 155–76.

CHAPTER ELEVEN

Contacts

The word "contact" has many implications: electrical, as in throwing a switch to start the engine of a single-propellor biplane in the era when pilots were heroes and able to fly above the carnage in the trenches; adventurous, as with the meeting of Livingstone and Stanley deep in the African continent; inspiring, affirmative, or fraught with challenge, as in an encounter with the unknown. In its most literal sense *Kontakte* the music is about a meeting of two worlds, the temporal reality of a live performance, and the timeless reality of music on tape. For Stockhausen there is also the personal aspect of a meeting of minds: reaching a practical and intellectual accommodation between the Karel Goeyvaerts vision of an ideal, absolute world of perfect harmony to which he aspired, and the divided real world of imperfect instruments and unstable performance with which he had to contend. Here at last is a music where the theoretical and philosophical statement is fully congruent with the musical action, giving *Kontakte*'s symbolism the same kind of currency as Monteverdi's 1610 *Vespers*, that other triumph of musical diplomacy that manages to reconcile the timeless world of religion with the new dynamic of Renaissance progress. As a statement of the relationship between the temporal and the eternal *Kontakte* has only been matched in the present era by Boulez's aptly-named *Répons* of 1981, a companion achievement of the early digital era to complement Stockhausen's monument to the analogue age.

A personal mythology of radio can be reconstructed from a number of defining views expressed by the composer over the years. They include the value the composer attaches to the imitation of events and songs heard on the radio or on tape, from reproducing hit songs heard on the radio as a boy, to jazz improvising for the magician Adrion as a youth, to the manipulation of shortwave radio imagery in *Hymnen, Kurzwellen, Stop, Mantra, Trans,* and beyond, in his maturity. A distinctive feature of Stockhausen's imitation aesthetic is an assumption of innocence, of neutrality in transmission, on the part of the message-deliverer, as in reproducing a Kurt Weill song without understanding the political or moral implications of the text, "delivering the mail without knowing what is in the letters," or characterizing oneself as a medium or radio receiver that implicitly has no control over the information it is fated to transmit,—a quality of transparency also associated with the philosophical detachment of John Cage. In Stockhausen's terms, imitation is the exact and accurate reproduction of a given signal to the limits of the available resource, whether it is a voice, acoustic instrument, or synthesizer: in effect, reproduction without question or interpretation. When the musical image has been captured and stored (memorized), it may then be transformed, but once again these alterations, as Stockhausen conceives them, amount to imitations of mechanical processes applied to the original signal, and do not normally involve the elaboration or follow-through of a musical content in a classical sense, such as adding a verse, or supplying a missing cadence. Strict adherence to external features is also a feature of baroque imitation, as in canon, fugue, or sequence, the whole purpose of preserving an original *gestalt* being to enable a listener to track the journey of a musical image through changes of key, or of chord within a key, and in fugue, through inversions and alterations of scale. (One remembers Stockhausen's criticisms of the relative poverty of Bartók's motivic elaborations in the *Sonata for two pianos and percussion* compared to the dense and integrated counterpoint of J. S. Bach.) Progression by imitation is also inherent in Schaeffer's concept of the "complex note" of musique concrète, and its associated transformations.

Stockhausen's image of the composer as a radio receiver also attributes an authority, divine or otherwise, to the medium of radio or audio reproduction. For a child growing up under a regime that was among the first deliberately to employ radio as a medium of social control, a relationship of unquestioning obedience to the disembodied voice of the nation may not seem very different from religious belief or filial duty. In Stockhausen's own experience the radio voice was manifestly an instrument of government intimidation, and did in fact issue orders that had to be obeyed. His own mother's noncompliance, in attempting to argue with the hidden voice, was interpreted as mental derangement, for which the penalty was incarceration and eventual euthanization.

To the disembodied authority of the radio voice can be added a sense of timelessness or permanence of a kind traditionally associated with the realm of the gods, a mythical immortality also accorded to popular "stars" of film and sound recording media. An orthodox perception of history receding while the information on a recording remains locked in an eternal present, —even though the disc or tape itself may wear out,—is a situation paradoxically reversed in the Faustian pact of Oscar Wilde's novella *The Picture of Dorian Gray*, where it is the portrait that grows old and its subject who is doomed to eternal youth. For these and many other reasons, a composition in which live and prerecorded elements interact is readily understood as a dialogue of the temporal and the eternal that in the nature of things imposes a petitionary or subordinate role on the living performer. In this connection the composer's dismay at the actual and potential deterioration of master tapes of *Gesang der Jünglinge*, *Kontakte*, *Telemusik*, and other compositions reflects the somewhat cruel irony that works of art conceived as ageless, at times also fall victim to premature decay. Ensuring their survival was a major influence in his decision to buy back his earlier recordings and issue them under his own label.[1]

Stockhausen's initial determination to control his electronic compositions (and ideally, all of his music) from the total form right down to the microstructure of every single waveform, and the compromises forced upon him by that determination, offer some insights into the relationship between the aesthetic task to which he was committed and the artistic persona and mystique that evolved, at least in part, in consequence of that commitment. His earliest efforts in electronic music, the *Konkrete Etüde* and the two Studies, were geared to the objective of producing "pure, controllable sounds," pure both in the scientific sense of mathematically ideal waveforms, and also in the idealistic or religious sense of images of transcendental perfection. For practical reasons the ideal could not be achieved, a disappointment leading the composer over time to a redefinition of that artistic purpose, and modification of the persona associated with it.

A second objective, specific to tape music, and inspired partly by medieval practice and partly by Le Corbusier's doctrine of scale and proportionality (in *Le Modulor*), called for the composition of sounds and timbres specific to every new work, each germinal waveform a configuration related to the macrostructure of the entire work. This objective likewise faded away, this time not for reasons of impossibility, but because the aural results did not justify the time and labor involved in fabricating complex microstructures. Years later, however, when fractal mathematics appeared on the scene in the 1970s, an early manifestation of the computer age, it could be read as endorsing not only Le Corbusier's aesthetic of proportionality, but also Stockhausen's principle of deriving an entire structure organically from a germinal cell.[2] Through constant reiteration of a simple mathematical formula, fractal software is able spontaneously to generate mysterious images resembling coastlines, landscapes, and other natural phenomena that also exhibit structural self-similarity at every scale from the largest overview to the smallest detail.

For Stockhausen the moral imperative of striving toward an ideal and frequently impossible goal came to be justified by the gift of unexpected insights discovered along the way. Hence the importance to him of *Einschube* or "inserts:" "found objects" discovered during the process of composition and attached to the finished work even though they are unaccounted for in the composer's original master plan.

> Bach, Beethoven, Brahms, Stravinsky and a few other composers of the past have recognized the supremacy of intuition, based on the quality of the composer being a medium. He is a mouthpiece of the divine. . . . The

whole *Einschub* technique goes back to the KONTRA-PUNKTE and even to the DREI LIEDER when I first started composing. In particular the DREI LIEDER which I wrote very fast during the college vacation in 1950, and which is based directly on the overwhelming experience of inner sound visions which are stronger than your own will, technique, style preferences, or whatever it may be.

On the other hand, you are an engineer, you do mental work, and there is sometimes a conflict between the two: you have overall visions, images which make demands of a kind you cannot yet realize, and they lead to the invention of new technical processes, but then the technical processes go their own way and become the starting point for other techniques which in turn provoke new intentions and you find yourself bombarded with images again.[3]

For a method allegedly more rigorous, both intellectually and in practical terms, than the twelve-tone system of Schoenberg, Berg, and Webern, there is all the same something perplexing about a serialism that embraces inspired additions that arise spontaneously during the course of composition. The whole purpose of following a serial regime,—or so one might suppose from reading Schoenberg, Webern, or even Boulez on the subject, —is to ensure that the structures that arise are specific to an initial set of conditions: fresh, new, and uncontaminated, even inadvertently, by aesthetic prejudices of any kind. By his own definition, Stockhausen's *Einschub* additions are parenthetical interjections that interfere with the ostensible purity and integrity of the serial plan in a number of ways: first, in that he is consciously attracted to them, second, in that they are deviations from the serial scheme, and hence affect the integrity of an original conception, and third, because they inevitably distort the outcome of the work as an expression of serial procedure, along with the listener's perception of its intellectual and aesthetic success.

In defense of the inserts, one could say that this is how it works in practice: the serial matrix is not an end in itself, but a method through which discoveries are made. Not to include the discoveries is missing the point. In effect the inserts manifest themselves as possibilities that might have been if the original set of conditions had been planned just a little bit differently. It is a long way from the conventional approach to the philosophy of design (at least among English-speaking cultures) of setting a limited goal and then finding the best way of attaining it; instead one starts with a theoretical goal, pursuing an inflexible method, and ending with a result that is not quite what you were looking for in the first place. But this is just the way that continental European minds typically work. We find it in Boulez's and Adorno's writing as well. Edmund Leach invokes a generic criticism of European reasoning in querying the underlying scientific method and associated prose style of the anthropologist Claude Lévi-Strauss:

> packed with oblique references and puns which recall Verlaine's Symbolist formula *'pas de couleur, rien que la nuance'*. Readers who find the precise meaning of Lévi-Strauss' prose persistently elusive should

remember this part of his literary background. . . . Many would argue
Lévi-Strauss is insufficiently critical of his source material. He always
seems to be able to find just what he is looking for. Any evidence however dubious is acceptable so long as it fits with logically-calculated
expectations, but wherever the data runs counter to theory he will either
by-pass the evidence or marshal the full resources of his powerful
invective to have the heresy thrown out of court. So we remember that
his prime training was in philosophy and law; he consistently behaves as
an advocate defending a cause rather than as a scientist searching for
absolute truth.[4]

It is not that perfectly valid analogies to Stockhausen's method of discovery
are hard to find, in scientific research, archaeology, movie acting, action
photography, or sculpture that is assembled from items discovered at random. Nobody is offended that classical architecture and painting are based
on rigid geometrical schemata concealed beneath the more flexible outer
envelope. It is simply to question the credibility of a method for which so
much is claimed, and yet one that fails satisfactorily to account for the
results it purports to deliver. "Erst kommt das fressen," as Macheath says to
Jenny; "dann kommt die Moral." One has the feeling at times that the initial complexities of a method are being used to disguise powerful creative
impulses that are relatively intuitive in operation.

Serialism itself is not the issue here. There are strong arguments in
support of serialism in the Boulezian sense, derived from de Saussure and
embedded in the structuralism of Durkheim and the structural anthropology of Claude Lévi-Strauss. That human beings exist and cooperate by
virtue of making distinctions, perceiving and interpreting continuities in
nature in terms of series or progressions of discrete values, is a story as old
as Adam and Eve; it also entails a moral, which is the loss of innocence (in
the holistic sense) attendant on discovering knowledge through making
discriminations: devising scales of pitch and dynamics, interpreting the
spectrum of a rainbow as bands of different colors, and organizing the
infinitely variable processes of vocalization into the vowels and diphthongs
of speech. Without the distinctions of notation and orchestration, Western
music would not have evolved in the way it has. Modern music after
Helmholtz, from the microtonal scales of Julián Carrillo and Alois Hába to
the microrhythms of Conlon Nancarrow, is characterized by attempts to
enlarge and refine the range of scale determinations available to the
composer. Schoenberg defended chromaticism as an advance of music to a
higher plane of awareness; Messiaen made similar claims for his theories of
rhythmic growth and diminution. Avant-garde composers of the *die Reihe*
era were encouraged and motivated by the claims and aspirations of communications science,—the domain of Werner Meyer-Eppler, André Moles, and
others with a professional interest in new music,—to pursue a scientific goal
of total quantification of the musical experience, leading to scales of
dynamics, timbre, time relations, and even degrees of intelligibility of a
musical *gestalt*. The underlying principles of postwar serialism and scale
generation are amply supported in rational and historical terms.

That is not to say, however, that agreeing on a scale (of touch, for instance, or dynamics) is an easy task. The microphone is a great teacher. Human performers are not precision instruments. Dynamics are necessarily approximate: a perception of loudness is always relative to frequency and timbre, and can be further compromised in notation by added accents and touch indications such as staccato. An additive scale of durations, as in Messiaen's *Mode de valeurs et d'intensités*, is not evenly balanced, the longer values taking precedence over the shorter. In *Spiel* Stockhausen attempts to compensate by increasing the loudness of a note relative to its shortness of duration; for *Gruppen* his alternative duration scale, based on progressive subdivisions of a unit beat, simply transfers the imbalance of Messiaen's mode to shorter values: a scale where, as we have seen, the median value corresponds to one-sixth of a beat, leaving no intermediate steps between half and maximum values. Similar inequalities arise in the composition of timbres from tape-loop sequences modeled as miniature replicas of serial form: again the longer and louder values in the microstructure overwhelm the remainder.

The term *parameter* employed in relation to avant-garde music made its appearance in periodicals such as *die Reihe* to mean an expressive dimension such as pitch, duration, tempo, or dynamics, one that in serial music is quantified and organized in a scale of graded values. Since it appears in a similar context, it is easy for a reader to interpret the word as an equivalent term, say, to *mode* in relation to the modes of Messiaen's *Mode de valeurs*. The term *parameter* refers however to a defining condition rather than to an ordered sequence, and is therefore properly employed in relation to music, and especially for those properties of rhythm, dynamics, attacks, and timbre, that do not exhibit the same degree of internal consistency as pitch or tempo, and can therefore only be sequenced in an arbitrary, or approximate, and essentially subjective manner. In Stockhausen's electronic music, for example, the term is properly used in connection with the tone quality associated with a given microstructure, which is liable to change dramatically in the course of transposition from bass to treble and beyond; one does not however speak of the timbre of a conventional musical instrument as a parameter, since the tone quality varies with pitch, but can still be recognized as issuing from the same instrument. It is reasonable to suppose that in setting out to construct individual waveforms in microcosm, Stockhausen expected to create ranges of tone colors specific to the work and also exhibiting the tonal consistency of conventional musical instruments. In reality, however, unlike a normal musical instrument, on tape the same initial waveforms give rise to distinctly different timbres at different scale transpositions.

Such a result leaves the composer with some explaining to do, given that conventional music of every culture relies on controlled modulations of pitch and tonal affect within perceived consistencies of timbre. And it was ever so. The basic sound materials of *Konkrete Etüde*, by his own admission, proved neither "pure" nor particularly "controllable." In order to achieve the blended and consistent tone-mixtures of *Studie II*, the working principle of

"pure, controllable tones" had to be set aside. In the early stages of work on
Gesang der Jünglinge it became painfully clear that the meticulous fab-
rication of artificial waveforms on tape guaranteed neither individually
distinctive nor consistently recognizable timbres, and furthermore, that
timbres of a specific voice-like quality could not be designed to order.
Indeed, by the time of his conversations with Jonathan Cott, Stockhausen is
ready to admit freely that the precise microstructure of a wave is no longer
as important in practice as he had once declared it to be in theory. Hence
the ambiguity of his remark:

> The secret of timbre composition lies in the production of very specific
> cycles of rhythmic changes. At first it's not so important what these
> changes are because you speed them up to such an extent that the re-
> sulting timbre is a newly perceived unity. It has a certain timbre
> characteristic, and you don't consciously analyze how it's composed in its
> micro-structure.[5]

In persisting after goals that go beyond the humanly possible, there is
always the risk of endorsing compromise as an inevitability. *Gesang der
Jünglinge*, which after all is a parable about keeping the faith when all
around you is in flames, set the bar much higher than the earlier Studies,
aiming to synthesize a vocabulary of electronic phonemes resembling the
fundamental particles of speech and song. It is a beautiful idea: the musical
message, underpinned by the boy's voice, is sufficiently clearly stated for an
audience to grasp the grandeur of the conception and appreciate the
virtuosity of its execution, despite the practical impossibility of the task. But
in coming to terms with the reality of synthesized waveforms giving rise to
complex timbres whose resemblance to speech sounds is more a product of
accident than design, Stockhausen's sophisticated explanation for this
uncertain result is to characterize the composer's role as following a divine
plan rather than manufacturing sounds to order. Suddenly this is no longer
science, but art. There are parallels between Stockhausen's new rationale
and the views of nineteenth-century Romanticism, that the artist's proper
role is rather the imitation, than the reproduction, of nature:

> The purpose of art, according to Ruskin, is to reveal aspects of
> universal "Beauty" or "Truth." The artist is one who, in Carlyle's words,
> "reads the open secret of the universe." Art is not "imitation," in the
> sense of illusionist representation, or an adherence to the rules of
> models, but Art *is* "imitation," in the older sense of an embodiment of
> aspects of the universal, "ideal" truth. . . . A man is not a good artist
> merely because he has good ideas, but, rather, the artist's apprehen-
> sion of good ideas is an intrinsic element of his artist's skill. The
> quality of seeing, the special quality of apprehension of essential form:
> these are the particular faculties through which the artist reveals the
> essential truth of things.[6]

A nature, redefined in terms of Darwin's theory of evolution, that creates an
abundance of species of which only a few are destined to survive by a
process of natural (or divine) selection. A generative process in music that

leads to diversity rather than unity is thus arguably closer to nature than one leading to predictable and consistent results. The Darwinian analogy, seductive in its own way, has the effect of diverting the focus of potential criticism from a flawed theory of timbre generation to a lack of historical awareness among ordinary mortals. It also lends a certain credibility to Stockhausen's canonical views of the artist's role as an instrument of divine authority, some of which still remain difficult for an ordinary mortal to grasp.

It is curious to reflect, all the same, that the causes of unpredictability of electronic waveforms are not at all difficult to understand. They arise from a misconception, fundamental to synthesizer design, that a musical timbre is defined by a waveform of a particular shape, whereas in reality constancy of timbre is a function of the interaction of an energy source with a resonating body. The consistencies audible in a standard instrument or voice can be attributed to a resonant structure vibrating the way it does in order to dispose of excess energy and return to an undisturbed state. An electronic microstructure or waveform can be compared in this sense to the action of a bow on a violin string: to achieve a timbre analogous to a violin, however, a passive reverberation circuit is required that reproduces the stable features of a violin's resonating body, its material, shape and volume, and radiation characteristic. Today, digital circuitry of this kind is a regular feature of domestic audio equipment, employed to impose (as it happens, superfluously) the ambience of a concert hall or concert chamber on an existing recording. Circuitry designed to reproduce in three dimensions the smaller-scale, more subtle resonances, say, of a Stradivarius violin, have yet to reach the mass market, however.

Because classic electronic synthesis does not extend to simulating the cavity resonances in a musical instrument (the tube or box), in cases where a sound sample is dilated or compressed in time (slowed down or speeded up) everything about the original sound is transformed, and nothing remains constant. Hence a change of playback speed is heard to alter the perceived personality of a recorded voice, as well as the pitch of the voice. Too great a distortion of speed, faster or slower, may also lead to undesirably comic effects. In the apotheosis of Ernst Krenek's *Spiritus Intelligentiae Sanctus*, a Cologne Radio electronic production from the same period as *Gesang der Jünglinge*, the tape speed of a quartet of singing voices is increased with the intention of producing an acoustic effect resembling a chorus of birds; the actual result, however, sounds more like a tremulous choir of mice. (A similar procedure is heard in "Montags-Abschied" from *Montag aus LICHT*). Stockhausen's avoidance of excessive pitch transformation of the boy's singing voice in *Gesang der Jünglinge*, is clear evidence of his awareness of the potential for distortion of recognizable sounds. Such a realization goes hand in hand with an awareness that the same qualitative inconsistencies are also likely to occur in the case of artifical waveforms. The peculiar genius of *Kontakte* arises from the composer turning the progressive distortion of an artificial timbre, under varying degrees of acceleration, from a practical and theoretical liability into a creative asset. The new work is a triumphant vindication of this new approach.

Kontakte (Contacts)

1958–1960: No. 12 (Realization score: Stockhausen-Verlag; cd SV-3)
Electronic music. Duration 34' 30.
No. 12½ (Performance score: Stockhausen-Verlag; cd SV-6)
For electronic sounds, pianist, and percussionist.
Duration 34' 30.
Percussionist: 2 African wood drums, marimbaphone, 3 tom-toms with plywood heads, guiro, bamboo chimes, 2 wood-blocks, 4 cowbells, 13 fixed antique cymbals, inverted cymbal, hi-hat, small tam-tam, Indian bells, bongo, 3–4 tom-toms, inverted bongo with dried beans, snare drum.
Centre stage: large tam-tam, large gong with dome.
Pianist also plays: bamboo chimes, 2 wood-blocks, 4 cowbells, 3 fixed antique cymbals, suspended cymbal, hi-hat, Indian bells, bongo.

Kontakte is the greatest of the "perfect three" compositions of this period, the other two being *Zyklus* and *Refrain*. Perfect in the sense that they are compelling musical statements, and also in the sense that they are perfectly imagined, both serially and also philosophically. In earlier works, as the composer himself has noted, miscalculations or discrepancies appear, on occasion conceptual errors, at other times more practical issues such as dynamics or instrumentation. In these three works, the culmination of a rationalist phase inspired by Meyer-Eppler and endorsed by Cologne Radio with Eimert as its spokesman, there are no fundamental errors, no excess complications, no tactical diversions, just exceptional ideas and dramatic visions, expressed with wonderful economy and precision, and conveying a sense of powerful energy and humor.

The more than two years of planning and production, from early 1958 to mid-1960, was a period in which Stockhausen became increasingly attentive to recent developments in American music, to composers Cage, Brown, and Feldman, to the pianist David Tudor, and to jazz. American influences in the scale and style of Stockhausen's musical utterance, and in his adoption of graphic notation, are outward signs of a profound transformation in artistic sensibility, of which *Kontakte*, by virtue of its lengthy gestation, is both product and documentation. During this time the Cologne studio was also being made available to other composers: among them the Hungarian exile György Ligeti for the creation of *Artikulation*, and to the Argentinian Mauricio Kagel for *Transición II*, in both of which Stockhausen was involved as an advisor.

Stockhausen's realization score of *Kontakte*, which took over a year to produce, with the help of Jaap Spek, is a unique document of analogue electronic music production methods, and a valuable guide to the composer's art of creative self-provocation. He had not produced a score of any kind for *Gesang der Jünglinge*, relying on isolated sketches in an unknown hand for the presentation published as "Musik und Sprache III."[7] At the outset Stockhausen's approach to the synthesis of basic tone material shows little change from the direct craftsmanship of his earlier electronic studies. Indeed, there is little in the earliest microstructures to identify them as specific to *Kontakte*, which may simply be because the composer is working to a matrix of time and frequency relationships that is already in place. After the experience of working with dynamically volatile speech sounds in *Gesang*, the focus of the synthesis process is directed away from previous ideas of "pure," "static," or "dead" sound materials in favour of microsounds having inner life, and demonstrating a capacity for movement in space.

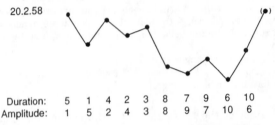

Duration:	5	1	4	2	3	8	7	9	6	10
Amplitude:	1	5	2	4	3	8	9	7	10	6

The first process detailed in the realization score, dated 20 February 1958, is a train of ten tone segments varying in amplitude and duration, though not in pitch, arranged as a symmetrical series. The pattern represents one cycle of a waveform, joined end to end as a tape loop and accelerated until the repeating pattern within each cycle is heard as a constant pitch of a particular tone quality. The visual shape recalls the symmetrical expanding all-interval series favored by Nono (in *Incontri*) and also recommended by Eimert (who claimed to have discovered it first). The actual sound "looks" different in both duration and amplitude, though the resulting pattern is a potentially rich source of combination orders of superimposed fives and sixes:

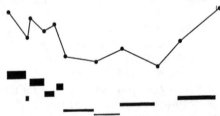

In the second entry, dated 25 February, the amplitude of segments is constant, a change reminiscent of the *Konkrete Etüde* experience, suggesting that the synthesis procedure is revisiting older material rather than following a preconceived work plan. Three months later in an entry dated 29 May 1958 the focus has moved from a ministructure of segments to an arpeggiated pattern of edited sine tones of equal durations and amplitudes similar to the source material of *Studie II*. The 5 cm. modular duration is easy to work with, and at a tape speed of 76.2 cm./second delivers a final periodicity very close to MM 60. In the realization score this pattern is represented as a contracting tremolo between an underlying pitch and three alternate

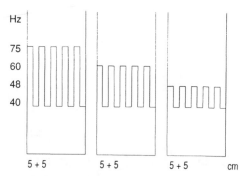

"partials" in descending sequence, each interval repeated five times. These pitch levels are related to Stockhausen's scale of tempi (40–48–60–75). Stockhausen may have been curious to discover if the 5 cm. repetition rate of the sequence would also be audible as a constant tone. The sequence can be heard in *reverse* order at a higher transposition as a warble tone punctuating section XIIB of the score:

[pitches approximate]

Entries dated 2.6.58 and 4.6.58 combine earlier methods in different ways, but always with an emphasis on the unifying qualities of structural symmetry (regularity of waveform) and sonority (production of "energized" timbres). The last of the 4 June examples is also the most complex, the so-called "*Zyklus* complex" of five pitch layers oscillating out of phase. Each dot represents a 5 cm. segment of tape: the pattern is so arranged that the sequence can be edited onto a single tape, which is copied and joined back to front to produce a symmetrical oscillation of great complexity.

The composer's craftsmanlike directness of approach up to this point is matched by his dependence on the traditional "cut and stick" method of editing. This multilayered microstructure has elements in common with Milton Babbitt's serial technique of time-sharing, or pulse code modulation.[8] The advantage of better coordination of partial components is offset, however, by a huge increase in preparation time. In the absence of a keyboard input, each "note" in the sequence has to be cut and edited together by hand. There is no dynamic shaping of tape as in the previous *Studie I* and *Studie II*; nevertheless this is a long and painstaking operation.

The resulting sounds are certainly vibrant, each with an inner motor, and they stand alone in section III (the original section I) of the performing score, where it had been Stockhausen's original intention to have the players controlling their movement in four-channel space with potentiometers. This section is very similar in character to the opening of *Carré*, where it had also been Stockhausen's intention to effect a similar movement of

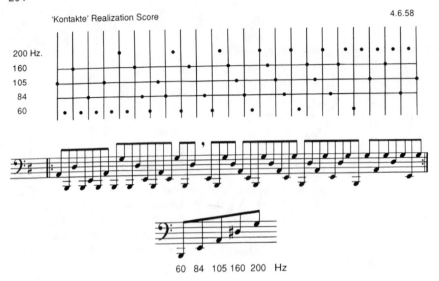

'Kontakte' Realization Score   4.6.58

60 84 105 160 200 Hz

relatively static live orchestral sound by having the conductors vary the dynamics of the four orchestras.

A less time-consuming method of building complex sounds layer by layer emerged from a discovery that the three contact heads on a studio tape recorder could be transposed. Whereas in domestic tape recorders the erase, record, and read functions are combined in a single tape head, in a professional machine these functions are assigned to three separate heads arranged normally in the sequence erase–record–play, the order in which the tape passes them, left to right. This means that a prerecorded tape normally passes the erase head and information already on the tape is erased prior to new material being recorded by the record head and detected by the playback head. If the wiring of the three-part tape head is changed to the order play–erase–record, however, the information on a continuous tape loop can be taken from the play head and reenter the record chain, rather than being lost, to combine with new layers in an accumulation process that in theory could go on indefinitely, but in practice is limited by a progressive accumulation of unwanted generational noise.

The "copy head," as this arrangement came to be called, introduced a new dynamic into the compositional process. The choice of materials needed no longer to be limited to serial distinctions of a pointillistic kind; with flexibility of manipulation comes a flexibility of choice. Thus the concept of a closed, theoretically integrated, and essentially speculative system of composition was superseded by a more open-ended, series-orientated range of options, governed in the final resort by an intuitive awareness of "the good sound." Soon after, entries in the realization score indicate the emergence of naturalism as a desirable criterion. Synthetic sounds begin to be given names, like "bell-like" or "skin-like." What makes these imitation sounds so different from the artificial phonemes of *Gesang der Jünglinge* is the sense that they are not deliberate simulations but spontaneous resemblances, intuitively recognized. In an effort reminiscent of the composer's 1952 analyses of ethnic instrument recordings in the Musée de l'Homme, Stockhausen's assistant Gottfried Michael Koenig was assigned the task of analysing the acoustic spectra of a number of percussion instruments (crotala, bongo) that figure in the instrumental version of the final work. Whether this research was really necessary, or done simply to provide scientific validation for essentially aesthetic choices, is difficult to say. What is certain is that many of the range of timbres represented by the live instrumentation can be adequately accounted for on the basis of intuitive resemblances to tape transformations of simple sounds. Here the instrumentation is chosen to imitate the tape, not the tape the instruments. Categories of "wood," "metallic," or "skin" sounds, though arguably scientific in an ethnomusicological sense, are certainly not scientific in any acoustic sense and do not imply complicated analysis or synthesis processes. The basic categories of sound audible in *Kontakte* arise from a combination of editing, reverberation, and transposition procedures with which Stockhausen was already familiar from earlier tape experiments.

In his experiments dated 4.7.58 Stockhausen varies the tape speed, and thus the density and pitch, of impulse aggregates while maintaining fixed filter and reverberation characteristics; a procedure corresponding to the separation of a source vibration (e.g., bow friction on the string) from the associated cavity resonance (the violin body). This marks a significant progression conceptually, recognizing the independence of these components of a musical sound. From this point on the technical processes described in the realization score become increasingly elaborate, and the source processes less and less precisely defined, in line with the more dynamic approach deriving from the "impulse-shower" processes of *Gesang der Jünglinge.*

The work begins and ends with cyclic gestures, imitated on gong and snare drum respectively, that suggest, perhaps unintentionally, the actions of a 78 rpm gramophone record starting and stopping. After a short hiatus of highly-reverberated whirring, a vigorous résumé of some of the principal types of electronic sound is heard, ranging from the dense flux of section IB to the comically nasal exclamation of ID and the solitary complex tone of IF. This introductory burst of energy gradually peters out in both electronic and instrumental parts, leading by a short passage of droning electronic sounds with built-in Doppler effects, sounding like distant light propellor airplanes, to section III, a more static and contemplative sound-world, a little like *Refrain*, except that the inner life of the electronic sounds makes them appear to issue outward in straight lines from a central source, like beams of light from a beacon. Here too the instrumental parts are spare and austere. Perhaps it should be mentioned at this point that the performers' score represents the electronic music in approximate but functional graphics, and is laid out to a timescale of about 7.5 mm. per second. For the most part the performers' music is without a regular beat or time-signature, and so cannot be sight-read (the score is also inaccurate in places). Since the timing of the live instrumental parts is conditioned by the electronic music, the tape has to be memorized in advance, provoking a distinguished British percussionist to observe in frustration, "One needs to listen to the tape alone for several hours to acquire even a passing acquaintance."[9] The performers' reliance on standard technique is further tried by a score that employs an approximate notation of whole and filled notes distantly related to the unmeasured preludes of seventeenth-century French harpsichord music.

After some four minutes of contemplation, a Saul Steinberg moment during which the tape sounds approach and recede like perspective lines to a far distant horizon, section IV cuts in with a second dynamic interlude similar in kind to IB–IF but more concentrated. Section V reverts to the Doppler sounds of II, beginning with a sound rather like an electric fan or air conditioning being switched on (an image looking ahead to the ignition moment of the "Helikopter-Streichquartett"). This time, however, the continuous transitions of II are dissected into shorter moments and reshuffled, creating distinct lines of sound that eventually converge in a single note that then divides again, a symbolic gesture of "contact" that recurs later in more elaborate forms.

In VB the solitary tones of III are overlaid on the continuous transitions of II; here again the music moves by increasingly rapid changes to a point where the two elements seem about to merge into a single tone color. Here there is another sudden cut to a further anticipatory passage, this time descending in pitch to the point of confluence to which the previous passage seemed to be rising, that is, the deep, loud "close-up" complex at VI through or within which staccato saxophone-like melodic fragments can be heard. Unexpectedly, this intimidating foreground is succeeded by an even louder, deeper, and "closer" leonine growl at VIIA, but that quickly recedes to merge into a series of animated exchanges between the instruments and their electronic mirror-opposites. Four such "sparring" episodes introduce a short fugato at VIIF, brusquely interrupted by buzzing signals. A series of musical gearchanges leads to a passage of more agitated and less sharply focused counterpoint at VIIID, which rapidly fades leaving only the high, tinselly rattle of a greatly accelerated complex. Following a passage of ornamental figuration of a kind already familiar from Piano Piece V, a second fugato begins, this time with the marimba, played out against an accelerando background that creates suspense. More aggressive ornamental figurations return at IXB, and in a lower register, followed by a sequence of short episodes illustrating different aspects of accelerated frequency, including bell-like pitches at IXD, and increased internal complexity and energy at IXF. They lead to possibly the most famous and most analyzed passage, at X, in which a siren-like train of impulses is slowed down and transformed into an undulating glissando that decelerates into separately-perceivable impulses of definite pitch, briefly audible as a bouncing ball of melody before settling down into a tolling reverberation on e below middle c. This brilliant episode connecting pitch to rhythm, and back to pitch again, expresses that sense of connection across frequency space from tone to rhythm and form that Stockhausen defends so eagerly in "The Concept of Unity in Electronic Music," "Four Criteria of Electronic Music," and other writings.[10] Contact is made in that final drop to e, where the electronic tone is joined first by the piano, then the marimbaphone. The electronic pitch itself passes into a timeless, resonant limbo out of which emerge low frequency pulses of an intensity so great that the listener feels rather than hears them—the ultimate contact, one might suppose, but one that closes the alternate cycle of rhythm (impulses) – tone – rhythm (low frequency vibration).

This deep volcanic rumble is crossed at sporadic intervals by brilliant ornamental gestures. A melancholy mood settles, reflected in complicated and sometimes angry transformations which follow in section XI. Here the music returns to the image of meeting and parting layers encountered in VA. From a stable train of impulses on f sharp above middle c, a succession of layers peels away, each time taken apart as we listen, to reveal an underlying process. The first layer breaks away and swings downward in pitch, descending in intervals of approximately a fourth, to turn into marimba-like single tones in the tenor range; at which point a second layer arches upward to crystallize into tones of a more metallic quality at XIB, again in fourths, this time in the treble.

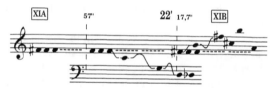

I am reminded here of the tremolo solo, on nearly the same pitch, and also undulating in fourths, in the third movement of Bartók's Violin Concerto No. 2 (a comparison to which the composer has objected, though the association of electronic impulses and tremolo strings is explicitly stated in *Carré* and has since reappeared in the fricative tremolos of the "Helikopter-Streichquartett").

Bartók: Violin Concerto No. 2

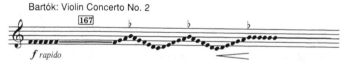

A third layer takes on a more noisy, wood-drum-like character. Further layers are stripped away as the music gathers momentum, the texture first thickening, then attenuating to allow deep metallic resonances of the kind first encountered in III to emerge into the foreground. Section XIIA, during which both instrumentalists move center stage to strike gong and tam-tam, marks a high-point, the first of many symbolic moments for these two instruments. In the lecture "Microphony" Stockhausen observes "You have probably seen the monster tam-tam being hit at the beginning of the movies, followed by a lion opening his mouth and roaring. I have always associated the lion's roar with this tam-tam," a juxtaposition innocently conflating the call-signs of the MGM and British J. Arthur Rank movie companies with his own star sign.[11]

In the event the gesture seems a shade portentous; relief comes with the explosive disintegration of XIIIC, featuring another low pitch dialogue structurally similar to VIIIF and IXB but more varied. Another acceleration in pitch and speed attains a peak of tension at XIV, where Stockhausen seems literally to "switch off" constituent frequencies from low to high, in a gesture reminiscent of the ending of *Gruppen*. This gesture signals a return to an earlier feeling of solitude, and the echoing melodic fragments heard through the electronic haze at this point have all the plaintiveness of the boy's voice in *Gesang*. (Here again, perhaps only for personal reasons, I hear a distinct echo in XV of the piano's valedictory "shama" call-sign of Messiaen's *Oiseaux Exotiques* of 1956.)

Time was indeed running out, as it had also run out for *Gesang der Jünglinge*. The listener senses that the music is coming to an end, though the mood is elevated and, in a strange way, exalted. The electronic sounds seem to lose their grip, breaking off and floating separately away, while the live instruments remain high-pitched, ringing, and generally tranquil. Sudden rushes of sound descend from the stratospheric turbulence to alight on the snare drum and take off again, and the work ends on a note of heavenward withdrawal.

Ended, but not complete. "The present finish seems to him very much like a dummy ending; it is only pretending that it could not continue," remarks Karl Wörner;[12]—while in his cover essay to the Wergo recording, Helmut Kirchmeyer refers to the approaching premiere date as the determining factor.[13] Stockhausen had planned two more sections and in theory could have continued adding to the work indefinitely. Today the ending seems so right it is hard to imagine a further continuation, but it is one of the saving graces of his approach to serial form that being modular it is open to truncation or extension without seeming deformed.

The final form is also far from the interactive composition he had originally conceived. In a letter to the author Stockhausen observed

> *Kontakte* in its first version was not only a combination of fixed parts of instruments and tape, but the instruments were to react freely during the performance in handling also individually the fading in and out of one channel per player of a multiple tape recording. Then I started to rehearse this and it was a real disaster. The musicians did not know what to do. From that moment on I began to fix entirely the parts of the players and I also did not want to change the tape any more.

The key ingredient was to have been mobility of the electronic sounds within the sound stage defined by four loudpeakers. In an image recalling Debussy's *Jeux*, Kirchmeyer writes of "a very clear image of a musical tennis match, with the players serving and returning balls of sound one to another." Such a concept goes some way to explain the occasional longueurs, as in sections III and XIIA, long sounds that one can easily imagine being pulled from speaker to speaker with each shift of the potentiometer. That loss of mobility at a late stage provided a stimulus to develop the "rotation table" by which individual layers of music are mechanically spiraled clockwise or anticlockwise among the speakers, in a process that adds a further layer of cyclical pulsation to the musical form.

This rotation table consisted of a horizontal-facing speaker, about 8 in. in diameter, enclosed at the wider end of a slightly tapering tubular baffle, and mounted on the solid carcase of an old turntable rotated by hand. The emerging sound is picked up in succession by an array of four microphones at the points of a square, facing into the center, and from there routed to separate channels of a four-track tape. Stockhausen was very proud of the result, despite an intrusive flap effect, because as he said the phase information within the manually rotated sound varies in a natural way, an effect that cannot be achieved by pan-potting or simply fading the sound from channel to channel. His use of the turntable in the studio also prompted Stockhausen to attempt analogous rotation effects in *Carré*, leading to the last-minute addition of the turbulent X-moments that are arguably the most exciting sequences of the four-orchestra work.

The image of spheres of sound moving in space like planets in a musical solar system, compellingly realized in the electronic music of *Dienstag* and *Freitag aus LICHT*, is first alluded to in the 1958 essay "Musical Impressions of an American Journey," in an account of a visit to a private recording studio where he heard an experimental recording of a Bösendorfer piano. "I heard a piano recorded as I had never heard it before in my whole life. Piano tones suspended like globes in the room; like an invisible sculpture. The room was full of sound, and yet I could not tell where the sound was coming from."[14] The effect was produced, it seems, by connecting series of microphones placed in concentric arrays around the piano, through delay lines to a control desk so that all line feeds were coincident and in balance. Stockhausen could not follow the technicalities, commenting "for me the acoustic example was enough," but the impression on him speaks eloquently of his intentions in having the players control the movement of sounds on tape in *Kontakte*.

Just as surprising is the revelation that at such an early date Stockhausen is already considering how to involve performers in the expressive shaping of a work, in the sense usually associated with *Prozession*, *Kurzwellen*, and the text pieces. The imitations he spells out in detail in the instrumental parts for *Kontakte* can be understood in this sense as blueprints for the exchanges more obliquely described in these "meta-musical" scores.

What makes a work great? In this case, I think, because despite the difficulties and changes forced on him, *Kontakte* remains true to the philosophical position that argues for unity, a continuity of tone-color, frequency, tempo, and form, that transcends the divisiveness of human perceptions. Human beings discriminate by design and by nature. As the composer himself says it so beautifully, "the ranges of perception are ranges of time, and the time is subdivided by us, by the construction of our bodies and by our organs of perception."[15] In the realm of science, or divine reality, however, these separate perceptions are united in a single frequency continuum that extends far beyond the spectrum of human sensibility to embrace the motion of the atoms, the planets and galaxies. That would be a merely fanciful notion if it were not for the fact that *Kontakte*, through the electronic sounds produced by acceleration of a range of microstructures, and their resemblances to, and "contacts" with actual instruments, clearly demonstrates the acoustic connection,—the only real connection, in principle, —between them. What the audience sees on the platform are different instruments with nothing in common; what the music describes is an overarching continuum in which they are all connected: each one a color, a location, a line on a spectrum.

Notes

1. Mya Tannenbaum, *Conversations with Stockhausen* tr. David Butchart (Oxford: Clarendon Press, 1987), 19–25.

2. Benoît B. Mandelbrot, *Fractals: Form, Chance, and Dimension* (San Francisco: W. H. Freeman, 1977).

3. *SoM*, 135–36.

4. Edmund Leach, *Lévi-Strauss*. 4th edn. rev. James Laidlaw (London: Fontana, 1970).

5. Jonathan Cott, *Stockhausen: Conversations with the Composer* (London: Robson Books, 1974), 86–88.

6. Raymond Williams, *Culture and Society 1780-1950* (Harmondsworth: Penguin Books, 1961), 142–44.

7. *Texte 2*, 58–68.

8. Milton Babbitt, "Twelve-tone Rhythmic Structure and the Electronic Medium," *Perspectives of New Music* I/1, 1962.

9. James Holland, *Percussion* (London, Macdonald and James, 1978), 250–60. Writing from the considered perspective of a sight-reading performing tradition, the author rightly draws attention to problems in the score that hinder the performer's task. For many composers, however, a reading, even by an expert, cannot do justice to the musical intention; only through memorization can such a music (or perhaps any music) be faithfully interpreted.

10. "Four Criteria of Electronic Music." *SoM*, 88–111."The Concept of Unity in Electronic Music." *Perspectives of New Music* I/2, 1963.

11. *SoM*, 76.

12. Karl H. Wörner, *Stockhausen: Life and Work* trans. Bill Hopkins (London: Faber and Faber, 1973), 110.

13. Helmut Kirchmeyer, "Zur Entstehungs- und Problemgeschichte der *Kontakte* von Karlheinz Stockhausen." Notes to Wergo lp 60006.

14. *Texte 2*, 228.

15. *SoM*, 95.

CHAPTER TWELVE

Theater

Meyer-Eppler's sudden death in 1959 deprived electronic music in Europe of a significant authority figure, and Stockhausen of a senior colleague and friend. The entry in Kurtz is eerily laconic. "In July of that year Meyer-Eppler died, quite unexpectedly, and Stockhausen finally abandoned the doctorate he kept postponing because he had too much other work."[1] This is the first mention of a doctorate. In 1954 Cologne Radio had given Stockhausen a grant to enrol for a higher degree in a subject related to electronic music, but it was always understood that this was only a mechanism to enable him to attend Meyer-Eppler's seminars in acoustics and communication theory, which he did from 1954 until 1956. A doctoral thesis related to the composition of *Gesang der Jünglinge* is plausible, since the decomposition and recomposition of the sacred text by electronic means is intimately related to the fondly remembered sessions in which newspaper articles were cut into progressively smaller segments, and analyzed for their degree of redundancy (a deconstruction and reconstitution of language the composer continued to pursue in the glossolalia of the *LICHT* cycle). Of *Gesang*, however, no score survives, apart from a few sketches in various hands. This is very atypical of a composer renowned for abundant documentation of every phase of the compositional process. And yet, the work notes conspicuously allude to a substantial portfolio of research, into the classification of speech sounds, the "degrees of comprehensibility" of the sung text, and so on. It is all a little strange.

> Meyer-Eppler was my best teacher, a true acoustician and phonetician. For that reason he had the same attitude as I against *Musique concrète*, namely that the method was fundamentally *dilettantisch*. He said, "Nothing will ever come of it." And he was right. . . . An acoustician, very logical, but with hardly a clue about music (that was obvious from the

start), he delighted in bizarre transformations of cello tones. But I had immense respect for his knowledge of physics and acoustics. He was the only one with any competence, you understand. Everyone else— journalists, administrators,—simply talked around the subject without knowing a thing about it.[2]

There is no hint of a rupture. In fact, Stockhausen mentions a conversation shortly before his death, during which, with typically dry humor, Meyer-Eppler observed that to make modern music more acceptable to the general public one would have to ban performances of old music.[3] Did Stockhausen stop attending classes in 1956 because his speech synthesis programme was not delivering results? In addition to Meyer-Eppler's class, as Kurtz also reports, he was also enrolled in musicology, in which subject Heike recalls at least one paper arousing controversy. Was there a score, later destroyed? Only Stockhausen can say; what can be said with reasonable certainty is that under university regulations it would not be easy for a thesis in the form of a musical composition, even one whose inquiry into the nature and perception of speech was of demonstrable scientific interest, to satisfy a panel of academics, in particular if there were residual doubts over the method of analysis and its success.

In Act I of *Donnerstag aus LICHT*, the first of the seven operas to be composed, the character of Michael submits to an examination for entry to the Academy (the School of Music). The result is a foregone conclusion: he is admitted by acclamation. In the next Act Michael embarks on a journey around the world. Why is the examination scene of special significance, if not for some hidden reason, known only to the composer, that gives it a deeper resonance? Did Stockhausen indeed face an additional "entrance examination" in the eighteen months prior to his first visit to America? It is a puzzle. If there had been an appearance before a Bonn University jury of information scientists in 1957, and it had not worked out, the scene in *Donnerstag* gains in dramatic point, and also a certain piquancy.

In the absence of a score of *Gesang der Jünglinge*, the realization score for *Kontakte* presents itself as an alternative thesis. A "postponed" doctorate is not abandoned, after all, and if a first attempt is withdrawn, a second based on the analysis and synthesis of musical instruments would seem like a sensible alternative: after all, percussion sounds are very much simpler in nature than speech sounds. How else is one to explain the hundreds of pages of analyses of percussion instrument sounds suddenly revealed to Marietta Morawska-Büngeler in 1986? Kirchmeyer's essay accompanying the 1963 *Kontakte* recording attributes analyses of instrumental tones to Gottfried Michael Koenig, but says nothing about any by the composer himself. And yet, years later, out of the blue, Stockhausen reveals the existence of a vast archive of instrumental analyses, clearly in his own hand.

Stockhausen: There are over 600 pages of sketches for KONTAKTE—I'll just get my file with the originals. . . . Before I began to compose KONTAKTE, I made analyses of instrumental sounds, recording different sounds and analysing and describing the different partial tones using a

tunable selective amplifier" (feedback filter). I made a tape loop of each
recorded sound and played it back at a slower speed, timing the duration
of each partial tone with a stop-watch. . . .
Morawska-Bungeler: So these were investigations in *psycho-acoustics*.
Stockhausen: No, physics. I measured everything exactly with precision
equipment. There was nothing "psycho-acoustic" about it.[4]

That Stockhausen finally abandoned his doctorate after Meyer-Eppler's
death means that he had not abandoned the idea of a doctorate prior to that
time, but implies that the loss of his friend and mentor was a blow to his
hopes of academic success. Alone among his close associates, Meyer-Eppler
understood the acoustics of speech and the implications of aleatoric procedures. He had been a prime mover in setting up the first electronic music
studio in Cologne, for reasons of science that most musicians, Eimert included, could not really grasp. It was Meyer-Eppler who recognized an intelligence and a purpose in the music of John Cage and his associates, and
provided Stockhausen with moral and intellectual support in his advocacy of
the New York school. While Meyer-Eppler was alive, Stockhausen's continuing contact with him, even informally, ensured that his reputation as a
composer grounded in science remained unassailable. With his death, Stockhausen found himself adrift, without an anchor.

Meyer-Eppler's interest in "bizarrely transformed instrumental sounds"
dated from 1952 when, following his successful tournée at Darmstadt, he
invited Bruno Maderna to visit his laboratory at Bonn University for some
experimenting, the outcome of which included a short piece titled *Musica su
due Dimensioni* for flute, cymbals, and tape, sometimes credited as the first
completed work for live performer and tape. The tape "background" consists
of prerecorded and electronically modified instrumental sounds. This study
by Maderna could be regarded as the first of a privileged line of compositions for flute and electronics extending via Otto Luening's *Fantasy in
Space* of 1953 to Stockhausen's "Kathinkas Gesang als Luzifers Requiem"
from *Samstag aus LICHT*, of 1984, and Boulez's version of . . . *explosante-
fixe* . . . for multiple flutes, dating from 1993–1994. In a special issue of Hermann Scherchen's *Gravesano Review* Meyer-Eppler explained his interest in
the acoustic coloration of "background" elements in electronic music:

> *Aleatoric modulation* allows one to distinguish parameters more clearly.
> To take a simple example, more or less aleatoric amplitude- and phase-
> modulations can be obtained by *reverberation* (using an echo-chamber or
> reverberation plate). Such measures within the realm of electronic
> music, as distinct from the reproduction of traditional music, are not
> done with the aim of adding a sort of spatial effect; the reverberation of a
> single note, tone, or noise serves much more to endow a sound event with
> a *distinctive character*. It might for example be desirable, when you have
> a composition of many "layers," all lying in the same range of frequen-
> cies, and difficult to tell apart, to use aleatoric enhancement to render
> them more easily distinguishable.[5]

He could be talking of the Maderna composition. (Or indeed, had he lived, of the tape background to Stockhausen's "Orchester-Finalisten.") In an interesting codetta, Meyer-Eppler also strongly recommends that such music be listened to in an anechoic chamber.

The cello to which Stockhausen refers is a rarity in the world of electronically-modified tone colors, so the question is why he should single out that particular instrument for comment unless he had heard an example for himself, and found it particularly unimpressive. One likely candidate is the cello part in Berio's *Différences* of 1957, a composition for flute, clarinet, harp, viola, cello and tape, in which the sounds of a live quintet performing on stage in front of a curtain are imperceptibly taken over by progressively distorted sounds of the same instruments on tape, issuing from stereo speakers concealed behind the curtain. Through Maderna, Meyer-Eppler had a connection with the Milan *Studio di fonologia musicale*, where Berio produced the original tape for *Différences*, and Henri Pousseur his *Rimes pour différentes sources sonores* of 1958–1959. *Différences* is as much a Meyer-Eppler influenced composition as *Gesang* and *Kontakte*. Even the title is related by inversion to Stockhausen's *Kontakte*. In the former instance, following Meyer-Eppler's precept of alienation of electronically modified sounds, Berio is focused on making distinctions; Stockhausen by contrast sees this analytical approach as an aesthetic of degradation; the more difficult (some would say, religious) task to which he was committed being precisely the opposite, the demonstration of essential resemblances, family relationships and underlying harmony among even the most disparate elements of acoustic and musical creation.

> There are many things in this world that are like unknown plants and animals in Nature. One simply doesn't know what they are, and some of them are pretty frightful to look at, like certain insects that make people afraid. All the same, we believe in them, and accept them, because they stand before us as real, not because they impress us as perfectly formed, or objects of beauty. Imagine [the life-forms] if we were able to visit all the stars and planets of the entire universe. We would be in perpetual shock. We earthlings are not at all prepared to contemplate such improbable and unique beings. In music it is the same.[6]

As with Boulez, Stockhausen's musical development in relation to Berio is a fascinating and compelling dialogue of minds and belief systems that has still to be fully explored. An intellectual, not inclined to religion, Berio was fascinated by the explorations in language of James Joyce, Samuel Beckett, and e e cummings, and gifted with an Italianate lyricism, via his teachers Ghedini and Dallapiccola, in realizing them. Berio's understanding of *Gesang der Jünglinge* is expressed in terms of his own literary models; neither in his music nor his published remarks does he signal any awareness of the deeper moral or aesthetic implications of the technology with which Stockhausen was even then constantly engaged. Berio was attracted to ideas, and to finding elegant and beguiling, if superficial musical solutions to fashionable issues in critical theory (e.g., "art in a technological age," "music as text") that for a time weighed so heavily on contemporary aesthetics. Nevertheless, in repudiating the pessimism of critical theory and demonstrating grace under fire, we should all be grateful to him.

Berio's fascination with riddles, mazes, and literary detective work (not to mention a forensic addiction to musical forms and idioms of a distant past) is of a piece with an embedded historical perspective that today, only a few years on, feels as dated as the bat-wing fenders on a 1959 Chevrolet. Stockhausen by contrast has scrupulously avoided the image of a modern literary intellectual, and his work remains fresh and enigmatic. Despite his early aspirations as a poet, and demonstrable prolixity as a writer and commentator, since his first encounter with Sartreian pessimism Stockhausen has deliberately refused, in his music at least, any explicit recourse to literary solutions to compelling philosophical or existential propositions: none of Kagel's wearisome and debilitating irony, none of Ligeti's political satire. And yet a sense of Berio's stage rhetoric, fluency with languages, and dramatic skills is refracted through Stockhausen's music theater from *Momente* to *Sonntag aus LICHT*. It is almost as though Stockhausen has applied Meyer-Eppler's "aleatoric modulation" principles not to the sounds of musical instruments, but to language and literature themselves.

Klavierstück IX (Piano Piece IX)

1954, revised 1961: No. 4 (UE 13675e; cd Stockhausen-Verlag SV-56)
Duration 10'.

Completed in 1961, Piano Pieces IX and X reinterpret sketches of 1954 and round off the first cycle of eleven piano pieces that represent Stockhausen's earliest project of major dimensions. Along with *Punkte 1952/62*, these revisions introduce a variety of textures and colours to clothe, and perhaps disguise, the functional austerity of originally pointillist structures. Piece IX is a work of 33 sections grouped by tempo into two major divisions, of 24 and 9 sections, hence in the ratio of 8 : 3, a ratio also expressed in the alternating tempi, MM 160/MM 60, of the first section. Herbert Henck has identified the series on which the work is based as a two-part symmetrical intervallic set of which the second half is the retrograde at the tritone, "a technique employed by Webern in his Op. 21 *Symphony* and regarded by him as guaranteeing a special consistency of integration." Stockhausen uses

4 5 3   1 2 : 2 1 3 5 4

the same row, Henck adds, in some of his other piano pieces, in particular the beginning of Piece VII and Piece X. It also clearly recalls the symmetrical formation of the first tape microstructure of *Kontakte*.[7]

The first episode of Piece IX emphasizes *measure*. It develops out of two basic elements, repetition (the famous repeated chord), and the sustaining and ornamentation of a chord: techniques of active and passive prolongation respectively. These two forms of extension intercut, overlap, and finally merge, creating an effect of a fundamentally simple pointillist structure subjected to various kinds of simulated electronic transformation. This is most explicit in the image of flap echo (very fifties, very musique concrète) plainly evoked in the lengthy introduction, then progressively modified by effects such as the gradual addition of pedal reverberation on page 3 (*allmählich ganz niederdrücken*), and in the manner in which the initial chord is slowly dislocated, as if left and right hands were tapes moving slowly but inexorably out of synchronization. These are live imitations of electronic processes.

Few legato indications are evident, but the work is clearly tightly edited, even to the measurement of pauses in seconds (a measured pause, by the way, is "silent music" and not the same as a rest). So exposed a use of the Fibonacci series of proportions (1, 2, 3, 5, 8, 13, . . .) is both innovatory and an undisguised allusion to his spiritual roots in Bartók and Le Corbusier. Out of the way in which the lengthy period of repetition and manipulation of pedaling (considered as controlled, artificial decay processes) interact with the natural tendency of piano sound to die away of its own accord, arises a quality of dramatic tension perhaps expressing a wish to have the power to reverse time. For many listeners it is just this periodic repetition that is so unexpected, given its sinister associations for Stockhausen of marching feet and loss of personal freedom. But this might well be exactly the point: repetition as an image of fear, of inexorable evil, or of a fist pounding the table in grief and frustration.

At measures 94–108, a sequence of chords, graded dynamically and juxtaposed in the manner of snippets of prerecorded tape, is presented over a pedal bass acting as a sort of artificial reverberation. Strict time yields to ornamental freedom in the section beginning MM 120. Linear and monophonic rather than chordal in character, the music here is also palpably more relaxed and fluid, also relatively undirected. The mood is not very distant from Boulez's constellations of motives within a fermata, such as we hear in the 1958 *Improvisations sur Mallarmé*, but the procedure also looks forward to the extraordinary suppleness and energy of Piano Piece X. In sum, then, a rigid, mechanical, vertical organization gives way to a music that is flexible, horizontal in emphasis, and *intuitively* timed:—a transition comparable with *Refrain* that in view of subsequent developments seems strangely prophetic: a Meyer-Epplerian triumph of "aleatoric" lyricism over deterministic structure.

Klavierstück X (Piano Piece X)

1954, revised 1961: No. 4 (UE 13675f; cd Stockhausen-Verlag SV-56)
Duration 23'.

Piece X unites the filigree intricacy of Debussy (e.g., "Voiles," measure 41, or "Feu d'Artifice," measures 43–45) with the energy and intensity of impulse-generated sound. The work is dense and delicate, technically and emotionally highly wrought, and carries an expressive charge in striking contrast to the composer's normally detached style. Among the instrumental works perhaps only *Zyklus* compares to it in sheer physical impact: at times ecstatic, at other times hugely enraged. The new outspokenness is most directly revealed in a boldly rhetorical employment of note-clusters, sounds that in previous works (*Gruppen, Kontakte*) are employed only discreetly and relatively nonaggressively. The expansion of points into clusters, also a feature of the recomposed *Punkte 1952/62*, creates an effect of shifting surfaces of sound, with repetition being used as a sustaining, rather than as a metrical or accentual device. Clusters add an important new dimension to the expressive range of the piano, and are here so subtly manipulated as to draw the listener into a state of elevated awareness. Sliding intervals had been employed, though more for atmospheric than dramatic effect, in the Piano II part of the slow second movement of the *Sonata for two pianos and percussion* by Bartók, at measures 70–71; by a strange coincidence, the staccato chords interrupting the final cadence of the same movement bear a strong family resemblance to the repeated chord that opens Piano Piece IX. Yet again this is a piece in which elements of retrospection combine with a sense of panic, or at least, of uncharacteristic urgency.

Clusters and cluster-glissandi also appear as new elements late in the electronic music of *Kontakte*, clusters as hammering points in section XIIIE, very difficult to synthesize, and actually drawn to look like nails in the score, and glissandi from XVIE, lighter in texture and associated with sensations of floating and withdrawal, their tapering shapes signifying diminuendos and not converging pitch. A further radiophonic element, also found in *Kontakte* but imbued in Piece X with the pathos of a distress call, is the morse-like repeated tone penetrating the quasi-electronic or shortwave maelstrom. (The same morse signals, with explicit symbolism, will return in *Kurzwellen* and *Mantra*.)

Silence is another element that acquires new and dramatic connotations, signifying not only an absence, or arbitrary failure of sound, but also (notably in *Punkte 1952/62*) a removal or erasure of existing material. If Piece IX's 139 initial repetitions seem designed to challenge the audience's stamina, then the sudden blackouts of Piece X (during which, as Roger Smalley has observed, the music may be imagined as continuing as it were underground) are just as dramatic.[8] These silences speak with all the urgency of a lost connection, not arrested motion or suspension of action, but breakdowns of perception.

Despite its outward ebullience, the quality of touch indicated for Piece X: light, quick, and consistent for all pitches in all dynamics, suggests an instrument combining the tonal uniformity of an electronic organ with the responsive action of a fortepiano. Tone homogeneity within the cluster is important. It enables the listener to hear Piece X not only as a form in constant evolution in the conventional sense, but also as a global sonority in constant exposition, the sonority in question being the total resonance of the piano itself. Such a way of hearing leads directly to the conception of music as derived or filtered sound, as experienced directly in a work such as *Mikrophonie I*, and implicitly in works such as *Momente, Stimmung*, and *Stop*. Lightness of touch and uniformity of timbre are less characteristic of the modern concert grand piano and its repertoire since the mid-nineteenth century, but are features of earlier keyboards associated with the late baroque and classical eras of Mozart, Beethoven, and Chopin, which raises the interesting possibility that Piece X may actually have more in common with an eighteenth-century sensibility than might at first be apparent.

Originale (Originals)

1961: No. 12⅔. Score published in *Texte 2*, 107–29.
"Musical theater with *Kontakte*."
Music: *Kontakte for electronic sounds, piano, and percussion.*
For conductor, director, pianist, percussionist, street singer (or violinist), performance artist, singer, poet, painter, lady of fashion, movie cameraman, lighting technician, sound engineer, theater costumier, newspaper vendeuse, child, six actors.
Duration 1 hour 34'.

"History falls handily if not quite precisely into decades," observed Andrew Porter.

> The next landmark is 1960, and specifically the 1960 ISCM Festival, held in Cologne, at which some practices of the fifties found consummation and some new compositional means still with us were first tried. . . . When the official concerts were done, we visited the Festival fringe: into Mary Bauermeister's studio, which twenty people could comfortably have filled, some two hundred people packed to hear Bussotti's graphic compositions played by Aloys Kontarsky, Cornelius Cardew, and the composer, [and] Nam June Paik's *Hommage à John Cage*, during which, while three tapes played, the composer chucked eggs at a mirror, flung a rosary at the audience, and ferociously attacked a piano with a pair of long-bladed scissors. . . . Stockhausen was perched on high in a loft, his eyes kindling to a wilder glow the more extravagant the manifestations became. . . .[9]

Stockhausen describes *Originale* as "musikalisches Theater," that is, as a composition of dramatic actions conceived in musical terms. He had been involved in nothing quite like it since *Burleska* and his student days, and it is possible to interpret what might be described as an "essay in spontaneous realization of a structure determined only in outline" as something of a gesture of relief, after *Carré* and *Kontakte*. In terms of his musical evolution it may be seen as a formal study in the kind of productive collaboration he had formed with David Tudor and others. In this sense the title reads as a return to the sources of creativity, to inspired play.

He was certainly used to composing with assistants: most recently in the studio, with Koenig and Jaap Spek on *Kontakte*, and with Cardew on the composition of *Carré*. In *Zyklus* too the boundary between "forming" and "performing" is deliberately obscured. The more radical approach of *Originale* can also be related to the difficulties Stockhausen experienced with the original *Kontakte*, when he found skilled musicians unable spontaneously to imitate events they were hearing on tape. In part the exercise is designed to acquaint the composer with the techniques of a related art in which such collaboration is taken for granted, namely theater, and in part to accustom his musicians to the new style of collaboration. He may well have been guided in this by the example of method acting, an approach to theater pioneered by Stanislavsky and revived by Lee Strasberg at the Actors Studio in New York during the fifties, a technique emphasizing psychological realism through improvisation based on total immersion in character and lifestyle.

Commissioned by the Cologne Theater am Dom, *Originale* was sketched out relatively quickly during a visit to Finland in August 1961, and performed twelve times from 26 October to 6 November. Many of the principal players came from the composer's circle of artist friends: David Tudor and Christoph Caskel (whose recording of *Kontakte* was soon to be released by Wergo), the Korean performance artist Nam June Paik, whose highly-charged appearances in happenings in New York had aroused media excitement, the experimental poet Hans G Helms, and artist Mary Bauermeister.

It was a project fraught with danger. Recalling Piscator's triptych-like simultaneous stage productions in Berlin during the twenties and thirties, Stockhausen envisaged the piece to be performed on three separate stages with the audience in the middle, to allow the polyphony of actions to be clearly visible. First, the management of the theater objected that such an arrangement would reduce audience numbers, and insisted that all the action take place on the single cramped stage. Then, after two controversial performances, the theater manager was instructed to suspend performances on pain of the theater's subsidy being withdrawn. Composer and players responded by taking on financial responsibility for the remaining ten performances. It was a time of strong emotions.

Stockhausen's conception is typically exuberant, opting for richness of aural effect and a high degree of visual activity, and drawing on his experience in handling large numbers that led Stravinsky to observe, as we remember, that the composer is at his best when he is busiest. The "improvising" in most cases is simple role-playing: actors act, an audio technician makes a recording, a street singer sings street songs, and the newspaper seller, a local identity, enters on cue and sells newspapers of the day. Only a few participants are entrusted with spontaneous invention on stage. Stockhausen's simplicity of characterization, and his readiness to respond to performer feedback, while all the time maintaining strict overall control, give *Originale* a direction and set it apart from the modishly laissez-faire. His notes describe *Originale* as translating moment-form from the concert hall to the stage, a preliminary exercise for *Momente*. "I = musical theater," the composer proclaims, echoing Kurt Schwitters:

> The goal he [Schwitters] had in mind was not so much the total work of art in the sense that [Hugo] Ball or even Kandinsky meant it—a synchronous combination of all the arts—but rather an unceasing obliteration of all borders between the arts and their integration into one, including the machine as "an abstraction of the human mind," including kitsch, chair legs, singing, and shuddering. In reality, HE, Kurt Schwitters, was the total work of art.[10]

In the opening scene, for example, two musicians begin to perform *Kontakte*. Their performance is simultaneously recorded, (translating the performance situation from "continuous present" to "future perfect"), while *as a recording session* it is also being filmed by a director and cameraman, becoming also an event in "future imperfect:" that is, a work "in action," or "in the making." Time itself is thus telescoped, expectation and memory meeting around a kernel of actuality, which is the music as it is unfolds. This is a play on temporal awareness of a high degree of sophistication, and it arises from deep reflection on the paradoxes of studio practice and the vast distinction between the hugely expanded, and multidirectional (forward and back) time experience of preparing a work for tape (or indeed film), compared to the compressed, unidirectional "real-time" experience of the audience.

In Karl Wörner's sympathetic but dispassionate account of *Originale* it is possible with hindsight to recognize elements and actions that are destined to grow and develop in the composer's future stage works. In the formal sense, Wörner observes a blurring of conventional distinctions between stage and musical actions and audience reactions; of the sense of where reality ends and theater begins, and vice versa; and the importance of those serially-inspired external controls: "the articulation, the differentiation, the variation of density"—that look ahead to a new kind of music theater. All of which is as one might expect; the real excitement however is in details, images, vignettes. Mirrored surfaces surrounding the stage area, in which the audience can see themselves reflected. A child, building with colored blocks on stage, oblivious to everything else (on alternate days, the composer's daughter Christel, and his son Markus). A scene where everybody on stage freezes for around two minutes: "Absolute calm, only the cooing of the doves. Each of the participants stares fixedly for about two minutes into the eyes of a spectator. (The public's solo, with astonishingly different reactions from one evening to the next.)" A disturbing scene where all the participants take flash photographs of the audience. The inclusion of actual Cologne characters (a street singer, a news vendor) in their real-life roles.[11]

In their way just as compelling are observations of the critic of the Munich *Süddeutsche Zeitung*, in a review omitted from Bill Hopkins's translation of Wörner, but from which a reader is able more precisely to gauge the temper of public reaction, something in which Stockhausen, unlike Cage, was deeply interested. The critic, Karl Heinz Ruppel, has no difficulty in connecting *Originale* to its origins in dadaist manifestations of the interwar years, associations that older members of his Bavarian readership might well construe as calculated to revive sentiments of cultural anarchy and political protest historically linked with opposition to National Socialism. Memories of the Berlin *Erste Internationale Dada-Messe* of 1920, or the Paris *Exposition du Surréalisme* of 1938, are evoked in his description of a stage set featuring an aquarium with goldfish, a balloon, a birdcage, and a number of stop-clocks suspended haphazardly from the ceiling; two doves "*à la mode de* Picasso" in a small wooden hutch in front of the rear curtain, and descriptions of characters changing costume as if in a shop window. Helpfully, he is able to identify and interpret a number of readings chosen by different participants: Mark Antony's speech from *Julius Caesar*, spoken deliberately out of character; Saint-Just's famous speech from Georg Büchner's *Dantons Tod*, delivered upside down, in a yoga position; and Hans G Helms ("G without the full stop") reciting his poem *Fa:m' Ahniesgwow* "in the role of speech demolition expert, after the model of James Joyce in *Finnegans Wake*." Ruppel found some aspects strangely beautiful: the release of the cooing doves, and Mary Bauermeister's painting in fluorescent colors that disappeared when the house lights were raised. Other aspects he found jejune or cliché, and a few quite disturbing, in particular questioning the propriety of participants reading real names from the obituary columns of the local newspaper published the same day and on sale during the performance.[12]

Like many others, Ruppel attributed Stockhausen's apparent conversion to dada to his association with Cage, and imitation of the latter's 1960 *Theatre Piece*, a work deriving from a series of pieces of more or less theatrical content relating to Cage's travels in Europe, starting with the *Music Walk, TV Köln,* and *Fontana Mix* for tape (originally titled "Performance Mix") of 1958; continuing through 1959 with *Water Walk* and *Sounds of Venice* (works for television performance based on the same transparencies as *Fontana Mix*); and culminating with the lecture performance *WBAI* and the four-lecture montage *Where are we going? And what are we doing?* early the following year. *Theatre Piece* is a composition for up to eight performers, the first public realization being for contralto, pianist (David Tudor), trombonist, tuba, dancers (Merce Cunningham and Carolyn Brown), actress, and lighting assistants.

Cage's driving principle for *Theatre Piece* is the substitution of stage actions for musical actions prescribed by chance operations. A set of parts establishes time frames within which up to twenty actions are to take place at any one time; the actions themselves are triggered by "a gamut of nouns and/or verbs chosen by the performer" and written on separate cards which are then shuffled. Among the instructions numerically encoded in the score are plus and minus signs: a plus sign signifying the insertion of a new action to the ensemble, a minus sign the removal of an action. The outline prescription is analogous to *Originale*; the notion of a "score for working out," incorporating the addition and subtraction of material, also prefigures Stockhausen's *Plus-Minus* and related works; in turn, the shuffling of materials is destined to reemerge as a feature of *Momente*.

The conventional view makes it seem as though *Originale* is "only" a happening, and that the happening was an aesthetic contrivance originally devised by Cage and developed from 1958 by Allen Kaprow and others. Such a view is not challenged by Cage, who in a 1965 interview is rather more concerned to distinguish his own aesthetic intentions for *Theatre Piece* from those of Stockhausen (presumably in relation to *Originale*, though Cage does not say). With a practiced deftness under interview conditions that is also a hallmark of Boulez and Stockhausen himself, Cage brings up the tricky question of mutual influence seemingly in order to preempt further discussion: "I had a conversation earlier that year [1960] with Karlheinz Stockhausen and he asked, 'If you were writing a song would you write for the singer or would you write music?' I said I would write for the singer. He said, 'That's the difference between us, I would write music.'"[13]

Stockhausen was considering writing a piece for the singer Cathy Berberian, wife of Luciano Berio. He was interested in having her whistle; Cage objected that she could not whistle, she did not know how. And that is all. "That is why I left the *Theatre Piece* unspecified. I didn't want to ask anyone to do something he couldn't do." It is an interesting, but not a very convincing distinction to make, and one that by drawing attention to a difference of aesthetic intention appears designed to establish that Cage had a better grasp of the artistic objectives implied by such an event, while conceding that in significant other respects the two composers were actually in agreement. (Unfortunately for Cage, the lesson of method acting is that realism in performance,—in *any* drama, for goodness' sake,—is created from a situation of stress and not absence of stress. That is what drama is about: hence paradoxically it is a Stockhausen making exceptional demands of a performer who is more likely to provoke a convincingly "natural" and emotionally committed action, than a Cage who interprets naturalism as letting performers "do their own thing.")

Cage's game of precedences is typical of the nuanced diplomacy of cultural negotiation of the era, cultivating an image of the artist as a critic or guru, observing contemporary life but intellectually detached from it, that is essentially Romantic in origin. Stockhausen himself is not immune. Not for nothing does he associate himself, even in fun, with a postcard image of Liszt at the piano surrounded by adoring fans.[14]

Stockhausen however already had a devilish sense of humor, and a particular interest in humor that arises spontaneously from formal procedures. As we know, an image of the composer as clown surfaces as early as 1950 with the lyric of "Der Rebell." As a student in Paris he experienced firsthand a musique concrète with a propensity to generate involuntary comic effects made even more funny by their seriousness of intention,—a vein of comedy to be taken up with agreeable success by François Bayle (e.g., *Oiseau-chanteur*), Luc-Ferrari, and the world of advertising. There was even a place for humor in Stockhausen's classes with Meyer-Eppler in which fragmented texts were shuffled and reordered; such activities connected in turn with a European cultural legacy extending from the nineteenth-century rebus to the free-association games of the surrealists. This was a depth and richness of context of which Cage and the Americans in general were unaware, or like Boulez, chose to ignore.

Stockhausen tells an illuminating anecdote that illustrates a certain ambivalence in his attitude to such spontaneous events. In a broadcast of October 1958 and in his Juilliard lecture later the same year he alludes to three moments in Ligeti's electronic composition *Artikulation I* at which the audience spontaneously bursts out laughing.

I talked about associations in electronic music and their effect on the

perceived quality of a work, and how important it was for the composer
to avoid associations that might distract the audience's attention from
the music. Then, without any hint of explanation, I played the electronic
piece "Artikulation" by Ligeti. In all three places the audience laughed;
at the first, strongly; at the second, somewhat less; and at the third,
resounding laughter. After they had all stopped laughing, with a straight
face I then read out the following prepared text: "When this composition
is played, people laugh (more laughter). The composer, and those working with him in the studio, would also laugh (still more laughter). In our
studio work we often come across sounds and noises that are not very
civilized (prolonged laughter). The reason for this is that certain sounds
and noises remind us of specific events that we have experienced at an
earlier time in a different connection (silence). Associations arise from
our experiences and then disappear again: they tell us nothing about the
form of a music or the meaning of such sounds or noises in a given
composition."[15]

The ambivalence arises from acknowledging that serious abstract music can
provoke involuntary laughter, but not knowing quite what to make of it.
Shortly after this experience he was to encounter in Birdland a genuine and
uncontrived "happening" for himself, a piece of impromptu music theater
featuring an unnamed and intoxicated female vocalist, an audience, a Lilliputian interlocutor, and Count Basie and his orchestra.

If high art was uncertain of its relationship with the public, low art was
beginning to respond appreciatively to the avant-garde. The enthusiastic
presence of English critic Andrew Porter at the 1960 ISCM fringe event in
Mary Bauermeister's atelier is itself testimony to a growing interest in the
avant-garde among the British public, a trend inspired by the happily-
named Gerard Hoffnung. Affectionate parodies of modern music in the
fifties did a great deal to prepare English audiences for the Glock/Boulez
regime at the BBC during the sixties, and Stockhausen's triumphantly
successful British tours of 1971. Already in 1956 the first Hoffnung Festival
had paid him indirect homage in a "Duet from the Comic Opera *The Barber
of Darmstadt* by Bruno Heinz Jaja" (Humphrey Searle, a former pupil of
Webern); in the Hoffnung Astronautical Festival of 1961 came the more
explicit tribute of a work titled "Punkt Contrapunkt" by the same fictional
composer. Among other musical conceptions that continue to resonate are a
"Mobile for Seven Orchestras" by Lawrence Leonard, Malcolm Arnold's
"United Nations" for full orchestra and multiple military bands, and an
innovatory "Introductory Music Played in the Foyer" by Francis Chagrin.

Surrealism's public image had been rehabilitated for American audiences by the 1951 Disney animated feature *Alice in Wonderland*, a work of
nineteenth-century literature through which the US art of animation could
signal ties of natural affinity with the high art of Dalí, Miró, and Ernst, and
the theater of the absurd of Jarry, Artaud, and Ionesco. *Alice* had everything: a children's story unfolding as a theater of dream in disconnected
scenes of varying degrees of irrationality involving magic mushrooms,
changes of physical scale, parodies of social rituals, a mock trial, and a
demented head of state. The original tales were not only conceived by a

highly intellectual Oxford mathematician, but underpinned by the most abstruse paradoxes of modern science and formal logic.

After a decade that also saw the emergence of MAD magazine and pop art, *Originale* can be seen as a personal turning point for Stockhausen, involving a new sense of the composer's relationship to the performer and the public, and a commitment, to the idea, at least, of a music of direct action. It was the nearest he would get to embracing pop art, and though he has continued to express regret at pop art's sacralization of the banal, it is possible to see in the emergent imagery of Warhol and Lichtenstein at this time a highly stylized and formal expression of the commonplace that is able to aspire to the same spirituality as a found object by Duchamp, a *Merzbild* by Schwitters, or a Picasso *Bull's Head*. As a young artist in 1958 Roy Lichtenstein attended several Cage-inspired happenings by Allan Kaprow and was deeply impressed. His adoption of comic-book imagery a few years later offers its own witty and very "New York" rejoinder to Stockhausen and his approach to music theater:

> The comics from which Lichtenstein takes his women are no longer "the funnies," but instead entirely humorless epics dealing with the emotional extremes of daily life. As most people do in daily life, these figures take themselves extremely seriously and are only funny in an unintentional way, unknown to themselves. This is what makes them so appropriate for Lichtenstein. He operates from another level of consciousness and it is this difference in awareness that may actually be the real subject of his comics paintings.[16]

Notes

1. Michael Kurtz, *Stockhausen: A Biography* rev. tr. Richard Toop (London: Faber and Faber, 1992), 108.
2. "Elektronische Musik seit 1952: Gespräch mit Marietta Morawska-Büngeler." *Texte 8*, 399–504.
3. *Texte 2*, 239.
4. *Texte 8*, 472–79.
5. Werner Meyer-Eppler, "Die elektrischen Instrumente und neue Tendenzen der elektroakustischen Klanggestaltung" (Electric instruments and new tendencies in electro-acoustic tone production). In *Musik: Raumgestaltung: Elektroakustik*. Special edition of *Gravesano Review* (1955): 88–93.
6. *Texte 4*, 483.
7. Herbert Henck, "Karlheinz Stockhausens Klavierstück IX: Eine analytische Betrachtung" In *Musik und Zahl: Interdiziplinäre Beiträge zum Grenzbereich zwischen Musik und Mathematik,* ed. Günther Schnitzler (Bonn–Bad Godesberg: Verlag für Systematische Wissenschaft, 1978).
8. Roger Smalley, "Novelty and variety." *Musical Times* (1968): 1046–1048.
9. Andrew Porter, *Musical Events. A Chronicle: 1980–1983* (London: Grafton Books, 1988), 386–87.
10. Hans Richter, *Dada: Art and Anti-Art.* Cited in Udo Kultermann, *Art-Events and Happenings* tr. John William Gabriel (London: Mathews

Millar Dunbar, 1971), 37. The David Britt translation is less emphatic (London: Thames and Hudson, 1965 rev. 1997), 152.

11. Karl Wörner, *Karlheinz Stockhausen, Werk + Wollen 1952–1962* (Roden-kirchen: P. J. Tonger, 1963) 189–92.

12. K. H. Ruppel, "Neodadaisten" (Neo-dadaists). Munich: *Süddeutsche Zeitung* (3 November 1961).

13. Michael Kirby and Richard Schechner, "An Interview with John Cage." *Tulane Drama Review* Vol. 10 No. 2 (Winter 1965), 50–72.

14. A montage (some distance after Max Ernst) in which Stockhausen has inserted a photograph of himself as conductor of a musical séance into an engraving from the painting "Liszt am Klavier" by Josef Danhauser (1805–1845). *Texte 2*, facing 263.

15. *Texte 2*, 225–26.

16. Janis Hendrickson, *Roy Lichtenstein* (Cologne: Taschen, 1994), 26.

CHAPTER THIRTEEN

Uncertainty

It fell to me to synthesize all these different trends [in twentieth-century music] for the second half of the century, perhaps in a similar way that Heisenberg, in the first half of the century, had the role of bringing together the discoveries of Planck and Einstein in atomic physics.[1]

At the heart of twentieth-century culture lies a debate over the nature and representation of reality that in seemingly analogous ways informs the sciences, the arts, linguistics, and philosophy. The sixties counterculture is often perceived as a postwar, social and generational reaction against continuing political instability and the threat of nuclear annihilation; a movement against war and bureaucracy, and for love and individual free-dom. Though expressed as civil disaffection toward an institutional social order enforced through the literal interpretation of a written legal code, social unrest on the part of a younger generation of students was also fueled by doubts of a more fundamental kind that had been articulated with varying intensity by an earlier generation of scientists and philosophers between the two world wars. These doubts concerned the possibility of ultimate truth, the existence of an objective reality, and certain knowledge. They were current in Europe when Stockhausen was a child, and came to exercise a significant influence on the thinking of a cold war generation growing up in the shadow of the atomic cloud. As a logically "meaningless" activity, music is supposedly incapable of dealing in such matters as truth or necessity, though the same body of conventions that says so has little difficulty in identifying the absence of harmony in twentieth-century music, to take a banal example, with the expression of a peculiarly Western sense of collective anxiety or guilt. Among English-speaking thinkers, the idea that music is capable of making or supporting statements of naïve belief,

—for instance, in the power of harmony, collective action, and so on,—is relatively uncontentious, but also trivial; the notion however of employing music to convey statements of a particular philosophy is simply inconceivable. Among the cultures of mainland Europe a rather different perception prevails; there the representational potential of music, not only in the emotional sense, as in opera, but in an abstract or philosophical sense, as in the Bach preludes and fugues, is more readily accepted. As a student at the University of Cologne in 1947 Stockhausen read philosophy and also philology; we should not be surprised therefore if in order to reach a sympathetic understanding both of his music and of his worldview, it may be necessary to consider the impact on his musical thinking of contemporary discoveries in physics, and their epistemological implications.

His 1955–1956 studies of statistical form in Debussy, and of probability in Webern's String Quartet Op. 28, though viewed with disdain by orthodox musicologists, are nevertheless informed with ideas from the world of science, as though intended as examples of a new analytical method for twentieth-century music,—or indeed, for Mozart. In his casual description of Piano Piece XI as "simply a sound in which certain partials are behaving statistically," it is possible to detect an allusion to Max Born's statistical interpretation of the charge and spin of electrons in relation to the nucleus of an atom, the permitted states of which can be understood (perhaps naïvely, but positively) in terms of the same laws of motion that govern the frequencies of partials in relation to a fundamental tone. Again, in revising four early pointillist compositions after Meyer-Eppler's death,—*Kreuzspiel*, Piano Pieces IX and X, and *Punkte 1952/62* for orchestra,—Stockhausen seems to be reassessing an originally determinist aesthetic in the light of concepts of indeterminacy in quantum physics. In Piece IX, for example, a statistically aperiodic music is invaded and threatened with obliteration by a counterimage of absolute determinism (the repeated chord). In Piece X, the image of a precise organization of musical quanta in serial terms is energized and dispersed with varying degrees of scatter directly related to the intervention of the performer/observer (an inference, perhaps, from Niels Bohr); and in *Punkte 1952/62* the position of each elementary particle in the original score is represented anew as a field of increasing or decreasing probability (in partial accordance with the uncertainty principle of Heisenberg). To this day, when Stockhausen compares his position in the universe to an atomic particle, it can be interpreted not only as identifying his affinity with the concerns of particle physics, but also as signaling the impossibility of his own position and direction of movement ever being precisely determined.

That music can be influenced by abstruse discoveries in science need not alarm us. To say that abstraction in modern art took inspiration from the discoveries of new technology is a noncontroversial statement. The improvisations of Wassily Kandinsky awaken the same sense of a mysterious natural order as the alien worlds of diatoms and microorganisms revealed in black and white by pioneering studies in microphotography; Malevich's architectural arrangements of rectangular shapes derive their overwhelming sense of space, in part, from the new art of aerial photography, while the dynamics of Balla's futurist art are clearly derived from motion pictures, and in Delaunay's *Circular Forms* the color theories of Michel Chevreul are implicitly combined with the dynamics of the gramophone turntable. A qualitative distinction can be drawn between *abstraction* and *surrealism*. Abstract art is paradoxically "realistic" in seeking to represent essential or subliminal relationships in isolation from the distracting appearances of actual objects. Surrealism, as endorsed by Carl Jung and Sigmund Freud, and practiced by Max Ernst, Marcel Duchamp, and others, cultivates a form of directed intuition inspired by a world of dreams and conscious and unconscious symbolism, and dynamically embodied in the movie fantasies of Georges Meliès, Luis Buñuel, and Jean Cocteau. Both abstract and surrealist art are arguably representational, in deriving from individual sensory experience or visions; the difference between them, that whereas abstraction is implicitly concrete and familiar, surrealism is explicitly strange and elusive. The fact that it is heard rather than seen is often advanced as a reason for concluding that music too is abstract, or surreal, or non-representational; but music is just as capable of representation in the acoustic domain as the visual arts, of the realm of the visually real or imaginable.

Naturally, art is not necessarily limited to the representation of invincibly subjective perceptual processes or mental states. In exploring protocols for the graphic expression of spatial relationships in four and more dimensions, the cubism practiced by Picasso, Gris, and Braque was engaged in a task of visualization of a scientific interest equivalent to perspective in the Renaissance.[2] There is no earthly reason why Stockhausen's studies in indeterminacy should not be characterized, in a similar way, as exercises in the acoustic realization of concepts in physics for which music arguably provides a more precise and appropriate medium of expression than symbolic language, and from which conclusions of universal application can be deduced.

Stockhausen was not trained in physics. His interest in science is perhaps closer emotionally to Goethe and his theory of color than to Einstein's general theory, a reminder that for German speakers the word for science, *Wissenschaft*, is also the term for knowledge in general. Heisenberg was his archetypal tragic hero. In Goethe's *Faust*, as in Beethoven's musical portraits of Coriolan and Prometheus, we encounter timely philosophical (and not psychological) reflections on the ethical consequences of absolute power and absolute knowledge, handed down from an era that still recognized cultural heroism. And like Beethoven, Goethe was a high intellectual, a powerful figure of the Age of Enlightenment, who also confronted, and had to adapt to, the destructive consequences of social revolution on the progress of human knowledge. The stories of Goethe and Beethoven were part of every German child's education. For a young adult of Stockhausen's generation, renewed social upheaval in the late fifties was once again bringing into question the role of the visionary in relation to the people's state. In the thirties, heroism had remained a defining principle of nationhood, but it was a heroism reconfigured to endorse the aspirations of National Socialism and the moral authority of the Nazi leadership. It was not difficult to perceive Heisenberg as a tragic figure, a leading scientist and seeker after truth, brought down by a government "of the people" whose ideological rejection of "Jewish science" ironically contributed to the eventual failure of the German initiative to produce a nuclear bomb. At the same time, the regime's policy of public ridicule and suppression of "degenerate" abstract and surrealist art had been designed to vitiate popular confidence in the moral independence and authority of artists, a leadership that had been a continuing legacy of eighteenth-century classicism.

Stockhausen's awareness of Heisenberg came from reading popular science; he refers to the writings of Carl Friedrich von Weiszäcker, an associate of Heisenberg whose *Der Geschichte der Natur*, published in 1948, was followed in the mid-fifties by *Physik der Gegenwart* (Contemporary Physics) and *Die Verantwortung der Wissenschaft in Atomzeitalter* (Responsibility of Science in the Atomic Age).

Quantum physics is concerned with weights and measures on the microcosmic scale of elementary particles; a science deeply involved therefore with the Faustian dilemma of unlocking the secrets of nuclear power. What Heisenberg discovered is that both the position and the momentum of an electron cannot simultaneously be accurately determined: if its position is measured, then its speed and direction of motion cannot be ascertained, or its momentum can be measured, in which case its position can only be approximately estimated. The wider implications of Heisenberg's discovery were shattering. The uncertainty principle entered popular mythology as a formal statement of the ultimate unknowability of a real world.[3]

> Heisenberg's own breakthrough, which was accompanied by an experience of the intuitive vision of the new theory, made a tremendous impression on him. As he puts it himself (in *Der Teil und das Ganze*, 138), 'the most important criterion of truth' is the intuitive vision of the simplicity of the solution which 'at the very end' illuminates everything.[4]
> . . . I think that this vision of an 'illuminating simplicity' was decisive. It made him feel 'this is *it*': this was the end of the road, the final truth. He used the German word 'endgültig.'[5]

To a nonspecialist, the issue of indeterminacy seems little more than a restatement of Zeno's classic paradox concerning the position and velocity of a moving arrow. Since an arrow can only occupy a space equal to its size at any given moment, and there is no measurable lapse of time between one moment and the next, Zeno concludes that the arrow does not move.[6] What the paradox actually implies is that for the position of the arrow in flight to be accurately determined, an observer is obliged to reduce the time dimension to zero, whereas the speed of its motion (which in any case is not constant) can only be averaged between arbitrarily chosen points in the arrow's trajectory. The situation is further complicated by what Thomas Kuhn might have called a convergence of paradigms. A paradigm is a template for thought, rather than the thought itself; however if we consider the model of inference expressed in Heisenberg's uncertainty principle, a family resemblance can be observed with Wittgenstein's theory of meaning, and also de Saussure's linguistics. In every case a total determination of a fundamental datum of meaning cannot be made with respect to its evolution in time. Surprisingly, the dominant paradigm, as Karl Popper observed, is not so much words and their definitions as images or pictures: i.e., the movies.

> Heinrich Hertz said (and Wittgenstein repeated it) that in science we make for ourselves *'pictures'* (*'Bilder'*) of the facts, or of reality; and he said that we choose our 'pictures' in such a way that 'the logically necessary consequences' (*'die denknotwendigen Folgen'*) of the 'pictures' agree with 'the necessary natural consequences' (*'die naturnotwendigen Folgen'*) of the real objects or facts. . . . Mach, in discussing Hertz, suggested that we should interpret Hertz's 'pictures' as 'concepts'. Bohr's view seems to be similar when he speaks (as he so often does) of the *'particle picture'* and the *'wave picture'*; in fact, his way of speaking indicates strongly the (at least indirect) influence of Hertz and Mach.[7]

Today it is difficult to comprehend the extraordinary challenge of film technology to the preconceptions of Western science and philosophy. Until the arrival of stop-motion photography in the late-nineteenth century, barely a generation before Heisenberg, the phenomenon of motion had remained a matter of abstract speculation. Before Muybridge and Marey it had been impossible to determine the pattern of leg movement of a galloping horse, or the wing movement of a bird in flight. "It would not be improbable to say that by chance Muybridge had brought about a change in human consciousness. In much the same way as the telescope and microscope had done, his sequences opened up a world to the eye that the eye formerly had been unable to see."[8]

Surprisingly, many intellectuals found the evidence of motion revealed by moving pictures difficult to believe, and it is this unwillingness of intelligent people to accept the objective truth of the movement of living creatures revealed by mechanical means that resonates with the later controversy over detection of the motion of invisible particles. For many the issue was not whether the evidence was credible, but whether it was morally defensible to believe a machine in preference to a human being capable of rational thought. The historian of photography Aaron Scharf tells the story of the sculptor Auguste Rodin arguing against the veracity of Muybridge's representations of motion, declaring "it is photography that lies, for in reality time does not stop," when he clearly knew otherwise.

> In conversations with Paul Gsell, the *St. John the Baptist* was compared with instantaneous photographs of walking figures. The manner in which such photographs arrest movement is described by Gsell: "They never seem to advance. Generally, they seem to rest motionless on one leg or to hop on one foot." And Rodin agreed, pointing out that the striding St. John has both feet on the ground, inconsistent with photographic truthfulness but which, as art, more successfully conveys the idea of a progressive development of movement.[9]

Scharf illustrates Rodin's argument with a Marey chronophotograph of 1887 of a walking male in which only one foot is flat to the ground at any one time. However, a recent article shows the sculptor's source of inspiration is undoubtedly an original sequence from Muybridge, showing a bearded elderly man walking with head downcast, in at least two frames of which the subject is clearly shown with both feet flat on the ground at the same moment: left before right, as in *St. John the Baptist,* and right before left.[10]

Residual doubts concerning the realism of motion picture imagery also surface in a pioneer study by Hugo Münsterberg, the same Harvard University colleague of William James who was also tutor at different times to Gertrude Stein and Harold Stetson. Münsterberg "came to the conclusion that films, *by their nature,* observe the laws of the mind rather than those of the outer world, . . . overcoming the forms of the outer world, namely space, time, and causality, [and] adjusting the events to the forms of the inner world, namely attention, memory, imagination, and emotion."[11]

According to the the movie paradigm, what we see as movement is an illusion arising from the sequential presentation of still photographs or instantaneous samples. The time dimension is simulated as a consequence of the limitations of human perception (persistence of vision) confronted with the exactly synchronized repetition rate of the shutter mechanism. To a filmgoer it is axiomatic that every frame in a movie is a still; if it were not, and movement were to occur during the exposure, a smearing of the image would result, and it would be difficult to know what image was being represented, as well as where exactly it might be located within the frame. It is also axiomatic that an observer cannot know with any certainty, from the evidence of an individual frame, what the future disposition of images within any succeeding frame is going to be.

A theory of existence that is also a theory of knowledge, one that deals in elementary quanta variously described as "particles," "waves," and "wave packets," is bound to have profound meaning for a young composer of an idealistic electronic music assembled from musical elements (pure vibrations) that share the same ambiguities of definition: note or point, impulse or aperture, rhythm or collection of sine-tone segments, etc. But though he may have seen his work as fulfilling a similar role in music to Heisenberg in physics, and though the two activities have intriguing elements in common, Stockhausen is careful not to claim any deeper historical significance from resemblances that are clearly more poetic than scientific in nature.

Punkte 1952/62 (Points 1952/62)

1962 rev. 1964, 1966: No.½ (UE 13844, 13844a (1964), 13844c (1966); cd Stockhausen-Verlag SV-2).

For orchestra: 3 flutes (also piccolos; 3. also alto flute), 3 oboes (1. also oboe d'amore, 3. also cor anglais), 3 clarinets (e flat, b flat, bass), 3 bassoons (3. also contrabassoon); 3 horns, 3 trumpets, 2 trombones, 1 tuba; 3 percussionists: tubular bells, glockenspiel, vibraphone, marimbaphone, 2 pedal timpani; 2 harps, 2 pianos (2. also celesta); strings 8.8.8.6.4 ("all solistic").

Duration: 27' 30.

Punkte in its post-1962 guises is one of only a few Stockhausen compositions for unadorned orchestra of symphonic dimensions available in the public domain after the withdrawal of *Formel, Spiel,* and *Punkte 1952.* The pitch material of the original score (which had also served as starting material for *Kontra-Punkte*) is embedded in the new score, and subjected to a treatment that effectively blurs its original distinctions.

The recomposition is primarily concerned with the linking together of predetermined tonal "constellations" into tractable lines and textures. The orchestra is enlarged, especially in the brass and string divisions, but also in percussion, though the latter is still confined to instruments of equal temperament. The resulting music is complex, scintillating, and densely written (and it is worth noting that the composer's subsequent modifications of 1964 and 1966 add more material than they take away). The original point-structure is fleshed out into sound masses that, particularly in the writing for strings, are able to produce effects of palpitating lushness. Such unaccustomed sensuality is of a piece with the composer's developing personal relationship with Mary Bauermeister; it also emerges at a time of change of focus from point to texture composition among avant-garde composers in general:—Ligeti, Xenakis, Penderecki,—a shift inspired in part by the example of *Carré,* and enhanced by a renewed appreciation of texture and shape in earlier composers such as Debussy (*Jeux*), Charles Ives (the Fourth Symphony) and Alban Berg (for example, the Op. 6 *Three Orchestral Pieces,* in "Reigen" at measures 17–20, and "Marsch," at measures 25, and 36–37.

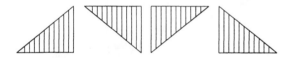

In the new version the "points" of the title are rarely simple note-points. To distinguish the original points I used four formal types: a point expands upwards, or it expands downwards; or a vertical aggregation narrows upward or downward to a point. Both expanding and narrowing types have characteristic textures (sostenuto, tremolo—repeating on the same note or notes—, trill; staccato, portato, legato; glissandi, chromatic melodies, etc.), also characteristic timbres, intensities, and relative speeds, [which] remain constant for set durations and so link up to form larger structures.

During composition so many layers of sound sometimes accumulated that the mass of sound became too great for the available space. (Why must we always conceive music simply as note-structures filling empty space, instead of as carved out of a homogeneously filled acoustical space, its musical figures and forms revealed with an eraser?) So I composed negative forms as well, to correspond with the positive forms mentioned: holes, pauses, cavities of various shapes and sizes, sharply or vaguely defined. At a further stage of composition I changed these back and forth: shaping leftover areas in one case, or making an empty space resound in another.[12]

The simplicity and relative freedom of textures in *Punkte 1952/62* in comparison to the structured shapes and textures of *Gruppen* (Cardew having intervened in the instrumentation of *Carré*) might seem to suggest a trial run or sketch. Despite false starts (a Ligeti-like page "0" added, then withdrawn), hiccups, and afterthoughts that to a publisher do not come without a price, the music as finally issued on disc—to this listener, at least—is very feminine, shimmering, coruscating, unexpectedly delicate, and wonderfully ductile. The 1964 version makes some minor adjustments for ease of performance, such as the transposition of high trumpet trills at 27, and trumpet and horn parts at 35, to a more comfortable range, and some reshuffling among woodwind parts at 139. To these may be added changes mainly of string dynamics, for balance or accentuation, mostly between rehearsal numbers 79 and 115. The structured shimmy on a unison f that constitutes page 0 is an interesting representation of chaos and related in pitch to the f – e "cadence" at the very end, but does not sit easily with page 1; though it revisits the "splitting of the sound" in *Kontakte* at XI, it may have more to do with Stockhausen's project for a Scelsi-like orchestral composition on one note titled *Monophonie*, later abandoned; a more elaborate initiation on one note recurs with interest, in any case, in *Inori*.

Interrupted cadence from Punkte 1952/62 (revision 1966).

Among the more interesting changes undertaken in the 1964 revision, given Boulez's involvement in a number of premieres and his correspondence with Stockhausen on the subject, are changes that have to do with timing, a liberal introduction of pauses, and a raising of the overall tempo by one degree in Stockhausen's scale of tempi: that is, MM 60 becomes 63.5, 63.5 raised to 67.5, and so on. The added pauses, in many cases offset by artificial echoes, seem designed to break the continuity, and so provide points of orientation—literally, interrupted cadences,—for performer and audience alike. Interruption, one recalls, is also a device associated with Boulez, in particular the combination of a long fermata enclosing, as it were in parentheses, an aleatoric re-shuffling of parts (though Boulez in turn adapted it from Berg, notably the coda of Berg's *Kammerkonzert*).

In the revision of 1966, Stockhausen has removed all but a few of the pauses, and retains only the feedback repetitions at 66 and 114, substituting focal harmonic or melodic elements (as above) into some of the remaining fermatas, including string accents at 51 and 71, the trumpet signal at 58, and woodwind interruptions at 129. Harp and piano parts are strengthened, and background harmonies added in brass and woodwind parts, restoring material removed in 1964, especially from 133 to the end. Perhaps the most unexpected innovation, however, is the filling-out of remaining "points" into melodic lines. This appears in the first six pages of woodwind material, and again at rehearsal numbers 20, 92, and 123; for the strings at 8, 26, 30, 35, and 48; and in piano and harps at 4, 15, 48, 54, and 58. The 1966 version reverts, in fact, to the 1962 concept of a generally uniform, musical flow, but retaining enough of the pauses of 1964 to clarify and aerate the structure.

A transition, so it appears, from post-Webern pointillism to post-Berg; from the pole of absolute purity to the opposite pole (or rather, equator) of undisguised expressionism. Disappointed at what appeared to be the avant-garde's premature abandonment of Webern, and what he may have seen as Boulez's influence on the change of aesthetic, Stravinsky complained "I hear everywhere now that Webern's series are too symmetrical, that his music makes one too conscious of twelves, that *la structure sérielle chez Berg est plus cachée. . . .*"[13] So why keep the name? What is "Punkte" now supposed to mean?

Throughout the fifties Stockhausen had valued his reputation as a seriously determinist composer whose passion for total control led to musical results that were often (deliberately or otherwise) unexpected or out of control. Electronic music was a method of forming, of synthesis. Aleatory, as it was taught by Meyer-Eppler, concerned analysis,—essentially destructive intervention, that is,—applied to systems or structures, such as language or sounds, in order to reveal or introduce perceptual unpredictables normally hidden or otherwise unperceived. Cage's indeterminacy, on the other hand, concerned the natural uncertainty of organic processes that, given their binding relationship with human observers or performers, were necessarily human in scale and perspective. After Meyer-Eppler's death Stockhausen became increasingly alert to the wider social and political implications of indeterminacy, as new disciplines such as sociology entered the cultural arena with a view to ascertain, and ultimately impose, collective norms of artistic expression.

Cage's 1958 "Lecture on Indeterminacy," in which he talks about friends, mushrooms, and other things,[14] is a selectively anecdotal portrait of the reality of the unexpected in everyday life, to be understood perhaps as an outwardly unintentional statement of the necessary reality that exists beyond human will or intention (which goes some way to explaining Cage's appreciation of the expressionless aesthetic of Erik Satie). Issues of indeterminacy are raised in three significant papers published by Stockhausen at this time. Together with Boulez's lofty *Penser la musique aujourd'hui,* (and aided and abetted by Kagel's sardonic *Sur Scène*), they offer a vigorous and concerted intellectual defense by European musical leaders of a philosophy of uncertainty that was coming increasingly under popular attack as an expression of negativism, doubt, and despair (or, if you like, of nihilism).

Stockhausen's several contributions consider the issue from a number of carefully-defined intellectual perspectives. In "'Chances' de la musique electronique" (Chance elements in electronic music) (1959) he outlines a program for electronic music in the dry tone and matter-of-fact terminology of Shannon and Weaver's information theory:

a) Determination of elements: Discovery of elemental groups, with which each element can be transmuted into each other;

b) Determination of connective laws: Maximum coincidence with the connective laws of musical thinking;

c) Determination of results that are not permitted: Elimination of everything that is already known. Maximum information.[15]

On the surface, "Erfindung und Entdeckung: ein Beitrag zur Form-Genese" (Invention and discovery: a contribution on the subject of the genesis of form) is a review and rationalization of ten years' development in his own musical researches.[16] Its title, however, can be read as a reference to Carl von Weizsäcker's defense, after the war, of the morality of scientific research, in which the scientist makes a distinction between the discoverer, a Galvani or Volta, who cannot predict the practical consequences of his work and therefore cannot be held morally responsible for the abuse by others of that contribution to knowledge, compared to the inventor, whether of the telephone or of firearms, who may be said to have acted in accordance with the wishes of society at large.[17] A hint of moral anxiety is underlined by the German word "Beitrag," which in that language also carries the implication of a payment on an insurance policy.

The alarm is well and truly sounded in "Vieldeutige Form" (Multivalent form), an outwardly Cage-like lecture also formed of a collection of personal reflections capable of being read in more or less random order, delivered at Darmstadt in 1960 by Heinz Metzger in the absence of the composer.[18] Stockhausen had learned that pressure had been put on Wolfgang Steinecke to have Cage excluded from Darmstadt that year. Meanwhile, in Cologne, serialism itself was under attack. The audience response at the premiere of *Kontakte* at the Cologne ISCM Festival had been less than ecstatic. Even Boulez did not know what to make of the new masterpiece. Then, at a gathering in Mary Bauermeister's atelier only five days after the less than happy premiere of *Kontakte,* looking Stockhausen straight in the eye, Metzger had delivered the so-called "Cologne Manifesto," a "commitment to a 'negative aesthetic'—to the end of any kind of generally applicable musical language,—and to John Cage and his compositional anarchy."[19] Stockhausen could see that this expression of support for Cage was also a covert (and to be honest, unprincipled) attack on himself. Even delivered at second hand, his response is untypically ferocious. It was a matter of life and death.

We know from animals that the ones with the strongest horns and sharpest tongues are those that survive. Especially distasteful in all of this ["uncertainty"] is undefinable applause. It makes no difference who says what, as long as it is said with the necessary authority. In the name of discipline, order, class, progress: In the name of Universal Likeness, always different, always new, seen in the same light: we have words reduced to farce; distinction to conformity with the wishes of a hundred thousand brown- or blue- or gray-shirts.[20]

To do justice to the cultural and historical resonances of this extraordinary, passionate polemic would take a volume in itself. It is a remarkable, highly nuanced critique that works on many different levels. As a portrait of the composer it is of particular value as a restatement of faith (belief in self-determination), of artistic priorities, and, most significantly, of the position of the artist in relation to German society and cultural history. In many ways the lecture is a key to all of Stockhausen's subsequent development.

The high emotion is partly due to the change in rhetorical style forced on him by events. For Stockhausen, as for many intellectuals at that time, to have to justify one's actions in the public arena was distasteful on a number of counts, among them: 1. the futility of trying to explain in words what is manifest in the music itself; 2. a reluctance to accept the "right to know" of a public that is more interested in exercising its authority than profiting from the knowledge that might thus be obtained (the very phrase "right to know" investing public ignorance with the power to suppress any knowledge of which it does not approve); and 3. veiled intimations of the same public hostility to science that had emerged in the Weimar era, or even of a return to the era of censorship under National Socialism.

A flavor of the public unrest articulated in Europe in the aftermath of the 1914–1918 war, and of the patrician disdain affected by an intellectual élite, is tellingly evoked by the Gestalt psychologist Wolfgang Köhler in the introduction to his William James Lectures, given at Harvard University in 1934 and subsequently published as *The Place of Value in a World of Facts*. Köhler's opening chapter, "The Case Against Science," addresses the public concern at a *Krise der Wissenschaft* (Crisis of Confidence in Science) arising from a perceived failure among intellectuals to take account of the social consequences or moral implications of their "truth-seeking" investigations. The public's representative mentioned in Köhler's account is the editor of a popular German periodical. "Although my friend has had a university education," writes Köhler, "he is far from being a professor."

> "Why this strange impatience in the faces of professors when we ask our questions about man, society, and history? We laymen do not understand this attitude. We fail to see any reason why learned men should assume an attitude of disdain with regard to certain subject-matters. Was the world created to fit a set of given scientific methods? You seem to presuppose just this when you look down upon some phases of creation, because their appearance is not that of neat scientific material."
>
> Although I was seriously annoyed (says Köhler) by the crudeness of this attack I suppressed my resentment and calmly gave the man all the explanations which his *naïveté* made obviously necessary.[21]

Stockhausen was faced with a dilemma. For many Germans after the 1939–1945 war, specialist knowledge, divorced from a concern for social utility or welfare, had troubling moral implications. On the other hand, National Socialism had demonstrated all too clearly the dangers of investing the fate of humanity in the political manipulation of mass opinion. The same public who criticized science had embraced Hitler, and in consequence been betrayed, demoralized, and wasted a second time. Winning popular approval through the power of rhetoric was simply using Hitler's tactics, since inevitably the message would be lost in transmission. Either one remained silent under attack, in which case one connived with the forces of unreason, or one resisted, in which case one had to employ the methods of the demagogue. Cage's silence had never seemed so eloquent. The paradox of speaking out in defense of the right thing was also implicit in the very cause it was intended to serve. If Cage's "indeterminacy" seemed the abnegation of responsibility, how much more were Stockhausen's "determinism" and "determination" tainted by distinctly negative and oppressive overtones.

The term "vieldeutige form" is a neologism. That new knowledge entails new words is a truism of science that, under the influence of de Saussure and Wittgenstein, leads to gridlock: an entropy or disorder of many small meanings. (In English, "the devil is in the detail.") Set in the wider context of the early sixties, a period in which Boulez produced *Pli selon pli*, a "portrait of Mallarmé," and Berio *Circles*, a setting of the American poet e e cummings, a disciple of Gertrude Stein, the text of "Vieldeutige Form" reveals yet more, purely etymological epiphanies:

determine	*to find out, delimit, order*
terminology	*language of science*
determination	*objective, decision, moral courage, leadership*
indeterminacy	*uncertainty, indecision, disorder*
termination	*finality, final solution*

. . .

zweideutig	*ambiguous*	uncertainty	
vieldeutig	*manifold*	many-fold	*Pli selon pli*
bedeuten	*to mean*		
deutlich	*precise, to the point*		
deut	*deuce, duple*	deuterium, duplicity	
deuten	*to point at, out*	point	*Punkte*
Deut(schland)	*Germ(any)*	living cell, protozóon	

Adding to the challenge to his intellectual authority was a burgeoning sense, arising from his deepening relationship with Mary Bauermeister, of the precariousness of his own position in relation to the traditional institutions of marriage and the Roman Catholic church. For Stockhausen, the old dichotomies of good and evil no longer applied. Self-determination was now the rule. Evil actions needed to be distinguished from the evil inherent in a leadership based on illegitimate tactics of persuasion, and brought to power out of the ignorance of society at large. For a while Stockhausen briefly entertained the idea of an opera based on the character of a peasant, a simple artist, who rose to power and was overwhelmed by the appalling consequences of his own single-minded vision.

I once wrote that the function of music must be spiritual. That doesn't mean religious. I make a distinction between "geistig" and "geistlich" even though my etymological dictionary says both mean the same and are derived from the same original meaning of ghostly. To me the concept of spirituality comprehends both the spiritual and the unspiritual (and you'll always find the devil lurking in there as well). . . . "The same, always different" is a spiritual phenomenon: at the same time understandable and damnably elusive.[22]

For a young German artist, after the travesty of Chaplin's *Great Dictator* ("too sentimental") seriously to entertain the idea of treating the failure of National Socialism and its leadership in terms equivalent to Greek tragedy, provides a clue to the depth and intensity eventually invested in the sacralization of good and evil as positive and negative influences in the virtual universe of *LICHT*. And for Metzger, the propagandist, to be charged with delivering Stockhausen's message of divine multiplicity to Darmstadt's waiting audience, must have seemed an apt and delicious irony.

Momente (Moments)

1961–1964, rev. 1972: No. 13 (UE 13816; cd Stockhausen-Verlag SV-7).
For soprano solo, 4 choir groups, and 13 instrumentalists.
Each choir of 3 or 4 × SATB; Choir 1 play tuned cardboard tube drums, Choir 2 tuned claves, Choir 3 shot-rattles, Choir 4 tuned metal claves.
4 trumpets, 4 trombones, 2 electronic organs (e.g., Hammond (or Lesley) organ, Lowrey organ); 1 large and 1 small tam-tam, vibraphone, 3 tom-toms, 5 suspended cymbals, 5 antique cymbals (f–c). kidney drum, 3 tambourines (3 percussionists).
Duration 80'–90'.

Stockhausen's reflection on Hitler should be understood in terms of the cosmic irony of atomic power itself: that the meanest indefinable particle can come to exercise such destructive power on a world scale. In an atomic reaction, the "moment of truth" is triggered by the attainment of *critical mass*. It is the same for political power. After the angry rhetoric of "Vieldeutige Form," *Momente* is Stockhausen's "critical mass," or sacred provocation. The watchword henceforward is *engagement*: no longer the passive resistance of a Gandhi (or a Cage), but positive action in the spirit of Sri Aurobindo. The small boy whose simple poem of defiance ("we will hold up our faith") had so angered the Gestapo and terrified his own father,—a teacher!—could no longer be content to rely on faith as a means of insulation from the heat of public opinion, as in *Gesang der Jünglinge*. It was necessary to confront social disorder in the spirit of Martin Luther King. And the message of defiance, like King's, is a message of love.

Apart from his charming brief setting of "On cherche . . ." as a gift to Heinrich Strobel, subsequently transformed into the opening of *Zeitmasse*, *Momente* is Stockhausen's first live vocal work since the *Drei Lieder* of 1950, and only his second major work, after *Gesang der Jünglinge*, in which the voice and text play an overtly programmatic role. For serial music the problems associated with composing for the voice are partly technical (how to determine the components of language), partly practical (how to choose an appropriate text), and partly philosophical (a residual suspicion of propaganda in all its guises). In the mid-fifties, when Boulez produced *Le marteau sans maître*, a suite of fragments and reflections (according to Stockhausen "mere variations") on surrealist verses by René Char, Stockhausen's response was an electronic exercise in the serial fragmentation and reconstitution of a traditional sacred text. A few years later, Boulez having virtually eliminated all traces of the poet from "Don" and "Tombeau," the remaining movements of *Pli selon pli*, his icy, ultra-refined "portrait of Mallarmé," Stockhausen responds with a garrulous and heated portrayal of womankind. *Momente* is a cantata with radiophonic and theatrical overtones; it is like Berio's *Visage* of 1958, and *Thema–Omaggio a Joyce* of 1961, in being a portrait of the thoughts of a woman in emotional turmoil, but also different, being a staged performance and not a studio tape creation (hence, requiring the soloist to imitate the effects of a tape creation, but in the flesh). *Gesang's* image of boyish innocence prevailing against the fiery blast, is transformed in *Momente* into its opposite, a portrait of mature female experience embracing the temptations of mortal delight. When Stockhausen writes for solo voice we may be sure he has a personal message to convey; that message corresponds here to a reversal of polarity, already noted in *Kontakte*, from abstract to natural form, from the ideal, that is, to the real.

If *Momente's* literary antecedents include the stream-of-consciousness novel and the radio play (James Joyce, Samuel Beckett), the work's unusual form also acknowledges Mallarmé, Alexander Calder (via composer Henri Pousseur) and Claude Lévi-Strauss. Its spiritual content and persona pay tribute to the black American gospel tradition, and the image of leadership personified in Martin Luther King (whose name can also be interpreted as a synthesis of the names and spiritual aspirations of the philosopher *Martin* Heidegger, religious leader Martin *Luther*, the founder of Protestantism, and Jesus Christ). Another, perhaps surprising influence is the J. S. Bach of the cantatas. *Momente* is a cantata rather than an opera, since the text is a meditation and there is no action, and Bach's is the archetypal Protestant cantata, distinguished from traditional Roman Catholic ritual by involving the public (the congregation) in the service.

In a radio play, which is like a dream or a prayer, events are organized by association, not by temporal sequence, from a store of images in memory. Just as the human mind draws on a store of words and sounds to create ever-changing sentences, so this music is laid out as a network of formal units, each reflecting a different combination of serial determinants, capable of being read in a variety of sequences. These musical events are the "moments" of awareness, epiphanies in waiting: "For most of us, there is only the unattended / Moment, the moment in and out of time" as T. S. Eliot expresses it.[23] A programme note for *Kontakte*, omitted from the *Texte*, offers the following definition:

> The musical events do not take a fixed course between a determined beginning and an inevitable ending, and the moments are not merely consequents of what precedes them and antecedents of what follows; rather the concentration on the Now—on every Now—as if it were a vertical slice dominating over any horizontal conception of time and reaching into timelessness, which I call eternity: an eternity which does not begin at the end of time, but is attainable at every *moment*.[24]

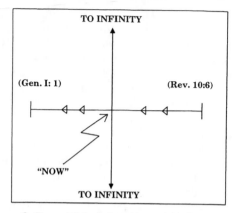

C. F. von Weizsäcker: Now and Infinity

The idea of taking a slice of time as if it were a piece of fruitcake, and reading the configuration of fruits as a datum *laid out in time*, (rather than the expression of a temporal process) goes back beyond Cage and his transparencies to the world of physics and astronomy, and the commonplace observation that the pattern of the constellations visible on earth is an image limited not only by the location of earth but the relative instantaneity of human existence in comparison to the timescale of the universe. In fact, at the time of *Momente,* John Cage was composing *Atlas Eclipticalis* (1961 –1962), a music based on actual star maps that posed the question of how such an instantaneous,—and classically pointillist,—image should be translated into the time domain. (Sight reading a piece of fruitcake, by the way, was one of David Tudor's peculiar abilities.) Stockhausen's definition of the NOW (since when his work titles have continued to appear in apocalyptic capitals) draws on Carl von Weizsäcker:

> The pattern of two lines thus crossing, one representing the horizontal passage of TIME and the other the vertical NOW-ness of ETERNITY, allows us to carry the figure one step further in the service of setting forth the truth. The horizontal line moving through history continues to flow by us until, according to scripture, it will one day come to an end. Time will then have entirely passed away, and the vertical line of ETERNITY will no longer intercept it. . . . TIME will have ceased to exist. *Intensity* of experience will replace *extensity*.[25]

Originally *Momente* was envisaged as a kind of cubist essay in gospel worship, led by the solo soprano from a central dais, silhouetted against the large tam-tam, with the two organs and two groups of percussion at her feet, and the four choirs, each accompanied by a trumpet and trombone, distributed in a semicircle around the platform periphery. The tight cluster at the center, and empty space between the central group and the outlying choirs, suggests a scaled-down version of *Carré*, with electronic organs substituting for strings, and the whole transferred to a single stage so as to be manageable by a single conductor. Dramatically, it is also a sequel to

Carré,—and indeed, to *Kontakte,*—if one imagines the soloist as composer *qua* preacher at the hub of the vocal and instrumental and vocal turmoil deciding to stand up and talk back, seize control of the flow of events and channel that energy toward a higher purpose. Much of *Momente's* drama hinges on the suggestion of open confrontation between the composer and his public detractors. As Stockhausen remarked in an interview with the *New Yorker,* "The reaction to my music in Germany is as violently hostile as ever. Last year, for example, when I conducted my *Momente* in Cologne, the audience made so much noise I just gave up—stopped the performance. After about five minutes, I started again, and went through to the end, although they were yelling so that even *I* couldn't hear anything. At home, it is always that way."[26] The sound-vocabulary of the work is cleverly designed to incorporate the kinds of noises and interjections of a hostile audience, drawing the unsuspecting public into the compositional mêlée and thus under the composer's control.

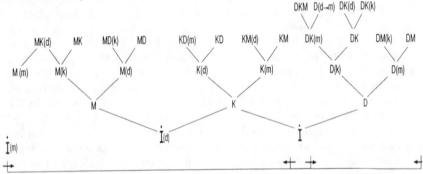

Momente: the moment-structure. Moments I and I(d) link the three M, K, and D moment-structures. K is the central pivot around which M and D structures turn; likewise M(k) and M(d) structures may rotate about M, and higher branches around their respective centers.

The formal structure of *Momente* is an ingenious mobile, governed by affective rather than purely quantitative criteria. The structure is a network of three principal lattices, issuing respectively from the elements K, M, and D (*Klang, Melodie,* and *Dauer,*—terms also associated with the personae Karlheinz, Mary, and Doris). K-moments are homophonic, emphasizing the vertical, including timbre and harmony. They are associated with male voices, solo and group, with the physical connotations of metal and skin percussion instruments, and with spoken consonants and noises that both define speech and interrupt it. M-moments are melodic, emphasizing the horizontal, the dynamic line; their characteristic elements include glissandi, and heterophony (a feature of folk music where several voices follow a similar but not identical path, and are permitted a measure of self-expression along the way). The solo soprano, both singing and speaking, other speaking voices, and the four trumpets and trombones are identified with M-moments, together with a certain type of randomness associated with heterophony. Finally, D-moments signify extension in time: duration, or waiting, are associated with polyphony and mensural notation, and also with silence. These moments are identified with female voices, of high pitch and pure tone, and with the electronic organs, which are able to sustain pitches indefinitely without dying away (and can thus dissolve a sense of time passing).

Linking the main K, M, and D branches are I-moments (meaning

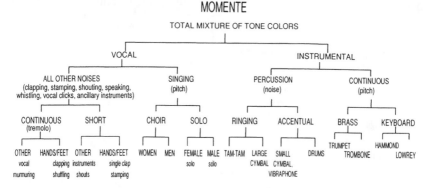

amorphous or indeterminate) that are intended to neutralize distinctions between them, and create a bridge between the musicians on stage and the audience. Interjections, hissing, clapping, and foot-stamping add unpredictable color and texture to the musical fabric. The multiple schemes of music and gender relationships and associations formalized in *Momente* (which by an odd coincidence, also shares a 3 × 7 structure with Schoenberg's Op. 21 *Pierrot Lunaire*), describe a continuum folded over on itself so that the highest and most subtle distinctions of the D-moments merge imperceptibly with the lowest in the I-moment flux (as in *Zyklus*, but this time on the vertical rather than the horizontal axis).[27]

In 1961 no composer, not even Xenakis, knew how to explain multivalent form. In his paper "Vieldeutige Form" Stockhausen comments that Boulez likens the concept to the image of a labyrinth, whereas he thinks of it more as a rabbit warren.[28] Ever-practical, Berio coined the term "opera aperta" (open form) and did his best to defend the concept, at a conference in Toronto, by appealing to examples from contemporary life: in literature Joyce, Mallarmé, Brecht, Proust, e e cummings; in sculpture Calder, and also in modular furniture and architecture:

> There are now many works in which the performer is no longer a means, an intermediary, but also a collaborator. He is given a plan of action, more or less precise, a certain number of structures which he can arrange in a way most congenial to himself. The composition . . . is no longer something ready-made, but rather to be made, made to fit. From being a means of communication, it becomes a means of cooperation.[29]

In *Circles,* Berio draws on the allusive character of e e cummings's syllabic free association to recreate on the platform a distributed landscape of players whose instruments make sounds that, like *Momente*, refer to individual speech sounds, and among whom the solo soprano is free to move. By association with *Circles* and Boulez's *Pli selon pli* the reader of *Momente* is drawn back to the post-Saussurian enigma of reality as text, and arising from de Saussure, the mysterious "Livre" or book of everything envisioned in the late-nineteenth century by the French symbolist poet Stéphane Mallarmé, whose poem "Un coup de dés" creates a narrative laid out on the page

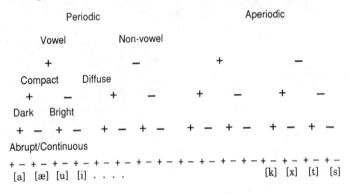

Structured classification of speech sounds (after Halle and Jakobson, Distinctive Features Theory) [30]

in such a way that it can be read in a number of different orders without its meaning being compromised. The formal and musical implications of the poet's final objective had been identified by Berio as long ago as 1956, in the elegant and genial phrase "le vers qui, de plusieurs vocables, refait un mot total, neuf, étranger à la langue" (the line of verse that, from a plurality of speech sounds, reconstitutes a word complete, new, unknown to the language).[31] The implications of the Mallarmé model address the paradox entailed by the Saussurian model of knowledge, namely the logical impossibility of saying or discovering anything new.

For Stockhausen this was familiar ground. The "plusieurs vocables" of *Momente* were like tape-recorded syllables, capable of infinite rearrangement. In real life, however, the syllables of ordinary speech influence one another according to their order of succession: every consonant is colored by a vowel, and every vowel shaped by a consonant. For a composition modeled on spoken language (bravely upholding the banner of Abbé Rousselot and Stetson) the implication was clear: ideally each choice of sequence should incorporate pre-echos and post-echos. For Stockhausen, degrees of phonic influence were also a metaphor for emotional influences arising from degrees of contact among the musical personalities represented by K, M, and D. It was all getting rather complicated. His interpretation of pre- and post-echos (known in phonetics as "coarticulation effects") was the *Einschub* or insert, here a virtual off-cut of a larger moment, originally to be overlaid on the score as a transparency (a brilliant idea, subsequently changed to the present much more complicated arrangement of slots and interpolations).

Because it is not always possible to tell the inserts apart from the moments into which they are inserted, I am not sure that the inserts work in their present form (they certainly complicate matters for all concerned), and it is perhaps relevant to note that inserts in the later *Mikrophonie II* are tape recorded and thus belong audibly to a different space-time. Today of course the organizational problem need not arise. Digital technology has made it possible to store a work of this complexity on cd-rom, meaning that a conductor in future should in principle be able to play with the score as a computer game, listen to a synthesized playback, choose a preferred configuration for live performance, and then have the parts and score printed to that chosen configuration. And that is surely the point: that what Stockhausen and others were grappling with in 1961, we can now spontaneously recognize in the format of a computer game. (Not for nothing do images of war, space travel, myth, and the labyrinth proliferate in the domain of interactive computer literature).[32]

At its 1962 premiere, the "Cologne" version, only about a third of the structure had been realized, consisting of the central K-structure, moments M(m), M(d), and the three I-moments (in which the audience is involved). This performance was the source of great controversy. The remaining M- and D-moments were realized during the summer of 1963 and early 1964; aided by a change in the stage disposition of solo and players, a good-humored and much less confrontational 61-minute "Donaueschingen" version, omitting the D-moments, was premiered in October 1965 and subsequently released on disc. The dramatic effect was to transform an image of an isolated woman haunted by unseen voices, into a true gospel celebration of a preacher and her community.

By 1969, when he resumed work on moment I(k) with a new series of performances in prospect, Stockhausen was once again riding high in public esteem, and his conception changed yet again. What had started as private, intimate theater, even cabaret, was now transformed into a Hollywood Night with the Stars. The soprano character of the Beloved, beset on all sides by a threatening public, has mutated into a matronly "Mother Earth surrounded by her chickens." The glowing orb of the central tam-tam is turned on its edge, almost invisible. Introducing the new Europa Version of 1973–1974 is a new moment I(k), a Fellini-like Introduction (—with a *beat*, for goodness' sake!) wherein choirs and brass, summoned to the stage by a cheerful "Komm' doch herein!" (Come on down!—containing the letters K, M, and D), process down the aisles to take their places on stage. It seems to contradict the very basis of moment-form,—that is, a work with no formal beginning nor ending,—as well as conveying so complete a change of mood, from intimate and reflective to a public event. It seems a pity if, in adapting the work to accommodate a more conciliatory worldview, he has turned this exceptional dramatic form against itself.

Notes

1. *SoM*, 33.
2. Linda Dalrymple Henderson, *Fourth Dimension and Non-Euclidean*

Geometry in Modern Art (Princeton: Princeton University Press, 1983).

3. Karl R. Popper, *Logic of Scientific Discovery* (Revised edition, London: Hutchinson, 1988), 453.

4. Werner Heisenberg, *Der Teil und das Ganze* (New edition, Munich: Piper, 2001).

5. The word *endgültig* also implies a "final solution." Karl R. Popper, *Logic of Scientific Discovery*, 8.

6. Colin A. Ronan, *Cambridge History of the World's Science* (Reprint, London: Book Club Associates, 1983), 79–80.

7. Karl R. Popper, *Quantum Theory and the Schism in Physics*, ed. W. W. Bartley, III (Reprint, London: Routledge, 1992), 44–45.

8. Eric Rhode, *History of the Cinema from its Origins to 1970* (Harmondsworth: Penguin Books, 1978).

9. Cited in Aaron Scharf, *Art and Photography* (Harmondsworth: Penguin Books, 1968), 224–25. Gsell, of course, was pushing his own agenda, and Rodin was perhaps just being polite.

10. The unnamed Muybridge sequence is illustrated in Robert Kunzig, "Falling forward: Why humans move like an imperfect pendulum." *Discover* Vol. 22 No. 7 (July 2001): 24–25.

11. Hugo Münsterberg, *Film: A Psychological Study* (Reprint, New York: Dover Publications, 1970). (Emphasis added.)

12. *Texte 3*, 12.

13. Igor Stravinsky and Robert Craft, *Memories and Commentaries* (London: Faber and Faber, 1960), 104.

14. John Cage, "Lecture on Indeterminacy." In *Silence* (Cambridge, Mass.: M.I.T. Press, 1966), 260–73.

15. "'Chances' de la musique electronique" (1959). *Texte 2*, 233–34.

16. "Erfindung und Entdeckung: Ein Beitrag zur Form-Genese." *Texte 1*, 222–58.

17. http://www.spartacus.schoolnet.co.uk/GERweizsacker.htm. (01/07/2004.)

18. "Vieldeutige Form" (Multivalent form) (1960). *Texte 2*, 245–61.

19. Michael Kurtz, *Stockhausen: A Biography* rev. tr. Richard Toop (London: Faber and Faber, 1992), 103–11.

20. "Vieldeutige Form." *Texte 2*, 245.

21. "The Case Against Science." Wolfgang Köhler, *The Place of Value in a World of Facts* (Reprint, New York: Mentor, 1966), 15–38.

22. "Vieldeutige Form." *Texte 2*, 249.

23. T. S. Eliot, "The Dry Salvages" (line 207), from *The Four Quartets*. In *Collected Poems 1909–1962* (London: Faber and Faber, 1974), 212–13.

24. Karl Wörner, *Stockhausen: Life and Work,* tr. Bill Hopkins (London: Faber and Faber, 1973), 46.

25. C. F. von Weizsäcker. Original source untraced. Quoted by W. H. Thorpe in *Beyond Reductionism: New Perspectives in the life sciences. Proceedings of the Alpback Symposium 1968.* ed. A. Koestler and J. R. Smythies (London: Hutchinson, 1969). On website http://www.custance.org/old/sci-faith/ch3sc.html (07/24/2003.)

26. Interview in "The Talk of the Town," *New Yorker* (18 January, 1964).

27. *Ein Schlüssel für 'Momente.'* Kassel: Edition Boczkowski, 1971; from 1981 published by Stockhausen-Verlag.

28. "Vieldeutige Form." *Texte 2*, 249.

29. Luciano Berio, in "Form," a symposium of the International Conference
     of Composers, Stratford, Ontario, 1960. 140–45 in *The Modern Composer
     and His World* ed. John Beckwith and Udo Kasemets (Toronto: Univer-
     sity of Toronto Press, 1961).
30. Roman Jakobson and Morris Halle, *Fundamentals of Language* (Second
     edition, Berlin and New York: de Gruyter, 1971).
31. Luciano Berio. "Aspetti di artigianato formale." *Incontri Musicali* 1
     (1956), 55–69.
32. Robin Maconie, "Opera Aperta." *Canzona* 1991, 3–8.

CHAPTER FOURTEEN

Process

Classical stave notation is a musical map, with pitch as latitude and time as longitude. As the earth rotates, lines of latitude remain constant while those of longitude move past an external observer from west to east. It is the same for a musical stave; as a performer reads from left to right, so the music becomes sound in a reciprocal movement, passing from right to left, while pitch relationships remain constant in the vertical plane. The grid of a musical map is a consequence of agreement on universal measures of pitch and time, embodied in the necessary compromises of tempered tuning and mensural notation, abstractions that transcend particular limitations of intonation, instrument, and memory. Standard notation evolved to its modern form at just about the time that the science of cartography was coming to maturity, so it is not surprising that sixteenth-century European keyboard composers should have expressed the same interest as their sea-going contemporaries in charting the course of a melodic shape moving at will across the musical map, often into remote regions of chromatic tonality, inhabited by wild and strange dissonances.

A philosophical interest in timbre as a constituent of meaning can be inferred from medieval monotone plainchant in which the vocalization of a text provides the only dynamic. That medieval composers were also aware of transformations of time and tone-color is clear from the example of vocal works such as the "Viderunt Omnes" by Pérotin, in which the infinite grandeur of the Almighty is addressed in a music of superhuman timescale that opens up the syllables of the sacred text to lay bare the inner quality of every vowel. As Messiaen taught, composers of the era of Guillaume de Machaut were also devoted (—it was, literally, an expression of faith) to the idea of setting the Mass to a trivial and familiar melody formula that determined the external structure of the entire rite as well as the thematic content of its constituent parts. Learned composers of the baroque era also experimented with transformation processes in alternative parameters, for example dynamics (echo-canon, crescendo and decrescendo, and as stratified dynamics on upper and lower keyboards), as well as relative timescale (unmeasured prelude, ornamental figurations "hors tempo," accelerando and ritardando, and augmentation and diminution). Among all of these transformations, modulation of key came to assume primary importance in the classical era as the natural expression of the restless and exploring spirit of eighteenth-century Europe. Even today, modulation remains synonymous with the idea of musical progress, considered as movement in the comparatively vast frame of reference of pitch.

Navigating in a multidimensional musical space is the theme of a number of meta-musical process compositions that make up an important strand of Stockhausen's composing activity in the sixties. But if classical modulation or sequencing resembles the movement of musical shapes on a map-like plane, Stockhausen's is more like learning to navigate in conditions of weightlessness. Lacking the gravitational attraction of conventional tonality, his process compositions operate within scale coordinates not only for pitch and duration, but also for magnitude (expansion and contraction), dynamics, timbre (tone into noise), probability, and even movement in physical space. The composer's repertoire of transformations draws on a range of sources, from Schaeffer's expansion and contraction of a "grosse note," and Messiaen's growth and diminution of a "cellule rythmique," to stop-motion photography, Piaget's structuralism, and electronic music. In a literary sense the transformational aesthetic also alludes to the transformation of meaning implied by wordplay and word evolution, and more distantly to the mantric verses of Gertrude Stein, who defended her own poetic of reiteration by declaring "Any two moments of thinking it over is not repetition... as I said it was like a cinema picture made up of succession and each moment having its own emphasis that is its own difference and so there was the moving and the existence of each moment as it was in me."[1]

Stockhausen's misadventures with *Kontakte* in its original conception, and his desire to exploit techniques of spontaneous invention in *Momente*, had also persuaded him of the need for a repertoire of study exercises in the realization and transformation of musical entities. Among the first of his priorities was to develop suitable notations to communicate degrees of transformation in these various dimensions.

Plus-Minus

1963: No. 14, UE 13993.
"2 × 7 pages for working out."
For solo or ensemble.
Instrumentation and duration unspecified.

As its name implies, *Plus-Minus* is a process based on the polarities of attraction and repulsion, growth and decay. In 1963, with the support of the rival Konservatorium, across town from the Musikhochschule, Stockhausen directed the first of the series of "Cologne New Music Courses," which took place annually until 1968 and were conceived as a longer-running and more productive alternative to the two-week Darmstadt summer courses (which in the composer's view had been infiltrated by unfriendly musical and political influences). Devised as a test piece for composition students, *Plus-Minus* has features in common with Cage's arithmetical rules for *Theatre Piece* as well as Roman Jakobson's plus-minus classification matrices for speech sounds, and those in Lévi-Strauss: "mutuality (=), reciprocity (±), rights (+), and obligations (–)," applied to tribal attitudes and affinities.[2] The work consists of seven pages representing form-schemes, laid out in a manner resembling a board game, and an additional seven pages of pitch constellations. Each page of form-scheme is assigned a page of pitch materials; the plan also provides, in the event that two or more pages are realized, for sample moments to be exchanged, like the inserts in *Momente*, in a superimposed performance. This is not a music that can be rendered directly from the published notation: a score has to be prepared,—like *Zyklus*, but more so,—before it can be performed.

Such a conception of music is like a statement in algebra, or a computer program, in proposing a transformational logic independent of its musical content. A complicated score, the complexity of *Plus-Minus* is part of the composer's message: serial music is hard work.

Each form-scheme page consists of a cycle of 53 time frames or moments, read in the conventional manner from left to right, and top to bottom (unlike other mobile scores of the day, which can be read in any direction from one frame to the next). Each moment within a frame consists of a standard formula comprising symbols for a "central sound" and "ancillary notes"—the latter standing in ornamental relationship to it,—or indeed, in the manner of the *anacrouse* and *désinence* in relation to the central *accent* of a complex note in Messiaen. The central sounds define the formal process, while the ancillary notes define the central sounds. Each of the seven central sounds of each form-scheme is assigned a corresponding ancillary note group. Other controls extend to the duration and envelope curve of the note formula, its rhythm, accentuation, reverberation, clarity, and liaison with the following event.

The formal significance of the title lies in the systematic accretion or erosion of material from the combinations of central and ancillary notes, as in a game of chess; a clue perhaps to the conception of the work as a prototype "glass bead game" in the spirit of Hermann Hesse's mystical game of abstract knowledge. Central notes are able to expand to a point where they are promoted into a new identity, or be reduced to zero and be replaced by an alternative "negative" entity; ancillary notes likewise proliferate and permutate, or simply disappear. During the course of working out, the musical events associated with the choice of symbol content wax and wane, eventually leading to the annihilation or accumulation of material.

As a compositional game, *Plus-Minus* probably operates at a level too elevated and abstract for most composers, let alone performers. This is a game for initiates, and ultimately for the "Magister ludi" himself; that qualia K and D are distributed in the form-scheme pages, but not M, suggests that on another level the play is about an actual transformation process in the composer's personal relationships, and one that in principle could go either way.

On the other hand, K and D could well be a covert allusion to Friedrich Froebel, the nineteenth-century philosopher of child education, for whom, as we recall,

> *Play* is the highest phase of child-development—of human development at this period; for *it is self-active representation of the inner—representation of the inner from inner necessity and impulse.* . . . The inner being is organized, differentiated, and strives to make itself known (*Kund thun*), . . . and this tendency is expressed fully in the word *Kind* (child) *K-in-d*, which designates this stage of development. . . .
>
> Variously designated as the law of development and the law of unification, [Froebel's Law of the Connection of Contrasts] furnishes the following systematic presentation of all development, in which (–) designates fixed or constant, and (+) fluid or variable elements, and (±) the connection of the two. . . . In their modality, contrasts are temporal, eternal, or combine the two. The "mediation," or connection, of contrasts is either *direct* or *indirect* (true "mediation"), and the former is either more *external* or more *internal*.
>
> Every thing and every being, however, comes to be known only as it is connected with the opposite of its kind, and as its unity, its agreement with this opposite, its equation with reference to this is discovered; and the completeness of this knowledge depends upon the completeness of this connection with the respective opposite, and upon the complete discovery of the connecting thought or link.[3]

In principle *Plus-Minus* is intended to extend the composer's own horizon of possibilities. "For many years (says Stockhausen) I had the idea of writing a piece having such powers of metamorphosis that I might come across it one day and hardly recognize it as my own." In 1964 Frederick Rzewski and Cornelius Cardew each prepared one page of *Plus-Minus* for a joint performance on two pianos. Both decided to realize the "negative-band" material on a second instrument, Rzewski opting for a cluster played on the harmonium, and Cardew for shortwave "static" on a transistor radio. Stockhausen, who had not been consulted about these choices, was astonished.

> When I heard the tape of the Cardew-Rzewski version of *Plus-Minus* for the first time, I was, in a truly unselfish sense, fascinated by it. . . . Sounds and sound combinations that, while recognizing their use by other composers, I had personally avoided (prepared piano and radio music), were now being brought by performers into my music, and in exact accordance with the functional sound requirements laid down in the score. The result is a highly poetic quality, reached as a result of the way *Plus-Minus* is constructed: when such a result is obtained, detailed considerations of sound and material become unimportant.[4]

Stockhausen's debut as an independent teacher is deliberately fashioned in

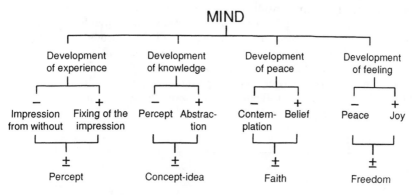

Part of Froebel's representation of the Law of Connection of Contrasts (1829).

the model and spirit of traditional German educational philosophy. The goal, the method, even the terms of reference are strikingly similar. An unexpected citation of William Blake in the text of *Momente,*—alongside private letters from Mary Bauermeister, Martin Luther's translation of the "Song of Songs," and excerpts from Malinowski's *Sexual Life of Savages,* —can all be read as a signs of a new commitment to the holistic counter-culture of early nineteenth-century Romanticism. "Education consists," said Froebel,

> in leading man, as a thinking, intelligent being, growing into self-consciousness, to a pure and unsullied, conscious and free representation of the inner law of Divine Unity, and in teaching him ways and means thereto. . . . There is no other power but that of the idea; the identity of the cosmic laws with the laws of our mind must be recognized, all things must be seen as the embodiments of *one* idea.

Froebel called his method *science of education*, and its objective, "knowledge of that eternal law, the insight into its origin, into its essence, into the totality, the connection, and intensity of its effects," the *science of life*.[5] Such a science of education situates itself in direct opposition to the tradition of Meyer-Eppler.

As one might expect, Stockhausen's conversion is total. Young Karl re-invents himself as Carl Jung. A life that started out as a search for knowl-edge (*Wissenschaft*) is henceforth rededicated to the fulfillment of dreams (*Wunschträume*). "I have a dream," said Martin Luther King. To a prag-matic English-speaking readership raised on the plain reality of Samuel Johnson and his dictionary, holism,—the embrace of esotericism by an elder generation of intellectuals, Jung, Huxley, Weizsäcker among them,—speaks of moral evasion: a retreat from the language of hard reality into guilt-free alliances with organic belief systems of preindustrial cultures, as a way of acknowledging the failure of Western science to deal with pressing issues of social accountability. The same had happened before, after the 1914–1918 war. A similar retreat from reality marked an earlier period of revolution when eighteenth-century intellectuals cultivated fantasies of the "noble savage" to divert attention from social injustices in their own backyards, an intellectual sleight of hand that at the same time provided surrogate justification for a continuing belief in the improvement of humankind and their own privileged situation in the eternal plan. For students of Stockhausen it just adds another layer of etymological complication to the interpretative task: the significance of the pun, the verbal pictograms, the possibility of coded meanings.

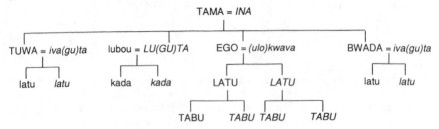

Part of Malinowski's diagram of relationship.
From The Sexual Life of Savages.

[Malinowski] rejected the emphasis which had been devoted to studying kinship terminologies, particularly as a means of reconstructing historical kinship and marriage regulations. Yet he himself regarded the few words printed in capital letters on the only genealogical diagram to appear in *The Sexual Life of Savages* as providing 'the key to the whole terminology of kinship and . . . the foundation both of the sociological system within native culture and . . . its linguistic expression.' . . . Writing on kinship in more general terms, he depicted the 'initial situation' of a child within the supposedly universal nuclear family, gradually extended through the addition of further kinship relations. Each person thus constructs kinship for him- or herself; there was no notion of [Pitt-] Rivers's covert, enduring system of socially recognized relationships.[6]

So if this is the game, and the word *Kund* is to be taken as signifying "K-in-D," and *Kind* (child) with the English "kind" and "kind-ness," then presumably *Mund* (mouth) relates to "M-in-D", and also the English word "mind," and "Mother Earth" to (M+Erde)—not very polite—, and we are supposed to hear the invocation "Komm' doch herein!" as a coded reference to K-M-D-H. Analysis has turned into a potentially endless play of mix and match. (So why the H? Because ultimately M-K-D *has* to mean "(m)an(k)in(d)." Add the syllable "Hu," meaning the spirit of creation, to make "Humankind." The magic syllable "Hu" first appears explicitly in *Ylem*, and thereafter in *Inori*.) After all of which a *process* composition, by the same token, signifies a *Prozess*, or trial. That, too, one can understand.

Bending the rules, or making them up to suit a personal vision of the truth, is a charge leveled at different times against a number of pioneers in the human and social sciences; Lévi-Strauss came under fire from Edmund

Leach, as we have seen; and the credibility of Freudian psychoanalysis has lately been reduced to a charred wreckage. As the daughter of an anthropologist, Mary Bauermeister encouraged Stockhausen's research into kinship relations and it is typical that he should only indirectly signal his interest in Lévi-Strauss,—to whom above all the motivation for inventing mythical structures of kinship permutations in *Momente* and the *LICHT* cycle is almost certainly due,—by crediting Malinowski as a source for the earlier work. (A hint: there are many relationship schemata in Lévi-Strauss, but only one in Malinowski.)

Mikrophonie I (Microphony I)

1964: No. 15 (Realization score: UE 15138)
For tam-tam, 2 players, 2 microphonists, 2 filter and potentiometer operators.
1965: No. 15½: "Brussels version" (Performance edition: UE 15139; cd Stockhausen-Verlag SV-9)
Duration: at least 20'.

A noisy but infinitely fascinating work. After the total abstraction of *Plus-Minus*, here is a composition of inescapably real, concrete, physical sound. Stockhausen describes this first composition of "live electronic music" as a personal breakthrough. The work uses only one source of sound, the large tam-tam, purchased for *Momente,* from which is drawn the entire rich and allusive range of sounds of which the work is composed. The "breakthrough" lies in the fact that since all the sounds are derived from a common source, they are all inherently in harmony with one another. If harmony in the conventional sense is conceived as a human task of reconciling differences, —as in the case of a broken consort in Renaissance times, where the instruments are not all of the same family,—then *Mikrophonie I* resembles its opposite, an image of divine creation of which all the diversity of sounds presented are by definition partial spectra, like colors from a prism. That the tam-tam is not an instrument of harmony in the Western tradition is neither here nor there; it was certainly an instrument of power and authority in oriental civilizations. For Stockhausen the tam-tam also has a personal association, via J. Arthur Rank, with the lion of MGM, and both in turn with gaining admission to the world of dreams that is the movies.

Stockhausen may have been prompted to experiment with the tam-tam from an encounter with an old musique concrète composition by Pierre Henry, *Tam Tam IV*, dating from 1950. The latter work is mentioned in the first of a series of radio broadcasts on music for tape made by Stockhausen for Cologne Radio between 1964 and 1966.

> I understand by the title that for this piece Henry recorded sounds of a tam-tam on tape and then proceeded to work on the taped material; a tam-tam is a very noise-rich and resonant metal percussion instrument, which according to the size and material of beater produces a sound of greater or lesser depth and complexity. . . . It is thus clear that quite new sounds are obtainable through the transformation of natural (or rather,

"familiar") sounds.[7]

Technically, drawing a vocabulary of different sounds from one primary resonator is a procedure analogous to electronic tone generation by filtering noise from a white-noise generator. The advantage, in theory, of filtering a noise source rather than trying to build up complex timbres from superimposed sine-tones, is that with the aid of filters a composer can create a continuum from white noise to sine-tone, while to create white noise from sine-tones is not possible. Either procedure in studio terms would be impossibly laborious, but something very close to it is feasible if a tam-tam is substituted for the white-noise generator, and different materials are applied against the tam-tam to act as substitute filters.

To conceive of such a process, it helps to have an aural image in one's mind. Stockhausen was not only familiar with the sound of the tam-tam, —which up to that time he had employed in a relatively limited, if climactic fashion, in *Kontakte* and *Momente*;—he was also accustomed to filtering and varying the speed of tape-recorded sounds, either to transcribe them, or just to experience their inner modulations in close-up. For example, when a voice recording is played back at half speed or less, a point is reached where the words being spoken are no longer recognizable: the voice becomes a modulated and guttural growl, not unlike a lion's roar. (A similar technique is used to disguise the voices of anonymous crime victims or witnesses on television.) It would not be in the least surprising if, in listening to the Pierre Henry piece, Stockhausen was reminded of his own experiments with the human voice, and suddenly realized that here was a means of exploring the possibilities of a music of slow motion.

The tam-tam is also similar to a reverberation plate, a metal resonator employed in a studio to add a sense of space and depth to voices and instruments. By that token, drawing sounds out of a tam-tam is arguably like reversing time, or reversing a tape of reverberated sounds and imitating the way distinct and recognizable sounds emerge out of the reverberant haze and eject at full force into the foreground.

In operating directly on a single resonating body, *klangfarben* effects of liaison and continuity that are difficult to achieve electronically (and indeed, in Webern, instrumentally) will tend to occur as a matter of course, so that the focus of performer effort can be diverted to developing techniques of intonation and control. The music of *Mikrophonie I* is a music of gestures, notated graphically and more or less conventionally for live performers in relation to timing and pitch. New ways had to be found for specifying and notating timbre. Stockhausen initially experimented at home, beating, rubbing, and dragging a variety of kitchen implements across the surface of the tam-tam, which was hanging in the garden. His assistant Jaap Spek, inside the house and out of view, moved filter controls and faders at random while recording the sounds on tape. After they listened to the results and were astonished at the richness of effects that they heard, the task began of structuring that potential into a workable notation. Stockhausen settled on a vocabulary of descriptive terms,—"rumbling", "hooting", "whirring", etc.,

—as a timbre and action notation to be interpreted by the performers using materials of their choice.[8]

The six players are organized in two teams of three, operating one on each side of the tam-tam surface. The first member of each team draws out the required sound by activating the surface (which is coated in dissolved rosin for added friction) with various materials. These sounds are monitored by the microphonist, who stands close by and moves the microphone in and out like a movie cameraman. In the auditorium, seated either left or right of center, the third member of the team further modulates the sound by means of a sliding filter with independent treble and bass attenuators, and a poten-

I		**II**		**III**	
$\widehat{=}$	entsprechend *similar*	$+$	unterstützend *supporting*	$\nearrow$	zunehmend *increasing*
$\#$	verschieden *different*	$\vert$	neutral *neutral*	$\rightarrow$	konstant *constant*
$\parallel\!\!\!\!\text{-}$	gegensätzlich *opposite*	$-$	zerstörend *destroying*	$\searrow$	abnehmend *decreasing*

Mikrophonie I: *symbols of relationship*

tiometer. The resulting modulated sound from each team is sent to speakers to the left and right of the auditorium.

A further element of sophistication arises from the fact that the sound created on one side by one team, is also picked up by the microphone wielded on the other side; likewise the various noises produced by each team influence the modulation of sounds of the other team. These incidental contributions are however *in reverse phase*. The implications of a two-channel composition of which each channel contains a muted image of the other in reverse phase, are that the stereo effect will be three-dimensional, with sounds appearing to leap and dance in front of the loudspeakers.[9]

The score of *Mikrophonie I* consists of thirty-three "moments" played alternately by each team. The sequence of moments may vary, but must conform to a fixed scheme of triplet relationships, symbolized as shown. The work tends, as it unfolds, to move from "identical" sound-events to contrasts; in the middle events sound "similar," and at the finish, "opposite." In one moment only, "Tutti 157," both teams of players come together in a passage in which "*all* moment-types are heard simultaneously and in succession." As a *process* of articulation, *Mikrophonie I* resembles speech; if the tam-tam represents the vocal cavity or resonator, the filters correspond to "lips" (modifying the aperture), and the actions of the sound-makers, the larynx. In that sense, the combination of noise source and modulators is designed to imitate, in real time, what the analogue vocoder, Meyer-Eppler's and Eimert's pride and joy, was only able to do in a much slower process with a limited sample of only a few seconds' duration.

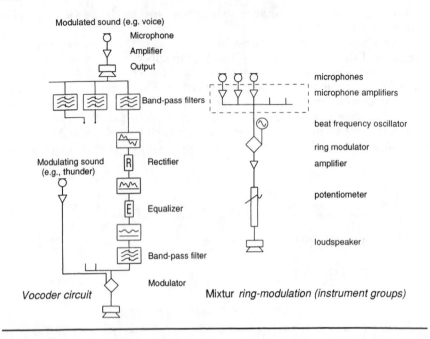

Modulated sound (e.g. voice)

Microphone

Amplifier

Output

Band-pass filters

microphones

microphone amplifiers

beat frequency oscillator

ring modulator

Modulating sound
(e.g., thunder)   R   Rectifier   amplifier

potentiometer

E   Equalizer

Band-pass filter   loudspeaker

Modulator

Vocoder circuit   Mixtur *ring-modulation (instrument groups)*

Mixtur (Mixture)

1964: No. 16 (UE 14621; cd Stockhausen-Verlag SV-8)
1967: No. 16½ for smaller ensemble (UE 13847; cd SV-8)
For 5 orchestra groups (woodwind, brass, percussion, plucked strings, bowed strings); 4
ring modulators, 4 sine-wave generators, 7 loudspeakers.
Large orchestra: 3 flutes, 3 oboes, 3 clarinets (bass clarinet), 3 bassoons (contrabassoon);
5 horns, 3 trumpets, 3 trombones, tuba; 3 percussionists, each 1 suspended cymbal, 1
tam-tam (with contact microphones); harp, strings 12.12.10.8.6.
Reduced orchestra: flute (piccolo), oboe, clarinet (e flat, bass), bassoon (contrabassoon), 2
horns (high, low); trumpet, trombone; percussionists as above, strings 4.4.4.2.2.
Duration: 28'.

After the exciting experience in *Mikrophonie I* of shaping sounds in real
time, Stockhausen was understandably eager to find out if the same procedure could be applied to orchestral sound. Working with electronically modified real sounds in real time had distinct advantages over traditional studio
practices of working direct to tape: saving time, developing techniques more
quickly, and the benefits of team feedback. *Mixtur* is the first work of this
new genre of live electronic music for ensemble. Stockhausen had encountered ring-modulation in Varèse's *Déserts*, back in 1954. As originally conceived for an orchestra of large numbers, the composer's intention seems to
have been to create a music in which the real sounds of the full orchestra,
heard as a totality, are simultaneously divided and refracted electronically
to create a complex "hall of mirrors" antiphony. (It may also have been his
original intention in *Mikrophonie I* to balance the natural sound of the

instrument with the two channels of modulated sound.) The version for small ensemble alters the balance in favor of electronics, so the role of the instruments in the 1967 score is geared more specifically to the production of cleaner ring-modulation, than to create a balanced dialogue of live and electronic components.

The essentially exploratory nature of the work is expressed in a loose form consisting of twenty named "moments" representing specific gestures, textures, or musical interactions, written in a simplified graphic notation seemingly designed to produce a range of desired effects with a minimum of explanation and with the active cooperation of the players. (In this respect the score looks like, as well as back to, some of the early graphic scores of Morton Feldman, and a number of Stockhausen's moments in *Mixtur* (e.g., "Ruhe" (calm), "Vertikal" (vertical), "Holz" (woodwinds)) also carry Feldman-like titles.)

The role of the percussionists is to mediate between the real and electronically modified tonal worlds. Each amplified suspended cymbal and tam-tam combination covers a wideband frequency range, and the notated actions contribute alternate structures of naturally modified metallic resonance to match the somewhat abrasive sum and difference complexes of the ring-modulated instrumental groups. The implication is that the ring-modulated sound should resemble cymbals and tam-tam. (In the version for smaller ensemble the mediating role of the percussionists is less pronounced, since the live instrumental sound is considerably weaker.)

Though the instrument and pitch composition of each moment is serially determined, its essential shape is sketched out with pictorial directness and simplicity. "I wrote the score fairly rapidly and without interruption in July and August 1964, obeying only my intuition, since experience was lacking; I hope that the music has captured some of the freshness and gaiety of those adventurous days."[10] Each moment incorporates a speculation about the influence of ring-modulation on instrumental sound. In some moments, "Ruhe" for instance, or "Blech" (brass), ring-modulation is not so much a given as an added expressive coloration, like a color wash on a line drawing. Other moments, such as "Translation," play on effects that are specifically foreseen; in these the instrumental score without modulation has little independent meaning, and so the role of ring-modulation is more structurally significant.

Mixtur thus continues the trend away from static structure to dynamic process that began with *Kontakte*. Boulez was troubled by the score, which seemed to him rather rough and ready. Any child of the fifties, growing up with children's radio stories of talking train engines, jet planes, and Jack Benny's talking violin,—all vocoder produced,—can understand a desire to achieve similar effects in the orchestral domain. Ring-modulation, however, is a risky affair: the side effects can be excruciatingly loud and acoustically dazzling, not to mention difficult to control. That Stockhausen took the plunge into ring-modulation knowing the risks, but convinced of the ultimate potential of real-time intermodulation, tells its own story of visionary recklessness; that he succeeded, in *Mantra*, in containing the problem of intermodulation distortion, is more than sufficient justification for having taken that step.

Problems in rehearsing and performing *Mixtur* led to a rift in relations with Boulez, who one suspects did not fully appreciate what Stockhausen had in mind. Many of the work's key issues remain unresolved, and have not been ameliorated by the new version for smaller forces, which conceptually is a different work. The main issue, of a technical nature, is how to soften and control the harsh consequences of ring-modulation. The glare of high frequencies, distressing to ordinary listeners, can be reduced by electronically filtering and compressing the sound of each instrumental group, to eliminate high frequencies from the signal before it passes to the ring modulator. That such a relatively simple procedure was not attempted says something about the composer's determination to accept the outcome as a foregone, and in some way authorized, conclusion.

Mikrophonie II (Microphony II)
1965: No. 17 (UE 15140; cd Stockhausen-Verlag SV-9)
For choir (6 sopranos, 6 basses), Hammond organ, 4 ring modulators and tape.
Duration: 15'.

After the inconclusive experience of *Mixtur*, this follow-up essay in live electronics is designed to test the malleability of ring-modulated voices. From *Mikrophonie I* is borrowed the successful idea of specifying sound types by name; the Hammond organ however is a change from *Mixtur*'s relatively unwieldy orchestral forces to a reliable analogue keyboard instrument, capable of changes in register, and under the dependable control of Alfons Kontarsky. The twelve voices are divided into first and second sopranos, and first and second basses, three in each group. Each group is individually ring-modulated with music played on the organ, the resulting four channels of modulated sound passing to four speakers on the platform. Though smaller in scale, *Mikrophonie II* is richer in sound potential, with voices and organ alike capable of considerably greater flexibility than the corresponding instruments and monophonic oscillators of *Mixtur*. A more volatile expressive potential combines with greater immediacy of response, and improved scope for self-monitoring and adjustment of technique.

Like *Mikrophonie I*, the modulating sound is "agitated" as it were by the four voice-groups, working independently. The effect of ring-modulation on the voice was not an entirely unknown quantity, since Eimert had employed a ring-modulated speaking voice in his 1962 *Epitaph für Aikichi Kuboyama*. Stockhausen himself had had recent experience writing for the Hammond organ for *Momente*, in which the instrument functions as a substitute string orchestra, in much the same way as the synthesizers of the "modern orchestra" of *LICHT*.

The subject matter of *Mikrophonie II* also derives from *Momente* 1964 and its portrayal of crowd scenes that, in the early version at least, act the part of a skeptical German public, interrupting, cajoling, and harrassing the solo soprano. This time, however, the solo soprano is silent, or present only in echo, in a tape excerpt of moment MK(d) that, along with flashbacks from *Gesang der Jünglinge* and *Carré*, breaks open the dark and congested fabric to let in a little daylight. The image is one out of Bruegel, of the crowd jostling and haranguing Christ on the road to crucifixion. It is a dark, introspective world, in stark contrast to the bright optimism of earlier times. The text is taken from the poem *Einfache Grammatische Meditationen* (Simple grammatical meditations) by Helmut Heissenbüttel (1921–96), the German poet and playwright whose long association with Stuttgart Radio led to an attitude to speech sounds and their meaning that offers some insight into Stockhausen's own resynthesis of language, especially in *LICHT*:

> The radio play was a natural medium for a writer interested in the distance between language and the visible, material world. In the modern, post-realist world language was no longer able, in Heissenbüttel's view, to reflect or penetrate a reality beyond itself. . . . What was needed was "a new and radical nominalism . . . that takes words as objects, structuring words to form a new reality, not figuratively standing for something, but like a second reality."[11]

Heisenbüttel is like a darker, more serious Raymond Queneau, but does not attain (or perhaps aspire to) the utter purgatory of some of Samuel Beckett's later monologues. Indeed, in some ways this particular poem evokes the spirit of a lecture by a slightly weary John Cage.[12] Stockhausen has protested, somewhat half-heartedly, that the work is humorous in intention, but the spirit of the musical action seems closer to Goya than to Thomas Rowlandson, and follows publication of a despairing text by the composer in which he speaks of Germany reverting to a nation of blockheads and Philistines ("verdammtes Pflaster"). Stockhausen's selection of fragments from Heissenbüttel, together with his own additions, emphasises enclosure and withdrawal: phrases such as "environments and landscapes and either," "to have been circumscribed," "swarms of enclosures" (6–7). Dualism is another refrain: darkess/ light, being/ not-being, association/ disintegration, movement/ fixity, arrival/ departure,—though in his *Momente* text Stockhausen at least declares for conjunction: "and" as mediator between "either" and "or."

In a gesture foreshadowing the bastard creations of *Freitag aus LICHT*, the singers are asked to produce a range of voices, some real, others mechanical: "like a typewriter," "solemn Levite chant," "birdlike—pigeon, parrot," "like a Sicilian street vendor, choked," "like a confused toothless old crone, enraged." Each type of voice brings forth a particular combination of inflection, timbre, and rhythm, and the musical sense in which this range is exploited emerges in indications to modulate from one voice to another, as in the passage where basses are asked to repeat the phrase "oder und oder" (or and or) initially like plucked string basses, gradually changing to the style of "an affected snob" (probably an Englishman). In contrast, the word setting is unexpectedly literal; on page 9 of the score the phrase "hesitating diagonals," for example, stammers in short bursts of a descending scale. On the same page, the phrase "blacknesses of blackness and the chromatic of the bright-lit patches," the tone, at first "menacing, horrifying," shrinking to "timid, frightened," is illuminated by a taped extract from *Momente,* heard over a fifth loudspeaker as if coming from a great distance like a radiance from heaven. Light at the end of the tunnel, but from the past: i.e., from behind. Orpheus's descent is only just beginning.

Stop (Stop)
1965: No. 18 (UE 14989)
For orchestra, divided into 6 distinct, mixed groups of about the same size.

1969: No. 18½ "Paris version" (UE 14989; cd Stockhausen-Verlag SV-4)
For eighteen players in six groups, e.g.: I: oboe, piano, trombone; II: electronium, trumpet, 2 cellos; III: vibraphone, bass clarinet, cello; IV: basset-horn, 2 violas, bassoon; V: clarinet (e flat and a), violin, trombone with extension; VI: flute (alto), violin, horn. Duration: 15'.

A test piece composed for the Cologne New Music Courses, the title *Stop* suggests radio static ("obliteration by noise") as well as prevention or absence of movement. The sketch score is proportioned to a simple Fibonacci series, like *Mikrophonie II.* The musical actions "work" on two levels: production of background noises of varying textures, and within them signals of a melodic character that emerge from the backgrounds at different times and with varying degrees of clarity. There are melodies buried deep in the fabric of *Mixtur* like fragments of hidden treasure, and in *Stop* they rise to the surface and seem intended to release a strong emotional charge.

Boulez had no time for buried treasure, even in Berg, but Stockhausen seems here to be considering how it might be possible to bring images of popular (tonal) music into the serial equation. For the time being, the only device by which he can do so is in simulating shortwave radio, an image evoking strong memories of listening to the radio in secret, late at night, as a schoolboy. From the example of radio, it is logical to interpret the distinct orchestral groups as adjacent channels, each of specific character, and each distinct in collective timbre. This is not a music of dramatic gestures; it is a music intended to evoke poetic situations of secret radio communication and reception, and its emotional quality rests on the radio operator's heightened dependence on maintaining links with "the outside world." It is an imagery to be developed further, in *Adieu, Telemusik, Kurzwellen, Hymnen, Kurzwellen mit Beethoven,* and *Trans.*

Solo (Solo)
1965–1966: No. 19 (UE 14789; cd Stockhausen-Verlag SV-45)
For melody instrument with feedback (4 assistants).
Duration 10'–19'.

It seems sometimes as though structural ideas arise of their own accord, like epidemics. *Solo* is arguably a Stockhausen project; it fulfils a technical brief, it fits into the larger context of his live electronic music at this time, and it develops a tape-loop device for generating and manipulating complex multilayered sound,—the "copy head,"—that was first discovered and put to use at the time of *Kontakte*.

Reel-to-reel tape recorders usually operate by delivering tape at a constant speed from a storage reel on the left to a pick-up reel on the right, reading the stored information as it passes by one or more tape heads in between. This is a finite, linear process with a beginning and an end. Alternatively, a length of tape can be joined end to end to make a loop of information that orbits endlessly past the playback head in a periodic cycle. If the information on the tape is simply rerecorded as it passes the playback head, so that it becomes a copy of itself, and then a copy of a copy, and so on, noise will gradually accumulate, and the recorded sound will deteriorate in quality. If however something happens to alter the recorded information in between cycles, the repetition process will lead to a change in content, or quality, or complexity, or perception, or all of these, as the process continues. Both of the above are degenerative processes, since both involve a continuous reduction of information quality or content over time. A poetic analogy with the effects of a mechanical daily routine on quality of life and physical well-being is self-evident. If such a process is applied to recorded speech, as Steve Reich discovered in 1965, in experiments that led to *It's Gonna Rain* and *Come Out*, something very interesting happens: the consonantal definition, and thus the literal meaning of what is being said, is worn away, leaving only a music of rhythmically-inflected intonation.[13] So, by a type of erosion, one layer of meaning is lost, but another fully revealed —precisely the layer of gestural meaning that Harold Stetson and Abbé Rousselot argued, contrary to de Saussure, to be more significant than word content (and both Stetson and Rousselot, as we recall, based their contention on the evidence of continuous but degraded speech that was all they could discern on the primitive cylinder recorders available to them).

Tape loops and their possibilities for instrumental music were a source of interest and inspiration for Terry Riley, the composer in 1964 of *In C*. Riley was not so interested in the fairly obvious poetics of deterioration; an improviser, he saw the tape loop as a storage device of fixed duration, providing a template for creating and modifying musical shapes or structures in real time, layer by layer, in a manner analogous to a laser machining a prototype component out of wax, layer by layer. In tape loop music of this kind, each additional layer adds to the information already there, and since the additive process is being monitored by a real person with an interest in discerning and helping to define an emerging image, the inevitable decline in tape content and quality, relating to the mechanical process, is offset by a deliberate process of redefinition and renewal, relating to the intervention of the perfomer.

In a more fundamental sense, however, the tape loop is a mechanism for extending the moment of intuition. The options available as the tape content develops can be understood in much the same terms as the difference signs in *Mikrophonie I*: a player can add to a pattern already recorded, or make it more complex, or by imposing a contrary pattern, seek to counteract or destroy it, like Picasso painting on glass in the famous 1956 documentary movie by Henri-George Clouzot.[14] With each additional layer, the player's strategy also becomes more apparent, and the composite image acquires a personality of its own: the question then is to know when to stop. If the player's strategy is infirm or ill-defined, on the other hand, the effect will be negative, and the cumulative result will become less and less coherent. In his last years even Stravinsky was drawn to the conception of a music of cyclically accumulating layers, in the five-part solo superstructure to the Prelude of *Requiem Canticles*, where it is offset by pulsating ripieno strings; he went on in 1966 to recompose the Finale from *Firebird* as a multilayered *Canon* of different speeds, transpositions, and directions (at the same time drawing attention, in this last composition for orchestra, to the roots of canon in baroque practice).

In tape-loop music, as for the partials of a complex wave, there are certain freedoms, and also certain rules, if the resulting aggregate is to work harmoniously. When a recorded natural sound is filtered into frequency layers, and the layers heard in succession, the rules are not always apparent. Working with the vocoder, Eimert and Schütz took apart a spoken phrase and revealed it as seven layers of distinct rhythms at specific frequencies, with no obvious relationship to one another; but that when added together again, miraculously restored the original words.[15] Human performers are limited, by contrast, to periodic structures. To expect an image of coherent speech to appear spontaneously in a tape loop composition is asking a bit much.

Solo adds a further refinement, or complication, taking advantage of the two channels of a stereo tape recorder to allow for the generation and modification of two layers of music at the same time. A line of music is laid down by the performer on one or both tracks of a two-channel feedback circuit or tape loop. After a predetermined lapse of time the recorded material is played back and may be rerecorded with an additional layer of live music superimposed. Two factors govern the superimposition process: the number of times a cycle repeats, prescribed by the score, and whether or not the accumulated material is added to each time round, which requires two technicians to switch the recording microphones off or on as the score requires. With two feedback circuits instead of one it becomes possible to regulate the structure and density of the resulting polyphony, from a continuously-evolving canon in two parts at the most basic level, through a hierarchy of intermediate levels of complexity (such as generating an ostinato accompaniment alongside a constantly-renewing theme), to an uninterrupted accumulation of layers into a dense band of sound. The score plan also provides for any continuous material to be interrupted or segmented by rapid opening and closing of the faders on each channel, to isolate slices of accumulated layers for an effect of "blocks" or chords (the shorter and more instantaneous the segment, the more it will tend to sound harmonious). The relatively unsophisticated nature of these modifications arises from the fact that they are performed in real time, and not under studio conditions where the basic circuitry can be changed at leisure from one layer to the next. How the resulting two channels are projected as a stereo mix is a significant additional layer of aesthetic choice.

The work offers a choice of six form-schemes, varying in duration between some 10½ and 19 minutes. Each form-scheme is divided into six subsections, or "cycles," whose duration is governed by the length of the loop. The form-scheme defines a layer-structure and the quality of integration within the layers to be aimed for. These imposed specifications, which require a sophisticated understanding of Stockhausen's philosophy of relative difference, are hardly calculated to make the live performer's task any easier, and lead to an impression that the written score is itself the result of an analogous loop process that has perhaps been allowed to accumulate more layers of instruction than are really helpful.

Telemusik (Telemusic)
1966: No. 20 (UE 14807; cd Stockhausen-Verlag SV-9)
Electronic music.
Duration: 17' 30.

Small, polished, beautifully precise, *Telemusik* stands in jewel-like contrast to Stockhausen's generally sombre and rough-hewn music of the mid-sixties. The piece was realized in the electronic music studio of NHK Tokyo during the first quarter of 1966, a remarkably short period of time that seems to have concentrated the composer's mind wonderfully and, together with the eager assistance of technical staff, contributed to the music's effective simplicity of gesture and high degree of finish. *Telemusik* is composed of 32 sections, varying in duration from 13 to 144 seconds (once again, structured to a Le Corbusian Fibonacci scale), each section a moment designed to be realized in one studio day.

The Tokyo studio made available a custom 6-track tape recorder, an advanced instrument for the era, allowing up to five tracks to be laid down independently and then mixed down to mono on the sixth track. Copying from one track to another did however introduce a delay of about 0.3 second, corresponding to the distance between replay and record tape heads, a delay that was only noticeable however if there were prerecorded tracks playing alongside. This "Zeitverzögerung" or time-delay effect proved an interesting challenge and analogous effects would later appear in *Hymnen* and *Tunnel-Spiral* as expressive devices. In addition to ring-modulators of conventional type, the NHK studio also offered a linear amplitude-modulator, enabling the amplitude envelope (or underlying rhythm) of one prerecorded signal to be imposed on a second signal already on a second channel. Whenever the information on one of the six channels was ring-modulated or amplitude-modulated, and the result copied onto a third channel, the 0.3 second delay effect played havoc with the channel alignment, as might be expected.

With one minor exception, the later addition to track I of sections

24–25, the composition was produced and assembled in the same order as the published score, which means that a listener equipped with the score is in a position to follow the train of Stockhausen's thought with unusual clarity. The composition can be understood as a study on two levels: technically, as an examination of attack and resonance relationships, resuming the percussion-oriented research of *Studie II*, and also as a series of further investigations into the possibilities of controlled ring-modulation, this time relatively free of unwanted side effects. Stockhausen's form-scheme is given a ritual and radiophonic character through the inclusion of instrumental sounds, and the modulation of electronic frequencies by excerpts of folk and ritual music from a variety of world cultures. Each new section (each new day's work) is introduced by the recorded sound of a Japanese ceremonial drum or gong: dry-sounding bokusho or taku beats for shorter sections, ringing rin or keisu strokes for longer sections, and the characteristic accelerating beat-pattern of the mogukyo drum from time to time injecting an element of dynamic momentum. It follows that each initiating drum or gong stroke signals the passage of time, and a change to a new procedure of intermodulation, or style of resonance. The work as a whole is designed to resemble a radio transmission from another planet, or the sounds of earth as they might be picked up from an approaching craft.

From the outset the printed score indicates a marked debt to *Studie II*: the same rectangular formations, the same opposition of short and long events, and of attacks and resonances, and the idea of attacks as "hard-edited" or interrupted resonances. An emphasis on cymbal-like radiances is another point of contact, the score's rounded art deco shapes revealing a new level of control over the phrasing and shaping of events, and a higher priority given to continuity of gesture and flow.

In *Telemusik* Stockhausen pushes the limits of modulation to greater extremes than *Mixtur*, taking the modulating frequency as high as 10 or even 12 kilohertz, and below 15 hertz, into the crossover region between pitch and rhythm (by coincidence, the same two frequency zones, of the auditory nerves and the heartbeat, famously identified by Cage from his experience of an anechoic chamber). This strategy, coupled with advanced processing, have contributed to the impressive cleanness of the *Telemusik* sound.

Though a significant presence, the traditional music woven into the musical fabric, including examples of gagaku music for the Imperial Court, folk music of Bali, the Amazonian Shipibos, and the South Sahara, tends to be well concealed and only rarely audible on the surface. A similar reticence in acknowledging borrowed material has already been noted in *Mixtur*, and would persist in the composer's ban on the use of unmodulated source material in *Kurzwellen*. After the absurd claims that followed his incorporation of a boy's voice in *Gesang der Jünglinge*, a reluctance to having the new work identified with the decorative aesthetic of musique concrète is very understandable. In declaring that "*Telemusik* is *not* a mere collage," Stockhausen wishes it to be known that what he recognizes in these borrowed examples of music from other cultures are universal models of vibrating structures, and not collector's items or mere cultural artifacts. The message, rather, is one of universal acoustical principles (pulsation, interference, inflection, transition) intuitively adopted by world cultures for ritual purposes, and thus valid expressions of binding realities.

Telemusik resembles *Mixtur* in many ways, for example passages where statistical point-complexes are attenuated and compressed, and in the similar role assigned to percussion. In all of Stockhausen's ring-modulated compositions from this period, the modulation process itself carries a strong emotional charge; in *Telemusik* for the first time, however, one hears electronic ululations in direct association with real sounds of lamentation of traditional cultures. Likewise in sections 15–17, layers superimposing material taken from sections 1, 4, 6, 7, 9, and 14, are lifted upwards one by one to merge into a hissing chroma of sound at the upper limit of audibility. This "resonance of consciousness" as we may call it (adapting Cage's metaphor) is sustained, with minute interior adjustments, into 16, a twilight sequence in which tiny arpeggiate figures are heard descending like flames of Pentecostal fire, and seem to alight on the listener's head before retreating upward once more. Similar gestures occur in *Kontakte*, but what makes them so wonderful here is the knowledge that the effect is not contrived, but a process discovered in real time with the actual material. Though coda-like in mood, it is followed at 29 by a regular "instrumental" recapitulation in which bokusho, mogukyo, rin, and keisu come together to beat a series of measured, cadential responses. A long (144-second) meditation on the sound of temple bells follows, and the piece ends with a sudden rush of upward glissandi like a flock of birds taking off, and the "Yo-ho!" cry, in this context distinctly triumphant, of a Noh percussionist.

Adieu (Adieu)

1966: No. 21 (UE 14877; cd Stockhausen-Verlag SV-4)
For wind quintet: flute, oboe, clarinet, horn, bassoon.
Duration: 11'–15'.

Written in memory of a young musician killed in a motor accident, *Adieu* draws on the speaking and breathing associations of these instruments. More explicitly than *Stop*, its dramatic form is based on images of interrupted movement:—incomplete cadences, simulated breaks in transmission, imitation of tuning from shortwave channel to channel in search of signs of life,—to express the idea of separation and bereavement. The work imitates "live" the studio manipulation of a "dead" tape recording, in doing so provoking reflection on the transience of experience. Often a listener has the impression of listening to a tape that has jammed, freezing the continuity of the music, and abruptly suspending perception of time, an effect capable in theory of being produced by the rotating-head "Springer-machine" in the Cologne studio,[16] or the equivalent *phonogène* developed by Jacques Poullin for Pierre Schaeffer.[17] These sudden arrests, which Stockhausen compares to the right-angle intersections of Piet Mondrian's paintings, add to the sense of unexpectedness (though a fatalism might be read into the fact that the interrupted fragments of music are themselves tonal cadences).

Long, drawn-out chords with microtonal fluctuations resemble those passages of *Telemusik* that sound like weeping. The instruments are all partials of a harmony of mutually supportive and destructive interference, for which individual amplification may be desirable, so that every possibility of intermodulation between the instruments can be clearly heard (as in *Stimmung*, where the six singers have separate microphones, and are also facing one another in a circle).

The work is constructed very simply in four sections of 144 time-units, three of which are subdivided in Fibonacci ratios:

$$
\begin{array}{cccc}
\overbrace{144} & \overbrace{144} & 144 & \overbrace{144} \\
89:55 & \underset{4}{55}:55:34 & 144 & \underset{8\ \ 4\ \ 4\ \ 4}{34}:\underline{13}:\underline{8}:\underline{34}:21:34
\end{array}
$$

Each division, represented by a barline in the score, marks a change affecting the whole ensemble (similar to *Telemusik*); the more frequent the changes, as towards the end, the more the time-structure imposes a shape and uniformity on the expressive content.

Stockhausen adds another expressive dimension in his composition of fermatas. Each "General Pause" in the score [ ] occupies the end element of a symmetrical formation, rendering it incomplete. At 6 the structure of subdivisions is 8–13–21–13–[8]; at 17, 2–3–5–(3+3)–(5+5)–(8+[8]); the "sehr lang" (very long) after 25 connects with the following formation: [13]–8–5–8–13; while the fermata at 29, together with the four pauses of varying length at the work's final cadence, may be interpreted as a descending series of silence durations [8–5–3–2–1] interlocked with a series of increasing music durations (5–8–13–21–34).

Right at the end there is a little hint of Bartók, the valedictory piping high b on piccolo in the final section of *Adieu*, that echoes the same gesture, also by piccolo, at the end of the melancholy third movement of the *Concerto for Orchestra*. Says Stockhausen,

> The music looks simple enough on paper, but I found out in 1969, rehearsing it for the first time myself in Paris, how difficult the work actually is. The dynamic balance between the instruments, free glissandi around a pitch, synchronized groups and fairly frequent fast changes of playing technique, require an ensemble in complete understanding and agreement. On top of that, the musicians have to be able to experience deeply and form into notes, the sense of closeness to death that vibrates in this music.[18]

Notes

1.   Gertrude Stein, "Portraits and Repetition." *Gertrude Stein: Writings and Lectures* ed. Patricia Meyerowitz (London: Peter Owen, 1967), 105–7.
2.   Claude Lévi-Strauss, "Language and Kinship." In *Structural Anthropology* tr. Claire Jacobson and Brooke Grundfest Schoepf (New York:

Basic Books, 1963), 49.

3. Friedrich Froebel, *The Education of Man* tr. W. N. Hailmann (London: Appleton, 1906), 42–43; 50–55.

4. *Texte 2*: 40–43.

5. Friedrich Froebel, *The Education of Man*, 2–3.

6. Mary Bouquet, *Reclaiming English Kinship: Portuguese Refractions of British Kinship Theory* (Manchester: Manchester University Press, 1993), 54–57.

7. *Texte 3*, 224.

8. *SoM*, 76–87.

9. It is not altogether clear that the technical production of the recorded version has taken account of the fact that the two channels of sound are effectively in opposite phase. An improved three-dimensional effect may be experienced by listening to the cd recording with one or other of the speaker outputs inverted, achieved by switching white and red connectors at the amplifier.

10. *Texte 3*, 52.

11. "Helmut Heissenbüttel," obituary by Philip Brady. *Independent*, London (25 September 1996).

12. Helmut Heissenbüttel, *Einfache Grammatische Meditationen* (Freiburg: Walter-Verlag, 1955). In English "Simple Grammatical Meditations" tr. Michael Hamburger. In *Texts* (London: Marion Boyars, 1977), 30–31.

13. Michael Nyman, *Experimental Music: Cage and Beyond* (London: Studio Vista, 1974), 131.

14. Henri-George Clouzot, *Mystery of Picasso* (1956).

15. "Musik und Sprache." Vocoder study by Herbert Eimert and Heinz Schütz. In Herbert Eimert, *Einführung in die elektronische Musik*, vinyl disc Wergo WER 60006, 1963.

16. A. M. Springer, "Ein akustischer Zeitregler." *Gravesaner Blätter* 1 (1955), 32–37.

17. Jacques Poullin, "Von der musikalischen Transmutation zur Klangprojektion aufgenommener Schallvorgänge." 97–102 in *Musik, Raumgestaltung, Elektroakustik* ed. Werner Meyer-Eppler. Mainz: Ars Viva, 1955.

18. *Texte 3*, 93.

CHAPTER FIFTEEN

Anthems

Two telling images sum up Jean Cocteau's magical film *Orphée*. One is the famous scene where Orpheus passes through the mirror to reach the underworld. Orpheus is the musician of classical mythology; his journey across the frontier of reality into a spiritual netherworld is no gratuitous act of tourism but a quest to recover his lost muse from limbo by the eloquence of his music and restore her to the land of the living. In a memoir Cocteau describes staging the scene where the surface of the mirror is magically transformed into a liquid allowing Orpheus and his companion to pass through to the underworld.[1] Today such a scene would be effected by computer, but in the austere postwar days of black and white such illusions had to be fabricated in real life. Orpheus looks at himself in a mirror. In the next shot the mirror has become a tank full of mercury, very expensive and highly dangerous. Orpheus's extended hands, protected by surgical gloves, are seen to approach and pass through the reflecting surface. This single shot is over in seconds but took an entire day to accomplish. Among many difficulties, the mercury tended to cloud over and had to be periodically polished to restore what Cocteau describes as its "soft, heavy" reflective surface. Working with mercury, there is also a danger of breathing in vapor or of stray mercury coming into contact with the skin. "Why go to these risks?" Cocteau was asked. "Because mercury shows only the reflection and not the part that has penetrated into the mirror, as water would have done. In mercury the hands disappear, and the gesture is accompanied by a kind of shiver, whereas water would have produced ripples and circles of waves. On top of that, mercury has resistance."[2]

To create a poetic illusion can involve great risks and feats of organization to achieve apparently casual effects. But hard work can make all the difference: to the viewer Orpheus *does* go through the mirror, because you see it happen, and that makes his journey into the underworld believable.

Cocteau's existentialist imagery summons up the mysterious vision of the artist di Chirico, in particular the famous canvas, like a backdrop to an empty stage, in which a Greek statue suggesting an enduring memory of time past and a rather large bunch of bananas representing a transitory present are discovered side by side in a timeless urban piazza rendered in the distorted perspective of opera with a departing steam train silhouetted on the horizon.[3] The image of travel hints at the same promise of escape from the logic of history to a new beginning and a new world as the movie of Honegger's *Pacific 231* and Pierre Schaeffer's pioneering sound effects composition *Étude aux chemins de fer*. The journey across cultures is also a subtext of *Hymnen*.

In another famous scene in *Orphée*, Orpheus is travelling by car through the mysterious landscape of the underworld. It is the dead of night, but the scene of night outside is actually a negative print, the mysterious antithesis of a daylight view down a tree-lined avenue. As the car speeds silently along, delphic remarks are heard from a radio in the dashboard, obscure clues in a secret code that heighten a viewer's sense of alienation and anticipation. That sense of embarking on a dangerous journey, travelling in the dark toward an unknown destination guided only by coded fragments of messages relayed from another world is the 20th-century equivalent of Arthurian legend, where the gods are represented by radio and the task of the hero is not only to achieve a particular goal but to learn how to navigate safely and interpret the messages encountered on the way. The myth extends from Saint-Exupéry's *Night Flight* to Stanley Kubrick's *2001: a Space Odyssey* (another journey that ends enigmatically with the sound of heavy breathing), and from the fictitious endless journey of *Star Trek*, to real-life dramas of search and rescue.

For Cocteau's Orpheus tale mercury is the reflective medium by which the hero gains entry to the underworld. But in his guise as messenger of the gods Mercury is also the god of radio communication, not just of the mobile phone, and it is through the medium of radio, both as radio drama and also as telecommunication, that we discover a perspective on Stockhausen's *Hymnen* (Anthems), a rich composition for four-channel tape which takes the listener on the flight deck for an epic journey where the only means of orientation in the aural stratosphere is radio and where survival depends on recognising call-signs and making connections. Whether Stockhausen is a fan of Cocteau or not I have no idea. There are echoes of the motorcycles of Cocteau's messengers of Hades in *Orphée*, in the rotating sounds of landing and liftoff in Stockhausen's "Close encounters" space oratorio *Sirius*, and a real moped makes an appearance in the composer's gagaku-inspired *Der Jahreslauf* (The Course of the Years)—now Act I of *Dienstag aus LICHT*. These could be just odd coincidences. But the radiophonic connection with myth and dreams is absolutely certain: they are the message of the medium, to paraphrase McLuhan.

The point was vividly brought home to me on a visit to Cologne some years ago when I stepped out of the train late at night and into a cab, an old

Mercedes bristling with aerials and reeking inside of diesel and cigarettes. It was midwinter, just after midnight and miserably cold. The taxi dashboard, a miniature landscape of lights of every color, looked like an airplane cockpit display, and the intercom speaker emitted a continuous stream of overlapping transmissions as if monitoring every available radio channel simultaneously, some voice, some music. The idea of navigating through this communications maze added an extra dimension of excitement to an otherwise routine journey. Who else could the driver be listening to? Was he on the alert for distress calls? What could be happening at this normally dead time of night to generate all of this electronic activity? It was like stepping into the opening shortwave chaos of *Hymnen*, and I realised that the composer was not simply making it up: this was a chaos he must have experienced many times in real life.

The essential parameters of radio drama were outlined as long ago as 1924 in a curious little book, *Broadcasting from Within*, designed to win over a skeptical public to the idea of public service broadcasting. Its author was Cecil Lewis, the last survivor of the original management team of the fledgling British Broadcasting Company—in fact he died in 1997 at the ripe old age of 98.[4] A poet and playwright, Lewis saw exciting potential in the new medium, applications far ahead of what technology was able to deliver. In a chapter called "Stereoscopic broadcasting" he writes of the possibility of listening to a Shakespeare play or an opera performance in stereo using two transmitters broadcasting on different frequencies, adding that the listener would be put to the expense of obtaining two crystal sets, one for each channel. Elsewhere he develops the idea of a new art of radio,

> largely narrative in form, given in a series of sound pictures and linked up by a Voice which carries story and action forward, depending largely for its effect on the realism of the various atmospheres produced by the noises transmitted. . . . Scenes can be set from one end of the world to the other. They must develop quickly, each character being sharply contrasted in tone; for the listener, blinded as he is, cannot concentrate indefinitely on any [one] theme, however enthralling it may be. There must be, also, a very limited number of characters or else the hearer soon becomes mazed in a whirl of voices and argument out of which he can make no order or purpose.[5]

Hymnen (Anthems)

1966–1967: No. 22 (formerly UE 15142, now Stockhausen-Verlag; cd SV-10)
Electronic and concrete music.
Duration: 1 hour 53'.

Hymnen mit Solisten (Anthems with soloists)

1966–1967: No. 22 ½ (formerly UE 15143, now Stockhausen-Verlag; cd SV-10)
Electronic and concrete music, with five solo musicians.
Duration: 1 hour 53'.

Hymnen (Dritte Region mit Orchester) (Third Region of *Hymnen* with Orchestra)

1969: No. 22⅔ (formerly UE 15145, now Stockhausen-Verlag; cd SV-47)
Electronic and concrete music with orchestra.
For 2, 3, or 4 × flutes, oboes, clarinets, bassoons, horns I (high), horns II (low); trumpets, trombones; 1 or 2 tubas; strings 10.10.10.5.5, or in proportion.
Duration 38'.

In 1965 Stockhausen had taken over the artistic directorship of the WDR electronic studios from Herbert Eimert. After the austere perfection of his earlier electronic music, which was only then becoming available on disc, his new involvement in ring-modulation, in *Mikrophonie II* and *Mixtur*, seemed to be playing with dangerously complex material and deliberately taking risks in the hope of unforeseen results. Despite *Hymnen*'s more congenial agenda and cleaner sound, it was still not easy at the time to discern any procedural or intellectual consistency between the earlier, "purer" electronic works and the new work, in which the composer was overtly employing the very kind of ready-made musical images he and Boulez had publicly renounced so many years before.

Hymnen started life as a sequel to *Kontakte* in which a tape was to play a continuous backdrop of radiophonic and electronic sounds and a small number of players on stage would react to them and bring them as it were "down to earth." Stockhausen was building on what he had originally intended for *Kontakte*: a relationship of tape as database to musicians as independent operators, able to select, imitate, and freely combine musical tones and gestures continuously available on tape. On that earlier occasion in 1959 it was clear that the players were uncomfortable working in such a way with unfamiliar material, and so the idea was abandoned for the time being and a fixed score of instrumental parts composed for the version of *Kontakte* with instruments. Stockhausen's adoption of national anthems for the new composition could thus be interpreted as a device to provide his soloists (and audience) with easily recognizable materials of a kind that classically-trained musicians would relate to and be able to transform freely in an ongoing process of musical dialogue.

Aesthetically *Hymnen* shares a heritage of radio drama not only with *musique concrète* but also with Berio and the neorealists such as Cage whose chance compositions are a calculated rejoinder to the permanence of recording. The world of radio drama is a world of interior monologue. It is the same world of memory as can be experienced by anybody reading a novel. The logic of any narrative event or argument is somebody else's interior monologue. Either you enter into that perception of events or you hitch a ride on it and find an alternative interpretation that fits what you want to discover. Art is like that. There is nothing special or novel in the underlying idea that the tape or the radio or the interactive disc inhabits a different world, or parallel universe, and that what we make of that information defines our interior world.

But we all know too that the world through the looking glass is one where time runs differently or not at all and normal distinctions no longer obtain. It is true of all looking glass worlds, whether it be Orpheus's silver screen, or Lewis Carroll's mirror over the mantelpiece, or your neighbor's wide-screen television, or the computer games arcade at a motorway service station. In all of these worlds things are not what they seem: they change shape and assume different, sometimes menacing identities. In *Hymnen* the national anthems that act as navigational beacons are liable to slip, slide and change from moment to moment. In television we know it as "morphing:" Constable Odo turns into a hatstand, a thermos flask into an unspeakable alien. We observe real-life morphing in speeded-up nature films where a pupating caterpillar dances a jig and changes into a butterfly, or a dead mouse on the sand evaporates in a flurry of maggots to become a scrap of carpet. A line such as Shakespeare's "Bare ruined choirs, where late the sweet birds sang" derives its poetic force, as William Empson reminds us in *Seven Types of Ambiguity*, from the fact that in poetry we do not grasp words such as "choirs" or "birds" simply by their literal meanings but interpret them as multiple images capable of oscillating from one meaning to another.[6]

Hymnen is Stockhausen's fifth major electronic composition and his first to employ prerecorded material on a large scale. Composed in 1966–1967, it is a product of the 1960s, and by virtue of being based on national anthems combined in various hierarchies and transformed one into another, may be understood in superficial respects as music with an overriding political message of reflection and reconciliation at a time of student revolution, Vietnam, the Cold War, and other issues of mass protest and mass celebration. For listeners who remember those times *Hymnen* may arouse familiar memories. For a younger audience these associations are less relevant. But for any listener the musical meaning of Stockhausen's concrete sounds is not just what they say or signify but what they are acoustically; —indeed, in order to grasp what the sounds are in acoustical reality, the ideal way of listening is to empty one's mind of what the sounds represent. The same applies to the anthems themselves. In that way a listener can become aware of certain sounds not just as high-pitched, but as fast-moving, and other sounds not only as low in pitch but as slow-moving, and from that understanding move on to realize that sounds that are low in pitch can be transformed into sounds of high pitch, and vice versa, by a change of speed. In one particularly famous sequence a tinselly rattle slows down and becomes recognisable as a cheering crowd and then slows down further to merge with the sound of quacking ducks, and at the end of this sequence (Region II, 2' 30; cd 1, track 14) the composer mischievously adds a solo duck quacking the "Marseillaise": this is after all a part of the music where the French anthem is in the ascendant.

The work consists of four regions, the term a spatial analogue to "movements" in the classical sense. As originally conceived, there were going to be many more, the present state containing only some 40 of the 137 anthems originally collected. So, like *Gesang der Jünglinge* and *Kontakte* before it, *Hymnen* is complete but unfinished, a journey to be resumed in

1978 with "Michaels Reise um die Erde."

In a spirit of reconciliation, each of the four regions is dedicated to a friend and composer. Region I, the most uncompromising in its use of alien radiophonic material, is dedicated to Boulez, whose own rallying cry "Il faut considérer le délire, et, oui, l'organiser" (One should take delirium seriously, and, yes, organize it) from the 1958 essay "Son et Verbe" could stand as its epigraph.[7] Out of a confusion of radiophonic distortion (which the fastidious Boulez had disliked intensely in *Mixtur*) emerges a sense of definition and form, thanks to the saving grace of serialism. Boulez is the figure of discipline, the intellectual imposing order on chaos.

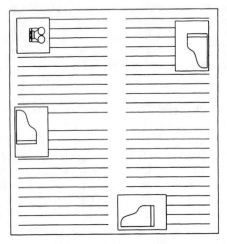

Hymnen: *Stockhausen's sketch of an early conception of the work for tape and three pianists, suggesting a tetrahedral speaker array.*

Pousseur, dedicatee of Region II, is associated with the character of the casino croupier who breaks into the musical action from time to time with a "Faîtes votre jeu, Mesdames, Messieurs." The usual form of words is plural, "Faîtes vos jeux," the singular form perhaps alluding to an initial conception of *Hymnen* as an open-form composition available to be cut and rearranged to suit a movie or ballet, but only by one group at a time. "The work (as originally announced) is composed in such a way that different libretti or scenarios for films, operas, and ballets can be compiled for this music. The arrangement of the individual parts and the total duration are variable. Regions can be interchanged,—depending on dramatic requirements,— extended, or omitted."[8] (These options were later withdrawn). As well as recalling the Ringmaster in Berg's *Lulu*, and the card-playing devil in Stravinsky's *Jeu de Cartes* (another work of humor that incorporates "found objects"), the croupier is also a pivotal figure in Pousseur's open-form opera *Votre Faust*, to a libretto by Michel Butor, during which the audience is invited at key points to vote on how the plot shall continue. (The Belgian composer had been struggling with the ramifications of a plot with multiple outcomes since 1961; the opera was finally completed in 1969). Another interruption, the spoken "Rouge, rouge" moment (at 9' 25,5" of Region I, track 5 on cd 1) during which the composer and three colleagues are heard reciting variations on the color red (for Russia) in several languages and also in mock plainchant,—on the surface sounds like a private joke at the expense of Pousseur, who had decided to embrace Marxism: it recalls the litanies on "Hélas!" in Pousseur's *Électre*, a ballet from 1960, and on a street name in the composer's *Trois Visages de Liège* of 1961.[9] (Pousseur returns the compliment in *Le Tarot d'Henri*, a piano solo from his opera in which the character Henri Faust, a composer, makes a not very convincing stylistic journey from Bach to the serialism of the sixties.)

The dedication of Region IV to Berio is easy to understand in terms of the Italian composer's devotion to James Joyce; at this time Berio was in the process of adding further movements to *O King* to make *Sinfonia*, of which the third movement, "In ruhig fliessender Bewegung," is rightly celebrated as a virtuoso exercise in the stream-of-consciousness integration of musical themes from Bach to Stockhausen. Cage, dedicatee of the Third Region, which has a US center, is associated (rather loosely, one would think) with the Region's "fleeting collages and pluralistic mixtures," but there are alternative US connections as well, in particular with pioneer experiments by researchers at Bell Labs into the development of computer software to allow for the transformation of melody *gestalten* by probabilistic means.

Stockhausen acknowledges *Hymnen* as "electronic and concrete music," a gesture apparently reconciling the old antagonisms between Paris and Cologne. To be sure, a national anthem is the perfect example of a Schaefferian "musical object" for transformational analysis: a composition of limited length having a distinct identity; a music symbolizing nationhood and capable of triggering all kinds of emotional responses; also a music that functions as a call-sign or communications signal both at a live event and on radio. All of this allows us to see Stockhausen's musical interests in *Hymnen* in terms of the wider issue of information science through the fifties and sixties, as exemplified in the US researches of Max Mathews, Hiller and Isaacson, John von Neumann and others. This was a wide-ranging collective investigation into the deconstruction and reformulation of coherent musical sentences, and it focused quite deliberately on national anthems and folk melodies as sources of the basic units of musical speech. A paper by Max Mathews and L. Rosler of Bell Labs presented at the Fall 1966 San Francisco Joint Computer Conference deals with the transformation by computer of the United Kingdom military anthem "The British Grenadiers" into the corresponding US marching song "When Johnny comes marching home." In a second example, titled "International lullaby," a familiar Schubert melody is "transcended" (the authors' term) "by means of time-varying weighted averages of frequency and duration functions" into a pentatonic Japanese melody.

> The title is a fitting one as this example combines lullabies from distinctly different cultures, Japanese and German. Instead of playing both

tunes simultaneously—as Charles Ives would probably have preferred
—Mathews transcends [sic] between them by means of time-varying
weighted averages of frequency and duration functions corresponding to
each melody. While the Schubert cradle song is in the ordinary Western
key of C, the Japanese lullaby is written in a pentatonic scale using only
the notes C, D, E flat, G, and A flat.[10]

These examples, produced in Bell Labs, are musically speaking unbelievably
banal: they have perhaps some psychological interest but no aesthetic merit
whatever, and the barren Music IV square-wave sonorities in which they
are recorded are equally impoverished. The whole point of the exercise lies
in the transformation process of one melody into another. (Stockhausen's
equivalent scene,—in Region III, 2. Center, cd 2, tracks 6–7,—involves a
transition between British and Japanese anthems, by way of the US "Battle
Hymn of the Republic," a juxtaposition to be read in a number of ways.)

   In this context one can also interpret *Hymnen*,—a major-length tape
composition dating from exactly the same period and sharing exactly the
same intellectual premises as the Mathews/Rosler paper,—as a magisterial response from the German musical and intellectual tradition to a US
cold war agenda of speech recognition and translation, the difference being
that whereas the US effort is focused on one thing only (the process) and is
deliberately lacking in aesthetic or human interest, from the same starting-
point Stockhausen has generated an extraordinary musical composition that
at the same time comprehensively addresses the same underlying issues of
melody synthesis by interpolation and substitution programming.

   The banality of Mathews' musical examples is deceptive. In *Hymnen*
also. Simple subjects, as in a fugue, are chosen to allow for transformation,
and also to allow the listener to follow the transformation process. The
melody transformation processes employed in *Hymnen*, in versions both for
tape alone and tape with soloists, are dramatically and musically analogous
to techniques of improvisation from the silent movie era. (In fact one has to
wonder about the influence of the silent movie era on the musical perceptions of information scientists of the fifties.) A technique of creating hybrid
anthems by the forcible interpolation or interpenetration of one into another
may seem about as fantastical as creating a Frankenstein out of body parts,
—and as dependent on the life-giving power of electricity. But one does not
have to look far for a musical, albeit low-art, precedent for Stockhausen's
melodic transformations both here in *Hymnen*, and as specified in *Prozession*, *Kurzwellen*, and thereafter. Mention of the movies is a reminder of the
art of montage and its basis in the psychology of memory, as elaborated at
some length by Sergei Eisenstein in his classic text *Film Sense*.[11] Once
again the thought arises of Stockhausen drawing inspiration from an
earlier era of mechanical art.

   The procedure might be described, from one point of view, as "free
   variation" form, but the term "metamorphosis of theme" is more correct,
   as the procedure necessitates the *development* of ideas with continuity.
   The theme should contain phrases or "figures" which, taken as separate

"fragments" will provide material for development. In "metamorphosis of theme" the player will either devise variants of the theme itself, or utilise portions—"fragments"—which lend themselves to development, such metamorphoses being designed in accordance with the characteristics of the scene portrayed. [The player] must be able to bring his mind completely *en rapport* with the photo-play; to quickly "size up" the scenes, and seize upon the important idea and the "point" of the scene. Skilful "timing" of the music to the action is essential; even a second is often of vital importance in this, and a second lost in introducing a dramatic effect can ruin a dramatic scene, and even reduce it to an absurdity.[12]

One's immediate response to a work of music with national anthems as major characters is to think conflict, conflict-resolution, peace, love, the sixties,—and leave it at that. But the roots of *Hymnen* penetrate deep into the art and film of the twentieth century, from the fantastic visual anamorphisms of Meliès to the collages of Picasso, Braque and Schwitters, and the frottages of Max Ernst. Stockhausen has spoken of the visual artist's powers of illusion and in particular of Jasper Johns's painterly transformations of the map of the United States and the Stars and Stripes; also of Robert Rauschenberg's ability to create new associations from juxtaposing the most unlikely objects: a tire, a stuffed goat.[13] In many ways *Hymnen* can be seen as applying the techniques of these artists,—the incorporation of "real" objects into the artwork, the deliberate distressing and distortion of the familiar,—to musical objects which have equally strong powers of association. In that sense *Hymnen* seems closer to Dalí than Schwitters, its poetry through-composed metamorphosis, and not simply cut and stick.

The characters in the dramatic landscape of *Hymnen* are national anthems. Some are relatively familiar: those of the USA, France, Britain, Germany, Austria; a greatly-expanded Russian anthem provides a superstructure; other melodies are less familiar, those from African nations: Egypt, the Gambia. There is a moment of tension when the "Horst Wessel-Lied" unexpectedly surfaces, and in one of several interruptions of the musical flow the composer, in his role as the Voice, is heard to observe that despite its painful associations the Nazi rallying song is also part of the German national heritage: it is a memory ("Es ist eine Erinnerung"). These anthems with their familiar historical and cultural associations meet and interact, and from time to time they seem to exchange identities or merge to produce hybrid offspring. The audience follows this celestial debate as it were from a distance. Stockhausen's experience of long-distance flight over the United States is a helpful guide to the timescale of a work where instead of modulating from key to key the music travels from continent to continent, a movement expressed as a change in musical perspective from anthem to anthem,—even though a journey that begins, as in this case, with the "Internationale," and ends with the Swiss anthem, is one that starts from a music that represents everywhere but nowhere, and ends at a place that is politically neutral, a point of no return.

The work's grand scale is also closer to the fifties than the sixties: one thinks of the huge tapestries of Jackson Pollock and the monumental canvases of Robert Motherwell as well as the vast prairies of the films of John Ford. In years to come the spirit of Stockhausen's cinemascopic soundscapes will re-emerge in the "Unsichtbare Chöre" of *Donnerstag aus LICHT* and the "Orchester-Finalisten" of *Mittwoch*, but it also looks back to the surreal dance interludes of Vincente Minnelli musicals of the fifties, or ballet sets of the same period by Noguchi where the world is a flat plain with lines converging on the horizon, dotted with silent cactus-like figures out of Henry Moore and Hans Arp that cast long shadows in the twilight. Nor is the landscape entirely bleak either: at times the listener is transported into a sketch by Saul Steinberg where a thumbprint becomes a grizzled face, and a french curve a mysterious cloud in the sky. In "Third Region of *Hymnen* with Orchestra," a region dominated by a synthesized Russian anthem, one is able to hear Stockhausen connecting with the tradition and timescale of Bruckner and Mahler, as well as with the humor of Beethoven (of the *Variations on "God Save the King"*).

In a conventional symphony the instruments and tempos are a listener's points of reference, and themes and key changes the variables; here in *Hymnen* the anthems are your guide and what one might call "ways of hearing" the variables. The anthems are glimpsed, then hidden; stretched and compressed in time; moved up and down in pitch; muffled, interwoven, overlaid, pulverised, sliced ("zerhackt") and recombined. From time to time the musical fabric is ripped asunder; at other times all there is to hear is ringing in one's ears, or something very close. Highly accelerated events can be discovered in the midst of the very slow, and moments of extreme stasis within a context of enormous turbulence. In Region II, Centre 1, having survived a brutal editing process to reach the first cadence of the Austrian anthem, the choir suddenly freezes in mid-chord, its harmony slowly pulled apart as if on a gigantic rack. Or Region IV, "Feed-back" (5' 47,3") a period of calm where the composer imagines himself once again as a boy, lying under a tree, listening to the sound of a small airplane circling overhead.

In the final part of *Hymnen*, Region IV, the clouds lift and the sense of landscape returns more powerfully. Stockhausen has expressed a liking for the films of Antonioni, whose *Blow-Up* expresses a kindred fascination with the possibilities of discovery in the technical enlargement of mundane images. It is possible to hear in the composer's voice calling "Ma-ka!"—an echo of the search for the lost girl in Antonioni's *L'Avventura*: "An-na!"—that in context is also a cry from the heart. Here too we feel closer to the composer of *Déserts* and *Poème électronique*, another kindred spirit and almost a father figure. The music is overwhelmed by a sense of desolation expressed in a paradoxical ever-descending cluster of metallic sonorities resembling the sound of a low-flying passenger jet passing overhead. An acoustic illusion adapted from Jean-Claude Risset,[14] it is based on an inversion of the ever-ascending "Shepard Scale" of 1964.[15]

In both *Hymnen mit Solisten* and "Third Region of *Hymnen* with Orchestra" the tape functions as a "silent movie" to which the musicians have to respond, and since the recorded material is itself musical, to select, imitate, and develop material. The procedures involved are akin to the later plus-minus scores. For the 1969 score for orchestra, composed for the New York Philharmonic, Leonard Bernstein's orchestra that had previously come to terms with graphic scores by Feldman and others, Stockhausen's notations for transformation, combining abbreviated verbal instructions and conventional symbols, are relatively uncomplicated, but generated considerable resistance from musicians unused to imitating sounds on tape.

> They have signs, such as T, which means, listen, pick out a single tone and repeat it. Then I give a sign to show how fast it should be repeated, whether the player maintains the pitch or transposes it, slowly upwards and downwards, or whether he repeats it periodically and then speeds up the repetitions or slows them down. The same applies to signs like IN —pick out an interval, or GR—pick out a group of notes, and so on. . . . And these strips form a polyphony with the music that is already on tape.[16]

Although imitative in a literal sense, the mass effects produced by the orchestra are undeniably poetic. Stockhausen treats the orchestra primarily as a *resonating* medium. There are no keyboards nor indefinite-pitch percussion instruments:—in fact, no instruments of invariant pitch at all. All players are required to make adjustments in tuning to harmonize with the frequent microtonal alterations of pitch on the recorded tape. The intention seems to be to create textures through multiplication of numbers, like sparks flying from a grindstone. The orchestral music as a whole is a succession of contrasting episodes cut to the proportions of the electronic music and completely dependent on it. The effect of the orchestral additions is to retard, sustain, divert, or enhance the tape imagery by "feedback" repetition, sympathetic resonance, progressive deviation of pitch or tempo, or in other ways.

"Third Region" begins at the third Center of Region II, following the pregnant pause after the spoken words "Wir können noch eine Dimension tiefer gehn" (we can go one dimension deeper still). A number of African anthems are imitated, first discreetly, then more confidently. After some three minutes, an immensely distended Russian anthem moves into center stage, reflected by the orchestra in constantly-changing instrumental colors. At 17, the entry of the Cameroon anthem, 7' 19" in the score, the pointillistic surface texture against sustained electronic harmonies is reminiscent of *Spiel* and *Punkte 1952*, with the difference that the "points" are now melodic fragments repeating over and over, gradually disintegrating into the flux.

At 7' 39" an upward surge in the tape is accompanied by a three-part glissando of string harmonics, the first of several appearances of a high radio static effect that doubles as a change-of-waveband signal. This marks the end of Region II and a hiatus during which, in performances of the version for tape alone, there is a short intermission. After the break the music re-enters with a 27-second downward surge, as though the reverse of the previous upward movement, as the music "tunes in" again to a continuation of the Russian anthem. Into this silence Stockhausen inserts a specially-composed section for orchestra alone, called the "Russian Bridge." Between four and five minutes in duration, the Russian Bridge consists of three principal musical processes, 1. a sustained, slowly expanding chord played by muted strings, leading out of the previous fade-out of the Russian anthem, 2. woodwinds and brass repetitions of these same pitches at irregular intervals, gradually diverging in pitch and periodicity to create a halo effect (not dissimilar in principle from *Ylem's* image of an expanding universe), and 3. anthem fragments, also played by woodwind and brass, sporadically inserted into the glissando texture. Like figure 9 in *Adieu*, which it closely resembles, this is played at an ethereal pianissimo, and even the anthem fragments are played "just loud enough to be recognizable." The slow and powerful impact of this huge transition is like the uncertain feeling associated with lifting off in a great aircraft, a sense of hiatus between being earthbound and airborne. One consequence of the loss of tonal fixity is a change in character of the anthem fragments, which now appear to be radio call-signs, emotionally and spatially detached.

Prozession (Procession)

1967: No. 23 (UE 14812; cd Stockhausen-Verlag SV-11)
For four-part ensemble (e.g., tam-tam, viola, electronium, piano, 2 microphones, 2 filters and potentiometers; 6 performers).
Duration 30+'.

A programmed structure of transformations, indeterminate in length, *Prozession* is the first of a series of compositions in which the idea of object displacement takes precedence over definition. The score, published in separate parts, and principally notated in plus, minus, and equal signs, reduces the complicated symbolism of the original *Plus-Minus,*—and even that of *Mikrophonie I*, with its nuanced conception of relative difference, —to a bare minimum. The work is designed to allow performers to build on earlier Stockhausen compositions, drawing figures from memory and subjecting them to transformations of scale, dynamic, rhythm, timbre, and other dimensions. Although these source works are not specified, *Kontakte* and *Hymnen* are the obvious candidates for transformation; by not singling out these two works Stockhausen may however be indicating that *Prozession* has its own distinct agenda.

Since content is lacking, discussion is bound to address the implications of a system of notation that deals only in interval relationships, and that only in a very general sense. Standard notation is essentially points on a graph; the music being realized by a performer results from joining the points to create a pattern of modulated gesture in which an audience may discern emotional or physical significance. Stockhausen's plus-minus notation here looks back to the transformational processes available in musique concrète and described by Schaeffer as "new musical processes . . . discovered in the alignment of a series of musical objects bearing an intrinsic relationship one with another. . . . A complex note, a point in the scale, a letter in the alphabet of sounds, a whole word, or even a phrase of a new musical language, . . . heard once, twice, three times in succession, describing any desired gradient of intensity, [that] could amount in itself to a miniature work, or at least the self-contained fragment of a work."[17]

Plus, equal, and minus signs correspond, in the domain of musical content, with the onset, steady state, and decay in the domain of the musical envelope, and indeed, to *anacrouse–accent–désinence* in the structure of a unit syllable. The conception of a music of modified repetitions also revisits Messiaen's simple processes of growth and diminution in "Reprises par Interversion" (not to mention Stravinsky's in *Le Sacre du Printemps*,—or, better still, the Introduction to *Firebird*; Scene 3 and Finale of *Petrushka*; and the second of *Three Pieces for String Quartet*). Such a conception is based on two fundamentals: 1. reiteration of material, and 2. continuity independent of the musical action. Reiteration is self-evident: something that is not repeated cannot be perceived to change. Continuity independent of the musical action is harder to grasp, and involves a conception of time relating to mechanical models. Conventionally, a musical performance, in addition to whatever other meanings it may convey, is a description or depiction of a temporal process. A movement (fast, slow) is just that, an image of human action with temporal implications. A dance movement by Rameau in principle is a template for people to move to; likewise a song by Schumann controls the pace and intensity of delivery of a text, and thus its emotional impact, which is also an experience of time.

A notation of plus, minus, and equal signs can imply either relationships that obtain between independent entities (first subject, second subject), or alternatively, represent dynamic changes of state (before and after). Sometimes the distinction is not always clear. Beethoven created a style out of insistent repetition, for rhetorical effect, for emotional effect, and also because he was deaf. Wagner's greatest contribution to musical technique is arguably his genius for conveying emotional development in real time, rather than episodically, in snapshots, in the classical manner; but to do so he also introduced the *leitmotif*. Varèse employs transformational repetitions, for instance in *Intégrales*, and is perhaps closest of all to Stockhausen in this respect. (All the same, one cannot escape an Orwellian sense of hierarchy in a system according to which some things are more positive, greater, or more equal than others.)

Plus, minus, and equal signs in *Prozession* are interpreted in the following way:

+ higher *or* louder *or* longer *or* more sections (*Glieder*: limbs);
− lower *or* softer *or* shorter *or* less sections;
= the same pitch (register) *and* volume *and* duration *and* tone-color *and* number of sections.[18]

"Higher" and "lower" denote exact pitch transpositions; "louder" and "softer" refer to amplitude, but as a mechanical conception (volume control), rather than a change of emphasis (action), that would result in a change of timbre.

"More" and "less" (fewer) sections, which might seem to imply a change of overall duration, in fact refers to *tempo*:

> A length can be subdivided into any desired number of sections. When relating a sign to this number, + means an increase in the number of sections (the rhythm accelerates within the constant length); = the number remains the same; – the number of sections is decreased [the length remaining constant]. Furthermore, under + the rhythmic and melodic subdivisions should become more complicated, under – simpler, and under = they should remain more or less the same.[19]

Perhaps "density" would be better than "number," likewise "complexity" than "rhythm." Much of Stockhausen's terminology is actually counter-intuitive. The sign "Per" stands for "periodic," but what is actually required is not exact repetition of a phrase, but a gradual elimination of inequalities in the internal rhythm, leading to all notes being the same length—a Messiaen "interversion," in other words, or gradual simplification of the mode of vibration, corresponding to the behavior of a vibrating string after it has been struck or plucked.

In order to clarify the interactive process which is what *Prozession* is all about (interacting with oneself, and with others), it would certainly be useful to provide each instrumentalist with a personal feedback, *Solo*-style tape loop or sampling device in order to hear back what has just been played, over sound-transparent headphones, after a short delay; perhaps even to see it displayed as a graphic on a laptop as well. (The process is easier to imagine in graphic than acoustic terms.) In some such way the player would be helped to control the imitation and mutation process, and to keep track of the development of changes within the individual voice, and within the group. From the score an ideal performance can be envisaged, in the manner of a dance of musical objects, moving around one another, interacting, and mutating; a process analogous to interpolation in computer animation. That Stockhausen does not express his intentions in quite these terms is not altogether his fault: in 1967, personal computing was still a long way off.

No full score was originally published because the four parts are not always synchronized; nevertheless they are equivalent in structure and "work-load," each consisting of 250 symbols or symbol combinations representing successive stages of transformation, and gathered in turn into multiples of ten symbols: 18 (or 19) for viola, 19 for tam-tam, and 20 each for piano and electronium.[20] These major subdivisions are indicated by heavy barlines, and visible changes in the pattern and combination of symbols. At different times one instrument gives the lead, and the others imitate it, either in register (R), or dynamic envelope (I), or duration (D) or internal rhythm (G: meaning *Glieder*, or number of components). On occasion two or more parameters are simultaneously imitated. These episodes act like cadences, counteracting a tendency toward fragmentation and dispersion inherent in the process.

The individual part-writing is deceptively simple, with a marked predominance of simple changes, relating to only one parameter at a time. Symmetrical formations are abundant. One two-layer structure "Im gleichen Parameter" (in the same two parameters) occurs once in each part and appears to function as a kind of refrain. Another recurrent structure consists of a collection of ten plus signs followed by ten minus signs, though

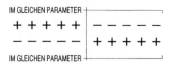

a change of lead instrument at the critical juncture can introduce a rogue element.

Mirror-image relationships between parts are unexpectedly abundant, though in the circumstances these are bound to be speculative rather than real. Their purpose appears to be to emphasize an underlying organization that strongly conforms to human perceptions of sameness or difference, rather than as the result of a purely mechanical or permutational process. The evidence of "intention" is itself clearly intentional.

The idea of *Prozession* is appealing in theory but incomplete in practical terms. An ever-present danger, given the freedom of choice, is loss of coherence. If, as the composer may have originally intended, all four performers were to draw material from the same ongoing source, such as a tape of *Kontakte* or *Hymnen,*—even if the audience were unable to hear it,—it seems there would be a good possibility of synchronized if divergent dialogue, and a better probability of spontaneous connections. (That in fact is one conclusion to be drawn from the comparative success of "Third Region of *Hymnen* with Orchestra," with the tape as a unifying presence and aided by more specialized notations.) A second difficulty and reminder of Stockhausen's problems of serial dynamics since the *Konkrete Etüde*, has to do with noncompatabilities of scale among the various parameters, something that Messiaen had already understood at the time of *Mode de valeurs*. And although arithmetical signs imply a logical process, what is actually depicted in musical terms is a succession of states in strict linear relationship, like a movie, or a legal argument in which there is no room for ambiguity.

In 1966, however, Mathews and Rosler were adamant that their software marked a significant advance toward the automatic generation of music by computer. The algorithms involved were robust, easy to use, and required neither learning programs nor random processes.

> We expect that much of the music of the future will be scored graphically. . . . Many of the details of generating individual notes need not be completely written out. The composer can control the loudness, tempo, and number of voices by simple global functions that directly express his musical intentions. . . . However the result is sequences of sound that are unplanned in fine detail by the composer, even though the over-all structure of the section is completely and precisely specified. Thus the composer is often surprised, and pleasantly surprised, at the details of the realization of his ideas.[21]

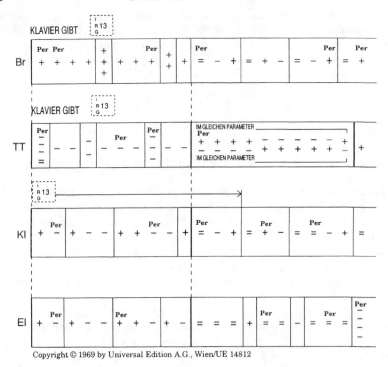

Prozession: *reconstructed section of a "full score."*

Less obvious to the reader is that Mathews and Rosler's paper ultimately has to do with *grammatical* structure. The authors are not composers and not interested in music per se, only in music as a simplified model of a generalizable linguistic process. A software that allows new musical melodies to be created spontaneously suggests the possibility of an analogous language software being created to enable a mechanical device to communicate intelligently with a human being, like a speak your weight machine, or an airline booking service (or voicemail, which rather spoils the joke). The test of an intelligent machine, in René Descartes' definition, was whether it had the ability "to use speech or other signs as we do," and above all "[to arrange] its speech in a variety of ways in order to reply appropriately to everything that may be said in its presence, as even the lowest type of human being can do."[22]

At this point Stockhausen's earlier studies under Meyer-Eppler assume a deeper significance. What the composer recalls as "exercises demonstrating the principles of the Markoff series,"[23] can now be seen as studies in the grammatical logic proposed by Shannon and Weaver to allow the meaning of a sentence to be decided in purely structural terms. A grammatical sentence in a language is defined as a succession of states, and the meaning of a sentence, in terms of the gradient of transitions between successive states. The "finite state Markoff process" assigns a probability to each transition from state to state, a freedom of selection increasingly limited as a sentence nears completion. To understand the intention of *Prozession* as the creation of new musical sentences by transformation processes from existing material, (which is what the work in fact is), is thus to see the work as a musical critique of communications research having implications for linguistic theory. A theory of language that accounts for the production of new sentences is also a theory of mechanical (artificial) intelligence.

> Thought, chaotic by nature, has to become ordered in the process of its decomposition. . . . Language is a system of interdependent terms in which the [truth] value of each term results solely from the simultaneous presence of the others. . . . Even outside language, all values are apparently governed by the same paradoxical principle. They are always composed:
>
> > (1) of a *dissimilar* thing that can be *exchanged* for the thing of which the value is to be determined; and
> >
> > (2) of *similar* things that can be *compared* with the thing of which the value is to be determined.
>
> Although both the signified and the signifier are purely differential and negative when considered separately, their combination is a positive fact. . . . In language, as in any semiological system, whatever distinguishes one sign from the others constitutes it. Difference makes character just as it makes value and the unit.[24]

In 1950 A. M. Turing asked the question "Can machines think" and devised the "Imitation Game" to answer it: a game in the form of an imaginary dialogue conducted by keyboard between a discrete-state machine (a digital computer) and a hidden human questioner. If the answers typed by the machine were indistinguishable from those of a human being, so that a third party could not tell which was the machine, then (said Turing) there was no basis for distinguishing the processes by which their respective sentences were produced.[25]

In *Syntactic Structures* Noam Chomsky came to a different conclusion: "English is not a finite state language. . . . No theory of linguistic structure based exclusively on Markov process models . . . will be able to explain or account for the ability of a speaker of English to produce and understand new utterances."[26] Mathews and Rosler inclined to a more positive outcome. Today, a generation later, computer programs are readily available that allow nonmusicians to compose songs by numbers, starting from randomly chosen sample phrases, or even snatches of existing music. It can be done. The advantages of a program offering limited and artificial transformations (for example, a maximum six degrees of growth in any direction), in the manner of *Prozession*, could well lead to very interesting results, and also provide a model for live performers to attempt interpretations of this fascinating composition with confidence and flexibility.

Notes

1. Jean Cocteau, *Cocteau on the Film, a Conversation recorded with André Fraigneau*, tr. Vera Traill (London: Dennis Dobson, 1954).

2. Jean Cocteau, *Cocteau on the film*, 113.

3. Giorgio di Chirico, *The Uncertainty of the Poet*, 1913.

4. Cecil A. Lewis, *Broadcasting from Within* (London: Newnes, 1924).

5. Cecil A. Lewis, *Broadcasting from Within*, 119–21.

6. William Empson, *Seven Types of Ambiguity* (Reprint, Harmondsworth: Penguin Books, 1961).

7. Pierre Boulez, "Son et Verbe." 57–61 in *Rélévés d'apprenti* (Paris: du Seuil, 1966).

8. "Spiritual Dimensions." Stockhausen, in interview with Peter Heyworth, *Music and Musicians* (May 1971): 31.

9. "Litanies de la Rose" by the French poet Remy de Gourmont also comes to mind: "Rose rose, pucelle au coeur désordonné, rose rose, robe de mousseline. . . . "

10. M. V. Mathews and L. Rosler, "Graphical Language for the Scores of Computer-generated Sounds." 84–114 in Heinz von Foerster and James W. Beauchamp ed., *Music by Computers* (New York: Wiley, 1969).

11. Sergei Eisenstein, *Film Sense* tr. Jay Leyda (London: Faber and Faber, 1943), 18.

12. George Tootell, *How to play the Cinema Organ: A Practical Book by a Practical Player* (London: Paxton, 1928), 89–92.

13. Jonathan Cott, *Stockhausen: Conversations with the composer* (London: Robson Books, 1974), 213.

14. "An endlessly descending tone." Sound example 4.5 in John R. Pierce, *Science of Musical Sound* (New York: W. H. Freeman, 1983), 230.

15. "Shepard Scale." Acoustical Society of America website http://asa.aip.org/demo27.html. (01/19/2004).

16. Peter Heyworth, "Spiritual Dimensions," *Music and Musicians* (May 1971): 31.

17. Pierre Schaeffer, "L'Objet Musical." *La Revue Musicale* 212 (April 1952), 69–71.

18. *Texte 3*, 103.

19. *Texte 3*, 103.

20. A section bar-line seems to be missing from the viola part at the point corresponding to "Im gleichen Parameter" in the tam-tam part in the composite score as illustrated.

21. M. V. Mathews and L. Rosler, "Graphical Language for the Scores of Computer-generated Sounds." 105–106.

22. Keith Gunderson, *Mentality and Machines: A Survey of the Artificial Intelligence Debate.* (Second edition, London: Croom Helm, 1985), 1–38.

23. *SoM*, 50.

24. Ferdinand de Saussure, *Course in General Linguistics* ed. Charles Bally and Albert Sechehaye in collaboration with Albert Reidlinger, tr. Wade Baskin (Glasgow: Collins, 1974), 112–21.

25. Alan M. Turing, "Computing Machinery and Intelligence." *Mind* Vol. LIX No. 236 (1950). Reprinted in *Minds and Machines* ed. Alan Ross Anderson (Englewood Cliffs, N.J.: Prentice-Hall, 1964), 4–30.

26. Noam Chomsky, *Syntactic Structures* (The Hague: Mouton, 1957), 23.

CHAPTER SIXTEEN

Figures

When asked for whom he composed, Stravinsky replied "For myself and the hypothetical other." This is not what an advertising executive likes to hear. If the meaning of a piece of music is known only to the composer and a hypothetical listener who is simply the composer in disguise, then as an information transaction it quite clearly has severe limitations. If the function of language, as J. Z. Young expressed it, is "to communicate information that is useful for living" (already a fairly limited definition), it would seem to follow that a medium of expression of which nobody can be sure what is being communicated is neither very efficient, nor terribly useful,—indeed, it could be objected, as Plato said, that music was a willfully perverse antithesis to language, whose use should be carefully restricted.

Naturally Stravinsky does not exclude the possibility that somebody else, at some point in space and time, might understand exactly what he means by a particular piece of music. All he is saying is that he cannot know for sure whether if ever his musical statement will make exactly the same sense to a listener as it means to him, or originally meant to him at the time he composed it, though it may still mean something. A musical transaction has even less chance of error-free transmission given the presence of the performer as intermediary, which introduces a whole raft of uncertainties, from wrong notes and wrong tempi, to a total lack of sympathy with the composer's personal and cultural context. And yet composers continue to write music, and critics and audiences continue to listen to it and express a variety of opinions about it. The puzzling inference to be drawn is either that listeners (you and me) are illogical and do not see the futility of having a view of, or even listening to, an information about which no agreement on the meaning is possible; or alternatively, that music *does* communicate information, but of a primitive kind that is irreducible to statements of language and logic. In addition to alleging a debilitating if not fatal imprecision in musical notation as a system, a predisposition to believe that music is unable to convey exact information is entailed by the Saussurian position that all subjective statements are dangerous, and inherently meaningless, since meaning is conferred by society. That is the nineteenth-century bourgeois view underlying the same European anticultural tradition, born of the industrial age, that continues to regard artistic activity of *any* kind as suspect, and potentially subversive. According to the bourgeois view, art is destabilizing since it implies 1. that communication of meaning through art is in fact possible, 2. that such communication lies outside the jurisdiction of society, and further, 3. that the *potential* of art to communicate unauthorized information is as damaging to society, in effect, as the challenge of any message that might be read into a particular artwork. It would not be the first time. Plato said much the same. Criticism of the propriety of Gabrieli's music, and of Galileo's science, had been expressed by the presiding cardinals of the Inquisition in similar terms.

That way, of course, lies the paranoia of a socialist realism that sanctions the persecution of artists and composers. That so many significant European artists and composers were forced into exile in the thirties, and found safety and acceptance in the United States, perhaps says as much about the survival of eighteenth-century enlightenment hierarchies and values in America,—the duty of patronage, and respect for art as research, —as about any political commitment in America to freedom of expression. In his music, in his own way, Stockhausen confronts "socialist realism" as a (literally) evil *doctrine*, and defends art and artists, in particular "modern" artists from the late nineteenth and early twentieth century, whose alternative visions were sufficiently understood, even by their oppressors, as protestations of a personal perception, and thus amounted to acts of individual courage.

The above ungainly reflections are by way of a personal admission that even though the given work itself may appear incomplete, or his account of it frustratingly elusive, something in Stockhausen's ideas persistently engages and illuminates, and has significance. To me that quality of wider relevance is the (unprovable) mark of genius: and not "sui generis," in just his own terms, but in a universal sense. It is why, for example, I have a special liking for *Prozession* even though I cannot be sure that it works. As a student of the Second Cologne New Music Courses in 1965, I was one of a class under Stockhausen that witnessed rehearsals of *Mikrophonie I* and got to study Makoto Shinohara's hand-drawn page proofs of the score of *Mixtur*. Early in the course, we were set exercises in *gestalt* composition, to invent and modify three-, four-, and five-part musical objects expressed as combinations of symbols projected on a rudimentary three-zone pitch space. In the first example, of a three-part *gestalt* and three alternates, the "similar" alternate is one degree softer and one degree longer; the "different" alternate represents a lessening of contrast from extremes to middle, and reduction by one degree of duration and dynamic of the final part (otherwise they would all be the same, which is the complete elimination of difference, and not consistent with the definition); finally the "opposite" alternate variously inverts position, pitch, dynamic, and duration values for low and high, and transforms the central value into a complex of possibilities, dynamically linked. Clearly a highly specialized intuition is at work here.

G	entsprechend ≙ similar	verschieden ≠ different	gegensätzlich ↔ opposite
High　　　'f	m̄f	m̄f	p̂
Medium	m̄f　　　　p̂	ṗ	m̄f<f̂>ṗ<mf
Low　　p̂	p̣p	m̄f	'f

↑　　　↑　　↑
beginning　middle　end

For a boy from the Bronx (in a manner of speaking) the exercise raised more issues than it solved. It was unclear to me on what principles a *gestalt* was defined (and yes, I was struggling to get to grips with Köhler's *Gestalt Psychology* at this time). If a *gestalt* can have three, four, five or more segments, I wondered why a segment could not also be regarded as a *gestalt*. In the very act of defining a segment, a certain autonomy is accorded to the part. I was also not convinced by the division of a *gestalt* into beginning, middle, and end components. Like any other music, serial music unfolds in a seamless and continuous time, and in the absence of the consistent rhythm and beat structures of classical music, or even of Webern and Stravinsky (e.g., strong, weak, medium, weak), how I wondered is the listener to hear where one *gestalt* ends and another begins. I was also not too convinced by the definition of difference; while intriguing in theory, it too seemed arbitrary in practice.

At the time, one had to conclude: 1. that while Stockhausen's terms might be arbitrary they could still be justified in terms of a larger system or method, and 2. that such distinctions might not have to be transparent to the individual listener, being technical aids to composition. But even in that respect, however, to me they were not explanatory in a general sense, no more than Boulez's analysis of Stravinsky's rhythms, for comparison, is explanatory of Stravinsky's purpose in constructing them (in fact Boulez's interpretation, like Messiaen's, substitutes a loose aggregation of unequal cells for a dynamic of syncopation). My own modest critique of the class exercise (shown overleaf) took the form of a triplet which, being interpreted, Messiaen fashion, would signify that all three elements are identical, differentiated only by relative speed. (If a low-pitch, long-duration, soft sound is recorded on tape, and the tape then gradually speeded up, it will be transformed first into a sound of medium pitch, medium length and *mezzoforte* dynamic, and ultimately into a high-pitched, short, loud sound.)

As a compositional aid, there is nothing to object to in a *gestalt* system of organization. All language systems are arbitrary, after all, and writing systems too: the ideographs of Chinese and Japanese appearing closer to *gestalten* in Stockhausen's sense than letters of the Greek alphabet. But the experience did illustrate in a vivid manner just how deeply Stockhausen's compositional processes seemed to be informed by latent historical and cultural assumptions: for example, the German language's disposition to form

compound words, the form of a logical statement, Froebel's Law of the Connection of Contrasts, and so on. The reader will also notice a structural affinity between a *gestalt* and a unit of speech as described by Harold Stetson ("a consonant that releases the syllable pulse, a vowel that emits the syllable pulse, a consonant that arrests the syllable pulse"),[1] or a Messiaen cellule rythmique, or a "note" of electronic music that consists of an onset, a steady state, and a decay.[2] In Stockhausen's own history the act of editing a group of note segments to tape, and then subjecting that composite group to various treatments (acceleration, filtering, reverberation, etc.) makes his concept of a *gestalt* plausible in his own specialist terms. If the definition of a unit of speech includes a beginning, a middle, and an end, then that would seem to justify defining a unit of musical speech in the same terms.

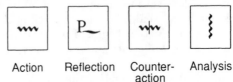

Action   Reflection   Counter-   Analysis
                          action

In 1965, knowing nothing about computers, I was all the same intrigued at the possibility suggested by Stockhausen's *gestalt* process that a symbolic logic might be invented to allow for the uninterrupted manipulation of a freely chosen musical entity, in the manner of a medieval disputation. This was after *Plus-Minus*, but before *Prozession*. It occurred to me that a minimum of four signs would be necessary: a sign for (new) action; a sign for reflection; a sign for counteraction, and one for analysis. Action is assertive, and corresponds to new material; reflection is supportive; counteraction is oppositional; and analysis tends to separation and fragmentation. It looked promising, but when I tried to imagine a normal conversation taking place, and describe it in terms of these symbols, it quickly became apparent that no dialogue was possible without the deliberate introduction of error, or ambiguity, or multiple identity.

So it was with a great deal of excitement, when I finally got to see the score of *Prozession,* to find that Stockhausen had simplified and reduced his original notation to relationships, just as I had envisaged. It appeared that he had solved the problem until a closer look at the score revealed that the composition did not after all amount to a continuously unfolding conversation, but more to a succession of statements of limited transformation that reach a point and are then replaced by new opening statements. Something in me says that the problem of extended transformation is inherently solvable, or has been solved, by research in artificial intelligence; in that context the plus, minus, and equal signs of *Prozession* begin to resemble logic gates: plus corresponding to AND, minus to NAND, and equal to OR (leaving NOR unaccounted for).

Ensemble (Ensemble)

1967: Collective composition by members of Stockhausen's composition course, International Vacation Courses for New Music, Darmstadt.

For twelve instrumentalists: flute, oboe, clarinet, bassoon, horn, trumpet, trombone, percussion, Hammond organ, violin, cello, double bass; also tape recorders and short-wave receivers (4 mixing desks).

Duration: 4 hours. Edited version on lp, Wergo 60065, 65'.

Stockhausen began teaching in earnest during the sixties. During that time much of his music assumed a deliberately adventurous and speculative character. During the fifties, under the watchful eye of Meyer-Eppler, his vivid musical imagination remained grounded in science, and his notation, though demanding, was punctilious and explicit. A performer might not find the task of interpreting a Stockhausen score either easy or grateful, but the technical challenge was its own reward, and the musical results, individually and collectively, were new, intriguing, and often breathtaking. Meyer-Eppler's untimely death, coinciding with an unexpected decline in public and institutional confidence in a determinist aesthetic, were factors contributing to an adaptation of method to allow, as they say, "more participation in the creative process." Though his explorations of open form could lead to startling results, they also forced Stockhausen into a dependence on the good will and high level of technical skill among performers, a situation with which he was only comfortable if the performers were close acquaintances and completely trustworthy.

Open form is a dangerous game, and dedicated exponents in the musical arena are few and far between. "Free jazz" in the United States is one outstanding exception; classical Indian practice and the communal music of African and Indonesian nations are others. These traditions of spontaneously invented music belong to oral cultures, however. It seemed that Western classical music had only achieved the enormous social and organizational advantages of notation by suppressing individual qualities of resourcefulness, imagination, self-awareness, and sense of personal worth among rank and file musicians. The task facing composers of modern music,—not just Stockhausen, but since the time of Mahler,—was how to reawaken a sense of emotional responsibility among musicians whose professional attention to executing precisely notated instructions had inured them to stereotype expression, or no expression at all.

> *R. M.: Stravinsky once complained of his difficulty in persuading orches-*
> *tral players on occasion to interpret crotchets marked* portato *as sforzato*
> *and* staccato *semiquavers with accents, depending on the style.*[3]

> Kh. S.: Then he should specify. I don't agree with that at all. I don't want
> any accents if I do not write accents. . . . One should study very carefully
> the meaning of the symbols in specific scores. My scores are, I think,
> exceptionally rational in their use of notation.[4]

In 1981, when the above was recorded, Stockhausen is still insisting on the
accurate performance of notation as a value higher than individual interpretation. The question then arises of where and how a musician-collaborator is
permitted to contribute to the realization or extension of a Stockhausen
open-form composition. The answer lies in the scores themselves, and the
freedoms made available, which are at times very specific.

Open form exacts a price, not just on the performer, but on the composer, who has to define its freedoms in other ways than notation. It leads to
a situation toward the end of the sixties where there is more prefatory
advice and instruction on how to interpret the score than there is music
itself. In some cases, such as *Mikrophonie I* and *Stop*, the composer has had
to provide a performing version of an open score, as he had previously been
obliged to do in the case of *Kontakte* when plans for a more open score
proved unworkable.

The greatest obstacle to successful realization of graphically or procedurally open-form compositions, however, has to be a combination of lack of
training and active resistance among the musicians involved, which is all
the more ironic since the community of musicians (more accurately, would-
be composers) was at one time leading the call for greater creative involvement in the interpretation of contemporary music. The task of explaining
what he wanted became a task of explaining himself.

Though his role in *Ensemble* is more that of régisseur than composer,
this collective work produced by members of his 1967 composition seminar
at Darmstadt deserves consideration as a precursor of his own large-scale
simultaneous works, and also as a trial assessment of what types of music
are best suited for such multilevel enterprises.

> *Ensemble* is an attempt to transform the traditional concert format into
> something new. We are accustomed to comparing compositions played
> one after another. In *Ensemble*, "pieces" by twelve different composers
> are performed at the same time. . . . These "pieces" are not perfectly
> worked out musical objects ("works"), but images in sound produced on
> tape or by short-wave receiver, with individual rules, forms of action
> and reaction, and notated "events," which their composers bring into
> play in the process of the collective performance. . . . The resulting four-
> hour process is more than the sum of its "pieces"; it is a composition of
> compositions, fluctuating between the total isolation of individual
> events and the total interdependency of all levels, mediating also
> between extreme determinacy and unpredictability."[5]

The twelve members of the composition group (Tomás Marco, Avo Somer, Nicolaus A. Huber, Robert Wittinger, John McGuire, Peter R. Farmer, Gregory Biss, Jürgen Beule, Mesias Maiguashca, Jorge Peixinho, Rolf Gehlhaar, and Johannes G. Fritsch) were asked to bring either a tape recorder and tape containing around 25 sound events, or a shortwave radio receiver. Stockhausen took charge of the overall form plan and responsibility for "inserts leading to occasional synchronisation."[6] During the four-hour event the audience was free to move around the auditorium (the assembly hall of the Ludwig-George Gymnasium), while tape-recorded and radio sounds were distributed from four mixing desks among four pairs of speakers (allowing for movement of the sound between left and right speakers). During the course of the evening, each composer in turn, performing a different instrument, became the soloist of the moment. Stockhausen took charge of the dynamic disposition of the ensemble within the auditorium space, including the entrance foyer, and limited movement in the vertical plane (up and down stairs). From the materials provided, Stockhausen thus "composed" (put together) a spatial polyphony of soloists and radiophonic sources offering considerable scope for experiencing live and electronic perspective effects. Although the totality appears very complex, the combination of live and not-live elements is carefully controlled and relatively sparse. The spatial disposition of loudspeakers, which is highly unusual, is designed to distance live players from the speakers associated with them. There is thus a graduated hierarchy from live sound through live (reproduced) to purely reproduced sound. The spatial distribution of players and speakers also allows plentiful opportunity for imitation and dialogue.

A degree of uncertainty emerged over whether the collective composition was to be regarded as an aggregation of autonomous works, or as a single compartmented structure, a matter of concern for those participants anxious to make personally identifiable statements. Within the composition seminar, and reflected in Stockhausen's overall schema, a focus of study was the interpretation of varieties of contrast, most notably "difference," as expressed symbolically in the scores for *Plus-Minus* and *Mikrophonie I*. On this matter the composers evidently had views of their own:

> It must be emphasized that "difference" is a very specific relationship; not any old *different* thing, but different in *relationship* to something. An elephant, for example, is in this sense not different from a tree, but is "something else." To make the "similar" relationship clear, one must show that there are only two extreme possibilities, a dualistic approach [*sic*]; the "different" relationship is pluralistic and demonstrates that there are many possibilities. . . . Both "opposite" and "different" must display a certain "similarity" to the structure to which they relate, in order to be perceived as relating at all.[7]

This bears the hallmarks of a classification struggle, generated in part by a mysterious lack of specifically musical criteria for difference relationships (an elephant? a tree? Is there a Linnaean schema for oboes?)—or rather, an equally mysterious avoidance of conventional (classical or serial) criteria of difference. Many participants expressed a preference for the simpler symbolic language of *Prozession*; said Gehlhaar "it became clear through this composition it is very effective to indicate the changes in direction with one sign only, to say *shorter*, *softer*, etc., rather than to notate many differentiations, like *a little* or *much* shorter, etc.; this allows the musician to make an intelligent decision every time."[8]

Stockhausen's interest in the spatial disposition of multiple musicians and sound sources happened to coincide with the publication of an update of Henry Brant's 1955 paper, "The Uses of Antiphonal Distribution and Polyphony of Tempi in Composing," of which Stockhausen had been aware at the time of composing *Gruppen*.[9] Brant's new and greatly expanded essay, "Space as an Essential Aspect of Musical Composition," detailed a number of subsequent researches into the articulation and perception of spatial relationships among both live musicians and multiple loudspeakers, and became a useful ongoing resource for Stockhausen during the *LICHT* years.[10] In his earlier paper Brant had insisted on the need for "an exactly specified plan" for the distribution of players. His experiments since then had shown the acoustical and musical benefits arising from distributing the orchestra throughout the auditorium for the composer's *Voyage Four*, benefits including increased volume and resonance, a greater sense of height and depth, improved balance, and above all, greatly improved separation of coincident voices: even spatially separated unisons appearing unrelated.[11]

In subsequent spatial and multilevel works Stockhausen would examine three distinct categories of plurality. In *Musik für ein Haus* he revisits the concept of a simultaneous concert, the musical content of which has a strongly-defined signaling character. In *Musik für die Beethovenhalle* (the concert event incorporating *Fresco*), "active" signaling items (music performed within the concert halls) are offset by "passive" reverberating complexes (*Fresco*) performed in the corridors and public spaces. Finally, the outdoor multigroup *Sternklang* explores the possibilities of maintaining coordination among groups widely separated in a park. Years later, in *Lichter-Wasser*, the poetic of *Ensemble* would once again be revisited.

Stimmung (Tuning)

1968: No. 34 (UE 14805; cd Stockhausen-Verlag SV-12)
For six vocalists, microphones, speakers, sound projection.
Duration 70'.

Stockhausen's works do not exist in isolation. *Stimmung* in particular. The work is arguably unlike any other work Stockhausen had previously composed, or has written since: a leisurely, very "cool" meditation for six voices, and at the same time an extremely rarefied and methodical investigation into speech as a process of harmonic modulation. Temperamentally it makes a welcome sortie out of the twilight of *Mikrophonie II* into the clear light of day; as research, it marks a continuation of *Telemusik*'s interesting line of development into the field of timbre synthesis, and the integration (by intermodulation) of folk elements from other cultures,—speech acts, sacred names, rather than musical idioms,—into the overriding harmony.

But these resemblances are content relationships. To understand where *Stimmung* really comes from is to understand more clearly what it represents. Consider the seemingly fractious experience of *Ensemble*: 1. a group of composer-instrumentalists, each doing their own thing but not able to work as a team; 2. events distributed in a real space within which the audience is able to move freely and experience different perspective effects; and 3. a programme of events directed in time. Now imagine its total opposite: 1a. a group of singers completely integrated as performers, and working in harmonious cooperation in the interpretation of preformed material within a perfect harmony (but allowing nevertheless for variation, dialogue, and give-and-take within that context); 2a. a *negation* of exterior space, and exploration of a meditative, interior space to which the audience only has imaginative access; and 3a. a *negation* of time-directedness: music that takes place in an "eternal present." Now *that* is a true definition of *Stimmung*. In other respects the argument is well laid out by Hermann Helmholtz:

> In English the phrase *out of tune*, *unstrung*, and in German the word *stimmung*, literally *tuning*, are transferred from music to mental states. The words are meant to denote these peculiarities of mental condition which are capable of mental representation. I think we might appropriately define *gemüthstimmung*, or *mental tune*, as representing that general character temporarily shewn by the motion of our conceptions, and correspondingly impressed on the motions of our body and voice. Our thoughts may move fast or slowly, may wander about restlessly and aimlessly in anxious excitement, or may keep a determinate aim distinctly and energetically in view: . . . The listener may thus receive a more perfect and impressive image of the 'tune' of another person's mind, than by any other means.[12]

Helmholtz also draws attention to a lack of sense of natural harmony among trained opera singers, in consequence of the introduction of temperaments that are strictly out of tune: "At the present day few even of our opera singers are able to execute a little piece for several voices, when either totally unaccompanied, or at most accompanied by occasional chords. . . . The chords almost always sound a little sharp or uncertain, so that they disturb a musical hearer. . . . The singer who practises to a tempered instrument has no principle at all for exactly and certainly determining the pitch of his voice."[13]

Stimmung is an exercise, or programme of exercises, in voice training, very much in the spirit of self-improvement of the nineteenth century. That makes it seemingly as private, and about as interesting, say, as a book of Czerny exercises for the pianist, but being Stockhausen it is more than that, too, the names of divinities of a variety of world cultures being substituted for the nonsense vowels of regular speech exercises. Into the routine of vowel practice,—now an avowedly "celestial" routine, given the sacred nature of most of the text material—is insinuated a distracting element of erotic meditation in the form of intimate verses to accompany lovemaking, which enter spontaneously into the meditative routine like pleasant images into the consciousness of a person humming while engaged in some aspect of daily routine, like shelling peas, or putting on makeup.

Insistence on the spirituality of everyday conduct is a feature of instructional texts of the Romantic era, and goes hand in hand with the dutiful,

Cavity resonances of the human voice (after Helmholtz).

cyclic repetition, over and over, of outwardly meaningless exercises—like a piece by Philip Glass, for example. That a person acquires virtue through an unquestioning practice of speech acts that, if done in public, would run the risk of arousing suspicion as to one's mental state, or otherwise causing alarm, is a precept associated above all with Stockhausen, and yet it has its roots in accepted educational practice of an earlier time. The teaching of singing is a respectable, indeed a noble vocation; there is a certain poetic justice in discovering a perfect advocate of *Stimmung* in the writings of an English choirmaster of the Victorian era:

> Speech differs from singing in its want of *sustained* musical tone. In *singing* the vocal cords are drawn to certain degrees of tension, and are held in the required position as long as necessary. . . . The moment we fix the voice to a definite note or succession of definite notes, we change from speaking to singing.
>
> The voice must be cultivated in such a way that, at the will of the speaker, it may rise and fall in melodious cadence suitable to the sentiment of the words. It must be made to "ring" till its rich vibrations can penetrate the farthest recesses of "monstre" halls, courts of justice, churches or theatres. It must be so completely under control as to be capable of expressing every emotion of the soul, whether of joy or sorrow, admiration or disgust, pity or contempt, courage or fear, praise or prayer. Then, and then only does the speaker *really* speak, then only does the reader read, the pleader plead, or the preacher preach.[14]

Stockhausen's return to harmonic simplicity corresponds to a switch from a primarily gestural expression, in which uncertainty of intonation, whether systemic (tempered tuning) or expressive (vibrato) connotes *physical* emphasis, to an intimate, nonrhetorical mode of utterance, more sociable in tone, in which a deviation from harmonic agreement is signaled more discreetly. Phonetically, *Stimmung* marks a change of emphasis from inflected and fragmented imitation of consonantally-directed speech (as in *Mikrophonie I*) to a music of continuity-in-stasis, and the affective connotations of vowel

sounds, e.g., "Ahh. . . ," "Ohh. . . ," "Ooh. . ." etc. Stockhausen's choice of harmony incidentally makes an interesting resolution of an earlier "endless
chord" in music; not the Prelude to *Das Rheingold*, as it happens, but "Farben," III of the *Five Pieces for Orchestra* by Schoenberg:

The work is in 51 sections, defined by a fixed order of harmonic combinations of the basic pitches; these "carrier harmonies" are modulated by "Modelle" (models)—speech elements invoked by a succession of leaders, taken up
by the other singers, and assimilated into the prevailing harmony. The
leadership of a given section is indicated in the form-schema by a thickening
of the note-line, which also suggests that the indicated singer sings a little
louder than the others. The order of "Modelle" is not fixed; the three female
vocalists have eight each to choose from, the three male voices nine, and
leaders are free to adjust the model to the prevailing harmony.

Subordinate singers, acting as "resonators," may choose from three
possibilities of tuning in to the leader, according to circumstance. If cued in
after a silence or caesura (double bar), the singer follows precisely the tempo
and inflection of the leading voice. Should a change of leader occur while a
subordinate voice is singing, but there is no barline in the subordinate part
to indicate it, the new leader's inflection is ignored, though the intonation of
the subordinate part may change. Third, if there is a change of leading voice
while a subordinate voice is singing, but the change is indicated by a
barline, then the subordinate voice makes a gradual transition to the new
tempo and inflection (Stockhausen suggests a linear substitution process,
first tempo, then vowel content, then accentuation, as it were on a sliding
scale).

The duration of a section is determined by the number of cycles
(repetitions of the leading model) that are needed for the group to attain the
desired condition of harmoniousness, a process that can be held up on occasion, for example by a late entry. The harmony is also subject at times to
"tuning *out*" distortion, indicated by the sign "var." This involves a gradual
phasing in and out of unison, in imitation of the beating effect when two
electronic oscillators move out of tune with each other.

Twenty-nine of the 51 sections are marked with the letter "N." In these
sections, after total harmony has been achieved, the leader invokes a
previously selected "magic name" and those already singing one by one
incorporate the sound into their singing. Up to six such magic names,
contributed in rotation, the leader last, may be introduced into an "N"
section, so these tend to take somewhat longer than unmarked sections in
performance.

One female voice and each of the three male voices has a part with a poem attached as a coda to one model. The poem is inserted into the music by the voice indicated as a replacement for a magic name, or to preempt the introduction of a magic name by another singer. The poems are inflected, but not sung: "the speaker of the poem (says Stockhausen) should make pauses of varying lengths in order to follow the integration of his text"—i.e., to render the poem in manageable chunks. Finally, at a number of places,

Exercise XIX.

Y and U.

2 2 2 2 2 2   2 2 2 2 2 2
e–a yah e–ah yah   e–aw yaw e–o yo

e–oo yoo e–u yu e–i yi e–oi yoy e–ay yay e–y yy.

ye ya yah yaw yo hoo yu yi yoy yay yy.

Speech exercise (after Helmore, 1874).[15]

singers are assigned empty staves, in which they are at liberty to move freely among the pitches in use at that time, and introduce random deviations of intonation, rhythm, and accentuation from the prevailing model.

All of these various degrees of modification are to be understood in the terms of "degrees of difference" in *Mikrophonie I*, thus as tending to *sameness, difference*, or *opposition*. To these equivalent alternates is added a hierarchy of spirituality as well: the divine, highest state of harmony represented by the magic names, the human level by the poems, and destructive forces by the consequences of the empty staves: there is a multilevel poetry going on here that clearly invites comparison with the operation of arithmetical signs in *Prozession*.

Since *Stimmung* appeared in 1968, public awareness of voice modulation in world music has grown enormously. Concerts of Tibetan chant attract a large popular following, particularly in the United States, and jaw harp and throat music as practiced in the Tuva region and remote Mongolia have also become more widely known and accepted by listeners of all ages and musical interests. In these musical traditions, manipulation of the resonances of the voice is often associated with closeness to nature,—provoking a response from the environment,—and also with magic and spirituality, since it is possible by manipulating the vowel resonances to emit a ghostly whistling melody that moves independently of the intoning voice. It is worth noting that Stockhausen does not imitate, theatricalize or require the deep voice techniques of these traditions. His objectives are essentially Western, practical, and nonanachronistic: the training of the singing voice in consciously directed modulation of pitch—a higher consciousness of the abstract beauties of sung words that gives meaning to monotone plainchant in the Ambrosian and Gregorian ritual, and indeed to any tradition of monotone chant.

Stimmung is performed, unusually, in an "around the campfire" staging, with the singers in a circle, facing inwards, their voices picked up by microphones and relayed to external speakers. The impression of a private ritual is deliberate. This is a musical environment appropriate for the expression, as Helmholtz said, of inward states of being. At an Amsterdam concert in 1969, a group of disaffected composers, objecting to being left out, as they felt, broke up a performance to stage their own protest against the "authoritarian" style of the music. Stockhausen wrote, "*Stimmung* will yet reduce even the howling wolves to silence."

Kurzwellen (Shortwaves)
1968: No. 25 (UE 14806; cd Stockhausen-Verlag SV-13)
For four instrumentalists, microphonist, and sound projectionist (e.g., piano, electronium, tam-tam with microphone, viola with contact microphone, 2 filters, 4 potentiometers, 4 loudspeakers, 4 shortwave receivers).
Duration: 50'–65'.

Kurzwellen mit Beethoven (Shortwaves with Beethoven)
Also known as "Opus 1970 / Stockhoven-Beethausen."
1969: No. 25 (UE 14806; lp DG 139 461)
Score and performance requirements as above, except tape recorders and prepared tapes substituting for the shortwave receivers.
Duration: 54'.

The new work is richer, more polyphonic, and more susceptible to ambiguity than *Prozession*, and the trend that sees the earlier "individual memory" component replaced by the "collective memory" of shortwave radio, then with prepared tapes of Beethoven related sound material, can be interpreted in one way as a progressive enrichment of relational possibilities, and in another way as progressively limiting the freedoms of performers. The transformational patterns composed are more complex, for a start, but in addition Stockhausen asks his musicians to imitate, transform, and exchange shortwave events, which like the national anthems in *Hymnen* are recognizable musical figures or sound objects (or "facts" as Braque aptly described the starting pistol, typewriter, and foghorn in Satie's *Parade*), colored and distorted by intermodulation. In identifying shortwave sound as a common denominator, Stockhausen is setting up a natural convergence in the ensemble, toward a neutral shortwave quality. This in turn appears calculated to encourage a perception of the different instruments as quasi-electronic transformations of one another, a return to the original poetic conceit of *Kontakte*.

In his account of the interrelationship of four myths of the origin of water (a structured comparison in which corresponding elements may be designated by a plus sign in one tribal narrative and its analogue by a minus in another), Claude Lévi-Strauss writes pertinently about the persistence of structural relations between myths, even where the narrative contents seem totally at variance with one another. Stockhausen was not only aware of Lévi-Strauss,—whose influential writings were widely understood as an important intellectual validation of music in general, and serial music in particular,—he was also profoundly interested in the application of Lévi-Strauss's discoveries to music. In relation to Stockhausen's plus-minus compositions, the French anthropologist's daring account of the origin of water myth suggests a conception of the role of instrumentalists, in *Kurzwellen* and comparable works, as analogous to storytellers or mythmakers, each from a different cultural tradition. In effect, a performance of *Kurzwellen* amounts to an intertribal conference, or Chaucerian *Parliament of Fowls* in which different interpretations of creation are exchanged, and perhaps reconciled. Interpreting the four myths, superimposed, as creating a kind of musical harmony despite following different paths, Lévi-Strauss also lays out the pattern of myth relationships in a score form that asks to be considered as a model for Stockhausen's metamusical forays into oral memory. Speaking of myths "so different in content that any comparison between them would seem unthinkable," Lévi-Strauss observes:

> The anomaly can be accounted for, if it is made clear that the contrasting elements . . . relate only to the messages, which are transmitted with the help of codes. The latter, in their turn, comprise both a grammar and lexical material. . . . The grammatical armature of these codes remains invariable in the case of all the myths we have studied. But the same is not true of either the messages or the lexical material. . . . The more partial the transformation of the message, the more blurred the initial lexical material tends to become, so that it is made unrecognizable when the transformation process brings the messages back to a state of identity.[16]

Kurzwellen is a more open form than *Prozession*, but one in which time coordination of the four players is more firmly controlled. It has 136 symbol units (compared to the 250 of *Prozession*), divided into sequences of 5, 20, 25, 35, and 51 units. At the end of each sequence, indicated by a heavy barline, each player repeats the last sign until everyone has "caught up." The newly designated leader then gives a signal to proceed, in synchronization, for a specific number of events, after which they are at liberty to diverge. By placing the first such "cadence point" after an introduction of only five unit events, Stockhausen enables the players to come quickly to an appreciation of their relative speeds of transformation, and thus to pace themselves for the remainder of the performance. As the performance proceeds, and the distance between coordination points increases, so the individual paths of all four instruments will tend in theory to diverge; on the other hand, the number and placing of interactional cues will tend to bring players back into line, a process of regulation also inherent in the imitation of shortwave materials that are the same for every player.

Stockhausen's notation of performer interactions is also tighter. The co-ordinative repeat, indicated by the sign [W] ("Wiederhole") is neater and a more natural usage than [Per] though its meaning is not exactly the same. The latter sign is omitted, along with *Prozession*'s compulsory imitations of Register, Number, and Duration. The presence of shortwave radios, the programme materials of which will tend to be quasi-periodic (speech) or periodic (music), largely compensates for these omissions; in addition the limited frequency range of radio material will tend to support a drift of sonority toward the higher frequencies. If one considers the possibilities of imitation available for each player, taking the piano as an example:

1. Imitation of oneself (piano) on the piano;
2. Imitation of oneself (radio) on the piano;
3. Imitation of oneself (piano) using the radio;
4. Imitation of oneself (radio) using the radio;
5. Imitation of another (2, 3, or 4: instrument) on the piano;
6. Imitation of another (2, 3, or 4: radio) on the piano;
7. Imitation of another (2, 3, or 4: instrument) on the radio;
8. Imitation of another (2, 3, or 4: radio) on the radio;

—it becomes clear that purely instrumental interactions are vastly outnumbered by interactions involving the imitation of radiophonic events. "When and how often a player alternates between shortwave and instrumental events is left to his discretion; he should, however, aim for a balance," says the instruction. The implication is that, left to their own devices, the musicians will come to rely on the shortwave source material. Clearly this will tend to bind the ensemble into an acoustic unity, and reciprocally limit the function of each instrument to that of an imperfect resonator of the radio-wave continuum.

The score is tighter, then, and also more complex. Its introductory section quite clearly features a canonic sequence of miniature symmetries, as if introducing themselves, by players II, III, and IV. In contrast to *Prozession*'s opening trail of minus signs, here the material remains virtually constant in all parameters. The imitation principle exposed in the introduction is pursued in the first major section, of 20 units (or section A, if we designate the five sections of the score as Introduction, A, B, C, and D). It is not difficult to identify blocks of three equal signs [= = =] disposed at successively later stages from I through IV, each preceded by an aggregate of five events composed exclusively of plus signs (in II interrupted by a 4-event insertion), and followed by a sequence of minuses, of which I and III (the former interrupted by an equal sign) make an evident pair. Bracket signs, used more frequently than *Prozession*, create new and intricate internal symmetries. For example, the underlying 4×5 division of section A is rendered by I as 1–4–3–2 : 2–3–4–1, whereas in II the substructure is incremental: 2–3–4–5–6. Symmetries of signs and between parts are also more sophisticated here than in the earlier piece. An example is the reciprocal relationship of III and IV toward the end of section A.

Section B, of 25 events, divides into 5 × 5; here the symmetries are more regular, and a fair degree of unanimity can be found among the four parts: an opening string of 4 × 3 minuses in IV, followed by an equal sign, balanced by 4 × 3 plus signs and an equal in III. There is renewed canonic imitation between I, II, and IV; after which minus-sign symmetries follow in all four parts, a vertical group of four minus signs passing IV–III–II–I, and so on. In section C a basic grouping by fives is counterpointed by fours and threes in II and III. At first the balance of plus and minus is fairly constant, but each part suffers one major and one minor deviation. In I, measure 4, the pattern is: major decline, minor rise, minor decline, major rise; in II, beginning at event 12, the pattern is: moderate decline (4 events), major rise (5 events), moderate decline (6 events), minor rise (4 events); in III, from event 16: attenuating decline, major rise, major decline, minor rise—all in fives. Finally in IV the symmetry is "looped" as it were, end to end, with an intervening three measures of moderate decline, and the minor symmetry, bracketed, likewise dislocated:

Completing the section, the final five-unit group is mirror-symmetrical as between I and IV, and reciprocal for I and the previous 5-unit group of II.

Section D continues the pattern of plus-minus symmetrical orders, varied this time by the interpolation of "wild card" equal signs. By and large there is less obvious reciprocity than in previous sections, partly because the barlines, after 10 units, progressively diverge from 5-unit groupings, and partly because changes are less elaborate. A degree of complementarity can be seen between I and IV, and between II and III, in terms of complexity of changes. This ends toward the middle of the section; at 17 before the end, I and II form a retrograde symmetry with III and IV. The final measures of each part recapitulate processes (or their negative identities) from near the beginning. Part I's final 14 units reflect the first 14 units of A; the final four measures of II are a variant mirror image of measures 2–4 of its section A; the final two measures of III recapitulate the final two measures of its section A, while the final minus grouping of IV recalls the close of section A, in part I, and measures 2–5 of section A, in part III.

Invited to contribute a lecture on Beethoven as part of the city of Düsseldorf's celebration of the composer's bicentenary in 1970, Stockhausen devised an evening-long meditation on Beethoven together with his performing ensemble (Aloys Kontarsky, piano; Johannes G. Fritsch, viola; Harald Bojé, electronium, and Rolf Gehlhaar, tam-tam). Stockhausen imagined an ideal performance situation for *Kurzwellen* in which every shortwave channel would be transmitting speech or music related to the composer. In order to recreate this ideal situation, special tapes, all different, were compiled, to be "tuned in and out" in the manner of the shortwave receivers.

These tapes consisted of excerpts of recordings of selected Beethoven compositions, interspersed with recorded readings (by Stockhausen) of passages from the Heiligenstadt Testament. To give the effect of shortwave transmissions, this material was subjected to a variety of electronic transformations based on processes previously employed in *Hymnen* and *Telemusik*. Related innovations in ring modulation made at this time led directly to the development of the Modul 69B modulating circuit, and thus prepared the way for the composition of *Mantra*.

Opus 1970 is closer perhaps to the original conception of *Hymnen* than to what *Hymnen*, even *Hymnen mit Solisten*, ultimately became. Instead of a single polyphonic tape playing continuously and "commented on" by the players, there are four separate mono tracks, each a simulation of a different radio transmission. Though they do run continuously, these tapes are heard by the audience only sporadically, when players come to the end of a line of transformations and tune into fresh material.

That Stockhausen felt confident enough to undertake a performance of *Kurzwellen* involving "totally unmodulated realistic shortwave events," says a great deal for his confidence in the players with whom he was working.

> Chance played a remarkable role in the decision [to include in the published recording] the *fourth version*: [in which,] 2 minutes after the beginning, exactly the same timpani motif emerged in one of the radios, with which, one year earlier, the [premiere] version in Bremen had begun. This STATION IDENTITY SIGNAL (one of the performers discovered that it was from the *BBC*)[17] led in both cases to lengthy instrumental transformations and developments, each of which subsequently took a completely different course.[18]

To listen today to the *Kurzwellen* recordings of 1968 and 1969, and to consider what Stockhausen and his group achieves in relation, self-evidently, to John Cage's *Imaginary Landscape No. 4* of 1951, a work for twelve radios, lasting only a few minutes,—is to appreciate the huge chasm, artistic and technical, that had opened up between the two composers.[19] With Stockhausen there is always a reason, a process, a genuine argument, and an outcome: always a reality to set alongside the myth. However it happens, the musical result is invariably gripping, intense, and disciplined.

Sadly, the harmony was not to last. "He himself sits at the electronic controls and when any idea he considers inappropriate is produced, he promptly phases it out by the twist of a knob. Not surprisingly, this has sometimes caused resentment, which reached explosion point last year [1970] at Darmstadt. Several of his players parted company with him and Stockhausen confessed himself surprised and deeply hurt."[20]

Notes

1. R. H. Stetson, *R. H. Stetson's Motor Phonetics* ed. J.A.S. Kelso and K.G. Munhall (Boston: College-Hill Press, 1988), 61.
2. Robin Maconie, "The French Connection: Motor Phonetics and Modern Music. Serialism, Gertrude Stein, and Messiaen's "Mode de valeurs."

http://www.jimstonebraker.com/maconie_lingtheory.html. (01/23/2004).

3. Igor Stravinsky and Robert Craft, *Conversations with Igor Stravinsky* (London: Faber and Faber, 1959), 120.

4. *SoM*, 169–70.

5. *Texte 3*, 212.

6. Rolf Gehlhaar, "Zur Komposition 'Ensemble.'" *Darmstädter Beiträge für Neue Musik* XI (Mainz: Schott, 1968).

7. Rolf Gehlhaar, "Zur Komposition 'Ensemble,'" 47.

8. Rolf Gehlhaar, "Zur Komposition 'Ensemble,'" 50.

9. Henry Brant, "Uses of Antiphonal Distribution and Polyphony of Tempi in Composing." *American Composers Alliance Bulletin* Vol. 4, No. 3 (1955): 13–15.

10. Henry Brant, "Space as an Essential Aspect of Musical Composition." 223–42 in *Contemporary Composers on Contemporary Music* ed. Elliott Schwartz and Barney Childs (New York: Holt, Rinehart and Winston, 1967).

11. Henry Brant, "Space as an Essential Aspect of Musical Composition," 228. See also Robert Erickson, *Sound Structure in Music* (Berkeley: University of California Press, 1974), 139–93.

12. Hermann Helmholtz, "The Tonality of Homophonic Music." *On the Sensations of Tone* tr. Alexander J. Ellis (Reprint, New York: Dover Publications, 1954), 250–51. See also "Vowel Qualities of Tone," 103–119.

13. Hermann Helmholtz, "Disadvantages of Tempered Intonation." *On the Sensations of Tone*, 326.

14. Frederick Helmore, *Speakers, Singers, and Stammerers* (London: Joseph Masters, 1874), 49–50.

15. Frederick Helmore, *Speakers, Singers, and Stammerers*, 86.

16. Claude Lévi-Strauss, *Raw and the Cooked: Introduction to a Science of Mythology* (London: Pimlico, 1994), 210–12.

17. The BBC call-sign at this time was the same "V for Victory" motive from Beethoven's Symphony No. 5, recorded on timpani by James Blades, that was broadcast to the European resistance during the 1939–1945 war.

18. From Stockhausen's liner notes to compact disc SV-13, 11.

19. Henry Cowell, "Current Chronicle." *Musical Quarterly* (January 1952). Reprinted in Richard Kostelanetz ed., *John Cage* (London: Allen Lane, 1974), 94–105.

20. Peter Heyworth, in the *Observer* (25 April, 1971).

CHAPTER SEVENTEEN

White Space

As an apprentice lithographer, Ben Shahn ran errands and practiced making letters "until I should know to perfection every curve, every serif, every thick element of a letter and every thin one, where it belonged and how it related to the form of the letter to which it belonged." As his mastery of the letter-forms grew, so did his dissatisfaction. The foreman made him look at the spaces between the letters. Shahn struggled to find a means by which to regulate the spacing between the different shapes, so that they might make a perfect line. Finally the foreman told him the secret: to imagine a small measuring glass of water that held just so much water, and pouring water into the spaces between the letters, so that every space contained exactly the same amount, and the water level was constant, whatever the shapes.[1]

Fifty years later, Volkswagen ran a very successful and durable advertising campaign for the original VW Beetle, based on the image of white space: a full column, or a full page, containing little more than a badge, a modest caption in plain sans serifs, and just occasionally a hint of small-scale detail of the actual car. Absence of content engaged very successfully with the reader's expectation of content, and the message worked on a number of different levels, for instance, 1. the car speaks for itself; 2. in a perfect relationship, words are superfluous; 3. small is beautiful; and 4. less is more.

The fifteen *Aus den Sieben Tagen* text pieces, composed during a period of retreat in May 1968, are open to interpretation as the point of no return in the composer's progress toward a music of essential statements, or "elementary propositions" (Sachverhalten) in the sense attributed to the Wittgenstein of *Tractatus*.[2] As the philosopher sought ultimate meaning in the limits of language, so the composer seems to be reaching here for the ultimate meaning of music, beyond the limits of conventional notation. For musicians only just getting used to the disciplines of plus-minus notation and imitation of shortwave radio transmissions, the conceptual leap has the hallmarks of a critical moment in catastrophe theory. Stockhausen has said that after composing *Kurzwellen* he came very close to suicide, and that the experience of retreat, meditation, and fasting that inspired these new compositions, was personally liberating. At this time, we learn, he was also introduced to the writings of Sri Aurobindo, the Indian philosopher and guru of active resistance to the forces of oppression.[3]

There is something not quite right, however, in this account of the emotional circumstances surrounding the composition of *Aus den Sieben Tagen*. The composer is not in the habit of volunteering information relating to his sources of inspiration, and there are other issues of historical interest already in the public domain. For anybody with a passion for new music, the issue was not why Stockhausen would choose to compose text pieces, but why it had taken him so long to do so. Cage's silent piece *4' 33"* for a pianist had been a subject of earnest debate since its composition in 1952. Another American, LaMonte Young, had studied under Stockhausen at Darmstadt in 1959, composed text pieces in 1960, and been a featured composer at Mary Bauermeister's soirées.[4] That Cage's composition has no words, and Young's text pieces are of indeterminate purpose, compared to the texts of *Aus den Sieben Tagen*, is precisely the point. By taking them into account, one is better able to appreciate the nature of the challenge, both intellectual and musical, that Stockhausen faced, and the quality of his solutions. If the idea of composing at this level of rarefaction seems like staring into the abyss, then it was an abyss the composer had lived with for a good many years. So it would appear that 1968 (not a good year in many respects) may rather have provided a combination of circumstances and the incentive for Stockhausen to make the imaginative leap.

1968 was certainly not a good year for Boulez, whose conducting career had left him little time for composing: this was the year of the *Livre* for orchestra, a reworking of the twenty-year-old string quartet inspired by Mallarmé, and *Domaines*, a pale reflection of Berio's *Circles* of 1961. Berio himself completed *Sinfonie*, a major work likely to be of both technical and thematic interest to the composer of *Momente* and *Hymnen*. Its stream-of-consciousness third movement incorporates passages from Samuel Beckett's *L'Innommable* (The Unnameable), notably a recurrent exhortation to "keep going!" Writing of a certain relevance since, in the words of David Lodge, "all we have is a narrative voice talking to itself, or transcribing its own thoughts as they occur, longing for extinction and silence, but condemned to go on narrating, though it has no story worth telling, and is certain of nothing, not even of its own position in space and time."[5] Like Shakespeare's Hamlet, Beckett was very much obsessed by the agony of being, the mind of a consciousness arrested in the present moment; but as a poet and dramatist of the spoken word, his impossible task was to convey in continuous speech the discarnate timelessness of the printed word. To do so he adopted a technique of verbal scanning, in which the low-resolution image emerging from speech is always in the process of forming.[6] Cage was to adopt a very similar mode of discourse in his Harvard lectures.[7] In the visual arts, by comparison, representations of being and nothingness had long since acquired a currency and sophistication denied to much of literature and music, through the pioneer work of Malevich and the Russian suprematists, via Mondrian and Barnett Newman, to Mark Rothko, Ad Reinhardt, and Clyfford Still: color-field works of an emotional intensity the Europeans, Yves Klein for example, were unwilling or unable to match.

In music, as in drama and the fine arts, the expressive possibilities of silence are available, ready-made, through the familiarity of the ritual, the cooperation of an audience, and the provision of an appropriate environment and instruments. The reverse logic of Cage's or LaMonte Young's philosophical position is that whereas the role of music in a conventional concert situation is to *limit* the freedom of thought and movement of an audience, their compositions were designed to *extend* it by creating a sense of the potential for expression available in such a ritualized context. In effect, their compositions are "white space." The burning issue in such a situation is how to color the space, as it were, with just enough information to prevent chaos, and create and maintain an elevated discourse. American composers were not very good at this, he thought. Nor was Stockhausen terribly impressed at the intellectual sleight of hand of having performers and audience exchange roles, so that a concert event such as *4' 33"* revealed itself to be a performance of spontaneous noises by unsuspecting members of the public for the composer's amusement. What attracted,—and, given the long delay, may also have baffled him,—is the idea of a music that, by its power of suggestion, is able continually to sustain an audience's sense of expectation, while at the same time not delineating objects or processes to satisfy it. That essentially is a definition of abstract art; and also of prayer.

In another interview Stockhausen refers to the circumstance of the *Aus den Sieben Tagen* texts as a near-death experience. A near-death experience can also be construed as a rebirth experience. April 1968 saw the premiere of Stanley Kubrick's movie epic *2001: A Space Odyssey*, the enigmatic but visually compelling translation of Arthur C. Clarke's parable of technological and human progress. For perhaps the first time in the history of the movies a director incorporated avant-garde music into a soundtrack with an intelligent awareness of its dramatic purpose. Ligeti's music (*Atmosphères, Requiem, Lux Aeterna*) is employed deliberately to convey the impression of a mysterious and intelligent presence, one that fortunately we never get to see. The most controversial and difficult scene in the movie depicts the end of the astronaut's final journey to a resting-place where past and future are superimposed, and space is reduced to a framework of appearances. There is no music in this episode, only the sound of the space-suited astronaut breathing, broken from time to time by the heightened clatter of accidental noises. It is a scenario startlingly close in mood to the "Pluramon" ending of *Hymnen*,—and for added symbolism, the initials of the actor playing the solo astronaut are K and D.

The subtext of Kubrick's journey is evolution and human progress, and how the latter is perpetuated through the genetic code. When a spermatozöon penetrates the egg, its tail detaches and only the head, containing the male genetic material, continues the journey. In the movie, survivor Keir Dullea,—having disabled its intelligence system, which has turned against mankind,—detaches himself from the spaceship, which looks like a gigantic spermatozöon, and is drawn through the wormhole at enormous speed to the sound of a rather makeshift montage of Ligeti's music, eventually to arrive at the place where his genetic identity is to be transferred to a new and higher form of being. For a younger generation of the Vietnam era, Kubrick's message of human progress being directed away from militarism and reliance on technology, through transcendence and rebirth, to a higher level of intelligence, is self-explanatory. For Stockhausen to feel identified with the astronaut K. D., both in his personal situation, and through the final scene's allusion to *Hymnen*, also makes sense.

The inspiration for Stockhausen arising from this crucial episode in the movie can be imagined: how to convey in music a sense of past and future superimposed, and how to signal through music the imminent rebirth of a transformed humankind. He takes himself off into retreat, and comes up with fifteen *text* pieces: music involving no technological apparatus, and no "program" of conventional notation.

Kubrick's reaction can also be imagined. All would have been rejected. The will is too overpowering. All fifteen texts are ultimately about directed intuition. Kubrick would have been searching for a music beyond the human will. He opted instead for startling, heightened, incidental sound effects, sounds that are real because they have been produced by chance.

Aus den Sieben Tagen (From the Seven Days)
1968: No. 26 (UE 14790 in German, 14970e in English, 14790f in French; cd Stockhausen-Verlag SV-14: 7 cds).
15 text compositions: "Richtige Dauern" (Right Durations), "Unbegrenzt" (Unlimited), "Verbindung" (Connection), "Treffpunkt" (Meeting-point), "Nachtmusik" (Night Music), "Abwärts" (Downwards), "Aufwärts" (Upwards), "Oben und Unten" (Above and Below: theater piece), "Intensität" (Intensity), "Setz die Segel zur Sonne" (Set Sail for the Sun), "Kommunion" (Communion), "Litanei" (Litany), "Es" (It), "Goldstaub" (Gold Dust), "Ankunft" (Arrival).
Durations unspecified, from 4' to 60'.

From the time of its composition this collection of works has lived, somewhat uncomfortably for English-speaking audiences, with the image of a catechism, or series of spiritual exercises, to be practiced religiously for the good of one's soul. The mind-altering connotations have to be understood in the context of a potentially disastrous rise in the use of LSD as a panacea for the ills of society, encouraged by the demented evangelism of Dr. Timothy Leary. The moralistic implications of Stockhausen's studies have tended to overshadow their undoubted practicality as group exercises in mental gymnastics, of a kind already familiar to students of acting, who are taught to take mental and psychological preparation for a role extremely seriously, indeed, to a degree that makes Stockhausen's demands almost too simple.

Of the fifteen texts, only one, "Litanei," refers to mental attitude. In "Ankunft" he admonishes "Give all that up, we are going about it the wrong way;" in "Es," the direction "think nothing" takes many by surprise. The other texts refer, in different weights and intensities, to recognizable Stockhausen objectives:

1. *Extension of the time perspective* (concentration, endurance):
   Richtige Dauern, Unbegrenzt, Intensität;
2. *Extension of frequency perspective* (pitch, rhythm):
   Verbindung, Nachtmusik, Abwärts, Aufwärts, Kommunion;
3. *Translation from one focus of awareness to another*:
   Nachtmusik, Abwärts, Aufwärts, Kommunion;
4. *Reconciliation of opposites*:
   Abwärts–Aufwärts (considered as a pair), Intensität–Setz die Segel zur Sonne (considered as a pair), Oben und Unten;
5. *Convergence–divergence*:
   Treffpunkt, Oben und Unten, Setz die Segel zur Sonne;
6. *Extension of influence*:
   Intensität, Setz die Segel zur Sonne, Kommunion;
7. *Freedom from external influence*:
   Richtige Dauern, Es, Goldstaub, Ankunft.

Weeks later, at Darmstadt in August, Stockhausen introduced a new group of composition students, and a band of highly experienced performers, to the discipline of composing and interpreting text pieces. It was not an easy task.

> "Play a vibration in the rhythm of your thinking" [—a line from "Connections"]. When I gave a seminar that same year, 1968, in the Darmstadt International courses for Contemporary Music, none of the fourteen young composers knew what I could mean by that. . . . Another example: it says here "Play a vibration in the rhythm of the universe." [Aloys] Kontarsky, who is an extreme intellectual, . . . said, what do you mean by the rhythm of the universe? What is all that mystic stuff here? And I said, I mean, have you never had dreams where you fly from star to star? . . . And he was saying, I don't know, let's stop and you can get somebody else. I said, well Aloys, you see, perhaps the constellations, think Cassiopeia or the other constellations of the stars. He said, Oh, you mean Webern? I said Yes! He said, well okay, let's start.[8]

Stockhausen's candor and humor in discussing the rehearsal and interpretative problems of the text pieces creates an impression of boundless confidence that sits interestingly alongside the evidence of Fred Ritzel's report of the Darmstadt sessions,[9] and the very different images aroused by the 1969 recordings as a whole, which are at times Dante-esque in their depiction of raw emotion and suffering, an experience that led to the withdrawal of the trombonist Vinko Globokar from the ensemble, and removal of his name, at his insistence, from the recording credits. Part of this intensity of effect may have to do with the composer's assertion of control, and assumption of responsibility for the outcome, a decision somewhat at odds with the music's ostensible message of following one's inner promptings. At other times, it worked, as at the Fondation Maeght, where after a series of concerts the Stockhausen group created, on the spur of the moment, an intuitive music accompaniment, based on "a verbal direction, like a text from AUS DEN SIEBEN TAGEN," to a documentary film about a French sculptor in welded metal.[10] Stockhausen was determined to eliminate any trace of selfishness from group performances, having realized that some musicians were unable to resist the temptation to follow their own inspiration at the expense of everybody else. The texts created situations able to bring out the worst, as well as the best, in a performer. The number of players in the group multiplied relationship issues exponentially; four or five seemed to be the optimum. After his initial hopes were dashed that it might provide a model of cooperation for his musicians, Stockhausen reserved a special odium for the influence of free jazz: "What they did this year [1971] at Donaueschingen . . . was just chaos. Everyone played as loud and as fast as possible, and everyone at once. There were hardly any solos, and when there were they were full of unconscious citations of idioms I would rather get rid of."[11] He goes even further in the lecture "Intuitive Music," describing some musicians' behavior as aggressive, totalitarian, and destructive.[12]

Musik für ein Haus (Music for a House)

1968: Collective composition of members of the composition course, Darmstadt International Vacation Courses for New Music, directed by Stockhausen; composers Jorge Peixinho, Clare Franco, Rolf Gehlhaar, Thomas Wells, Fred van der Kooy, Boudewijn Buckinx, Jaroslav J. Wolf, John McGuire, David Ahern, Mesias Maiguashca, Gregory Biss, Costin Miraneau, Junsang Bahk, Jens-Peter Ostendorf, Satoshi Nozaki.

All the same, there has to be a certain irony in the fact that in the photographic record of the *Aus den Sieben Tagen* text pieces, the presence of audio processing technology is overwhelming. Indeed, the composer's specification for *Musik für ein Haus* at Darmstadt is, if anything, more dependent on electronic relays than for *Ensemble* the previous year. This performance event, occupying two floors and a basement of a four-room lodge on the Darmstadt estate, once again overlays a technological superstructure on the primary issue of individual and group interpretation of intuitive music, now texts for meditation. The ritual nature of the texts is superseded, it appears, by the creation of a miniature communications network allowing instrumentalists to converse with one another as if over great distances, identifying themselves by musical call signs and planned limitations of gesture. Out of an exercise in collective intuition Stockhausen has created an electronic simultaneity of chamber concerts in which unity of spiritual purpose is somewhat distracted by a maze of possibilities of accidental conjunctions, mediated by microphones, mixing desks, and loudspeakers.[13]

In a new century, the texts of *Aus den Sieben Tagen* no longer seem difficult or controversial. Television, in particular documentaries designed to reveal, with remarkable technical ingenuity, the lengths to which nature will go to enable living creatures to stalk, kill, and eat one another, has shown itself to be an ideal medium for instantaneous sound images evoking alarm, helplessness, and pain. Initially targeted on composer-performers, the texts now seem especially apt objects of study for Hollywood special effects composers, and might be reclassified as "a breviary for foley artists."

Hinab-Hinauf (From the depths to the heights)
1968–1969: Unrealized project for an intuitive music and light composition.

> Das Tier ist ein Mensch geworden.
> Der Mensch wird ein Geist werden.
> (The beast has become a human being.
> The human being is destined to become a spirit.)[14]

The first intimation of a sound and light composition comes in a text styled in the manner of a press release, dated Darmstadt, 25 August 1968, announcing the composer's participation in the 1970 Osaka World Exposition, in a music programme for a German Pavilion designed to showcase music and technology, to be open to the public daily from 14 March to 14 September. The prospect of overseeing an unprecedented series of daily concerts of his own music over a continuous period of six months was thus already known to Stockhausen at the time of the 1968 Darmstadt composition course, and almost certainly contributed to the direction of the course, its focus on intuitive techniques, and unabashed emphasis on technical relays and effects. This was a remarkable turnaround in fortunes from the events of May.

The planners' original proposal called for a circular auditorium in the style of a stadium, within which a variety of light and sound equipment, distributed freely around the periphery, would form a sculptural landscape of working exhibits of German manufacture. Stockhausen was almost certainly the only composer in Germany with the experience and imagination necessary to undertake the task of bringing life, high art, and creative excitement to a display of items of equipment over such a long period, and it is to the organizers' credit that they accepted the composer's alternative proposal for a geodesic dome to operate as a fully functional electronic concert chamber. The composer's 25 August text does not explicitly refer to a spherical auditorium, but does mention architect Fritz Bornemann's "new model that conforms to a considerable extent with Stockhausen's proposals and drawings."[15]

Consideration of the form and content of Stockhausen's proposed music and light presentation, both in the technical sense, and in the aesthetic dimension, is incomplete without some reference to precedent. Stockhausen would remember Pousseur's unfortunate experience with *Trois Visages de Liège*, a work commissioned by the Liège city fathers in 1961 to accompany an abstract light show by the sculptor Nicolas Schöffer, only to be taken off the programme after just a few days. The German organizers for Expo 70 were almost certainly mindful of the success of Xenakis's *Polytope de Montréal*, a light and sound installation for the French government pavilion of the 1967 Montreal Expo, involving four orchestras and an intricate light show, and lasting all of six minutes. At 13½ minutes, the allotted time-frame of Stockhausen's *Hinab-Hinauf* was scarcely long enough for the composer to draw breath; even so, he is eager to reassure the commissioning body, in terms reminiscent of Froebel, that "spontaneous play directed to a specific outcome is an absolutely essential enrichment, and guarantees, —within predetermined limits,—variation of the music, so that over the course of several months it will evolve like a living thing and not turn into a petrified object."[16]

Naturally it is important for any such project to make a statement, and send a message of the quality of Germany's cultural and technological achievements, at least impressive enough to match the impact and prestige of the Xenakis initiative at the French pavilion at Montreal. For Stockhausen himself, the benchmark would have been set much earlier, by the Philips Pavilion of the 1958 Brussels World Fair, designed by Le Corbusier and featuring the *Poème électronique* by Varèse, a fresh reminder of which had just become available in Fernand Ouellette's biography of Varèse, newly published in English translation in 1968. The Philips sound and light presentation was an event in which the three channels of Varèse's tape composition were independently distributed along prefigured pathways traversing an installation of over 400 loudspeakers attached to the under-side of the tent-like structure, controlled from signals recorded on a multi-track tape recorder. The Philips installation had features in common with the RCA-Bell "Fantasound" system developed for Disney's movie *Fantasia* in 1940 (and its visualization, to be sure, with the movie's more abstract representations of the music of J. S. Bach). Varèse's music was accompanied by projections, chosen by Le Corbusier, and in the words of Howard Taubman of the *New York Times*, images of "birds and beasts and fish and reptiles; . . . masks, skeletons, idols, girls clad and unclad. . . . The score is not compounded of recognizable instruments. It is the work of a man who has been seeking for several decades to return music to a purity of sound that he does not believe possible in conventional music-making."[17]

The elaborate and dynamic distribution of sound, the nature of the imagery, and the humanitarian impact of Varèse's organized sound are in accord with Stockhausen's own proposal; elsewhere another review of the 1958 Philips presentation had expressed sentiments with which the composer could also identify: "Here, one no longer hears the sounds, one finds oneself literally in the heart of the sound source. One does not listen to the sound, one lives it."[18] On the other hand, there are clear oppositions in design if the two are compared. Whereas Varèse had relied on tape, Stockhausen would also employ live performers; where Varèse's sound projection was mechanically controlled, Stockhausen's would be manually controlled; where the relationship between Varèse's sound images and Le Corbusier's visual projections had been arbitrary and unplanned, in Stockhausen's pro-posal the counterpoint of music and visual imagery was through-composed.

In contrast to Le Corbusier's tensile structure, a mathematical statement of positive and negative curvatures, Stockhausen was opting for a geodesic dome, also mathematical, but expressing a rigid and inflexible sphericity. In the Philips pavilion a moving public had been led physically by the sound projection system; for Stockhausen, the rotational movements of his music were designed to lead the audience upward, spiritually, and even make them dizzy. Le Corbusier had conceived his pavilion as "un estomac"—a stomach, taking in, digesting, and expelling a continuously moving audience; for his part, Stockhausen envisaged the German pavilion as a sound-transparent electronic womb, within which his audience would be seated in relative stillness, and from which they would depart feeling reborn.

Varèse had had mixed feelings about Le Corbusier's selection of light images, for which he was unprepared and about which he had not been consulted. Albert Jeanneret, the architect's brother and himself a musician, expressed the problem succinctly: "the two lessen and dissipate each other, . . . whereas the music on its own is truly a spontaneous creation endowed with that infinity toward which all music tends."[19] (The same criticism could also be made of the dynamic visual effects accompanying the worm-hole scene of Kubrick's movie, compared to the "Overture" of the same movie, where all one can see as accompaniment to the same music, apart from the word itself, is a luminous darkness.) As Stockhausen's first project to involve a visual scenario, *Hinab-Hinauf* is a significant indicator of his aesthetic priorities in the visual domain; but one has also to remember that the visual aspect was a given, so the difficult creative task facing the composer was how to arrive at a suitable accommodation of music and light.

Working very rapidly, as he had done for *Mixtur* and would do again for *Trans*, Stockhausen had prepared a working plan for the composition of *Hinab-Hinauf* by the second week of September, along with a detailed technical specification for the complicated sound projection system.

> It is a model of musical, visual, and sculptural/environmental (raum-plastisch) integration. . . . The title "Hinab-Hinauf" signifies a dynamic movement passing continuously through eight levels of consciousness of appearance and experience. Beginning with bright, exalted, nameless happenings, a first phase of concerted light, sound, and spatial movement leads through a panorama of abstract forms, then technical-objective images, then living-organic forms, then surreal and dreamlike, then flora and fauna, then mineral and inorganic images, through to the unimaginable world of the atoms. In subsequent phases, sound, light, and spatial movements diverge more or less from one another, passing independently through the various levels, meeting from time to time and ultimately coming together in a long, contrapuntal upward movement out of the deepest sphere of dead and lifeless things, finally reaching the highest attainable level, a region of calm, pure, lasting brightness of sound and light. . . .[20]

It may well be that Stockhausen was so preoccupied with the technical issues of sound projection that he did not take time to consider the full impact of such a visual conception on visitors of other world cultures.

Mindful perhaps of the power of intuitive music to unlock the most debased as well as the most sublime elements of a musican's persona, Stockhausen has devised a modern *Gradus ad Parnassum* in which, responding directly to visual images, as to a silent movie, performers articulate the fall and rise of the human spirit, leading upward to a transcendental state that, over a period of months, may continuously transcend itself. While drawing on tendencies already expressed in the writings of Kandinsky, in *On the Spiritual in Art,* and *Der gelbe Klang* (the Yellow Sound), and also Schoenberg, in *Die Jakobsleiter*, Stockhausen's visual program can all too easily be read as endorsing a resurgent neosuprematist ethic associated with the *Ganzheitslehre* sympathies of a still powerful intelligentsia.

> Sri Aurobindo emphasized that evolution was moving the race toward a Superman and Superwoman species. Paramahansa Satyanada . . . refers to the Animal/Man becoming the God man. He emphasized that at the next level of evolution we would become Junior Gods. Gopi Krishna categorized this transition as evolving from Human to Transhuman Consciousness . . . [maintaining] that by the application of various psychotechnological practices this innate mechanism can be fully activated, leading to an acceleration of an individual's evolution, resulting in expanded consciousness, greatly increased creativity and a profound state of happiness.[21]

Gopi Krishna's *Biological Basis of Religion and Genius* appeared in print in Germany in 1968, with an introduction by Carl F. von Weizsäcker.[22] Whatever its intellectual merits, the undisguised Nietzschean overtones of a philosophical message dedicated to the renewal of the master race were unlikely to be welcomed by Japanese audiences, let alone representatives of the international diplomatic and business communities. Though lightened by touches of humor including images of flying carpets, Stockhausen's exposition of spiritual growth and human perfectibility,—music aside,—now seems terribly dated, like a color-engraved evolutionary chart on the wall of a classroom, or in the back of a family encyclopedia. What makes the project interesting in a purely musical sense is the composer's idea of using visual stimuli as a means of guiding and coordinating the intuitions of his musicians. Abandoning his original plan released Stockhausen from the constraint of a 13½-minute time frame, allowing a more varied repertoire, to include alternative pieces, provisionally entitled *Duo* and *Trio*.

Spiral (Spiral)

1968: No. 27 (UE 14957; cd Stockhausen-Verlag SV-15, SV-45, SV-46)
For soloist with shortwave receiver; 3 microphones, 2 × 2 loudspeakers, mixing console.
Duration: 135'.

This composition arose from a request from a young American guitarist, which accounts for the nice distinction in subtitle between *Solo*, "—for a melody instrument," and *Spiral*, "—for a soloist" (though the new piece is also performable by a melody instrument or voice). The score provides new

1. Intensification of material (nondevelopment)

OR	(ornament) intensifying Duration	D
POLY	(polyphonic) intensifying Register	R
PER	(periodic) intensifying Gestalt	G
E	(echo) enhances intensity/loudness	I/L

2. Nonlinear transformations (performer-centered)

⊕	(expand in all dimensions) equivalent	+
⊖	(contract in all dimensions) equivalent	−
✳	(repeat an element) equivalent	=
▯	(spiral-sign repeat and transcend a previous event) equivalent	±

3. Diffusion of material (partial development)

❘: 7 :❘	Repeat previous event as often as indicated, applying the given sign
←⌒•	(retroactive)
⌒•→	Permutate a previous sequence to make a polyphonic continuum
PERM-POLY	(anticipatory)

4. "Freeze" signs (semi-automatic)

(AKK)	Make the previous note-succession into an arpeggio or chord in the rhythm of the previous event ↕ (vertical "fix")
(BAND)	Play parts of the previous event singly, then in a chosen sequence, so fast that they blur into a band of sound ↔ (horizontal "fix")

Spiral: *A new vocabulary of transformation signs and their meanings*

possibilities for a harmonic instrument, but the change of focus from instrument to performer is more interesting, and may be explained in the first instance as an effect of Stockhausen's meditative texts. *Spiral* brings to the plain arithmetical notation of *Prozession* and *Kurzwellen* a supplementary vocabulary of performer-orientated signs, and a flamboyance of style, that create new expressive ambiguities (and tautologies) to be exploited by the interpreter. In fact, the new piece is much more "improvisatory" in a real sense than either earlier work, or *Solo*. The supplementary signs, some restored from *Prozession*, others derived from *Solo*, fall generally into groups of four, categorized as variants of the original plus-minus signs. From time to time, special emphasis is laid on particular types of event. Here too a selection of four signs is available: P (points), Gr (groups), M (mass texture), and "Mix," a mixture of categories.

Of all the signs in this new array, the most provocative is certainly the "spiral sign" indicating that the performer should go beyond the limits of the attainable. In an unusually fulsome introduction to a piece consisting of a single page, the composer explains with examples how the first eight symbols are to be interpreted. It is clear that what he has in mind are changes of scale corresponding to mechanical operations, such as expansion in time, expansion (or decompression) of amplitude space, expansion of frequency range (and interval steps, as in *Studie II*), and expansion of intervals of rhythm, as in Messiaen (also a mechanical, additive process).

Spiral: *symmetrical and "exponential" sign-groups*

The new richness of vocabulary permits a range of quasi-symmetrical formulations of great suggestiveness. There are familiar juxtapositions of groups of plus and minus signs, and also reciprocal pairings of different types of sign; paired elements can also be separated by intrusive elements, as in *Kurzwellen*, but in more complicated permutations. The options of transformation suggest an extraordinary capacity for expansion and diminution of scale: a preponderance of three- and four-sign aggregates that could simply be mischievously intended, but could also relate to the cosmic scale of the *Aus den Sieben Tagen* texts, to be interpreted "mit der Gewissheit/ dass Du beliebig viel Zeit und Raum hast" (with the certainty/ that you have an infinite amount of time and space).[23] Two additional features testify to that grandeur of concept, and a compulsive forward urge far exceeding the precise, point-to-point alterations of the earlier pieces in this group. One is the "exponential group," an expansion process differing from the spiral sign, and taking a number of forms (as above); the other, also exponential in effect, is cyclical: its most striking example, the following "super-symmetry:"

Spiral: *example of a "Super-symmetry"*

Spiral is Stockhausen's most closely reasoned, and the most baroque in conception, of the plus-minus group of compositions. It exposes a formidable intensity of will, given added edge from his encounter with the writings of Sri Aurobindo. Now adopted for the composer's work-list, the spiral emblem has many connotations: natural power, as in a tornado or maelstrom;

physical strength, as in the tattoo on the buttock; resistance, as in a screw
or spring; authority, as in the facial tattoo; transcendence, as in the spiral
dance of the whirling dervish. A spiral shell is emblematic of continuous
growth, certainly a relevant consideration. As a musical statement, *Spiral*
articulates the promise of a new dynamic, but one with attendant risks: of
disorientation, or destruction. The same spiral path that leads to the
summit of the sacrificial mound, may also lead to the unfinished chaos of an
abandoned Tower of Babel.

Dr. K.–Sextett (Sextet for Dr. Kalmus)

1969: No. 28 (UE 19914; lp "A Garland for Dr. K." UE 15043)
For flute, bass clarinet, piano, vibraphone (tubular bells), viola, cello.
Duration 3½'–4'.

In January 1969 the London office of Universal Edition requested a number
of the firm's house composers to compose a short work, suitable for the
ensemble "The Fires of London," to be performed at an eightieth birthday
celebration for director Dr. Alfred Kalmus. Stockhausen's offering, sketched
on the back of the letter from Universal Edition, is a tiny masterpiece: a
slow-motion study of a wave, caught in 26 eight-second "frames" (or alternatively, blowing up a party balloon in 26 eight-second "puffs"). The image
of a shock wave emitted and reflected back through itself is caught in words
in the text "Waves" from the collection *Für Kommende Zeiten*. Here it is
expressed in a structure of eights: eight voices, eight dynamics, eight divisions of the fundamental pulsation (which, though notated graphically, may
be interpreted as a duration series 1–2–3–4–5–6–7–8 inserted in a time
module of 3 × 12 unit subdivisions, first foward, then reverse).

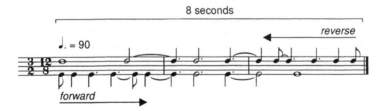

The unit measure is treated as an expanded rhythmic cell or time frame, to
be scanned at regular intervals at a constant speed, like an oscilloscope. At
first the measure is divided into a decelerating pattern of beats, like the
mokugyo drum in *Telemusik*. An initially compacted cluster of tones is
gradually dispersed, like the petals of a flower cast into the sea. The
initiating attack is fortissimo, to signify the wave-making shock; the second,
in pianissimo, the aftershock, and the intervening duration, the
fundamental periodicity (like a wave flowing from one end of the bath to the
other). Thereafter the wave motion becomes progressively audible as a
bending out of shape of the opening vertical chord. One by one, perhaps

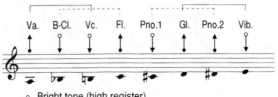

o Bright tone (high register)
• Dark tone (low register)
↑ Ascending
↓ Descending

more like a string of corks than separate petals (one has to hear them as connected, after all), the notes played by bell, vibraphone, viola, cello, piano (right hand), bass clarinet, piano (left hand), and flute detach themselves from the downbeat to create a gradually widening arpeggio. The greater the distance from the downbeat, the louder the note, so the time frame is defined by both a deceleration and a crescendo. This genially simple process is enhanced by unexpected accents, trills, prolongations, and little "mistakes" of pitch or dynamic in measures 7, 11, and 18, to make it more interesting.

The widening process reaches its maximum at measure 9, to fill out the entire time frame. It is then "reflected" back in time, the leading instruments *accelerating* (i.e., a backwards ritardando) to overtake those still on the outward path—a very beautiful conceit, elegantly worked out (a pity that the timbres of the instruments could not also be reversed). As each voice rejoins the downbeat, it sounds fortissimo once again. What began as a logarithmic ritardando is reflected as a delayed accelerando (like a bouncing ball), all the while the note cluster continuing to expand, finally reaching a six-octave span. At maximum expansion the cluster, now a harmony of sorts, repeats in triumphant fortissimo, like the final chord of a Beethoven symphony, suddenly collapsing like a balloon, with tremolo sound effects, to end in a terminal beep. One really wants the last chord to fly uncontrollably around the room like a red balloon that has been blown up and then mischievously let go.

For all the fun, this is not an easy piece to perform. The composer offers some hints:

> Notes short, but not staccato.
> No body-movement between notes. Play each note facing in a
> different direction and hold the body rigid in the same
> attitude until the following note. The performance should not
> be conducted.

This composition is a textbook case for distributing the players in a circle around the audience, to achieve the separation of individual voices, noted by Brant, that is needed here; and also to ensure that members of the audience are unable to see all of the players at once, so the expansion pattern impacts directly. When Stockhausen returns to this type of expansion process, in *Ylem*, the performers do indeed execute an expansion movement from the center to the margins, and back again.

Fresco (Fresco)

1969: No. 29 (UE 15147)

"Wall sounds" for orchestra divided into four distinctive, mixed groups, and four conductors, located in four foyers or separate rooms of the same auditorium, and arranged from low to high in pitch, e.g.:

Group I: tuba, 2 trombones, 2 bassoons, 3 horns, percussionist (2 pedal timpani, marimbaphone), conductor (oboe), 2 oboes, 2 trumpets, 2 clarinets, 2 flutes, vibraphone (soft sticks);

Group II: 2 contrabasses, 3 cellos, 4 violas, conductor (harmonium), 5 second violins, 6 first violins;

Group III: conductor (piano), trombone, 2 contrabasses, 1 bassoon, 2 cellos, 2 horns, 2 violas, oboe, trumpet, 2 second violins, clarinet, 2 first violins, flute;

Group IV: 2 contrabasses, 3 cellos, 3 violas, conductor (accordion or chromatic mouth organ), 4 second violins, 7 first violins.

Duration: 5 hours 40'.

The title refers to walls, but also to fresh air and the idea of an artwork created in real time in perfect calm. The composition arose from an invitation from the principal conductor of the Bonn Symphony Orchestra, that Stockhausen take over the entire recently-opened Beethovenhalle in Bonn for an evening of music. Funds and rehearsal time were limited, but apart from that (and a discreet hint that an event resembling *Ensemble* and *Musik für ein Haus* would be welcome), the offer was unconditional. After a conducted tour of the new building, which comprises a large auditorium, two concert chambers, service rooms, and interconnecting passageways allowing free flow of movement:

> I agreed at once, and the same evening drew up a plan for four-hour, nonstop performances in each of the three rooms of the Beethovenhalle, . . . already hearing in my imagination orchestra musicians playing quiet "wall sounds"—starting at the entrance foyer, through the cloakrooms, along the lengthy promenades, from the cross-bridges leading to the balconies, right through to the entrance to the most distant studio. . . . The idea of "wall sounds" intends no irony. What I had in mind was that for once, instead of the usual concert story, the whole area, from cloakroom to seat in the auditorium, could be made an experience in sound, so that the listener could begin listening, if he wanted, from the moment of entry, making his own selection from a timetable placed at the entrance giving details of the three programs to take place simultaneously in the three auditoria.[24]

There were no shopping malls to speak of in Germany in 1969, but there were air terminals, with their multiple interconnected transit lounges, hours of waiting, and piped music. *Fresco* is Stockhausen's gift, not to the concertgoer, but to life's airline passenger, caught between connections, with several hours to kill. Rather than seeking, as Cage had done in his musical "environments" *Variations IV* and *Variations V*, to compose a sound system within which performers were to interact freely (a procedure guaranteed in the circumstances to generate an experience of major tedium and minor sociological interest),[25] Stockhausen aims for exactly the opposite: live musicians creating low-level, controlled, colored resonances of musical sounds, but expressing no immediately perceptible form. Such sounds are designed to have a soothing effect, discreetly blanketing the drone of air conditioning and the clutter of conversation. Over four hours the sound atmosphere will slowly change, so that an audience member coming out of one concert hall will sense a difference in the air.

A four-hour session starting at 7:10 in the evening, before the audience has begun to arrive, and continuing until 12:40 am, long after the cleaners have departed, and performing very slow up-and-down scales, is not calculated to be enjoyable for the members of the orchestra, who generally prefer to perform in a concert hall than on the street, even if the street in this case is a comfortable corridor. But this is part and parcel of the composer's keen didactic and disciplinarian approach. (One imagines that the orchestra's union representative saw it as an opportunity to claim overtime, for an evening of musical actions simple enough to be sight read, so it could work both ways.) The "wall sounds" themselves consist of slow, alternately rising and falling clusters of glissandi or scalewise progressions, expanding or contracting in range, with ample rest periods between. The closest familar example of such an effect would be the orchestra glissandi in The Beatles' "A Day in the Life" from the 1967 album *Sergeant Pepper*, but unimaginably slower, and without the back beat. Another image to be borne in mind is the descending cluster of *Hymnen*, Region IV, with the difference that *Fresco*'s clusters have the humanity and variation of acoustic instruments as opposed to the unyielding metallic sheen of electronic sound.

On to the matt surface of group clusters the composer has etched a variety of textures, following a procedure similar to the noises in *Stop*. These textural effects, carefully graded, follow their own symmetrical patterns of rising and falling complexity, e.g.: continuous tones–trills–agitated tremolos–irregular repetitions–continuous tones, and back again.

The four orchestral groups were disposed along walls and corners in different locations, the instruments in line, in order of tessitura from bass to treble, and positioned to allow eye contact between the conductor and every player, which is not as easy as it seems. There were no electronics, which might have created safety complications in public areas. Like the orchestration of *Punkte 1952/62*, all instruments are of precise pitch. In such a situation the acoustic behavior of different instruments becomes a significant issue. Heavy carpet on the floor absorbs a great deal of the sound energy that would be reflected from a concert platform, so for most instruments, playing in a corridor or foyer has the effect of drastically dampening their individual sound level. For some instruments, however, such as horns or tuba, with their bells pointing toward the wall or ceiling, the reflections will be stronger and earlier, so their sound will be noticeably more penetrating. The issue of ensemble balance cannot be improvised away. Most modern orchestral instruments have been adapted for power: concert halls are large places, and even the distance from platform edge to the first row of seats is a corridor wide. The questions of balancing an ensemble to be listened to from close quarters were fully addressed in the baroque and classical eras, before the invention of the nineteeth-century mega-auditorium; logically the best range of instruments for "wall sounds" are to be found among the renaissance and baroque: viols, recorders, cornetts, shawms, organs, lute, theorbo, harp and spinet—all out of the question in the circumstances. Ironically, the acoustic result Stockhausen had in mind might best be realized, in the long run, by a multichannel recording, studio recorded and balanced, with coordinated images of the performing musicians viewable on television monitors.

Tunnel-Spiral (Tunnel-Spiral)

1969: description in *Texte 3*, 188–93.
Composition for solo performer, 3 temple bells, shortwave receiver, and feedback relay.
Duration unspecified.

John Mizelle, a student in Stockhausen's composition seminar at University of California, Davis in 1967, invited the composer to contribute a work for the Los Angeles Junior Arts Center "Sound Tunnel," a rectangular tube 40 feet long, 6½ feet high, and 3½ feet wide, lined with a programmable relay of 100 speakers, and with large Altec monitors facing inward at either end. Stockhausen's suggestion creates a spirally rotating delay line, specifying an incremental delay of 80 ms. between speakers 1–12, rising to 300 ms. between speakers 90–100, giving an acoustic impression of a continuously expanding spiral in the shape of an old-style conical megaphone.

Since he could not travel to Los Angeles to test the structure in person, Stockhausen has kept the sound-material deliberately simple: 1. a reading (by a male bass voice) from Sri Aurobindo's *Synthesis of Yoga*, punctuated from time to time by: 2. strokes on three rin tuned to adjacent semitones (Japanese temple bells, heard in *Telemusik*); 3. sporadic bursts of shortwave signals, for preference "scarcely comprehensible speech," faded in and out; and 4. very occasional single handclaps (two hands). Some imitation of shortwave speech by the speaker is also indicated.

Pole für 2 (Poles for 2)

1969–1970: No. 30 (Stockhausen-Verlag; cd SV-15)
For 2 players or singers with 2 shortwave receivers, 2 microphones, 2 × 4 loudspeakers, mixing console.
Duration: 23'.

Stockhausen's "Duo" and "Trio" for the Osaka Expo, renamed *Pole für 2* and *Expo für 3*, complete the sequence of plus-minus process scores with a return to simplicity. As the title suggests, *Pole für 2* revisits the dialogue of opposites first encountered in Stockhausen's early pieces inspired by Hesse's fictional Glass Bead Game. As one might expect, mirror-image processes form the basis of a symmetrical composition plan that might almost be described in the terms of a medieval formal courtship dance where male and female partners execute complementary patterns of movement, sometimes alternately, sometimes in parallel. Compared to *Spiral*, the score appears neither tentative nor burdened with symbolic overkill; however the introduction of higher and lower orders of plus and minus signs (like an "Arrow" study score) is an interesting development. The work is in seven sections and ends with a "Da Capo" allowing for indefinite continuation. The instrumental dialogue is reflected, after the manner of *Mikrophonie I*, in separate parts for sound projection, designed with the Expo 70 dome in mind, but adaptable to smaller loudspeaker installations (the composer specifies a minimum of eight separately-addressable outputs). At places where the two voices form a symmetrical duo, the implication is that their opposite natures are emphasized; these sections always terminate with oppositely-charged "spiral-sign" cadenzas. Alternating dialogue, on the other hand, suggests convergence and exchange of material; the point of maximum reconciliation, at measure 17 toward the end of section 3, followed by a codetta in which echoes of the previous event predominate.

Expo für 3 (Expo for 3)

1969–1970: No. 31 (Stockhausen-Verlag)
For 3 players/singers with 3 shortwave receivers; 3 microphones, 3 × 2 loudspeakers, mixing console.
Duration: 21'.

Closely synchronized gestures and canonic imitation feature prominently in this altogether more relaxed piece in which solo leads and synchronized accompaniments suggest a high level of mutual understanding. A combination of factors gives the score its cheerful aspect. One is the hybrid sign language, combining conventional verbal and symbolic notations of rhythm, accent, and dynamics, along with plus and minus signs. Another is the relative simplicity of individual parts; these are individually characterized, and involve a lot of bantering mutual imitation. There are also touches of humor: a lengthy solo passage for III consisting of single plus signs followed by quadruple minuses that looks suspiciously like self-parody (suggesting the performer implicated had too fertile an imagination); another passage where all three players synchronize to a common periodicity, and repeat, with syncopations, a fragment from a previous event, implying a joke beng repeated until everyone has got the point. The seven-times repeated cadence leading to "Da Capo," coming after all three players have been independently playing in a blur at top speed (BAND) has the mock finality of Satie. As Stravinsky said of *Zyklus*, "one almost wishes it didn't have to be *translated* into sound but were a kind of hand-drawn photo-electric sound (after a spectrum)."[26]

Notes

1. Ben Shahn, *Love and Joy about Letters* (London: Cory, Adams & Mackay, 1964), 13–14.

2. Ludwig Wittgenstein, *Tractatus Logico-Philosophicus* tr. C. K. Ogden and F. P. Ramsay (London: Routledge and Kegan Paul, 1922).

3. Jonathan Cott, *Stockhausen: Conversations with the Composer* (London: Robson Books, 1974), 26.

4. Michael Nyman, *Experimental Music: Cage and Beyond* (London: Studio Vista, 1974), 68–71.

5. David Lodge, *Art of Fiction* (Harmondsworth: Penguin Books, 1992), 21–22.

6. Samuel Beckett, *Ping.* In *Encounter* Vol. 28, No. 2 (1967): 25–26. See also David Lodge, "Some *Ping* Understood." *Encounter* Vol. 30, No. 2 (1968): 85–89.

7. John Cage, *I–VI* (Cambridge, Mass: Harvard University Press), 1990.

8. *SoM*, 117–19.

9. Fred Ritzel, "Musik für ein Haus." *Darmstädter Beiträge zur Neuen Musik* (Mainz: Schott, 1970).

10. *SoM*, 144–45.

11. Peter Heyworth, "Spiritual Dimensions," *Music and Musicians* (May 1971): 38–39. See also Jonathan Cott, *Stockhausen: Conversations with the Composer* (London: Robson Books, 1974), 198–99.

12. *SoM*, 122.

13. *Texte 3*, 216–21. See also Jonathan Cott, *Stockhausen: Conversations with the Composer*, 206–8, 214–17.

14. "From the notes for *Hinab-Hinauf.* September 1968." *Texte 3*, 164–65.

15. "Licht–Raum–Musik *HINAB-HINAUF*: (Das ursprüngliche Projekt)." *Texte 3*, 155–58.

16. *Texte 3*, 156.

17. Howard Taubman, *New York Times* (July 8, 1958). Cited in Fernand Ouellette, *Edgar Varèse: A Musical Biography* tr. Derek Coltman. (London: Calder & Boyars, 1973), 201.

18. "J. O.", "Poème électronique." *Radio et T.V.* No. 5 (May 1958): 349–55. Cited in Fernand Ouellette, *Edgar Varèse: A Musical Biography*, 202.

19. Fernand Ouellette, *Edgar Varèse: A Musical Biography*, 202.

20. *Texte 3*, 156.

21. http://www.philosophy.org/webarticles/text/gopi1.htm. (07/24/2003).

22. Gopi Krishna, *Die Biologische Basis der Religiösen Erfahrung*. With an introduction by C. F. von Weizsäcker (Munich: Wilhelm Heyne, 1968). In English, *Biological Basis of Religion and Genius* (New York: Harper and Row, 1972).

23. From "Unlimited." *SoM*, 116–17.

24. *Texte 3*, 143–44.

25. James Pritchett, *Music of John Cage* (Cambridge: Cambridge University Press, 1993), 150–56.

26. Igor Stravinsky and Robert Craft, *Memories and Commentaries* (London: Faber and Faber, 1960), 118n.

CHAPTER EIGHTEEN

Findings

In German the word for cathedral is "Dom." Say "cup" in England and you mean afternoon tea, but say "dome" in Germany and you mean a sacred space. The sacredness of a dome is not so much external and fetishistic—the feminine analogue to the campanile—as internal: the dome interior is at once a representation of the dome of the heavens, and an acoustic lens. In reinstating freedom of movement and access to areas normally out of bounds, the growth of tourism has revived public awareness of the acoustic significance of historic interiors, spaces, and materials. Standing underneath a cathedral dome and looking upward,—a combination of location and attitude usually denied to the congregation and reserved only for authorized religious dignitaries,—one is exposed to the curious acoustic effect of elevation whereby the singing of the choir is brought to a focus and reflected as if from heaven above. That the effect was well-known and regarded as sacred can be inferred from the situation of the altar, installation of public seating beyond the dome periphery, and restriction of public access to the zone to the most sacred moments of social and religious life. Dome interiors are typically decorated with images of the Ascension, heavenly hosts, and singing angels, to reinforce the *acoustic* illusion of an elevated and heavenly space. In the eighteenth-century era of secular humanism, wealthy landowners redesigned the landscape and installed small domed gazebos as listening posts in which to sit and enjoy the sounds of nature.

One of very few historic buildings to be spared by Allied bombing, Cologne Cathedral stands in the center of town, opposite the Hauptbahnhof, the main railway station, on the west bank of the Rhine, Germany's main waterway leading from Switzerland to the south, to Holland and the English Channel to the north and west. A devoted Catholic, Stockhausen was a regular churchgoer as a young man; as a composer and fabricator of sounds, he paid great attention to the acoustics of religious buildings, the movements of religious ceremony, and their powers of suggestion. To the mind of a poet there is meaning and symmetry in the close juxtaposition of a great building, dedicated to the eternal values of religion; a great river, emblematic of time; and the railway station, a surrealist icon representing human industry, commerce, and directed movement in space.

In Cologne, they call it "the Dom"—but the Cathedral *has no dome*. It has everything else the word implies: doom, domination, domain, dominion, domicile; but not the acoustic. The north German gothic cathedral is a vast and complex interior space, but not the same kind of acoustic space as the basilica of St. Mark in Venice where Gabrieli and Monteverdi conducted their spatial experiments in the early years of the seventeenth century.[1] The interior shape and complexity of a building created for sound influences the music created within it. Domes or spheres are not good containers for direct sound, and architects are taught to avoid them. Curved walls, as in baroque architecture, create unexpected zones of sound reinforcement and reflection; but parallel walls, as Palladio knew, reinforce the divisions of a wavelength corresponding to the distance between them, and so establish a preferred tonality for a given rectangular space.[2] Sound radiates outward in spherical waves, hence the music of the spheres as an image of celestial order and stability; but a spherical reflector, or even a part sphere, such as a Roman amphitheater or a dome, creates acoustical chaos.[3]

Although Stockhausen had called for the introduction of "new halls for listening," including spherical auditoria, in the article "Musik im Raum" (Music in Space) published in 1959 in *die Reihe 5* and reprinted with additions in *Texte 1*, there is nothing in the article to suggest either that he had practical experience of the acoustics of dome structures, or that he was aware of their musical implications, other than in a formal sense of allowing flexibility of positioning of an orchestra or of loudspeakers.[4] In a rather opaque summary, suggesting he does not quite understand what it implies either, Karl Wörner explains "the spherical form seems to him favorable on account of the fact that one would be able to hear from all directions; the sphere should have scarcely any resonance of its own, for this would already be given by the loudspeakers provided."[5] The symbolism of the sphere is noted by Fred K. Prieberg. "A dangerously explosive idea," he observes, then goes on to suggest that Stockhausen's essentially idealistic conception is "streng akustisch gedacht" (conceived on strong acoustic principles).[6]

The question is whether, in opting for a geodesic dome, Stockhausen was aware of the acoustic risks. Given the celebrated engineering debacle over Jørn Utzon's Sydney Opera House, a structure of great visual charisma but debatable acoustic merit, it would be very surprising if Fritz Bornemann, the architect of the German Osaka Pavilion, had not alerted Stockhausen to the practical implications of a spherical structure. That the composer regarded a sphere as a perfect shape for the music of the future is a matter of record. Stockhausen may well have been inspired by the symbolism of the 1770 sphere of Claude Nicholas Ledoux, designed as an image of classical perfection and reproduced in Prieberg's monograph as an eighteenth-century prototype of what Stockhausen had in mind.[7] Or, more famously, Étienne-Louis Boullée's internally spherical cenotaph, devised in 1784 to commemorate the life of Isaac Newton and the triumph of reason. That the French author of a recent textbook on architecture can refer to the perfect symbolism of Boullée's sphere without mentioning that, if built, the structure would have been a disaster acoustically, is perhaps an indication of the profession's continued reliance on visual priorities:

> The universal character of these volumes hardly needs to be empha-sized, and one wonders whether such spatial layouts should not be reserved for exceptional buildings whose public significance really deserves it. The project for the cenotaph of Newton by Boullée, a monument dedicated to the glory and universality of science, perfectly illustrates this correspondence between the intrinsic qualities of the form and the meaning that is conferred on it.[8]

Newton's law of the motion of the planets is derived in part from Pythag-oras's doctrine of the music of the spheres, but the issue is not about the perfect sphere of the universe, which is a figure of speech, but the relation-ship of vibrating components within a stable and orderly system. As well as being acoustically inharmonious, the spherical monument somehow misses the point.[9]

Stockhausen's comments on his Osaka experience, in the lecture "Four Criteria of Electronic Music," while not intended to be exhaustive, are nevertheless of interest. "It was a geodesic construction with a plastic skin, very well made. And it worked acoustically: everyone said a sphere never works well, you get sounds bouncing up and down, but the sound was wonderful, very good acoustics and good reverberation." In the same lecture he talks in some detail about the acoustical cues that distinguish a sound that is near at hand, from one that is heard from miles away; and he also laments the fact that most people have difficulty in dissociating visual appearances from acoustic realities: "they say, well, the walls have not moved, so it is an illusion." Although spatial effects have been exploited in the past, for example by Mahler placing a trumpet at the back of the audi-torium, they are primitive compared to the multilayered perspectives that are possible by electronic means (the allusion is specifically to *Kontakte*).[10]

Such remarks are contentious, and also fascinating. Contentious be-cause it is customary to "listen out" for sounds in a world that is implicitly out there; hence, we use sounds primarily as a means of verifying the exis-tence of an external world and locating ourselves in relation to it and them, and only secondarily out of interest in identifying them by name. Fasci-nating, because what Stockhausen appears to be saying is that nearness or distance in a sound are inherent in the coloration and relative complexity of the sound itself, and not in how a person hears it. A recording engineer may well agree: as you bring the microphone closer to a buzzing bee or a violin, the spectrum of the sound and its dynamic range both increase, and the balance of direct to reflected sound shifts dramatically in favor of the direct sound. For listeners with normal hearing, however, the direction and distance of a sound are determined spontaneously by comparing the input at one ear with the input at the other, in loudness, time of arrival, and relative clarity. This is done automatically: it is a "primitive" survival mechanism of all binaural creatures, and does not involve the higher brain function of giving a name to the sound. (In fact, since hearing is an ongoing process, dissociating a sound from its environmental context and giving it a name are operations that can only be done after it has already been processed as an unidentified flying object). At this point one is bound to recall that Stockhausen's hearing in one ear was damaged in infancy by a childhood infection. Since a perception of location in acoustic space (the processing of extremely subtle differences between two coincident signals) relies critically on the high frequency sensitivity of both ears working together, any serious imbalance in sensitivity between the two ears is bound to impair a person's spatial discrimination to some extent. Hence the emphasis at Osaka, perhaps, on dynamic movement and the rotation of sounds at speed while the listener remains motionless.

Since the world prior to Gutenberg was modeled on acoustic rather than visual phenomena, it would be strange indeed if composers in earlier times had not devoted attention to images of space. In the thirty years or so since Osaka, a resurgent early music movement has restored to public notice a repertoire and instrumentation of preclassical music, unheard and unappreciated for many centuries, that obliges us to think afresh about the conceptual bases of post-1950 avant-garde music as essentially and exclusively modern. Those who deny the past, as the saying goes, are forced to relive it: but to be fair, it was in part the ferocious determination of the serialists to take music back to its origins in acoustics and hearing that inspired the authentic early music movement to take a much deeper forensic interest in the documented sounds and structures of music of historic times, including the relationship of music to its acoustic surroundings. Musical perspective was first systematically investigated in Italy, in works associated with the church, and within acoustic structures such as the basilica of St. Mark in Venice, that were equipped with domed resonating chambers. Thanks to composers of Stockhausen's generation, and Stockhausen himself in particular, it is possible to appreciate the acoustical virtuosity of the Venetian masters and their successors, including Heinrich Schütz, who brought the techniques to Germany, and Giovanni Priuli, who brought them to the Austria of Heinrich Biber and his contemporaries.

Mantra (Mantra)

1970: No. 32 (Stockhausen-Verlag; cd SV-16)
For 2 pianists, with woodblocks and antique cymbals; 2 sine-wave generators (sweep frequency oscillators), 2 ring-modulators, 2-track tape recorder; 6 microphones, 2 × 2 loudspeakers, mixing console.
Duration: 65'.

This is a masterpiece. It defines Stockhausen's aims for the seventies as surely as *Mikrophonie I* for the previous decade. In his great work for solo tam-tam Stockhausen addressed the audio-tactile qualities of sound, and the achievement of exactly defined musical ends by flexible and collaborative means. With *Mantra* the polarity is abruptly reversed. The music is synthetic rather than analytic, active not passive, and detached rather than involved. There is a coolness and reserve implied in the composer's return to the neutral sonority of the piano, to the world of equal temperament, and to a rigorously conventional notation which uses verbal indications for tempi and offers few excursions into irrational values. The payoff, however, is music of high action and high spirits which by some marvelous alchemy succeeds in "tuning in" to a succession of different classical and modern idioms.

The mantra, or basic formula, is a thirteen-note melody in the form of a decorated series that ends on the note it began. The melody is ornamented in such a way that each segment becomes the seed of an expansion process; it is divided in four phrases by rests of unequal length, and accompanied in the left hand by a form of mirror inversion of itself. At the very beginning one hears the mantra compressed into a fanfare of four chords. Following a brief tremolando on the note a below middle c, the pivotal tone on which the entire compass of the work turns, the mantra is stated in open form for the first time, as a melody confined within the interval of thirteen semitones. The entire work grows out of this kernel of rhythm and interval, image and reflection. Woodblock signals, antique-cymbal flourishes, sine-wave glissandi and tremolando ostinati (derived from the repetition of the first note of the mantra) in their several ways all articulate different expansions of the mantra in pitch and time, the maximum time-expansion corresponding to the duration of the entire work (excepting the inserts and coda, which are genial afterthoughts). The greatest pitch expansion of the mantra is three and one-half octaves, half of the piano keyboard being allotted to each hand. Naturally, the greater the expansion of the mantra, the more "vertical" and intervallic the music; the less the expansion, the more "horizontal" the music is, and more contrapuntal in idiom. Of more than just incidental interest is the power of the music to evoke the piano styles of other composers, simply in terms of the degree of expansion of the mantra itself. In tempo, mood, counterpoint, and interval content, the first statement of the mantra and its inversion connect unexpectedly with the opening measures of Schoenberg's Op. 11 No. 2 for piano. Soon afterward, mid-range repeated notes combined with a modest expansion of the mantra in dotted rhythms, conjure up the neoclassical era of the Stravinsky of *Concerto for two pianos*, to be followed shortly after by a statement of the mantra at maximum expansion that, not unexpectedly, evokes Boulez's *Structures 1a* for two pianos. (After Richard Voss's inquiries into the randomness of different types of music, these stylistic allusions can now be explained as relating to the fractal dimension, or scale of allowable fluctuation, of melodies of different idioms.)[11]

The tone of each piano is also audible in electronically modified form, a refinement of ring modulation for which a device called the "Module 69B" was created. In a process which has features in common with the natural voice modulation technique of *Stimmung*, the piano tone is electronically subjected to the influence of a pure sine tone, such that the notes of the mantra are more or less colored in proportion to their degree of dissonance with the sine tone. Ideally the sine tone component should be completely inaudible when its pitch coincides with that of the piano; in practice, owing to the vagaries of tempered tuning (not to mention the conventional distuning of multiple strings in a piano for warmth and reinforcement of tone), some electronic coloration leaks through the circuit most of the time.

The concept of tempering the tuning of acoustic instruments by electronic means had already been indicated in the moment "Spiegel" of *Mixtur*, and the first structure of *Mikrophonie II*. In both scores, the notation of live instruments or voices tuning in and out of consonance with electronic modulating pitches suggests that at moments when the two coincide exactly in frequency the resulting tone should sound purer and also louder, by mutual reinforcement (like finding the eigentones of an empty room by playing up and down the scale). In these earlier works, positive reinforcement does not occur as clearly as one would like, because of too much residual noise in the live sound; the cleaner sound of *Mantra* is the result of adding a compressor and a filter to the ring-modulating circuit, suppressing the rogue second and third harmonics of the modulated consonance, and filtering out the metallic high frequency halo generated by the piano. Where the modulating sine tone is of medium or high pitch, additional resonances are created; if, however, the modulating tone is at a low frequency, the intermodulation takes the form of a pulsation agitating the piano tone. Such a passage occurs at 132, where piano II lowers the sine frequency to around 7 hertz, and the effect is mesmerizing.

Electronic modulation introduces a new, quasi-tonal factor into the familiar conjunction of opposites; not just in the mirror-imagery of the two piano parts, but in the relationship of each piano with its electronic transformation, and between the two transformations as well. The latter symmetry is beautifully expressed at measure 110, where a slow descent in the piano II part is followed by a slow rise by piano I, each accompanied by its electronic mirror-image. Stockhausen has described working on *Mantra* as "the happiest composition time I have ever spent in my life," and the elation bubbles to the surface in spontaneous inventions like the Zen-inspired target practice at 212, which arose from his own difficulty in playing notes at either end of the keyboard simultaneously,—or at 329, where he mimics the sound of a tape-loop being switched on and off with a wood-block acting as the switch. There is high exultation at 421, where gigantic chords, as huge as glaciers, are scanned back and forth by both oscillators, and intersected unisons seem to leap forth from the sustained resonances.

At the end of the formal exposition of the mantra in its serial transformations, Stockhausen adds a concentrated reprise, like a tape rewind, in which "all expansions and transformations are gathered, extremely fast, into four layers, gradually condensing into vertical harmonies." The texture here is Boulezian *avant la lettre*: the object of comparison, Boulez's *Sur Incises* of 1996–1998. More significant, perhaps, is the inauguration of a new era of melody-based serial composition, more approachable to the public and more confident in itself.

Für Kommende Zeiten (For Times to Come)

1968–1970: No. 33 (Stockhausen-Verlag; cd SV-11 "Ceylon")

17 texts for intuitive music: "Übereinstimmung" (Unanimity), "Verlängerung" (Elongation), "Verkürzung" (Shortening), "Über die Grenze" (Across the Boundary), "Kommunikation" (Communication), "Intervall" (Interval), "Ausserhalb" (Outside), "Innerhalb" (Inside), "Anhalt" (Halt), "Schwingung" (Vibration), "Spektren" (Spectra), "Wellen" (Waves), "Zugvogel" (Bird of Passage), "Vorahnung" (Presentiment), "Japan" (Japan), "Wach" (Awake), "Ceylon" (Ceylon).

Stockhausen composed several more texts at the time of the Darmstadt seminar in August 1968, and these, together with others written at various times between then and July 1970, presumably with the Osaka ensemble in mind, have been gathered into a further collection under the title "For times to come." By and large these new texts have little of the emotional tension of the earlier sequence; a number seem to be exercises in musical haiku (short in text, long in contemplation). True to form, as his self-confidence returns, so the pathetic tone diminishes, and his thoughts take on a more practical turn. An exception is "Über die Grenze," an invitation to play (and possibly a self-portrait) that might almost be translated as "over the top":

> Imagine you are a HIGHER being
> which comes from another star
> discovers the possibilities of your instrument
> and proves to your co-players
> that in its homeland
> it is a "Humorous Master-Interpreter."
> The shorter pieces in its repertoire
> Last roughly one earth-hour.[12]

Other texts in the new set range from expressionist studies closely related in objective to *Aus den Sieben Tagen*, to pieces like "Ceylon" whose form and instrumentation are determined in some detail, and verse miniatures in which the musical implications are not immediately obvious, like "Wellen," which may have helped to inspire *Dr. K.–Sextett*:

WELLEN	WAVES
Überhole die anderen	Overtake the others
Halte die Spitze	Hold the lead
lasse Dich überholen	Let yourself be overtaken
Seltener	Not often

The image of movement, and pausing between movement, as in a suspended upbeat, is quite novel, as is the implication of a latent repetition (also found in "Schwingung" and "Zugvogel"). Here too, as in the earlier set, one encounters reciprocal pairings: "Verlängerung" and "Verkürzung," for example, the one addressed to eternity in the moment, the other to the momentariness of long durations. Both of these relate to the text "Übereinstimmung," in which long, quiet sounds are reconciled with short, loud sounds,—a relationship of intensity to time familiar from the pointillist fifties and embodied in the duration series of a number of works. Here Stockhausen appears to be trying to recreate spontaneously the contrived fireworks of some of his earlier works. In turn, "Übereinstimmung" appears to have inspired "Intervall," a 1969 tongue-in-cheek duo four-hands for robotic pianists playing with their eyes shut.

Sternklang (Star Sound)

1971: No. 34 (Stockhausen-Verlag; cd SV-18)
Park music for 5 groups (21 singers and instrumentalists); 21 microphones, ca. 10 synthesizers, 22 loudspeakers, 5 mixing consoles.
Duration 150'.

Interviewed by the BBC after the announcement of Stravinsky's death, neither Boulez nor Stockhausen had very much to say. Boulez complained that Robert Craft had put words into Stravinsky's mouth. Stockhausen, who had a secret fondness for *Petrushka*, ventured that the Russian-born composer's greatest achievement had been in living so long. Both were clearly in shock. At the invitation of the periodical *Tempo*, Boulez went on to compose . . . *explosante-fixe* . . . , an ingenious mobile for chamber ensemble in the image of a planetary system orbiting around the letter "S," which is also e flat in German (and the word "It," so perhaps also a play on Stockhausen's text piece "Es"). Stockhausen did nothing so public, but it is entirely in character that he may have intended *Sternklang* as a form of disguised tribute to the master. Given the European fondness for puzzles and wordplay,—one thinks of Berg's coded references to himself, Schoenberg, and Webern in the Chamber Concerto, or Boulez's to Paul Sacher in *Messagesquisse*, (not to mention Kagel's *Anagramma*)—one has only very slightly to permutate the name

IGOR STRAVINSKY

to discover the message

STAR VIGOR IN SKY.

Most outdoor concerts in the summer tend to be noisy affairs: a Fourth of July celebration, with the "1812" Overture and coordinated fireworks, or rock and roll in the name of world peace, free love, and illicit medication. *Sternklang* is neither of these; it is not even Handel's *Fireworks* or *Water Music;*—though a listener may discover echoes of the contemplative mood and oscillating harmonies of Schoenberg's "Farben" (Chord-colors) from the *Five Pieces for Orchestra*. It is five vocal and instrumental groups in separate locations within a park setting, picking out the constellations in music, and translating the peaceful inner resonances of *Stimmung* into a harmonious evening celebration, in the open "during the warm summer weather, under a clear starry sky, preferably at a time of full moon." A taste for outdoor spaces comes to the fore in 1969, having started with an evening-long performance of the text composition "Unbegrenzt" at St. Paul de Vence in July, in an open-air setting, and including three versions of *Spiral*. Then in November, the concert at the Beethovenhalle in Bonn, featuring *Fresco* for four orchestral groups performing "wall sounds" in the public spaces, continued the process of freeing up spaces for live music and relocating performers from their traditional private enclosures into more pastoral and publicly accessible settings. Scarcely a fortnight after *Fresco*, Stockhausen and his group were involved in a series of open-air concerts in the massive underground caves at Jeita in Lebanon,—again, featuring the intuitive repertoire to be performed at Osaka the following year.

For intuitive works as concentrated in feeling as the *Aus den Sieben Tagen* texts to be translated into the open air, has the effect of altering their original focal range, and with it their function as private meditation. *Sternklang* builds on the earlier intuitive works, and on *Stimmung*, but is designed with collective meditation in mind. This is a notated music with modest opportunity for intuitive additions, bearing in mind the number of players (grouping in fives is also prudent, given Stockhausen's experiences with larger numbers). The first performance took place in the English Gardens of the Berliner Tiergarten, a park in a city, a public recreational space dedicated to the quiet enjoyment of nature. The five groups are distributed in planetary fashion around a central percussionist acting as time-keeper. The groups are close enough to hear their nearest neighboring groups and the percussionist, but do not have eye contact (though if they did, it would not help much, given the time delay between seeing and hearing actions in a park). Because of the relatively slow speed of sound, the groups would hear signals from the percussion player in the middle more or less at the same time, but not one another. Giovanni Gabrieli encountered the same problem of coordination of separated groups of brass instruments in a much smaller enclosed area, and devised complex imitative canons to cope. *Sternklang*'s music is not directly imitative in that sense; indeed, it is a genuinely innovative solution to the problem of coordinated but independent harmonic groups that can be experienced without loss of definition or quality from completely different perspectives.

Having said that, the music performed by the five groups is of a similar kind; each group harmonizes on a different eight-note harmonic series of which one pitch, e 330, is common to all. As in *Stimmung*, members of each group take turns in leading their group in intoning the names and vowel constituents of zodiacal constellations, the vowel intonations transforming the names into *klangfarben* monody. Instruments are required to imitate these latter timbral configurations. As the group reaches a satisfactory integration and harmonization of a constellation name, a signal is given to move on to the next name and the process is repeated.

Isolation of the groups, and the freedom of timing within each group, create problems of intergroup coordination that cannot be solved, as in *Fresco* for example, with reference to clock time. Coordination is restored in

Sternklang in three different ways: 1. by group-to-group signaling, followed by a general pause (like the follow-my-leader signaling in *Prozession*); 2. by the percussionist in the middle beating out a regular pulse that can be heard by all (again derived from *Prozession*), and 3. by chosen members of the group *running* from one group to the next, bringing new pitch and rhythm material to be shared with the destination group. This latter poetic invention is a charming reminder of the composer's boyhood experience of delivering messages, and in addition to providing an opportunity for a few to stretch their legs, it introduces an element of orbital motion into the otherwise static constellation of musicians.

Stockhausen's innovative combination of five harmonic spectra, tuned to a common reference frequency corresponding to harmonics 5 though 9, is

e' = 330 Hz. Each chord comprises partials 2–9 of a harmonic series.

tonal thinking of a very high refinement, requiring assistance in maintaining exact tuning (electronic or prerecorded). If synthesizers are employed, as in the cd version, their default tuning, which is equal-tempered, has to be disabled to allow the exact harmonic pitches to be obtained. How this can be done, if at all, will vary with the instrument. There is no mention of tuning problems at all, however, neither in the sleeve notes to the original vinyl recording, nor in the composer's published notes; and only criticism by the composer,—a mite severe, in the circumstances, one would think,—of the tuning of instruments in a recording compiled from a series of independent 1984 performances given in California, which also does not mention problems of tuning electronic keyboards.[13] (Given a choice, the ideal instruments for *Sternklang* would seem to be the *tromba marina* among stringed instruments, and the trombone among brass.)

On conventional instruments subject to microtonal adjustment, like the violin, by finger position; woodwinds, by changing the fingering; or valve trumpet, by adjustment of the tuning slide; sharper intonations tend to sound brighter, and flatter intonations darker, qualities influenced by a perception of respectively forcing or depressing the tone. Either way, the gradual upward progression through *Sternklang* from chord A to chord E seems calculated to be heard as a gradual lightening of mood from an initially dark sonority through to an elevated brightness.

Stockhausen's model incantations are also structured to correspond in tempo with the harmonic frequency structures of the pitch material. Each group has a set of six "models" representing harmonic divisions of a fundamental pulsation: MM 16, 18, 20.6, 24, and 29 for groups I–V. As for the pitch material, all tempi are harmonically derived from a common frequency, in this case MM 144. The way in which time and pitch structures are self-similar is unexpectedly reminiscent of *Gruppen*.

Each fundamental tempo unit, by repetition, is also revealed as a partial frequency of a fundamental of 60 seconds' duration. The entire structure of oscillatory patterns can thus be seen as a subtle and far-reaching network of proportional relationships affecting both pitch and duration values. In an outdoor environment it is difficult to imagine pitch and time relationships of this refinement being accurately executed, maintained, or perceived. Certainly for the musicians' sake, a combination of click tracks for timing and prerecorded tuning resources would now be indicated. Although difficult to achieve in practical terms, the precision of Stockhausen's schema is neither arbitrary nor aesthetically superfluous. The mathematics of this musical art correspond to the geometry of Naum Gabo: arrangements of lines warped into curves, or of moiré transparencies, regular grids that when superimposed reveal interference patterns of a mysterious beauty.

At sections in the score marked K (for constellation), performers break off intoning the names of constellations to sing or play their shapes in the heavens, interpreting the configuration of stars as distinctive vocal signs notated in a cosmic version of Daniel Jones. As might be anticipated, the selection of constellations favors the Northern Hemisphere; that of Leo, Stockhausen's birth sign, appearing twice, once for north-facing groups, once for those facing south (though not in the southern hemisphere). Leo Minor also makes an appearance as a Group I model; a jocular upward-leaping figure, it is ingeniously merged with the "yo-ho!" cry of the Noh percussionist, which having already been heard in *Telemusik* and *Mantra*, seems to have been adopted as a kind of musical signature.

Trans (Across)

1971: No. 35 (Stockhausen-Verlag; cd SV-19)
For orchestra divided into four wind and percussion groups, and strings with organ.
Group I: 4 flutes, bass clarinet; celesta; 5 cinelli, Indian bell garland.
Group II: 4 oboes, trombone; vibraphone, low cowbell, sizzle cymbal, hi-hat.
Group III: 4 clarinets, bassoon, contrabassoon; tubular bells, 2 gongs with domes.
Group IV: 4 trumpets with cup mute, tuba; 3 tom-toms, bass drum, tam-tam, infantry drum.
Strings 22.0.8.6.4; electronic organ with low c (32 hertz).
Duration 26' 15.

After *Sternklang*, music out of doors and in the round, the new work, for conventional orchestra treated unconventionally, is music back indoors and severely longitudinal in orientation, corresponding to the sight line of conventional perspective, and suggesting overlapping planes at increasing distances. Stockhausen thought about the title "Jenseits" (the Other Side), and, more grimly, "Musik für den Nächsten Töten" (Music for those who are about to die), before settling on *Trans*, a prefix suggesting "trance" as well as "transition," "transparency," and "transcendental." This is another in a series of works examining particular aspects of physical (longitudinal) and musical (vertical) space. Later, in *Inori*, Stockhausen will go on to redefine pitch as a lateral dimension, left to right; in *Musik im Bauch* the musical action articulates a space of lines and circles round a center, while in *Sirius* audience attention is directed outward, and the musical action takes place at an imaginary periphery. "*Atmen gibt das Leben . . .*," *Harlekin*, *Ylem*, and *In Freundschaft* are other works through which the composer systematically examines the musical choreography of linear and rotational actions on a plane, around a point, and even in the air.

The stage and lighting plan of *Trans*, which includes suffusing the auditorium in a reddish-purplish light, represents musical space as a multilayered aural perspective that cannot be seen and can only be intuited, one that seeks to draw the listener out of the inner space of an auditorium, through a perceptual gateway, into a mysterious auditory hinterland. Despite suggestions of Hamlet-like resignation (". . . to die, to sleep, perchance to dream . . ."), the musical effect is intensely physical. Not here the diaphanous shades of Ravel, Debussy, or Boulezian impressionism. Rather, a combination of tunnel vision and interiorized, amplified polyphony. The audience hears and sees a wall of string players, playing as if in a trance, bathed in red-violet light; behind them unseen musical forces can be discerned, surging and writhing in response to a measured flagellation of amplified moves of the shuttle of a mechanical loom that fly across the auditorium from left to right and back, above the audience's heads. It is imagery comparable in its fashion to the haunting pessimism of the artist Francis Bacon. The sound of the amplified shuttle can also be heard as an amplified slide projector, or the automatic shutter of a spy camera capturing the evidence of a crime; all having the effect of sectioning time into frames.

Trans contrives an initially suspenseful situation out of confounded expectations and ambiguities introduced into the conventional orchestra-audience dynamic. Normal visual cues are reduced or eliminated; there is no conductor visible; and, interpolations apart, very little performer action to be seen. It is interesting, after *Fresco*, to find Stockhausen once again creating "wall sounds," but with massed strings and organ rather than a mixed group of timbres. Organ clusters had been employed to similar effect in *Momente*, in moment I(d):—the sound is a conventional term of reference for dream in the specialized world of radio drama. Here the web of string and organ sound also functions in imitation of the colored noise of shortwave radio, through which the listener strains to make out the distant inflections of big band jazz, a reference to Stockhausen's cadet experiences of listening in secret to American jazz on the radio late at night, during the war.

Stockhausen was also well aware of the use of dense harmonic mixtures in Japanese gagaku, associated with the shô, a form of mouth organ that plays mixtures rather than single notes, with an intensity of effect described by Messiaen as "féroce mais immobile" (motionless ferocity). In gagaku music, these changes of mixtures are always synchronized with percussive attacks. (Interestingly, in the movement "Gagaku" from *Sept Haï-Kaï* Messiaen recreates the sound of the shô with multiple violins.) Here, the imagery of a static trance persists only as long as the listener perceives the foreground cluster as a featureless tinnitus, which is revealed not to be the case. Stroke by measured stroke, the cluster (which to some listeners may sound like the effects of a migraine) varies in density, now attentuated, now compacted, now notched and pierced to allow more of the masked layers to be heard. These changes in density are themselved masked by the whizz and crunch of time's guillotine clacking above the listener's head (or, for a listener wearing headphones, through the skull itself). But they are discernible all the same, and they change the dramatic balance of the music significantly, from what the composer describes as "tragic,"—the working-through of a preordained situation of conflict,—to a subtler, measured, and potentially "comic" (i.e., humanly influenced) dialogue between concealment and revelation, "hearing" and "the heard."

As the listener struggles to penetrate the visual and acoustic screen to make sense of what is going on behind it (it sounds like several radio channels at once), so too the hidden instrumental groups divide and combine among themselves in a suggestion of musical ideas in ferment, trying to assert themselves, and trying to break through into the consciousness of the listener. In this respect *Trans* is more actively engaged with the imagery of shortwave than Berio's altogether more congenial "In ruhig fliessender Bewegung" from *Sinfonia*, in which multiple strands of music are interwoven without any suggestion of mental conflict or strain.

Each of the four concealed instrumental groups comprises a bass instrument, representing a fundamental, or a second, or a fourth harmonic (Stockhausen's registrations are octave-transposable, like an organ), above which is superimposed a cluster of four higher harmonics or their equal-tempered equivalents; thanks to the foreground clusters, their precise tuning is not clearly audible and therefore not critical. The principle is similar to the tuning in *Sternklang*: for example the first "frame" of music incorporates groups of harmonics relating to the fundamental pitch e 1 (41.25 hertz); here the four flutes of Group I form a cluster corresponding to harmonics 14, 15, 16, and 18; the four oboes of Group II, to harmonics 13, 15, 16, and 19 of the same fundamental, the four clarinets of Group III to harmonics 16, 17, 21, and 22 of a fundamental e 0 an octave lower (20.6 hertz); and the four cup-muted trumpets approximate to harmonics 20, 21, 23, and 28 of a fundamental e –1, yet another octave lower (10.3 hertz). The bass notes of each group are prominent and the role of the higher instruments is self-evidently coloristic. Stockhausen's transposition of the melody register into the sub-bass is a remarkable innovation: the melodies remain articulate and volatile, and despite the interval gap separating bass and upper harmonics, the latter in the middle of the audible range, group identity and internal balance are consistently preserved (he revisits this region in "Luzifers Tanz" from *Samstag aus LICHT*). On the other hand, it does seem a shame that the upper harmonies move in parallel where Stockhausen might have taken the opportunity to treat them as formant mixtures, after the manner of voice harmonics. When a voice sings a vowel up the scale, the formant or resonance associated with the vowel does not always move in the same way, preferring to remain within a narrow frequency zone. Stockhausen seems to have modeled his harmonies here on Messiaen's mixture stops and not the human voice.

Under repeated assaults from the hidden instrumental groups, the string and tonal fabric suffers a variety of stresses, changes in the texture of pitches, and temporary ruptures. Out of view, the hidden groups themselves also show signs of stress, if that is the way degrees of loss of co-ordination and disintegration are interpreted. Tension and anger spill over, however, into laughter, as one by one the group harmonies dissolve into fragments gently floating down or upward through the pitch space, in imagery similar to *Fresco*. And in the music's only overt manifestations of theater, the visual action is interrupted from time to time by solo cadenzas seemingly in spontaneous reaction to the tensions of the situation, of having to sit still and play like zombies, or at least like mechanical dolls.

These episodes create larger divisions in the six-part form. They are actions that could almost be snapshots of the composer's experience of the discipline of school life at Xanten. To signal the start of part II, a military drummer marches onstage to inspect the strings. He fixes his attention on a hapless viola, who stands to attention and promptly goes berserk, playing a wild parody of a cadenza until rescued by the next shuttle stroke. Part III, cue 12, is prepared by an orchestra tutti during which an assistant enters with a stand and music for the principal cello, whose smooth performance is switched on and off along with the light on the music stand. Part IV, cue 17, involves the leader of the strings apparently succumbing to a nervous tic, his bowing arm breaking into a mechanical twitching on a high-pitched harmonic. All other musical action grinds to a halt; one by one the other violins turn to face him with reproachful eyes, while he in turn averts his gaze as if to dissociate himself from the behavior of his bowing arm.

Finally at cue 23, the beginning of Part V, a solo trumpet appears from behind the wall of strings and mounts a ladder to play a joyful reveille. Wake up, wake up, it's a dream, the gesture seems to say, ending with a flatulent noise directed at strings and audience alike in the spirit of Richard Strauss's Till Eulenspiegel. But even this is not the climax of the work. Two strokes before the end of Part V, on a stroke of the shuttle at 21' 13, all music stops. After twenty seconds of stillness, another shuttle stroke. The silence continues. It is like the intimidating moment in *Originale* where the performers turn and stare at the audience, and though the silence in *Trans* is less than a minute in total, in the concert recording on compact disc the vacuum is predictably filled by audience protests that have been building up from the opening bars. It is as though the music were winding up the audience as well as testing the stamina of the string players, but to future listeners the audience noise has the effect of opening a door to the past, as though one is experiencing the work *in reality* "from the other side." The piece resumes and concludes with a coda bringing the entire ensemble, including the recorded time-strokes, into a dignified unity as telling as the coda of Stravinsky's *Symphonies of Wind Instruments*, which it passingly resembles.

Alphabet für Liège (Alphabet for Liège)

1972: No. 36 (score not yet available)
13 "Musical scenes" for soloists and duets with electro-acoustic equipment.
Installations in separate rooms of the same building, e.g., an art gallery. Filmed in 1972 by RTB Liège. Film duration 60'.
Duration: 4 hours.

Am Himmel Wandre Ich (In the Sky I am Walking)
(Indianerlieder)

1972: No. 36½ (Stockhausen-Verlag; cd SV-20)
12 songs based on American Indian poems, for 2 voices; 2 microphones, 4 loudspeakers, mixing console.
Duration: 52'.

As *Originale* eleven years earlier had turned the composer's spotlight on the self-revealing spontaneous actions of a number of his artist friends and colleagues, so in *Alphabet für Liège* Stockhausen has composed a musical installation that observes natural phenomena, including the actions of a number of musician friends. This time, however, it is not so much what they do, as how they respond to musical vibration. People and inanimate matter alike can be altered by the vibrations they receive and transmit. The quality of being a medium, as expressed in the text pieces in acoustic terms, is now demonstrated visually.

The composition brought together science, meditation, and music in a simultaneous exhibition of thirteen "situations" in different rooms of the basement complex of the newly constructed Liège RTB radio and television headquarters in the Palais de Congrès, a resonant labyrinth of concrete and breeze-block walls and ceilings still awaiting the arrival of office furnishings, windows, doors, and carpets. Of the thirteen situations, only the first, "Am Himmel wandre ich. . ." for two singers, is fully notated. The others, in the composer's paraphrase, are manifestations of the influence of sound vibrations on the physical world. They make an interesting mixture of practical science and esoteric belief.

2. Tone vibrations made visible in fluid, light rays, and flames. Generate visible models in fluid by the influence of specific sound vibrations and project them on a screen.
3. Make sound spectra visible in solid material (flour, iron filings, etc.).
4. Bring glass to breaking point with the aid of tones.
5. Magnetize foodstuffs with tones, making the magnetization visible with the aid of a pendulum.
6. Massage a human body with sounds (a female dancer translates the vibrations of a musical instrument into her body, which becomes a living loudspeaker).
7. Self-extinguishing tones (for example, by bringing the bell of a

trumpet ever closer against the wall, which is bare or hung with a variety of materials).

8. "Make love" with tones (e.g., generate beat frequencies of varying speed and intensity by bending the unison vibration of two opposing recorders and/or voices, possibly showing the beat frequencies on an oscilloscope).

9. Bring the seven centers of the body into harmony with the aid of tones (Mantra-technique).

10. Use tones to repel thoughts and keep thinking at bay [compare "Es"].

11. Use tones to vary continuously the respiration and heartbeat rhythms of living creatures (fish).

12. Invoke and supplicate the spirits of the dead in tones (until in a trance).

13. Pray in tones (sometimes intelligibly); listen to and study sung prayers of all religions from tape recordings.[14]

The title "Alphabet," with its overtones of primary school and learning the language, arises from a program of actions associated with the letters of the alphabet (Anrufen, Begleiten, Chaos, Dudeln, etc.). These actions, allocated at random, are the basis of hourly excursions by the human performers to visit other designated players or situations, communicate in tones something of what they are doing, and bring back tonal or rhythmic information from the visit to be incorporated in the musical actions resumed thereafter (actions transforming the hide and seek of *Musik für ein Haus*, and the message deliveries of *Sternklang*, into more of a shopping expedition). Events are coordinated to a master time-plan by acoustic signals given by the leader: Japanese chimes marking the minutes, sustained tones the moment sequence. Twice every hour the action stops and everybody freezes stock-still; these moments are signaled by camel-bells (a string of nesting cup-shaped bells of diminishing size, similar to a Chinese bell tree). Bundles of tiny Indian jingles are shaken at the end of sustained tones to "erase" any memory of them.

In his programme notes to *Mantra* Stockhausen mentions that sound can kill: immediately before an earthquake, the earth resonates infra-sonically, and farm animals can sense the vibrations. In an infamous series of experiments, French scientists during the sixties tested a super-whistle that generated powerful pure tones in the 5–8 hertz region, frequencies that interfere with the internal biorhythms of living creatures, and in this case were able to kill cattle. Less hazardous demonstrations of a nonorganic nature, such as sand patterns formed on a Chladni plate when its edge is bowed at different points, or the movement of talc powder in a Kundt tube, are small manifestations of vibratory behavior associated with nineteenth-century science. What such demonstrations tend to overlook is the fasci-nating acoustical science embodied in music itself, and musical instruments, much of which is normally invisible, such as the complex vibration of a piano string, or the flexing of a violin body as it is played: processes argu-ably deserving of wonder, but more difficult to render visible in real time.

On the surface, the twelve *Indianerlieder* are an austere collection paying homage to an ancient culture and performed in the style of a ritual incantation. The verses are English translations from an anthology, *The Winged Serpent*, edited by Margot Astrov.[15] Stockhausen treats each word as a shaped sound, playing with it until it loses all connection with sense (something of the sort happens to the word "spool," a word that becomes an object of beauty in Samuel Beckett's play *Krapp's Last Tape*). The songs gradually unfold a twelve-note series, note by note, song by song. The first song is thus monotone, the second on two notes, the third on three, and so on up to song number twelve, embracing all twelve notes of the chromatic scale. The two singers sit facing one another and are required to sing with precision in a manner stripped bare of conventional expression. The subtext of this show of ritual is the behavior of vocal sound in the space between the two singers, starting with the mystery of the unison and developing from there to explore the nuanced world of stereo movement and interference that is created when two signals from opposite directions meet and combine. Stockhausen himself compares the *Indianerlieder* sequence of songs, and gradual accumulation of tones, to a history of Western music from monotone to chromatic music (he was later to make a similar claim for *Inori*, which unfolds in an analogous way).

Like the other exhibits on display, in order to appreciate the delicacy and beauty of what is happening in the space between the two singers, one really needs the aid of sensitive monitoring equipment, though this in turn may create feedback problems. As it is, Stockhausen's choreography of gesture and movement in relation to pitch and inflection provides a fore-taste of the lyric and dramatic expression of melody to be further explored in *In Freundschaft* and after.

The title "Alphabet," and composition of musical actions, all present the appearance of a new style of simple learning from factual sources, at the opposite extreme from the transcendental evolutionism of *Hinab-Hinauf*. Stockhausen's list of exhibits is sketchy, the sort of material one would pick up from a children's encyclopedia—there is (alas) none of the "music therapy with chickens" the composer encountered at the State University of Arizona in 1966,[16] or the "piano of pain" he discovered at the University of Penn-sylvania, where the pain threshold of rats was tested with the aid of a keyboard.[17] "Vibrating flames" could be a reference to Koenig's manometric capsule, invented in 1862, a burning gas jet that vibrates in response to pressure variations in a sound wave.[18] "Making sound waves visible in light rays" could be a description of the arc transmitter of Valdemar Poulsen, invented in 1902. "Making sound spectra visible in solid material" seems to refer to Chladni figures, discovered around 1800, though these are not strictly images of spectra but rather of modes of vibration specific to the plate material. "Making a wineglass break with sound" is simply about the energy in a sung tone; by contrast, making music with wineglasses is about assisted resonance, and would be perhaps more instructive,—though again, we are dealing with phenomena investigated long ago. "Self-extinguishing tones" as the composer describes them only demonstrates that if a tube (trumpet) is stopped completely (by pressing the bell against the wall), the

instrument can no longer function as an acoustic piston; the more interesting acoustic consequence of bringing a *noise* source toward a wall, is that
the reflected noise and direct noise interact, and a comb filter effect is
produced, that is, the noise becomes "tuned" to a moving pitch corresponding to the changing wave-length of the distance between the source and the
wall. A trumpet, or better still, a slide trombone, is appropriate to excite the
eigentones specific to a rectangular room: eigentones are the fundamental
frequencies that correspond to the wavelength between parallel surfaces,
and to their harmonics. "Make love with tones" is a romantic description of
what the *Indianerlieder* are actually designed to demonstrate. To "bring the
seven centers of the body into harmony with the aid of tones" is an esoteric
concept that would be difficult, and possibly hazardous, to attempt, since to
do so scientifically would involve experimenting with physical vibrations
coordinated to biological and brain rhythms. The "use of tones to repel
thought" is a conventional function of monotone chant in religion, and of
white noise in experiments in sensory deprivation, while a proposal to modify the behavior of fish through exposure to tones might today attract the
attention of animal welfare pressure groups,—though in the event, the
demonstration amounted to not much more than synchronized gill movements. The entire display seems haphazardly conceived, which is a pity,
because the underlying theme is worth pursuing.

It is possible to construe the composer's poetic conceit of the history of
music consisting of a gradual accumulation of more and more pitches in the
scale,—an image having more to do, it appears, with mastery of the alphabet letter by letter by a small child, than the growth of civilization,—as a
return to the tired old alphabetical (hence, serial) epistemology of de
Saussure. This is disconcerting, since the concept of knowledge reducible to
words and letters is not only a backward step in Stockhausen's own philosophy, but also directly at odds with the evidence of natural behavior on
display. Nevertheless, it offers a framework for understanding the thrust of
Ylem, Inori, "*Atmen gibt das Leben . . . ,*" and eventually *LICHT*: in all of
which "theories of growth and development" are expressed in terms of
evolutionary processes from simple to complex, and sustained by a self-
reflexive and deliberately ahistorical narrative or language code.

The works after *Mantra* elevate technical issues of recording and sound
projection to a new level. Stockhausen's singers on the recording of the
Indianerlieder are under the composer's direct supervision, as is the
recording itself, and yet the whole point of the composition, to capture the
vibrations in the air between the two singers, seems to be lost. The tempi
are much too fast, and the vocal techniques inappropriate, especially after
the example of *Stimmung*, which uses a focused and radiant voice. In order
to reveal the subtle interplay of sung speech, the microphone must be
brought very close to the singers' open mouths, and they should be sitting
very close to one another.

Even greater practical issues arise in recording a work such as *Sternklang*. A studio recording, while a valuable performance guide, is unable to
recreate an authentic impression of space, which may account for the

recording being originally issued on DG's medium-price Polydor label. A music that has no central point, or ideal listening location, is clearly a challenge to any producer and balance engineer; added to which, an outdoor environment is relatively dead in acoustic terms. A solution is possible, certainly in today's multichannel studio environment, by recording and balancing each group individually and then assembling the entire poly-phony at the mixing desk (a procedure strongly advocated by Henry Brant for poly-orchestral works, and even mooted by Robert Craft for a projected recording of *Gruppen* that remains unrealized). Stockhausen has nothing to say about the recording of *Sternklang* in *Texte 4,* which is unusual; in *Texte 5,* however, he describes in some detail the layout and microphones for two *indoor* performances that took place in the Bonn Beethovenhalle in July 1980, which by definition is a controlled acoustic environment of limited size. The seats were removed from the Great Hall and a great many potted trees brought in to create atmosphere and provide an element of natural screening of the five groups, an arrangement which, in addition to simpli-fying the coordination and balancing within and between groups, is self-evidently more suitable for recording in the round.[19]

In speaking of the recording of *Trans,* one is dealing with issues of balance and sound distribution associated with concert performance as well as on tape. What the wall-of-sound scenario suggests is a sound-transparent barrier beyond which the rest of the orchestra can be heard only distantly. Distance effects are a normal incidental feature of orchestra rehearsals; as one waits for the players to take their places on the platform, one can be aware of string players practicing at their desks and creating a haze of sound while trumpets and woodwinds can still be heard warming their instruments in corridors behind the platform. An equivalent distance effect is not what the audience hears in *Trans,* perhaps because having the strings seated on stepped podia at the front of the platform creates a real acoustic barrier as well as a curtain of sound, preventing the wind groups beyond from being heard. However, in amplifying the concealed orchestra groups, and relaying their sound from cinema-style loudspeakers suspended left to right above the proscenium arch and on or in front of the plane of the strings, the composer is contradicting the perspective illusion implied by the staging and the music itself. In his program notes Stockhausen makes a rhetorical point concerning the ambiguous nature of these musical layers, imagining the audience to be wondering whether the concealed orchestras are really there, or only tape recorded,—and by implication, whether the concert is value for money. But that is to divert attention from the larger contradiction between what the music appears to profess and what it actually delivers. The polyphony of layers at different physical distances is effectively interiorized, and a perception of real spatial perspective trans-formed into a cocktail effect of musical actions distinguishable not through a natural instinct for the disposition of sources in space, but only by internal musical relationships of timbre, rhythm and melodic contour. That Stock-hausen fudges the acoustic issue does not altogether invalidate the musical conception, and there may be practical imperatives relating to the concert hall in this particular case. But it does change the rules. (One should really hear *Trans* performed at Bayreuth, with the strings on the platform, the winds in the pit, and the soloists concealed in the wings.) It is all the same instructive to see how the composer deals with the same kind of distance effects in subsequent works: in *Jubiläum*, by the use of offstage wind bands and normal distribution of strings on a flat platform, and in "Luzifers Abschied" (from *Samstag aus LICHT*) by locating the performance in a church.

Notes

1. "Space." 101–17 in Robin Maconie, *Second Sense: Language, Music, and Hearing* (Lanham, Md: Scarecrow Press, 2002).

2. Rudolf Wittkower, *Architectural Principles in the Age of Humanism* (Fourth edition revised, London: Academy Editions, 1988).

3. Michael Forsyth, *Buildings for Music: The Architect, the Musician, and the Listener from the Seventeenth Century to the Present Day* (Cambridge: Cambridge University Press, 1985).

4. "Musik im Raum." *die Reihe 5*, 59–73; reprinted with additions in *Texte 1*, 152–75.

5. "New Halls for New Music." Karl Wörner, *Stockhausen: Life and Work* tr. ed. Bill Hopkins (London: Faber and Faber, 1973), 160–62.

6. Fred K. Prieberg, *Musica ex Machina* (Berlin: Ullstein, 1954), 167–68.

7. Fred K. Prieberg, *Musica ex Machina*, plate facing 208.

8. Pierre von Meiss, *Elements of Architecture: From Form to Place* (London: E & FN Spon, 1990), 115.

9. D. P. Walker, *Studies in Musical Science in the Late Renaissance* (London: Warburg Institute, University of London, 1978), 26. See also Robin Maconie, *Science of Music* (Oxford: Clarendon Press, 1997), 110–11.

10. "Four Criteria of Electronic Music: Splitting of the Sound." *SoM*, 97–108.

11. Martin Gardner, "White, Brown, and Fractal Music." *Scientific American* Vol. 238 No. 4 (1978). Reprinted in Martin Gardner, *The Night is Large: Collected Essays 1938–1995* (New York: St Martin's Press, 1996), 375– 93. See also Robin Maconie and Chris Cunningham, "Computers Unveil the Shape of Melody." *New Scientist* Vol. 94 No 1302 (1982): 206–9.

12. Published under the title "Music Fiction" in Fred Ritzel, "Musik für ein Haus" *Darmstädte Beiträge zue Neuen Musik* (Mainz: Schott, 1969), 40.

13. *Texte 7*, 185–98.

14. *Texte 4*, 194–95.

15. Margot Astrov ed., *The Winged Serpent: American Indian Prose and Poetry* (Reprint, Boston: Beacon Press, 1992).

16. Jonathan Cott, *Stockhausen: Conversations with the Composer* (London: Robson Books, 1974), 127–28.

17. Jonathan Cott, *Stockhausen: Conversations with the Composer*, 132–33.

18. Dayton C. Miller, *Science of Musical Sounds* (New York: Macmillan, 1916), 73–75.

19. *Texte 4*, 170–80; also *Texte 5*, 60–70.

CHAPTER NINETEEN

Rites

In his setting of "Deposuit de sede," a verse of the *Magnificat* lasting a mere two minutes, Monteverdi succeeds in depicting a multidimensional universe. Solo instruments invoking the same music to left and right, express the horizontal, and corresponding echo instruments in the background, the longitudinal dimension; the vertical is displayed by placing higher-pitched instruments in upper galleries to either side, and lower-pitched instruments in the center and on the floor (also good recording practice). Length, breadth, and height, the three dimensions of visual perspective, are offset and complemented by subtler associations: to one side cornetti send out call signs emblematic of external reality, the world of other people out there; to the other side the less powerful, more volatile timbre of violins conveys a sense of inner reality, the world of individual human feeling. To the three dimensions of objective space and the two dimensions of subjective space are added the imaginary vertical and horizontal musical dimensions of pitch and time, embodied in the new visual notation of a printed text. Finally, the coexistence of traditional plainchant and modern instrumental counterpoint expresses the intersection of a traditional concept of eternity, and a new renaissance consciousness of humanly-measured space and time, articulated in the device of the echo canon, which is both a time delay effect and a manifestation of acoustic space.

Much of the same poetry of spatial symbolism and awareness is implied by Stockhausen's music of the mid-seventies. Carefully choreographed, outwardly very simple movements by musicians are designed to achieve the same awareness of movement in external space, as *Stimmung* achieved for voice sounds in harmonic space.

In 1962 Ligeti composed a *Poème symphonique* for 100 clockwork metronomes set to different tempi. It seemed like a charming enough caprice; a tongue-in-cheek commentary on music of multiple tempi, and on the unreality of mechanical time in relation to a human perception of time. On another level the work could be regarded as a genuinely interesting, if rudimentary, experiment to hear: 1. what happens when a hundred precisely different tempi are superimposed, and 2. the effect of a mechanical rallenando over a relatively long period of time, as the machines wind down. Ligeti's metronomes are presented all together on the platform, indicating an interest in pattern that is rhythmic and temporal rather than spatial. It sounds like child's play until the image of a geiger counter comes to mind; at that instant the music becomes a parable as the listener is confronted with the awful reality of the time it takes for the radioactive signature of an atomic bomb to decay.

Ylem (Ylem)
1972: No. 37 (Stockhausen-Verlag; cd SV-21)
For 19 players/singers and conductor, e.g., flute, oboe, cor anglais, clarinet, bass clarinet, bassoon, horn, trumpet, trombone, violin; 4 synthesizers, electric cello, acoustic cello, piano, harp, vibraphone. 6 microphones, 2 × 2 loudspeakers, mixing console. Duration: 26'.

Ylem takes a fresh look at a recurrent image in Stockhausen's oeuvre, the attenuation and compression, over an unusually long duration, of a constellation of musical "points." It first appears in 1952, in Spiel, again fourteen years later in Mixtur: "Translation," in Adieu at 9, and yet again in the "Russian Bridge" interpolation of "Third Region of Hymnen with orchestra." The name Ylem comes from Aristotle via physicist George Gamow, and signifies the flux or plasma of elementary particles out of which all matter and life in the universe has condensed. Its secondary meaning, arising from observation of the red shift of the galaxies, is the period of oscillation of the entire universe.

> The famous red-shift of the spectral lines of galaxies is most likely explained by the assumption that they are all receding from each other —not unlike the pieces of an exploding bomb shell. . . . If there is real motion it defines a time-scale. . . . The distances of galaxies are roughly known, and the red shift, if interpreted as indicating a velocity, gives the numeric value of the velocity: hence we can calculate the time of the first explosion. It turns out to be roughly 15,000,000,000 years ago.[1]

Once again, this is an outwardly very simple piece, but one requiring considerable imagination in concert presentation and even more so in recording, as it involves an expansion movement of musicians playing portable instruments, from an initial cluster in the center of the auditorium, to positions to the sides, and back again. The expansion process is disc-like rather than spherical, so Stockhausen's image of creation is also implicitly an image of cataclysmic destruction, calling to mind archive footage of atomic tests in the Pacific Ocean, a mushroom cloud in the center of a shock wave radiating outward across the surface of the ocean at enormous speed.

In the recorded "London" version by the London Sinfonietta the musical action begins literally with a "big bang" on the tam-tam, synchronized with rapid repeated notes of either e flat or a natural:

The players of portable instruments immediately begin to act out an expanding shell of sound, retreating outward from the tam-tam and dispersing across the auditorium, eventually taking up positions along the side walls, while the nonmoving instruments including keyboards monitor their movements on the platform as if from an observation bunker. As the players move outward, their individual notes also move away from the starting note, the idea being to convey an impression of an expanding globe of pitches. Like the expanding universe, during the process the pitch material also cools and diversifies: becomes less loud, slowing down, and at times condensing into particles of melody: two, three, or four-note groups, with occasional staccato flourishes, like *Sternklang* constellations in miniature. During the eleven minutes of this part of the cycle, electric keyboards and amplified instruments on the platform observe isolated pitches in different locations and improvise melodic connections between them. Players in the hall are required to maintain a ritardando throughout the eleven minutes, without reference to anybody else; this will give rise from time to time to strange and unexpected conjunctions and oppositions from different directions. The conductor's role in all of this is to maintain coherence and signal suggestions.

At the moment of greatest spatial and temporal expansion, by which time the overall density of "points" should have thinned to about one new note every six seconds, one of the players on the platform calls the syllable "Hu!" and is answered by the other players (the cry "Hu, Hu" is also heard in *Telemusik*, taken from a Suyai Indian chant). From this time the musical density begins to increase again, and the moving players very gradually begin the process of return and slow acceleration back to the original pitch and speed of repetition of the beginning. At this climax a second "big bang" occurs, but suddenly a tone higher, as if in a new dimension. In this second expansion cycle the players withdraw, including those on the platform, who leave their keyboards behind and take up alternative instruments that they can carry, all moving out of the auditorium and out of the building, leaving the audience in an empty hall with only the retreating sounds of the players to be heard.

This is another composition about which the composer has relatively little comment to make. Technical information on the recording is omitted from the original DG record sleeve, and is also missing from the *Texte*, which normally carry detailed information of this kind. The tam-tam, an instrument with which the composer identifies himself, that symbolizes the sun, creation, light, and also the light of inspiration, and which plays a starring role in the London Sinfonietta version of the score, is now missing from the list of instruments in the composer's catalogue,—also not a good omen.

It seems like a repeat of the *Indianerlieder* experience. Strip away the outer shell of cosmology and what is left is a brilliant kernel of an idea that has yet to be solved in a technical sense. If the purpose of the exercise were merely about a noisy tremolo slowing down and condensing into pitch and melody, then we have been there before, in the marvelous transformation of impulses into pitch in *Kontakte*, at moment X, 17' 0,5, year 1960, *aetat* 32. It would certainly help if the performers of *Ylem* understood the electronic process and were able to imitate it. But the real point is spatial. To simulate the continuous movement of sounds *across* an auditorium space, using live players and traditional instruments, had also been Stockhausen's intention for *Carré* (1958–1960). In *Allelujah II*, the "exploded version" of his earlier *Allelujah I* for five spatially separated orchestral groups, Berio had already demonstrated in 1958 that it was in fact possible to "pan" sounds from front to back, and side to side, using the dynamics of conventional instruments. It was as though Monteverdi had invented the crescendo all over again. For *Kontakte* as originally conceived, the same control of continuous movement of sounds in space across the auditorium was to have been achieved through manipulating four channels of electronic music on tape. As we recall, neither process succeeded at the time, neither instrumentally, nor on tape. (Which is not to say in the least that these processes cannot be made to work, only that they require technical and production skills specific to the task.) So what *Ylem* is about, the same as the *Indianerlieder*, is finding a way to specify and reproduce the movement of sounds in a three-dimensional space.

As a programmed action, the expansion process is something a group of elementary school children could do, playing a variety of toy instruments including panpipes, plastic mouth organs, and clickers. Doubtless it would be fun for them, and their parents in the audience would get the point and enjoy it too. Older school children already perform maneuvers of much greater complexity in marching bands, playing instruments all the while. Such actions however are not usually asked of members of a symphony orchestra, especially when they are carrying expensive instruments. Stockhausen's heterogeneous choice of instruments for the London version, it has to be said, does not really help; it is as though he has selected one of each kind in order to try out as many timbres as possible at one and the same time. A similar situation arises with *Stop*, with which *Ylem* is coincidentally paired on the original Sinfonietta recording. In *Stop* the ensemble is divided into "characteristic groups" of composite timbres in imitation of adjacent but distinct channels on a shortwave receiver. The ordinary listener's problem with that is not being able to distinguish one group from another as a distinct and composite timbre (the composer finally reaches a solution in 2003, with "Hoch-Zeiten" from *Sonntag aus LICHT*). With *Ylem* the problem is more of perceiving the mobile part of the ensemble as a dynamic unity rather than a loose collection of fragments of very different color, weight, and density of tone. Such issues are normally dealt with by uniform instrumentation: a group of flutes, of double reeds, of horns, of muted strings, etc. If a heterogeneous ensemble is to be perceived as an acoustic unity, in the absence of tonality some form of unifying modulation is needed, as for the two pianos of *Mantra*. These are not insoluble issues. Perhaps the presence of so many synthesizers in the Sinfonietta lineup can be read as the composer speculating, after the success of *Mantra*, about the possibility of an instrumental companion work to *Mikrophonie II*, in which the sounds of the mobile instruments are transmitted to synthesizers and modulated by them. (That would imply at least ten transmitting microphones, multiple loudspeakers, and lengthy technical rehearsals, all adding to the cost. But it would also mean a mixing console in the middle of the performance space, and a clearly leading role for the conductor.)

By his own admission, recurrent difficulties in managing the internal balance of mixed instrumental groups, have brought Stockhausen to a point where every instrument is now amplified and its movement within the auditorium shadowed by a sound projectionist.[2] What that means is a loss of the very dialogue between a sound and its environment that is one of the primary aspects of navigating in the real world, and its substitution by a virtual world of only limited connection to a concert hall acoustic.

Inori (Adorations)
1973–1974: No. 38 (Stockhausen-Verlag; cd SV-22)
For one or two soloists and orchestra. The orchestra is divided into two groups:
Group I: 4 flutes, (2. piccolo), 4 oboes, 4 clarinets (2. e flat); 4 trumpets; violins 14.12; antique cymbals, vibraphone, glockenspiel, rin (Japanese temple bells).
Group II: 8 horns (4 high, 4 low), 3 bassoons, contrabassoon; 2 trombones, bass trombone, tuba; piano, bell-plates, strings 0.0.10.8.8.
Duration: 67'.

Vortrag über HU (Lecture on HU)
1974: No. 38½ (Stockhausen-Verlag)
"Musical analysis of *INORI*."
For a singer; 1 transmitter, 2 × 2 loudspeakers, mixing console.
Duration: 52'.

"Kontarsky recently told me (remarked Stockhausen in 1971) that Ligeti spoke of being fed up with his works up to now—he wants to compose clear melodies. I heard him at Darmstadt and he spoke like a man who weaves clothes, talking about *threads* and how the characteristics of threads were like certain textures, more or less dense, and about how they could be superimposed or intermingled."[3]

In 1973, after examining a range of possible options including Moog and Buchla devices, the Cologne electronic studio acquired a voltage-controlled EMS synthesizer developed in London by Peter Zinovieff. Stockhausen had previously been wary of abandoning the "hands-on" culture of the classical studio, but had seen smaller EMS synthesizers in action, in groups that had taken part in the creation of *Sternklang* and *Ylem*, and he had also visited Zinovieff's studio in Putney, and been impressed at the inventor's willingness to develop specialized modules in accordance with Stockhausen's particular needs, notably the Synthi 100 sequencer that promised to relieve him of the serious time burden of crafting and accelerating tape loops.

> When a portion of a melody or a single part of a composition has been prepared it can be played and remembered by this [memory] unit. At any time then a touch on the "start" button plays the melody back. What is stored, however, is not the actual wave form, but the control voltages involved. . . . The [Synthi 100] synthesiser memory and sequencer unit can store up to three different melodies and will play them back together when required so that sound textures can be built up and the relative timings are easy to achieve. . . . The same system may be used for producing all kinds of controlled wave forms for psycho-acoustic experiments.[4]

(That ability to store no more than three simultaneous melodies would ultimately have some bearing on Stockhausen's decision to opt for a triple formula in *LICHT* rather than continuing with the fourfold personae of *Sirius*.) On receipt of the new Synthi 100 Stockhausen began at once to create formulae of complete melodies, and to explore the implications of representing a melody as control voltages, including the new concept of a dynamic melody expressed as a fluctuation of loudness alone. The Synthi 100 offered unprecedented control over dynamics. It took the labor out of melody creation and fine-tuning while enabling the composer to continue working manually with tape as he was accustomed to do. The improved sensitivity of the Synthi 100 in the domains of interval and amplitude control was inspirational. As late as 1989 Stockhausen was continuing to voice reservations about the imprecision of traditionally notated dynamics, by comparison with the unprecedented precision of the Synthi 100: "For nearly 40 years I have been trying to find sensible solutions for the composition of dynamics. The unbelievably primitive method of composing with [a] dynamic scale having about 7 Italian abbreviations ppp – pp – p – mp – mf – f – ff supplemented by a few tricks of instrumentation and register, must finally be placed on a par with the composition of pitch and duration. INORI is a well-functioning example of composing with up to 60 dynamic levels. The new synthesisers have scales of up to 100 levels, which is realistic."[5]

Inori is a meditative work for soloist and orchestra. The Japanese title signifies "adorations" or prayer gestures. The solo part is composed as a melody and is theoretically performable by a melody instrument; however the relationship between solo gesture and orchestra response is so complete that the solo melody is invariably interpreted in silence by a dancer-mime, employing a vocabulary of gestures drawn from a variety of religious practices. Audiences are accustomed to following the gestural language of a Karajan or Bernstein, modeling and manipulating the expression of a symphony orchestra; there is a direct relationship between arm, hand, and body movement, and the quality of sound: a rallentando, a crescendo, a diminuendo. That sense of power and connection is essentially what makes a conductor a star in the eyes of the public. The gestures of the *Inori* soloist are just as intimately related to the dynamics of the orchestra; in fact, they are designed to convey movement in pitch as well as in loudness and tempo. In relating the solo movements to prayer gestures, the composer appears to be making a further statement about the higher duty of the conductor to serve music, which is a divine ritual, rather than to use the performance of music as a means of self-glorification.

Playing solo in *Inori* is not for the fainthearted. The soloist is required to perform on an elevated podium without safety rails, accessed by aluminium steps without hand rails. Rectangular at the back, rounded to a point at the front in the form of a shield, the podium is some 5' 3" (1.60 m) wide, 8' 3" (2.50 m) front to back, and raised 8' 5" (2.56 m) above floor level. Whereas a conductor normally performs with his back to the audience, the *Inori* soloist faces the audience like a high diver about to take the plunge. It is all somewhat precarious, and more than a little suspenseful: in addition, the actions of the soloist are open to interpretation as intending to conduct the audience members, or at least manipulate the minds of the audience. What message, one wonders, is silent gesticulation in front of an audience designed to convey? That members of the public are deaf, or that they are not really listening? If so, the widely reported impression after the first performance that the dancer-mime was simply making it up, would suggest that the message was not getting through. In subsequent performances, the soloist has been replaced by two soloists in complete gestural unison, an effective demonstration that the melody of gestures is fully composed.

The work is composed around a series of thirteen attitudes of prayer. Each attitude is associated with a pitch, a vowel sound, a tempo, and a dynamic level, the series notated as a melodic line simply designated as *Beter*: the one who prays. Each pitch in the solo part is associated with a specific harmonic spectrum, and each incantatory vowel with a particular distribution of orchestra instruments and registers. The music is modulated in 60 dynamic levels, representing combinations of notated loudness and instrumental numbers and mixtures, of a complexity of definition far exceeding Ravel's orchestrated scale of dynamics in *Bolero*. Dynamics are indicated in the solo part by the amplitude of the gesture: the arms outstretched for louder, folded inward for softer sounds. Pitch level is indicated by the position of the hands relative to the floor of the podium, raised for higher pitches, lowered for lower pitches. The central pitch is g 392, above middle c, associated with the tempo MM 71 in Stockhausen's tempo scale, as near as maybe to the standard heart-beat frequency of a person at rest.

Like *Mantra*, the composition of *Inori* derives from an *Urgestalt* or musical germ (now called a "formula"), in this case a melody of expanding intervals, variously decorated, reaching the octave and quivering on the higher c (c 512) before returning to the starting pitch, ultimately to be elevated to a higher pitch, in a dénouement akin to *Ylem,* on the mysterious signal "Hu!" The melody formula is divided into five segments or *Glieder* forming a sequence leading from pure rhythm ("In the beginning was rhythm"—Hans von Bülow), via dynamics, melody, and harmony, to polyphony:—hence, a progression from the primitive origin of music to a condition of pure intellect. The entire work is a projection of this basic formula onto a duration of about 70 minutes. Technically the music is a continuation and expansion of the hermetic formal processes so brilliantly expounded in *Mantra*, expressed in an elevated and refined traditional notation. Philosophically, *Inori* extends the conception of a musical composition into the realm of choreographed gesture, and thus looks forward to the total integration of movement and music in *LICHT*.

The first section, "Rhythm," is an orchestral study on one note that some may interpret as an extended meditation on the implications of Berg's famous "Interlude on the note B" from *Wozzeck*, much discussed in the golden Darmstadt years of the fifties. Indeed, the whole of Act III of *Wozzeck* follows a comparable if less completely integrated plan to that of *Inori*, comprising "six 'inventions,' respectively on a theme, on a note (B), on a rhythm, on a chord, with an interlude in the form of an 'invention on a tonality,' and, lastly, on a steady quaver pattern (*Perpetuum mobile*)."[6] This first section of *Inori* incorporates a "tempo melody" or sequence of tempo changes corresponding to the pitch changes of the formula.

The second major segment, dedicated to the unfolding of a dynamic scale, signifying action, emotion, and also aural perspective, introduces a surprise. The orchestra is disposed on the platform in an unusual arrangement designed to enhance a sense of acoustic perspective, arising from the regulation of dynamics by addition and subtraction of instrument numbers. It means that as the dynamic level of the ensemble is lowered, the density of the instrumentation is also "evacuated," as it were, from the center out to the periphery, so that the quietest music also sounds farthest away, and is played by soloists, including the concert-master, who are actually situated toward the rear of the platform. It is a genial analogy of the gradual attenuation of an expanding sound wave, clearly audible to the conductor at the dais, but less obvious to the audience. To a listener of the compact disc, in stereo, this orchestral fluctuation of amplitude, which one imagines should give the impression of undulating gracefully in and out like a sea anemone, is just as difficult to detect,—though it should not be technically impossible to achieve.

In the "Melody" section, which begins after about half an hour of gracefully modulated monotone, elaborations of the formula as a melody begin to appear. Here the composer's lateral organization of instruments by pitch, —bass instruments to the left, treble to the right,—comes into its own in the form of a spatialized left-hand, right-hand antiphony (recalling the keyboard-related graduations of pitch in *Kreuzspiel*, *Spiel* and *Punkte 1952/ 62*). Sections four, "Harmony," and five, "Polyphony," develop the formula by transposition and expansion in different dimensions with progressively greater complexity, to a symbolic cadenza or "Spiral-moment," in "Polyphony," where the orchestral texture and hierarchical structure are heard to dissolve in a teeming ejaculatory flux, culminating in the "Hu!" call that restores calm. Twice during the music, at moment VII of section two, and again in moment XX, the "Adoration" moment of "Polyphony," small layers of music (two horns, two trumpets) detach from behind the orchestral texture and rotate discreetly around a system of four loudspeakers, above the heads of the audience; a rotation controlled by the players themselves approaching and withdrawing their instruments from nearby microphones.[7]

As in *Trans*, there are moments of disturbance or drama that break the mood: the "Spiral" moment, for example, is initiated by a tuba interrupting the musical action at a moment of high ritual, with a repeated musical oath in the sub-bass (i.e., from the "pits"). This rude gesture, harking back to the jovial but unwelcome drunk, also a bass, who interrupts the soprano in *Momente* with loud comments in broad Cologne patois, is met with a baleful stare by the soloist, who brings him to silence by stamping her foot. Then, as the soloist descends the staircase as the ceremony draws to a close, she seems to stumble and fall at the last step, again breaking the tension. But it is all in the script: as quickly as she loses her balance, she regains it, falling on to a springboard that immediately bounces her back to an upright stance. In such gestures,—many of them as here inspired by events in real life, —the composer reinforces the point of the fragility of the spell of ritual.

Stockhausen's orchestration is uncharacteristically sexy and gorgeous, smooth, and harmonized to a degree of opulence and sensuality at an opposite extreme from the austerity and literally elevated spirituality of the prayer gestures above. Echoes abound of Mussorgsky (the "Death of Boris"), Debussy (*Jeux*), Stravinsky (*Zvezdoliki*), even Gershwin: (though thankfully no hint of the added-sixths of Messiaen's "Chant d'Amour" in f sharp major from the *Turangalîla-Symphonie*). Stockhausen's indebtedness to the anonymous specialism of American salon orchestration is every bit as remarkable, however, as any imagined debt to a named composer. In retrospect, *Inori*'s seductive harmonies are Stockhausen's statement, not only of his complete mastery of the orchestra, but also of his total rejection of the idiom as unworthy: a message driven home in 1977 by the ostensibly corrupting "entertainment music," with accompanying stripper, comprising the Fourth Temptation of *Der Jahreslauf*.

Stockhausen's meanings are elusive, complex, and often involve contradictory positions. If the title "Adorations" is intended to be read as a profession of the composer's personal loyalties, it has to be said that the music in its entirety sends a complex of mixed, if not diametrically opposed messages. The elevated platform raises the soloist, or pair of soloists, far above the earthly level of the orchestra and its implicitly degraded music; so what then is the soloist doing? Could it be that the soloist is inviting the audience to identify completely with the sensuality of the music, or contrarily is she/ are they engaged in a rite of exorcism? There is no definitive answer. The image of a stairway to a higher plane of being speaks clearly of Schoenberg's unfinished oratorio *Die Jakobsleiter* (Jacob's Ladder), a biblical allusion to Jacob's dream of struggling with an angel for his soul, and his vision of a stairway to heaven.

Schoenberg could not write an oratorio merely because it is beautiful to pray. He asks immediately: "So we pray?—Who does?—When?—Why do we pray?—What is the root of praying?—Its aim?—Its effect?" Praying becomes a fundamental problem to him—but a general one. He must understand it universally, as action and fulfillment of the human soul —and in all its possibilities. He thinks it through in all its forms. . . . And a choir sings from the highest point of the ladder: "Union with Him awakes magnetically the currents of the mind by induction"—giving an ultra modern interpretation of the same phenomenon.[8]

This last is an apparent reference to the theremin, an instrument from which an undulating melody appears by the mere proximity of the hands to the apparatus. Schoenberg's improbable appeal to "magnetic (—read, electrostatic) induction" brings the history of *Inori* full circle. Invented in the twenties and brought to New York by its Russian-born inventor, the musician and electrical engineer Leon Termin, the theremin is an instrument producing a voice-like tone of unearthly power in response to the mysterious hand movements of a performer in the space around a plain wooden cabinet outfitted with two aerials, but without touching them. The spiritualist implications of an invisible energy force combining with highly ritualized hand and body gestures to conjure a wordless and ethereal melody out of thin air, held the popular imagination in thrall for over two decades. All of which added together: a melody instrument, controlled by hand and body gestures in the air alone, associated with a high degree of spirituality, come to focus in *Inori*. Stockhausen would have known of the theremin, if not through professional contact with Robert Moog (an enthusiast and manufacturer of a transistorized theremin), then certainly through Varèse, who supported the theremin in its early days and incorporated two customized instruments in the original version of *Ecuatorial* (1932–1934) in order to reach a climactic high e (5280 hertz) unattainable even by piccolo.

In 1930 Termin developed a new instrument, the terpistone, to enable the movements of dancers to be transformed into melody. The new device involved an aerial in the form of a metal sheet laid on the floor, providing the dancer with a podium-sized area in which to move. The combination did not work very well, since the equipment was sensitive to the slightest body tremor. Fred Prieberg's 1960 monograph cites a contemporary description of a performance of the "Aetherophone" at Carnegie Hall in 1932, in its new guise. "A dance area was underlaid with antennae of the 'Aetherophone' to enable a female dancer to accompany herself musically through a variety of steps and attitudes. A pupil then demonstrated the same. Before the astonished gaze of the public she moved sedately over the stage, gracefully moved her head, and swung her arms . . . in response to which, as if by magic, sounded the exact tune of the "Ave Maria" of Bach-Gounod."[9]

That "pupil" was theremin virtuosa Clara Rockmore, drawn unwillingly into an art of body movement with which she was ill at ease, but for which her exceptional skills as a concert thereminist proved ideal. It was she who devised standing and kneeling postures, and a variety of delicate head, hand, and finger movements, of a sufficient refinement to be translated by the terpistone into viable melody. To all intents and purposes, Rockmore's repertoire of movements devised for the theremin terpistone corresponds to Stockhausen's repertoire of prayer gestures for *Inori*, with the difference that Rockmore's actually work, and were acquired from practical training and experience in manipulating the body within an electrostatic field to realize a controllable melody. Remove the superstructure of mysticism from the solo part of *Inori*, and what is left, however convincing, is a skillful simulation, by association of programmed gestures with a richly colored and expressive orchestral texture.[10]

A technical appreciation of the handling of the orchestra in *Inori* puts the new work several light-years ahead of *Carré*. Whether or not the tidal approach and retreat of sound from margins to center and back is perceived by an audience as a continuous movement, of filling and evacuating an acoustic space, it is still the case that Stockhausen's painstaking attention to orchestral dynamics is a huge advance, inspiring a music of enormous allure and plasticity that one instinctively feels was the composer's intention also for the earlier work. This greater suppleness is due, as the composer has said many times, to the example of the Synthi 100 providing experience in working with fine dynamic distinctions, and providing a model for emulating the same in real terms. The solo role of the dancer-mime can be interpreted as a literal expression of Stockhausen's conception of the conductor's role, and in the longer view, of the composer as a vessel for receiving and transmitting cosmic vibrations. In this respect the mute mime stands at the opposite extreme from the cheerful garrulity of *Momente*'s solo soprano, representing a real-time manifestation of the divine spark of the boy's voice in *Gesang der Jünglinge*.

Publication of the "Vortrag über HU," a substantial lecture text containing the solo score or "Beterstimme" and intended as a performance score in its own right, as a preconcert initiation into the mystery of the prayer gestures, introduces the delicate question of the mystical or religious significance that may be read into *Inori*. It is one thing to admire and be affected by a skilled and graceful performance from a tradition one knows nothing about; it is quite another matter to be warned in advance that anything one imagines in response may be taken down and used as evidence of a spiritual experience. For a number of reasons, the composer's ritual protestations of piety do not quite add up. In the first place, the solo role was originally conceived to be performable by a melody instrument. Stockhausen's subsequent publication of the "Vortrag,"—which means a report as well as a lecture,—implies that henceforth the solo part is to be performed only by one or two mimes, and not by any other instrument. That is a reasonable deduction to make, since no solo instrumentalist would consider mounting a precarious set of steps onto a narrow elevated platform, playing for seventy minutes without a break, and without eye contact with the conductor, let alone undertaking a staged prat fall at the bottom of the stairs with a valuable instrument in hand. That being the case, the stairs and platform have to be an inspired afterthought, now defended by a publication in effect claiming that this was the composer's intention all along.

The solo score is so completely adapted to a mime that even if the prayer gestures are completely discounted, it is hard to imagine how it could be realized by any alternative instrument in its present published form. In its own terms it is a very interesting score, one that allows a reader to interpret the later *Harlekin* and *In Freundschaft* as studies designed to develop an appropriate gestural language (including foot-stamping) to enable the solo part of *Inori* to be undertaken by a clarinet or basset-horn. The process continues well into *LICHT* with the development of additional techniques and notations for microtonal scales and glissandi, first for the solo trumpet, later for flute, clarinet, and basset-horn (in *Xi* and "AVE" from *Montag aus LICHT*). These techniques are all prefigured in the graphic notations of the "Beterstimme" of *Inori*.

A second, more difficult obstacle to belief in the mystical or spiritual connotations of the solo score (which is now somewhat implausibly described in the official catalogue as a "Musical analysis of *INORI*"), is the composer's own profound distaste for the musical idiom. Using religion as a smoke-screen arouses suspicion at what is being concealed. From a religious point of view, *Stimmung* was already in danger of giving offense, not just by taking the names of divinities representing world religious beliefs for use as "sanctified phonemic units" in an invented ritual, but at the same time in exposing the sacred names to his own private verses in celebration of the pleasures of the flesh. Again in *Inori* the composer, once more with magisterial insensitivity to their indigenous significance, appropriates a motley collection of prayer gestures for his own use as a hybrid sign language for a quasi-theosophical initiation rite;[11] action difficult to equate with a profession of religious sensitivity (and also having the effect of diverting public attention from the formidable beauties of *Inori*'s orchestration).

The magic syllable "Hu!" is another ambiguity. In performances of *Sternklang* and *Ylem* audience members of a skeptical or unruly disposition were in the habit of responding spontaneously to the call "Hu!" with their own shouts of "Hu! Hu!" According to Stockhausen (who refers the reader to his notes for the recording of the text composition "Goldstaub" (Gold Dust) from *Aus den Sieben Tagen*), the syllable *Hu* is sacred and comes from a reading of the Sufi philosopher Hazrat Inayat Khan: "*Hu* is the only name of the nameless . . . this alone is the true name of God; . . . *Huma* the fabulous bird (*Hu* = spirit, *mah* = water), *Human*, the God-conscious man, God-realized, (Hu = God, man = mind, ordinary 'man')," etc.[12] A citation, as he says, "from memory," embroidered by the addition of the composer's own definition of "Hu-man," carefully signaled by the absence of italics (boldface in the original). A Western reading of the Sufi text suggests that the significance of the syllable "Hu" in that cultural context has at least partly to do with its association with the act and sound of breathing in and out. There is nothing to suggest that the name retains its sacredness when called out loud and in public. In considering Stockhausen's intended meaning, however, one must never forget that the syllable also has significance as a sound, and the meaning of the sound is not always congruent with the meaning of the word. In nature, in Europe and the Western world, the call

"Hu! Hu!" is associated with the owl, a bird of negative as well as positive spiritual associations. In ancient Greece the owl was the emblem of Athens, a symbol of wisdom, and a messenger of Hecate. Among Christians the owl signifies the Devil. In German the syllable also means "Ugh!"—expressing disgust. Given the composer's past history (most recently in *Trans*) of venting contempt (or at least, a cocky disrespect) for his audience, it would not be entirely out of character for the ostensibly sacred syllable, coming when it does, to be construed as a double-edged gesture, the hoot of a Till Eulenspiegel. That would at least be consistent with the composer's attitude to the musical idiom of *Inori*, as well as with the character and name (Owl-mirror) of the mischievous antihero of German folklore.

Appealing to an audience's respect for religion in order to ensure the public's undivided attention runs the greater risk of exposing the artist and his work to irrelevant accusations of hubris or apostasy. *Inori* is not about religion, but about the expression of musical relationships in an abstract but coherent language of gestures, some of which happen to coincide with prayer attitudes. Without the music, the religious symbolism of the gestures is incoherent. With the music, the contemporary message of a solo dancer on an empty stage is powerful enough in its own terms. Imagine, for instance, a rediscovered scene from Wagner's "Ring" cycle in which the hero, dressed in white, white-faced like the Pierrot of Jean-Louis Barrault in *Les Enfants du Paradis*, but with a touch of Harpo Marx, all alone on an empty stage, gesticulates to the Bayreuth audience like a spirit figure trying to communicate from Valhalla, but whose voice can only be heard as a strange and beautiful slow-motion music issuing from an unseen orchestra below the stage. The emotional territory of such a conception unites Wagner and Samuel Beckett with the desperate but also sublime silence of a Garbo close-up from the silent movie era. (It would also make gripping television.) Outside the movies, the authentic poet of self-contained movement who comes readily to mind is choreographer Merce Cunningham, who not only looked a little bit like a more athletic Harpo Marx, but who also composed his ballets in quasi-serial permutations. Cunningham's notations for the 1953 solo *Suite by Chance*, for instance, build to a climax of spiral movements and describe spatial trajectories in a graphic language directly comparable with Stockhausen's for the movement of sound in space.[13] (The list of movements notated for Cunningham's 1969 ballet *Canfield*, as a matter of interest, also includes "stumble.")[14] Of course it will be said that in all of his published *Texte* Stockhausen does not once mention Merce Cunningham: the only reference to him in the entire series being a holiday photograph taken on vacation in Königswinter in 1964 in which the dancer appears.[15] Cunningham does not even figure in the Jonathan Cott conversations, though the composer says a great deal about Cage, and expresses admiration for painter Robert Rauschenberg, Cunningham's two collaborators.[16] Where Stockhausen is concerned, however, the very absence of discussion, of an artist whose work you know he knows, and in whose collaborations with Cage and Rauschenberg you would expect him to be keenly interested,—can be read as a statement of some significance, like the dog that didn't bark in the night (Sherlock Holmes, in *Silver Blaze*).

Cunningham might well have been an ideal soloist for *Inori*, and he would have done so without any reference to religion, except that the dancer's aesthetic is at an opposite remove from Stockhausen, his choreography resolutely indifferent to its musical and scenic environment. His style of gesture, still viewable on video, nevertheless provides an observer with a conceptual analogy from which it is possible to appreciate the nature and scale of Stockhausen's achievement: a choreography totally integrated with its music, and, for all its limitations, notated with a completeness of definition unknown to the world of ballet.

"Atmen gibt das Leben . . ." ("Breathing gives life . . .")

1974–1977: No. 39 (Stockhausen-Verlag; cd SV-23)
Choir opera (SATB, solistic) with orchestra or tape; for performance with 2-track tape; 2 × 2 loudspeakers, mixing console.

This composition has an unfinished feel to it, and might best be described as a prototype or draft in which the composer is seen to be playing with a number of ideas that he will go on to develop more fully in subsequent works. The work is described as a "choir opera" although there is no plot as such and next to no action. It is apposite to recollect the defense of another twentieth-century composer criticized for composing an actionless opera to a text from ancient history, that "a text for music might be endowed with a monumental character by translation backward, so to speak, from a secular to a sacred language. . . . I wanted a universal plot. . . . I thought to distil the dramatic essence by this, and to free myself for a greater degree of focus on a purely musical dramatisation. . . . (and adding) A great deal of the music is a *Merzbild*, to borrow Schwitters' term." In that case the composer was Stravinsky, the composition *Oedipus Rex*.[17]

The work is in two parts. The first section began life as a model for a student assignment for the composer's composition class at the Musikhochschule, in response to a request from the director of an amateur choir for a work suitable for nonprofessionals. Its title, another citation from Hazrat Inayat Khan, suggests a covert message about finding inspiration as well as staying alive: "Breathing gives life/But singing gives the form." The text is hardly great poetry; its significance to the composer, I suspect, lies in the fact that the composer's name incorporates "ein" and "aus," as in the act of breathing, and so the text provides independent justification for a signature study in four-part vocalized breathing that from time to time requires a soprano to hiccup, male voices to "piff" noisily in and out (colored noise, an interesting sound), and the choir to sing while inhaling, which is neither easy to do nor recommended for professional singers (in *Stimmung* words are murmured while inhaling, but not sung). In the original version, an alternative opening line "Schlafen ist erquickend" (Sleeping is reviving) was available, but later discarded; however the intimate murmurs and sibilants of waking sleep are a vital element of this opening scene, and already suggest a need for close-microphone amplification.

In the expanded score this first part becomes more of a rhetorical prelude or wake-up call; the second, more substantial part, taking the form of a mini-cantata in which particulate quasi-recitatives (a scrapbook of citations from Socrates, the St. Thomas gospel, Meister Eckhart (misspelled), haiku by Shiki, Issa, and Buson, and comments by the composer from the world of particle physics), alternate with choral *ritornelli* of an affirmative but excitable nature to the text refrain "Das ist wahr, das ist schrecklich wahr" (That is true, that is so frightfully true). The transition from the intimate vocal noises of the first part to the more strident head tone of the second is a challenge in live performance, but makes perfect sense as a radio opera, where the interplay of inner and outer voices is routinely exploited for dramatic effect. Under studio microphone conditions, or recorded in the lively acoustic of a baroque church, consonants dissociate from vowels, and the consonantal noises of the refrain in German, sung in canon, with voices all around, are calculated to create a marvelous surround sound energy flux:

d s st fv rr h d s st sch k kh fv rr sz fv rr
das ist wahr oh das ist schreck lich wahr so wahr

Could this mean Stockhausen is entering a neoclassical phase? It certainly does indicate a renewed interest in what used to be called harmony and counterpoint, arising from the possibilities of melody composition and combination available with the Synthi 100. At the heart of *"Atmen . . ."* is a four-voice refrain consisting of canonic variations of a single theme, the prototype of Stockhausen's "Zodiac" melodies, with an underlying serial structure and clear indications of star configurations.

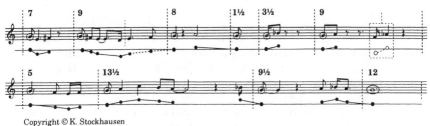

"Atmen gibt das Leben . . ." *Analysis of theme of four-part canonic inventions.*

Stockhausen's theme looks and sounds relatively diatonic, and it is interesting to note that in its four-voice permutations it still retains a sense of chromatic tonality and movement very similar to Stockhausen's student choral compositions under Hermann Schroeder (like them, the new work is also dedicated to the composer's first wife, Doris).

It is illuminating to compare the flat contour and limited intervallic movement of Stockhausen's theme with Webern's in the Op. 27 Piano Variations, second movement, which is much more angular and far-reaching. The advantage of flat melodies is that they are easier to follow in counterpoint: it's what one is taught in first-year choral harmony classes. That does not make such melodies any more interesting, compared with (say) the theme and combinatorial possibilities of the *Art of Fugue*. Indeed, several of Stockhausen's refrains contain suspect parallelisms that in another context, —*Mantra* comes to mind,—he might have wished to conceal; and two successive transpositions terminate fleetingly on surreptitious b minor and g flat major concords, which suggests that his point of departure for these exercises in voice transposition might actually have been the end point: literally, "ma fin est mon commencement." But Stockhausen also appears to be working toward the possibility of creating melodies out of figures corresponding to the *neumata* of traditional plainchant: the *porrectus, clivis, scandicus, torculus* etc. of Messiaen's classes at the Conservatoire. There are many ideas floating round in the primal alphabet soup.

Webern: Interval constellations from the Piano Variations *Op. 27, II.*

Another consideration peculiar to the twentieth century, arising from the rotational complexes of *Carré*, is the idea of melodic chains passing from layer to layer of the four voices, and varying with each transposition of the layers. Such twitchiness in line is a feature of melodies derived from independent scale melodies rotating among four voices. A melody of restricted compass, on the other hand, can also be thought of as a form with potential for intervallic expansion, as with the formula of *Mantra*, and later with *Aries*.

The published score incorporates photographs from the German premiere performance in 1979 that show the members of the choir disposed in different configurations and facing different directions at various points in the performance. Although the score is copiously annotated with additional instructions on what individuals and groups are to do, the present layout, including optional orchestra parts, is certainly in need of considerable clarification if the work is to be performed without the composer's active intervention. The impression created is of a work of incomplete or unresolved scenic actions for which a viable notation has still to be fully worked out. My own personal and unauthorized view is that the scenic actions correspond to a ballet after Merce Cunningham, in which the dancers perform canonic variations on sequences of moves, from time to time in unison, like the movements of sub-atomic particles (images of sudden encounters and spiral trajectories) as captured in a particle accelerator. These actions, ideally on a platform in the center of the auditorium, to be accompanied by live solo voices and *pre-recorded* choir ritornelli and orchestra, the choir canons having been discreetly vari-speeded on tape to achieve the exacting tempo and frequency changes required, and the whole balanced and relayed to loudspeakers surrounding the audience. Considered as a post-*Ylem* exercise in the manipulation of dissociated sounds in a three-dimensional acoustic space, the composition makes exciting sense as a significant precursor of the spatialized textures of *LICHT*.

Notes

1. Carl F. von Weizsäcker, *Relevance of Science: Creation and Cosmogony* (London: Collins, 1964), 147.

2. For example, the 1991 lecture "Electroacoustic Performance Practice." *Perspectives of New Music* Vol. 34 No. 1 (1996): 74–105.

3. Jonathan Cott, *Stockhausen: Conversations with the Composer* (London: Robson Books, 1974), 74.

4. Charles Taylor, *Sounds of Music* (London: British Broadcasting Corporation, 1976), 120–21.

5. "On the Evolution of Music." *Finnish Music Quarterly* No. 3 (1989): 8–13.

6. Luigi Rognoni, *Second Vienna School: Expressionism and Dodecaphony* tr. Robert W. Mann (London: John Calder, 1977), 136.

7. *Texte 4*, 224–25.

8. Berthold Viertel on Schoenberg's *Die Jakobsleiter*. In Merle Armitage, ed., *Schoenberg: Articles* (New York: Schirmer, 1937. Reprint, Westport, Conn.: Greenwood Press, 1977), 165–81.

9. Fred K. Prieberg, *Musica ex Machina* (Berlin: Ullstein, 1960), 203–207.

10. Steven M. Martin, *Theremin: An Electronic Odyssey*. VHS videotape; MGM Orion Classics, 1993.

11. "Neophyte Signs" in Israel Regardie, *Golden Dawn: A Complete Course in Practical Ceremonial Magic*. (Sixth edition, St. Paul, Minn.: Llewellyn, 1995), 133–34.

12. "Abstract Sound." 64–67 of *Sufi Message of Hazrat Inayat Khan*, Vol. II. http://www.murshid.net/mysticism-of-sound/abstractsound.html. (02/12/ 2004).

13. Merce Cunningham, *Danseur et la Danse: Entretiens avec Jacqueline Lesschaeve* (Paris: Belfond, 1980), 109. Compare Stockhausen, "Musik im Raum," *die Reihe 5*, reprinted with additions in *Texte 1*, 152–75.

14. Merce Cunningham, *Danseur et la Danse*, 139–42.

15. *Texte 3*, 248. "Ausflug zum Drachenfels, Königwinter, Sommer 1964" (Excursion to the Dragon Rock, Königwinter, summer 1964). The party comprises Carolyn Brown, Merce Cunningham, John Cage, Doris Stockhausen, David Tudor, Michael von Biel, Steve Paxton, Karlheinz Stockhausen, and Robert Rauschenberg.

16. Susan Sontag and others, *Dancers on a Plane: Cage, Cunningham, Johns* (London: Thames and Hudson, 1990).

17. Igor Stravinsky, "On 'Oedipus Rex.'" *Encounter* Vol. XVIII No. 6 (1962), 29–35. Reprinted in Igor Stravinsky and Robert Craft, *Dialogues* (London: Faber and Faber, 1982), 21–32.

CHAPTER TWENTY

Stagecraft

Stockhausen's increasingly focused interest in the choreography and scenic presentation of music theater (or music *as* theater), draws on established German conventions of radio drama and documentary that are little appreciated and easily overlooked. These conventions began to evolve in the twenties, when broadcasting began: there are traditions of the *Hörspiel*, and also the *Hörfilm*. As defined by Hans Heister in 1924, a *Hörspiel* is "any form of dramatic literature which cannot exist without the apparatus of radio, but which, as a text, resembles more a musical score than anything else." In 1929, the year of transition from silent movies to sound, Alfred Braun offered a definition of *Hörfilm* as a production consisting of "short scenes, in reported style, coupled with music, poetry, and particular sound effects, which is intended to reproduce a narrowly-defined piece of reality."[1] In general, Stockhausen's sense of music theater tends to favor the documentary reality of *Hörfilm*, though he also subscribes to the principle of an artistic studio creation corresponding to a higher and more truthful reality.

These radio arts of audio presentation, combining speech, music, and sound effects, were greatly enriched following the invention in Germany of a coated paper tape for magnetic tape recording in 1934. In the late twenties, the BBC had invested in the Marconi-Stille tape recorder for use in delayed newscasting to distant countries, but its expensive steel tape was designed for information storage rather than as an editing medium. The new German paper-based magnetic tape, however, could be cut and spliced as easily as film. For more than a decade the manufacture of tape-recording equipment, and development of associated editing skills, remained an exclusively German preserve. Progress in this area was to lead, during the 1939–1945 war, to audio reproduction from tape of a quality indistinguishable from a live news broadcast, making possible the routine simulation of wartime *Frontberichte* for propaganda purposes, incorporating prerecorded sounds of artillery fire, aircraft, and bombing. By the end of the war, German radio had built up an enormous technical and skills lead in the art of radiophonic scenic creation, with applications in documentary reportage as well as dramatic fiction.

Both Herbert Eimert's electronic music studio at Cologne Radio, where Stockhausen acquired and practised his skills, and Pierre Schaeffer's Paris-based *Club d'Essai*, the home of musique concrète, were founded as adjunct research departments of radio drama. Schaeffer's art of musique concrète, however, drew on a tradition of disc recording hugely inferior to tape in acoustic quality, and far less versatile in practical terms. Furthermore, the formal and aesthetic criteria of musique concrète were fatally conditioned to a defective medium, disc sound effects, for which no consistent or qualitative standards were in place: even today it remains an intuitive, impressionistic and essentially subjective art. The difference between electronic music and musique concrète does not reside in the fact that one uses prerecorded sounds and the other does not. Whether based on pure electronic or concrete sound materials, German electronic music draws on a longer tradition of creating mixed audio imagery in a superior recording medium.

Having written about the desirability of preserving endangered oral traditions of music, in *Herbstmusik*, a play of seasonal actions anticipating the *Sirius* cycle, Stockhausen extended the conception to sounds and customs of his adopted locality that seemed to be on the verge of extinction. For a composer now living out in the country, in a house built to his own design situated on a hill slope planted with young trees, the music of autumn belonged to the sounds and rhythms of harvesting and building. Autumn is a mysterious time, a time of stillness, when sounds carry, hovering between an end and a beginning. The activities of autumn are rites both of consummation (gathering in the harvest), and of preparation for winter (providing storage and shelter). "I looked for a musical link between autumn and the typical sounds which accompany that season, noises with an emotive resonance."[2]

Herbstmusik (Autumn music)

1974: No. 40 (Stockhausen-Verlag)
Autumn actions for four players; 16 microphones, 4 × 2 loudspeakers, mixing console.
1. "Nailing a roof" (duo with accompaniment);
2. "Breaking wood" (quartet);
3. "Threshing" (trio);
4. "Leaves and rain" (duo).
Duration: 62'.

Laub und Regen (Leaves and rain)

1974: No. 40½ (Stockhausen-Verlag)
Closing duet of *Herbstmusik* for clarinet and viola; 2 transmitting microphones, 2 × 2 loudspeakers, mixing console.
Duration: 11'.

Unlike *"Atmen gibt das Leben . . ."* which is an imaginative creation evoking
the mysterious interactions of subatomic particles on a microcosmic scale,
Herbstmusik is more in the nature of a documentary of traditional activities
on a human scale. Both works however are essays in fundamentally the
same radiophonic genre of choreographed sounds in space creating imaginative pictures of reality. Stockhausen's "choir opera" corresponds to a
fanciful animation in sound of the infinitely small; by comparison the
actions of *Herbstmusik* are on a human scale, and self-evidently real. But as
always with Stockhausen the message of the sounds is all-important, and
the visualization perhaps only a distraction. On the surface *Herbstmusik* is
about country life. The composition's audible poetry however lies in the
latent association of the four actions with specific evolutionary processes at
different frequency zones:

Action	Pitch	Material	Structure	Sound quality	Process
1. Nailing a roof	Medium	Metal	Periodic	Clangorous	Ascending in pitch
2. Breaking brushwood	Medium/high	Wood	Aperiodic	Snapping, cracking	Ascending in pitch
3. Threshing grain	Low/high	Batons, straw	Periodic/statistical	Pounding, rustling	Descending in pitch
4. Rough and tumble in the rain	High/low	Bodies, leaves	Aperiodic/statistical	Thudding, crushing	Descending in pitch

There is a slight hint of mischief in Stockhausen's translation of an intrinsically non-visual radiophonic idiom on to the stage, virtually guaranteeing
that the work will be misconstrued as a piece of visual theater. (There is a
slight suggestion of narrative, like a mime show with incidental noises, but
certainly no story-line in the conventional sense.) The comedy does not end
there. Sound images in radio and television tend to be static elements of a
developing external narrative: a door slam, a cork pops, a phone rings, etc.
In *Herbstmusik* it is the actions that tend to be visually static or repetitive,
and their associated acoustic processes that convey the passage of time, a
reversal of the conventional relationship of vision and sound. Some of the
more theatrical elements are also meant to be heard as equivalent to documentary actions, for instance the marching and heel-clicks of the "soldier on
parade" character, sounds that echo earlier hammer actions. At other times
a foretaste or aftertaste of one action is introduced into another, like an
insert in *Momente*.

Natural sounds, like the phonemic particles of *"Atmen . . . ,"* represent a
vast forgotten repertoire of material for art, made accessible through sound
recording, and only neglected by composers in general as a consequence of
outdated and unnecessary taboos. The first action, "Nailing a roof," is literally a two-part polyphony of nailing boards into the roof of a wooden shed.
The size of the nails, the type of hammer, and the pattern of rhythms
between the two players, are prescribed in detail. Hammering, of course, is
the physical equivalent of the composer's beloved electronic impulses, as
well as an action associated with memories of his childhood. There is also
hammering in the recording of the text "Intensität" from *Aus den Sieben
Tagen*. One can even discern an ironic obeisance to the elegant pointillism of

Boulez's *Le marteau sans maître.*

In the second action, four players seated on chairs break sticks from piles of dry brushwood, material chosen for its sharp percussive snap. The sticks are graded so that the thickest branches, producing sounds lowest in pitch, are at the top and broken first, followed by thinner and thinner twigs as the process continues. In this action the sound texture is percussive but aperiodic, gradually rising in pitch and thinning out. For a composer of electronic music there is the added attraction of selecting "real" processes that spontaneously transform in pitch, amplitude, or texture in real time. (Stockhausen has incorporated a "campfire scene" with breaking twigs in a version of *Hymnen mit Solisten* performed in London in 1985. The effect was magical.)

The third action, "Threshing," involves beating seed grain from straw using heavy flails of the size and weight of police batons, but roughly hexagonal in cross-section. The slow-motion pounding action produces a crisp-sounding reaction that becomes gradually less pronounced as the straw is compacted. The fourth and final theater action, "Leaves and rain," is like a scene from a French pastoral movie of a young couple relaxing and tussling in the hay, though in this case the hay is a pile of autumn leaves. As the pair tumble, the dry leaves rustle like a large-scale version of maracas being shaken, but this combination of synchronized thumping and rustling is gradually changed under the white noise of a sprinkler that plays on bodies and leaves. Over a period of time the crisp, dry sound texture is transformed into the sharper slap of wet bodies on damp ground. The acoustic transformation is perhaps more entrancing than the visual actions. Rather improbably in real-life terms, the physical play stops abruptly and the two take up clarinet and viola to perform a charming and witty final duet, also called "Leaves and Rain," corresponding to a continuation of the action-dialogue in musical terms.

In 1950 John Cage was asked to provide music for a documentary film *Works of Calder*, directed by Herbert Matter, showing the sculptor at work in his blacksmith's workshop. Cage's prepared piano sounds desultory and insipid compared to the exciting physicality and clangorous music of Calder methodically going about his work, cutting, hammering, and welding metal. Though artfully contrived and at times over-stylized, *Herbstmusik*'s actions are sufficiently consistent with reality to impress a listener in the same way as Calder with his hammer and anvil. Such documentary sound-actions have a truth and a moral concreteness that makes a refreshing change from the preciousness of conventional virtuosity. In its own terms as scenic sound actions *Herbstmusik* is Stockhausen at his most engaging and self-effacing. Once again a "silent movie with sound effects," it is a work as much for enhanced film or television reproduction, as for the concert hall.

The exception is the closing duet, which could stand as a separate work in its own right, and is eminently performable out of costume (and perhaps against a silent filmed backdrop of the actions). It seems a shame that no arrangements for alternative instruments are yet available, as for the *Tierkreis* melodies. The musical dialogue has an attractive lightness of touch, a glimpse of the composer in high spirits, and apart from a few token high notes the score is grateful to read and of limited compass.

Another lingering regret is that *Herbstmusik* of all works is unavailable in recorded form, especially ironic in view of the composer's earlier insistence, at the time of *Aus den Sieben Tagen*, on the vital importance of recording as a guide to interpretation: "A sound recording is important to me for building a new tradition for my compositions. For works of mine that are only approximately describable in the score, a disc is just as essential as the score itself. All of my works are cleared for publication only after I have proved them through many performances and they have been recorded."[3]

Musik im Bauch (Music in the belly)

1975: No 41 (Stockhausen-Verlag; cd (Leo+Aquarius+Capricorn) SV-24)
Musical action for six percussionists and musical boxes.
A life-size mannequin with the face of an eagle, garlanded with Indian jingles; 3 × 2-octave chromatic scales of crotala, sounding $c^5 - c^7$, mounted on boards; stick glockenspiel; 3 switches; bell plates, humming-top in e^3 (or tubular bell with very long resonance); marimbaphone, 3 musical boxes (chosen from the 12 *Tierkreis* musical boxes). Duration: 38'.

Tierkreis (Zodiac)

1975–1976: No. 41½ (Stockhausen-Verlag; cd SV-24 musical boxes, SV-35 trio version)
Twelve melodies of the Signs of the Zodiac for voice, melody or chordal instrument. 1. Aquarius; 2. Pisces; 3. Aries; 4. Taurus; 5. Gemini; 6. Cancer; 7. Leo; 8. Virgo; 9. Libra; 10. Scorpio; 11. Sagittarius; 12. Capricorn.
Separate editions for solo voice, chamber orchestra (clarinet, horn, bassoon, strings), clarinet and piano, trio (clarinet, flute/piccolo, trumpet/piano).
Duration of individual melodies: 24.4"–30.4", concert versions: 24'–30'.

The twelve zodiacal melodies introduce a new flexibility of scale and expression to the concept of a melody formula. Like the vibraphone formula of *Formel*, and the mirror formula of *Mantra*, they are designed for growth, and expansion into larger forms. There are however intriguing differences. The new melodies are longer and more consistent in tempo, and through note repetition and phrasing they correspond more closely to diatonic classical or folk melodies. They also omit serial dynamics and attacks, and abandon the stop–go structures, with interpolated silences, of earlier melody formulae. The absence of characteristic tempo variations, rests, accents, and decoration within the melodies may relate to limitations of the Synthi 100 sequencer, Stockhausen's major compositional aid. On the positive side, these melodies are designed to a different specification.

Considering their celestial names, one thinks of *Sternklang* and the dramatic advantage of substituting composed melodies at the points where the players look heavenwards and improvise melodies to the shapes of the visible constellations. Such an idea implies a collection of melodies designed to make musical sense in any combination or sequence, which is an attractive challenge. The wider implications of being able to choose from a range of interrelating melodies, instead of only one, are of particular interest. In an operatic context, for example, characters could be associated with specific melodies, and their dramatic interactions be reflected in appropriate contrapuntal combinations. In that sense alone, the *Tierkreis* melodies are an essential precursor (not *leitmotive* but LIGHT-motives) to the conception of *LICHT*.

The inner consistency of each melody seems remarkable for a composer of Stockhausen's serial pedigree, but it has a point. The individual melody corresponds not only to a formula, but also to a tape loop, that is, a wave form, and in the latter regard, consistencies of amplitude and tempo, and an absence of rests (connectedness) are standard features. Assigning each melody to an individual musical box is a clever touch, since it provides a rationale for omitting most of the expressive variables one has come to expect. The musical box is also an interesting mechanism in itself, since in addition to producing a pure and crystalline tone and repeating itself with clockwork precision, it is an instrument through which an audience senses a connection between the electronic music of the twentieth century and mechanical music of the era of Mozart, Haydn, and Beethoven. Each *Tierkreis* melody is composed as an indefinitely repeating cycle, based on a different tonal center ("Aquarius" on e flat, ascending by semitonal intervals via "Leo" on a natural to "Capricorn" on d), and each melody pulsates at a different degree of a tempo scale from MM 71 to MM 134 (consistent with the composer's regular tempo scale of MM 60–120 from c to c).

The inner structure of a melody follows the same basic principle as the choir melody of *"Atmen gibt das Leben . . ."* though without the rests; it might more accurately be described as a rhythm on one note with melodic appendages.

> In the LIBRA melody, B is the central pitch, and all of the other pitches swing out from it: up, down, up, etc. The durations of the measures are as follows: 2, 6, 6, 7, 5, 3, 1. Think of LIBRA, the balance, and how this large rhythm swings out and back over the entire melody. . . . Now let's see what makes this melody so rhythmically special. Always short, long, short, long. . . . The "new" [i.e., added] pitches . . . have the following progression of intervals in respect to the central note B: + 1, – 2, + 3, – 3, + 4, – 6, + 7, – 8, + 5, – 5, + 2, – 4, 0. . . . The principle is that in each *limb* there are two new pitches. This aspect is also like a balance.[4]

"Music in the belly," the story of a magic eagle-headed figure with three musical boxes concealed inside its torso sounds like a blend of fairy tale and American Indian tribal myth (it is a single-headed eagle after all, and looks and is dressed suspiciously like the composer himself). Its composition was inspired, Stockhausen tells us, by an occasion some years before, when his daughter Julika, then two years old, was surprised by noises inside her stomach. The present scenario came to Stockhausen in a dream. In Stockhausen's terminology a dream is a spontaneous and unaccountable solution to a technical problem in the form of a myth, just as the myth or fairy tale in the terms of a Claude Lévi-Strauss amounts to a secondary manifestation of musical relationships destined to remain hidden (to all, that is, apart from the author). In this case the composer was looking for a form with which to demonstrate the remarkable combinatorial properties of the twelve basic melodies. The mythical significance of *Musik im Bauch* is somewhat elusive, and the manner in which music is retrieved from the mute and suspended figure, a combination of sacrificial evisceration and caesarian section, a tad intimidating, especially since the underlying message is rather closer to the biblical story of Samson finding a honeycomb in the dried-out body of a lion. It is interesting to observe that Stockhausen's ahistorical myth-creating intuitions appear to be in general agreement with the methodology of Malinowski and his followers, who, if Lévi-Strauss is to be believed,

> refuse to consider any historical information regarding the society under study or any comparative data borrowed from neighboring or remote societies. In this way they claim to achieve, through inner meditation, those general truths [of social organization]. . . . Many an anthropologist of the younger generation . . . disdains study of any source materials or regional bibliographies before going into the field. He does this in order not to spoil the wonderful intuition that will enable him to grasp eternal truths on the nature and function of social institutions through an abstract dialogue with his little tribe.[5]

Creating stories as a way of bringing musical relationships to life for one's own family tribe is also a way of assigning meaning and value to musical (i.e., moral) imperatives that are hidden to the rest of society. There is a philosophy at work in the composer's deliberate progress toward a narrative idiom with which he can be comfortable, starting with *Mantra* and leading, via intermediate steps including *Herbstmusik*, *Musik im Bauch*, and *Sirius*, to culmination in the mythopoeia of *LICHT*. Stockhausen's translation of musical relations into ritualized human actions begs the question of what music can be said to represent, that is, to what reality it conforms. This is not a trivial issue. At the time of *Kontakte* the clearly imitative (and subordinate) role of the live musicians conveyed a Platonic message of human activity as imperfect and the world of human perceptions (instruments, categories) as affective splits or refractions of an incomprehensible universal continuum of being (frequency, timbre, material, etc.) represented by the electronic music. The musical boxes and robotic actions of *Musik im Bauch* can be interpreted in this context as covert commentaries on the Cartesian determinism of traditional music, not to mention the mechanistic no-mindedness of orthodox musical interpretation. In the seventies, however, Stockhausen's choreography of theatrical actions, whether "realistic" as in *Herbstmusik*, or enigmatic as in the present fairy tale, appears more inclined toward a Heideggerian "hermeneutics of everydayness" or representation of the nature of reality in the context of some meaningful activity, even though "we do not need to introduce a mental representation of a goal at all. Activity can be *purposive* without the actor having in mind a *purpose*. . . . The world, i.e., the interlocking practices, equipment, and skills for using them, which provides the basis for using specific items of equipment, is hidden. It is not disguised, but it is undiscovered."[6]

To the music itself. A version of *Musik im Bauch* can be created from any combination of three *Tierkreis* melodies, chosen perhaps to celebrate the birth-signs of three of the six performers, or of principal guests or patrons. Since there are twelve melodies, and each selection of three melodies can be combined in different hierarchies, the possibilities are endless. On one side of the stage two performers acting in extreme slow motion like automatons, play a stretched version of one melody on the marimba, lasting the entire length of the performance (a tempo of about one eighth-note every fifteen seconds). On the opposite side of the stage the three melodies are performed one after another in slow-motion on bell-plates, at tempi in the region of MM 10–15, each melody determining the length of one scene. Superimposed on this formal skeleton of clockwork actions are the flesh-and-blood ritual actions of the remaining three performers. Their actions suggest a Grimm-style fairy tale of three brothers on a quest to discover three magic caskets.

In the first scene, the three are seated at the rear of the platform, each performing a selected melody on antique cymbals in an ever-changing polyphony of brightly resonating points of sound. In the second scene the three leave their positions and take up switches that swish in the air with a whistling sound of varying pitch. (Normally a switch in music refers to an early form of drumstick now known as a "brush": these however are more like thin headmaster's canes). They advance on and circle around the mannequin, "Miron," suspended by a wire from the crown of the head at center stage, and bathed in light. Wielding their switches and grimacing like practicing samurai, they circle and swish, each in the rhythm of his original melody, taking care not to hit one another. At first tentatively, then more vigorously, they begin to pat, then swat the Miron figure with increasing force, provoking a crescendo of thuds and a coruscating sound of garlands of tiny bells adding to the swish of the switches through the air.

On a loud signal from the tubular bell (or spinning top in e), everyone freezes in typically Stockhausen "erstarrt" pose. Followed by the fixed stares of his companions one of the three runs offstage in a straight line with a clatter of footsteps (an action familiar to an older generation of British radio listeners from a famous episode of the BBC *Goon Show* of the fifties, "The Teahouse of the August Goon"). After a short pause he returns, and while the humming top continues to sound, produces an enormous pair of shears, as big as those of the Scissor-Man in Heinrich Hoffmann's fable of Johnny Suck-a-thumb in *Struwwelpeter* (Shock-headed Peter). Deftly inserting the blades between the buttons of Miron's shirt, he makes a couple of giant snips and reaches into the belly cavity to remove a small musical box. Moving to a low table at the left front of the stage, he opens the box, and lo and behold, it begins to play his melody. Kneeling at a glockenspiel, he begins to play along with the musical box until a loud bang from a bell-plate signals his time is up, and he runs from the stage.

The second player repeats the action of extracting a musical box, and places it on a table center stage, and again plays along with it on a glockenspiel. He sets the two musical boxes playing before also leaving on cue. The third retrieves the final musical box from the belly of the mannequin, advances, stops the other boxes, sets his own playing on a low table at stage right, and again plays along with it on a glockenspiel. With a flourish he rewinds the first box, sets all playing once again, salutes Miron with an elegant bow, and exits. Gradually the boxes run down, like Ligeti's metronomes, and their music disperses into hesitant and isolated tones (a little like *Ylem*, perhaps). As their own music reaches an end, the two marimba players perform a left turn and also take their leave, walking with the exaggerated stiffness of mechanical dolls. The music ends with the three musical boxes running down against a backdrop of tolling bell-plates.

So what does the story mean? Since the three glockenspielists already know their melodies at the start, it is not about discovering an identity, but receiving confirmation of the musical gift each possesses. The swishing of switches and the sound of the scissors are transitional noises, interesting in themselves, also associated with the penalties suffered by the young who willfully stray, though hardly more menacing than Lewis Carroll's "Speak roughly to your little boy/And beat him when he sneezes." Having received mechanical endorsement of their musical gifts, the players are encouraged to practice to a point where their playing is completely synchronous with the mechanism. All in all, about obedience to one's inner melody, not about freedom of invention. Stockhausen's choice of marimbaphone for the melody of greatest magnification is intriguing, since the sound is resolutely mid-range and does not suggest a transformation of speed in the way that crotala imitate accelerated tones, and bell-plates sound like a tape recording of a musical box played back at one-eighth speed. If the sound has to be dry and wooden, I would have thought a combination of temple blocks, woodblocks, and log drums perhaps more evocative.

Harlekin (Harlequin)
1975: No. 42 (Stockhausen-Verlag; cd SV-25)
For clarinet.
Duration: 45'.

Der Kleine Harlekin (Little Harlequin)
1975: No. 42½ (Stockhausen-Verlag; cd SV-25)
For clarinet. Shortened version of the above.
Duration: 9'.

Harlequin is the personification of mischief and magic, a human (and feminine) counterpart to the austere divinities of *Sirius* (of whom more anon). These pieces dedicated to Suzanne Stephens are affectionate portraits of virtuoso high spirits, and further developments toward a more fluid, secular art of music theater, in which visual and spatial actions are fully and consistently integrated with the musical gesture.

Harlekin is the musical expansion of a waveform, filled out in music and action. It begins in the high register, expands downward to cover the instrument's full pitch range, descends to lurk briefly in the low register, and ascends once more to the extreme upper register by a reverse process. The transformational journey across the registers, retracing a journey that began in the era of *Kreuzspiel,* is measured by a series of staging posts at which a principal formula, "Der verliebte Lyriker" (the enamoured lyricist) is presented at different registers and tempi, in effect enacting the transitions of a melody formula through the frequency continuum. This transposable but invariant eleven-note melody consists of a relatively tranquil legato sequence of long notes intersected and set in wavy motion by loud, short accents:

Harlekin: *Eleven-note formula "Die verliebte Lyriker."*
In this transposition there is no b natural.

Connecting these transpositions in musical space and time are cyclic *moto perpetuo* figurations based on the pitches of the formula, condensing out of an initial trill *Ylem* style and gradually increasing in number of pitches and dynamic spread to fill the entire pitch space of the instrument. These cyclic processes are also associated with rotational movements by the performer, which cannot be easy to do; in turn the rotations emulate the spiral movements and rotary processes of *Kontakte,* and as reproduced manually by Stockhausen's "sound mill" at the Osaka Expo in 1970.

Stockhausen's humor demands courage and a great deal of stamina. One's first impression of the introduction, entitled "Der Traumbote" (Dream Messenger) is of a cartoon character out of Looney Tunes (either Road Runner or the Tasmanian Devil, who arrives of course in his own whirlwind). This is very physical music indeed, with no respite and no rests, requiring circular breathing and continuous movement. Although it looks and feels like Henry Miller's interpretation of Czerny exercises, seemingly verging on the maniacal, what the gestural language appears to be based on is a combination of mechanical transformations. The music begins with a high trill that slows down to an undulating glissando, then to a sequence of repeating figures that by stages open out into wider and wider cycles. There is a lot in this sequence to compare with the "spindizzy" effect of Stockhausen's improved and more powerful "rotation turbine" that can be heard at the introduction and end of *Sirius.* A subsequent page of up-and-down arpeggio exercises looks like a strict transcription of a sawtooth melody entered on the Synthi 100 and repeated over and over while the baseline pitch is gradually lifted, compressing the interval of fluctuation from over three octaves to just under one octave in the highest register. When the music attempts to compress the interval space beyond a major seventh, the arpeggio starts to flatten out. The fact that Stockhausen doesn't introduce microtones at this stage suggests that he is describing a mechanical process. Among the "numerous scenes of humorous and cheeky play" is a "Dialogue with the Foot" in which the clarinetist alternates short rhythmic phrases with foot-stamping in the same rhythm. Even this I suspect is a transferred musical epithet from the example of the new rotation turbine which as it slows to a stop emits rhythmic pounding and grinding noises (also audible in the *Sirius* recording).

The humor here is childlike, of the classic circus clown variety, arising from vain human attempts to imitate larger-than-life processes. What makes it a little more interesting is that the imitation is in two stages: the first stage being the composer transcribing these mechanical processes as accurately as possible in order to realize them in notational terms, and the second stage the performer having to reproduce these notations,—probably without knowing where they are coming from. Then out of the performer's struggles with the notation emerges a human dimension which is then incorporated in the composition as the official interpretation.

Long-term, the interest of *Harlekin* resides in the challenge of recording and reproducing continuous circular movements with the correct phase information. The composer returns to this issue yet again in the realization of the electronic music of "Kathinkas Gesang" from *Samstag aus LICHT*. What seems a little surprising in the circumstances, given Stockhausen's recent and technically successful experience with *Inori*, is his reluctance to develop the possibilities of a new style of heterophony in which two, three, four or more instruments of the same family (say, clarinets) perform the same basic music in total synchronization, but with variations in attack, amplitude, and position in space that together create an impression of a single line of music moving in a three-dimensional space. What the brass instruments of *Gruppen* achieved, and the four orchestras of *Carré* failed to achieve, could certainly be attempted by smaller groups of the same instrumental family, and it is baffling that Stockhausen does not pursue such an obvious and potentially fruitful line of inquiry at this stage.

Sirius (Sirius)
1975–1977: No. 43 (Stockhausen-Verlag; cd SV-26, electronic music SV-76)
Electronic music and trumpet, soprano, bass clarinet, bass; 8-track tape recorder, 4 transmitting microphones, 1 microphone, 8 loudspeakers, mixing console.
Duration: 96'.

Aries (Aries)
1977/1980: No. 43½ (Stockhausen-Verlag; cd SV-33)
For trumpet and electronic music; 8-track (or 2-track) tape recorder, 1 transmitting microphone, 8 (or 2 × 2) loudspeakers, mixing console.
Duration 15'.

Libra (Libra)
1977: No. 43⅔ (Stockhausen-Verlag; cd SV-32)
For bass clarinet and electronic music; 8-track (or 2-track) tape recorder, 1 transmitting
microphone, 8 (or 2 × 2) loudspeakers, mixing console.
Duration: 33'.

Commissioned by the government of the Federal Republic of Germany in
honor of the United States bicentennial in 1976, *Sirius* is Stockhausen's
most grandiloquent statement to date, and in many ways the most challenging, both technically and scenically. Somewhere on the way from its origin
as a collection of musical signals (or zodiacal anthems, to pursue the metaphor of *Hymnen*) the work has acquired a cosmic gravitas not only in
keeping with the traditions of US national celebration but, in its capacity as
a cultural visitation from Europe, seriously reminiscent of the colonizing
spirit of Columbus and Cortez. Boldly dedicated "to the American Pioneers
on Earth and Space," *Sirius* delivers a visionary message of interstellar
greeting as baffling in its own way as Steven Spielberg's in the 1977 movie
Close Encounters of the Third Kind, wherein the curiously passive inhabitants of a giant spinning top greet the pastoral society of Copland and Virgil
Thomson with a musical sign language out of Zoltán Kodály, including hand
signals. As a rhetorical statement, *Sirius* appears to be offering a rather
heavy-handed tribute to the dark side of the American dream, that Lindisfarne subculture of spiritual inadequacy embodied in movie fictions of
hapless victims of malign governments, covert intelligence operations, and
flying saucers, now fortunately overtaken by the amiable escapism of *Men
in Black*.

    We need to remember that even in the mid-seventies personal com-
puters and the internet did not exist. In the era of the first Voyager space
probes, popular interest in science was fixated on the political and environmental mess human progress had gotten the world into, and on the possibility of intelligent assistance from beyond the solar system. In a duplicitous
climate of political stalemate where the only certainty to be believed in was
that of mutually assured destruction, answers were sought in myth. In the
words of US astronomer emeritus Carl Sagan, "Once intelligent beings
achieve technology and the capacity for self-destruction of their species the
selective advantage of intelligence becomes more uncertain. And what if we
receive a message? Is there any reason to think that the transmitting beings
—evolved over billions of years of geological time in an environment vastly
different from our own,—would be sufficiently similar to us for their messages to be understood? I think the answer must be yes."[7] It was, to be sure,
a millennial, grandiloquent time.

    In general, Stockhausen's invented scenarios, beginning with *Mantra*
and applied retroactively to works such as *Kontakte* and *Momente*, are
designed to provide a scenic or philosophical rationale for musical processes
otherwise difficult to perceive as coherent or meaningful. Naturally the
composer, as ringmaster, will insist under interview,—even at risk to his
own long-term credibility, on the literal truth, in the case of *Sirius*, of the

composer's role as an extraterrestrial *geist* with a mission to deliver a message of reassurance. The danger in maintaining such a position is that it offers no escape in the event of the message being taken literally, or giving offense. It must seem only too obvious, on reflection, that commemorating two hundred years of independence of a friendly nation and superpower with an oratorio pitting Nietzsche against Superman is not the best form of diplomacy. (There is certainly room for further discussion of the finer social and political distinctions that divide working-class American sci-fi cults and conspiracy literatures from the holistic alliances of high-ranking European intellectuals. Fortunately in the present case they are not much help in identifying the particular merits of the music itself, and may be safely ignored.)

Portentous though it may appear to English and American sensibilities, Stockhausen's message is intended as an expression of hope. It proceeds, furthermore, out of a German culture with a record of centuries of deliberation on the ratios of good and evil represented by a history of violence and destruction entailed by scientific progress. Stockhausen's utopian vision is not very different from that of the poet Novalis, who wrote (in "Wenn nicht mehr Zahlen und Figuren"):

> *Since quantity and definition*
> *Cannot determine God's creation,*
> *And love and music's sweet designs*
> *Exceed the best of human science,*
> *When boundaries are set asunder*
> *And human hearts to joy and wonder,*
> *And shade and light in due equation*
> *Proclaim the clarity of creation,*
> *Know then the everlasting truth*
> *Of poetry and sacred myth,*
> *And by a* single *word of mystery*
> *Annul the whole perverted history.*[8]

Stockhausen's progress toward a suitably protean narrative style is a fact to be recognized in terms of changes and developments in his musical thinking. He had successfully resisted the temptation to explain himself for over two decades. Though they might be technically difficult for a listener to assimilate, works such as *Gesang der Jünglinge, Momente, Telemusik*, and *Stimmung* were in essence self-explanatory. During the seventies, however, as radio continued to decline and television continued to gain in cultural influence, a composer with an eye to the future would be aware of the need both to adapt, and to find an appropriate visual or scenic expression of musical relationships. Stockhausen's response is typical: refusing to subject his necessary musical goals to the imaginative fictions of scriptwriters. But while its attendant risks may be considerable, public misunderstanding can still have a positive side. Because ordinary human beings do not look beneath the surface, an abstract narrative, even at its most revealing, can act as a protective cloak or disguise to distract critics and deflect prying commentators. Zealous unaccountability was a ploy adopted out of necessity by artists of protest in the Europe of the years of tyranny:

> The grounds for abstraction were not purely political, but reflect a tendency in many different arts to favour the material used, rather than external plot or content, as a focus for experimentation. In France, the influence of Artaud and absurdist drama was manifested in an increased emphasis on the theatricality of theatre; similar motivations lay behind the *nouvelle vague* in film, in which the *mise-en-scène* became more central than the plot. Inherent in such movements is a fascination not with the external world, but the reality of the artwork itself, and the specific nature of each art form.[9]

Stockhausen's message in *Sirius* could also be understood as a covert tribute to the visionary protagonist of *L'Astronome*, a planned but never executed musico-dramatic narrative from 1928 concerning an astronomer who makes contact with intelligent life on Sirius and is publicly vilified for exposing the world to the dangers of invasion by a superior intelligence. From the composer's notes, vivid images remain: "The sound of a drill again. The beam from the star twists down suddenly, transfixes the astronomer, disintegrates him, absorbs him. . . . The mob is turned to stone." The unfinished libretto, by Antonin Artaud, is titled "The Firmament is Gone." The composer and visionary: none other than Edgar Varèse.[10]

Jonathan Cott is very direct. Was Stockhausen aware of Varèse's plans for *Espace*, and by association, *L'Astronome*. Stockhausen demurs. He knew Varèse, and had visited the composer in his New York apartment. In the last ten years of his life Varèse had been "more interested in astronomy than in music," and Stockhausen had regarded him with affection. "I always felt as if he were a good father."[11]

Sirius opens with "die Vorstellung," or presentation of the soloists, whose fixed stage locations occupy the four points of the compass at the periphery of the circular seating plan: bass at the colder north, soprano at the warmer south, the male trumpeter at east heralding a new dawn, the female bass clarinetist at the west, the region of Eve: night and rest. Their appearance is signaled by whizzing bursts of sound, whirling around the audience like a cyclotron, creating weird aural illusions. Each rotational descent is marked by a final burst on the throttle reminiscent of Cocteau's motorcycle-riding messengers of the gods in *Orphée* (and revisited in "Helikopter-Streichquartett"). As they mount their platforms to the north, south, east and west, the four celestial visitors are accompanied by recorded natural sounds of snow and ice, a crackling wood fire, rushing water, and the whistling and howling of the wind:—aural talismans of a rich seasonal tapestry.

After stiffly formal greetings, the centerpiece of the work begins: "Das Rad" (the Wheel), a musical cycle of the seasons that can start at Spring, Summer, Autumn, or Winter as occasion may demand. This section lasts an hour. Each season is distinguished by its appropriate zodiacal melodies in different degrees of prominence and transition. "Each of the four main melodies reigns for approximately one-quarter hour, and all twelve melodies divide the hour like the twelve numbers of a clock."[12] The music is Stockhausen in contrapuntal guise, a four-voice solo and accompanying electronic music forming a dense continuous sound web demanding the greatest listening concentration. The experience is a good indication of just how much direction and ambience contribute to an audience's appreciation of the interweaving strands of melody, and to allowing the listener (not to mention the music) room to breathe: a reminder of Henry Brant's careful inquiries into the acoustic implications of spatialized composition, and that the mid-seventies was an era in commercial recording history when the industry was tearing itself apart over competing four-channel analogue recording and reproduction technologies. Naturally the reduction of *Sirius*'s eight tracks to two-channel stereo for commercial release does not aid appreciation of the spatial dimension, but an equally powerful factor is the penetrating, seemingly invariant intensity of the electronic sounds themselves, which glister in the acoustic darkness of multi-track tape with the disorientating brightness of chrome and neon.

It is surprising to reflect that much of *Sirius*'s electronic music in its present state could actually be performed by a string orchestra. That he had problems with the Synthi 100 Stockhausen later acknowledged: "the Synthi 100 has never performed wholly satisfactorily, because it is terribly unstable and the filters are very bad."[13] According to Berio, who at the time was involved in, and equally squeamish about, IRCAM's putative digital synthesis programme, the Synthi 100 "nearly drove him crazy, and he ended up using it as a generator of sound structures which he then elaborated, edited, and superimposed on tape in the traditional fashion."[14] Berio goes on to pay generous tribute to Stockhausen's contribution to

> one of the most difficult and interesting (and least discussed) aspects of the musical theatre of all ages, . . . this question of inventing temporal conventions that extend the relationship between words and dramatic action on one hand, and music on the other. . . . The most significant realizations in electronic music (such as Stockhausen's) are still those that make use of hybrid, open electro-acoustic systems.[15]

Sirius ends controversially, after the turning of the wheel, with "die Verkündigung" (Annunciation): a sublimely tactless message of population regeneration transmitted long since from out there to down here via Jakob Lorber (1800–1864), Austrian violinist, music teacher, mystic and self-styled "Scribe of God."

The work is a significant precursor of *LICHT* and consistent with the style and content of the opera cycle to a degree that makes it a dramatically logical precursor event, in the role of messenger of the gods, to a festival of the operas. *Sirius* serves as a useful introduction to Stockhausen's characterizations of male and female, their alternate identities as instruments, and the symbolic apparatus attaching to natural distinctions of biological function, voice range, speech gestures, and seasonal associations (a world of simple oppositions where men are naturally hard and icy, and women soft and warm, etc.). After the experience of listening to *Donnerstag, Samstag,* and *Montag aus LICHT* it comes as a surprise to listen to *Sirius* over again and discover how much less complicated the music is to follow. Stockhausen's progress in strict counterpoint is a major item, and the relative transparency of the writing and uniformity of timbres are as much to the advantage of study here as the plain sounds of the harpsichord to an appreciation of Bach's preludes and fugues.

Stockhausen's conception of strict counterpoint is the simultaneous appearance of more than one melody having the possibility of moving in or out of synchronization in tempo or rhythm, or of exchanging elements, or of merging to create hybrid melodies. One looks in vain for the classical variants of traditional counterpoint through to Schoenberg and Webern: inversion, retrograde, and retrograde inversion of a theme. For reasons that are probably more technical than philosophical, Stockhausen's formulas do not normally invert or reflect, and while that may have something to do with a fear of mirrors, the more likely explanation is that the composer's workbench, the Synthi 100, is not set up to make these transformations. Stockhausen's model in any case is *Hymnen* and its basis in linguistic transformational rules for national anthems that are only recognizable as inflected melodies in a single orientation. In *Sirius* the real-time vocal and instrumental components demonstrate the combinational possibilities of melodic formulas in terms largely of fragmentation and recombination, editing processes after the Max Mathews model and beyond that to Messiaen and the movies. To this human dimension of surgical reconstruction out of Frankenstein, the electronic music brings much the same additional powers, of continuous acceleration, rotation, compression, and simulated transformation, already familiar from *Kontakte* and *Hymnen*. Yet again, the real-time, human participants are presented as flawed and imperfect fragments of a higher state of being represented by the electronic music.

For all his student protestations of allegiance to the contrapuntal tradition of J. S. Bach, Stockhausen's multipart writing has more in common with the technical features he criticizes in the folk traditions of Bartók than those he admires in the master of the *Art of Fugue*. The parallel harmonies of the Synthi 100, an unexpected reminder of the hidden orchestra groups of *Trans*, are one example. For much of *Sirius*, the four soloists give the impression of talking very loudly at once and not listening to one another, like a Cage simultaneous lecture set to music, or a group of high-profile American attorneys arguing on prime time television. To be fair, the sense of congestion is also a consequence of mixing down and hearing in stereo a spatialized composition conceived in at least four channels, and possibly more. This is one Stockhausen composition, however, where to hear a solo version of the music is a real advantage and not an impoverishment.

There are wonderful moments. The trumpet solos in "Aries" at 2, 10, and 27; in "Cancer," the coda for bass clarinet from 26 to the end; a *Hymnen* moment in "Libra," from 10 to 21; the trumpet-bass clarinet duo in "Capricorn" from after 19 to 21, a precursor of the love-duos of *Donnerstag aus LICHT* that for once comes across as witty and genuinely affectionate, and that also works well against the electronic background. By and large the two instruments are more congenial than the two voices, whose considerable difficulties seem to be asking for special acoustic treatment, oscillating between the megaphone style of a political rally, a vocoder simulation, and ring modulation in the style of *Mantra*. Despite its pedantic manner, Boris Carmeli's recording of "Vorstellung" preserves a remarkable impression of Stockhausen's own voice and personality, both also reflected in the unforced and resonant timbre of the bass clarinet. The mysterious sounds of whirring and of breaking ice are also highly effective and very tangible.

One often has the impression that the burden of ritual significance associated with Stockhausen's narrative constructs is in inverse proportion to the difficulties of the particular project. In addition to its stated confidence in a technological future, *Sirius* intends a message of a renewed serial determinism, and of a new prowess in counterpoint, but for him personally the task was endlessly frustrating, in consequence of which he regards the published scores of *Sirius* as study scores only, and has not issued a detailed technical score,—in part because it would amount to a chronicle of mechanical breakdowns and artistic compromises. In *Hymnen* Stockhausen took a number of disparate musical objects (anthems) and forced them into association by interpenetration, creating hybrid objects of an appealing anonymity. In *Sirius* the anthems have become signs of the zodiac, signposts of astral navigation (—though surely only for earthlings, since neither the star configurations of human history nor their animal analogues would be familiar to inhabitants of the alpha star of the Sirius double star system located "at the center of our local galaxy"). In place of *Hymnen*'s utopian program of miscegenation in the spirit of *Hair*'s "chocolate colored people by the score," the more benign message of *Sirius* is one of celestial harmony, of coexistence, and seasonal change.

The relationship of the four soloists to the electronic music is much the same as for the live performers of *Kontakte* or *Hymnen mit Solisten*. Like the melodies with which they are identified, they are represented as human incarnations of a transcendental reality expressed in the proportions of the electronic music. This is a music whose transformational range extends further than ever before, across and beyond the time and pitch scales of the original melodies to become as fast as the wind or as slow as the seasons, and as slight in inflection as the buzzing of an insect or the swaying of grass. As in *Hymnen*, the electronic anamorphism of recognizable themes is impelled by a dynamic of speed, rhythmic and melodic exchanges, and melody compression. Cyclic formations dominate the work at every level: the cycle of the seasons, of the zodiac, of the elements of air, earth, fire, and water, even of human life itself, woven into a terrestrial fabric of existence and belief that connects with a universal order of cycles within cycles mediated by the electronic polyphony. Stockhausen's "characteristic texts" for each of the zodiac melodies are verbal signposts and inscriptions, documentary facts rather than poetry or literature, uncompromising and also unanswerable, and a hint of the *LICHT* texts to come. What they evoke is a robotic rather than human intelligence, with a vocal style to match: slightly skewed, detached, unoperatic.

On the composer's own terms, *Sirius* has symbolic importance as a statement of faith in technology, specifically in the Synthi 100, purchased at great expense by Cologne Radio on the composer's recommendation. Almost all of the technical interest is focused, however, on the performance of the Zinovieff sequencer and the combinational and manipulative possibilities of the slender material of the twelve *Tierkreis* melodies, which are coming more and more to resemble Messiaen's birdsongs, just as their persistent recombination in cyclic layers returns the reader to Messiaen's isorhythmic constructions (as in *Chronochromie*, for example).

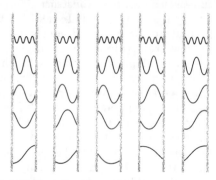

The distinctive "spindizzy" sounds of arrival and departure (to borrow the name of Robert A. Heinlein's antigravity gyroscope) are the sound of Stockhausen's new and improved sound rotation device, a speaker turbine capable of speeds of up to twelve revolutions per second. Referring to the earlier rotation table developed for *Kontakte*, he speaks of manual rotations of up to seven per second played back over four speakers at double speed, at which the sound "starts dancing completely irregularly in the room—at the left, in front, it's everywhere,"—even changing pitch depending on where the listener is standing.[16] With the new device in use for *Sirius*, rotations of twelve per second in real time, reproduced on eight-track tape, create more complex aural strobe effects.[17] Mysterious transformations in pitch of the same sound at different locations within the auditorium, are a consequence of the impulsive segmentation of the sound as it passes from speaker to speaker: a "flap" effect from *Kontakte*, but raised to audible speed. A rotating sound is only present in any one speaker for a short period of time, which at high rotational speed may not contain a sufficient number of lower-frequency oscillations to be heard as a continuous tone. In addition, zones of tone reinforcement can be encountered at points along a line between two or more speakers, creating an impression of standing columns of sound.[18]

The acoustic and musical implications of high speed rotation in *Sirius* are of great interest, especially by comparison with "Kathinkas Gesang als Luzifers Requiem," the electronic rotations of which were digitally synthesized at IRCAM, and do not produce as dynamic an effect. For not only diplomatic but also musical reasons, Stockhausen is at pains to defend the Cologne analogue devices, both the Synthi 100 and the new rotation turbine, despite their mechanical crudity; the former for its hands-on control, and the latter because the rotating sound preserves natural effects of phase-shifting, unlike analogue or digital pan-rotation effected by joystick control. A critical distinction between sounds that are spinning when recorded and sounds that are simply pan-rotated very rapidly from speaker to speaker in the studio, is that the partial tones of a naturally moving sound are alternately compressed and stretched, creating a dynamic alteration of the tone quality that is frequency specific and unobtainable in any other way. The best source of the effect is arguably the most primitive musical instrument known to man, the bull-roarer of the Australian native people, a spinning aerofoil on a cord readily familiar to moviegoers from a mesmerizing performance in Paul Hogan's movie *Crocodile Dundee II*. By sheer coincidence, the bull-roarer is also an instrument for transmitting messages.

In 1980 Stockhausen made a concert version of "Aries" for trumpet and tape, with the following description of the processes of melody transformation:

> This version of ARIES begins with the ARIES melody heard with the rhythm of CAPRICORN. It is increasingly sped up, and the CAPRICORN melody is added to, or mixed with, the melody of ARIES. During this accelerando process, the rhythm of CAPRICORN is transformed to become the ARIES rhythm, and the rhythm and melody of CANCER is slowly introduced. After about two minutes the melodies disappear and a hissing sound appears, because it is no longer possible to analyze either the melody or the rhythm: they are too fast.[19]

The sound divides into two layers, one is further accelerated, throwing off bright fragments of the "Aries" melody like sparks, while the other dense band, a polyphony of melodies "Cancer," "Capricorn," and "Aries," is slowly compressed until only a monotone a 440 is heard pulsating in the melody rhythm. Then, in a process reminiscent of Messiaen, the shorter rhythmic values are gradually lengthened and the longer values gradually shortened, to leave a regular pulsation. This too slows down, and the individual pulses are gradually lengthened until they merge into one continuous timbre:

> Here at last is the great survivor, the timbre. And the timbre disappears like the wind which whistles behind the corner of a house. [Be] careful here not to lose the residue of melody which conceals itself between two vowels, within the timbre, precisely between the i and the u. . . . Then from the depths of the progressive annihilation, the timbre rises once more, and this time with a completely different melody.[20]

Stockhausen's frustration over *Sirius,* and with the Synthi 100, assume added piquancy in the context of Boulez's preparations for the launch of IRCAM on the promise of digital synthesizer technology of unparalleled power, an enterprise with which Stockhausen, no doubt influenced by his commitment to Cologne Radio and analogue technology, was not publicly involved. There is a sense in which the studied invariance of *Sirius*'s metallic timbres can be read as a direct response to the barren square-wave

timbres of Max Mathews and his colleagues (at the time of *Hymnen*), not to
mention the equally persistent, though softer, matt aluminium tones shortly
to emerge from Pepe di Guigno's 4X synthesizer. Stockhausen's attention to
melody transformation stands in direct opposition to Boulez's aspirations,
which were centered at the time on Xavier Rodet's *Chant* software: "As I see
it (said Boulez) the most important underlying area of inquiry capable of
leading to a practical solution is the relationship of *continuity between
timbres*, however precarious its chances of success, and vulnerability to disruption by any number of factors as yet poorly understood."[21] It is only right
to recall the primitive nature of all synthesizer music in the seventies,
together with the widespread feeling that a computer revolution was just
around the corner. The music of *Sirius* may glare and dazzle, but as with all
of Stockhausen's musical achievements it is authentic, unforgiving, hard,
and above all real.

Notes

1. Cited in Stefan Bodo Würffel, *Das Deutsche Hörspiel* (Stuttgart: Metzler,
    1978).
2. Mya Tannenbaum, *Conversations with Stockhausen* tr. David Butchart
    (Oxford: Clarendon Press, 1987), 81.
3. "Interview III" with Hanspeter Krellmann, June 1969. *Texte 3*, 326–29.
4. Karlheinz Stockhausen, *Stockhausen in Den Haag*. Documentation of the
    Karlheinz Stockhausen Project (English edition) ed. Michael Manion,
    Barry Sullivan, and Fritz Weiland (The Hague: Koninklijk Conserva-
    torium, 1982), 19–20.
5. Claude Lévi-Strauss, *Structural Anthropology* tr. Claire Jacobson and
    Brooke Grundfest Schoepf (New York: Basic Books, 1963), 11–13.
6. Bruce I. Blum, *Beyond Programming: To a New Era of Design* (New
    York: Oxford University Press, 1996), 95–101.
7. Carl Sagan, *Dragons of Eden: Speculations on the Evolution of Human
    Intelligence* (London: Coronet, 1978), 230.
8. Free rendition by the author.
9. M. J. Grant, *Serial Music, Serial Aesthetics: Compositional Theory in
    Post-War Europe* (Cambridge: Cambridge University Press, 2001), 21.
10. Fernand Ouellette, *Edgard Varèse: A Musical Biography* tr. Derek
    Coltman (London: Calder & Boyars, 1973), 115–17.
11. Jonathan Cott, *Stockhausen: Conversations with the Composer* (London:
    Robson Books, 1974), 208. Also cited in Fernand Ouellette, *Edgard
    Varèse: A Musical Biography*, 131. Varèse adds, "What should be
    avoided: tone of propaganda as well as any journalistic speculating on
    timely events and doctrines" (e.g., National Socialism.)
12. *Texte 4*, 305.
13. *SoM*, 133.
14. *Luciano Berio: Two Interviews*. With Rossana Dalmonte and Bálint
    András Varga. Tr. ed. David Osmond-Smith (New York: Marion Boyars,
    1985), 40.
15. David Osmond-Smith tr. ed., *Luciano Berio: Two Interviews*, 48, 129.
16. Jonathan Cott, *Stockhausen: Conversations with the Composer*, 98.
17. *SoM*, 148–49.

18. The *Sirius* rotation turbine is illustrated in Maria Morawska-Bungeler, *Klingende Elektronen: Eine Dokumentation über das Studio für Elektronische Musik des Westdeutschen Rundfunks in Köln 1951–1986* (Rodenkirchen: P. J. Tonger, 1988), 73.

19. "Musikalische Metamorphose." *Texte 5*, 701–36.

20. Mya Tannenbaum, *Conversations with Stockhausen* tr. David Butchart (Oxford: Clarendon Press, 1987), 62.

21. Pierre Boulez, "Perspective–Prospective." 23–33 in Brigitte Marger and Simone Benmussa, ed., *La Musique en Projet: Le Premier Livre de l'I.R.C.A.M, Direction Pierre Boulez* (Paris: Gallimard, 1975).

CHAPTER TWENTY-ONE

Allegories

In 1959, with his career on the crest of a wave, Stockhausen joined other young composers in a vigorous response to a widely publicized complaint by Professor Friedrich Blume, the eminent musicologist and editor-in-chief of the encyclopedia *Die Musik in Geschichte und Gegenwart* (Music Yesterday and Today). Coming from a distinguished representative of the musical establishment, Dr. Blume's attack, on a "scientific" modern music he ventured to describe as both inhuman and blasphemous, carried considerable weight, despite its outraged tone and absence of substantive argument. Stockhausen's response, published in the periodical *Melos*, is tactically intriguing. In reply, to a convincing resumé of citations from Pascal, Goethe, the poet Christian Morgenstern, Schoenberg, Webern, Le Corbusier, Mondrian, and Paul Klee, he appended a strange couplet of his own devising, in the style of a nursery lullaby with overtones of Lewis Carroll, pointedly making a play on the name Blume (flower).

> The little *blooms*, in moonshine bred
> Nod each a sleepy little head
> At Man above who tends their bed.
> When axe upon the root they hear:
> "'Tis but a dream, I do declare"—
> *Dream on, your time is drawing near.*
>
> The Devil from below emits
> A serial shower from the pits
> Of electronic spots and spits.
> And, disbelieving, flowers yawn
> "Surely it's just a bit of fun"—
> *Sweet dreams, your time is almost done.*[1]

Since the argument, such as it was, was Stockhausen's to win, why bring it up now? For two reasons: first, the manner in which Stockhausen structures his defense, and second, the moral and aesthetic implications of the composer's terms. For an artist at the vanguard of the vanguard, Stockhausen has an unexpected habit of slipping, under duress, into the indulgent tone and style of a nineteenth-century schoolmaster. Here he evokes a satirical world of nursery tale where people are reduced to decorative but thoughtless flowers (or maybe, vegetables) equally at risk from the Great Cultivator above ground or volcanic destruction from below. That he so readily identifies electronic music as the work of the devil may simply be indulging the prejudices of his attacker. Then again, perhaps not. To Blume he seems to be saying, this is your vision of contemporary music: you deal with it. But underneath all of that there lurks the suspicion that, technically and philosophically, the objectors have a point, and science and electronic music are indeed local manifestations of the curse of knowledge that introduced disorder into the Garden of Eden. These points acquire significance as potential indicators of a narrative technique, aesthetic attitude, and latent Luciferian sympathies shortly to come together in *LICHT*.

Amour (Love)

1976: No. 44 (Stockhausen-Verlag; cd SV-27)
Five pieces for clarinet: 1. "Sei wieder fröhlich" (Cheer up); 2. "Dein Engel wacht über Dir" (Your guardian angel watches over you); 3, "Die Schmetterlinge spielen" (Butterflies are playing); 4. "Ein Vöglein singt an deinem Fenster" (A little bird is singing at your window); 5. "Vier Sterne wiesen Dir den Weg" (Four stars light your way).
Duration: 26'.

1976/1981: No. 44½ (Stockhausen-Verlag; cd SV-28)
Version for flute.
Duration: 29'.

This is a far cry from the sober factual titles of days gone by. These five character pieces continue Stockhausen's exploration of formula transformation as a vehicle for figurative representation of a kind more usually associated with children's studies than twentieth-century serialism. Unlike genre romantic studies, however, these are not so much inventions inspired by the object of affection as musical discoveries that awaken and apply procedural associations to particular individuals, who in turn provide musical processes with a personality. We are not quite back to the aesthetic of Schumann or Liszt,—Stockhausen's tempi are still more often numerical than verbal,—but the choice of illustrative titles evoking the sentimental world of music lessons is clearly designed to direct the sympathies of the solo performer in a positive way.

Judging by its range and pitch centers, corresponding to the open strings, "Sei wieder fröhlich" reads more like a short, melancholy folk melody for violin, than a piece for clarinet. Though the idiom and plaintive tone call to mind a half-remembered Romanian melody collected by Bartók, the fact that the piece was composed in N'Gor, in Senegal, may suggest an echo of local music heard on the African continent. (In matters of phrasing and technique all five pieces, needless to say, ask to be considered alongside Stravinsky's *Three Pieces for Clarinet* of 1919.)

"Dein Engel wacht über Dir" is a more alert, even jumpy, two-part invention in which initially widely separated versions of the same formula, one low and expansive, the other high and compressed into homogeneous time values, gradually merge and interact. It is not a difficult piece to follow; once again, the pitch range is limited to two octaves. Though freer in treatment, this piece resembles a draft for the more formal *In Freundschaft*. A musical image of courting butterflies is the visual referent of "Die Schmetterlinge spielen," an extended study in fluttering intervals in rising and falling scales. Dedicated to Jaynee Stephens, the younger sister of Suzanne and a flutist, the idiom is more suited perhaps to the timbre and breathy quality of the flute, although certainly effective when transposed into the clarinet range. In "Ein Vöglein singt an Deinem Fenster" a four-limb formula floats on the surface of a fluctuating tempo-melody with added verbal indications (slower, faster, moderate, poco rit., etc.). From an initially stretched-out configuration, the formula gradually converges in on itself, into a gently bobbing middle-range, with internal trills at the same time gradually teasing out into grace-note figures. "I remember sitting for hours, for days, at a pond when I was very small. I used to throw stones into the pond and watch my reflection become completely distorted. Processes like this have never been possible in music."[2] In this case, the effect is similar to nature, but time-reversed: the ripples closing in rather than expanding outward.

The fifth and last piece, "Vier Sterne weisen Dir den Weg," is a technical study in the continuous transformation,—in pitch content and rhythm, —of a cyclically repeated four-note phrase. The player is asked to discover nuances in transition from periodic to rhythmicized repetitions that are too subtle to notate. The distillation of rhythm from rapid periodicity imitates the digitally controlled Synthi 100 sequencer, which eliminates distinctions of duration and dynamics as a consequence of time compression (gradually all values shrink to 1).[3] By implication, a study of this kind looks ahead to a form of dialogue between clarinet and synthesizer in which formulae are transferred one to the other and continue their processes of modification without a break. The piece is dedicated to Doris Stockhausen, the "four stars" signifying their four children. However, it is hard to ignore what might be construed as a sardonic allusion to his first wife's own aspirations to musical stardom. While this bumblebee buzzes and forages, unable to take flight, far above it a larger version of the same interval pattern effortlessly soars.

In *Harlekin*, and again in *In Freundschaft*, Stockhausen puts special emphasis on the articulation of musical movement in space: rotational in the case of *Harlekin*, and lateral in the case of *In Freundschaft*. In the five pieces of *Amour* the listener's attention is focused more precisely on movement in the vertical plane, in terms of the coexistence of themes at the bottom and the top of the range, gradual transformations toward the center, and so on. Stockhausen's remarks on the subject of reproducing vertical movement in stereo balancing are perhaps worth mentioning in this context: "The sounds should brighten in the high frequencies as they move upward, and lose brightness as they move downward."[4]

Jubiläum (Jubilee)

1977: No. 45 (Stockhausen-Verlag)
For orchestra and conductor. 4 flutes, 4 oboes, 4 clarinets, 4 bassoons, contrabassoon, 4 horns; 3 trumpets, 4 trombones, 1 tuba; 2 glockenspiels, glass chimes, 5 triangles, chromatic bell-plates (or gongs and tam-tams) c^2–c^3 sharp; piano, celesta; strings 8 (10). 8 (10). 8. 6. 6.
10 microphones, 6 loudspeakers, mixing console.
Duration: 16'.

This brilliant, short, festive piece for orchestra was a commissioned for the 125th anniversary Jubilee of Hannover Opera. To obtain an idea of its sound imagery, we may borrow the example of a football crowd (one of the structured noises Stockhausen employs in *Hymnen*), a combination sound-event that can be perceived as a process of multiple layers. First there is a layer of general applause, a dense noise filling the frequency spectrum, within which the sound of individuals clapping at different speeds can be heard, some increasing in speed, some slowing down. Against this background a second layer may appear from time to time, as groups begin to synchronize their applause in periodic or rhythmic clapping, often to the chanting of slogans; these spontaneous structures also revert, either by acceleration or disintegration, back into mass applause. At times there is music playing, which some parts of the crowd may clap and sing along with, or clap against, depending on mood or team loyalty or other factors.

Imagine such a sound-event with its layers of speeds, degrees of noise and music, degrees of indeterminacy and integration, and superimposed transitions from more disordered to more orderly and back, all expressed in orchestral terms, and that is the kind of music Stockhausen has composed here. The orchestra is divided into four mixed-instrument frequency layers. At the top of the range, harking back to the "star-sound" quality of *Formel*, two glockenspiels, piano (treble only, with sustaining pedal), and celesta; flutes, clarinets and muted violins constitute a second layer in the mezzo-soprano range; trumpets, horns, violas and cellos form the tenor layer, and bassoons and contrabasses, aided by tuned bell-plates, sitting securely in the bass. All instruments are tuned to the chromatic scale, with the exception of glass chimes and five triangles, though these are employed as pitch collections.

The banded divisions of the orchestra are expressed in a stage layout that once again organizes treble instruments to the right and bass instruments to the left, like a piano keyboard as seen from the audience. Technically, the musical structure of *Jubiläum* is an orchestral realization of a four-layer polyphony of formulae in perpetual motion and perpetual transformation. The essence of the melody transformation is an acceleration process from *Spiral* by which a melody fragment is repeated over and over until it is smeared into a bandwidth; this is combined with a Synthi 100 *Sirius* deceleration process by which a sequencer melody as it slows down is gradually transformed from a string of unit values into a fully rhythmicized formula. By adapting originally solo processes to the multiple voices of an orchestra Stockhausen is able to increase the density of sound in each band, and add depth and variety of texture unavailable in the solo or electronic domains. The controlled asynchronicity (or "crowd effect") thus achieved corresponds to the role of reverberation in electronic music (*Studie II* for example), and also to the triangular randomization of points in the recomposed *Punkte 1952/62* (which is also composed for a well-tempered orchestra). At the work's epicenter is a solemn, harmonized formula, punctuated by pauses filled with the whoops and whistles of horns and string overtone glissandi, "in the character of a hymn."

Not since the coordinated accelerandi and ritardandi of *Zeitmasse* has Stockhausen addressed with such care,—and concern for notational clarity, —the problem of combining multiple tempi in continuous variation, and he does so in quite a different manner from Boulez, Elliott Carter, or anyone else. In a number of respects *Jubiläum* can be understood as a companion piece, or scherzo counterpart, of *Trans*, aiming for the same intuition of depth perspective as the earlier work, but with none of its paralysis; in particular the free mobility of the "background" represents a huge advance on the earlier work.

Each layer in the composition is effectively a loop, and each loop is a sequencer-style transformation in pitch and time of the (unharmonized) hymn melody.

> It's very hard, in a music of more modern character, to move the listeners out of their middle region into another, let's say into a very fast region, for long enough for the fast to become normal and everything that was medium before to appear slow. Or the other way around, to slow an audience down with music like Japanese Gagaku music, which is very much slower than traditional western music, so that having listened for a long time to this very slow music, everything medium in speed is perceived as fast.[5]

At the beginning audience attention is directed to the two-minute long hymn, played fortissimo at MM 30 against turbulent, glittering, and also breathy layers of high keyboards, woodwinds, and muted violins. The reader is surprised to see that each upper layer is composed in parallel octaves, though since the players are out of synchronization, the effect is not strictly discernible. Each 15-note melody loop emphasizes upward-leaping fourths to begin, and closes in a descending quasi-trill on a diminished triad, ending on what eventually becomes a cadential upward leap of a fourth, so there is a latent tonality in the formula, stretched almost to breaking point in the actual harmonization. As the tenor instruments accelerate away from the opening tempo of MM 30, the higher layers gradually decelerate and ultimately coalesce in a higher transposition of the same formula. At 33 the texture is interrupted by the first of two "sound windows;" through an open door at the rear of the platform a quintet of trombones and tuba is heard playing the harmonized hymn at the new MM 60 tempo. This break in the continuity is dramatically effective and a useful tactic for covering both the synchronization of flute and violin layers, and an otherwise tricky transition of the tenor layer from harmonized synchronization to a unison about to

Jubiläum: *Transition of Flute 1 and 2 parts (in octaves) showing the gradual emergence of rhythmic identity from unitary values.*

dissociate into independent voices. Having briefly synchronized with the tenors, the mezzo layer begins to accelerate once again toward a second moment of truth at 94, where a different "sound window" opens, this time to the opposite rear right side of the platform. "Nobody moves!" says the score, echoing *Trans*, while behind the treble instruments a quartet of oboes sounds the harmonized formula at a higher pitch.

By now the treble keyboards have slowed to a tempo in synchronization with the bass-line cantus firmus, at its higher speed of MM 60; these two extreme layers continue to slow down to the original MM 30 while the two middle layers accelerate back to their original high speed, at the same time compressing their rhythms back into single unit values as before. At the end of this process the orchestra comes together in a gesture of unity similar to *Trans*, saluting the audience with a final chorus, highlighted with triangles and glass chimes, at a briskish MM 50.

After the premiere Stockhausen made a few discreet changes of texture and balance to enhance the formal divisions, among them adding viola and cello string tremolos at 17 to signal the start of the acceleration process of the lowest group. The originally bare architecture of the hymn is also enhanced with decorative embellishments, that in addition to injecting some action in the manner of the *Trans* inserts, also do useful duty to coordinate the rank and file, in the manner of a the concert-master in a baroque concerto grosso. Stockhausen also adds considerably to the polyphonic texture from 107, incorporating a birds' chorus for flute, oboe, and violin based on fragments of the melody formula, and scalic flourishes for piano to enhance the brilliance of triangles and glass chimes. The work lives up to its name, being truly jubilant in character, but what is most exciting is Stockhausen's notational solution to the coordination of multiple tempi, and the potential that discovery offers for exploiting shifting patterns and effects in future works for orchestra.

For anyone of Stockhausen's generation any imagery of mass jubilation has a sinister shadow. Compared to the mechanical toys of *Musik im Bauch*, where the different states of being of the formulae, slow and fast, are presented as simultaneous but unchanging, and the only hint of a transition in speed occurs when the musical boxes run down at the very end, in *Jubiläum* the emphasis is definitely on continuously varying processes that as they gather collective momentum also gather definition and accumulate power; as a point of interest, furthermore, the transitions of speed are all within a human (i.e., nonelectronic) frame of reference extending from an upper limit of four triplet eighth-notes per second to a lower of a whole note lasting sixteen seconds. It is also noteworthy that the premiere version of the score is balanced entirely acoustically, requiring no microphones; it is only as a result of the composer's subsequent additions of solo decoration (which in a sense change the plot) that the score has acquired further layers of stage direction, rehearsal complication and amplification.

Spiral images of powerful natural forces are associated in art with Leonardo's visualization of the Flood, the clouds and night skies of Van Gogh, and J. M. W. Turner's visions of rain, steam, speed, and storm-tossed seas. For children of the industrial age they also arouse memories of the awesome power of Nikola Tesla's light-creating turbines, as well as nature's tornado that, in the movie *Wizard of Oz*, has the power to transport the pure of heart from an impoverished reality in black and white to a technicolor world of dreams. As an exercise in crowd control the message of *Jubiläum*, appropriately enough, seems to be that we should all come together in a hymn, though even a hymn has acted in the past as a call to arms.

From a technical viewpoint Stockhausen's solution to the challenge of representing a turbulence comparable to wind and waves may be more readily appreciated in comparison with the "Flood" scene of Stravinsky's *Flood*, composed in 1962, and the cadenzas of Boulez's *Rituel in Memoriam Maderna* of 1975. In the Stravinsky depiction a listener is aware of the coexistence of the very fast and the very slow, but no attempt is made to describe a formal continuity between the rapid actions of wind and spray (flutes and cymbal), the turbulence of the wave-tops (fluttertongue flutes, tremolo violins), and the surge of the tide and creak of the hull, which manifest much slower, and also more powerful tidal forces (low winds, low strings, harp, piano, tuba). To that extent Stravinsky's flood is a realistic image of a passive experience on different levels of the same natural force; compared to which, Stockhausen depicts the harnessing of outwardly unrelated manifestations of energy through an imaginative grasp of their continuity in nature, one that allows them to be reconciled to a uniform structure and timescale.

Though temperamentally at an opposite extreme from the physically demonstrative and celebratory mood of *Jubiläum*, Boulez's *Rituel*, a solemn memorial for the composer and conductor Bruno Maderna, also addresses many of the same technical issues of balancing large-scale unity and small-scale independence of movement, and employs directly comparable strategies in realizing them. The visual image that comes readily to mind is overlapping ripples in a pond; acoustically the image is of multiple tape-loop echoes of the kind so beloved of French musique concrète in the fifties. Like *Jubiläum, Rituel* is based on a polarity between a "disorder" of multiple undulations, and a ritual image of order, expressed in the recurrent slow processional of dense harmonies for brass instruments sustained by gongs and tam-tams (virtually the same instrumentation, one notices, as the "hymn" of *Jubiläum*). Whereas Stockhausen superimposes fast and slow layers and brings them all into relative synchronicity, Boulez alternates his solemn choruses with verse counterpoints of independent orchestral groups, accumulating in density from one to seven in number, that rather than accelerating or retarding, are required to maintain strictly independent tempi within the same moderato range. The effect required is of pebbles cast into a still pond creating patterns of overlapping ripples that all the same do not coincide. These moments in the score are unconducted. They also do not work.

They do not work, in practice, in live performance on the platform, because musicians are not trained to maintain independent but closely related tempi, but tend to fall into a common rhythm. It is human nature to do so. To deal with this Boulez revised the score of *Rituel* and assigned a percussionist subconductor to every group, each one tapping away on a different instrument to provide a clearly audible beat. Not only is this solution counterproductive, introducing active visible and audible controls into the simulation of what should be perceived as a passive reverberation process, but the clicks and clacks of the percussion instruments also bring a makeshift and noisy disturbance into what should be an atmosphere of contemplation. (Stockhausen's solution today is to provide the leader of each instrumental group with a click track via an earpiece, so that a separation of tempi can be maintained without the intrusive presence of percussion.)

One could also criticize Boulez's notation of the free cadenzas, in which grace-note anacruses and terminal flourishes are written in strict tempo, making the essential continuity of the longer note-values harder both to grasp and to articulate. All of which serves to underline the comparative sophistication of Stockhausen's decisions in *Jubiläum*, for example the simplicity of his "layer" melodies, the good judgement of his orchestration of temporal layers, and also his restriction of the number of layers to preserve their audible separation within the frequency spectrum. And although Boulez may not have intended to exploit changes in speed in the context of a memorial piece, it has to be acknowledged that independent groups within an orchestra are better able to control a speed that is uniformly increasing or decreasing, than to maintain the same strict tempo. If Boulez were to object to using click-tracks for his seven independent groups, it would be

possible to employ the subtler method of incorporating a discreet but
tangible fluctuation of tempo within each layer,—as he does in the miniature refrains of "Une dentelle s'abolit," for example.

In Freundschaft (In Friendship)
1977: No. 46 (Stockhausen-Verlag; cd SV-27)
For solo clarinet.
Alternate editions for flute (cd SV-28), recorder, oboe, bassoon, basset-horn (or bass
clarinet), violin, violoncello, saxophone, horn, trombone.
Duration: 15'.

Stockhausen's reworking of earlier pointillist themes to take account of the
principles of formula composition finds particularly clear expression in this
solo work for the clarinet of Suzee Stephens. Though the musical apparatus
is very different, the formal principle of *In Freundschaft* is similar to
Schlagtrio, the music describing a coming together of two melodies from
opposite extremes of range, and a resolution (though not a leveling-out) of
the differences between them. Imagery that is difficult to recognize in a
pointillist idiom of constantly-changing attack, duration, and dynamic indications, emerges clearly and unmistakeably in a melodic setting. The reconciliation of the two extremes is effected through a seven-fold repetition of
the double formula as alternate voices of a two-part invention, of which the
lower voice is a retrograde version, compressed in time and at the opposite
dynamic from the treble voice—a conjunction of shortened duration values
with higher dynamics familiar from the early fifties. In a sense we are back
in the world of the Glass Bead Game, but with the difference that the "polar
opposites" of earlier times have given way to polar transpositions of the
same material. This changes the nature of the Game from *object* transformation to transforming the *perspective* from which the object is viewed.
And since that new objective is achieved more or less automatically by
closing the register and dynamic gaps between the two layers, the dramatic
interest of the interplay is also shifted from the process of evolution itself to
the expressive potential that arises along the way, and how it may be exploited, in keeping with Stockhausen's remark "We should have composed
many more point pieces and gone into point music more thoroughly."[6]
    In this study Stockhausen continues to develop a vocabulary of spatial
actions corresponding to the movements of voices and registers, events
developed from the lower layer being directed to the performer's right (and
audience's left, the bass register of an imaginary keyboard), and those from
the upper layer to the right,—irrespective of their actual pitch, which is an
interesting refinement. Pitch is indicated by the angle of elevation of the
bell, the nominal midpoint corresponding to a 440, indicated by a trill that
also serves to divide alternate events from upper and lower initial layers.
    In addition the constituent limbs (numbered 1 through 5) of each layer
of the formula are subject to order transposition from one cycle to the next,
like changing partners at a barn dance. In these *Veränderungen* or cycles of

transformation, as in his frequent figural or textural elaborations of the underlying structure, Stockhausen allows himself considerable leeway to shape his material in ways consistent with aesthetic or expressive object-ives: avoiding octaves or repetitions, exchanging phrases, and cutting and shaping the material emerging from the transformation process to make it sound more effective, freedoms to be further elaborated in the melodic for-

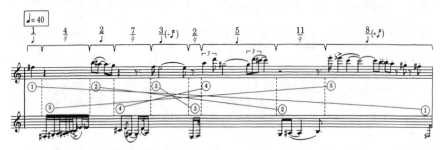

In Freundschaft: *the mirror-formula.*

mulae of *LICHT*. Twice the musical tension springs apart: an "explosion" inserted between cycles IV and V, and a trill cadenza after cycle VI.[7] The different versions of the score are by no means the same music. Each is adapted to the expressive potential of a particular instrument. Rather than trying to adapt every instrument to fit the same musical character, *In Freundschaft*'s multiple editions are deliberate recompositions of an initially severe and formal structure, designed to enhance features deemed char-acteristic, but not necessarily of the same musical personality. Such an extended exercise in adaptation of formula material to suit a variety of dramatic and musical personae can be seen as vital preparation for the challenge of multiple formula identification in *LICHT*.

Der Jahreslauf (The Course of the Years)
1977: No. 47½ (Stockhausen-Verlag; cd SV-29)
Scena for gagaku dancers, gagaku instrumentation, and tape; alternatively for concert performance by Western instruments and tape.
Stage dancers and actors: 4 dancer-mimes, actor, 3 mimes, little girl, beautiful woman (artist's model).
Gagaku orchestra: I. 3 shô; II. 3 ryuteki; shoko; III. 3 hichiriki; kakko; IV. gakuso, biwa; taiko; 2-track tape recorder, 2 × 2 loudspeakers.
Western concert ensemble: I. 3 harmoniums (sampler synthesizers); II. 3 piccolos; anvil (iron pipe); III. 3 soprano saxophones; bongo; IV. electric harpsichord (synthesizer); electric guitar, bass drum; 3 transmitter microphones, 7 cable microphones, 2-track tape recorder, 2 × 2 loudspeakers, mixing console.
Duration: 46'.

Jahreslauf vom Dienstag (Course of the Years, of *Tuesday*)
Scene from *Dienstag aus LICHT* (see commentary on *Tuesday from LIGHT*).

On his visits to Japan, Stockhausen was greatly impressed at that country's harmonious assimilation of a Western industrial lifestyle, alongside its own more organic culture of timing, based on the contrast and tensions of an extreme stillness giving way to sudden and decisive action. In Japanese arts he found many analogies to his own serially derived preoccupation with extremes of scale: for example, the juxtaposition of superhuman bulk and quickness of reaction of Sumo wrestlers, or the calm, motionless waiting followed by seemingly instantaneous gestures of traditional fine calligraphy. At his first encounter with the Japanese tea ceremony, he was fascinated to discover that the ceremony was not so much about manners, or even about tea, but rather about rightness of timing, of knowing precisely when and how to drink, in order to savor the moment of perfection.

This is another small-scale masterpiece, commissioned by Toshiro Kido for the Japanese National Theater, Tokyo, and composed very rapidly in the late summer and early autumn of 1977. What makes it more or less unique in Stockhausen's oeuvre is that the music is deliberately conceived for a traditional Japanese ensemble of timbres and gestures, a sound vocabulary that subsequent adaptations of the work to Western instruments have sought to preserve. "I had the vision (says the composer) of a musical year-counter. I wanted to realize that vision in contemporary form." The words *Lauf* and *Läufer* convey not only a sense of the *course* to be run, and of the action of *running*—in English, "loping,"—but also of the *barrel* shape of an odometer, as in a car, that provides the driver as it rotates with a constantly updated indication of the distance traveled. Stockhausen's initial vision translates into a scenic action in which four traditional actor-mimes enact the movements, and thereby the timescales, of the four columns of an imaginary date-tabulator. A four-column timer is also visible behind the musicians at the rear of the platform, its numerical display coordinated with the musical action from behind the scenes. The front of stage is marked out in four narrow promenades in the shapes of the digits of the year in question, in the initial instance 1–9–7–7. Behind each digit is a group of instruments whose music is timed to correspond with the associated speed of change. For the thousand-year column, the timeless harmonies of the shô; for the centuries, the shrill ryuteki, playing with long breaths, the skoko (anvil) as timer; for the decades, the reedy hichiriki, notes that can bend or sway, and kakko (hourglass drum) as timer; finally for the years, the gakuso (thirteen-string zither) and biwa (lute), whose sharp attacks suggest immediacy and speed. The entire Japanese instrumentarium is vivid and pungent in timbres and intensely tactile in the manner of tone production.

The entire scenario, influenced no doubt by the formalized actions and superb sense of timing of gagaku tradition, can be read as a commentary on the adaptation of a culture of instantaneous action to a Western (German, industrial) culture of continous progression. In the same way as the musical actions of *Jubiläum* are processes in constant acceleration and deceleration, here too the dramatic principle is the message of a universe in constant flux, the end of movement as signifying the end of time, and the end of time, the ending of all existence. Of Goethe it has been said that perhaps the deepest of his intuitions was that "man is movement within movement. . . . For all his attachment to the human scale and his dislike of abstraction, he would surely have been fascinated by particle physics, where extreme abstraction from 'reality' as we know it visualises minute worlds within worlds and translates inert matter into movement, true to [his] own dictum '"State" is a foolish word, because nothing stands still and everything is in motion.'"[8] After which, it comes as a surprise to find this play of time-scales is open to comedy, or even farce, as the four dancer-mimes, without specific direction from the composer, strive to reach an accommodation with the prescribed variations of metabolism between extremes of torpor and nervous agitation. (Stockhausen himself offers an interesting case in point; in reviewing a number of his 1971 filmed lectures and subjecting them to "fast forward" and "fast reverse" on an editing machine, it was possible to see the composer's own body movements conforming to stratified and distinct time layers, the face and mouth moving fastest, hand and arm gestures less rapidly, and lower body movements more slowly still, —though relatively periodic, to which the entire lecture span from the composer's entrance onstage to exit offstage added an equivalent "thousand-year" timescale.)

Though his scenario may not seem calculated to defer to the dignity of high-ranking Japanese artists, it is certainly possible to conceive gestures appropriate to Stockhausen's multilayered timescales that are not at risk of courting ridicule: for the highest speeds, for example, rapid tremors and movements of facial expression, hands and fingers. While there is certainly an element of broad comedy in the four "temptations" that threaten to bring time to a stop, as of the four "incitements" that set time in motion once again, the music is striking and severe enough in itself to complement an elevated rather than a comedic choreography. Anyone who has seen a thousand-fold speeded-up nature film of seed sprouting, a crystal growing, or a caterpillar spinning a cocoon, will appreciate that fast motion does not always have to be funny (though for Stockhausen the idea of solemn actions teetering on the brink of farce is very much in character).

The first of four temptations is signaled by the appearance (in the staged version) of a giant devil's mask from the wings at stage right—the side at which Hell is represented in a religious triptych. On tape a ship's bell is heard, and three sets of footsteps enter from the right, officials in evening dress bearing flowers. A voiceover (the composer) comments, with great care: "Blumen für den Jahresläufer:—er will sie nicht." (Flowers for the runner of the years:—he does not want them.) In the disguise of a congratulatory bouquet the ghost of Friedrich Blume rises again, threatening to put a stop to the proceedings. One by one in turn all of the runners refuse the flowers, and after some angry stamping the footsteps depart and the skipping clogs of a little girl enter from the left. She claps her hands rapidly in a variety of ways and pitches. "Applause!" she cries, "Applause for the artists, so it may begin again!" A magic moment ensues, as sporadic clapping begins and is taken up by more people on the recording (and by the real audience). It is magical in that the rapid, periodic clatter of the little girl's footsteps is seemingly taken apart and transformed into the aperiodic texture of hands clapping.

A second temptation is the arrival of a canteen trolley, bearing food improbably described by the voiceover as "exquisite eating." Once again the musical timekeeping is interrupted until the temptation to take a meal break is chased away by the sound of a lion roaring, and the music resumes (the live actions here are straight out of *commedia dell' arte*). The third temptation is a Hoffnung moment in which an ape, mounted on a Vespa moped fitted with multiple klaxons, drives on stage left and whirls to a stop in a parody of the whirring flying saucer sounds in *Sirius* (which in turn are linked to the motorcycle-riding messengers of the underworld from Cocteau's *Orphée*).[9] By this time the composer seems to be running out of moral inducements to continue; a girl enters with the announcement of a prize of 100,000 yen (or 10,000 marks) to the "winner" of the course of the years, now mutated into a race, though how it is possible to race against time and in the role of mere digits in a counter is hard to understand.

The fourth and final temptation is the distraction of sex: to the accompaniment of sultry noncopyright (and nonidentified) big band music (an allusion to the earlier Japanese commission, *Inori*), a spotlight picks out a female nude (described variously as "a beautiful woman," "a naked woman," and "a nudist," but clearly intended to represent a nightclub stripper), who in the actual staged event poses chastely like an artist's model rather than dancing erotically to the soft jazz accompaniment. The composer in his role as voiceover comments "Ho ho ho ho, stark naked!" For the Imperial Gagaku Ensemble performances in 1977 a more discreet representation of female temptation was arranged, and of course the concert version relies entirely on the music and voice to convey a message of debauchery. It is in fact the temptation to sins of the flesh that summons forth Stockhausen's most powerful incentive to virtue, the sound of a thunderstorm, the voice of the gods. This too is a slightly teasing threat of retribution by nature against human nature, and in a subsequent essay Stockhausen acknowledges that the sinful or virtuous implications of his chosen temptations and incentives are not always clear-cut,—especially on the subject of money.[10]

> When visions such as this come to me, I write them down and take them on board simply as they are. It is only when I tell others or when they experience a performance, that I find myself in difficulty, since everybody wants to know "What does it mean?" So it was on this occasion. Above all, my Japanese co-workers—the program director and his assistants, translators, dancing masters, staging masters, lighting technicians, and so forth—would ask me the meaning of each and every detail. I had no idea myself how to explain in words what the individual events of my vision stood for. Most people build a totally false impression of an artist and believe him to be in the business of making meaningful images (Sinnbilder) out of abstract ideas. That is simply not true in my case. I function throughout as a medium. Sometimes I find myself laughing or astonished or perplexed, but I do know that such meaningful images can be interpreted in any number of ways, without limit.[11]

Seemingly conceived on the spur of the moment, the composer's impulsive choices of dramatic insertions function in the same way as the puppet actions of *Trans*. In the earlier work the insertions are musical actions that arguably reflect prevailing attitudes towards musicians and audiences; in *Der Jahreslauf* the insertions are concrete sounds arguably designed as glimpses of the composer's attitudes to distractions that get in the way of an exaggerated (and perhaps demonic) work ethic. The fourth temptation and associated jazz take the listener back to the youthful *Drei Lieder* of 1950, in particular the conclusion of "Frei" and its bitterly sardonic association of freedom with the jazz lifestyle. That the comically avenging lion is the composer in disguise is patently obvious, so too the accompanying representations of hunger as sinful, of woman as the temptress, and of money as a just incentive, all tending toward a conservative, even reactionary canon of good and evil to be carried forward into the dramatic symbolism of *LICHT*.

The greatest triumph of the Devil, one is told, is in the power of sex to make the creative spirit "drunken," perhaps meaning lethargic and incapacitated. If in adopting *Der Jahreslauf* as the first instalment of the *LICHT* cycle the composer is implicitly endorsing the moral polarities superimposed on an essentially simple procedure, it is perhaps not because they are easily delimited, but because they are as powerful, as subject to recombination, and as elusive as the charged particles, neutrinos and muons of *"Atmen gibt das Leben . . . ,"* his earlier sketch for an opera of four characters, including Adam. Stockhausen's attitude to Luzifer provides a clue: "We should remember that the Devil is himself a fallen angel, 'Lightbearer,' as the name says, and that he turned rebellious, wishing to tempt the greatest possible number of spirits to resist, to hold back, to deny, —even to *stop* the very flow of time."[12] It is certainly a change of perspective from the evangelical instantaneity of *Momente*, one is bound to say: abandoning the timeless constellations of yesteryear in favor of a self-validating continuum of action.

Notes

1. Though he adheres more closely to the original rhyme scheme, I suspect that Richard Toop's free translation (in Michael Kurtz, *Stockhausen: A Biography*, 105) has missed the bite of the original, not to mention its Khrushchevian threat ("we will bury you").
2. "Musikalische Metamorphose." *Texte 5*, 734.
3. *SoM*, 133–34. Stockhausen's concerns over the limitations of the Synthi 100 can be judged from the detailed improvements he specifies in its replacement, including extending the manual faders from the normal 7–8 inches in length to twelve or even eighteen inches.
4. *SoM*, 150–51.
5. "Four Criteria of Electronic Music: the Splitting of the Sound." *SoM*. 100–101. Stockhausen's observation, from 1971, considerably predates the composition of *Jubiläum*.
6. *SoM*: 38–42.
7. "Die Kunst, zu Hören" (The art of hearing). *Texte 5*, 669–700.
8. From a letter dated 23 November, 1812. In T. J. Reed, *Goethe* (Oxford: Oxford University Press, 1984), 52–53.

9. An interruption reminiscent of Gerard Hoffnung's inspired idea of staging Wagner's "Ride of the Valkyries" on motor scooters.

10. *Texte 4*, 356.

11. *Texte 4*, 354. The term "Sinnbilder" echoes Wittgenstein.

12. *Texte 4*, 357.

CHAPTER TWENTY-TWO

Mysterium

In 1977, at the age of 7 × 7 years, Stockhausen embarked on the project *LICHT* (Light), a cycle of seven operas,—or more accurately, mystery plays or passion plays, one for each day of the week,—that was to absorb virtually all of his creative energies for the following 26 years. The ground plan for the entire sequence was published in the year of its conception, like an architect's sketch, in the form of a three-layer "tone-formula" or triple series, divided vertically into seven tranches. These triplet segments of varying groups, tone quantities, and intervallic shapes, assigned to successive days in the week, would determine the distinctive actions, colors, and degrees of relationship of each opera. While the principle of determining the form and disposition of an entire composition from an initial series of intervallic relationships is fundamentally serialist and open-ended, and can be traced at least as far back in Stockhausen's oeuvre as the electronic *Studie I*, the alternative approach of deriving an entire work from a closed system of melodic formulae dates more precisely from *Mantra*. Such a conception, distantly relating to the *ars nova* mass, or Bach's *Art of Fugue*,—the conception, that is, of a large-scale, polyphonic masterwork based on a theme corresponding to the "found object" of twentieth-century art, lays down a daunting challenge to the ingenuity of the composer to realize a universe of musical possibilities out of the barest of essential causes.

    LICHT is a statement: a monument in a tradition of literary monuments: Homer, Virgil, Chaucer, Dante, Milton, Goethe, Tolstoy, Joyce; it is also a mystery in the sense of the Bach *St. Matthew Passion*, Mozart's *Magic Flute*, Wagner's "Ring" cycle, or Schoenberg's *Jakobsleiter* and *Moses und Aron*, and not forgetting Hindemith's *Harmonie der Welt*. Not only the nature of the task but also the shape and content of *LICHT* suggest a second, hidden agenda for the composer as a facilitator of visions, a destiny to fulfill the prophecies of twentieth-century abstract and surrealist artists previously thwarted, suppressed, denied, outlawed, or condemned as degenerate by unbelieving collectivities of governments, orchestras, institutions of learning, philosophers, critics and journalists.

There is certainly no shortage of prophecies and anticipations, from Scriabin's apocalyptic and thankfully unfulfilled dream of a Final Mysterium to last seven days and nights,—"a quest for *oneness*, . . . [combining] a multitude of aesthetic experiences into a single all-consuming focus"[1]—to *Der gelbe Klang*, Kandinsky's partly-realized conception of a transcendental theater of pure light, music, and abstract syllabification which, as the artist's notes reveal, also extended to further episodes in purple, green, and black and white.[2] Or indeed, John Cage's Zen-inspired mission, announced in 1953, to commit the remainder of his composing life to a single, all-encompassing work in thirteen proportionally-determined pieces amounting to a total of 10,000 measures, a number associated in Chinese philosophy with the infinite,—touchingly described in a letter to Boulez as "a large work which will always be in progress and will never be finished; at the same time any part of it will be able to be performed once I have begun. It will include tape and any other time actions, not excluding violins and whatever else I put my attention to."[3]

"The first principle of evidence," observed Marshall McLuhan,

> . . . is that things have to be approached on their own terms if any understanding is to be attained. Edgar Allan Poe was the first to stress the need to begin with *effects* and to work backwards, in poetry and detective fiction alike. . . . Wyndham Lewis noted that "The artist is engaged in writing a detailed history of the future because, 'older than the fish,' he alone can live in the inclusive present." In Symbolist art, connections are deliberately pulled out in order to involve the public in a creative role.[4]

By the end of the twenties the new poetic of radio drama predicted by Cecil Lewis in 1924 was beginning to emerge across Europe.[5] The nonvisual medium was perfectly adapted to the exploration of states of mind and surrealist fantasy. For a brief few years sound recording, radio, and the movies together inspired forms of music theater playing on the divided and intensified modalities of hearing and vision: sound recording expressing images of an idealized perfection in an eternal present; radio, a collective actuality without past or future; and the silent movie, a choice: on the one hand of tribal anarchy, in the aptly if ironically-named "Western," and on the other hand, of the remote past of mannerist historical romance, an idiom delightfully satirized in the 1952 Gene Kelly and Stanley Donen musical *Singin' in the Rain*. The explosive impact of sound recording, silent film, and radio media provoked a sustained outpouring of unconventional works of music theater on variously expressionist, anarchic, neoclassical, and radical neorealist themes. They included Schoenberg's *Die Glückliche Hand* (1913), Satie's *Parade* (1917), Stravinsky's *Histoire du Soldat* (1918), Richard Strauss's *Schlagobers* (1922), Milhaud's *Christophe Colombe* (1923),

Krenek's *Jonny Spielt Auf* (1926), Walton's *Façade* (1926), Hindemith's *Hin und Zurück* (1927), Martinu's *La Revue de Cuisine* (1927), Hindemith again, with *Neues vom Tage* (1929) and Schoenberg, with *Von Heute auf Morgen* (1929).

The aesthetic revolution triggered by the introduction of simultaneous sound in 1927 in the Warner Brothers' movie *The Jazz Singer*, and perfected in 1929 with the arrival of totally synchronized optical sound, found expression in a sardonic realism merging the formality and fatalism of neoclassic drama with the bleak, anarchic immediacy of life in a postwar Europe headed for economic collapse. Sound on film also brought the newsreel and documentary, cinematic media endowed with alarming powers of information management and social persuasion not only within, but also beyond national boundaries. Two among the most successful and enduring of the neorealist operas, *Die Dreigroschenoper* and *Aufsteig und Fall der Stadt Mahagonny* by Bertolt Brecht and Kurt Weill, are all the same reinterpretations of traditional forms, the old German *Singspiel* and the eighteenth-century pamphleteering idiom of John Gay's *Beggar's Opera*.

Reflecting on this remarkable period of musical experiment and innovation, the English critic Ernest Newman ventured to prophesy (his word) that the future direction of music would be decided on the operatic stage rather than in the concert hall, and above all in Germany. "Instrumental music will become far less speculative, and opera much more so. . . . Opera can experiment with "life" in a way and to an extent that absolute music cannot; and the audacity with which the new German opera is getting to grips with life will in time endow the musical side of opera with new resources."[6] For Stockhausen and his immediate predecessors, the interwar culture of music theater gave voice to a modernist movement of political opposition and defense of artistic freedom, its weaponry the irrational and the superreal. In Germany above all, opera rallied public opinion in support of the individual, human and emotional connotations of *la parole* against the intellectual and bureaucratic tyranny of de Saussure's *la langue*, the printed word, and its offspring: censorship, industrialism, and war. In its opposition to a mechanized collective reason, opera appealed for a return to an age of innocence and freedom represented (somewhat naïvely, in hindsight) by preindustrial cultures, typically identified with black American Dixieland jazz and the lyric sexuality of Josephine Baker, childhood play (scat and nonsense lyrics), and the higher reality of dreams. Following a long period of suppression under National Socialism, the freedom agenda finally resurfaced after the war with such amiable conceits as Poulenc's *Les Mamelles de Tirésias* (1944), a theatrical entertainment to verses by Apollinaire (on a theme of gratuitous fertility to be revisited in *Montag aus LICHT*), and the young Boris Blacher's *Abstrakte Oper Nr. 1* (1953), to a libretto by fellow composer Werner Egk, in which a benign Gestaltist wordplay, containing elements of both scat and babytalk, takes the place of traditional dialogue. Clearly the incorporation of actions based in real life, and an attraction to "nonsense" dialogue and wordplay, both distinctive features of Stockhausen's libretti for *LICHT*, are in keeping with broader

tendencies in the theater of social commentary following in the tradition of
Albert Jarry, Karl Kraus, and Eugène Ionesco.

The question arose, whether it is possible to portray fear, love, pain,
negotiation, and panic, without having to link them to a specific person
or individual life? No more the love of Leonore or the agony of Acuzena,
but pain and love in themselves. . . . To express the fundamental
situations new words were created, for the specific purpose that from
their sound quality an association with the subject would be depicted, for
example:

Fear:	a u a u a u A-gatta gatta gatta
Love:	La-ga, Ba-ba, La-ga-ga, Ba-bu-na,
	O Curru, Curru, Curru, Curru,
	Te-te-re, Pe-pe, Li-li, Li-ti-ti, Lo-no, No-no. . .
Pain:	a a - - - i a - - - a i a a i a i a i a i a a
Negotiation:	Patschemu How are you ot wetschai o.-k. (*in English*)
	I hope that statements were made schlu-schai-te
	weather is permanent, Pagoda, ha-ro-scha
Panic:	A-zi-da-zant A-dy-na-zit, A-zit
	A-ni tronit, A-ka-plo-zit, A-clo-ro-gur, A-po-da,
	A-po-da-lip. . .[7]

Stockhausen's association of light with a series of proportions dates
from the 1953 essay "Orientierung,"[8] a piece coinciding with his discovery of
Le Corbusier and his book *Le Modulor*, in which the Swiss architect,—who
incidentally was not a trained mathematician, but was led to the Red and
Blue series of humanly-proportioned measures purely by experiment and an
artist's innate sense of proportion,—compares the Modulor to the equal-
tempered scale in music, allowing the user flexibility in the design of objects
and structures, while at the same ensuring their ergonomic fitness for use,
and their aesthetic compatibility with one another as elements of a larger
human environment. Mathematics, Le Corbusier declares, is the gateway to
a realm of numbers by which the universe reveals itself to a mankind
"entranced by so much dazzling, all-pervading light." Music, on the other
hand,—citing Rameau,—"is not a part of mathematics; on the contrary, it is
the sciences which are a part of music, for they are founded on proportion,
and the resonance of the body of sound engenders all proportion." Music
rules all things, the architect avers; harmony "is the spontaneous, indefati-
gable and tenacious quest of man animated by a single force: the sense of
the divine, and pursuing one aim: to make a paradise on earth."[9] It is not
just Le Corbusier's mystical metaphor of light that touches Stockhausen,
but the architect's association of light with dimension and proportion, his
analogy of music with architecture, and ultimately his method of architectural design, which Stockhausen adapts as a method of composition. As
for a medieval town, or a cathedral that takes shape organically over many
generations, the design process works from the outside in, from master
structure (the week) to individual habitations and interiors (the opera days
and divisions of days). Even Stockhausen's seemingly arbitrary choice of

dramatic content to fit the opera's prearranged scheme of durations and serial determinations, is consistent with the pure cubism of Juan Gris, who "constructed all his paintings on the basis of *a priori* regulating lines of great geometrical power, into the interior of which he pressed, thrust, moulded and forced his guitars, fruit bowls, glasses, bottles, fruits and figures."[10] *LICHT* is manifestly conceived in the image of Hermann Hesse's *Glasperlenspiel* (Glass Bead Game) in which we recall not only a character endorsement of Lucifer, for having the courage to fail, but also a fictional "Swiss musicologist with a passion for mathematics . . . [who] invented the principles of a new language . . . so that it became possible to combine musical and astronomical formulas, to reduce mathematics and music to a common denominator, as it were."[11] A prophetic allusion, if not to Frank Martin, no doubt to an amalgam of Le Corbusier the architect and Hermann Heiss, the Swiss composer and advocate of the theories of Josef Matthias Hauer, the latter based in turn on a mystical reading of Goethe's *Farben-lehre*. It all comes together rather nicely.

Stockhausen's full title, of course, is *LICHT: Die Sieben Tage der Woche* (LIGHT: the seven days of the week), a title connecting the emotional symbolism of illumination with the reality of planetary motion and its influence through the ages. As in *Sirius*, the composer's musical schema is in the image of a natural cycle in the earthly calendar, this time the cycle of the week, and its seventh partial, the day. The order of composition of the seven operas,—*Dienstag, Donnerstag, Samstag, Montag* etc.,—is unexpected and contains an important clue. The naming of the days of the week can be traced back to the ancient Babylonian tradition of dedicating the hours of the day to the seven major planetary bodies, ranged in an order related to their respective orbital periods, thus: Saturn—Jupiter—Mars—Sun—Venus —Mercury—Moon, from the longest period to the shortest; in musical terms, from bass to treble, or lowest to highest in frequency. The maintenance of the planetary system of interlocking frequencies in stable and perpetual motion is a mystery to be explained by the doctrine of the "music of the spheres," understood as meaning that the movements of the seven planets conform to the partial tones of a resonating system, and for that reason are necessarily locked in harmonious relationship. This then is the "astrological" universal law of motion that connects astronomical behavior with music, and music in turn with frequency relationships in the domain of color.

The first hour of the day gives its name to the day, each successive hour taking the next name in the planetary order. Like a tape loop, the sequence recycles endlessly, and since for the Babylonians as well as ourselves there are only twenty-four hours in a day, at the end of the day there are names left over, like a ring dance where one always ends with a different partner. This explains how the names of the days of the week are a permutation corresponding to every fourth name in the planetary cycle, i.e.: *Sun*day— (Venus, Mercury)—*Moon*day—(Saturn, Jupiter)—*Mars*day etc.—in the manner of a note-row permutation by Alban Berg.[12] The original order forms an interesting symmetry, by the way, like a triptych, with on the left three solid and slow-moving *masculine* divinities (Saturn, Jupiter, Mars), balanced on the right by two *feminine* divinities (Venus, Moon) and one of indeterminate gender (Mercury), with the sun arbitrating in the middle:

SUN

Jupiter   Mercury

Saturn   Mars   Venus   Moon

For the sake of dramatic progression, Stockhausen has rotated the sequence like a seven-note row: Sun—Venus—Mercury—Moon : Saturn—Jupiter—Mars, and then reversed it, so that it now ends with the sun, thus: Mars—Jupiter—Saturn : Moon—Mercury—Venus—Sun. Or, in German, *Dienstag, Donnerstag, Samstag, Montag, Mittwoch, Freitag, Sonntag*. It makes dramatic sense to have the opera cycle appear to begin with *Donnerstag*, the day of Jupiter and of Thor, god of thunder, associated with the lion's roar, and in turn with the composer himself, born under the sign of Leo,—and for it to culminate with *Sonntag*, the day of light. How then to account for *Dienstag*, the day of Mars, of war, and of service (*Dienst*), his wartime experiences in fact being the primary motivation of the opera cycle? Stockhausen literally saves the day by coopting the 1977 scena *Der Jahreslauf* (which by a happy coincidence is about starting and stopping time) to form Act I of *Dienstag aus LICHT*, which allows him to launch the cycle of performances with *Donnerstag*, the first opera to be completed, while maintaining that *Dienstag* is actually the first opera to be started. The same logic explains the numbering of earlier compositions. So apart from the minor hiccup of *Mittwoch* and *Freitag*, which appear in reverse order, the authorized sequence, as a serial entity, is faithfully preserved "as it is written."

In this way an ostensible polarity is set up between Jupiter and the sun, the persona of the highest demigod in the hierarchy (and his alter ego Luzifer) in opposition to the source of all being and all illumination. Ostensible only, since the hidden polarity, with Mars in opposition to the sun, modeled in the image of the sixties banner "make love not war," can also be read as a covert acknowledgement of war as the primary motivation for human progress toward enlightenment. (And the color of Mars, as we will see, is Windsor and Newton *red*.) The remaining planets are named after divinities with specialized qualities or human weaknesses, and all of them shine by reflected light, making them "luciferous" or "light-bearing" rather than light-generating, further setting the stage for a drama or conflict of beings each of which expresses a degree of partial illumination.

The harmonic interval represented by the ratio $1:7$ is also the interval of the dominant seventh, which in conventional tonal practice has very special properties. As a natural consonance,—already encountered in *Stimmung*, for example,—the seventh is inherently stable; within the tonal tradition, however, the seventh interval and chord have come to embody a sense of directed movement or progression toward a goal or final resolution, expressed in the formula V^7–I. Such complementary associations, embracing both the horizontal and the vertical, movement and stasis, purpose and fulfillment, are in paradoxical accord with the triple characterization of Stockhausen's dramatis personae: Michael, Eva, and Luzifer, representing not only spiritual absolutes in human guise, after the conventions of medieval mystery, but also charged in the manner of subatomic particles with different valencies of positive and negative, being and time, or even "strangeness, charm, and color." Stockhausen returns to the device, previously encountered in *Momente*, of a human trinity as playfully symbolic emanations of a mystical and musical unity. The three characters of *LICHT* are subtler essences, and their relationships are both physically and musically realized. It becomes clear that the multiple valencies of each character are intimately related to the syllabic permutations of each name: a symbolism already encountered in the "K in D" symbolism of Friedrich Froebel, as well as modeled on the tribal myths investigated by Malinowski and Lévi-Strauss, and musically authenticated in the mythology of Wagner.

Michael is a composite emanation of St. Michael (the German equivalent of St. George), of the artist Michelangelo, and various associations of the syllable MIK,—e.g., *meek*, *microcosm*, etc.; the triple composition of the name MI-KA-EL also signifying that there is a bit of Stockhausen and Luzifer in him as well. Says Stockhausen, "Michael is the creator of our local universe" (i.e., of the *Mikro-cosm*). And of the opposition of Michael and Luzifer, "There are constantly two influences: the one is, 'Go on, in spite of everything,' and the other one is 'Stop, because of everything.'"[13] This is the message of *Der Jahreslauf*, but with the added layer of implication that "to define is to stop, hence, to kill,"—an image of continuous progress toward a higher destiny as a necessary alternative to striving for closure, imposing a judgement, or coming to terms with the present, the effect of which is to stifle further action or debate. Eva (whose name has prevously been heard in *Carré*, *Momente*, *Hymnen*, and *"Atmen gibt das Leben . . . ,"* is Eve, the first woman (and betrayer of man), *evening*, and *Erde*, mother earth, a persona associated with continuity, changeability, temptation (carnal knowledge), and fecundity, but also honored as the sacred embodiment of motherhood; the syllable EV- also hinting at *evolution* (EVA + LU-zifer), *ewig* (eternity), and *evangelium* (the Gospel, EVA + Michael-ANGEL).

Luzifer, admonishes the composer, "is not at all the character whom the English see through their bibles. Lucifer *is* brilliant, intuitive, extremely progressive, but at a crucial moment he was disobedient, against the principle of hierarchy on a universal level. . . . In *LICHT* Lucifer denounces death, reincarnation, heavy materialization: he is the spiritual purist: he wants the evolution of pure *light*."[14] That sounds like a condemnation of the scientist's dedication to pure knowledge,—for instance, nuclear fission,—in denial of ("de-nouncing") the consequences, both human (death, rebirth) and contamination of the environment ("heavy materialization"). But there are other, more transparent associations, including madness (*lunacy*), clarity (*lucidity*), and mastery of the game (Hesse's *Magister ludi*), not forgetting the various connotations of "number" (lu-*Ziffer*): measure, fragmentation, quantification, and pointless abstraction (as in mathematical philosophy). The German word "Ziffer" also means *cipher* (a secret message with a concealed

meaning, or a deliberate obscurity) and *clock-face* (time or temporal values
as opposed to eternity or the eternal values). Of all three names, Luzifer is
certainly the richest and most potent in allusion. The three names are
endlessly fractured and recombined, as if passed through a prism; their initial letters adding up to MEL, the root of *melic* (Greek: of music or poetry),
melody, and melodrama.

Myth has to have a special resonance for a survivor of the Nazi regime,
which fostered its own mythology as a consequence of its rupture with the
past. Stockhausen's invention of myth flows from his generation's willful
break with history and neoclassicism, and has a similarly defensive motive.
Invented mythologies are traditionally a means by which a disillusioned
West has sought refuge in imaginary constructs of tribal cultures living in
untainted union with nature. Among some of a less idealistic persuasion
there remains a suspicion that the holism defended by Western intellectuals, Stockhausen among them, is little more than a cover for perpetuating
a worldview ironically manifesting the very prejudices (for example, against
women, native cultures, and the environment) holism professes to repudi-
ate. Respect for the music and religious symbols of other cultures is a case
in point. We have already referred to the delicate issue of propriety in the
use of sacred music or invoking the sacred emblems of non-Western cultures
in art, as in Stockhausen's names of the gods in *Stimmung,* the Omizutori
ritual in *Samstag,* elsewhere even the most potent rites and emblems of
Christian belief (the holy family, the crucifixion, the ascension).

Nor is it entirely surprising if the narrative and symbolic content of so
monumental a defense of the ideals and practices of surrealism, not to mention an ample, even overwhelming support documentation, should appear to
defy rational interpretation, since in the drama of *LICHT* reason itself is
portrayed as the archenemy of sacred intuition. In numerous statements
over twenty-five years, as in the music itself, Stockhausen has shown remarkable agility in deflecting the attentions of musicologists and the
musical press; furthermore, through an outwardly assiduous cultivation of
the occult, he has succeeded in confounding the interpretative intentions of
a wider community of otherwise well-disposed music professionals. Impenetrability is either a necessary byproduct or an essential ingredient of the
message. As in his earlier citations, of Jakob Lorber in *Sirius,* of Sri Aurobindo in support of the generative principle of *Mantra,* and of Hazrat Inayat
Khan for *Inori,* the composer's words and his musical creation present a
coupled system. What this entails for any critical or interpretative discussion of *LICHT*—of especial interest given that "illumination" is the topic at
issue,—is a play of language that under the pretext of explanation creates
an impregnable armature against it. The missing member of the cast of
LICHT, so to speak, is the composer himself in the role of interlocutor (or
Minister for Propaganda): his function, alternately affecting the rancour of
an André Breton and the paranoic-critical indifference of a Salvador Dalí,
being to preserve the mystique, ensure that the message reaches only the
faithful, and repel all attempts by the enemy at breaking the code. "I wanted
to write a cosmological composition that answers to the truth from now and

always; I wanted to flee from the temptation to write a historical work; I did not want the merely terrestrial; so, Mythological only in the sense that it restores to daylight something that is always valid; not in the vulgar sense of a nebulous mythology drawn from the dim and distant past where it languishes as a sort of pre-history, not eternal truth."[15]

In his English lectures of 1971, Stockhausen draws a number of analogies between varieties of serialism and familiar conventions of dramatic and poetic form. These remarks in passing reveal a perceptive appreciation of the poetics of classical literature, and an acute philosophical interest in the genesis of form and its moral implications concerning the nature and purpose of life itself. He speaks of the composer's role as that of a visionary or augur in the sense understood in ancient Greece; elsewhere he speaks of the radical finality of Shakespearean tragedy, an *ex nihilo* starting and stopping of time, concisely formulated as "a particular inital moment and a very particular final moment; and then the drama so to speak in between."[16]

Stockhausen's triple attributes of voice, instrument, and mime, for the principal characters of Michael, Eva, and Luzifer in *Donnerstag aus LICHT*, signal a return to the authentic tradition of *moûsike*, the unified art of poetry, music, and dance, that flourished in ancient Europe before literary conceptions of narrative reality and historical determinism came to prevail. The same imaginative reconfiguration of the real and mythical, juxtaposing scenes of a symbolic spirituality or magic alongside images of the composer's personal life (and indeed, members of his family), is also arguably in keeping with the old traditions of epic poetry. Among oral cultures the epic poem is traditionally an instrument for reinstating or strengthening national and cultural identity, especially when that identity is under perceived threat. In the case of *LICHT*, renewed dedication to the spiritual life, commitment to progress, belief in original sin and a transpersonal destiny, and a vigorous defense of previously persecuted art forms, are all part of the composer's moral agenda.

The epic poet was traditionally permitted, in the name of inspiration, to reinvent popular myth and legend, reinterpret the actions of gods and heroes, and introduce supernatural causes for events unable to be accounted for in reality,—much in the manner of the cinema epic of today. Expressing the prejudices of a newly literate, scribal culture, Socrates criticized epic poets for sacrificing historical accuracy for the sake of a good story. Aristotle, a more sympathetic observer of human nature, better understood the persuasive significance of a good story, and assigned a higher moral value to the dramatic recreation of powerful human experience. Actions that really happened, said Petronius, are for historians: epic poetry should deal in enigma, divine intervention, and a fanciful interweaving of motives expressing the oracular revelations of a mind in the grip of a powerful vision.

For German poets, epic is historically the form associated with the recurrent theme of national identity. Friedrich Gottlieb Klopstock (1724–1803), author of *Der Messias* (The Messiah), defined the poet's role as a combination of prophet, educator and religious leader of the nation's people. Goethe and Schiller, mindful of their moral responsibility to establish exact

criteria for the poetic treatment of epic subject matter in an age of unprecedented intellectual and social upheaval, jointly published the influential
essay *Über epische und dramatische Dichtung* (On epic and dramatic poesy)
in 1797.

For his part, Stockhausen makes a clear distinction between dramatic,
epic, and lyric forms, but interestingly in terms of their temporal implications: "If I speak of a musical development as dramatic, when it is strongly
directional, and epic, when it is sequential, then I could use the term lyric to
describe a music in which the forming process is instantaneous."[17] In the
sense that prior musical considerations absolutely determine its visual and
poetic content, *LICHT* attaches as much to the lyric as to the epic tradition
of classical poetry.

Typically conditioned by rigid formal constraints, the earliest lyric
poetry is said to have emerged from religious ceremonies such as the prophecies of Delphi, a "speaking in tongues" more celebrated for abstract sensu-
ousness of texture than for clarity of meaning. Among certain cultures the
lyric impulse is said to be most fully articulated in vocalizations that have
no literal meaning, including the imitation of birds and animal calls, taboo
and gestural expletives, nonsense refrains and syllables, as in lullaby and
children's verse, and magic incantations (e.g., *Abracadabra!*, *Shazam!*). The
impulse persists in nonsense poetry from Lewis Carroll and Edward Lear to
the allusive rich text of Marinetti, Apollinaire, Breton, Gertrude Stein,
Huelsenbeck, and Schwitters, and on to scat in the jazz era, and even hip-
hop in the present. Stockhausen has frequently spoken of the importance of
imitation, both in music and as a sign of genius; in different ways imitation
provides the formal basis of *Gesang der Jünglinge* and *Kontakte*, and the
entire plus-minus series of compositions is predicated on imitation and
development. The Meistersinger tradition celebrated by Wagner and familiar to every German musician and poet, conforms to that same lyric strain of
nationalist verse in which a strict adherence to narrowly-defined rules of
form, number, and a limited selection of preordained melodies, combines
with freely invented religious, profane, impious, and didactic subject matter.
It is manifestly clear that the distinctive poetic and aesthetic features of
LICHT—its structure, its tight adherence to a limited repertoire of themes,
its fantasy, even its serialist principles—conform all the same to a very rich
and ancient, one might even say timeless, body of conventions. Hegel himself argues in *Vorlesungen* (Prefaces) that drama is especially marked by a
combination of lyric and epic characters. Hegel also declares the expression
of nationalistic sentiment to be a proper role of epic poetry. That nationalism is also an underlying theme of *LICHT* cannot be discounted.

Myth is normally supposed to be social rather than individual in origin,
arising from collective oral traditions of storytelling connecting the inhabitants of a specific locality to their history, identity, customs, the natural
environment, and the universe. Epic poetry may appear to sanction the
invention of myth, in the sense of rewriting tribal memory, but to render an
existing tradition in more memorable form, not to the extent of dreaming up
an entirely new set of tribal identities, which is a kind of fiction peculiar to

literate societies. Mythtelling today has more to do with the intuitions of twentieth-century art, the paintings of Max Ernst for example, whose austerely haunting and essentially personal images do not ask, but are simply available to be interpreted as coded intimations of the suppressed desires and anxieties of an entire social group. If ancient myth is diachronic, concerned with preserving the continuity of social identity, then modern myth by contrast is synchronic, intended to find meaning in the chaotic reality of a particular moment in time.

The anthropologist's search for a concordance of linguistic and social hierarchies is itself an exercise in myth creation. In a move inviting credibility by association and the protection of legitimate science, Lévi-Strauss seizes on an unguarded observation of Niels Bohr on the resemblance of relational terms shared by the social and physical sciences, to claim intellectual kinship for structural anthropology with the economic theory of John von Neumann and Otto Morgenstern, the systems theory of Norbert Wiener, and Shannon and Weaver's Mathematical Theory of Communication.[18] The problem is that once all pretense of interest in the indigenous significance of tribal mythologies is stripped away, what is left is an intellectual game of reconciling competing models of social systems imputed to different language codes. Hailing the dawn of a new era of cooperation between previously warring factions, Lévi-Strauss blithely matches von Neumann's theory of economic behavior and A. L. Kroeber's comparison of social institutions with "the play of earnest children," adding "As Von Neumann [sic] puts it, 'The game is simply the totality of the rules which describe it.'"[19]

> The objectivity aimed at by anthropology is on a higher level: The observer must not only place himself above the values accepted by his own society or group, but must adopt certain definite *methods of thought*; . . . Anthropology aims to be a *semeiological* science, and takes as a guiding principle that of "meaning." This is yet another reason . . . why anthropology should maintain close contact with linguistics. . . . When the anthropologist endeavors to create models, it is always with the underlying motive of discovering a *form that is common* to the various manifestations of social life.[20]

A strange and disturbing statement, one might think, and in resonant accord with Stockhausen's manifest belief in a unified musical cosmos extending to the finer protocols of individual behavior. The statement is noteworthy, first for the ease with which specifics are discarded in the interest of a higher unity, and second, in creating a pretext for rule-seeking between disciplines in preference to rule-derivation appropriate to a specific social context. It leads to a situation where the object of research has turned away from inside knowledge toward the all too dazzling light of a prescriptive "universal harmony." It has happened before. The Pythagoreans declared that all things are number, meaning that everything is known in terms of relationships best defined in "natural" musical intervals and concordances. All the same, the implication of a common language is not the same as a theory of everything. In the present digital age we take for granted the idea that all kinds of knowledge can be stored and transmitted in the same binary code, forgetting that a universal software in the image of the Glass Bead Game is a very recent discovery. We should not be surprised therefore if prominent thinkers of the precomputer era sometimes blur the distinction between an information code and the information stored, or construe the limitations of the code as limitations to human knowledge. More to the point is the anthropologist's naked determination to seek harmony at any cost, in the interests of a cold war agenda entailing not only the elimination of war, but inevitably the stifling of all intellectual debate.

In *LICHT* Stockhausen is arguably starting from a perception of music as original science, and its accompanying Pythagorean worldview of a universe expressible in terms of tonal, i.e., number relationships. Like Juan Gris, he begins with an abstract outline structure (the super-formula), from which, by a combination of deduction and intuition, he derives a series of connected microcosms that, while enacted on a human scale, correspond only incidentally to a coherent narrative in what the composer calls "historical" terms (i.e., "earthly," or conforming to the way human beings normally behave or interact in a connected history). The actions and images of *LICHT* are contrived in accordance with musical formulae on the assumption that human actions ideally aspire to the same degree of abstraction but are prevented from achieving it for either selfish reasons or spiritual inadequacy ("sins of the flesh").

Unlike the sciences, which seek some kind of unifying pattern in their different experiences of data management, Stockhausen begins with his own pattern and then fits events and actions into it. He would call that a "polar opposite" approach, I daresay. For an artist or dramatist, the issue to be sure is not whether the pattern corresponds exactly to mundane reality, but whether it is essentially plausible enough to compel attention and thus permit the ultimate recognition of a determining pattern. On the other hand, there is a certain interest in observing what subtleties of behavior actually emerge out of a reverse procedure of this kind. After all, the case for twelve-tone composition in part is that it is able to give formal expression to a more highly nuanced (and therefore ambiguous) range of emotion than conventional tonality.

Goethe's presence in *LICHT* is both general (German lyric and epic poetry from the Meistersinger tradition via Klopstock and Schlegel),—and particular, in relation to *Faust* as an allegory of knowledge and power covering the transition from eighteenth-century Enlightenment Europe via the Napoleonic social revolution to early Romanticism. More specifically, Goethe's theory of color which, as a scientist as well as a poet, he defended with irrational fervor against the Newtonian account of light refracted through a prism.[21] Goethe objected to Newton as a scientist and leading member of a closed group (the Royal Society) determined to exclude holistic thinkers such as himself. The triumphalist message of Alexander Pope's memorial encomium "God said, 'Let Newton be!' And all was LIGHT!" had been promulgated, revered, and translated across Europe for the best part of a century. Goethe however was *morally* offended at the notion of colors, which he regarded as "dark light," being identified as component frequencies of white light, which had always been understood as the pure and absolute emanation of the divine. Newton allowed a pinpoint of sunlight to pass through a prism and be refracted as a band of color on a whitewashed wall. He then measured the width of each part of the spectrum corresponding to a perceived color, observed that some areas of color were broader and others narrower, and determined that their different angles of refraction expressed differences in what he called the corpuscular density of light, and which we now know as frequency or wavelength.

Goethe's objection was founded on a fundamentally different approach. Looking *through* the prism, he observed fringes of color at the borders of adjacent dark and light areas, and was led to conclude that colors *as the human eye perceives them* are the consequences of varied interferences or contaminations of light with darkness, its antithesis. "Colors (he said) are the deeds and sufferings of light, the deeds and sufferings of light with darkness." Through such an interpretation such sacred mysteries as the rainbow are explained as an effect of divine light interacting with the sins of an otherwise doomed humanity. It is poetry and not science. From this and other like-minded scriptural analogies emerges the notion of human characters and actions forming a continuous spectrum expressing states of relative virtue poised between light and darkness, a concept of moral relativity of some relevance to German science and philosophy in the aftermath of the first, then the second world war. We make essentially the same point when we say that nothing is ever completely black or white. (The connection between color (in a Newtonian sense) and music, one need hardly point out, has little to do with synaesthesia as intuitively practiced by Scriabin, Kandinsky, Messiaen, or Rimbaud. As a description of frequency relations, a theory of colors already has musical implications; if not the simple ratios of the common chord and its derivatives, certainly the timbres of bells, or Messiaen's unorthodox note mixtures, or the serial combinations of Stockhausen's electronic studies, not forgetting Boulez's computer-synthesized harmonies.)

In parts of Europe Goethe's theory of color still has its defenders.

> Goethe's and Newton's respective approaches to color illustrate two very different approaches to experimental research. We call them theory-oriented and exploratory experimentation. . . . Exploratory experimentation often results in the establishment of a hierarchy within a realm of phenomena. At the pinnacle are those phenomena—Goethe calls them primordial—that involve only the essential conditions and that are therefore attributed a special status. All other effects can be deduced or explained from those elementary ones by progressively complicating the experimental arrangement and adding new conditions. The connection between experimental arrangement and an elementary phenomenon is revealed by establishing a chain of intermediate effects.[22]

Goethe's resistance to Newtonian rationalism comes out of a longstanding philosophical opposition to specialist knowledge, the pursuit of a knowledge perceived as fragmented and lacking in humanity, a view persisting to the present day and described by historian Peter Gay, in alliterative turn of phrase, as "a myth of a prosy, presumptuous precision, of a cold rationalism, invented by the German Romantics."[23] Popular opposition to the indifference of science to the wider needs of society and the relief of suffering, a conviction shared by Goethe's English contemporary William Blake (a poet and visionary also acknowledged in *Momente*), continued to burn through the nineteenth and into the twentieth century, provoking a surge of anti-establishment irrationalism and surrealism in literature and the arts, movements even now resonating in the terrifying counterculture of *l'acte gratuit* of the present day. In Germany, the mutual antagonism of arts and sciences came to the fore as an urgent political issue in the period between the wars when Stockhausen was a child; and in England, as late as 1959, with the muted "two cultures" controversy of C. P. Snow and F. R. Leavis. However difficult it may be for a non-European to understand, the penetration of German science by nationalist sentiment was sufficiently powerful to justify (for example) the calculated persecution of Einstein's "Jewish science" by the National Socialist regime, on the grounds that theoretical physics, in denying the existence of matter, was undermining public confidence in ultimate reality.

For a young schoolboy and son of a teacher growing up in Nazi Germany, Goethe was the heroic incarnation of scientific humanism, and Newton an emblematic figure of unemotional, petty, relentless, and vindictive determinism. For reasons perhaps including maintaining public confidence in the integrity of German science, Goethe's *Farbenlehre* has continued to be vigorously defended, among others by two of Stockhausen's intellectual heroes, Werner Heisenberg and Carl Friedrich von Weizsäcker. The mixed media assemblages of the artist Mary Bauermeister, illustrated on the sleeves of Stockhausen's DG recordings *Momente* and *Kurzwellen*, are self-evidently meditations on Goethe's experiments in looking through lenses and the perception of color fringe effects.

The ultimate clue is a line from Region I of *Hymnen*, the words "Windsor and Newton's artist's watercolors," spoken innocently enough by Stockhausen's American assistant David Johnson at the end of that longwinded (and to be honest, not terribly funny) polyphonic incantation on words for the color red. Hitherto one has always interpreted this inspired interpolation as a rumination on the color of Communism,—the Red flag, the Red banner, Rudi Dutschke etc.,—in opposition to the freedom of movement allowed, as the message of *Hymnen* implies, to citizens of Western democracies. It accords with the composer's own account: "At the time (1966–1967) the word *Red* was associated with socialism, communism, and oddly enough the Social Democrat party. . . . Among West German intellectuals and a few 'advanced' artists in the West it was fashionable to be *red*. I *deliberately chose* (he says, my emphasis) a text expressing *no political orientation*, the color catalogue of the English firm Windsor and Newton." But in a classic example of Stockhausen wordplay, behind the neutral façade of a "found object" another message is concealed: *red* implying not the Soviet hegemony, but the color of the British Empire, *Windsor* the British crown, and *Newton* the tradition of British empiricism. In a second studio commentary, the composer defends his incorporation of the Nazi anthem the "Horst Wessel-Lied" in a composition of national anthems, and observes, with great care and precision, "es ist eine Erinnerung"—"it is [after all, only] a memory." In German, the word *Erinnerung* implies "an internalization."[24]

The dramatic subtext of *LICHT* can now be seen as an artistic and holistic manifesto, drawing on a specifically central European conception of structural affinities affecting the organization of language, the family, and the state, and expressed with particular force in the theories of Ferdinand de Saussure and Claude Lévi-Strauss, and the surrealist writings of André Breton and Max Ernst. These same views are informed in turn by a now forgotten but intense and protracted debate from the early years of international broadcasting concerning the social role of the mass media, and the relative truth value of documentary observation compared to poetic fiction and political propaganda. It allows us to understand *LICHT* as a drama not so much of actions as of latent tensions, a drama that sees choices not as between good and evil, rather as between alternative conceptions of reality, among which a Newtonian science perceived as arid, fragmented, and obsessed with exact quantification is clearly the underdog, represented in part by the counting that afflicts Luzifer (as it afflicted Bruckner, no less) like a nervous tic. The same skepticism is revealed in the composer's ambivalence toward his former mentor Werner Meyer-Eppler, and his dry and overly cautious approach to an information science the young Stockhausen had found hugely exciting and inspirational.

LICHT's imaginative reconfiguration of the real and mythical, juxtaposing snapshots of the composer's personal life with superreal visions, and incorporating the active (if intermittent) participation of members of his own extended family, is arguably in keeping with the old tradition of epic poetry, defined by Schlegel in *Prosaische Jugendschriften* (Youthful prose writings) as a sequence of chance events, loosely connected, appearing from a primordial flux and returning thereto. And there are echoes of Goethe here as well: of the novel *Die Wahlverwandschaften* (Elective Affinities), in which human couples are split and recombined in new compounds like chemicals in a laboratory, or of *Faust*, where the single persona of one aspiring to total knowledge, the possession of beauty, and ultimate power, is refracted in alternate identities manifesting self-doubt and temptation. In the poet's *Trilogie der Leidenschaft* (Trilogy of Passion) a new mythology is forged in the spirit of Romanticism: "But where they proposed bizarre mixtures of science, philosophy, European literature and legend, and oriental myth, he has built one from motifs of his own making . . . in which love takes its place in a considered scheme along with the other moving forces of life: the individual daimon, chance, compulsion, hope."[25]

John Constable, the English observer and painter of clouds, remarked that seeing nature was almost as great a challenge as reading the Egyptian hieroglyphics. For the Romantic artist, the Rosetta Stone and its successful decoding by Jean-François Champollion represented contact with an alien intelligence from the dawn of creation, in precisely the same way as the fictional slab of Stanley Kubrick's *2001: A Space Odyssey* appeared to the generation of Vietnam, or as we imagine the inscribed plaques of the Pioneer spacecraft are destined to appear to civilizations beyond the solar system. Perhaps *LICHT* is not meant for our time after all, but, in the words of Claude Lévi-Strauss, for those archaeologists of the future coming from another planet, who in trying to decipher human script "would soon discover that a whole category of books—music—did not fit the usual pattern."[26]

Notes

1. Hugh Macdonald, "Alexander Scriabin—Towards the *Mysterium.*" In *Scriabin: Preparation for the Final Mystery.* Realization by Alexander Nemtin. Decca 289 466 329-2.

2. Ulrike-Maria Eller-Rüter, *Kandinsky: Bühnenkomposition und Dichtung als Realisation seines Synthese-Konzepts* (Hildesheim: Georg Olms, 1990).

3. James Pritchett, *Music of John Cage* (Cambridge: Cambridge University Press, 1993), 96–97. Cage later drastically modified his original plan, outlined in a letter to Boulez; then abandoned it altogether. The full text of the original letter is reproduced in Jean-Jacques Nattiez ed., *Boulez-Cage Correspondence* tr. ed. Robert Samuels (Cambridge: Cambridge University Press, 1993), 142–44.

4. "To The Listener, October 8, 1971." From H. M. McLuhan, *Letters of Marshall McLuhan* ed. Matie Molinaro, Corinne McLuhan, and William Toye (Toronto: Oxford University Press, 1987), 443.

5. C. A. Lewis, *Broadcasting from Within* (London: Newnes, 1924), 122–23.

6. Ernest Newman, "The Spirit of the Age." Reprinted from the *Fortnightly Review* (1930). In *Testament of Music: Essays and Papers* ed. Herbert Van Thal (London: Putnam, 1962), 235.

7. "Abstraktion in der Oper?" Friedrich Herzfeld, *Musica Nova* (Berlin: Ullstein, 1954), 264.

8. "Orientierung." *Texte 1*, 37.

9. Le Corbusier, *Le Modulor* tr. Peter de Francia and Anna Bostock (London: Faber and Faber, 1961), 71–74.

10. Le Corbusier, *Le Modulor*, 217–18.

11. Hermann Hesse, *Glass Bead Game* tr. Richard Winston and Clara Winston (Harmondsworth: Penguin Books, 1972), 15–48.

12. John D. Barrow, *Artful Universe: The Cosmic Source of Human Creativity* (Boston: Little, Brown, 1995), 150–56.

13. From the unpublished transcript of an interview with Edward Fox, for the article "Light fantastic." *Independent Magazine*, 7 August 1993.

14. Private communication, November 1, 1988.

15. "Licht-blicke" (Glimpses of Light). Interview with Michael Kurtz. *Texte 6*, 203.

16. *SoM*, 54–55.

17. *SoM*, 59.

18. Claude Lévi-Strauss, *Structural Anthropology* tr. Claire Jacobson and Brooke Grundfest Schoepf (New York: Basic Books, 1963), 283.

19. Claude Lévi-Strauss, *Structural Anthropology*, 198.

20. Claude Lévi-Strauss, *Structural Anthropology*, 364–65.

21. Johann Wolfgang von Goethe, *Zur Farbenlehre* (Goethe's Color Theory) (New York: Van Nostrand Reinhold, 1971).

22. Neil Ribe and Friedrich Steinle, "Exploratory Experimentation: Goethe, Land, and Color Theory." *Physics Today* Vol. 55 No. 7 (July 2002).

23. Peter Gay, *Enlightenment: An Interpretation; The Science of Freedom.* (Reprint, New York: Norton, 1977), 625.

24. "Rouge, rouge." In *Hymnen* Region I at 9' 31,5"; also Region II, 8' 07,3", "Studio conversation." Booklet to cd Stockhausen-Verlag SV10, 162–68.

25. T. J. Reed, *Goethe* (Oxford: Oxford University Press, 1984), 90–91.

26. Claude Lévi-Strauss, *Structural Anthropology*, 212.

CHAPTER TWENTY-THREE

Donnerstag

As the first completed opera of *LICHT*, the day in which, drawing on his own life experiences, the composer lays out his philosophical agenda for the entire week, *Donnerstag aus LICHT* is at once the most personal in its declarations and the most troubling and controversial in its ethical and spiritual implications. In as much as the opera has a theme, the theme is *Kindheit*: education, upbringing, self-determination, and spiritual growth. More than ever before, the message to be discerned, in a deliberately elliptical and fractured, but nonetheless intellectually coherent libretto, expresses views consistent with the idealism of German primary educational theory of the nineteenth century, views deeply imbued in turn with nationalistic aspirations. As the son of a country teacher, it would be natural for the com-poser's idealism to be formed, not only by direct instruction and guidance, but also by texts on the theory of childhood education that a country teacher would be expected to possess, and that would be among the few books avail-able for reading to a gifted and precocious child of an impoverished house-hold. Be that as it may, such sources of instruction offer needed insights into the pastoral mindset of a distant age, one that emerges with increasing clarity in Stockhausen's notes and public commentaries during this period. "Education (says Froebel) consists in leading man, as a thinking, intelligent being, growing into self-consciousness, to a pure and unsullied, conscious, and free representation of the inner law of Divine Unity, and in teaching him ways and means thereto." And he goes on, "Every human being who is attentive to his own development may thus recognize and study in himself the history of the development of the race to the point it may have reached, or to any fixed point."[1]

Children's education was also seen, in Germany as in other countries, as a bulwark of national sentiment:

> If we inquire how the German people has obtained the first principles of
> its present knowledge, we discover unequivocally that those principles
> always came from a distance, from foreign parts, or were even forced
> upon it from without. Therefore, we have not even a generally accepted
> term in our own mother-tongue for these first principles, elements, or
> rudiments. . . . For thousands of years we have worn these fetters. . . .
> Shall we never cease stamping our children like coins and adorning them
> with foreign inscriptions and foreign portraits, instead of enabling them
> to walk among us as the images of God, as developments of the law and
> life implanted in them by God and graced with the expression of the
> divine? . . . The German mind can no longer be satisfied with the lifeless
> extraneous knowledge and insight of the time; . . . a culture of mere
> external polish can no longer suffice, if, indeed, we are to become self-
> centered, worthy children of God.[2]

Stockhausen does everything for a reason. The libretto of *Donnerstag* is
deliberately contrived. Fragments of dialogue from the composer's childhood; nursery rhymes used as word-play and as mnemonics; more or less
rhetorical statements; statements in the form of subtitles. It is a vision or
dream in which only certain events of the composer's life are recalled, and
the recollections tend to be painful. The composer, his mother, and father,
are a distorted image of the holy family, led by a driven father, the caricature of a man of knowledge, whose understanding of history is reduced to
rhymes, and who has a counting fetish. His very first words: "Aufgepasst!
Jetzt kommt das grosse Einmaleins der Elf!" (Pay attention! Now for the big
one times table of eleven!) would be recognized immediately by a German
speaking audience as a reference to the Witch's riddle, the "Einmaleins" of
Goethe's *Faust*, which begins "Make one into ten, *let two go*, let three make
three"—a trick sum adding either to thirteen, the magic number associated
with Michael, or (interpreted as taking away two) to eleven, the imperfect
number associated with Luzifer, and perhaps also with its English homo-
nym "elf" (in German "Elfe") or wizened servant of the devil.[3]

Simultaneous monologue in which no party is listening to any other is a
convention of operatic comedy taken apart in the simultaneous lectures of
John Cage with the more relevant purpose of creating a fabric of voices in
which the listener is aware of isolated clues emerging out of a vocal chaos.
Here, as for Samuel Beckett, the comic routine is skewed toward a generalized expression of suffering. One is reminded of T. S. Eliot's expiatory remarks on Baudelaire: "He could not escape suffering and could not transcend
it, so he *attracted* pain to himself. But what he could do, with that immense
passive strength and sensibilities which no pain could impair, was to study
his suffering."[4]

The meaning of "light" in *LICHT* can be read on a number of levels.
First, intelligence: light as illumination, in the sense of enlightenment,
understanding, revealed knowledge, or spiritual growth (as in *Hinab-
Hinauf*). Second, light as structure: in the sense of an all-embracing series
of proportions that ensure harmony of size and scale. This has to do with the

determination of form. Third, light in relation to darkness, considered from a philosophical standpoint of truth and falsehood, good and evil. This concerns the action of the drama and its moral implications.

In the course of a conversation with Jonathan Cott dating from 1971, a reader notices Stockhausen's train of thought moving from the musical significance of "light" to a notional drama in which the same actors appear in a number of different characters:

> By the "same light" I meant a set of proportions—no matter what appeared in these proportions: the relationships became more important than what was being related. . . . You can take configurations in the same light and write, for example, theater pieces where one and the same actor is for some time Macbeth and afterward Lady Macbeth, then an animal—I mean that he really changes: always new people appear and others disappear, nobody goes through the entire play. But the way they behave, the way they're related to each other, the tensions or the constellations of these beings—*that* is the constructive element, rather than the figures, the *personalities*.[5]

Cott is prompted to mention the seven-hour-long theater piece *Deafman's Glance* by the American playwright Robert Wilson, whose work the composer feigned not to know. Only a year later, the Shiraz Festival in Iran programmed Wilson's week-long happening *Ka Mountain and Guardenia [sic] Terrace* alongside performances of Stockhausen's *Hymnen, Mantra*, and the text composition "Spektren" from *Für kommende Zeiten*. Inspired by the author's experiences, first as a director of movement therapy in New Jersey, and subsequently in drama at the Byrd Hoffman School, an art therapy commune in New York, *Ka Mountain* represented a genre of behaviorist theater addressing the real actions of individuals of a disoriented intellectual or social competence: real-life equivalents, one might say, of Samuel Beckett's outcasts. Despite uncomfortable echoes of nineteenth-century voyeurism, a theater that arguably deserves to be recognized as an authentic form of drama and a valid extension of method acting. To object that theater conceived as therapy for the mentally impaired is inappropriate for public consumption, is to miss the point that drama and ritual have always been exactly that: collective therapeutic strategies to enable the community to recognize and come to terms with essential issues of human and social existence. Ritualized actions of great simplicity and purity are a natural characteristic of those in mental or physical pain, and can have a containing and healing effect not only for the sufferer, but also for the audience, as models of how to behave, or of how to understand suffering.

Ka Mountain was staged on Haft Tan, a mountain named after the seven sufis buried at its foot, and followed an ascending path, symbolically

> divided into seven levels, each surmounted with an historic emblem —the Sphinx, the Trojan Horse, the Parthenon, rising at the top to New York itself which was due to go up in flames on the final day. . . . Pressed for explanations, the Byrds say we are all living in apocalytic times. . . . For most people, *Ka Mountain* meant assembling at midnight

on Level One to watch a play. For many this was an event of stupefying vacuity. . . . Now and then the figures made imperceptible movements; walking somnambulistically round the platform with a knife; speaking detached words into a telephone. . . . Dialogue consisted of detached grunts and falsetto squawks; except toward 2 am when Mr Wilson staggered schizophrenically toward the front-stage scaffolding and pointed outward with an accusingly dislocated gesture: "Why are you-oo lee-ee-vv-ing?"[6]

It is not hard to see this as a significant encounter. Indeed, Stockhausen could hardly ignore the message of a play not only on so vast a scale but also an event *named in his honor*, the syllable *Ka* (for Karlheinz) being one of his personal signs. Wilson's conception of theater is an immersion experience in mysterious accord with Stockhausen's own seven-day retreat and meditation in May 1968: not only on a scale attuned to such ultimate intuitions as the sense of having infinite time and space at one's disposal, but exemplifying an approach perfectly suited to the kind of stylized action for which he was seeking: an oblivious, autistic grace, that at the same time is grounded in reality and deeply compelling. A style moreover requiring a special attitude to interpretation: not dazed and confused, as in comedy, but rather entranced, manifesting an intensity and economy of gesture totally free of the usual operatic mannerisms, including vibrato and other indicators of artistic self-awareness. It is in fact a familiar movie-style psychological realism, applied to participants whose external behavior has already been rigidly conditioned by a permanent alteration of consciousness. The critic's description of Wilson's play as "stupefyingly vacuous" is exact in this sense, since it applies to a drama whose conscious purpose is to be both "stunning," and also "empty."

In 1976 Stockhausen saw Wilson's *Einstein on the Beach*, with music by Philip Glass. This proved to be theater of few words and very little action, nearly five hours of ritualized meditation on a theme of how music can coexist, or is even possible, in a world capable of mutually assured destruction. The play's simple message is encapsulated in the figure of Einstein (who in real life was an amateur violinist and lover of Mozart) playing the violin against a backdrop suggesting nuclear annihilation. The team of performers included actors, male and female singers (who also danced), a speaking chorus, and an orchestra of electric keyboards, synthesizers, three saxophones, flute, clarinet, and electric bass, an ensemble not far removed from the chamber orchestra of the future envisaged by Josef Matthias Hauer, and eerily anticipating the solo instrumentation and "modern orchestra" of *LICHT*. Choruses, after the manner of Gertrude Stein, chanted an imperturbable libretto consisting largely of number sequences: 1, 2, 3, etc., offset by longer melodies intoned to their corresponding tonic sol-fa names. Dramatic content aside, the formality and remoteness of Wilson's theater aesthetic was again very much to Stockhausen's liking: a world away from the instantaneous encounters of the happening era.

Had Stockhausen wished to construct a conventional drama out of the events of his boyhood, he could certainly have done so. Act I of *Donnerstag*,

"Michael's Youth," makes a promising beginning and is the nearest to conventional opera in character delineation through dialogue. But a great deal
of the real life is missing. His mother's vain remonstrations with the voice of
the radio, a telling image of absence of communication; or the boy's innocent
delivery of leaflets seeking donations to the *Winterhilfe* and other charities
sponsored by the government, that in reality were only fundraising devices
for the Nazi party; or the occasion when, in honor of a visiting church
dignitary, he recited a poem defending the faith only to have his father
visited by Blackshirts later in the day and accused of putting the boy up to
it. The absence of any explicit reference to National Socialism in the fragmentary account of a family life so clearly modeled on his own may seem
like a denial of the reality of good and evil as the composer experienced it;
on the other hand, it is at least arguable that in Stockhausen's view the
historical causes of human suffering are local distractions from the timeless
nature of suffering as a dimension of all human experience. The particular
life is seen as just one example of a universal human condition.

Relative absence of human drama, and of the naturalistic rendering of
human expression in the interpretation of a text in a musico-theatrical
work, have been aesthetic considerations for operagoers since the time of
Bach and Handel. That Stockhausen's preference is for extreme stylization,
formality, and ritual, connects him not only with Bach but with more
ancient forms of ritualized behavior that inspire awe and embody a philosophical rather than a simply dramatic message. And while Stockhausen
deplores the content of pop art, he also recognizes a certain kinship with the
enigmatic canvases of Roy Lichtenstein, austerely iconic images of crisis
caught from anonymous romance comics of the fifties.

In the past century the same objections—to apparent absence of plot, of
character development, of narrative interest,—were also raised against
early documentary films. "It has no story," bridled C. A. Lejeune, film critic
of the *Observer*, at the release in 1935 of the American filmmaker Robert
Flaherty's classic *Man of Aran*. "It barely recounts the movements of a
nameless father, mother, and son through their daily life. . . It is a sealed
document, the key to which is in Flaherty's mind." At the heart of that
debate, not only in Germany but throughout Europe as a whole, lay the
ethical and philosophical issue of the truth that one had a right to expect
from documentary media portraying the real lives of working people. Critics
objected that a film dealing with the islanders of Aran, a barren rock off the
west coast of Ireland, ought to acknowledge the political and social realities
these people were suffering, in this case the islanders' struggles against
eviction and religious persecution. Others saw the function of documentary
rather differently. John Grierson responded that Flaherty's intention had to
be seen as "the story of mankind over a thousand years . . . a simple story,
but . . . an essential story, for nothing emerges out of time except bravery."
Pure documentary required total detachment. What mattered was not the
individual situation but the pattern. Paul Rotha agreed. "Flaherty's approach is wholly impersonal," he said. "What really happens on Inishmore is
not his or our concern."[7] It is also the approach of the anthropologist, if not

the dramatist. The same approach to the elemental family is also indicated in Stockhausen's story of *Donnerstag*. Although the actions are from a real life, the life itself is an illustration of myth.

Donnerstag aus LICHT (Thursday from LIGHT)

1978–1980: No. 48–50 (Stockhausen Verlag; cd SV-30)

Opera in three Acts for soprano, tenor, and bass voices, 8 solo instrumentalists, 3 solo dancers, choir, amplified orchestra, and tapes.

Orchestra: 2 flutes (alto flutes), 2 oboes (cors anglais), 2 clarinets (II. also basset-horn), bass clarinet, bassoon, contra-bassoon; 2 horns, 2 trumpets, 2 trombones, bass tuba; strings 3.0.2.2.1; harp, harmonium (or synthesizer), piano (with optional ring modulation), electric organ (or synthesizer); 3 percussionists: ① large tam-tam, 2 Thai gongs, Geisha-bell, bongo; ② vibraphone, keisu (Japanese temple bell), cymbal, 3 tom-toms; ③ large tam-tam, 2 congas; 4 transmitter microphones, 37 microphones, 6 × 2 loudspeakers, mixing console.

Duration: 4 hours.

Donnerstags-Gruss (Thursday Greeting)

1978: No. 48½ (Stockhausen-Verlag)

For 8 brass instruments, piano, 3 percussionists (conducted).

Alternative title: "Michaels-Gruss" (Michael's Greeting).

Duration: 11'.

The opera begins with a music of greeting performed in the entrance foyer. It is a conventional overture to a far from conventional opera. After an opening fanfare for brass of appropriate solemnity, a selection of highlights follows, like a movie trailer, focusing on the Balinese segment of Act II "Michael's Journey," music of upbeat character for a reduced instrumentation of imaginative mixtures and new and fascinating timbres for piano and percussion. The recording is close and somewhat inert, as is natural in a carpeted foyer, but ends with a burst of reverberation suggesting a transition to a cathedral-like acoustic.

Act I: Michaels Jugend (Michael's Youth)

KINDHEIT – MONDEVA – EXAMEN

1978–1979: No. 49 (Stockhausen-Verlag; cd SV-32 "Tanze Luzefa!," "Mondeva," SV-43 "Examen")

For tenor, soprano, bass; trumpet, basset-horn, trombone, piano; electric organ (or synthesizer); 8-track and 2-track tapes; 6 transmitting microphones, 2 microphones, 8-track and 2-track tape recorders, 10 loudspeakers, mixing console.

Duration: 64'.

Unsichtbare Chöre (Invisible Choirs)

(Act I and Act III)

1979: (No. 49 extract) (Stockhausen-Verlag; cd SV-31)

For prerecorded unaccompanied choir (16 to 8- or 2-track tape)

Duration: 50'.

Act I, "Michael's Youth," opens against a backdrop of a suspended and distant harmony recorded by muted trumpet, clarinet, and trombone, the significance of which is both as a musical "color" specific to the day, and as a means of imposing a static quality on the stage proceedings. An effect more remote than *Stimmung*, more nocturnal than the prelude to Wagner's *Das Rheingold* (which is not static at all, rather a description of the ceaseless movement of a river), this pedal point is perhaps closer to Schoenberg, and beyond him to the dream world of Sigfrid Karg-Elert (the *Sieben Idyllen für Harmonium*),—manifesting, in short, a peculiarly Gothic fascination with the endless chord. Under the barely audible unseen watch of the recorded *Invisible Choirs*, Act I plays out in a sequence of intimate, dream-like, stream-of-consciousness vignettes that establish the three essential characters. Like the three *personnages* of Messiaen's "Reprises par Interversion," one character is destined to grow, one to diminish, and one to stay the same. Michael, incongruously already a full-blown tenor, is seen as the innocent child eager to learn and play; Eva as woman and mother, the nurturing spirit; and there is an awful sense of finality in the character of Luzifer, a personification of worldly knowledge whose hold on life is reduced to counting numbers and reciting a tribal litany of historical facts, in rhyming mnemonics, about ancient heroes of battle and the numbers of dead. From the very beginning a heightened emotion can be detected in the volatile Eva melody, and ironic laughter and disillusion in the guttural tone and staccato rhythms of the Luzifer melody. Stockhausen associates the upper extremes of pitch with the superreal, and voices and instruments of low register with those who are deemed to have fallen from grace. The association of voice tessitura with spirituality tends to an excess of tension in the Michael and Eva vocal lines, and a perhaps deceptive appearance of relaxed, sardonic realism in the Luzifer role. Stockhausen's image of boyhood is strangely altered from the idealized purity of the boy's voice in *Gesang der Jünglinge*. We see Michael as a dispassionate observer of the human tragedy, and inheritor by birth (by assuming mortality) of a genetic predisposition toward war, furthermore as a creature easily led and seduced by adult figures, and thus inherently corruptible.

Elements of *Donnerstag* including the role of the Invisible Choirs are vividly foreshadowed in Kandinsky's notes for *Der gelbe Klang*:

> The stage is filled with a dark-blue glow, in the middle of which is a white light, that has the effect of deepening the blueness. In the suspenseful atmosphere a choir is heard, from where it is impossible to say, singing its hermetic, mysterious tunes, with which it evokes the borderland of the Unnameable. . . . A music begins, slowly descending from a great height, while simultaneously the dark-blue background is hemmed in by blackness. A stiffly-sounding choir emits wordless sounds. . . . As the choir's singing becomes more audible, the front of stage is once more submerged in a blue mist, and the orchestra "struggles with the choir and overwhelms it."[8]

The composer's disorientating and seemingly pathological addiction to echolalia, e.g., "Mi-che-va (i e a)" introduces a modulation of vowel tone acting as

a transitional stage between sung speech and instrumental music, in particular the vowel coloration of the Michael trumpet tone with the aid of mutes
and extended playing techniques, some of the latter originally associated
with the virtuoso trombone of Vinko Globokar's impersonation of Grock the
clown in Berio's 1966 showpiece *Sequenza V*.[9] (Interesting, then, that Stockhausen should retain the trombone as an instrument of Luzifer.) When
consonantal noise is eliminated, the harmonious vowel content is left
exposed, like a coin rubbed smooth so that the edges are eliminated and
only the essential curvatures remain, in a musical imitation of the wea-
thered appearance of Henry Moore's sculpture, or of Rauschenberg's faded
gray paintings. To the naked eye, Stockhausen's notation of vowel melodies
is a reminder of the convention in plainchant, of notating the closing text of
the Doxology "et in saecula saeculorum amen" as vowels only (e u o u a e);
though from his own religious upbringing, as well as from his studies with
Messiaen, Stockhausen would be perfectly aware that the complete words
are always sung, and not just the vowels. Fracturing a text is a familiar
Stockhausen device in any case; what makes the word-setting in *Donnerstag*
more than usually interesting is the sense in which the voice and trumpet
are heard to meet and merge in an intermediate zone that is neither purely
instrumental nor purely vocal. Here too, Kandinsky has interesting ideas of
his own: in Bild 3 of *Der gelbe Klang* "An anguished tenor voice breaks the
tension-laden atmosphere with meaningless fragments of vocal sounds, such
as 'Kalasimunafakola'—speech employed as pure sound, as the first steps of
something musical;" another interesting convergence of contemporary studies of anthropology on the aesthetic vocabulary of the fine arts as early as
Schoenberg's time.

Kandinsky's symbolism of the trumpet is also very clear: for him the
color yellow (as of gold, or of brass) is associated with the dauntless striving
of the human spirit onward and upward "bis zur Aufdringlichkeit" (to a
height of imperiousness). The message conveyed in the keen sound of an
approaching trumpet, or of a fanfare at its highest pitch, is (he says) one of
radiant warmth and power, rousing all around to activity, lifting a people's
vision and courage of purpose to new heights of endurance, and, most notably, infusing the physical and moral relationships of mankind with *light*.[10]

In this first act of *Donnerstag* Stockhausen's account of childhood
education,—snatches of syllabic exchanges, singing, clapping, and dancing,
taken straight from orthodox sources,[11]—is of crucial importance in establishing the drama and the message of *LICHT*, and it is unfortunately the
case that a heroic rendering in conventional operatic style (as in the composite premiere recording, for example) is more likely to belabor the roles than
bring out their sympathetic human qualities. Given that the fragmentary
words of dialogue *are* meaningful and potentially dramatically effective, the
question is how these relationships may be satisfactorily communicated
within the terms they are composed. In a revealing interview with Jill
Purce, the composer admits being uncomfortable with word-setting in the
conventional sense of subordinating his music to the demands of a text, even
when the text is his own. In his own view,—formed as long ago as *Gesang*

der *Jünglinge*, and consistent with an appreciation of the *Lautgedichte* of Schwitters, Marinetti, and Heissenbüttel,—it is not words that communicate meaning, but the musical qualities of speech itself.[12] That might appear to suggest that the surface meaning of the Act I libretto is less important than the syllabic texture that arises from it, a valid enough observation of the composer's consistently effective word-setting for multiple voices, but perhaps less so for solo roles with a clear message of their own. Both in live performance and in balancing his recordings in the studio Stockhausen has spoken of adjusting his own prescribed tempi and varying the internal balance of part-writing, for the sake of improved transparency. As in the case of *Momente*, the dramatic conviction of Act I might arguably be enhanced if the solo voices were indeed individually amplified and thus heard "in close-up" as it were. They offer a rare glimpse of real human beings, not the mechanical dolls of *Trans* or *Musik im Bauch*. The dramatic context of "Michael's Youth" is intimate rather than public, frequently subsiding into interior monologue. An amplified voice is less artificial, less easily fatigued, easier for an audience to listen to, and can draw on a greatly extended range and expressive flexibility, to create the right radiophonic mix of inner voices and exterior reality.

It is important clearly to establish the reciprocal emotional valencies of the three characters, in their first appearance as a nuclear family, in order for the qualities they embody to be appreciated in alternative characters and other disembodied manifestations. Luzifer's counting is a persistent aesthetic challenge for instrumental performers, and I do not know why Stockhausen finds it necessary to insist on the actual words being articulated, when nonverbal counting routines of equal transparency are available, such as the statement of a duration series, as employed by Messiaen in *Cantéyodjayâ* for piano, and by Stockhausen himself in the percussion parts of *Kreuzspiel*—and indeed, as an introduction to "Drachenkampf." Counting by numbers is an uncompromisingly plain alternative to the shepherd's tally of Harrison Birtwistle's opera *Yan Tan Tethera*, and it also introduces uncomfortable echoes of the "Abzählen!" scene of Schoenberg's *A Survivor from Warsaw*, set in a concentration camp. Perhaps that is the point.

Unlike the characters of classical drama,—or indeed any theater about people who always have something to say because, according to the convention, without dialogue there is no drama,—real people, and especially the poor and suffering, usually have very little to say, and much of what they do say, they repeat to themselves, as we know from the pathos and gallows humor of the early songs: "Der Saitenmann" in particular. If Stockhausen is indeed attempting, as I think he is, to model a new kind of opera after the example of Beckett, or Heissenbüttel, or even the mesostic ruminations of Cage, the challenge of dealing with necessary inarticulateness is alleviated by the presence of music as an alternative form of self-expression. This is certainly true of *Donnerstag*, in which the major source of emotion lies with the solo instruments. All the same, there is a hint of Hamlet's tragic indifference about Michael, not to mention a touch of Polonius in the father figure, and of the madness of Ophelia in the mother.

His portrayal of a family adds a further gloss to the mystical "Hu!" prefix, the connotation of "*hu*miliation," a poverty inflicted, we may think, not simply by an oppressive regime, which is never explicitly mentioned, as by the economic conditions imposed on Germany that made the regime possible. The father is a hunter, killing for food, at one point serving up a cat instead of a hare, a mysterious intimation of Kathinka Pasveer's appearance as a cat-demon in *Samstag aus LICHT*. Meantime, the mother rather frantically teaches her son to sing and dance with nervous claps and irregular rhythms, singing in that alien version of the English language associated with German attempts at emulating American popular songs of the twenties,—an innocent rite of initiation, implicitly through radio, into the morally uncertain world of *Mahagonny*, Josephine Baker, the Al Jolson of *Der singende Narr* (The Singing Fool), and not least the banal lyrics of Ernst Krenek's musical *Jonny spielt auf*, the original staging of which, by an interesting coincidence, featured a black violinist standing in triumph on top of a massive globe of the world.[13]

Death is a continuous presence. "Are you dead, little deer? Where do you go from here?" asks the boy Michael in a *Bambi*-like moment, not the only allusion to Disney in *LICHT*. But death is also desensitized to a degree more disturbing and less innocent than Wozzeck's orphan child. The sounds of rifle fire and of battle are crude rimshots from a silent movie; and in Scene II, "Mondeva," we see the moonstruck youth, abandoned to his own devices, engaging in a bizarrely mannerist love-duet with Mondeva while in the background we see a fatal injection being administered to the mother in a sanitorium, and the father repeatedly shot on the front line.

In every opera of the *LICHT* cycle, certain actions and tendencies recur, in imitation of the layered polyphony of the triple formula: an upward process, a downward process; an orbiting or rotational process; an argument; a confrontation; a fight; a sevenfold process; a mystical union. In *Donnerstag* the focus of attention is on Michael, his growth as a human being, and his ultimate return skyward. Act I Scene 3, "Examination," is a *Magic Flute* rite of passage, an obstacle to growth to be overcome, and also an induction into the human community of musicians. It is noticeable that at moments of high tension the Invisible Choir surges into prominence like an aura. The examination does not seem very dramatic, despite deliberate stumbling by the pianist's left hand. Dedicated to the composer's sixteen-year-old daughter Majella, Piano Piece XII is a test piece to end all test pieces, composed in the image of Glenn Gould with added vocal and incidental noises, and a work of didactic formalism so completely out of character with Pieces I–XI, not to mention the piano writing in *Mantra*, that it is hard to imagine it as a Stockhausen composition, unless the composer is now telling us that the piano itself is a musical invention of doubtful virtue. (Though on reflection, indeed, that would actually make sense, Bach's well-tempered clavier being a product of Galileian science that divides the sacred continuum of pitch into a tempered scale incapable of pure harmony.) But if it were really the composer's intention to revisit the world of Stravinsky's mechanical nightingale, a rhythmically impossible piece for pianola after the fashion of

Conlon Nancarrow would perhaps have made the same point in a more entertaining fashion. Alternatively, if the solo were a way of reminiscing on Stockhausen's skills as a magician's accompanist, one might have appreciated some real magic to fill the music's many lacunae, an option set aside for use in *Samstag aus LICHT*. For Stockhausen in 1980 to be reduced to such *démodé* actions as picking and strumming inside the piano, even if they are new for him, seems a poor substitute for the inventiveness of old.

In a remix of "Examination" for television, issued as cd SV-43, Stockhausen rotates the piano part so that left and right stereo channels correspond to left and right halves of the keyboard, despite the fact that the piano is heard (if not seen) in the center middle distance, side-on to the audience. The dramatic purpose of the examination scene is to show Michael's transformation into art of his childhood experiences, an earthly metaphor of the redemption of human suffering through an idealized human life. All the same, it is hard to discern either genuine virtuosity or any drama; the four-person jury, who one would prefer to be wearing masks, or at least hats, since they have confusingly already appeared in other roles, is evidently not in any mood to criticize; there are no hard questions, no unexpected requests to transpose into five flats, nor even any internal disagreement among the jury members themselves.

Act II: Michaels Reise um die Erde (Michael's Journey Round the Earth)

1978: No. 48 (Stockhausen-Verlag; cd SV-32 "Mission und Himmelfahrt," SV-43 "Eingang und Formel," SV-60 "Halt")
For solo trumpet, solo basset-horn, and orchestra: 2 clarinets (II. also basset-horn), 2 flutes (alto flutes), 2 oboes (English horns), bass clarinet, bassoon, contra-bassoon; 2 horns, 2 trumpets, 2 trombones, bass tuba; strings 3.0.2.2.1; harp, harmonium (or synthesizer), piano (with optional ring modulation), electric organ (or synthesizer); 3 percussionists: ① large tam-tam, 2 Thai gongs, Geisha-bell, bongo; ② vibraphone, keisu (Japanese temple bell), cymbal, 3 tom-toms; ③ large tam-tam, 2 congas; 4 transmitter microphones, 37 microphones, 6 × 2 loudspeakers, mixing console.
Duration: 50'.

After Act I Stockhausen seems to have abandoned all pretense at plot and character development, in favor of a masque-like sequence of stylized set pieces with summary announcements. Act II, "Michael's Journey Around the World," takes the form of a massive one-movement concerto for trumpet, large orchestra, and mandatory sound distribution system requiring up to 41 channels of surround sound. The writing for orchestra is so arranged that elements of the music issuing from the platform can also be heard gradually moving around and over the heads of the audience in real time, an effect discreetly reminiscent of the original RCA "Fantasound." Building on the casual rotational effects at certain points in the musical action of *Inori*, in "Michael's Journey" for the first time the musical experience is simultaneously a conventional concert, a theatrical event, and a demonstration of surround sound in confident anticipation of DVD. In fact, the very technical sophistication that makes "Michael's Journey" so interesting an engineering and acoustical challenge, also runs the risk of confusion for the normal concertgoer and home listener, on the one hand through a dislocation in hearing of the real from the reproduced sounds, and on the other hand from the impossibility of satisfactorily reducing a surround sound experience to stereo.

The visual action centers on a large globe of the world into which Michael as trumpeter climbs and reappears at different locations. (Stockhausen's fascination with physical exits and entrances merits a study in itself, and is all of a piece with the paradoxical presence-in-absence of prerecorded sounds and their interaction with live performers; it even affects Boulez in *Répons*, in how one is being asked to interpret the relations of orchestra and soloists to one another, and to the transforming power of the 4X computer.) Superficially, "Michael's Journey" is a magical mystery tour based on Stockhausen's travels in different parts of the world and his encounters with the musical idioms of different cultures. At each stage in the seven-part journey the formulae of Michael, Eva, and Luzifer are injected into a musical context intended to emulate the host culture, a rather obvious gesture suggesting the insemination of less developed idioms with the genes of a higher alien civilization. (Michael's personal mandala, by the way, which we are told represents a bud or flame, is no less than a stylized four-way *lingam*, just as Eva's sign is a vulva, and Luzifer's a redrimmed fundament or full stop.) This sort of behavior is not very tactful, of course, but it is in keeping with the composer's fervent belief both in the perfectibility of humankind, and in the historic duty of the more highly developed and mobile civilizations of the first world to impose the benefits of superior intelligence on everyone else. We observe the tendency to colonize other cultures at will in *Telemusik* and *Stimmung*, not to mention the evolutionary theories of language of de Saussure, or of tribal myth in Lévi-Strauss.

More controversially, the travels of Michael are also presented as a ritual along the lines of the Stations of the Cross; in "Mission and Homecoming,"—in the aftermath of the seventh and last "Jerusalem" stage, that is,—are brief and easily overlooked episodes dealing with the trials and Crucifixion of the Messiah, hidden from view perhaps out of deference to the Jewish poet Reicha Freier, who commissioned "Invisible Choirs." It is indeed a strange altar-piece that conceals its central image of human suffering and death from public contemplation, but at least it allows the mystical "Ascension" of Act III to be understood in context.

In a note to the score, Stockhausen invites the listener to consider the seven terrestrial locations of "Michael's Journey" in relation to the colors associated with the seven days of the week, from the bright green of Monday through to the gold of Sunday. That is as much as to say, in the sense defended by Goethe in the *Farbenlehre*, that each culture represents a different level on the road to enlightenment, and can incidentally be associated with the moral and human qualities identified with each opera. Perversely, all of this programmatic and symbolic apparatus only serves to distract attention from the very powerful qualities of the music, to superficial issues that, for the time being at least, are hardly calculated to inspire affection.

"Eingang," the beginning, is marked by low register growls and little MGM lion's roars from the trumpet and trombone, hints of a prehistoric world. The mechanical rotations of the globe are expressed musically by flickering rotations of fragments of the solo melodies, like the orbiting reflections of a mirror-ball at a high school prom. With "Abfahrt" the journey begins, a texture visually reminiscent of the layered canons of *"Atmen gibt das Leben . . ."* The first station, "Cologne," is associated with Monday, and thus with nurturing. The instrumentation revisits the deep-freeze of Stockhausen's youth with hints and textures of *Formel* and *Spiel*: vibraphone, harp, and string harmonics. (Those who wonder why the composer includes a bravura solo for virtually every instrument except the violin may recall that in addition to being the instrument of the leader of the orchestra, the violin is an instrument much beloved of the devil, as we know from Stravinsky, Tartini's "Devil's Trill" sonata, and Einstein.)

Station 2, "New York," introduces groups of the same sonority playing parallel seconds, thirds, and sevenths, which some may hear as having more to do with New York as the home in exile of Mondrian and Bartók, than as a culture in its own right. New York's day is Tuesday, meaning war. Added cymbals and tom-toms are small Varèse-ian gestures, and bursts of American wind band orchestration anticipate the Luciferian visage of *Samstag*. The relationship of orchestra to solo players appears very Cage-ian, a simultaneous polyphony in which everyone works at a small, specific task, but essentially independently. But this too could be read as a memory of the trials and textures of "Third Region of *Hymnen* with orchestra," associated with the New York Philharmonic.

Station 3 is "Japan," and its day is Wednesday, signifying reconciliation. For once the overall dynamic is relatively quiet. Yet again the cultural allusions to Japanese music are crudely drawn, though the music itself is fascinatingly rich. As in *Der Jahreslauf*, the textures and sonorities of gagaku music are imitated by Western instruments: the shô by harmonium and Hammond organ, biwa and koto by harp and pizzicato strings, and the reedy hichiriki by oboe and English horn. Commendably, Stockhausen avoids any temptation to reinterpret the gliding tones of Japanese classical music in the manner of the excitable glissandi in the Eva formula. There is a quite wonderful solo for viola, and at a certain moment the music shimmers almost to a stop, in a 3 × repeated phrase of unexpected magic.

Station 4 is "Bali," and its day, auspiciously, is Thursday, which may account for the fact that this segment is among the most vital of the entire concerto. Composers as different as Poulenc, Colin McPhee, and Britten have been inspired by the tranquil complexity of gamelan, and even Stockhausen on a much larger scale manages to imbue this segment with a quality once happily described by a student as "waitlessness." Representing Station 5, "India," is a strongly heterophonic music for flutes, violins, violas, and bass clarinet, with descending harp glissandi and parallel sliding cellos the only obvious concessions to the subcontinent's figures of musical speech. Its day, Friday, is associated with miscegenation, an allusion no doubt to the interpenetration of species depicted in the mythology of the culture.

Tom-toms and elephant calls in the style of fifties jungle music introduce Station 6, "Central Africa," a music of full and shimmering sound that would be much more comfortable to listen to if it were not for the fact that it is music exploiting the very lowest registers of the orchestra, and thus signifies an essentially primitive level of human evolution. The breathtaking insensitivity of such a view, previously intimated in the sketches for *Hinabhinauf*, and strikingly at odds with the attitude to African art of Picasso, Braque, Modigliani, Klee, and others, is further compounded by association with Saturday, the day of death, with Luzifer, and with blackness of skin as well as of spirit. All that can be said in justification is that the composer has a mission impartially to record the full range of symbolism as it is manifested in Western myth and ritual down the centuries, however unpleasant that may be.

At 345, "Umkehr," a ceremonial high basset-horn call is heard, as if to say "we can't go any lower than this." In a moment of sublime tastelessness and dramatic effectiveness, the globe revolves backwards to return Michael to civilization. Station 7, "Jerusalem," is associated (a little incongruously, perhaps) with Sunday, the color gold, and the principle of mystical union. The music is dense, rich, and full, with premonitions of "Luzifers Tanz" from *Samstag*. "Halt" which follows is an interlude between trumpet and string bass, a gesture of affection to trumpeter Miles Davis, an unlikely advocate of Stockhausen's intuitive music and a notable influence on the trumpet playing of Markus Stockhausen. A slight but atmospheric glimpse of a jazz style familiar to Stockhausen from his visit to Birdland in 1958, it feels like a discarded sketch for the New York segment of "Michael's Journey."

The mystical union previously heralded by the Jerusalem music is realized in the joining of trumpet and basset-horn melodies in "Mission," a rite of horizontal integration interpreted with deliberate charm and fastidious elegance on the recording (Michael is certainly no toreador). His musical journey now leads into ethically troubling scenes of "Ridicule" and "Crucifixion" from the Passion. In a mirror image of Act I, these references to cruelty, torture, and painful death are treated with resolute indifference. As a concession, the Michael and Mondeva soloists retreat offstage, and are replaced by a Punch and Judy couple, also trumpet and basset-horn, whose boisterous intervention can be read as an attempt to lighten the spell. The offstage drama of the Crucifixion scene is reduced to a mixture of "tone shots and salvoes" by trombones, connecting the cheap sound effects of rifle fire of Act I, and the death of the father like an animal, with the nailing of Christ to the cross—"with pointed, sharp tones they *nail* the distant Michael and Eva melodies so completely, that they almost cannot be heard" —and also to the original hammer-blows of "punktuelle Musik." It is quite a conceptual leap to construe any of these images in terms of pinning a butterfly to a card, or nailing an argument to a point where it ceases to live.

Seven solemn chords for brass herald the triumphant return of Michael and Eva in "Ascension," which paradoxically does not ascend in pitch, but in a continuation of the process of melodic integration, converges to a spiraling and quite beautiful trill ending on a unison g.

Act III Michaels Heimkehr (Michael's Home-coming)

1980: No. 50 (Stockhausen-Verlag; cd SV-43 "Drachenkampf")
For tenor, soprano, bass, trumpet, basset-horn, trombone; 2 soprano saxophones, electronic organ (or synthesizer); old woman; choir, large orchestra, 8-track and 2-track tapes; 8 transmitter microphones, 15 microphones, 8-track tape recorder, 10 × 2 loudspeakers, mixing console.

Donnerstags-Abschied (Thursday Farewell)

1980: No. 50 ³/₄ (Stockhausen-Verlag)
For five trumpets.
Alternative title: "Michaels-Abschied" (Michael's Farewell).
Duration 11'–30'.

Tactfully omitted from Act II, reintroduced by a Messiaen-like fanfare for woodwinds, "Invisible Choirs" returns with its message of benediction in Act III, "Michael's Home-coming," in which, restored to his triple guise as singer, trumpeter, and mime-dancer, the "son of light" is welcomed back to his heavenly abode. On the strength of this spirit's achievements on earth, which appear to consist in what he is rather than what he does (it is of course "he," beyond a peradventure), there is not much to celebrate in the way of good deeds or sacrifice: in fact in its own strange way the celebratory ritual resembles the return of the prodigal son. If this is the Protector of Mankind, he is not much of a role model. Behind the deliberately portentous greetings and statements of a kind familiar from the film chronicles of Leni Riefenstahl lies a moral oblivion that, as the description of a human personality, is transcendently sad.

This is a time when not to understand the language is a real bonus; which by an ironic twist may be what Stockhausen has in mind, to create *LICHT* as a time capsule, like the Rosetta Stone in Goethe's era, to be decoded and marveled over millennia hence when the world language is Inuit or Cantonese, and the mysteries of Judaeo-Christian belief are no longer even a memory. Stockhausen does his best to disguise his pronouncements by having them intoned in slow and painful syllables, as though the performers themselves are trying to decipher aloud a long-dead inscription.

"Festival" offers good visual inventions: the gift of the three trees (which my instinct tells me represent the three cardinal waveforms of electronic music: the sine wave, square wave, and ramp wave); and the gift of the three light compositions by Mary Bauermeister, artistic reminders of the composer's debt to Goethe and his holistic theory of color (to the words "Monde aus Glas, Glaslinsen, Glas-Sonnen"). In celebration of light composition 3, representing the heavens, the names of the constellations are invoked in a momentary reprise of *Sternklang* until ostentatiously interrupted by an old lady hobbling onto the stage like the witch from Hansel and Gretel to berate one and all and tell them to go home. Like the orchestra strike in *Samstag*, and the "real" spoken interruptions in *Hymnen*, it is another example of Stockhausen's use of anecdotal experience to break the illusion. Haydn also liked to keep his listeners awake. As we know, this particular event is inversely symmetrical (and therefore identical, in a Lévi-Straussian sense) to Robert Wilson's querulous "Why are you leaving?" admonition to the audience of *Ka Mountain*. But the old lady provokes a response from the choirs that is perhaps the most genuinely moving text in the entire opera, even though the way it is articulated is fragmented and nearly incoherent. They reply "Es gibt kein Zuhause; auch Engel sind ewig unterwegs" ("There is no 'at home' for angels eternally in transit").

Comic relief arrives in the wizened form of a little black devil, a Rumpelstiltskin bearing the gift of a blue globe to Michael, a gesture of commendation from his master Luzifer, the latter in his guise as teacher. Outwardly this blue sphere is a memento of the earth; but it also has a hidden significance as a prize awarded to a child who has achieved the lowest level of competence in kindergarten (which is why Michael promptly hands it over in a gesture of distaste to an attendant choir member). The inspiration of this symbolic gift, once again, is Friedrich Froebel, the pioneer of childhood education, who developed a reward system tailored to the mental and spiritual growth of the child. According to Froebel, the gift of a colored ball, or set of balls, symbolized attainment of the primary level of awareness: of color, selfhood, and sense of location.[14]

With a lot of huffing and puffing from the ringside choir, and heel-clicking from the combatants, a fight breaks out between the trumpet and trombone, the Michael-mime, and the Luzifer-mime, as between St Michael and the dragon (in English, St. George and the dragon). Musically this is more a show of force than a duel of skill, and is played broadly for laughs until two youthful angels bearing saxophones arrive to restore a partial sense of decorum. Once again, a truculent Luzifer, seemingly the worse for wear, harangues a resplendent Michael in a dialogue that might easily have been adapted from *Momente* (or indeed, from *Monty Python's Life of Brian*). It comes as quite a relief to hear the two masculine antagonists actually communicating in reasonably coherent sentences, and is interesting as an intimation of what the composer really has to say. We learn that Michael has come down to earth against Luzifer's advice (hence a double-negative, thus an act of virtue), not to save humanity, but to taste it. Neither emerges with any credit: Luzifer is abusive, and Michael frankly a prig, in a wordy exchange that, given the overwhelmingly sanctimonious tone of the rest of the scene, comes over not as philosophy, nor poetry, nor even as political rhetoric. "You have allowed your wisdom to be corrupted by your intelligence!" complains Luzifer. "You are a fool, a fool!" (*Ein Narr! Ein* [singende] *Narr!*) And he stomps off.

The final scene, "Vision," is cast in the style of a résumé and benediction. Its most engaging invention is a sequence of three shadow plays, after the manner of the Balinese, but charmingly upside down, like a slide show to which one has been invited by neighbors recently returned from an exotic holiday abroad (though there may be a more ominous meaning). Seven shadow plays are accompanied by brief audio clips of earlier scenes. An inverted bow of light mysteriously appears. The opera concludes with a peroration of pious sentiment but unfathomable significance. As it ends, and as the audience departs, a lingering farewell can be heard ringing out from five trumpets repeating segments of the Michael formula from high vantage points around the opera house piazza.

Notes

1. Friedrich Froebel, *The Education of Man* tr. W.N. Hailmann (London: Appleton, 1906), 2, 41 (emphasis added).
2. Friedrich Froebel, *The Education of Man*, 231–32.
3. John R. Williams, *Goethe's Faust* (London: Allen & Unwin, 1987), 96.
4. T. S. Eliot, "Baudelaire." In *Selected Prose* ed. John Hayward (Reprint. Harmondsworth: Peregrine Books), 1963, 178.
5. Jonathan Cott, *Stockhausen: Conversations with the Composer* (London: Robson Books, 1974), 224–26.
6. Irving Wardle, "Exclusive lines under the desert stars." London *Times*, September 12, 1972.
7. Arthur Calder-Marshall, *Innocent Eye: The Life of Robert J. Flaherty* (New York: Harcourt, Brace & World, 1963), 162–65.
8. Ulrike-Maria Eller-Rüter, *Kandinsky: Bühnenkomposition und Dichtung als Realisation seines Synthese-Konzepts* (Hildesheim: Georg Olms, 1990), 67–68.
9. Luciano Berio, *Sequenza V* for solo trombone, recorded by Vinko Globokar. DG 137 005.
10. Ulrike-Maria Eller-Rüter, *Kandinsky*, 73–75.
11. Friedrich Froebel, *The Education of Man*, 268–70, 323.
12. "Stockhausen—Sound International." 1978 interview with Jill Purce, published in three parts in *Sound International* October, November, December 1978. German tr. by Stockhausen, with additions. *Texte 6*, 347–66.
13. John Willett, *New Sobriety: Art and Politics in the Weimar Period 1917–33* (London: Thames and Hudson, 1978), 165–67.
14. "Synoptical Table of Gifts and Occupations." In Friedrich Froebel, *The Education of Man*, 285.

CHAPTER TWENTY-FOUR

Samstag

A century ago, reflecting on the implications of Richard Strauss's literary choices from *Tod und Verklärung* (Death and Transfiguration) to the opera *Salome*, and the composer's deliberate attraction to provocative or scandalous dramatic themes, J. A. Fuller-Maitland observed:

> As a philosophical treatise, 'Also sprach Zarathustra' may be a valuable addition to the literature of the subject, and it may be a commentary on, or a confutation of, the Nietzschian doctrines that suggested it; but here we reach the vexed question of what is permissible or possible to express in terms of mere music. . . . There is from henceforth the absolute necessity for elucidatory pamphlets on the subject of each composition. . . . The inevitable discussion on the legitimacy of the means employed and the composer's meaning has given fine opportunity to journalists and others, both admirers and detractors, to bring themselves into public notice; but each discussion has been forgotten as soon as the next work has appeared. . . . As it is never stated in so many words that the pamphlet is written by authority of the composer, one class of his admirers can always say that the explanation is far-fetched and goes beyond the composer's intentions, while the others can quote it as an authoritative explanation of the meaning of the work.[1]

While he shares Strauss's delight in the grotesque, and in pricking the bourgeois moral sensibilities of his audiences in ways merely diverting to his intellectual patrons (who are in on the joke), Stockhausen in the long run is both more endearing and more honest than his forerunner, firstly because his music speaks with admirable directness of what he really believes, and secondly because his music defends the renewal of our Western musical language in terms that are authentic in the highest degree: "authentic" in the sense he means by "universal." Weighed against the moral uncertainties of parts of the composer's message is the striking challenge represented by the integrity of the music itself, which by virtue of making no concessions to convenience or popular taste, is manifestly not for hire.

Samstag (Saturday) is Luzifer's day; not just the day of (feigned) death, as the composer says, but rather the Day of Judgement, or, as befits a compulsive counter, (and, I suspect, for the sake of a particularly atrocious pun), the Day of Reckoning. And the Day of Wrath. Luzifer is already guilty. That is the point. The same audiences who judge Michael as passive and unheroic and are unmoved simply by being told that he is a genius, have no problem in perceiving Luzifer as the bad guy despite the obvious power and brilliance of his music. That too may be the composer's message, since compared to *Donnerstag* the music of *Samstag* is mostly wonderful: inspired, hugely imposing, exciting, grotesque, magisterial, and at times intensely poetic. The positive qualities expressed in the music demand to be reconciled with the assumptions an audience is bound to bring to the sympathetic portrayal of a figure of unreconstructed hubris. The works of a devilish intelligence, even of the archetypal mad scientist, are all the same products of an exceptional mentality, and that in itself should command respect. Stockhausen's ideological point, that in a conflict of opposing philosophies, winning the physical battle does not automatically dispose of the intellectual argument, while less comfortable is just as necessary. Human perceptions of virtue, guilt, condemnation, and ultimate punishment are the issues here, and it is fair enough that amid the clamor, echoes of youthful protest are still heard, at the crude and self-righteous vengeance inflicted on the defeated, and at the casuistry of those who pass judgement on crimes of war committed by the vanquished, glossing over the starvation and the phosphor bombs delivered on a defeated civilian population and teenage conscripts in the trenches after D-Day. The moral and dramatic tensions of *Samstag aus LICHT* are those of the condemned prisoner in Death Row, contemplating his doom, and declaring unequivocal defiance. In his early notes, Stockhausen writes that Luzifer is not a musician, he cannot play an instrument, but has to persuade others to create music at his bidding. This is precisely the redeeming weakness of the devil in Stravinsky's *Soldier's Tale*, who also cannot play the violin, and whose evil consists in persuading the soldier to give up his fiddle, and thus deny himself access to the saving grace of music.

Two other composing spirits are present in *Samstag*. The first is Henry Brant, an authentic "American pioneer explorer of musical space" whose patient experiments into the effective distribution of static and moving sounds indoors and out of doors are a common thread connecting outwardly very different musical episodes. (One of Brant's inspirations, as a matter of interest, was hearing the "Tuba Mirum" of Berlioz's *Grande Messe des Morts* performed at the Invalides in Paris.) The other is Richard Wagner, whose opera *Parsifal* also attracted controversy over its reconstruction of the Christian gospel. In particular, the "Transformation Music" from Act I, and specifically, the awesome sound of the "Bells of Monsalvat," also known as the "Bayreuth Bells," that Wagner specified for the opera. Although the bells have not survived, their sound, heard on a 1927 recording made at the Festspielhaus by the Bayreuth Festival Orchestra under Karl Muck, and preserved on compact disc, in a version simulated by multiple piano bass strings, sounding like the extended bass register of a Royal Bösendorfer grand piano, and not like bells at all.[2] It is precisely the conjunction of these three elements: the idea of tolling bells, the theme of spiritual transformation, and the timbre of an immense piano, that provides an acoustic as well as a symbolic link between the piano as a stage prop, representing Luzifer's casket, the sound of the piano as the instrument of "Luzifers Traum," the electronic music of "Kathinkas Gesang als Luzifers Requiem," and the real bells that toll out at the end of "Luzifers Abschied."

If this is saying that the piano is Luzifer's instrument, that opens up a fascinating subtext relating to the piano as the initial instrument of pointillist music, and the association of Messiaen and the "star sound" of *Mode de valeurs* with the initially purist aesthetic of Stockhausen and Goeyvaerts, which was essentially an aesthetic driven by an intensely religious attitude. A determining feature of the purist aesthetic is its absence of emotional expression, a philosophical and moral detachment that emerges in the most abstract philosophy, in Webern, in the sublime indifference of John Cage, and the transcendental detachment of Erik Satie, whom Cage also admired. For Satie, Debussy and their contemporaries, absence of expression was protest and palliative against the corrupting influence of a nineteenth-century Romanticism perceived as exacerbating a spirit of aggressive and vengeful militarism among nations in the decades leading up to the 1914–1918 war. The rejection of Schoenberg by Cage and Boulez after the 1939–1945 war, and their embrace of a new music of total objectivity and emotional detachment can be read in the same way, as a rejection of the spirit of Romantic expressionism as it survived in the thematicism of Schoenberg.

But we know from the correspondence that the realist in Stockhausen rebelled very early on against the strict principles of pointillism enunciated by Goeyvaerts and envisaged in the fictional Glass Bead Game. Accepting the principle of total organization, Stockhausen pursued the idea of serial controls further than any composer before or since,—and then, when the acoustic results were not sufficiently compelling or exciting, unlike Goeyvaerts, he broke the rules, or sinned against the Webernian canon of divine perfection. As early as Piano Piece I, sensing that Messiaen's music of isolated points was already exhausted, Stockhausen began to organize points into groups; yet again, when the purist Goeyvaerts objected that it was not possible to employ conventional musical instruments because they were neither exactly controllable nor a comprehensive tonal resource, Stockhausen went ahead nevertheless and composed works for orchestra that he knew to be tonally and philosophically imperfect. Of all the instruments available to him, the piano was one of the purest, and of course we can see now that the serial doctrine itself is based on a perception of the family of keyboard instruments as musical data processing devices of deliberate precision and emotional neutrality, a perception that goes back at least to the time of the English virginalists.

So when Luzifer delivers his little homily about the facial distortions that arise from the independent actions of a contrary spirit, what the prefix "Kontra–" and the term *Kontrageist* actually evoke are the same rebellious emotions attached to the composition of *Kontra-Punkte* (and later, to the recomposition of *Punkte 1952/62*): both gestures of defiance against the pointillist ideals he initially set up for himself, and indicative of his pleasure in the success of the music and the sense of liberation that came with composing against the canon of perfection. Out of that paradox comes a statement of the human condition as necessarily imperfect, existing in an environment of constant change, unstable by nature and requiring expression for its very survival, hence incapable of attaining the stillness and tranquility of an ideal perfection.

Samstag aus LICHT (Saturday from LIGHT)

1981–1983: No. 51–54 (Stockhausen-Verlag; cd SV-34)
Opera for 13 musical performers: bass singer, flute (piccolo), basset-horn, trumpet (piccolo trumpet), piano, 6 percussionists, 2 dancers; symphonic band: 6–8 flutes (3–4 *ossia* alto flutes); 6 clarinets, 3 basset-horns (*ossia* alto clarinets), 3 bass clarinets; 2 soprano (sopranino) saxophones, 2 alto, 1 tenor, 1 baritone, 1 bass saxophone (*ossia* contrabass clarinet or tuba); 2–4 oboes, 2–4 English horns, 2–4 bassoons, 1–2 contrabassoon(s) (*ossia* contrabass clarinet or tuba); 12 trumpets with mutes, 2 alto trombones (*ossia* flugelhorns), 6 trombones (III. VI. bass trombones); 8 horns, 2 baritones (tenor horns), 4 euphoniums, 4 bass tubas; 10 percussionists: ① keisu, ② glockenspiel, ③ 2 alarm bells (tocsins), ④ 3 Japanese rin: temple bells, ⑤ 2 tubular bells, ⑥ 2 Javanese gongs, ⑦ (soloistic) 1 hi-hat, 2 susp. cymbals, 2 Thai gongs, 1 Chinese opera gong, 1 bell plate, 1 snare drum, 1 tom-tom, 1 bass drum with pedal, ⑧ 1 vibraphone, 2 cinelli, ⑨ 1 antique cymbal, 2 tam-tams, ⑩ 1 bowl-bell, 1 tam-tam; men's chorus, organ.
Duration: 3 hours 15'.

Samstags-Gruss (Saturday Greeting)

1984: No. 53½ (Stockhausen-Verlag)
For 26 brass instruments and 2 percussionists.
Duration: 8'.

After *Sternklang*'s docile and ineffectual polyphony of greeting to celestial visitors, inward meditations translated out of doors in the spirit of a pastoral frolic of the flower generation era, the robust monophonic signal emitted by Steven Spielberg's alien spacecraft in the movie *Close Encounters of the Third Kind* offered a salutory reminder that the gods speak a strong and unambiguous message, even when the message turns out to be a lesser catechism of the prophet Kodály. The lesson is learned in the opera's "Saturday Greeting," a powerfully intimidating, but jovial and exciting noise for four groups of brass players located at four compass points high within the auditorium. This is music very definitely gesturing *de haut en bas*, and not just with the roar of multiple lions of the movies, but a true war music, growling, braying, blaring, sneering and posturing musically in set piece gestures that are simple and extremely effective, even with a hint of parody of the lofty trumpets of "Michael's Farewell." This is a music that one could imagine bringing down the walls of Jericho, and it is also on a loudness scale to provoke the same fear and anticipation triggered by the sudden wail of air-raid sirens at times of major civil emergency. At the same time, however, the Greeting contains reassuring elements of dialogue, statement and counterstatement, suggesting the taking of sides. It is music not only on a scale to be performed in a vast arena or stadium, but totally appropriate for a public confrontation such as a major sporting event, and just the right length to sustain audience excitement.

Among contemporary composers, Henry Brant is one of the few other composers of Stockhausen's generation with the courage to attempt such a bold statement, and the skill to make it work. Composed in 1979, Brant's *Orbits*, "a spatial symphonic ritual" for 80 trombones, coloratura soprano, and organ, is a different kind of statement, more of an extended melody, but in its own way just as awesome.[3] The ritual music of Tibetan Buddhism, its resonant throat singing, braying long trumpets and incessant tintinnabulating percussion, offers a number of additional points of reference—in Stockhausen's case, not just to the scale and tone of the "Saturday Greeting," but also to the exultant clatter of "Luzifers Abschied."[4]

Scene 1: Luzifers Traum (Lucifer's Dream)

1981: No. 51 (Stockhausen-Verlag; cd SV-33)
For bass and piano solo; 2 transmitting microphones, 3 microphones, 2 × 2 loudspeakers, mixing console.
Alternative title: Klavierstück XIII (Piano Piece XIII)
Duration: 36'.

"The dimensions of art," said Paul Klee, "are dot, line, plane, and space," and dot, line, plane, and space define the four principal scenes of *Samstag* in turn. After the spaciousness of the Greeting, all attention focuses on a point toward a pit near the center of the apron from which the curved shape of a mock piano can be seen silhouetted like a tombstone in a shaft of light. Indeed, from certain angles, when the light plays on its thirteen keys it might even look like an anamorphic Neanderthal skull. This is Luzifer's piano, but he cannot play it: a *Hammerklavier sans maître*, its notes the hammer-blows of an inquisitive small boy and also the nails in the coffin of the inventive spirit. A tomb defines fixity in time and space; the composer's scenario calls for lighting and a combination of refracting and reflecting glass panels to create the effect of a hall of mirrors around the immobile figure of Luzifer and his pianist assistant, who in the original libretto is summoned as "Satanella" (child of sin), but for the premiere recording is addressed more politely by her proper name, Majella (Majella Stockhausen, now aged 20).

This is supposed to be a dream, and the piano part contains some of the noises associated with sleeping. The apparatus of microphones is intended not only to enhance actions that would normally pass unheard, but to create an impression of a piano interior of enormous size, in which every note has its clearly audible location in the stereo panorama. (I am quite certain, in fact, that the effect Stockhausen is seeking is the same "globes of sound suspended in space" that he experienced at the private studio in the midwest in 1958; these were Bösendorfer piano tones, picked up by microphones in series adjusted for phase coincidence at the mixing desk. At the time Stockhausen did not understand how the effect was achieved, but it made a lasting impression on him.) We are back in the realm of *Mikrophonie I*, where the vibrating body of the instrument is subjected to a variety of physical attacks and monitored as it were by stethoscope. After the (perhaps deliberate) tedium of Piano Piece XII, Piece XIII is more inventive in effects, and more convincing in a theatrical sense, though one cannot be sure that the intended possibilities of amplification or the implications of the incidental noises are yet fully realized. Ideally, they include the whizz of small rockets, (or remembered sniper fire) sharp intakes of breath, knocking on wood in the manner of Cage's *Wonderful Widow of Eighteen Springs*, whistling, and frantic counting—the effectiveness of which might conceivably benefit from the player's voice modulating the piano resonances in the manner of a vocoder.

Luzifer's role here is relatively modest: he is in a frozen, trancelike state, and everthing we hear in the scene is conceivably inside his mind. His initial words to Majella are disguised in the International Phonetic Alphabet so that their exact meaning is hidden, or slurred, as if spoken by a person in a semiconscious state: "[sh]play . . . more . . . one . . . try for me . . . [sh]pituesk (picturesque)," the figure says, nodding at the keyboard. The implication of the scene suddenly deepens as we realize these could have been the words spoken by a dying American soldier in the final days of the war, to the young Stockhausen himself as a pianist. The performer's additional noises can thus be interpreted as the sounds of fierce concentration and suppressed emotion. After some time the patient, Luzifer, heaves himself up and whispers "13 – 12 – 11 . . ." etc., but counting in reverse, as though counting down the seconds. Then, still in a slurred voice, a further sequence of syllables in which a few words seem to have meaning: "[sh]play . . . *schnell* . . . [rien ne] *va plus* . . . [ler] *vite* [ster] (Luzifer?) . . . slowing . . . soft . . . *lentement* . . . must die . . . in ecstasy . . ." And later, "less soft, . . . *plus faible* . . . *désire* . . . *plus forte*," after which the words become more comprehensible: "crescendo, decrescendo, *silence colorée, bruits, degrès, couleurs du néant*" (colored silence, noises, degrees, colors of nothingness). It is as though the patient were reviving or returning momentarily to consciousness as a consequence of the healing power of the music.

At the beginning, and again at around 25' 45" at the word "dreizehn" (thirteen) low bass notes toll powerfully. At first they are minor ninths, but later they become octaves (thirteen-note intervals), an unusual effect for Stockhausen, last heard in *Inori* and perhaps associated with that number. Around the piano are tiny rockets, fired off at irregular intervals. We are not necessarily being asked to take these requirements literally: rather they are indications of musical effects to be achieved in some way, perhaps to resemble the whispering sounds of flares set off by a lifeboat, or to represent the souls of the dead rising to heaven. They have the effect of expanding the audience's perception of musical space outward from the point into the void, like Hawking radiation from a black hole, perhaps. (There appear to be no rockets fired on the premiere recording, presumably for fire safety reasons.)

Technically the work offsets rapid decorations against these long tolling resonances, and in that respect rejoins the aesthetic of the Piano Pieces V–VIII, with some cluster additions from Piece X. Once again the performer has to weigh the composer's dynamic notations against the effects of amplification, and adjust the gestures of physical accentuation to any microphone present. The aesthetic issue, exactly as it used to be in the early fifties, is how to reconcile extreme dynamics with an essentially intimate musical scenario. In relation to his own *Sur Incises* for multiple pianos, harps, and percussion, which deals with the same issues, Boulez speaks of magnifying the internal acoustic of the various parts of a piano by multiplying the number of pianos and pianists, and introducing substitute instruments (such as steel pans) to convey the effect of knocking on the frame, and so on. In effect Boulez is redoubling and refracting the interior sound of one grand piano to give the impression of a cubist, multi-faceted polyphony. And by sharing the energy among a plurality of instruments and performers Boulez is indeed able to achieve a high degree of polyphonic complexity and fullness of sound, while at the same time avoiding the distortions to which a solo performer is susceptible. Multiple instruments and performers are clearly not appropriate in the present situation, since they imply a notion of space contrary to Stockhausen's requirement of concentration in a point. Nevertheless, there is the alternative possibility of prerecording the conventionally notated elements of Piece XIII on a disk reproducing piano, allowing the live performer to focus on the special effects.

The technical problem is to extend the dynamic range of a solo piano, without compromising the advantages of delicate amplification of transient effects. Multiple microphones are the best option, and contact microphones on the soundboard and elsewhere are one promising possibility to bring out the deeper resonances of specific structural members. It is certainly not unfeasible for additional microphone channels, set up at points beyond the casework of the instrument, to be monitored by noise gates set to open only when the energy level detected is higher than a set threshold. That would allow the loudest tones to be heard with added impact and resonance, but leaving the delicate noises of whistling or breathing unaffected. At present, the work gives an impression of crude violence out of keeping both with Stockhausen's normally astute handling of piano tone, and also out of character with the dramatic purpose of the music in this context. The appropriate way of handling this issue of balance, it seems to me, is by amplifying the piano to a pitch of sensitivity where the pianist is obliged to maintain excessive restraint and play with all the precision of a surgeon performing a delicate and painstaking operation.

In 1981, during the recording of the conversations of *Stockhausen on Music*, the composer mentioned that he was hard at work on "Luzifers

Traum," and that he had been evaluating a number of possible replacements or upgrades for the Cologne studio's Synthi 100, including the computer system at IRCAM. Surprisingly, he had rejected di Giugno's 4X system. What he required in an ideal studio, and what by implication the 4X could not deliver, was real-time control of every parameter: the information might all be stored digitally in a computer, he says, but it had to be accessible in real time, and the various parameters of individual timbre, speed, pitch, amplitude etc. had to remain independently controllable.[5] The implications for "Kathinkas Gesang" are very interesting, given that the remarks establish a consultative relationship between Cologne and Paris, hence between Stockhausen and Boulez, at the very time Boulez is working on the real-time interactions of *Répons* for keyboards and computer-generated sounds, and looking ahead to the possibilities of nonkeyboard instruments also in real-time dialogue with the IRCAM system. The difficulty centers on a midi detection system that allows the computer to "read" what the live instrument is playing. For keyboard instruments of tempered tuning such as the piano, vibraphone, harp etc., the pitches are always discrete, and (in theory at least) always in tune, thus reducing the margin of error in detection; for nonkeyboard instruments there is an expressive dimension incorporated that involves "bending the pitch," and this makes detection a more hit and miss affair. Nevertheless, the boffins at IRCAM were on to the task, leading to the creation in 1985 of Boulez's *Dialogue de l'ombre double* for clarinet and computer-generated sounds, with the technical assistance of Andrew Gerzso,[6] in 1993 to a version of . . . *explosante-fixe* . . . for midi flute, two acoustic flutes, instrumental ensemble, and computer-generated sounds,[7] and in 1997 to *Anthèmes 2*, composed for the most intractable instrument of all, solo violin and real-time electronic sounds.[8] (All three works, by the way, are derivations of the original . . . *explosante-fixe* . . . of 1971, which from the outset was always conceived as a work for live instruments and real-time electronic intermodulation: in effect, as Boulez's clean-burning alternative to *Mixtur*.)

Scene 2: Kathinkas Gesang als Luzifers Requiem (Kathinka's Chant as Lucifer's Requiem)

1982–1983: No 52 (Stockhausen-Verlag)
For flute and 6 percussionists; 7 transmitting microphones, 10 loudspeakers, mixing console.
Duration: 33'.

1983: No. 52½ (Stockhausen-Verlag; cd SV-28)
Concert version for flute and electronic music; 1 transmitting microphone, 8-track tape recorder, 10 loudspeakers, mixing console.
Duration: 33'.

That a third version of this work has been announced, for flute and multiple pianos, though without a date and not yet premiered, is food for thought. "Kathinkas Gesang" marks the debut of flutist Kathinka Pasveer, and with the addition of the flute sonority to the solo vocabulary of tone colors, Stockhausen's family of instrumental characters is now complete: the flute, basset-horn, and trumpet corresponding to the three cardinal synthesizer waveforms, of sine wave, square wave, and ramp or sawtooth wave. Kathinka is her real name, and, yes, Stockhausen introduces her into the opera as a Cat Woman, attended in this scene by six roaming percussionists identified in the libretto as the "six mortal senses," but whose one-man band costumes of assorted metalwork identify them clearly enough as six *tinkers*.

In this scene the musical point (or point of no return) becomes a line, and the line is a flute melody. Here is Henry Brant describing one of several experiments conducted at Bennington College in December 1964, and his impression: "In a room 20 feet by 20 feet and 12 feet high, a flutist walks round the walls, playing continuously. He takes various vertical positions while playing, by means of climbing ladders, standing on tables, and sitting on the floor. . . . *An unmistakable impression of travelling sound and of vertical positions.*"9 In Noh drama, and perhaps everywhere else, the flute signifies breath and continuity, the wind of change, the breath of life, and therefore life itself. The scene is effectively a vigil performed for the soul of the dead at a lying in state, so despite the apparent humor attached to cat suits, and the tradition of witches' cats (which the composer takes very seriously, of course), this scene needs to be enacted in the manner of a ritual, and under lighting and staging conditions appropriate to a religious setting. As a solo recorded performance the piece comes across as a further extended virtuosic exercise in the genre of *Harlekin* and *In Freundschaft* for clarinet. Certainly a piece of this kind seems to be Stockhausen's way of extending a welcome to those for whom he feels a special affection, even if the same pieces do seem to labor the point as solo concert items, in the absence of the dimension of choreographed movement.

The redeeming features, or potential features, of the piece as an opera scene having symbolic meaning, consist in the visual presentation, and especially in the sound distribution, which once again represents a challenge to the recording engineer or sound projectionist. Acoustically, the flute melody flickers like a candle-flame or a willow-the-wisp, and can be envisaged as a disembodied light dancing in the darkness, or on the tomb of an unknown hero. We remember the nineteenth-century dancing flame originally considered for *Alphabet für Liège* as a dramatically effective option, and it is easy to imagine, high in the air, a manometric capsule enclosed in a glass lantern with revolving mirror, in which the flame of a burning gas jet is seen vibrating in response to variations of pressure of the flute melody. Added to that is the element of movement of the soloist in space. In the normal course of events that movement would be executed by the performer and interpreted as a moving melody by the audience in the spirit of Paul Klee's "line going for a walk." Ironically, it is a visualization that demands to be seen in almost total darkness, or under ultraviolet light with small touches of fluorescence to guide the eye. In practice it is not quite so simple. The flute has a radio microphone, its sound goes into a sound distribution system, and is relayed back into the auditorium by speakers to either side, so that the real sound and movement of the flutist is electronically shadowed and panned by a sound projectionist, in a further instance of the paradoxical superposition of realities already noted in "Michaels Reise," except that this time the panning of the flute is intended to follow the flutist rather than move independently.

By way of justifying the scene dramatically, Stockhausen has devised a series of actions involving the flutist demonstrating in order segments of the chant music in front of two discs, to the left and right, upon which notations are reproduced. These discs are described as "mandalas" as though they were religious objects, but in reality these drab and didactic teacher aids are simply clock dials engraved with twelve figures of music instead of the numbers 1 to 12. In apparent reference to motor phonetics *and* Messiaen, the exercises are focused on the three cardinal elements of a waveform: the onset or initial accent (head period), the steady state (heart period), and the termination (tail period). The two dials are yet another allusion to the manifold implications of the name of Luzifer, this time the suffix word *Ziffer* in its meaning of a clock-face. The clocks have no hands, but nevertheless imply that the melody line unfolding in space is also unfolding in time. As if in confirmation, the six percussionists, dressed as one-man percussion bands, but adorned in unconventional and invented noisemaking devices, attend on the flutist with the whirring and clicking of clockwork mechanisms. The six musicians involved in the premiere were given a more or less free hand to come up with weird and magical sound effects, but the results do not sound particularly magical.

When the scene is viewed as a combination of an active agent, the flute (representing a sine sweep frequency oscillator) provoking the passive emission of mysterious metallic noises from a plurality of unseen sources, it becomes evident that Stockhausen's "six mortal senses" began life as the ring modulators of *Mixtur*, which emit metallic resonances provoked and controlled by sine waves; that they were transmuted in *Kurzwellen* into shortwave radio receivers, emitting mysterious and distorted signals as and when "tuned in" by sweep frequency oscillators; reincarnated as musical boxes in the new post-*Mantra* era of melody formulas (miniature caskets containing pure melodies reproduced in metallic tones, to be imitated by living performers), and are now transformed into tin drummers wound up and stirred into a semblance of life by the flute's animating spirit (needless to say, with a bit of *animus* included with the *anima*).

Stockhausen had neither the time nor the facilities to put in place a system to compete with the 4X of Boulez's *Répons*, which was setting a new benchmark, so instead he envisioned a music for flute at least to match, and perhaps exceed, Boulez's goals for clarinet and flute. Hence the manufactured opposition of solo flute and imitation toy instruments, and the eager exploration of unorthodox sounds for the flute, including simultaneous singing and playing to produce combination tones, an effect pioneered by Vinko Globokar, and actually described by Stockhausen as "ring modulation" in relation to the flute music of "Kathinkas Gesang," even though it is nothing of the sort.

These new flute sounds, a gamut of hums, clicks, and whistles culminating in eleven "trombone tones" in the tenor register that one feels ought to sound frightening but do not, are of potential interest to flutists. But they lack the power that makes the rest of the sounds of *Samstag* so compelling, while at the same time appearing to strive after the same awesome and transforming character. On the other hand, the effort required to create these quasi-modulated sounds is not quite able to match the attractively speech-like quality of Michael's trumpet, with its many mutes, and injects an air of restlessness out of keeping with the ideally serene image of a flickering flame.

In May 1983 Stockhausen devised a new version of "Kathinkas Gesang" for flute and electronic music. The electronic music was realized over two weeks at IRCAM in December 1983 and August 1984, with the assistance of Marc Battier. The electronic music consists of a sequence of six eight-channel digital whirlwinds of sound, like the flying saucer sounds of *Sirius*, but raised to a new level of acoustic complexity, and coming to focus in what one instinctively feels should be earth-shattering detonations, but in fact resemble plucked giant bass strings of the piano: a link with the bass sounds of Piano Piece XIII, and beyond that to Wagner's Monsalvat bell sounds from *Parsifal*. Stockhausen had been particularly fascinated by a demonstration by Giuseppe di Guigno, builder of the 4X, of the gradual dissociation of phase relationships of an overtone spectrum corresponding to the output of allegedly more than 700 phase-synchronized tone generators, an incredible number. From the time of *Kontakte* he had been well aware of the practical difficulties of synthesizing sounds that appear to move realistically in space, for precisely the reason that in real space, every partial frequency emitted by a moving sound source is affected to a different degree. The effect is familiar from the sound of a jet aircraft passing overhead, in the changing intensities and dynamic fluctuations audible within the sound. Although it could not deliver coherent rotation, at least the 4X offered a possibility of a rotation-like expansion and contraction effect similar in kind to that created in 1957 by Herbert Eimert and Heinz Schütz in "Zu Ehren von Igor Stravinsky," using techniques of vocoder and tape loops, (and in doing so, reinventing the message of "Kathinkas Gesang" in the childhood image of Dorothy's magical journey by tornado to the colorful world of Oz, there to encounter the formidable visage of the Wizard himself).

In theory the 4X offered 6 "boards" each of 64 programmable oscillators, in total 384, to a maximum sampling rate of 32 kilohertz, meaning an upper limit of 16 kilohertz. Sound generation was controlled by a PDP-11. In order to generate a continuous sequence of spectra, the boards had to be divided into two alternating groups, so that while one board was executing commands from the computer, the other would be loading fresh wave tables. The delay in loading and implementing commands, for operations of such complexity as long as six seconds, proved problematic, a difficulty reflected in Stockhausen's subsequent decision in favor of a hybrid digital/analogue system offering instantaneous access in all parameters.[10] The six spinning tones (on a frequency scale tuned to a 440 hertz, rather than the preferred a

442 hertz of Kathinka's flute) are modeled after frequency and amplitude analyses of existing prerecorded instrumental tones: K1: a piano, lowest c at 32.7 hertz, K2: a cello, lowest c at 65.4 hertz, K3 a bass clarinet, lowest c also 65.4 hertz, K4 a piano, lowest f sharp at 46.3 hertz, K5 a tuba, baritone f sharp at 92.6 hertz, and K6 a piano at the higher octave c 65.4 hertz:

Thus, six notes comprising a tritone, four in c, and two in f sharp, more or less conforming to the four principal tone colors: bowed string, struck string, brass, and woodwind. I suspect that Stockhausen would have preferred to simulate an organ pipe (flute) instead of a cello, and a trombone instead of a tuba, but perhaps he was limited in the choice of samples available. And while he is justifiably pleased with the result, it is likely that the result was not quite what he anticipated, since all six tones end up sounding like the bass strings of an oversized piano.

In a technical paper comparing three leading music processor systems of the early eighties, James Moorer identified some of the problems of the IRCAM 4X (4C) synthesizer at this time.

> Since the machine does no table interpolation, low tones often require enormous tables. Consider the problem of simulating the bottom octave of the piano by placing one period of the waveform into the oscillator table. We should perhaps explain here that the piano does not really exhibit a harmonic waveform, so the concept of a single period is not well defined. . . . Needless to say, it defeats the purpose of having 32 oscillators if we are forced to eat the entire wavetable for one tone, but this was the only way we found to obtain that particular sound. . . . Simulating a tone with 120 partials . . . came from the musical need of a serious composer. This was a limitation that this composer reached in the course of trying to realize his piece.[11]

Scene 3: Luzifers Tanz (Lucifer's Dance)

1983: No. 53 (Stockhausen-Verlag; cds SV-28, SV-57 "Zungenspitzentanz;" SV-35, SV-43 "Oberlippentanz;" SV-59 "Rechte Augenbrauentanz.")

For bass voice, piccolo trumpet, piccolo flute, symphonic band, stilt-dancer, dancer, ballet or mimes; 4 transmitting microphones, 22 microphones, 2 × 2 loudspeakers, mixing console.

Symphonic band: ca. 80 players, in 10 groups: ① 1 percussionist, 3–4 flutes, 3–4 flutes (alto flutes), 3 basset-horns; ② 1 percussionist, 3 clarinets, 3 clarinets, 3 bass clarinets; ③ 1 percussionist, 2 soprano saxophones (sopranino), 2 alto saxophones, 1 tenor saxophone, 1 baritone saxophone, 1 bass saxophone; ④ 1 percussionist, 2–4 oboes, 2–4 English horns, 2–4 bassoons, 1–2 contrabassoons; ⑤ 1 percussionist, 3 trumpets, 3 trumpets, 3 trombones (3. bass trombone); ⑥ 1 percussionist, 3 trumpets, 3 trumpets, 3 trombones (3. bass trombone); ⑦ Solo percussionist; ⑧ 1 percussionist, 2 horns I, 2 horns I, 2 horns II, 2 horns II; ⑨ 1 percussionist, 2 euphoniums I, 2 euphoniums II; ⑩ 1 percussionist, 2 alto trombones, 2 baritones, 4 bass tubas.

Ossia: Symphony orchestra of ca. 59 players; in group ③ strings 6.0.4.2–2.4.
Duration: 50'.

After the dot and the line, now the plane:—this time, the vertical. One of Stockhausen's most outrageously comic creations, "Luzifer's Tanz" is revealed with the parting of curtains as a giant face of instrumentalists, perched on narrow platforms raked almost vertically up the rear wall, towering over the audience. The idea of an animated face is Stockhausen's own, each of ten groups of players representing a mobile part of the face and coming to life in turn, starting on high with the flutes of a twitching left eyebrow, then one by one adding the right eyebrow of clarinets, saxophones as a winking left eye, double reeds as the right eye, and so on down to the tongue and chin.[12] Once again the musical interest of a vertical displacement of performers is argued by Henry Brant, who observes "If the players can be distributed vertically from floor to ceiling, playing simultaneously in an even spread over a substantial part of the area of an entire wall, . . . the entire wall space will seem to be sounding at once, an extremely vivid and concentrated directional effect." Brant illustrates this conception of vertical space with a string orchestra arranged 8.6.6.5 on four tiers.[13]

"Luzifers Tanz" was commissioned for the University of Michigan Symphony Band and its conductor H. Robert Reynolds. From his many visits to the United States, Stockhausen was aware of the high level of commitment and professional discipline of American wind bands, of their public role in major civic and sporting functions, and of their particular skill and inventiveness in combining music with movement in intricate patterns, on parade and in the sports arena. While wind band music conventionally draws on a nineteenth-century repertoire that has very little by way of a message to deliver to contemporary audiences, it provides a vehicle for the expression of a stylized teamwork of astonishing complexity, executed with clockwork precision. In the sports arena, both music and movement act as a foil to the improvised skills of opposing teams, and in combination make a statement expressing the values of teamwork as well as about laying claim to the stadium territory under dispute. So for American audiences, movement and wind bands go together. The telling difference in Stockhausen's design of an animated Luzifer mask, is that here the band's normal freedom of movement on the horizontal plane is reduced to the animated twitching of facial features on the vertical plane. The composer's earlier epigraph to "Luzifers Traum," spoken by Luzifer, speaks of "compression of figures of human music, extensions and pauses leading to the annulment of time." Here the unspoken subtext is annulment of space: restriction of the prisoner to a point where all that is left to move are the facial features, in accordance with the Luziferian imperative to bring all life and movement to a stop.

It is not that the facial expressions on this musical animation have any specific message. All that happens is that one by one the ten groups of instruments come to life until the whole ensemble is a mass of sound and movement. The message is about facial expression (and by extension, expression in general) as physical action driven by an emotional impulse, and distorting the ideal composure of the human face as depicted in classical art, and reinvented in the expressionless demeanors of Pierrot, Harry Langdon, Buster Keaton, and Stan Laurel. The negative associations of facial expression with distortion and emotion are what matters; the same Renaissance aesthetic of Michelangelo and Leonardo that placed the highest value on radiant composure and perfect symmetry, also devised ingenious distortions of the facial grid to account for the less than perfect symmetry of real faces in the real world, and for the distortions of morality they were assumed to reveal. In a word, this is about caricature.

Stockhausen also draws on the conventions of American big band jazz to bring his Luzifer visage to life. It is not just that the groups of players in different locations on the vertical plane come to life and play their music; they also gesture physically, using the conventional big band mannerisms of having momentary soloists or solo sections lean forward, rise, and sway from side to side. That these conventions are rooted in radio, and were devised to bring highlighted musicians closer to the microphone (and thus to give them greater prominence) has long since been forgotten. We just like the gestures, and Stockhausen takes advantage of the convention without assigning them any significance in terms of acoustic balance.

The music is feisty and hugely entertaining, even if it does tend to resemble a monster mechanism gone berserk rather than a choreographed realistic animation. On the one hand it contrives to give the impression of a Bach concerto grosso, but on an industrial scale; the baroque era, and especially Bach, embodies a new approach to modulation, the dynamic of time-keeping, increased density of real part-writing, and pleasure in mechanical intricacy for its own sake. Some of this fascination with cogs and wheels rubs off on Messiaen, of course, in isorythmic pieces like "Liturgie de Cristal" from the *Quartet for the End of Time*, and glimpses of battle pandemonium in the *Turangalîla-Symphonie*. Each group of winds is held together by a percussion timer beating on a clearly distinct metal resonator, a safety measure more successful in both practical and musical senses than the ad hoc percussions of Boulez's *Rituel: in Memoriam Maderna*, another rite of accumulation about death and transfiguration, and one that also involves the coordination of spatially separated groups at different tempi (though on the horizontal plane). The music of "Luzifers Tanz" descends from eyebrow to chin, each feature coming to life in music of a specific pulsation and character, but the process of filling out the musical space is essentially the same, and exciting in the same way, as the "Danse de la Terre" in Stravinsky's *Sacre du Printemps*—an excitement of accumulating complexity, of ever-increasing power, of an approaching tidal wave. Behind the jovial mask of the Wizard of Oz there lurks the more threatening and baleful image of Fritz Lang's Moloch, industrial god of sacrifice in the movie classic *Metropolis*.

In alternate guise as master of ceremonies, Luzifer admonishes the audience "If you have never learned from the distortions of the face that arise from a spirit of rebellion and independence, you cannot turn your faces towards the light." As we have come to expect, the message is simple but ambiguous, at the same time a schoolmasterly warning against the perils of succumbing to emotion, and a barely-disguised invitation to do precisely that,—because of course, the music itself is enormous fun. The only concessions to drama are solo cadenzas for piccolo trumpet and piccolo flute. The "Oberlippentanz" features Michael as trumpeter in lonely protest action against the curling upper lip, in an effort to calm emotions and restore harmony and decorum. It is a brilliant rhetorical solo and a moment of relief from the cascading deluge of sound. Soon afterward, riding on the tip of a suddenly mobile and extending tongue pointing toward the audience, the cat-figure of Kathinka emerges to exacerbate emotions in a brilliant solo clearly intended as a rude gesture, and incorporating the explicit insult "Salve, Satanelli!" (Hey there, children of Satan!), a rerun of the flatulent trumpet in *Trans*, but calculated to give particular offense to listeners of a nervous or religious disposition. (The extended tongue, by the way, can be taken as a knowing allusion to the Rolling Stones logo.)

That both interruptions are scored for solo instruments, is a perception of the individual, good or bad, as an isolated figure standing against the crowd. That both are piccolo instruments emphasizes even more the puny efforts of these two characters, literally "in the face" of the collective might of the symphonic band. Solo editions of these two dances are available on compact disc, but as monologues, like so many of Stockhausen's extended solos, their virtuosic qualities fall a little flat, like performances of soliliquies from *Macbeth* or *Hamlet* in a concert recital by a visiting thespian. Stockhausen's larger pieces, like "Michaels Reise" and "Luzifers Tanz," are certainly capable of standing very successfully on their own, but to make the shorter extracted pieces work as concert items, in the absence of any dramatic or musical backdrop, is no easy task.

In a *coup de théâtre* provoked by an industrial dispute with the choir of *Donnerstag* (though not forgetting earlier encounters with professional musicians' organizations in parts of America), the stage performance of "Luzifers Tanz" ends with a third interruption of an apparent strike: the ultimate indiscipline, one might think, of a face in revolt. Musically little is lost, and perhaps a touch of additional publicity is gained.

Scene 4: Luzifers Abschied (Lucifer's Farewell)

1982: No. 54 (Stockhausen-Verlag)
For men's chorus (13 tenors, 26 basses, all wearing wooden clogs), organ, 7 trombones, tam-tam, birdcage containing a wild raven or black bird, a bag of small coins, a large sack containing 39 coconuts, strong enough to withstand being cast down to the floor from a great height, a large stop-clock, various church bells, low and high in pitch; 26 transmitting microphones, 4 microphones, 5 × 2 loudspeakers, mixing console. 7 basses also play "Good Friday clappers," 6 basses "Mass bells" each of 6 miniature bells.
Duration: 58'.

Anyone who is simply thrilled by the solemn and deliberate pandemonium of Tibetan instrumental ritual will understand what this final scene is about. That it is a work of genius I have no doubt. Stockhausen's triple formula has left him with almost nothing to work with apart from half a dozen pitches, a few pulsations, and rising and falling major third glissandi. Out of this unpromising material he has conjured a rite of purgation and transformation of genuine power and, for once, a work from which all cynical, ironic, or trivial matter has been excluded. As recorded in the highly reverberant acoustic of a church in Cologne, this is a cleansing noise of a richness and penetration that, like its exotic models, is designed both to stun and to temper the spirit. "Luzifers Abschied" looks back to *Trans*, a work also conceived, as we recall, as a rite of passage of the spirits of those about to die; but in place of the static, wide-screen movie ambience of the earlier work, this is a musical maelstrom from which performers and listeners alike emerge squeaky-clean and ready to start over again, like used tapes fresh from the bulk eraser, to appropriate a studio metaphor.

Stockhausen has been accused of cynically forcing each new commission that comes along into the next available serial compartment, and in having considered a setting of the "Hymn to the Virtues," commissioned in celebration of the 800th anniversary of St. Francis, as suitable for the last scene of a work of music theater in honor of Lucifer, of a fatal misjudgement. But that is to ignore who Luzifer (the character) is in the opera and what he stands for in the Stockhausen canon, even before seriously considering the philosophical argument the composer consistently advances in justification of the role and significance of the fallen angel in traditional mythology. Stockhausen may question, and he may tease, but at heart he does not trivialize. Composers of new music have been living with the moral opprobrium of the majority for over a century. The same kind of objection is continually heard against the function of dissonance in the atonal music of a Schoenberg or Bartók. When supposedly intelligent musicians go on record as saying that twelve-tone music is nothing but the transient expression of the troubled psyche of a Europe during a time of conflict, or students of harmony are cautioned against emulating Bach's use of the accented passing note, it shows not only a musically inadequate grasp of the value of transitional dissonance, but an absence of intelligent awareness of the moral implications of dissonance in religious music, or in harmony of any kind. This attitude is frankly stupid. What music could be more harmonious than *Stimmung*? And yet, it is the surface movement, the modulations, the distortions, that give harmony meaning and the music a sense of moral and aesthetic purpose.

For Stockhausen, Luzifer is anything but the devil. He is the embodiment of deliberate disobedience whose destiny is either doom or redemption. For the conclusion of a work of music theater that has already meditated on the end of individual life, the survival of the spirit, and the arrogance of collective might, what could be more appropriate than the prayer of a virtuous sinner in hope of a better world?

Once again, Henry Brant comes to Stockhausen's defense. In the same paper already cited in relation to the perception of linear movement in "Kathinkas Gesang," and of the wall of sound in "Luzifers Tanz," the veteran composer further addresses audience perceptions of sound traveling

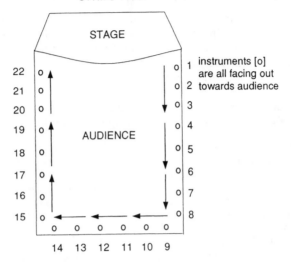

Henry Brant: Diagram illustrating an experiment of sound travelling around and filling space.

and filling up an acoustic space. This involved a line of musicians extending around the first-floor gallery of an auditorium; the musicians do not move, but begin to play one after another in sequence until all are playing.

> When instruments placed in fixed positions begin playing one at a time *accumulating* (staying in) as indicated by the arrows in the diagram above, there is a compelling impression of the hall tangibly *filling up* with sound, principally along the walls. . . . The impression of the sound *travelling* gradually down the first wall is very strong; this impression of moving direction becomes less well defined as the further entrances and accumulations occur.[14]

Brant goes on to discuss the impression of a performer walking through a large hall while playing or singing, an effect he finds inconclusive. His diagram illustrating this portion of the article, in the form first published in the *Bennington Review*, is startlingly similar to Stockhausen's diagram indicating the locations and movements of singers in "Luzifers Abschied."

After dot, line, and plane, this is music expressing space; with the final unfolding of space, time is also redeemed, and Luzifer's spell is finally broken. Once again Stockhausen has created a whirlwind of sound, making noises, which is what he does best. And in order for the audience to be in the middle of the whirlwind, it may be necessary, after "Luzifers Tanz," for listeners to leave the concert hall and move to an adjacent church, ideally with a continuous first-floor gallery, allowing the musicians to move freely around the periphery.

A number of commentators have seized on Stockhausen's account of witnessing the Omizutori (Water Consecration) Festival at the Todei-Ji

Temple in Nara, Japan, in 1966, and a particular episode, the "running moment," as a primary source of inspiration. One mentions the Ozimutori account not only because it is a vivid account of Stockhausen's perception of an exotic ceremonial, but in order to emphasize that "Luzifers Abschied" is not a mere copy but an autonomous invention with its own musical logic. Part of the excitement of the work arises, for this listener at least, from a sense of an originality that, perhaps for the first time, does not reflect unkindly on the cultures to which it pays lip service.

> It lasts for six weeks, with a climactic ceremony which goes on for three days and three nights without a break. Eleven priests take part. It's pure music: every movement, every piece of clothing which (with little discs and rings) can make sounds, every shoe, is a musical instrument. . . . When the running moment began, the priest [wearing clogs] ran around the altar, clock-a-lock, clock-a-lock! He had laurel leaves and when he passed the altar he would throw one and call out and then the second priest would join in. They made this crescendo, with two and then four feet . . . clack-a-lack, clack-a-lack, clack-a-lack! then four, five, six, seven, until all eleven priests were walking one after another irregularly, but in rhythm, and it was an enormous build-up, a crescendo of noise. . . . They would run faster and faster, and it became more and more periodic. . . . And when they reached a certain speed the first one threw one of his shoes against the wooden wall, and they all ran on until twenty-two shoes had been thrown against this wall. You can imagine the transformation from the enormous wooden sound to the slapping sound which they made on the floor with their bare stockings. It was a fantastic musical transition from harsh to soft.[15]

Equally powerful is the majestic noise of Tibetan ritual music, which has gained a devoted following in the United States, and has stimulated considerable interest in the techniques of throat singing, acknowledged here in the deep intonations of bass voices. But here too, Stockhausen introduces his own symbolisms, of the organ pedal point, which reaches back to the Byzantine era of Christian ritual, as well as the seven trombones, representing the forces of disruption.

The association of wooden percussion with the sound of trickling water becoming a torrent is echoed also in the vocal clicks of "Invisible Choirs," again a music of atonement and forgiveness that invokes the cleansing image of water. Here the crescendo of wooden clogs and wooden clappers (little mallets pivoting on handles) reaches a climax in the ceremonial release of the black bird (reciprocating the release of white doves at the end of *Originale* in 1961), and the bursting of coconuts at the entrance to the church, a brilliant stroke of head-breaking into consciousness that combines the crack of wood with a magical release of life-giving water (the coconut milk).

Certainly the music reintroduces Western audiences to the primal therapy of an intensely noisy experience that is both "ear-cleansing" for oral cultures, while at the same time finely judged acoustically so that those listeners who bring a focused consciousness to the event can still identify everything that is happening, despite the appearance of general clamor. In battle, which traditionally is a noisy hand-to-hand affair, maintaining composure is a lifesaving asset. Translating the acoustic image of battle into a ceremonial image of a life under constant seige, gives sensory and aesthetic point to a turbulence far removed from the anodyne serenity of scripture-based Western religion.

The musical score is clearly outlined, and in fact closer to the script of *Originale* than to conventional music. The entire event, to be totally honest, is closer to a radio or movie script than a concert item. Its nonreliance on conventional musical forces may ironically lead to the piece becoming one of Stockhausen's more popular items, since fate itself is a twisty and unpredictable affair. The outwardly neo-Gothick trappings of a rite of exorcism involving hooded monks in white, brown, and black gowns (crusaders, brown-shirts, and black-shirts, perhaps), together with the highly saturated ambience created by this music, certainly coincide with the rise of a cult Gothick popular music idiom, centered on suburban angst garage bands whose rave music cultivates images of demonic power, using distortion of the voice and dangerously intense levels of amplification for the sake of an ongoing adrenaline rush within a mind-altering (and clinically deafening) saturation experience. But there is nothing demonic about "Luzifers Abschied." Whether or not it becomes a repertoire item does not alter the fact that this extraordinary ceremony, ending with the release of a caged black bird into the dawn chorus, is a truly original and dramatic acoustic event that everyone should experience at least once.

Notes

1. J. A. Fuller Maitland, "Richard Strauss." *Grove Dictionary of Music and Musicians* ed. J. A. Fuller Maitland (London: Macmillan, 1911), 717–20.
2. Richard Wagner, *Parsifal.* 1927 recording cond. Karl Muck, reissued on compact disc Naxos Historical 8.110049-50.
3. Henry Brant, *Orbits*. Compact disc CRI CD 827 (1999).
4. For example, *Tibetan Buddhism: The Ritual Orchestra and Chants. Rituals of the Drukpa Kagyu Order.* Recorded by David Lewiston. Compact disc Nonesuch 9 72071-2 (1995).
5. *SoM*, 129–34.
6. Pierre Boulez, *Dialogue de l'ombre double* (1985). Compact disc DG 289 457 605-2 (1998).
7. Pierre Boulez, . . . *explosante-fixe* . . . (1971–1993). Compact disc DG 445 833-2 (1995).
8. Pierre Boulez, *Anthèmes 2* (1997). Compact disc DG 289 463 475-2 (2000).
9. Henry Brant, "Space as an Essential Aspect of Musical Composition." 223–42 in *Contemporary Composers on Contemporary Music* ed. Elliott Schwartz and Barney Childs (New York: Holt, Rinehart and Winston, 1967).
10. "Elektronische Musik zu KATHINKAS GESANG als LUZIFERS REQUIEM." *Texte 6*, 117–36.
11. James Moorer, "Synthesizers I Have Known and Loved." 589–97 in

Music Machine: Selected Readings from Computer Music Journal ed. Curtis Roads (Cambridge, Mass: MIT Press), 1989.

12. A play by Tristan Tzara, *La Coeur à Gaz* (1920), has the characters Eye, Mouth, Nose, Ear, Neck, Eyebrow. That is as far as it goes, though it is interesting to reflect that the ears of Luzifer's face take no part in the musical action.

13. Henry Brant, "Space as an Essential Aspect of Musical Composition," 231.

14. Henry Brant, "Space as an Essential Aspect of Musical Composition," 238.

15. Karlheinz Stockhausen, "Ceremonial Japan." *Times Literary Supplement* (1974): 1189–90.

CHAPTER TWENTY-FIVE

Montag

After *Samstag* and death (or oblivion), *Montag* and birth. Lots of birth. In this pastoral masque of Eve's day, women are honored, if that is the word, as human queen bees and cheerful worker bees, biological machines dedicated to the indiscriminate overproduction and nurturing of new members of the human tribe (sometimes not so human). The opera "is characterized principally by female voices. They have to be clear as well as high in range. . . . Also electric organs." Actually that prescription refers to the D-moments of *Momente*, an earlier celebration of "Mother Earth surrounded by her chickens." The dominant colors are luminous green and mother-of-pearl; the dominant imagery, of abundance, living creation, and the biological urge, rather awkwardly expressed, and infused with a certain fey eroticism. After the deep bass (i.e., base) musical emphasis of Luzifer's day, the tessitura of *Montag* is predominantly female and children's voices, considerably more elevated in register, richly harmonious, and inconstantly undulating, in smoothly articulated microtonal sweeps and glissandi, like the sea that forms part of the backdrop to the musical action. These transitional elements are the accent feature of the opera, a notational challenge calculated to provide the music of *Montag* with a distinctive vocabulary. The high prominence given to gliding tones also accounts for Stockhausen's replacement of the Hammond and Lowrey organs of *Momente* by programmable synthesizers, new keyboard instruments able to perform the gliding tones and harmonies that are so prominent a feature of the Eva formula. Synthesizers of the mid-eighties are a definite impoverishment in sonority, but at least they can handle glissandi.

Stockhausen's characterizations of the Michael, Eva, and Luzifer formulae are so intrusive, once they have been pointed out, that it seems a little sadistic to draw attention to them. Michael's is the heroic melody of rising and falling fourths, like a bugle call, and Luzifer's rhythmically distinctive, with staccato eleventuplets (and counting). Compared to them, the Eva melody is somewhat more interesting and "authentic," combining elements of temporal and positional uncertainty (ornamental figurations), with continuously rising and falling inflections, musical elements that have no "stable state" and thus no definable location in time or pitch space, other than vaguely within certain limits.

Transitional diphthongs and inflections are the paradoxical elements of spoken language that confounded the postwar denizens of visible and synthetic speech, including Werner Meyer-Eppler and the team from Bell Labs who devised the original vocoder.[1] The weight of significance still attached to continuous transitions in electronic music is reflected in the priority assigned by Boulez to research and development of interpolation software at the start of IRCAM in 1977, and the perhaps disproportionate importance associated thereafter to works that exhibit it: for example, Jonathan Harvey's *Mortuos Plango* and its transformation of a boy's singing voice into the sound of a bell.

Since according to this rather primitive "semeiological" approach (still reflecting, even at this late date, the linguistics of de Saussure), a "timbre" is defined as a momentary sample of a dynamically evolving harmonic spectrum, the difference between timbres is reduced to differences of amplitude relations between corresponding harmonics, and the interpolation process converting one "timbre" into another, into a transition between amplitude envelopes, a piece of mechanical sleight of hand that has to do neither with the physical nature of the instrument, nor with the natural dynamics of instrumental performance. So while it is tempting to interpret Stockhausen's interest in notating glissandi as simply a byproduct of a personal and limited serial exercise, the reality is that the challenge posed by the *LICHT* triple formula embraces an entire theory of articulate sounds and their interpretation that dates back to the composer's studies of information theory in the fifties, and in particular, to a problem area at that very time under active investigation by the software designers of the Souterrain du Centre Pompidou.[2]

It is nonetheless true that the cry or wail, as a unit of vocal expression, is a feature transcending language and arguably even species. Glissandi are the connective tissue of speech and a subtle and powerful indicator of meaning; inflected vowels in themselves are also musical emblems of transition, of uncertainty, and of suffering. Gliding tones express that range of sensations that literate (male-dominated) societies throughout the centuries have done their best to deny and suppress; needless to say, they are a consistent feature of female music, from the songs of the courtesans of ancient Greece, via the sacred love songs of Hildegard, to the wailing women at a funeral,—a music, in other words, that is originally therapeutic in purpose. Such unstable forms of expression are also not in accord with the basic conventions of classical music notation, which is founded on discrete pitches and quantities, and ill-adapted to cope with the moving target of human emotion.

Stockhausen conducts Haydn and Mozart
1985–1986: Cadenzas by Stockhausen. (Stockhausen-Verlag; cd SV-39)

In 1985 and 1986 Stockhausen took time out to record the concertos for clarinet in a major KV 622, and for flute in g major KV 313 by Mozart, and also the trumpet concerto in e flat major by Haydn, with Suzee Stephens, Kathinka Pasveer, and Markus Stockhausen respectively as soloists, and the composer himself conducting the Berlin Radio Symphony Orchestra. While of interest to the specialist for the sake of the cadenzas specially composed for the recordings, these interpretations deserve wider recognition on their own terms, not only for the understated eloquence of the solo performances, and their balance and grace as ensemble recordings, but for the insights they offer into the characters of clarinet, trumpet, and flute in *LICHT*, and into the roots of the triple formula in classical music. Clarity, contrast, and the long line are especially noteworthy. Says Stockhausen, "For the musicians the most unusual aspect of my interpretation was 'singing' the music in such a way as not to allow any section of a movement, passage, or single phrase to drop at the end, but rather to maintain the musical flow over the breaks, . . . to hold all the final notes before pauses for their full value, playing them neither softly nor with a diminuendo . . . [steering] each long musical period towards one particular note."

Among many beautiful features of the clarinet concerto, the carefully managed relationship of detached and legato lines, between the clarinet and violins, is a particular delight; a first movement cadenza draws attention to the scale passages that connect this work with the basset-horns of *Montag aus LICHT*, whereas the cadenza to a delicately nuanced and wonderfully poised slow movement is reduced to an austerely intervallic statement that manages not only to express a spiritual kinship with the idiom of *In Freundschaft*, but also to hint at an emotional distance that seems actually very poignant. The trumpet themes of the equally familiar Haydn concerto are suddenly perceived as prefiguring the Michael formula; a new second movement cadenza conveying military overtones, and the third movement attracting the longest and most elaborate cadenza of all three, very angular, accretive, and inspiring. Kathinka Pasveer's intensely focused interpretation of the flute concerto brings out the same detail of interval and attack modes as in "Kathinkas Gesang," while with wonderful transparency, Stockhausen as conductor reveals the complexity of rhythm and counterpoint in Mozart's orchestration, and the operatic relationship of solo and orchestra, in which the orchestra appears as the motivating agent, and the solo flute the active spirit. An austerely beautiful first movement cadenza opens a window into the musical world of *LICHT*, but assembled out of the Mozartean features Stockhausen admires. In a slow movement of gracefully managed transitions one hears as though for the first time that the flute is on a different temporal plane from the orchestra, while the demurely measured final movement rondo hints at the Pied Piper ending of *Montag* itself.

Montag aus LICHT (Monday from LIGHT)

1984–1988: No. 55–59 (Stockhausen-Verlag; cd SV-36)

Opera in three Acts for 3 soprano, 3 tenors, bass, choir, children's choir (7 treble, 7 alto voices); flute, 3 basset-horns, "modern orchestra" (trombone, percussionist, piano, 3 synthesizers).
Duration: 4 hours 38'.

Montags-Gruss (Monday Greeting)

1986–1988: No. 55 (Stockhausen-Verlag)

For multiple (or prerecorded) basset-horn(s) and electronic keyboard instruments; 8-track tape recorder, 4 or 5 loudspeakers, mixing console.
Alternative title: "Eva-Gruss" (Eve's Greeting)
Duration 34'.

Xi (Chi)

1986: from No. 55 (Stockhausen-Verlag; cd SV-28 for flute; SV-32 for basset-horn)

For melody instrument with microtones; 1 transmitting microphone, 2 × 2 loudspeakers, mixing console.
Duration: 6'.

The audience is drawn in to the sound of slow-motion foyer music performed by a quartet of basset-horns and synthesizers. The effect of submersion under water the music is intended to evoke is conventionally associated with the hollow timbre of the clarinet low register, but this very demanding study in waxing and waning sonorities places exceptional strains on the performers and for practical reasons is best prerecorded. The first and most celebrated example of an extended clarinet glissando in classical music was of course Paul Whiteman's sensational introduction to George Gershwin's *Rhapsody in Blue* of 1924. In contrast to the rich timbre of sirens in Varèse's more strident *Hyperprism*, composed in 1923, the clarinet two-octave glissando, achieved with a special jazz mouthpiece, is laid back and relaxed in tone. In a similar fashion the basset-horn glissandi of "Montags-Gruss" intend a hollow, cavernous timbre far removed from the petulant sneers of the trombones of "Samstags-Gruss," and different again from the textured tremolo glissandi of the "Helikopter-Streichquartett" yet to come. Having said that, the microtonal shifts that make up the basset-horn sweeps of harmony from low to high,—including quasi-tonal formations and near-parallel octaves,—are nevertheless audible as discrete pitches, albeit very close together. One is vividly reminded of the 16th-tone piano music of Julián Carrillo, and the interminable length of time it used to take for a soloist to descend an octave. For Stockhausen's part, however, interminability is a virtue, the slow pace of change drawing a listener's attention to every shift in pitch, however minute, and its distinct effect on an ongoing four-part harmony, especially when the progress of that harmony has unexpectedly tonal implications. To a critical listener, "Montags-Gruss" seems to incorporate occasional tiny elements of stress, squeaks and clicks, apparent glitches possibly to be heard as reminders of the living presence of the performer, though some, in what might be seen as an astute move on the composer's part, could also correspond to elements of the formula, disguised as performer errors.

The entrance music's relative absence of content, since its major challenge is of reproducing in real time the impression of a hugely distended tape recording, is arguably consistent with its function as background music in the sense originally conceived for the multiple orchestral groups of *Fresco*. The technical challenges of breathing and fingering on such a slow timescale are nevertheless valuable, though from a practical point of view the special fingerings required to obtain these fine divisions of a semitone do vary from instrument to instrument, and thus cannot be standardized. The effort is well repaid in the case of "Xi," the six-minute concert solo derived from "Montags-Gruss" and available in editions for solo basset-horn or flute. In this piece the slowing-down effect and exactly controlled inflections give rise to a music of a very feminine and transcendent serenity, to which the flute's superior ability to inflect a sustained tone adds a further touch of eloquence.

Act I: Evas Erstgeburt (Eve's First Birth-giving)

1987: No. 56 (Stockhausen-Verlag; cd SV-28 "Flautina," SV-37 "Geburtsfest," SV-38 "Geburtsarien," SV-63 "Luzifers Zorn")
For 3 sopranos, 3 tenors, bass, actor, choir, children's choir, 3 synthesizer players, percussionist; 16 transmitting microphones, 8 microphones, 8-track tape recorder, 12 loudspeakers, mixing console.
Duration: 1 hour 33'.

Terms like "tedium" and "soporific" are conventional journalistic responses to the contemplative framework of much of *LICHT* and the music's frequent recourse to serially-determined pedal points. An attitude to musical structure in which the time frame precedes the musical and dramatic content that has to be invented to fill it, is self-evidently out of kilter with classical stage conventions in which the timescale is governed by the actions and situations of the drama. On the other hand, the drama as a waiting game, controlled by the movement of the moon or stars, is a feature of more ancient rituals, as well as an increasing experience of a contemporary life of constant travel, of driving along endless turnpikes, and waiting at airports. After living with this music for some time, a listener adjusts to Stockhausen's timescale, which while on a par with the operas of certain highly bankable American minimalist composers, arguably offers considerably greater riches in imaginative content. Indeed, for any mother in the audience, the mere half hour of "In Hoffnung," which is about waiting nine months to give birth, must seem to go by very fast, especially when accompanied by amusing Meliès-like projected images flying across the sky. Waiting is a story in itself. It stills the mind. In this case, it sharpens perceptions. After the sacred turbulence of "Luzifers Abschied," it comes as a blessed (and timely) relief.

Stockhausen's text material for *Montag* returns to that primal syllabic plasma of which he is undoubtedly a master. In an ideal performance or recording, one in which, as the composer says, it is possible "to shut off the visual experience and return to a new kind of radio experience,"[3] the listener should feel as if in the center of a crowd, aware of the texture of a mass of conversation going on, but able to focus only on fragments at a time, that even when clearly audible, are only imperfectly understood. In one sense Stockhausen's choruses are a very literal interpretation of the random images and thoughts that crowd within the mind of a poet or dreamer. Compared to music, said the poet Paul Valéry, having to communicate through words is a terrible limitation on the creative process, since an image caught in words is immediately snared by sense and grammatical rules: "In no way does [poetic] language act, like sound, upon a single sense, the sense of hearing, which is, more than any other, the sense of anti-cipation and attention. On the contrary, it forms a mixture of perfectly incoherent sensory and mental stimuli."[4]

Unusual though it may seem to operagoers long accustomed to verbal messages delivered with exaggerated simplicity and inflection, Stockhau-sen's treatment of speech textures has a legitimate aesthetic as well as intellectual basis in symbolist and surrealist poetry. It also deserves to be interpreted effectively in a theatrical context. The microphone's absence of discrimination when placed in a complex acoustic environment,—the fact that it does not understand the "cocktail effect,"—makes it ideal for repro-ducing confused states of mind, or indeed dreams. Indeed, reproducing the hallucinatory nature of reality is part of the composer's reasoning behind the version of John Cage's *Variations IV* commemorated on vinyl recording.[5] While the image content of *Variations IV* is considerably more varied than the fragmented vocables of Stockhausen's simultaneous choruses, the goal in each case is to generate a trancelike experience in accordance with well-established radio and sound effects techniques. As an attractive and distant cloud of sound, Stockhausen's female choruses in *Montag aus LICHT* cap-ture that sense of a dreamlike event very well, except that at the kinds of distances experienced in an opera-house presentation, one is forced to rely on the programme booklet to know what texts are actually being sung, and since the texts are largely abstract, being able to read them in cold print is not much help. For much of the time the syllabic material is woven into textured noises that are meant to be listened to "in the round"; even the solo soprano text streams are meant to incorporate frequent changes of persona and voice style in imitation of tape montage, though they are not always so interpreted in the recording.

As for "Luzifers Traum" in *Samstag*, a more specific problem that arises is of reproducing the stream-of-consciousness of a play of inner voices within the large-scale ambience of an opera house. That function is normally assigned to a chorus, but to work effectively in a concert environment of opera-house size and complexity requires some of the tricks of radio drama, such as selective amplification and reverberation. The same objective of enhancing discrimination of multiple events in a monophonic acoustic space had been addressed by Werner Meyer-Eppler in an important early paper

on selective reverberation.[6] One reason why "Luzifers Abschied" is so powerful an experience is that an excessively reverberant environment isolates
and sustains accentual features while blending together everything else. To
achieve a similar effect in an opera-house acoustic, on the other hand, it
might conceivably be necessary to distribute a number of spot microphones
over the stage area specifically to intercept and amplify glimpses of text as
random highlights, contextual clues encountered in passing.

But Stockhausen is also determined to pursue a theoretical model of
childlike or "sing-song" speech, both as a more primitive form of human
utterance, and as a genetic birthright with which human beings are already
programmed (Noam Chomsky's "Deep Throat"—or is it, "Deep Structure"
doctrine). Not simply the idea that baby talk is a protolanguage or a metalanguage, but that somehow embedded in the meaningless babble of small
children and their nursery rhymes and games, is a grammatical (read:
serial) deep structure common to all languages and cultures, the meaning of
which humanity has either forgotten or never discerned. Through playing
with language, Stockhausen aims to release this layer of meaning, as
Heissenbüttel and others sought to release it, from the doomed specifics of
literal definition, and restore the sensuous delight in verbal consciousness
that is historically the dimension of lyric speech closest to music.

Another striking departure from reality, which this time one cannot
wholly blame on overexposure to radio at an impressionable age, is the
composer's unlikely aversion to representing actual pain and suffering. For
an artist of such moral determination it is a curiously scrupulous exclusion:
in *Donnerstag*, absence of the spiritual sufferings of the parents, and of the
physical pain of the Crucifixion; the numbness of "Luzifers Traum" in *Samstag*; and in *Montag* the avoidance,—it surely cannot be ignorance,—of any
physical suggestion of discomfort associated with childbirth (entailed by
having a statue give birth rather than a live human being). Despite bearing
twenty-one offspring during the course of the opera, the Eva statue never
once looks pregnant. To be fair, aversion to the representation of pain may
have something to do with the composer's having studied philosophy at a
time when the very existence of pain was seriously disputed: in Great
Britain in 1950, for example, by the distinguished zoologist and BBC Reith
Lecturer Professor J. Z. Young,[7] and again as late as 1984, by philosopher
and BBC Reith Lecturer Professor John Searle.[8] Since human existence is
normally predicated on suffering, and, more to the point, since the message
of human survival, in myth, poetry, and drama, is also predicated on overcoming both the reality, and also the threat of suffering, a scenario based on
a pain-free existence has to be a prescription either for farce, or for the
purgatory of situation comedy (which in fact is a great deal worse).

Stockhausen's centerpiece of *Montag* is a giant translucent female form,
a vast empty shell sculpted as though by Jacob Epstein out of Niki de
Sainte-Phalle. As we recall from his remonstrations with Michael, Luzifer is
against incarnation on principle. Nevertheless, a female playhouse is what
it is, an inert magic mountain of fecundity, an object again of many doors,
for which producing children is as painless and instant an operation as

shelling peas. "Montag is Christmas," says the composer with inspired lack of tact:

> Eve gives birth to new beings, initially in a rather modern, distasteful form, with a 'pop-star' conception of birth, a giant papier-mâché woman with her legs apart, through which babies pop out. That is the sort of image one sees nowadays in exhibitions—one can walk around in such female bodies (a modern conception of birth offering a number of options of play). But then later on everything has to start over again from the beginning, because even Luzifer is incensed at this vulgar form.[9]

Anointing a statue the size of a small hill as a rite of spring, while a developing moon-embryo glows overhead in the manner of Stanley Kubrick's apotheosis to the movie *2001*, and then to have the statue appear actually to give birth to the comforting noises of a team of excitable midwives, is the arresting fantasy of "In Hoffnung." Though only a single developing embryo is visible in the heavens, the *accouchement* leads to a rapid sequence of multiple births, each birth improbably preceded by its own "breaking of the waters," a poetic device to emphasize the association of water and womankind. In a scene evocative of the dreamlike montages of Max Ernst, the "Heinzelmännchen" born in this first round of multiple births are seven dwarfs, to be followed by seven chimeras, little monsters with animal heads. This first sequence of births is evidently a false start; in one of a number of fastidious omissions from the printed libretto (quite possibly a direct quote of Vinko Globokar from another context) the trombonist representing Luzifer calls out "Abortion! Get rid of it!"

While the layered vocal and choral glissandi of this opening scene are musically innovative and quite magical, and other passages are beautiful in the same way as passages of *Momente*, from early on the dramatic impulse essential to opera appears needlessly formulaic, despite the promising potential of a relatively large cast and some inspired visual inventions. There are just too many sevenfold rituals, too many repetitive processes, too many routines such as the speeding-up and slowing-down roundelays after the model of *"Atmen gibt das Leben . . ."*—in fact, altogether too many cyclical patterns that seem designed merely as padding or for reasons of number symbolism. Children's games are cyclical too, which is part of the idea, but the adult world,—the real world of giving birth, of feeding, of learning, and cultivation in general,—is infinitely more varied, structurally and morally, so that after a while the empty formality of taking turns begins to wear thin. It is simply not good enough to have the midwives in attendance repeatedly reacting to the birth of chimeras with *estarrt* expressions. Taken to excess, stunned reactions become a pathological symptom of passive disbelief and inability to act. A stunned reaction does not make an event wondrous by default: it just exemplifies collective unconsciousness. Once is enough. To be stunned more than once is unnatural.

As Rudolf Frisius perceptively notes, in a further concession to radio, Stockhausen incorporates prerecorded animal and other sound effects into the musical tapestry: breaking glass, a roller-coaster, a muffled explosion, a squeaking pig, a neighing horse, and so on. These sound elements appear out of an acoustic no man's land that bears no relation to the acoustical scale of the stage action, the music, or even the amplified musical continuum. Not all are appropriate: a screeching Australian parakeet does not emit the same sound as a pet budgerigar, for example, and while consistent with casting an adult tenor as the boy Michael, to juxtapose the birth of a boy centaur with the neighing of an adult horse is simply confusing. For so experienced a parent not to distinguish appropriate from inappropriate developmental and emotional signs in the prerecorded sounds of human babies crying, cooing, sneezing, and making other noises, has the effect of compounding the embarrassment of matching ritualized actions with ill-chosen realistic effects.

"Bastards before angels" is soprano 3's cheerful comment on the first round of births, though these child-dwarfs appear unusually well-behaved. The vocal textures become more brittle toward the end of the first Birth Aria; a second birthing and Birth Aria begin with a burst of applause, *Sirius*-like metallic electronic sounds, and the less than complimentary associated farmyard noises of a chicken, a cow, and a goose. Three sailors (three tenors, three wise men) row in across the water bearing provisions, their rhythmic staccato voices contrasting pleasantly with the women's legato *Momente*-like harmonies. Their withdrawal is cue for the "Knabengeschrei" (Hullaballoo) in which the children simulate crying to the accompaniment of sound effects including a young infant fretting. A cow's udder appears in the sky to the sound of a cow mooing. These women attendants are evidently not wet nurses; nevertheless, they plant bottles of milk rather than pacifiers in the children's mouths, and then deposit them in two sets of seven prams. This is the cue for a new rotational movement by massed prams, entitled "Baby Buggy Boogie,"—the title incidentally of a song by Spike Jones and his City Slickers, leading one to wonder whether the same composer's wartime hit "Der Führer's Face" was as familiar to clandestine listeners to American Forces Radio in the latter days of the war. The point is of more than academic interest given the fact that the pram dance gone haywire is based on actual movie propaganda footage of singing nurses and perambulators on parade, urging German womanhood to do her patriotic duty and produce new children for the fatherland.

The long acceleration of formation pram-driving is briefly interrupted by the first of two audio clips from the war that are calculated to freeze the smiles on a German audience's face. It is a muffled but clearly genuine archive recording of the music to introduce a *Sondermeldung* or special news announcement on the radio, greeted with sound effects of an aviary, and an attempt by a child-budgerigar to whistle "La Marseillaise." Seemingly unable to respond in any other way, the women and their prams continue to rotate faster and faster, until the abrasive scream of an otter and anachronistic whine of a chain saw provoke the sound of a massive tree crashing to the ground. This marks the start of "Luzifers Zorn" (Lucifer's Scorn) and the appearance of Luzifer in the persona of a double-bodied

gremlin, joined together in a black amoeba-like costume, and simultaneously singing and cackling, a genuinely inspired invention that manages to
convey the verbal aggression as well as the humor of the dadaist protest
poets Raoul Hausmann and Richard Huelsenbeck, during which the singing
voice of Luzifer intones a canticle in praise of the letters of the alphabet.
During this latter recitation the voice of the Führer is heard again, assuring
his people of imminent victory, a genuinely awesome moment immediately
(and unjustly) trivialized by the sound effect of a toilet flushing, yet another
curious moment of squeamishness in the face of a history the composer feels
compelled to acknowledge.

Somehow the protest of Luzipolyp becomes an excuse for the Great
Weeping ("Das Grosse Geweine"), the symbolism of which involves yet
another manifestation of water, women, and stress. In this scene the
recorded mix is closer than ever to radio drama. By now the longwindedness
of the actions has become less of an issue than the apparently improvised
choice and assembly of sound effects. While the live singers are made to
imitate tape syllabification effects without always realizing what they are
doing (which is one degree of separation), many of the sound effects chosen
neither accord with the visual actions nor with their scale, let alone the
stage acoustic (at least three degrees of separation). They are simply stuck
on like decals, without even the attention to matching of Max Ernst's collage
engravings of strange bird-headed men (in *Une semaine de bonté*), or
Salvador Dalí's composite image of the child actress's head on the body of a
lion in the 1939 *Shirley Temple, the Youngest Sacred Monster of Contemporary Cinema*. Hybrid figures of this kind are part and parcel of Western
art history, a pictorial imagery of strange and rude noises depicted (often as
aides-mémoire) in the margins of illuminated bibles, right down to the
gremlins of Hieronymus Bosch and Martin de Vos in the late sixteenth
century. A deliberate looseness in montage is perfectly defensible aesthetically, if that is what the composer wants; however, the more abstracted they
become, the more sound effects take on the symbolism of names for actions
rather than the reality of the actions themselves.

Act II: Evas Zweitgeburt (Eve's Second Birth-giving)

1984–1987: No. 57 (Stockhausen-Verlag; cd SV-38, SV-63 "Die Sieben Lieder der Tage,"
version for basset-horn SV-32 "Wochenkreis")
For 7 solo boy singers, female voice, girls' choir, choir, 3 basset-horns, piano, 3 synthesizer players, percussionist; 12 transmitting microphones, 16 microphones, 8-track tape
recorder, 8 or 12 loudspeakers, mixing console.
Duration: 1 hour 06'.

Klavierstück XIV (Piano Piece XIV)

1984: from No. 57 (Stockhausen-Verlag)
Piano solo; 1 transmitting microphone, 2 microphones, 2 × 2 loudspeakers, mixing
console.
Duration: 6'.

"Dear audience, make babies!" beseeches the Stout Lady in the final Act of Poulenc's *Les Mamelles de Tirésias*. The words are Apollinaire's, and the message is one of population regeneration after the 1914–1918 war. Act II of *Montag* is more of the same, but the message is of having the right kind of babies. The sea is frozen. Briefly the lights go out: another intrusion from real life. In an action recalling the new carnival introduction to the 1972 version of *Momente*, though more demure in tone, two lines of young girls bearing candles and dressed rather prettily as lilies, perhaps more modestly than the composer had originally envisaged, process through the audience toward the stage, singing a charming round. Once again a sevenfold ceremony substitutes for dramatic necessity as the adolescent singers (evidently physically and emotionally more developed than the small boys of Act I) gather round the Eva statue and ask for another round of children, and preferably beings of higher musical intelligence. By this time an observer is beginning to wonder whether the libretto's almost total reliance on ceremony to get ahead is a personal tic, a cultural trait, or a barely concealed reminder of how things used to be done in the good old days. And for once the undisguised eugenic message of the libretto prays for the improvement of the human race from its animal origins; please may we have "healthier, more beautiful, more musical human beings." Either intelligence is implicit, or not an option. It leaves a sour taste in the mouth.

Then, in a grotesque change of tone, the Eva-statue weirdly becomes the object of playful insemination by piano, an action on the surface about as poetic as conjugating cattle. The pianist entrusted in the recording with this symbolic act of musical procreation is Pierre Laurent Aimard, dressed as a budgerigar, a pianist whose name, the reader is astonished to learn in a footnote, coincidentally means *lover* in French.[10] Reassuringly, an upright piano is not required, and while the Freudian undertones (*Flügel*, bird, flight, wet dreams) are best left to the attentions of a future Adorno, others may regard this comic interlude as a missed opportunity to introduce, as it were, a conch-pink mother-of-pearl piano with candelabras and accompanying pianist in a Liberace outfit. In redefining the piano as a Freudian fetishistic object of manufactured rigidity after the style of Dalí (*Un Chien Andalou, Evocation of Lenin, Necrophilic Spring*) Stockhausen may intend to associate the instrument with the tyranny of the past while ignoring an equally strong (and contemptuous) bourgeois perception of the grand piano as a symbol of a despised class system. Later in the opera he extends the same treatment to the basset-horn, which becomes a flower-vase, while needless to say the symbolism of the flute comes ready-made in the story of the Pied Piper.

What the opera needs at this stage is a genuine infusion of life; one prays for the fertility of a Piano Piece VI, the energy of Piano Piece X, even (for heaven's sakes) the hammer-strokes of a Piano Piece IX. Instead the mountain receives the mouse of Piano Piece XIV. This after all is a scene inversely related, in time and imagery, to the *Gesang der Jünglinge* of Stockhausen's twenties, a work coinciding with his first experiences of fatherhood, and also a radiophonic ritual based on the authentic scriptural mystery of the survival of three young men cast into Nebuchadnezzar's fiery furnace, which on another level is about the pure ore surviving the smelter, and on yet another level about the pure in heart surviving the morally destructive consequences of sex. In the apocryphal text of *Gesang* the song of praise is to the Lord of fire and ice; in this scene fire and ice are literally present, and the womb of the ice mountain literally glows red. At the heart of the mystery of the survival of virtue, in the earlier case, is the reciprocal mystery of existence itself, a mystery that to the composer's way of thinking ultimately has nothing to do with the animal act of procreation.

"Wiedergeburt" would ordinarily mean "born again" in the sense of a religious conversion, rather than a second round of production-line births in the sense forecast by Aldous Huxley in *Brave New World*, which is what actually happens. This time the birthing is instant, and according to plan: seven boys dressed in seven colors, one for each day of the week. The transitional harmonies in this section are interesting: in fact the composer's freer use of microtones and microtonally altered scales and melodies is altogether more inventive than previously. A ceremonial melting and distilling of ice in glass retorts takes place while "Coeur de Basset," a Suzee Stephens persona (initially wearing a Rhine-maiden's blonde wig, which to her credit she later refused to wear) oversees the *Sirius*-style introductions of the seven newborns, who are magically capable of walking and singing.[11] The seven songs of "Wochenkreis" are gratefully composed and charmingly sung, their lyrics strings of nouns and gerunds like entries in an agency file, defining the characteristics of the seven days rather than the children, who are little more than ciphers assigned to them. During the singing, sound effects are heard: at the start of the Thursday song, for example, the bark of a sea lion (no doubt a marine version of Leo), and at the Sunday prelude, a *Hymnen*-like insertion of the composer's own voice from the control room announcing "Take seven." The song cycle ends to synthesizer arpeggios of a particularly cheap and nasty timbre, an intimation of the awful consequences of abandoning more conventional instruments in favor of nonrenewable electronic keyboards that, compared to the handcrafted tape sounds of the pre-Synthi era, sound not only anemic but permanently out of date.

Act II winds down to a conclusion with a multifaceted reenactment of the "Mondeva" seduction of the boy Michael in *Donnerstag aus LICHT*. That the action itself may be modeled on traditional adolescent initiation rites of tribal cultures does not entirely resolve issues of taste and propriety that arise when grown women, garishly costumed as *Mahagonny*-era hookers, playing instruments associated with Masonic ritual in Mozart and Haydn's time, are made to go through the motions of seducing small boys under the age of consent, while inside the Eva statue, transparent images of nude women also appear. Once again the composer's superego intervenes to suppress all amorous dialogue from the published libretto, except for the darkly significant remark "Turn off the LIGHT!" The dramatic point of the scene, once again, is to characterize women as skillful sexual predators and mercenaries; the effect, needless to say, is strangely repellent.

Act III: Evas Zauber (Eve's Magic)

1984–1985: No. 58½ (Stockhausen-Verlag; cd SV-32 "Evas Spiegel," "Susani," SV-35 "Ave," SV-57 "Entführung," SV-63 "Der Kinderfänger")
For basset-horn, alto flute (piccolo), choir, children's choir, 3 synthesizer players, percussionist, tape; 12 transmitting microphones, 8 microphones, 8-track tape recorder, 8 or 12 loudspeakers, mixing console.
Duration: 57'.

Montags-Abschied (Monday Farewell)

1986–1988: No. 59 (Stockhausen-Verlag)
For piccolo flute, tape (multiple soprano voice, electronic keyboard instruments); 8-track tape recorder, 7 or 4 loudspeakers, mixing console.
Alternative title: "Eva-Abschied" (Eve's Farewell).
Duration: 28'.

Ypsilon (Upsilon)

1989: from No. 59 (Stockhausen-Verlag; cd SV-28, SV-32 version for basset-horn)
For melody instrument with microtones; 1 transmitting microphone, 2 × 2 loudspeakers, mixing console.
Duration: 9'.

Act III contains some of the most attractive music in the opera, the action tending ever more to resemble a Grimm fairytale version of Jean Cocteau's *Parade* (to music by Satie with sound effects). It is helpful to bear in mind that the stage actions are selected to coincide with the musical processes, and that they have an ulterior purpose as a sign language by which future civilizations or alien visitors may be able to interpret the composer's musical terms of reference. "Evas Spiegel" for example is about a melody and its mirror image, dramatized with the rhyme of the wicked queen from the story of Snow White, "Mirror, mirror, on the wall," to the somewhat lugubrious accompaniment of a male voice choir. This and what follows could be read as a story of rivalry between the basset-horn Eva and her flutist mirror image Ave, a new arrival announced in the manner of a singing telegram as a "wonderful, tender, exciting Musikus with magic powers." Before the meeting, in a brilliant solo piece, "Susani," Eva displays her musical charms before the male singers, who sing her praises in a kind of listless unison plainchant. At least their voices have broken. The text is a poetic description of the function of the Eva-melody in the *LICHT* triple formula: "You gather together the limbs of the formula and divide them anew." In "Ave" Eva is joined by the flute mirror image in yet another set of seven canticles on the theme of the days of the week, the lyrics of which list the emotional characters and colors associated with each day. The disparity in tempo between solo instruments and choir recalls "Die Nachtigall," the first of the 1950 unaccompanied *Chöre für Doris*. But the musical invention is consistently interesting, with wonderful textures and effects, helped along by less strident dynamics. Once again Stockhausen embraces a microtonal idiom of inflected harmonies that teeters on the brink of tonality but does not strike the ear as out of tune, as is sometimes the case (for example, with the string quartets of Alois Hába). A lot of thought has gone into devising an idiom that allows for the meaningful incorporation of precisely judged fractions of a semitone; here the sustained underlying harmonies of the synthesizers come into their own as reference pitches, and the adoption of a quasi-unison for the men's voices not only gives their singing a suitably petitionary air, but also recreates the contrived awkwardness of intonation that is a pleasant feature of natural singers, a modern counterpart perhaps of the "realistic" unpolished voices of a Lotte Lenya or a Marlene Dietrich of Weimar era cabaret. (Fortuitously, Kathinka Pasveer's singing voice is another good example of a nonoperatic, plain singing voice able to draw on natural subtleties of expression.)

Altogether the mood of this sequence, temperamentally, vocally, and instrumentally, is strangely baroque, even the synthesizer sounding like a harpsichord. In part it arises from a polyphony of scale passages that inevitably gravitates toward the chromatic progression of the Pachelbel canon, but it is noteworthy that the techniques and timbres of voices and instruments best adapted to fine intonation should also correspond so evidently to the textures and sounds associated with the "authentic" early music movement. "Ave" ends gracefully in a manner very similar to the earlier trumpet and basset-horn duo in "Michaels Reise" from *Donnerstag aus LICHT*.

Sound effects come into their own in "Der Kinderfänger" (Pied Piper, literally "children-stealer"). In this scene the children return, their clear trebles a welcome contrast to the rather dour tenor voices of the previous scene. Stockhausen's inventiveness with children's voices is raised to a higher level, and the spirit of this music is altogether more buoyant and reminiscent of *Gesang der Jünglinge*. The scene consists of a sequence of imitation games (after Turing, I wonder?) in which the flutist sings and plays catch phrases from nursery rhymes or children's play, and the young voices imitate the flute. The melodic shapes are by no means simplified for small voices, but are presented in manageable phrase-lengths and with a sense of challenge that leads to chorus effects of an attractive freshness. Each imitation exercise is accompanied by a selection of sound effects comprising a "Tone-scene," strung together like a comic strip, the sounds also animated with characteristic movements within a lateral quadraphonic sound-space. Put together with the same high spirits as the musical sound effects of Spike Jones, it is a sequence to delight children and to intrigue and amuse sound-effects professionals. While the choice of sounds is partly determined by abstract criteria of register, tone, and texture, they also refer back to the more serious allusions of previous scenes: breaking glass, dive-bombers, military commands, a machine gun.

The opera concludes with the "Entführung" or abduction of the children by the Pied Piper, a scene amounting perhaps to the longest fade in history. The enchanted children follow the flutist away, their clear voices evoking the childlike faith of *Gesang der Jünglinge*, but also memories, of which we have already been reminded, of the fateful consequences of blindly following a charismatic leader. Here however the magic of "Eva's Magic" comes to fruition in the musical transformation of children's voices into birdsong, an apotheosis that in other hands might appear a little too obvious, but that on Stockhausen's extended timescale is very effective: as a listener one ends by willing rather than waiting for the transformation to take place. At the end of Boulez's *e e cummings ist der Dichter*. . . the choir is also transformed into a dawn chorus, which is exactly what the poem is about ("birds . . . inventing air"), but at the same time we understand it as also a tribute to Messiaen, the great teacher. Stockhausen is more discreet: a child runs back on to the stage to pick up his shoes, exclaiming "Are you still here? It's filthy outdoors!" to the transfixed audience. The text is given in German in the programme and cd booklets, but actually spoken in the recording in heavily accented French.

In a music that reciprocates the pitch-glissandi of the opening foyer music, "Montags Abschied" continues the analogous temporal transformation process ever onward and upward for another twenty minutes. During this time the (recorded) piccolo and children's melodies are gradually and very discreetly elevated in pitch, as though with the Springer-machine of earlier times, until by the twelfth minute one can just about detect the onset of a chirping quality associated with songs by the Chipmunks in the fifties. During the same transition, prerecorded birdsongs are gradually slowed down in time and descend in pitch until they become audible as animal-like grunts and whimpers, to merge with the occasional sounds of synthesizers. Of particular interest is the ascent of the piccolo to a point around 4 kilohertz (top c of the piano) and then beyond. At this point pitch discrimination in human beings ceases to function, which makes the listener's experience of transition interesting in itself, and meaningful as a metaphor of something more spiritual. These high sounds briefly connect with the sound world of short wave radio, another glimpse of the past and of the oracular status assigned to radio at different times in the composer's life: at school during the war, in *Kurzwellen*, in *Mantra*. At the same time as one shares in the composer's fascination with sliding timescales, there is perhaps a residual sense of disappointment that nothing miraculous happens, to compare with the St. Elmo's fire of *Telemusik* [16], for example. At around 18' 35" a female voice calls "E-va!" in an echo of the composer's cry "Ma-ka!" at the end of *Hymnen*, a gesture accompanied by *Kontakte*-like glissandi that vanish like the wind.

It is hard to choose whether *Montag* is myth, rebus, or charade. As myth, a figure representing mother nature or mother earth spontaneously brings forth children, first inferior beings (the seven dwarfs), then seven chimeras (animal children), then after a second bout of insemination by piano, seven geniuses who are among a group of children finally lured away to never-never land by an androgynous flutist. Among the mythical allusions are notably the Nativity or virgin birth, which is perhaps ultimately about how life first appeared on earth; and the Pied Piper, another emanation of the Stockhausen Harlequin persona adopted here not only for the flute but maybe also for its autobiographical implications: the story of a "Musikus" who rids the town of a plague of rats, but when the citizens refuse to recognize his magical talents and pay him accordingly, entices the children away. A rebus is a picture puzzle that adds up to a message, a use of images as words: at the end of the opera, the transformation of the Eva-statue into "an old mountain." A curious description, "old," of a mountain that is green and was beautiful:—a *Verdi*, a *Monteverdi*, a *Schoenberg*, a *Berg*, a *Weib* (Webern) even. Stockhausen's new thematicism has led him covertly to acknowledge the virtuosity of the master whose "Dance around the Golden Calf" he and Goeyvaerts once described as "du Verdi sériel." As an image of motherhood, there are also little verbal subtexts in German and French: *la mère, das Meer, mehren* (to increase), *La Mer* (Debussy), *l'amère* (bitterness), not forgetting *l'Amérique*. Note too that the trefoil or clover symbol devised for *Montag* is the German word "Klee," as in Paul Klee.

As a game of charades, the play of events in *Montag* is a sequence of mimed cues that add up to letters or syllables of a message. Counting behavior, whether in sevens, elevens, or thirteens, is part of the assembly process by which a manifestation of the triple formula is finally revealed. On the way, however, events and relationships in the composer's own life are also implicated: since *Montag* is a meditation on the female species it is only natural that the imagery of womanhood should be colored by personal recollections of how women are perceived: as vamps and hookers in the imaginative worlds of Georg Grosz, Alban Berg, Josef von Sternberg, and Bertolt Brecht, as biological mechanisms under National Socialism for renewing the race, and replenishing the population in time of war, and as muses and companions in his past and present life. That the tenderness and affection of a relationship between equal partners that emerges so movingly in *Momente* appears to have given way to a view of women as energetic sexual predators and males as helpless drones, such that the abiding image of the opera, as also with *Donnerstag aus LICHT*, is of withdrawal from the real world, is a matter of some regret.

Notes

1. "Reading Combinations of Glides and Other Sounds." Ralph K. Potter, George A. Kopp, and Harriet Green Kopp. *Visible Speech* (New edition. New York: Dover Publications, 1966), 246–69.

2. Pierre Boulez, "Perspective-Prospective." 23–33 in Brigitte Marger and Simone Benemussa, ed., *La Musique en Projet: Le Premier Livre de l'I.R.C.A.M., Direction Pierre Boulez* (Paris: Gallimard, 1975).

3. *SoM*, 147.

4. Paul Valéry, "Remarks on Poetry" (1927). In *Symbolism: an Anthology* tr. ed. T. G. West (London: Methuen, 1980): 48–50.

5. John Cage, *Variations IV*. Assisted by David Tudor. From a live performance at the Feigen-Palmer Gallery, Los Angeles, 1965. Double vinyl recording. I Everest 3132, II Everest 3230.

6. "The reverberation of a tone, timbre, or noise here has less to do with adding a sense of space, but rather to add a distinctive feature (*Unterscheidungsmerkmal*) to the appearance of the individual sound." Werner Meyer-Eppler, "Die elektrischen Instrumente und neue Tendenzen der elektroakustischen Klanggestaltung." *Gravesano Review* (July 1955), 88–93.

7. J. Z. Young, *Doubt and Certainty in Science* (New York: Galaxy Books, 1960), 116–18.

8. "Pains and other mental phenomena just are features of the brain (and perhaps the rest of our central nervous system)." J. R. Searle, *Minds, Brains, and Science* (London: British Broadcasting Corporation, 1984), 19.

9. "Stockhausen—Sound International." Interview with Jill Purce. *Texte Band 6*, 357. The composer may be alluding to the work *Hon* (She) by Niki de Sainte-Phalle, a mixed media installation in the form of a giant recumbent pregnant woman with walk-in pudenda, created in 1966 at the Moderna Museet, Stockholm.

10. A rather desperate coincidence, provoking wonder at whether earlier choices of Matthias Hölle (Hölle = hell) and Nicholas Isherwood (Old Nick) for the Luzifer role, and of Alain Louafi (louer = to praise) for the Michael mime role, may have been guided by their names as well as their musical abilities. The Act III tenor of *Donnerstag aus LICHT*, whose real name is Paul Sperry, is listed on the DG recording as "Michael Angel."

11. "Corno di Bassetto" was the inspired pseudonym of George Bernard Shaw in his professional role as a music critic.

CHAPTER TWENTY-SIX

Dienstag

Tuesday is the day of Mars, the god of war. The word "Dienst" in German means service, military or otherwise; for Stockhausen war service in practice meant helping the casualties as a young stretcher-bearer, and being someone to talk to the wounded and dying of both sides and to ease their sufferings with music. The message is more of a rhetorical statement than a vision or recollection of physical conflict. On the one hand two mock armies improbably outfitted in a cross between Arthurian shining armor and Robocop costumes, and armed with trumpets and trombones, snarl and occasionally yodel epithets at one another in an abstract kind of foul language (which by the way is an interesting and tactile use of syllabic materials for gestural effect); on the other hand the music provides more or less literal images of droning squadrons overhead, antiaircraft fire, and the sounds of planes shot down falling to earth. For all the action, the total picture is curiously uncompelling. It is a grimly inventive notion to transform the glissandi of the Eva formula into the whistle of shells and the whine of aircraft descending in flames, but in the opera these casualties of battle do not descend with the awful gathering speed and sudden silence of newsreel footage, but rather swoop and flutter to earth like autumn leaves, or biplanes from the Red Baron era. Stockhausen's battle-scenes combine the congestion of a Dürer engraving with the formal symmetry of a Uccello, but they are strangely static, as paintings are, even though they exist in time as musical events. There is one casualty in the entire opera, who becomes the object of a Pietà.

The end of the eighties turned into a period of multiple complication in Stockhausen's professional life. La Scala, who had nurtured the first three operas of the cycle, withdrew further support after a change of management; then when the composer's contract with Deutsche Grammophon came up for renewal in 1989, again a new management made it clear that they could not agree on a way to continue the relationship. Stockhausen had already lived through a crisis of separation from Universal Edition and had successfully created his own music publishing company. He now faced the immense challenge of taking on the production and dissemination of his recorded music. He had been in anxious discussion with DG over a number of years over the company policy of limited release of his recordings, so the new challenge was also an opportunity to ensure that they would be all be permanently available in the future, and also that the master recordings would be properly preserved. Whatever other reasons may have influenced the breakup, the major players in the hifi and classical record industry were already in decline after taking a number of serious hits over three decades from investments in new technology that had failed to secure industry-wide agreement or popular support, including cartridge, Elcaset, various types of quadraphony, laser disc, and Betamax. The industry was also very nervous over the new economic challenges of phasing out vinyl and reissuing the entire catalogue on compact disc, and the imminent prospect of mini-disc and DVD. As an analogue composer born and bred, and a pioneer in the field of multichannel sound recording and distribution, Stockhausen had serious reservations about the viability of the compact disc as a suitable medium, even for two-channel reproduction. Nevertheless, he reached an agreement to take over the DG backlist of his recordings to form the basis of the Stockhausen-Verlag cd series, and in 1991 began the process of re-releasing his entire archive.

A third crisis of a kind was the falling of the Berlin Wall in 1989, coincidentally for the composition of a major work predicated on conflict: not just memories of the 1939–1945 war, but also on the continuation of a standoff between the West and the Communist bloc. For Stockhausen personally the wars of 1914–1918 and 1939–1945 represented issues of ideological difference that were still unresolved. The cold war itself had played a powerful undercover role in support of avant-garde art and music. For over half a century the balance of power within Europe had lain in the hands of code-makers and code-breakers: "intelligence" experts in secret communication. The digital era as we know it came out of that covert form of warfare. After the end of hostilities in 1945, for a brief period through the fifties serialism in music was widely seen as holding the key to the language code, and thus to the structures of human thought. Electronic and concrete music had been set up and supported through state radio channels as a research activity with implications for the development of speech recognition technology. Whatever the aesthetic and intellectual merits of particular works (which is a separate issue), abstract expressionism as a genre acted as very effective propaganda for freedom of expression under democracy in those socialist regimes where art was expected to toe the party line and confine itself to positive proletarian subject matter. With the end of the cold war in view, the pursuit of an encryption aesthetic in music no longer commanded the same political attention, even though the radical abstraction of the music itself continued to attract envy and admiration across Eastern Europe.[1]

For musicians and art-lovers a test of great new art is its ability to transform our perception of existing modern and controversial works. That capacity to illuminate the past does two things: first, it demonstrates continuity, and second, it allows the observer to appreciate quality. Even for Stockhausen, the new segments of *Dienstag aus LICHT*,—the Welcome and Peace Greeting, and Act II,—are extremely noisy, and the noise is more saturated and more inflamed than the ecstatic high spirits of "Luzifers Abschied." Faced with a high-intensity musical ritual of strong oppositions, featuring multiple trumpets and trombones, electronic keyboards, and solo voices speaking in tongues, one recognizes an antecedence in the neglected great music of Varèse: the conjunction of strident forces of *Intégrales* of 1925, or *Ecuatorial* of 1934, which shares, allowing for the time difference, a very similar style and instrumentation, the earlier work written for multiple brass, grand organ, piano, 2 theremins (or ondes martenot, or sweep frequency oscillators), and percussion. Some of the symbolism is reversed. For example, Varèse's text, from the *Popul Vuh*, the Mayan Book of the Dead, is a prayer addressed to the gods by a people who have lost their way; Stockhausen's lyric to the "Peace Greeting," written by himself, and sung by a soprano, is a godly admonition direct to the audience, telling them to make peace. There are other points of complementarity. Varèse aligns himself with the archetypal Romantics Beethoven and Turner, whose art seeks to express the superhuman grandeur and power of natural forces: in his own case not so much the atmospheric turbulence of wind and storm, as the tectonic forces at play within the earth's crust. For Stockhausen, a similar sense of an opposition of natural forces, rather than between the forces of darkness and light, seems to be a new development in the composer's dramatic argument.

Dienstag aus LICHT (Tuesday from LIGHT)

1977: No. 47; 1987–1991: No. 60–61 (Stockhausen-Verlag; cd SV-40)
Opera for soprano, tenor, and bass solo voices, choir (2 conductors); 3 piccolos, 3 soprano saxophones; 3 solo trumpets (1. also flugelhorn), 6 tutti trumpets; 3 solo trombones, 6 tutti trombones; guitar, 3 harmoniums (or synthesizers), harpsichord (or 4. synthesizer), 3 percussionists; 4 dancer-mimes, actors, mimes; 7 transmitting microphones, 8–40 microphones, 8-track and 2-track tapes and tape recorders, 16–20 loudspeakers, mixing console.
Duration: 2 hours 36'.

Dienstags-Gruss (Tuesday Greeting)

1987–1988: No. 60 (Stockhausen-Verlag)
For soprano, 9 trumpets, 9 trombones, 2 synthesizer players; choir divided antiphonally SSTT (right), AABB (left), conductor and co-conductor; 1 transmitting microphone, 8 microphones, 4 × 2 loudspeakers, mixing console.
Duration: 21'.

Commissioned by Cologne University in celebration of its 600th anniversary, this suitably resplendent antiphonal chant between believers and

unbelievers (believers being sopranos, tenors, and trumpets to the audience's right and rear, unbelieving altos, basses, and trombones to the
audience's left side and rear), match claim for claim for and against freedom
under God in a blaze of brass that consciously or otherwise also evokes the
the same sense of challenge to received opinion as Gabrieli's stunning brass
canzonas to the ecclesiastical authorities of Venice in the late sixteenth
century, when the dawn of a new era of instrumental freedom inspired a
new Renaissance dynamic of action and competition, a secular music more
intricately organized and more powerful than traditional ecclesiatical chant,
and free of the limitations, and thus independent of the authority, of the
written word. That message of freedom of inquiry, of renewed competition,
and above all freedom from dogma sits a little uneasily with the composer's
message of reconciliation between the forces of unbelief (the Newtonists)
and those who stand for the true light of knowledge (the Goetheians). It is,
to be sure, a more elusive message than Schiller's "Ode to Joy," but a
stirring experience nonetheless. As Lady Irwin wrote of Handel in her diary,
"I was at the entertainment on *Tuesday*; 'tis excessive noisy, a vast number
of instruments and voices who all perform at a time."[2]

That slight but telling shift of attitude may have to be read in the
context of a parallel development in popular music, of which Stockhausen
was bound to become aware through his increasing focus on synthesizer
music as an alternative to the instruments of a conventional orchestra. His
younger son Simon Stockhausen had been a keen synthesizer player since
boyhood and acted as a conduit for new ideas in synthesizer sound. Early
Kurzweil and Yamaha keyboard technology was evolving rapidly and had
even infiltrated IRCAM. The combination of midi keyboards, 24–48 channel
multi-track mixing, and 16-bit digital encoding created new possibilities of
auditory complexity and intensity of experience. In 1990 a new kind of disco
"rave" music began to emerge out of the synthesizer idiom of the Kraftwerk
era, coinciding with a change from a singles-based popular music economy,
centered on the traditional 3–4 minute hit, to a cd album economy catering
for a new generation of extreme partygoers seeking the adrenaline rush of a
loud and immersive music at very high energies for much longer exposures.
Tracks of 12–15 minutes became the norm for a music saturated in content
and pushing the extremes of aural perception into ranges of fre-quency and
amplitude capable of provoking spontaneous and potentially hazardous
mental and physical reactions. Not unexpectedly, the sense of danger and
mind-altering power of music at these high intensities became a selling
point for individuals and groups of a neo-Gothick or "demonic" persuasion.
One such group was the Norwegian band Burzum (a name, believe it or not,
taken from J. R. R. Tolkien, and meaning "The Darkness")—a name calculated to attract the attention of the composer and defender of *LICHT*.
Burzum's erstwhile leader, the now incarcerated Varg Vikernes, went by
the stage name of Count Grishnaki, the name of an Orc in Tolkien's *Lord of
the Rings*. Taking advantage of multichannel technology and high-gain
digital compression and enhancement techniques, this genre of black rock
music creates an auditory saturation experience that hovers on the edge of

psychological torture and has the capacity to inflict permanent hearing damage over the long-term. The imagery of this music, and its physically rasping vocals, is of burning in hellfire. Though the music has been accused of provoking murder and mayhem, it is exposure to physical damage, in combination with the side effects of chemical stimulants, that gives cause for alarm, rather than any inherent threat in the music to a listener's moral well-being. Indeed, compared to the raw ring-modulated sounds of *Mixtur* or *Mikrophonie II*, the music of a group such as Burzum is not only easier to listen to, under controlled conditions, but manifestly well-crafted in a technical sense. From the 1992 album *Dunkelheit* (Darkness) tracks such as "Erblicket die Tochter des Firmaments" and "Rundgang um die Tranzendentale Saule der Singularität" are interesting examples of synthesizer-based musical processes coupled with a willfully Faustian commitment to knowledge through physical suffering that invite direct comparison with the newly saturated imagery of *Dienstag* and Stockhausen's own relentless confrontation of extremes. It is as though suddenly the battle is no longer between science and art, or number and beauty, as between suffering for the sake of knowledge, and suffering as an aesthetic experience.

Act I: Jahreslauf vom Dienstag (Course of the Years of Tuesday)

1977/1991: No. 47 (Stockhausen-Verlag)
For tenor, bass, 4 dancer-mimes, actor-singer, 3 mimes, little girl, beautiful woman; 3 synthesizer harmoniums, 3 piccolos, 3 soprano saxophones, guitar, synthesizer harpsichord; anvil, bongo, bass drum, 2-track tape; 7 transmitting microphones, 7 microphones, 2-track tape recorder, 4 x 2 loudspeakers, 4 optional stage loudspeakers. Duration: 61'.

This is a very different *Jahreslauf*. The original 1977 version, a spare and witty charade in the manner of *Musik im Bauch* and a delightful take on the solemnity of Japanese music theater, remains one of Stockhausen's most accessible and finished works after *Inori*. There was always a risk of perception attached to his decision to incorporate it in *LICHT*. The thematic link is not immediately obvious between a game of multiple time-layers, in which the goal, in Samuel Beckett's refrain, is "keep going!" and an opera cycle characterized not only by massive discontinuities in space and time, but also by a music in which the flow of time is all but brought to a halt. Since it predates the formulation of the all-embracing triple melody formula of the rest of the cycle, *Jahreslauf* is distinctly different in structure and idiom from the rest of *LICHT*, and also very different in instrumentation. To bring the work into line, Stockhausen has added sung commentary of a basic kind for tenor and bass, representing Michael and Luzifer in untypically relaxed mood, adopted a more Western instrumentation including four synthesizer keyboards, and increased the role of electronics and sound projection.

Prior to 1970 Stockhausen's promotional images focus on the composer as conductor, poised to give a downbeat, master of the podium. After Osaka, however, a new image begins to emerge, of the composer at a control panel or at a mixing desk. In practical terms the developing role of sound projection in the composer's output has introduced new and substantial layers of complexity, technical assistance, and cost to the performance of more recent works that put them out of the reach of many otherwise interested ensembles and individuals. To this technical complexity is added a dimension of interpretative explication and commentary that as well as being hard to read, is not always helpful and indeed can work against the composer's own interests. The information, including photographs, laid out in a Stockhausen-Verlag score adds considerably to its pagination, and thus to its cost to the purchaser, but it is not always clearly organized and at times can actually mislead. Such basic information as the number of players required, for a work such as "Luzifers Tanz," can be buried in the middle of an extensive résumé rather than routinely displayed opposite the title page. Descriptions of technical setups previously used, often in multiple options to cover non-staged or chamber reduced performances, are of limited value, since they relate to specific structures and acoustic conditions. In the 200-page booklet accompanying the cds of *Dienstag aus LICHT* three technical setups are illustrated, down to the rotary control and fader positions of up to 41 input channels, all of them completely different. What the producer wants to know is what the equipment is intended to do, and what effects the composer has in mind. Musicians of the here and now who would like to master and enjoy Stockhausen's music in a natural acoustic without technical apparatus are effectively discouraged from their traditional interpretative role as mediator between the notated score and the conditions of a particular environment. Even for those works that are more radiophonic in nature, or that rely on a technical infrastructure to achieve one-off illusions of static and moving sounds in space, not only the composer's technical demands (which can vary), but his aesthetic intentions (which presumably do not change) should be clearly laid out, and this is not always the case.

Given that a purchased broadcast recording can be changed after the fact by remixing a multichannel original, by manipulating the information content and definition of individual tracks, superimposing new material, inserting vocal introductions, adding artificial reverberation, and more, the work of a composer assuming full responsibility for the technical quality of a cd recording is open to assessment on a technical as well as a musical level. The radiophonic aesthetic of Stockhausen's music has its own set of priorities, many of them in opposition to the traditional goals of classical concert recording, which aims for a sense of natural ambience and disposition of players. But whatever the prevailing aesthetic, even for the music of high saturation of a group such as Burzum, technical standards continue to apply. So hearing distortion in "Evas Zweitgeburt" of *Montag aus LICHT* is a worrying sign, one that becomes even more worrying in the context of *Dienstag aus LICHT*, not simply from a before-and-after comparison of the 1977 DG edition and the 1991 remix of *Der Jahreslauf*, but in the context of an aesthetic intention to push the boundaries of complexity and loudness in recording. When it transpires that these episodes of overmodulation (in *Jahreslauf*, for example, of the three piccolos, around 4' 10" of track [12], and again in the piccolo solo at track [16]) are specific to the right channel, which is Stockhausen's bad ear, the inference to be drawn is that he is overriding the settings and perhaps the advice of technical assistants, which is not always a good idea.

The *Dienstag* version of *Jahreslauf* accommodates clip-on parts for Michael as tenor and Luzifer as bass (and master of ceremonies). Their dramatic purpose, to establish that the action is a form of contest, falls strangely flat in comparison with the enigmatic character of the original piece. The additions also add considerably to the original length of the work. To a clangorous prerecorded sound of geisha bells, a crystalline tone imagery reflected in the opera's glass and metal costumes and stage sets, the musicians enter in gagaku ceremonial style, now costumed in the colors of the rainbow. There is something not quite right about the abrupt fade of the geisha bells, a feature of both recordings, since the sounds are very realistic and it would seem to make sense for them to die away naturally. Newly added reverberation also affects different taped and added elements of the new recording.

The new instrumentation is certainly adequate but lacks the flavor of the 1977 recording, which though Western is largely unamplified and therefore acoustically more coherent and spacious. There is an authentic feel to the combination of laconic guitar and drum sounds, with the hot and spicy piccolo and saxophone sounds, and the bland harmoniums, a mixture of tastes that does not quite translate in the modern orchestra version. The four interruptions, each time a temptation to stop followed by an incentive to resume, incorporate recorded material. They include the composer as voiceover: "Blumen für den Jahresläufer: er will sie nicht"—in a nicely-judged neutral tone,—the skipping girl, the stamping feet, the clapping, the ape on a motor scooter, not to mention sexy noncopyright nightclub music ("I found it in the radio in Cologne and I don't know what it is, [or] where it came from"[3]). A great deal of this prerecorded material, seamlessly integrated with the original music in the earlier version, has either not survived, or is discolored in the new mix. The footsteps and stamping of the First Temptation, a model of fine recording of stereo movement, are reduced to a single gesture, and the magical transformation of skipping clogs into sporadic clapping, and the later arrival and departure of the moped also lack their original crispness.

Act II: Invasion—Explosion mit Abschied (Invasion—Explosion with Farewell)

1990–1991: No. 61 (Stockhausen-Verlag)

For solo soprano, tenor, bass; 3 trumpets (1. also flugelhorn); 3 trombones, 2 synthesizer players with 2 assistants, 2 percusssionists with 2 assistants, 6 tutti trumpets and 6 tutti trombones; choir and conductor, 8-track and 2-track tapes; 5 transmitting microphones, 8 (or ca. 40) microphones, 8-track tape recorders, 8 × 2 loudspeakers, 4 optional stage loudspeakers, mixing console.
Duration: 1 hour 14'.

Pietà (Pietà)
1990: No. 61½ (Stockhausen-Verlag; cd SV-60)
For flugelhorn, soprano, and electronic music; 2 transmitting microphones, 8-track (2-track) tape recorder, 8 × 2 (2 × 2) loudspeakers, mixing console.
Duration: 27' 45.

Synthi-Fou (Klavierstück XV) Synthi-Fou (Piano Piece XV)
1991: from No. 61⅔ "Tuesday Farewell"
For a player of electronic keyboard instruments, or as electronic music; 8-track tape, 8 × 2 loudspeakers, mixing console.
Duration: 23'.

At the end of *Jahreslauf* Michael and Luzifer salute one another as if what has happened were a form of recreational exercise before battle. Luzifer compliments Michael and Michael declares that he is not afraid. The stage setting for Act II is a defensive installation, described in the English language note as "a bunker." The conflict takes the form of a defense by the Michael forces against the Luzifer invading force. Three "Invasions" are mounted, preceded in each case by a musical "air defense" modeled after the shooting down of individual aircraft by antiaircraft fire. In these scenes the drone harmonies that have become so consistent a feature of the opera, take on the familiar and sinister character of night warfare bomber operations as heard from the ground. Although enacted in the futuristic livery of a Hollywood movie, this is a strangely anachronistic form of warfare, in the spirit of the movie *Things to Come* based on the H. G. Wells novel. The sounds and actions of war are out of time with present-day reality; the invading aircraft propellor-driven, and shot down by wartime ack-ack, not guided missiles. Once again, the ostensibly timeless myth of Stockhausen's narrative spirals inward to focus on the experiences of his own adolescence, events that, while terrifying enough in their own terms, offer only a partial account even of the 1939–1945 conflict, let alone wars of ethnic cleansing or nuclear annihilation as we understand them today.

Stockhausen's cube-formation "octophonic" surround sound is designed to simulate movement in three dimensions, and is therefore ideal for depicting dramatic events that move in the vertical as well as the lateral plane. The miniature rockets set off one by one around the piano in "Luzifers Traum" represent the expansion of a null-dimensional point into a three-dimensional space; now in a reverse scenario moving targets in a three-dimensional virtual space are picked off and collapse inwards, as it were, to a null-point of impact. It is a nice conceit in its own way, a mirror image of Luzifer's encounter with oblivion, but one cannot help feeling that the sounds depicting rising shells and falling aircraft have little in common with the effects even of the historic conflict they are supposed to represent, and which are widely familiar through surviving archive newsreels and location recordings.

Since the sounds of rifle fire in *Donnerstag* are also "unreal," in the sense of resembling silent movie effects, an ethical objection to imitating such sounds in a realistic manner might be assumed. That would be consistent with the composer's previously noted, perhaps stoical, avoidance of literal expressions of pain and suffering. The Greeks also had an aversion to spilling blood onstage, but even the Greeks were concerned to confront the real effects of bloody actions, if not the actions themselves. With Stockhausen neither the actions nor their effects seem to have more than token significance, which is rather strange in a composer who in the past has not shown the least reluctance to make his audiences wince in a good cause. It is not only that the behavior of actual antiaircraft fire and stricken aircraft falling to earth are not convincingly observed, but that the sounds themselves are relatively feeble. (And as we know from archive footage, an air raid can be a powerfully exciting, indeed, a paradoxical experience. Try to imagine, for example,—let alone depict,—the fall of a V2 rocket during the London blitz. Faster than the speed of sound, the bomb delivers an experience of time in reverse: first the explosive impact, and only afterward the terrifying sound of the same missile descending.)

It is not that suitably powerful sound-generators would be hard to find, from the sirens of Helmholtz and Varèse, to the wind machine of Richard Strauss, the simple electronic circuitry of Trautwein and Martenot, through to Stockhausen's own impulsive tape loops: sounds with complexity, texture, depth, and power. The massive turbine sounds of *Sirius* and the comical moped sound of *Jahreslauf* alike belong to that genre of motorized noises that plays a distinctive role in Stockhausen's entire oeuvre. So it would be a mistake to deduce that the composer is opposed on ethical or any other grounds to timbres of an abrasive or warlike character. Indeed, for the first Invasion, the synthesizers are asked to produce "earthly-realistic;" for the second Invasion, "metallic-electric;" and in the third and final Invasion, "crystal-glassy" timbres. These synthesizer sounds are evocatively described in the composer's notes, in vocabulary similar to the terms of *Mikrophonie I*, as "screaming," "crashing," "hissing," "whizzing," "rumbling," "detonations," and so on. "An unusually complicated flying object howls into the depths," the booklet says at one point, referring to an event on track [68]; it is followed in track [69] by "a third, gigantic explosion." But these effects in themselves sound anything but terrifying, gigantic, or realistic. The more plausible explanation has to be, not for the first time, that the synthesizers Stockhausen is relying on have failed to deliver. An explosion, after all, even a firework, is still an explosion.

Unlikely though it may seem, the surreptitious presence of ideas first aired in the series of Hoffnung concerts may again be detected. The same series that introduced "Introductory music in the foyer" by Francis Chagrin, a *Hoffnung Festival Overture* by Francis Baines, featuring "a violence of trumpets," and *The Barber of Darmstadt* and *Punkt Contrapunkt* by Bruno Heinz Jaja (the estimable Humphrey Searle), also inspired *The United Nations* by Malcolm Arnold, a remarkable hybrid composition in which a pastoral music for symphony orchestra is literally invaded by military bands from all sides, playing simultaneously and as loudly as possible. At the time this piece was viewed as a piece of fun, a sardonic commentary on the impossible dream of peace and harmony between nations. That Stockhausen knew this work I am reasonably sure, having asked Henri Pousseur in 1964 if the Hoffnung concerts were known and appreciated in Europe, and being assured in all seriousness that they were. Long before *LICHT*, the ghost of Arnold's *United Nations* was already hovering over *Hymnen*, and the spirit of Chagrin's foyer music, in *Fresco*. To listen more clinically to the recording of *United Nations* after half a century is better to appreciate the compositional and balance engineering skills involved in creating an impression of musical chaos that works both as a montage of discernible parts, and as a complex of static and moving ensembles. In particular, one begins to appreciate the roles of percussion at either end of the audible spectrum, bass drum and cymbals, as acoustic references to enable the listener to follow a movement from left to right, and from foreground to background.[4]

Stockhausen's works have a characteristically strong physical presence and a corresponding emotional absence (or rather, implicitness). From a physical, technical, and acoustical perspective the "Invasion" scenarios of *Dienstag* make sense as representations of lateral movements (side to side, and fore and aft) in real space by real performers, alternating with the up and down movements of missiles and aircraft depicted electronically in virtual space. The alternation happens three times, so it has structural significance, and the encounters between the two groups, led by trumpets and trombones, are manifestly episodes of combat. Stockhausen has been choreographing the movement of sounds in space from the time of *Gesang der Jünglinge* and *Gruppen*, so he understands the acoustical challenges involved. These are normally passive, in the sense of designing sounds of a density and richness that allow their movement in space to be clearly followed, both in performance and in a recording. In *Jahreslauf* alone, one can identify the opening and closing processionals of geisha bells, the running footsteps episode, and the ape on a moped, as textbook examples of choosing dense sound optimized for stereo reproduction. In *Kontakte, Sirius, Harlekin*, and "Kathinkas Gesang," the primary movements are rotational; in the cartoon episodes of "Evas Zauber" from *Montag aus LICHT*, prerecorded "concrete" sounds, of widely differing textures and frequencies, are electronically moved, shaken, and stirred in a variety of distinctive configurations. All of this previous experimentation leads up to the new combination of real movement of synthesized sounds in real space. Stockhausen's commitment to synthesizers is absolute. The challenge is to make it work.

There are three critical difficulties associated with the task. First is the instrument's flaccid tone, second the inadequate power of the synthesizer sounds themselves; third the logistical problems of moving them. Stockhausen has committed himself to manufactured equipment that while capable of producing gliding tones and harmonies, is dependent on processes of waveform generation and manipulation that exist only in terms of voltage relationships, and not in terms of physical and acoustical systems and energies. They are no different in this respect from Boulez's 4X computer sounds, though the latter are more powerfully computed and amplified, and are capable of producing more interesting aleatoric spatial effects. Not only do

Stockhausen's instruments produce weak and debilitated sounds, but these domestic keyboard synthesizers also require massive amplification, and in order to move about they have to be carried. And they are not designed to be carried around like bazookas, let alone to emit musical detonations of the impact associated with battlefield armaments.

Once again, it is not that suitable solutions do not exist, or cannot be found, but rather a matter of the composer's choices. If it were simply a question of discovering *any* suitable instruments to take part in simulated commando operations, one has only to refer back to the tubas, euphoniums, and bass and contrabass saxophones of "Luzifers Tanz" to discover a whole range of genuinely powerful, unusual, and *portable* instruments for the purpose. If the composer has a preference for alien effects after the style of the flute "trombone sounds" of "Kathinkas Gesang," or the pedal tones for flugelhorn in "Pietà," these techniques too are adaptable for use in genuine bass register instruments. Techniques of ring-modulation, intermodulation, or the electronically impulsive fragmentation of a continuous tone are familar from Stockhausen's music of the sixties: in *Kontakte* and *Hymnen* the use of a noise gate to "chop" a sound into pulses produces a very intimidating and effective simulation of Bren gun fire that would be open to manipulation in a variety of interesting and thematically appropriate ways.

> Massimilano Viel played a portable *YAMAHA KX 5* keyboard (hung over his shoulder) connected via a circa 3 m long *MIDI cable* to a *sampler*, in a rack, which was carried by an assistant. . . . The sampler, amplifier, and power-supply were inserted into a plywood (6 mm) rack which was carried like a backpack by the assistant. Fastened to its base was a metal pole reaching almost to the floor. The weight of the rack could be rested on it during rehearsals. The player carried the loudspeakers in a *WRANGLER* military backpack. . . . In the first performances, during the 1st and 2nd INVASIONS, synthesizer player 2 carried two loudspeakers on his shoulders. At some places in the music these loudspeakers were not powerful enough, thus necessitating the slight additional amplification of his sounds via transmitter-microphone, transmitter and receiver, and projection over the upper [*sic*] loudspeakers in the hall. . . . A tubular pole on a heavy base must be placed at a sufficient distance away from the corner seats of each block of [audience] seats. This acts to guide the electric cables—pulled by the synthesizer and percussion assistants—away from the feet and chairs of the listeners, and thus to aid the proper feeding of the cables. . . . The synthesizer and percussion players require electric sockets *outside* the side exits . . . etc.[5]

The basic point, of course, is that powerful sounds of a low fundamental frequency require exponentially higher amounts of energy to shift large amounts of air, and this means not only large surfaces in contact with the atmosphere (as in bass drums and loudspeakers), but heavy equipment to drive them. That heavy equipment is hard to carry. Is there an alternative? Well, yes there is. The answer is to conceal powerful low-frequency speakers at various locations within the hall where they will actually transmit vibrations into the structural members of the opera house or concert hall. In the low frequency zone (15–40 hertz) where power and impact are sensed, the wavelengths involved (the distances between successive pressure peaks) are of the order of 20–60 feet for the lowest octave of the piano to a fifth lower. At such wavelengths in the sub-bass human hearing can no longer determine position or distance, so the exact location of thudding and booming sounds is not an issue. Human ears are only inches apart and therefore attuned to pressure-waves that are only inches apart; that is why hearing relies on phase changes in the high frequency regions associated with cymbals, portable glockenspiels, snare drums, and triangles, for pinpointing position or following a moving sound target. Because low-frequency and structural vibrations are effectively omnipresent, it should be possible to simulate movement in real space using portable synthesizers, without having to rely on assistants to carry weighty speakers and battery packs on their shoulders; it is done by transmitting the signal to a mixing desk and sending the amplified bass component to one or more hidden subwoofers, allowing the mid- and high-frequency parts of the signal to be transmitted from light-weight "trumpet mute" sized speakers of any number of different materials and shapes.

As in other aspects of *LICHT* productions, what seems to be the case here is that the composer has an ideal situation or vision in mind for which he relies on others to provide a practical solution, as for example the idea of having Luzifer and Michael hovering above ground for their exchange of compliments at the end of *Jahreslauf*. That being the case, the challenge of turning portable synthesizers into truly effective mobile armaments would only remain a problem for as long as it might take for technology to catch up with the composer's demands. Somewhere along the way, however, the spectacle of armed conflict on the ground, commando style, has mutated into a rescue operation in which enfeebled synthesizers, representing an ultimately futile dependence on technology, are presented as deadweights to be carried to safety by mute assistants. At that point we recall Stockhausen's own war service, not as a combatant, but as a stretcher-bearer for the ambulance service. What we are now being asked to contemplate is not so much the actions of combat as their effects on those left to care for the casualties.

There is a scream, and a token death. The image of a young body cradled in the lap of a nurse is transformed into a Pietà that on the surface could be in the image of the last great sculpture of Michelangelo, but below the surface could also be seen as a shadow of the 1923 *Pietà, or Revolution by Night*, by Max Ernst. In this second, psychologically troubling image, the dead youth is cradled by a kneeling father figure. "In the *Pietà* Max Ernst takes up the iconographic theme of the Virgin Mary cradling the dead Christ in her lap. . . . But this father takes over from her only the gesture of protection. He is holding a dummy; there is no inner bond between father and son. In his father's arms the son is as cold as a statue."[6]

Stockhausen's "Pietà" provides a set piece for meditation on the reality of death, a reality that has been assiduously avoided in *Donnerstag*: in the stylized deaths of the parents, in the miraculous translation of Michael himself, and in the elimination in all but name of the image of the

Crucifixion. Also in *Samstag,* death for the archenemy is represented as a mere illusion in "Luzifers Traum." This episode of stillness, a Pietà in which the shade of Michael appears behind the figure of soprano Eva in the guise of a nurse, cradling the body of the young soldier, is filled by a music of eerily extended range for a specially constructed flugelhorn, played by Markus Stockhausen. The deeper conical bore of the keyed bugle is a change to a more mellow tone, and one that allows throaty, groaning pitches of a low fundamental to be produced. For once, in a curiously muted but also affecting scene, the brilliance of the solo trumpet is abandoned: a music cut unduly abruptly into music for choir that shares the valedictory significance as well as the title "Jenseits" (Beyond) originally considered for *Trans.* The lyric to this limpid and haunting music briefly alludes to the Urantia Book of prophecy, an esoteric publication the personal significance of which Stockhausen has vigorously denied more than once since the Cott conversations of 1971.

The visual transformation at this point is very strange. Within the glass bunker a control room appears, filled with white light. A transparent conveyor belt carrying silver and glass model soldiers, tanks, battleships and planes glides between two lines of people representing the two opposing forces. With croupier's long-handled sliders they draw items to either side. Presumably these are the trophies of war. On the wall digital dials after the style of the counters in *Jahreslauf* tally up the numbers. It is a strange combination of references. We see a conveyor belt out of Chaplin's *Modern Times,* with connotations of a mindless war generated by industry, located in a war operations bunker, in which models on a table are raked about by military planners like gaming chips. War is a gamble. The opposing lines also recall the underworld jury in Cocteau's *Orphée,* coldly acting according to the rules to decide if the young god of music will survive.

> When it became clear that the war was lost, the decline in human morality took me by surprise. . . . I learned that death was nothing I would ever be afraid of. I saw that when people are determined to win, as the Americans and English were then, they wouldn't hesitate to choose the most inhuman methods to win by. . . . It became clear to me that people acting collectively on a large scale could become completely impersonal and unconcerned, caring only to win, that's all.[7]

As the singing ends, with words suggesting the end, not only of suffering and death, but also, Messiaen-like, the end of time itself, female figures dressed as nurses join the male tally-masters, those for whom the conflict is seen as a battle of numbers and a Luziferian counting game. Their arrival coincides with the appearance of a bizarre musician on a motorized synthesizer. He wears green elephant ears and huge sunglasses, has a very long nose (as in Pinocchio), and plays with infectious happiness. Designed as a set piece for Simon Stockhausen, the composer's description of the character "Synthi-Fou" ("mad synthesist" rather than mad scientist) seems more like a caricature of Elton John. On the other hand, a keyboardist at this point in the narrative has to be a self-portrait as well, of the composer in his role as a pianist playing sentimental ballads and popular jazz to assuage the pains of the dying and keep up the spirits of the living.

This *Klavierstück XV* is a music of survival, of high spirits at having come through the ordeal alive and physically intact. But in an ironic twist, the exuberance is mixed with loathing: at defeat, at the debased music he was requested to play, and at the immorality he witnessed among the hospital personnel. It is as though in part he blames this music, and himself as its messenger, for stimulating this sexual frenzy in the midst of carnage to which his remark on the decline in human morality refers, and behavior to which the actions between the women and men on stage only hint at: "One after another they toss away their red cross nurses' caps, then also other parts of their glassy clothing."[8] Even the names of "Synthi-Fou" and his "foutouristic solo" [*sic*] are clues (in French) to an abandoned promiscuity. An image of traumatized and illusory happiness, it seems, and not much of a compliment to synthesizers in general, or son Simon. For all that, the music is genuinely exciting, of a good length, and a virtuoso showpiece that not only hints at an interplanetary Spike Jones, but also reminds us of the underlying exuberance of a postwar serial genre not normally associated with high spirits, in works such as Boulez's Second Piano Sonata. A nonelectronic version of "Synthi-Fou" for acoustic piano would be attractive.

During the Farewell music a listener becomes aware of glassy electronic sounds orbiting overhead. As "Synthi-Fou" counts down and slows down to a quasi d minor cadence (with unusually, a ritardando, and the only explicit counting in the entire work), one is left with a double system circling in the air, the larger orbit slightly abrasive, like a finger circling the edge of a wineglass (a Ben Franklin glass armonica sound), and a flickering central sound, hovering around a 440, that one suddenly imagines to be an entire melody sequence, perhaps of an hour or more, that has been accelerated over and over again until all that we can hear is a weird doll's cry: "w-w-w-ow-ow-ow-ow-ow-w-w-w . . . w-w-w-ow-ow-ow-ow-w-w-w . . . " Slow-motion transformations of electronic loops are a feature of black rock, whose acid sounds will return as the defining timbres of *Freitag aus LICHT*.

Notes

1. David Wise, "Spook Art: Was the CIA really behind the rise of Abstract Expressionism?" *ARTnews* Vol. 99 No. 8 (September 2000): 160–64.
2. Lady A. Irwin, in a letter to Lord Carlyle, March 31st, 1733. 108–9 in Norman Demuth comp. ed., *Anthology of Musical Criticism* (London: Eyre & Spottiswoode, 1947).
3. Note to the author dated 11.X.88.
4. Malcolm Arnold, *United Nations*. Unpublished score, reissued on cd EMI CMS7 63302-2.
5. *Dienstag aus LICHT*, cd booklet, 103–5.
6. Uwe M. Schneede, *Essential Max Ernst* tr. R. W. Last (London: Thames and Hudson, 1972), 56.
7. *SoM*, 22.
8. *Dienstag aus LICHT*, cd booklet, 90–91.

CHAPTER TWENTY-SEVEN

Freitag

Set in the dawning Renaissance fantasy world of Brueghel-land, a Europe decimated by the Black Death and deeply disorientated by advances in the astronomical sciences, Ligeti's satirical opera *Le Grand Macabre* provided a welcome antidote to millennial cultism in the late twentieth century, and a timely reminder that the Apocalypse and its attendant paranoias have been a part of civilized culture since the dawn of philosophy. Stockhausen's acknowledgement of rave music in *Dienstag aus LICHT*, and his decision to base an entire opera around a synthesizer-based idiom that had been shown to accompany altered states of mind, can be read in a number of ways. On the positive side, the electronic music of *Freitag aus LICHT* is an authentically dramatic experience and a marked improvement, it seems to me, on the impermeable glitter of *Sirius* and the flaccid plastic timbres of *Dienstag*. These are airy sounds with precisely audible movement and a variety of matt textures, combining the stiffness of the Synthi 100 timbres with a welcome range of finishes and reflectances. At the same time, the atmosphere seems heated, even radioactive, metaphorically speaking, to a point where breathing becomes difficult at times and a listener has the impression of being trapped inside a diving bell at the bottom of the ocean, or in a capsule lost in space.[1] Musically, the new idiom and its handling in a twelve-voice panoramic space are significant changes, and as one might expect, the result, both musically and technically, is considerably more nuanced and certainly less hazardous to listen to than acid house party music.

But this is Stockhausen, and the medium comes with a message. Friday (Frei-tag) is not just the day of Venus, Freya, Frigga etc., even though the libretto is sprinkled with words and phrases to do with nativity, women's liberation, eros, venery, sex, and so on. It is also the day of contemplation of the idea of freedom, and freedom for Stockhausen implies all of those

behaviors: addictive, sexual, demoralizing,—associated with a lifestyle without God and without self-discipline, *including* acid house music. Luzifer's
error, we remember, lay in defying the principle of hierarchy. Now it
appears that there is more at stake in this defiance than the future of music
under serialism: the composer is still pining after an ideal religious and
social order, perhaps even a caste system in the model of the latter-day
gurus of holism, one in which the enlightened few hold sway and the lower
orders, including dentists, lawyers, and music critics, are ordained to defer.
In 1981 his attitude to American abstract art, compared to Europe, was
uncompromising:

> The whole movement toward a so-called pop art, in the visual arts as
> well as in music, I see as a disaster, really shameful for mankind, once
> orientated toward the highest, whose only goal in art was to glorify the
> divine and the cosmic spirit, and for whom everything in the human
> world was related to these invisible worlds. That this is now replaced,
> generally speaking, by garbage art, which celebrates material imper-
> manence and decay, is a disgrace. . . . And what is true of the content is
> equally true of the form, if you base a whole way of life on do-it-yourself,
> and deliberately choose to express yourself in disposable materials,
> which are by design and definition of inferior quality, perishable, and
> even ugly.[2]

Freitag is Stockhausen's most explicit statement of Goethe's theory of color
as a theory of a universal spectrum of variable degradation, and it comes in
a dramatic and musical context of images representing the worst in anarchy, depravity, and social disorder. It is also shocking in its own way. The
world of mock depravity conjured up is a world of stuffed toys that, in an
inversion of Colette's libretto for Ravel's *L'Enfant et les Sortilèges*, instead of
suffering physical abuse at the hands of a spoilt and unhappy boy, to his
dismay stridently indulge their erotic fantasies in the name of freedom of
thought and action. They are creatures of dumb show, and they are also
machines symbolizing people and processes: a typewriter, a photocopier, a
pencil, a syringe: objects that penetrate, that mark, that give a thrill. They
also include a violin and bow. From photographs of the costumes designed
by Johannes Conen for the Leipzig Opera premiere, they look a lot more
interesting than the average drag ball, and are certainly not designed for
casual intimacy.

One is driven to wonder whether over the course of so many years
Stockhausen has changed his views toward, or become reconciled with, the
moral implications of his original *LICHT* scenario. For followers of his music
it may come as a shock to realize that the leading radical composer of the
fifties and sixties is at heart an old-world conservative and moral reactionary. For those who merely observe the progress of his operatic narrative
from day to day, the rapid attrition of text, musical forces, even partici-
pating members of his own family, tell their own bleak story of an idea that
is wasting away, like a statue of Giacometti, until all that is left is the
powerfully attenuated presence of a village fakir.

The moral and spiritual vacuum that accompanies liberation from a dictatorship of any kind was not only real for the students of Stockhausen's generation, furiously waving their cigarettes as though they were thuribles while intoning the dystopian mantras of Orwell and Sartre. The same intellectuals looked back to an earlier postrevolutionary era after 1792, and discovered a literature of equally troubling implications relating to sexual freedom as a metaphor for intellectual and political freedom, and sexual censorship under a new democratic social order as the new tyranny of the mediocre. Stockhausen's vision in *Freitag* does not merely reflect a personal distaste for the immorality of a younger generation, though that feeling, —ironically echoing the disdain openly expressed by expatriate German music faculty toward their "materialistic" American students that he noted during his 1958 tour of the United States,—is certainly part of the picture. More to the point is the celebration of freedom, among Parisian intellectuals at least, in the debauched persona and philosophy of the Marquis de Sade, compared to the more measured response, for a young German readership, of a Goethe whose novel *Die Walhverwandschaften*, set in the same pastoral landscape as Ingmar Bergman's 1955 movie *Smiles of a Summer Night*,—or indeed, Shakespeare's *A Midsummer Night's Dream*,—plays with the idea of romantic coupling and uncoupling among groups of individuals as an issue of choice between duty to the socially responsible roles assigned to them, or fidelity to their personal impulses or destinies. In Shakespeare's play, of course, the patrician gods (who have romantic issues of their own) are briefly entertained with a fantasy of love by their devoted but simple-minded servants, an interlude in a narrative whose potential for moral and social disorder reaches a climax with the intimidating contrivance of a Titania, under the influence of what would now be classified as a date rape potion, falling passionately in love with Bottom the weaver, who is not only way out of her class, but for the time being endowed with the head of an ass, and presumably equipment to match. So we are perhaps being unduly fussy in imputing a sour censoriousness to Stockhausen, when the composer's message of freedom and responsibility is a classic theme of art and literature, and one rich with comic potential.

Freitag aus LICHT (Friday from LIGHT)
1991–1994: No. 62–64 (Stockhausen-Verlag; cd SV-50)
Opera for soprano, baritone, and bass; flute, basset-horn, synthesizer player; 12 couples of dancer-mimes, children's choir, 12 choir singers; electronic music with sound scenes, sound projectionist.

Freitag–Versuchung (Friday Temptation)
1991–1994: No. 64 (Stockhausen-Verlag; cd SV-65)
Ten "Real Scenes" of Friday. For soprano, baritone, bass, flute, basset-horn, synthesizer; children's orchestra, children's choir, 12 choir singers, 12 couples of dancer-mimes; 16 transmitting microphones, 10 microphones, 24-track tape recorder, 12 loudspeakers, mixing console.
Duration: (cd) 1 hour 47'; (staged) 2 hours 25'.

For the Renaissance Italy of Shakespeare and Monteverdi, the rise of a new realistic art of opera coincided with the development of new instruments for expressing human emotion, and new formal principles of tone relationship, based on a scientific and mathematical understanding of equal temperament, that challenged the ideals of formal and moral perfection hitherto enshrined in religion. In order to arrive at a system of keyboard tuning that would allow freedom of modulation, the philosophers of the day had to wrestle with noncomputable numbers such as the square root of 2, and reconcile themselves and their clerical patrons to the fact that a tempered scale allowing modulation from key to key was a pact with the devil, a compromise with perfect harmony. At this time, similar theological and moral doubts attended the observation of planetary motion, which as an issue of steady-state cyclical vibration had always been regarded as an issue to be explained in terms of the acoustics of music. As astronomers came to grips with the reality of inconsistent motion of the planets, they were forced to a conclusion that the observed inconsistencies were in part due to orbits being elliptical rather than perfectly circular, and in part to the fact that the earth itself was in orbit around the sun, and not the center of the universe. So when either Shakespeare or Stockhausen is talking about harmony and dissonance in human relationships, the subtext of the discussion is by definition musical, and ultimately philosophical. Freedom in personal relationships implies a moral relativism; freedom in musical relationships (freedom to modulate from key to key) implies a relativism in temperament, and inevitably a compromise with ideal harmony; and acceptance of the real motion of the planets in turn implies a perception of order and organization that is relative to individual planetary or social (or indeed, religious) constituencies. In a strange kind of way, the issues of public concern surrounding Einstein's theory of relativity and Heisenberg's uncertainty principle in the early twentieth century can be seen once again as the historically predictable alarm responses of the adherents of a particular social order and associated belief system to the independent proponents of an alternative worldview that exposes traditional beliefs as ungrounded in reality and therefore irrational in principle.

Relativism in *Freitag* is expressed in three principal parameters: in the depiction of taboo human relationships; in the modulation of acoustic and musical identities (concrete sounds) by vocoder; and in the progressive dilation and compression of electronic tonalities in timescale, so that melody or rhythm structures imperceptibly emerge from apparently stable tones and fade back into them by a speed transformation process familiar from *Kontakte* and also a feature of electronic black rock music and the tape-loop music of the American minimalists of the sixties. Stockhausen has created *Freitag aus LICHT* as a work of three layers: an electronic layer in extreme slow motion, that plays more or less continuously, a layer of real-time actions performed onstage, to be interpreted *Kontakte* fashion as manifestations of musical relationships in human behavior and on a human timescale, and a third layer of intermodulated voices and sounds produced in the studio and visualized on stage as a surreal ballet of hybrid beings. Of the three, the so-called "real scenes" are perhaps the most controversial in their implications, and should be dealt with first.

The central action, and the most challenging, involves soprano Eva (who is now, for the first time, white-skinned and blonde), a bass Ludon, a Sarastro-like figure, and his baritone son Caino, who are both black. Eva always enters from the left (the side of a triptych associated with paradise), the two men from the right (the side associated with hell and damnation). Ludon and Eva greet one another. He then proposes that she unite with his son. She initially demurs, then after a series of musical games in which children of their respective tribes entertain one another, she concedes in the scene "Consent;" their union is consummated in the following scene "Fall," and is followed by a noisy "Children's War" and a ceremony of "Repentance."

Though naïvety and revanchist political incorrectness are certainly part of the mix, Stockhausen's dramatization of color in human relationships as the ceremonial miscegenation of an initially reluctant Aryan blonde Eva and a princely Othello figure named Caino is arguably faithful to the historic prejudices of white-skinned cultures of Europe, America, India, and Australasia, against people of color. One might have wished for a more tactful and high-minded treatment of a sensitive issue. (It is sad to see the composer abandoning his lifelong loyalty to Afro-American female singers and leading actors, in *Momente, Inori,* and previous operas in the cycle, for the sake of racial stereotyping, though it is equally possible that the switch of color between soprano and bass came about for reasons unconnected with race or gender superstitions. For example, the scene may also allude to the invasion and corruption of the motherland by black American jazz in the twenties and thirties (or worse, the white American jazz in blackface of Al Jolson's *Jazz Singer* and *Singing Fool*) that had such an impact on German music and morals.

However, a hidden dimension to this outwardly gratuitous act of droit de seigneur may be found in the structural anthropology of Lévi-Strauss and its musical implications. This is a crucial component of the opera since the entire purpose of anthopology is to establish the presence in primitive mythology of a universal code of permitted kinship relations. Two sets of myths examined in Lévi-Strauss are of particular relevance: one deals with the origin of water, and the other with the origin and transference of shamanistic powers. The Bororo myth of the origin of water is one source, as it were, of the multiple mythology (river of time, stream of consciousness) of Berio's *Sinfonia* of 1968, and fragments of Lévi-Strauss's text are cited in the first movement of that work.[3] Berio's appropriation of anthopological materials has been criticized, among others by Lévi-Strauss himself, as superficial and opportunistic. For Stockhausen (whose plus-minus scores of the sixties derive from the same sources in Lévi-Strauss) the structural relationships of myth have actual as well as symbolic significance, and the composer's task is to effect a reconciliation of relationship laws as they obtain in human culture throughout the ages, with the astrological laws on which they are based.

In mythical as in narrative terms the reconciliation process is both incomplete and manipulative. Stockhausen has his own fixation on water symbolism, and his adoption of Lévi-Strauss's account of American Indian mythologies of shamanistic succession (in which magical powers are passed between the generations) has perhaps more to do with accreditation of his son Simon's role as keeper of the electronic keyboards, than with perpetuating the tribe. Lévi-Strauss's analysis of the Pawnee myth of the pregnant boy exposes a series of oppositions, between the initiated shaman and the noninitiated shaman, child versus old man, fertility of the child versus sterility of the old man, etc.

> According to [J. R.] Murie, "the usual way to become a medicine-man was to succeed one's teacher at his death." The myth, on the contrary, is based upon a two-fold concept of innate power, which, because it is *innate*, is denied the boy by the master; because the boy's power is not taught him by the master, the master refuses to acknowledge him as his successor. . . . Among these tribes, societies are based on age-grades. The transition from one to another is achieved by purchase, and the relationship between seller and buyer is conceived as a relationship between "father" and "son." Finally, the candidate always appears in the company of his wife, and the central motif of the transaction is the handing over of the "son's" wife to the "father," who carries out with her an act of real or symbolic coitus, which is, however, always represented as a fertility act.[4]

Stockhausen has inverted the myth and thus converted it from a delegation of musical authority into a symbolic acknowledgement of a new generation of shamanistic power. That may redeem the gesture symbolically, but does not make it appear any less distasteful on the operatic stage in Wagnerian costume.

In practice it is not so much the mixed-race actions that seem calculated to offend, as the crudeness of the antique prejudices associated with the imagery:—of white and black, purity and defilement, of womankind as sinful by nature,—and the impression that these are perceptions with which the composer, while protesting his role as a messenger, silently concurs. The bad taste extends, through a succession of abbreviated comic book scenes of musical play and tribal warfare, to imagery of African culture, expressed in music and musical instruments, as primitive in manufacture and uncivilized in organization. In the scene "Kinder-Orchester" a European children's orchestra, consisting of a motley collection of instruments including guitars and piano accordians, earnestly playing simple music from score sheets, is presented as more sophisticated than the indigenous music of African peoples, a perception now recognized as not only offensive and silly, but manifestly untrue, even as it draws attention to the disparity between oral and literate cultures in their musical priorities, and by inference, the priorities in relationship and communication skills attendant on them.

But there is more to the African equation (which includes the appalling pun "Afro-dite") than a plot reduction of Shakespeare's *Othello* for listeners of limited comprehension and short attention span. (In fact we are closer to the symbolism of Sarastro and the Queen of the Night in this particular match, than to Shakespearean tragedy.) The intermarriage of black and white is already predicated in Goethe's theory of color,—a theory of human moral and character differences, that is,—as degrees of contamination of light with darkness. Goethe's theory is perhaps marginally more humane, since it is possible to argue that darkness in this case implies only absence of light, rather than moral perversity.

Clues to the wider musical implications of Friday's homily on the perils of unrestricted interbreeding can also be found in the given names of the male proponents, the Zoroastrian Ludon and his sidekick Caino. Confirmation of the ambiguous significance of the "Hu" call, previously speculated to carry the double-edged message of sacredness and contempt, is revealed in the nocturnal scene of Eva "yielding," as the booklet coyly puts it, to the advances of her noble suitor, in the upright position in the middle of a virtual lake, a sacrifice of comfort for the sake of an ongoing symbolic association of women and wetness. This scene is watched over by basset-horn and flute, and accompanied by various birdcalls, among which one is pleased to note the hooting of an eagle owl (in German, "zweimal schreit ein Uhu"). One might be forgiven for interpreting Ludon as an alias for Luzifer, and Caino as the Cain of the Old Testament, but a closer look suggests that Caino is actually "Ka-ino," as in "neutrino," a micro-version (DNA code, possibly) of the composer himself. If so, then Ludon (as in "muon") is also a fundamental particle, and the coupling taking place is metaphorically speaking a nuclear reaction, and the lake is poetic licence for a watercooled reactor. The same imagery is stated more explicitly in the composer's fragmentary libretto for *"Atmen gibt das Leben . . . ,"* an early sketch for *LICHT* in which Christ, the "secret messenger, disguised as a man with a normal body, [who] brought the news to the crew of the captured planet . . . that the Cause is not yet lost," rides in to earth on a ray of muons. Verse 7 of the text alludes unambiguously to the sex life of elementary particles: "häi Eva . . . och, Adam. . . . Wenn die Mesons . . . es mit den Muons . . . ensteht ein Elektron . . . doch erst die Neutrinos" (hey, Eva!—What, Adam?—When mesons do it with muons, you get an electron!—Yes, but first neutrinos).

The name Ludon can also be construed Ave–Eva fashion as a mirror image (allowing that the nasal [ō] stands for both [–on] and [–om]) of the word "Modul," as in Modul 69A, the device developed to produce cleaner modulated sounds for the tape of *Kurzwellen mit Beethoven*, or the further refined Modul 69B developed for the two pianos of *Mantra*. (Why these items were allocated the numbers 69A and 69B is anybody's guess.) So there is a further chain of reaction, as it were, connecting the defilement of the tribe with the mutations that arise from nuclear radiation, and the hybridization of voices and concrete sounds by intermodulation, that is, by vocoder. Coming from Stockhausen, the notion of intermodulation as unnatural, and by extension, of vocoder-based children's radio stories from the fifties, of Jack Benny and his talking violin, or Sparky and the talking engine, as literally perverse, is a bit over the top, though it might be fairer to interpret any intensity of feeling as covert frustration at not being able to emulate the magic of those early exercises by Herbert Eimert and Heinz Schütz from the fifties.

Komet als Klavierstück XVII (Comet as Piano Piece XVII)

1994–1999: No. 64/7 extract (unpublished: cd SV-57; electronic music SV-64)
For electronic keyboards ad lib and tape; 2-track tape recorder, 2 × 2 loudspeakers, mixing console.
Duration: 14' 30.

In what may be construed as a response to the growth of an internet "sample and download" culture, the new work authorizes a keyboardist or computer operator of composition software to create a personal work against the backdrop of the "Kinder-Krieg" music. The choice of title, a comet being a symbol of doom, and of the particular scene, in which the children of opposing tribes play at fighting among themselves, express a point of view also voiced in the tenor's terrible cry "Eva! Unserer Kinder!" (in other words, "What is the world coming to?"), and in the tolling bells of doom that accompany the tape. A realization of the composer's instructions is recorded on SV-57, and a version of the electronic music alone, incorporating a rehearsal tape of the voice parts, on SV-64. The player is instructed to compile samples, specifically the sounds of toys, on which to improvise decorations ("points, curved glissandi, tremoli, intervals, chords, short arpeggi") on the pitches of chords audible in the tape. The improvised elements should also "elucidate" [sic] the tempi and beat patterning of individual measures. Then again, as in "Mission Impossible" the follow-up to an invitation to play the game, "if you choose to accept it," is presumably the composer's fervent hope that "this recording will self-destruct." Though the relationship of performer to tape is arguably a return to Stockhausen's original plan for Kontakte, and again for Hymnen mit Solisten, by definition the workplan contains no new ideas, leaving the composer's presence in the new score as relatively unquantifiable.

Tonszenen vom Freitag (Sound Scenes of Friday)

1991–1994: No. 63 (Stockhausen-Verlag; cd "Elektronische Music mit Tonszenen vom Freitag aus LICHT," SV-39)
Tape music for soprano, bass, electronic instruments; 2-track tape recorder, 2 × 2 loudspeakers, mixing console.
Duration: 52'. Combined duration with electronic music: 2 hours 25'.

The twelve Sound Scenes form the most complex layer of Freitag (organized complexity, that is, as distinct from the complexities of the choruses, which are aleatoric to a large degree). They return to the familiar territory of intermodulated sounds that for Stockhausen started with his introduction to ring modulation in the taped inserts of Déserts of Varèse (the Sound Scenes are inserts too, of course), continued with his introduction to the original Bell Labs vocoder originally brought to Cologne by Werner Meyer-Eppler, and successfully employed during the fifties by Stockhausen's senior colleagues in the creation of a few demonstration pieces but, for reasons of sonic quality, temperament, or ideology, not by Stockhausen himself. In 1964 with Mixtur he took up ring modulation, adapted it to a smaller ensemble for cleaner results, then modified it for voices with some success in *Mikrophonie II*, the modulating agent being changed from sweep frequency oscillators to a Hammond organ capable of harmonies, though not gliding tones. At NHK Radio in Tokyo he worked with an envelope shaper, controlled by an external signal, to intermodulate tones and tone complexes with prerecorded voices and music, somewhat in the manner of shortwave radio. Based on his Tokyo experience of a modulating process, also using compression and filtering of the signals to produce a cleaner result (a technique strictly comparable with the Bell vocoder, but operating in real time), Stockhausen developed modified circuitry for the taped sounds of *Kurzwellen mit Beethoven (Opus 1970)*, and this experience led directly to the dramatic success and breakthrough of *Mantra*.

After that time, coinciding with the arrival of the Synthi 100, his interest in ring-modulation seems to have lapsed, and while it is possible that he was simply more excited by the creative possibilities of permutating and intermodulating rhythm, dynamic, and pitch sequences by hand using the sequencer, as in *Sirius*, it is also clear that it took some time for him to adjust to the EMS Vocoder that was also purchased by Cologne Radio at this time. It is in fact this relatively ancient item of equipment that plays a starring role in the Sound Scenes. It is an analogue device, of course, and although it is certainly true that the modulated *objets sonores* are uncontaminated with the side-band distortion that has previously been a feature of ring-modulation in general, it is also the case that the offspring of intermodulation are also not always recognizable in terms of their parent sounds, nor always well-behaved. The "bastard" quality so cheerfully attributed to genetic intermodulation has probably more to do with the world of electronic sound than the morals of the younger generation, or the creation of mutants as an unwelcome consequence of playing with radiation. There are mixed messages being given here. The twelve couples in order are:

1. soprano, bass (unmodulated);
2. soprano + cat, bass + dog;
3. soprano + photocopy machine, bass + typewriter;
4. soprano + racing car, bass + racing car driver (with added ramp wave oscillation);
5. soprano + pinball machine, bass + pinball player;
6. soprano + "soccer ball in flight," bass + kicking foot;
7. soprano + owl (Uhu), bass + rocket;
8. soprano + sighing woman, bass + syringe (and swarm of bees);
9. soprano + electric pencil sharpener, bass + pencil;
10. soprano + woman's mouth slurping, bass + ice-cream cone (and drops and bee);
11. soprano + violin, bass + violin bow;
12. soprano + bird's nest (dry twigs), bass + jackdaw (blackbird).

Not all of the couple sounds are recognizable sound effects. Some are live recorded, others are taken from studio effects discs. Some have undisguised erotic associations. Like the prescriptions for *Alphabet für Liège*, it is a loose collection, some of which are more like ideas for sounds that suit the composer's serial purpose. But those that are recognizable sounds, are in principle distinctively structured in pitch and rhythm:

cat meow: continuous wail;

dog bark: accentual/rhythmic;

photocopier: hum, regular clicking rhythm;

typewriter: irregular tapping, high density;

pinball machine: irregular clicking, low density;

kicking foot: low thud;

owl: intermittent rhythm on one note;

rocket: continuous dense noise, fading gradually;

sighing woman: muted descending glissando;

swarm of bees: cloud of pitches, mid-range;

electric pencil sharpener: high-pitched grinding noise;

slurping on an ice-cream: shaped high-frequency noise;

licking on an ice-cream: rhythmic;

violin: musical voice-like timbre;

bird's nest: cluster of high-frequency twig noises;

jackdaw: harsh birdcall, mid-range.

Of indeterminate nature are: racing car driver, pinball player, the movement of a soccer ball (a whizz effect), a drug syringe (puncturing sound), a pencil being sharpened, and a violin bow. Among the rest, the human sounds (kicking, sighing, licking) are acoustically problematic as sounds for modulating, while others (owl, violin) are rather too precise in pitch to modulate effectively. That they are symbolic as well as musical in implication is obvious, and this also complicates matters acoustically. Almost certainly this is the fundamental reason why the modulated sounds are projected in mono rather than stereo.

What a listener is led to expect from the intermodulation process in *Freitag*, however, is *at least* stereo, and potentially four-channel hybrid sound shapes spontaneously floating in space: this can be inferred from a process in which both original sounds are stereo recorded.[5] On the other hand, if the EMS Vocoder is only designed to produce a mono output, a multichannel result is clearly not feasible. Hence the unusual ceremonial twelve-speaker arrangement, which unlike the cubic octophonic array that allows the composer scope to move concrete sounds up, down, and around in a three-dimensional virtual space, seems deliberately organized to obviate it. Speakers are assigned, like television monitors, to particular couples; the resulting polyphony of locations evoking the pre-stereo, post-Gabrieli system in place for *Gesang der Jünglinge*, but more striking than the historical associations is the impression that the coupled sounds are lacking in plastic dimension and movement, are caged, and not for public release.

After "Fall" the pairs of sounds are interchanged, to produce new hybrid sounds. The exchanging of couples is linked in the opera to immorality in varying degrees, but all that serves to do is underscore the often arbitrary relations of most of the legitimate couples we began with. On stage the forbidden couplings are seen to produce offspring of an engaging surreality (instantly, with no birth pains, as in *Montag*), but they give voice in the closing "Chor-Spirale" as unmodulated female and male voices, which is a further puzzle.

The Sound Scenes of *Freitag* are typically rich and often seemingly stressful acoustic shapes that provoke attention and convey, I think appropriately, a sense of the grotesque and twisted. That such outcomes are invariably neuter, or misshapen, or morally indefensible, is not in principle so clear-cut, and one is left with a sense that in this case the eugenic argument of corruption of the gene pool is perhaps more of an alibi after the fact for a promising procedure in musical regeneration that just didn't work out.

It may seem needlessly unfair to criticize Stockhausen for not succeeding in processes that no other composer has accomplished, and of which most musicians and listeners are blissfully unaware. The peculiar virtue of Stockhausen's music, however, is that these are processes to which the composer is self-evidently committed, and for that reason the music arising from his numerous compositions involving intermodulation deserves the credit of being taken seriously. The fact that we know his intentions gives his music a focus and a fundamental integrity of purpose, even though the processes may lead to mixed results. That history defines this aspect of his musical evolution as "exploratory experimentation" in precisely the same spirit as Goethe's investigations into color and light.

Stockhausen's involvement in intermodulation processes started in 1964, four years after Meyer-Eppler's death. He was unable therefore to ask Meyer-Eppler's advice, and would be forced to rely on his notes from Meyer-Eppler's seminars at Bonn University. These seminars coincided with the composition of *Gesang der Jünglinge* (which is about the formation of sound elements into coherent speech), and their aims and objectives were similar. To describe the string of compositions beginning with *Mikrophonie I* and ending with *Mantra* as "exploratory experiments" after the Goethe pattern, is simply to say that they are informed by a vision of an outcome rather than an understanding of underlying processes. Taken as a whole, these efforts over the years come across as a series of hit-or-miss trials driven by intuition and involving too many variables from one to the next to allow definite conclusions to be drawn. Indeed, after *Mantra* they dry up completely, a consequence all the more remarkable considering that it is more than likely that Zinovieff built the Cologne EMS vocoder, as he did the Synthi 100, to Stockhausen's exacting specification.[6]

For Stockhausen the essence of a modulation process is the mutual interference of two contrasting signals to produce a hybrid, previously unknown signal. In *Mikrophonie I* the tam-tam is presented as a vibrating disc operated on from either side to produce left and right channels of a pseudo-stereo event. His intention can therefore be read as a musical inquiry into the behavior of the diaphragm of a bidirectional or "figure of eight" microphone. Since the left and right (front and back) outputs of the same diaphragm are the same, but move in opposing directions, the two signals added together tend to cancel one another. In addition the tam-tam is also behaving like a reverberation plate, prolonging and blending together the noises produced on either side, like the echo chamber in the electronic *Studie II*. In a classic sum and difference stereo operation the left and right channels are derived from front (A) and back (B) outputs of a bi-directional microphone by a combined addition and subtraction process leading in this case to the following distribution:

Left channel: A + (A − B reverb)   Right channel: B + (B − A reverb)

In *Mikrophonie I* of course, the A and B outputs are also manually shaped by special filters along the way. Ideally the end result is a vocoder-like modulated vibration that stands out against a reverberant background: —an acoustic equivalent, in effect, of a random-dot stereogram of the kind devised by Bela Julesz at Bell Labs in the sixties.[7]

After the noisy experiences of *Mixtur* and *Mikrophonie II*, a consequence of modulating electrical rather than acoustic signals, Stockhausen produced a very clean *Telemusik* in Japan with an alternative system of amplitude modulation in which the dynamic shape of one signal is reproduced on a second carrier signal. Based on the dynamic sound projection system devised by RCA for Disney's *Fantasia* of 1940, and adapted by Philips in 1958 for the Brussels Expo presentation of Varèse's *Poème Électronique*, it differs from ring modulation in subjecting a passive signal to the dynamic envelope (but not the oscillating content) of an active signal. In *Mantra* a compromise is achieved between ring modulation and amplitude modulation, using sine tones to color the timbre of electronically simplified piano tones.

With the *Indianerlieder* of 1972 Stockhausen returns to the essentially acoustic intermodulation process of *Mikrophonie I*, but with important differences. Two singers, seated face to face on stage, progress through a series of chants beginning with a modulated unison tone and gradually working up to a complete set of twelve pitches (a development from simple to complex also encountered in *Inori*). On this occasion the interference of the two voices occurs in the air space between them, which can be considered as a vibrating surface with no mass: hence, optimum interaction. In addition, the voices are tuned, relatively well matched, and controllable signaling agents whose degree of mutual reinforcement can be predicted and specified in a musical score. The artistic challenge (as yet unrealized) is of controlling the voices and listening to the plastic interactions that arise when two signals from opposing directions meet and combine. To succeed artistically implies voices of exceptional purity and focus, and dynamic control. The technical challenge (likewise unrealized) is of capturing the acoustic interaction taking place in the space between the two singers, using a bidirectional microphone.

Stockhausen has hardened his attitude toward electronic modulation since the early years. After lengthy trials of manual intermodulation of the triple formula, using the Synthi 100, and transferring the results to paper in heavily modulated solos for virtuoso trumpet, basset-horn, and flute, Stockhausen comes back to the EMS vocoder in *Freitag aus LICHT* in order, it seems, to characterize the device as a devilish contrivance that can do no good. That moral overlay tells its own story of dissatisfaction, but the mismatched and modulated "Couples of Friday" continue to pose the question, as it were, of how two complex signals may combine to produce a new hybrid result. (The mythical insemination of Eva by piano in *Montag aus LICHT* can be seen in this context as a desperate maneuver; unsuccessful too, since the musical children produced as a consequence of this symbolic act of genetic intermodulation do not stay around.) The challenge is ours to decide, whether the process can be made to produce other than bastard results. Since what we are considering is already exemplified in those initial children's recordings of the fifties, of talking trains, planes, and violins, the answer is surely yes. The interesting new ingredient is how, through classic Bell (not EMS) vocoder modulation, to arrive at genuine stereo—or even quad, or octophonic—results: a sort of abstract holophonic audio, equivalent acoustically in real space to computer 3D holographic modeling in virtual space, and considerably more interesting than the bouncing cubes and spheres that flex and dance across a sleeping computer screen.

Klavierstück XVI (Piano Piece XVI)
1995: ex No. 63½ (Stockhausen-Verlag; cd SV-57)
For piano (or electronic keyboards) and tape.
Duration: 7'.

Piano Piece XVI is a piece to be freely worked out by the pianist, an exercise of virtuosity perhaps corresponding to the realization of a figured bass in classical times. Once again, as in the original conception of *Kontakte*, the performer is bidden to create a piece through repeated listening to a tape, here an extract from the Sound Scenes, and by synchronizing accent notes with the same pitches on the tape. Not virtuosity, but imagination and a sense of humor are required, the composer advises. Any such humor is offset, however, by the composer's selection of a tape segment, in his own terms, of morbid perversity, and for the hapless performer, of unbelievable complexity: the ultimate pileup and dismemberment of Couples starting at Sound Scene 12A (track 54 of SV-39) through to 12B (track 72). Here as in Piano Piece XVII the composer seems to be abandoning the keyboard of his youth with an angry and defiant gesture.

Freitags-Gruss (Friday Greeting)
Freitags-Abschied (Friday Farewell)
1991; 1992–1994: No. 62 (Stockhausen-Verlag; cd SV-39)
Electronic music for 8-track tape; 8 loudspeakers, mixing console.
Duration: 1 hour 8'. 30 + 1 hour 18'.

The story of the electronic music is reminiscent of H. G. Wells's short story "The New Accelerator" in which two chemists take a potion that accelerates human metabolism, and with it the experience of time, to a point where the world around them appears hardly to move. Like most of Wells's fictions, the story is based on actual experience of time dilation in the movies and also in early sound recording, when the speed at which a recording was reproduced often differed, sometimes markedly, from the speed at which it had originally been made on camera or wax. In the early days of manual recording neither the industry nor the public paid very much attention either to constancy in the flow of recorded time, or to coordinating the running speed of movie and audio reproducing equipment, to ensure that these speeds conformed to real time. Consequently, early phonographs were equipped with simple varispeed controls and the general public quickly became accustomed to the idea of the time of a recording as a variable to be coordinated or varied at will in relation to real time. It is a very short step from that perception to the notion that if human existence were regarded in the same terms as the recorded voice, i.e., as an experience analogous to the movement of a stylus along a groove or time line, it might be conceivable to pursue the idea of altering the speed at which life itself is experienced. In effect, slow- and fast-motion movie photography in science have made this a reality, not only revealing patterns in natural movement that were not previously visible, but also sharpening real-time perceptions to a degree that previously subliminal movements are now routinely detected. For others, to be sure, the attractions of an accelerated lifestyle are sought after through the consumption of recreational drugs.

That different creatures "live" at different relative speeds is implicit in the comparative description of individuals as slow or fast in their reactions, and the common belief that larger and slower-moving animals experience time on a slower scale from butterflies or mosquitos. The slow-motion time-scale of Stockhausen's electronic music for *Freitag* may be intended, for that reason, to create an impression of time running down, or of human actions on stage viewed from the time perspective of a larger-than-life consciousness. It is only fair to emphasize that an imagery that for many people is synonymous with drug-taking has nothing to do with, and should not be interpreted as reflecting on, the composer's own lifestyle. The experience of modulating time or living at different relative speeds has been a constant feature of his composing life since his apprenticeship in Paris with Pierre Schaeffer. As an art of montage of prerecorded "found objects," musique concrète relies on vari-speeding and its associated perceptions as a primary dimension of musical expression, involving the simultaneous transformation of pitch, time, clarity, and character of an acoustic event. Stockhausen's theory of the unity of musical time, published after more than ten years of practical work in electronic music (involving the acceleration of tape loops into timbres), and theoretical work in instrumental music (as in *Gruppen*'s expansion of microscopic waveforms into macroscopic structures), is surely evidence enough of an intellectual clarity on the subject of relative time-scales and perceptions to a degree incompatible with any passive addiction to "mind-expanding" narcotics (which do no such thing).[8]

Despite its austerity, the electronic music of *Freitag* deserves to be better appreciated for a number of positive reasons. It has a new and welcome texture; it is formed in long lines of continuously modulated tone quality; it is conventionally harmonious, in a bleak kind of way, but nevertheless reaching out to classical tonality; and, through use of the vocoder, is also harmonious in the sense of emulating the vowels of modulated speech. The composer's own voice, unusually in bass register, sings through the Luziferian sequence of numbers in slow motion, as if synchonized with a recording originally synthesized at eight times the speed (and three octaves higher). That his actual voice is heard in real time at this unaccustomed low register, simulating the effects of a massive deceleration (including extended consonants and beautifully rolled trills) is in complementary relation with the boy's voice of *Gesang der Jünglinge*, which is also always heard in real time, though in a musical context of accelerated motion. The coexistence of timescales, previously associated with transpositions of the formula, is experienced literally in the composer's juxtaposition of this slow layer with dramatic interpolations (the Real Scenes) in real time, and vocoder-modulated tape events (Sound Scenes) emulating an accelerated perception. (That the slow-moving electronic music dominates is a way of reinforcing the impression that what we are witnessing is a universe in microcosm where the children are actually Lilliputian adults, and the adult relations depicted are as between positively- and negatively-charged elementary particles.)

Max Mathews was among the first, back in the late fifties, to address the noncomputability of violin tone, which does not reduce to a simple waveform. It is of considerable interest that the textured quality of the electronic timbres of *Freitag* shows a degree of success in developing a method of synthesis that goes beyond the limitations of standard waveform replication to introduce a notional resistance into the equation, as between bow and string. That more complex interactive process is also key to a more authentic modeling of the human voice. Both instruments involve modulated friction, the resistance of vibrating elements, and associated reverberation (which is also subject to modulation). The textured electronic sounds of *Freitag* look ahead to reentry of the string quartet, in an analogous role, in the "Helikopter-Streichquartett." The focus on texture and continuity make particular sense in the context of researches in the same area simultaneously taking place at IRCAM.

In a letter to Alexander von Zemlinsky Schoenberg objected strenuously to a proposed cut in *Pelleas und Melisande* on the admirable ground that:

> Brevity and succinctness are a matter of *exposition*. In this case the details are not conceived compactly; it is all long-winded. If I cut some such details, the other long-winded ones remain, and it remains a work of long-winded exposition. it will not take so long to play, but it *will not really be shorter*! A work that has been shortened by cutting may very well give the impression of being an excessively long work (because of the exposition) that is too short in various places (where it has been cut).[9]

Despite the music's chronological length, the impression prevailing from the over two hours of electronic music in *Freitag* is of a lyrical and essentially momentary experience. We are perhaps in the same emotional territory as the "Pluramon" episode in *Hymnen*, an ultimate waking dream in which remembered images reappear and vanish in a flash. The electronic music also returns, with less success, to the earlier motif of "Kathinkas Gesang," that is, of simulating the sound of Wagner's bells of Montsalvat, whose tolling forms the epilogue to *Freitag* and a departing memory for the audience.

Notes

1. "Weltraum" (Outer Space) is in fact the composer's title for the electronic music of the Greeting and Farewell when performed separately, without Tone Scenes or Real Scenes.
2. *SoM*, 140.
3. Claude Lévi-Strauss, "Three-Part Inventions." In *Raw and the Cooked: Introduction to a Science of Mythology* (New edition. London: Pimlico, 1994), 199–215. See also Célestin Deliège, *Cinquante Ans de Modernité Musicale: De Darmstadt à l'IRCAM* (Sprimont: Mardaga, 2002), 491–92.
4. Claude Lévi-Strauss, "Structure and Dialectics." *Structural Anthropology*, 235–36.
5. *SoM*, 150–51.
6. *SoM*, 130–31.
7. Bela Julesz, "Experiments in the Visual Perception of Texture." *Scientific American*, 232 (1975): 34–43.
8. *SoM*, 99–100.
9. Arnold Schoenberg, "To Alexander von Zemlinsky: Vienna, 20 March 1918." *Letters,* ed. Erwin Stein, tr. Eithne Wilkins and Ernst Kaiser (London: Faber and Faber, 1964), 54–56.

CHAPTER TWENTY-EIGHT

Mittwoch

George Antheil's *Ballet mécanique* is a work endlessly talked about but until recently rarely listened to. Years ago I discovered a special order Columbia vinyl disc in a record store, but there were no liner notes and I learned afterward that it was the composer's 1952 revised, heavily edited, and watered-down version of the score.[1] A new recording issued in 2000 is much closer to the original.[2]

Why should this music composed in 1924–1925, before Stockhausen was even born, be of interest to a student of his music? The evidence is circumstantial and mostly trivial. But it adds up. Let's make a list. In no particular order:

1. The score incorporates the sound of a propellor airplane.
2. The composer's "bad boy of music" image.
3. The work's connection to Parisian culture of the 1920s.
4. The futurist connection.

After seventy-five years Antheil's *Ballet mécanique* still manages to shock and intrigue, partly because people are better listeners, in part because the digital medium preserves the musical pandemonium in high definition. And as well as being entertaining, for listeners already acquainted with Stockhausen's "Helikopter-Streichquartett" the older work is a curiously familiar experience: not just for the propellor sound, but also the music's unremitting energy, its texture, not to mention the dramatic silences and movable clusters that make the pianola solo sound in places like offcuts from Piano Piece X. Anybody who knows and enjoys Stockhausen's music will find intriguing pre-echoes of it in this pioneer example of musical futurism, and anyone who is excited by Antheil's music will find reason to admire Stockhausen's clearly more sophisticated handling of comparable material.

Stockhausen's famous attention to the inner life of airplane sounds, experienced leaning against the window of a succession of propellor aircraft on his long 1958 lecture tour of the United States, finds an unlikely echo in Gertrude Stein, the celebrated literary American in Paris, who by her own account was moved to write *The Making of Americans* through a similar fascination, this time with the interior music of spoken language:

> I began to get enormously interested in hearing how everybody said the same thing over and over again with infinite variations but over and over again until finally if you listened with great intensity you could hear it rise and fall and tell all that there was inside them, not so much by the actual words they said or the thoughts they had but the movement of their thoughts and words endlessly the same and endlessly different.[3]

The Paris-based surrealists were revolted by war (recalling that their leader André Breton, like Stockhausen, also saw service as a medical orderly) and took refuge in dreams and the irrational. The airplane in those days was a machine of dreams. In René Clair's charming movie fantasy *Paris qui dort* of 1924, passengers alight from a small propellor airplane to discover a Paris where time has stopped, allowing them the freedom to scrutinize a world in suspended animation. In *Entr'acte*, Clair's movie interlude for Francis Picabia's ballet *Relâche* (to music by Erik Satie) we see images of a kind we have come to expect from Stockhausen: a camel-drawn hearse, a bearded dancer (Satie) wearing a tutu, a huntsman on the rooftops, and glimpses of Marcel Duchamp and Man Ray playing chess. There is a lightness of fantasy, a detached inconsequentiality in those early movies that chimes rather well with the spirit of *LICHT*.[4]

Mittwoch aus LICHT (Wednesday from LIGHT)

1995–1997: No. 65–71 (Stockhausen-Verlag)
Opera in a greeting, four scenes and a farewell. For bass voice (with shortwave receiver); flute, basset-horn, trumpet, trombone, string quartet; choir with singing conductor; orchestra of 13 instruments (or 2 × 13): flute, oboe, clarinet, bassoon, horn; trumpet, trombone, tuba; percussionist; violin, viola, cello, contrabass; synthesizer player; 2 dancer-mimes; electronic music; sound projectionist.
Duration: 4 hours 37'.

Europa-Gruss (Europe Greeting)

1992–2002: No. 72 (Stockhausen-Verlag; cd SV-64)
For multiple wind instruments (or synthesizers), 8 solo (e.g., trumpets), 2 tutti groups (treble), and 2 tutti groups (bass).
Duration 12' 30.

LICHT-Ruf (Call from LIGHT)

1995: No. 67 (Stockhausen-Verlag; cd SV-64)
Call-signal (e.g., an interval signal) for trumpet, basset-horn, trombone, or other instruments (may be prerecorded).
Duration: 5 × 22" (or more often).

Mittwochs-Gruss (Wednesday Greeting)

1998: No 65 (Stockhausen-Verlag; cd SV-66)
Electronic music. 8-track tape recorder, 4 × 2 loudspeakers, mixing console.
Duration: 54'.

"Middling" is the theme of *Mittwoch*: "mid-week," mediation, striking a balance, reaching a compromise, muddling through. Also reconciliation: this is Stockhausen in nostalgic vein, traveling back in time to 1952 Paris to relive the pioneer spirit of early musique concrète, and beyond that to the first three decades of the twentieth century, the period immediately before he was born in which so many ideas were launched that came to fruition in his lifetime and in his music.

Changes of numbering of works in the Stockhausen catalogue indicate some revisions in the planning and execution of this new opera. "Europa-Gruss" was originally composed in 1992 in response to a commission from the Étoile Sonore Europe Festival for a "Europa-Fanfare." With a full complement of eight solo trumpeters, an extra solo trumpeter (Markus Stockhausen) as director, and 240 other participants, Stockhausen imagined an immensely enlarged version of the Wednesday tranche of the three-layer *LICHT* superformula as an appropriately Henry Brant-scaled music for such a large ensemble. The piece is monumental and effective for outdoors, in a *Samstag* kind of way, and was initially assigned the work number 65. For some reason, perhaps related to its similarity to the music of "Samstags-Gruss," Stockhausen decided at a later point to replace it with electronic music, and in 2002 he made a reduced version of the score for 10 instrumentalists. It is this later version, now assigned the work number 72, that is available on compact disc. Then followed the insertion of "Licht-Ruf," a four-measure fanfare or interval signal, composed in 1995, and assigned work number 67. "Orchester-Finalisten" changed from work number 67 to work number 68, and "Helikopter-Streichquartett" from work number 68 to work number 69.

From the outset, the music of *LICHT* has been composed with a view to recycling its component parts as individual works in the manner of virtuoso transcriptions of symphonic works for solo piano in the nineteenth century. A part of this strategy has been the repackaging of entire movements: of *Der Jahreslauf* as Act I of *Dienstag*, of "Luzifers Traum" as Piano Piece XIII, etc. In *Mittwoch aus LICHT* the use of dual versions or remixes of the same music is elevated to a structural principle. The music of "Mittwochs-Gruss" is a remix of the electronic music of "Michaelion," the concrete music of "Mittwochs-Abschied" is a remix of the tape music of "Orchester-Finalisten," and "Orchester-Finalisten" was conceived as a work of two halves in which identical groups of soloists interpret the same scores in different ways. It is a bit like Alice through the Looking Glass, or a comparison of left and right stereo channels, or a meditation (after the intermodulations of *Freitag*) on the mystery of dual identity. In any event, it looks ahead to the twin perspectives of "Hoch-Zeiten" in *Sonntag aus LICHT*.

"Mittwochs-Gruss" is another all-electronic work, this time with a lighter touch; the sound has an overall metallic sheen of chrome and glitter, like an airbrush painting, but there is a greater bass presence, and more dance-like pan-rotation of the various layers (here limited to the lateral plane, while "Montags-Abschied" explores the vertical). The young synthesizer virtuoso Antonio Pérez Abellán is Stockhausen's collaborator and contributor to the new sound vocabulary. Stockhausen's music has always been "over-produced" from an industry point of view, and it appears he is driving the process to a great many generations in the digital domain. In the choice of materials one notices if anything a greater attention to shifts in temporal perspective, giving rise to the simultaneous appearance of pairs of sounds from a similar initial source but transposed to opposite extremes of pitch and timescale, "delving in" to the microstructure of a sound wave by a process of repeated digital sampling and transposition of preformed material. At 8' 50", for example, a heavily reverberated tolling bass, carrying a lot of noise, is accompanied by a bicycle bell-like glistening ring, with a matt texture, that seems to be a transposition of it. At times the music behaves like an electronic version of *Carré*, in which steady state sounds and accelerated textures take turns at hovering and gliding through space, and just as in the earlier work, it turns out that the more textured sounds, those with an inner pulsation or movement, are perceived to rotate more naturally, since the phase components are less critical.

Though still relatively saturated in high frequencies, and thus rather nasal in tone, the new superrealist aesthetic, like a bright and glossy photograph, is less fixated than the reddish slow burn of *Freitag*, more lively and open to sudden discovery. At 7' 24" a female voice (Kathinka Pasveer) is heard, but "through a glass darkly," as if to suggest a person trying to communicate from another dimension—a trait familiar from acid rock music. At 9' 58" the continuity is brusquely punctuated by the sound of a power drill, a clean and aggressive noise of welcome physicality that works in just the same way as the "ripping" sounds in *Hymnen* Region I, created by pulling the tape manually past the playback head. Such techniques are well advanced in commercial electronic music: an example the collective Future Sounds of London.[5] The rock idiom that is being acknowledged here is an art of managed distortion; its origins can be traced back to the tape music of Varèse, where through overcopying and other treatments, voices and natural sounds are deliberately and inevitably distressed. Stockhausen seems to be playing in the same idiom, employing voice distortion for effect, for example at 11' 06", and again at 16' 25". At other times there are hints of self-quotation: heavy reverberation at 12' 05" and again at 35' 00" that sound like outtakes from *Kontakte*, and a touch of morse code and shortwave from *Kurzwellen* at 31' 00". And allusions to more recent images too: deep string Monsalvat bells at 21' 00", and again at 25' 00" and 26' 30", the third time enhanced by very slow phasing of a kind familiar from the era of Rod Stewart and The Small Faces in the song "Itchykoo Park." At 37' 30" the composer announces the title "Mittwochs-Gruss . . . Wednesday Greeting" in a normal speaking voice, but very slowly, so as to bring out a similar but natural phasing effect in the pronunciation of the English words:

"Wens . . . dae__ee . . . Gurr . . . uu__ee . . . ts . . . ee__nng."

At 31' 40" a burst of laughing seagulls looks back to the famous quacking and singing ducks of *Hymnen*, and ahead to the equally amusing closeup world of insect imitations in "Orchester-Finalisten." All of these sounds, apart from the composer's voice, are locked into the electronic sound-world like specimens under glass. They have little or no independent life, and the effect is to create a thirst for real sounds in three dimensions. We are being set up for the "grand reveal" of reality sounds in the scenes to come. The Greeting ends very charmingly to crystalline chords sounding like multiple triangles, alarm clocks, or transposed and phase-distorted tubular bells: a kind of musical Wasabe sauce, sharp and hot, but also refreshing.

Scene I: Welt-Parlament (World Parliament)

1995: No. 66 (Stockhausen-Verlag; cd SV-51)
For choir SATB a cappella (with singing conductor and two speaking voices); 34 microphones, 15 transmitting microphones (staged performance only), 2 × 2 loudspeakers, mixing console.
Duration: 40'.

Purely subjectively, the composition of *Mittwoch* is more varied, more animated, and technically cleaner and more adventurous than *Dienstag* or *Freitag*. One has the impression of coming out from behind a cloud, even if the composer's newfound delight in digital editing and remixing gets a little out of hand from time to time. In the context of prerecorded sounds from nature, of a kind previously encountered in *Montag*, "Welt-Parlament" resembles a Messiaen-style aviary (a parliament of birds); nobody has much to say, other than banal pleasantries ("love is cosmic glue"; "love is faithfulness"; "talent must serve beauty"; "think positively" etc.). The keynote event, in fact, is the election halfway through of a *woman* to the presidency of this Roman assembly, whose real function, like so much of Stockhausen's ritual actions, is simply self-referential: "Greetings, Mittwoch!"

Since the message of "Welt-Parlament" is of harmony among nations and peoples, it is not surprising to find it organized in a similar fashion to *Telemusik*, which is about reconciling the music of different world cultures (as distinct from the forced integration of national identities in *Hymnen*). In his role as president, the choir conductor governs the timing (and, by implication, the content) of events by alternately banging a gavel and sounding a bell, in imitation of the percussion strokes that indicate the onset of each new moment in *Telemusik*.

The vocal combinations are rich and varied, and include a greater variety of quasi-tonal harmonic idioms that stretch through the spiculated textures of "*Atmen gibt das Leben* . . ." to close harmony in the style of Scriabin (altos "Eva Inana" at [79]), Schoenberg (a spine-tingling glimpse of the soprano sacrificial victims from "Dance around the Golden Calf" at [34]), and back to harmony exercises in the class of Hermann Schroeder (the soulful and rather sweet tenor chorale "Liebe tönt in deine Stimme" at [91], which ends in the key of f sharp with added seventh). Add the gavel, and the allusions go right back to the hammering games of early childhood.

Although they may not actually be needed, electronic ticking metronomes are required for all choir members except the tenors, and are heard as a pleasant texture accompanying the choirs as they process on to the stage at the beginning, and again as they exit the stage. Of two "real" interruptions of the scene, one is misjudged, and the other is misinterpreted. At [211] a "janitor" breaks the proceedings with a Woody Allen-style announcement (as from the overdubbed movie *What's Up, Tiger Lily*): "Would the owner of the car, licence plate MEV Mittwoch 1996, be advised that the vehicle is about to be towed." Oh, how we laughed.[6] (It would sound much funnier coming over a studio intercom.) The other, more sinister addition comes at the end, when a straggling member of the basses is made to stutter to the audience "Ja, und hier käme dann die nächste Szene!" (So now here comes the next scene)—a gesture that is simply clumsy in the recording, and also not very funny. More effective than a stutter would be a distended delivery, in keeping with the speaker's slow exit, as if the actual person, —like Stockhausen himself in slow-motion guise in *Freitag*,—were a hologram, an image from another dimension, like the anamorphic death's head in Hans Holbein's *Money-Changers*.

Scene II: Orchester-Finalisten (Orchestra Finalists)

1995–1996: No. 68 (Stockhausen-Verlag; cd SV-52)
For double chamber orchestra and electronic music.
13 (or 2 × 13) solo instrumentalists: flute, oboe, clarinet, bassoon, horn; trumpet, trombone, tuba; percussionist; violin, viola, cello, contrabass. 3 (6) transmitting microphones, 10 microphones, 8 (8 × 2) loudspeakers, 16-track tape recorder, mixing console.
Duration: 2 × 45'.

On the surface, "Orchester-Finalisten" deals with the end round of a competition to prove one's worth as a performer. A rite of passage to earn the authorization to play and instruct,—though not, it seems, to interpret. An orchestra player does not interpret. He or she follows instructions. I labor the point. The image of competition comes up more than once in *LICHT*. Michael submits to examination in *Donnerstag*, a conservatoire-like affair with undertones of the trial scene in Jean Cocteau's movie *Orphée*—a modern retelling of the myth about a Greek god of music obtaining permission to enter the underworld to retrieve his lost love, but other than mentioning that in Stockhausen's version the underworld is here on earth, we won't go into that again. In *Der Jahreslauf*, the gagaku-influenced scena now Act I of *Dienstag aus LICHT*, the Year-Runners are offered various inducements to leave off their labors and bring the music to an end, and after resisting temptation have prizes bestowed on them. So here we are, another competition.

At the time of its British premiere at the Huddersfield Festival in 1997 there was some relief being expressed that at long last the composer was beginning to write for a regular orchestra once more. Not much seemed to have happened in that domain since the orchestrated strike that throws the ending of "Luzifers Tanz" in *Samstag aus LICHT* into chaos, and that was (gosh) back in 1983. So a new piece for a mix of nonelectronic instruments for a change was good news. One might easily overlook the fact that the ensemble is nothing like an orchestra in the dictionary sense of the word, nor does it function in this case as a traditional team. Obedience is the key, and divide and rule the composer's tactic, the same as for "Helikopter-Streichquartett."

It is always a risk to take Stockhausen's titles literally, and this one is no exception. "Orchestra" does not mean a normal orchestra, and "finalists" has other meanings. What the composer might appear ironically to be saying by the title is "the end of the orchestra as we know it," an outcome from the composer's perspective perhaps devoutly to be wished. According to Merriam-Webster, however, a finalist "is a believer in or advocate of *finalism*" which is further defined under *teleology* as "a metaphysical doctrine explaining phenomena and events by final causes or affine relationships involving transformations that preserve collinearity (math.) or family or tribal relationships." So the work title carries a subtext that is philosophical and anthropological in implication, and has nothing necessarily to do with a competition for a music prize at all. Character relationships are worked out in the same terms of structural anthropology as previously in *Momente*, the composer's earlier exercise in tribal semiotics.

In "Orchester-Finalisten," affine or family relationships are based on imitation. As we recall:

> Musical training has nothing to do with musicality. You can train someone for years in a conservatoire of music and develop the ability to recognize pitch constructions, harmonies, chords, melodies, intervals —all intellectually. But what I call a musical person is someone who can imitate any sound that he hears, with his voice, directly, without thinking about hitting the right pitch, but just doing it. Great musicians always start off as great imitators. Afterwards, building on the talent of imitation, comes the talent to transform what you hear.[7]

—which paraphrases to "the test of a musical genius is someone who can imitate any sound after hearing it only once."

When one thinks of imitation in relation to Stockhausen's music one thinks for example of the hunt, of instruments imitating animal sounds in *Mikrophonie I*, shortwave events in *Kurzwellen*, trombones roaring like lions in "Samstags-Gruss" from *Samstag aus LICHT*, and the string quartet blending in with their helicopters in "Helikopter-Streichquartett," not forgetting violist Johannes Fritsch, renowned as a member of Group Stockhausen for his "superb animal imitations."[8]

In "Orchester-Finalisten" the test is imitation of nature, the outside world of living and industrial sounds and sound processes as presented on tape. Who is the jury? Is it the audience, or an unseen panel of divinities? In a sketch dated 2/7/95 the composer outlines a scenario in which twelve jury members are heard to bid and dismiss the instrumental soloists over loud-speakers in ring-modulated *sprechstimme*, a realistic but expensive addition set aside in favor of squeaky Harlequin-esque introductions by Kathinka Pasveer.[9] ("A suggestion for the next phase: a helium atmosphere can extend the range of human and other voices by more than an octave."[10]) Whoever is supposedly in charge, we sense that the players are being made to feel small. There is a moment in "Donnerstags-Abschied" where the level of sound of the taped "Invisible Choirs" is suddenly raised with the effect of masking and threatening to drown out the voice of Michael, the tenor solo. Stockhausen refers to the alteration of balance as a change of scale, the tenor being made to appear to shrink, like Alice in *Through the Looking Glass*, to the size of a flower or lizard. Something very similar seems to be afoot in the new piece, in part because of the constant presence of taped sounds in the background, and in part because the soloists are given so little material to perform, mere fragments of fragments of the formulae that make up *LICHT*'s genetic code.

A similar loftiness of vantage, though from a different perspective, is exploited by Boulez in *Répons*, wherein the gods reveal themselves in the computer-generated transformations of data sequences delivered as burnt offerings by solo keyboards. But if that is the analogy, for whom then are Stockhausen's soloists performing, if there is no response from the electronic world, and little to no interaction among the players as a group? Interestingly, the momentary tuttis that do break in from time to time are like doors opening into the light, and then slamming shut. They belong to the same family of gestures as the interrupted cadences of *Adieu*, another valedictory work for chamber ensemble, from 1966.

The composer's intention I think is to portray the players as insects, microbes, small-scale living creatures after the manner of Messiaen's birds, observed in close-up like a black-and-white nature movie from the thirties, creatures seen going about their business with unselfconscious economy and precision against an out-of-focus backdrop of the environment. One sign is the brevity of the motifs they have to play: the violin buzzes like a mosquito, the tuba, albeit entirely against character, charmingly plays a bumblebee foraging on a flower, while the trumpet, armed with a full panoply of mutes, sounds more aggressively like a wasp or blue-tail fly. Scale transformations and the interpenetration of macro- and micro-dimensions are part of the serial fabric of Stockhausen's work. If the violin indeed represents a mosquito, then what the composer is also saying, since the same instrument is involved in the "Helikopter-Streichquartett," is that the mosquito is also a tiny helicopter. Unlike Messiaen or Boulez, who in their different ways celebrate wild life as free spirits, the finalists in this time of trial are presented to view as specimens, pinned to a board but still alive, whose largely futile struggles are delivered for our amusement.

The tape montages that form the background to this haunting work are put together from sound effects discs and given the glossy overlay of an old photograph album. Heavy with nostalgia, they create an impression quite unlike the radiophonic burble of *Hymnen* and having none of the ribaldry of animal noises that punctuate *Montag aus LICHT*. They are the sound of dreams, the dream of making music with sound effects discs that gave rise to the musique concrète studios the composer encountered as an apprentice in 1952. Listen out for the the pip-pweep of the choo-choo train from Pierre Schaeffer's *Étude aux chemins de fer* of 1948, or the overhead passing jet from Varèse's *Poème électronique* of 1957. There is a deep poignancy here. The noises in the background are nonthreatening, even pastoral, with a few subtle highlights: a sudden echo, a hint of feedback. Children play and squeal, a distant ship's horn sounds. The nervous fidgeting of the solo players is offset by tape images evoking the stained glass and movie screens that to a poor child in Nazi Germany were windows to a better life and represented a higher truth than the wretched reality of despair and deprivation he endured as a child.

Scene III: Helikopter-Streichquartett (Helicopter String Quartet)

1993: No. 68 (Stockhausen-Verlag; cd SV-53)
For string quartet (solistic), 4 helicopters and pilots, 4 video cameramen; 4 television transmitters, 4 × 3 microphones, 4 × 3 transmitting microphones, monitor headsets; (auditorium) 4 towers of television monitors, 4 groups of loudspeakers, mixing console(s), sound projectionist(s).
Duration: 28'.

On the question of machine noises and music Luigi Russolo's 1913 Futurist Manifesto is startlingly prescient:

> We must break out of this narrow circle of pure musical sounds, and conquer the infinite variety of noise-sounds. . . . Let us wander through a great modern city with our ears more attentive than our eyes, and distinguish the purring of motors (which breathe and pulsate with an indisputable animalism), the throbbing of valves, the pounding of pistons, the screeching of gears. . . . We must fix and regulate the harmonies and rhythms of these extraordinarily varied sounds. To fix the pitch of noises does not mean to take away from them all the irregularity of tempo and intensity that characterizes their vibrations, but rather to give definite gradation of pitch to the stronger and more predominant of these vibrations. . . . Every noise has a note—sometimes even a chord—that predominates in the ensemble of its irregular vibrations. Because of this characteristic note it becomes possible to fix the pitch of a given noise, that is, to give it not a single pitch but a variety of pitches, without losing its characteristic quality—its distinguishing timbre. Thus certain noises produced by rotary motion may offer a complete ascending and descending chromatic scale by merely increasing or decreasing the speed of the motion.[11]

This wonderful work is an image of flight experienced as music. Imagery of flight is a recurrent feature of Stockhausen's music, and imagery specifically of propellor-like rotation involving impulsive textures can be found in a number of earlier Stockhausen compositions, and also in works by other composers with which the composer is known to have been familiar. Rotational motion and the sound associated with it also connect with other times and cultures. The weird whirring sound of a bull-roarer in the movie *Crocodile Dundee II*, rising and falling in speed and pitch, is not only a form of bush telephone used by native Australians to keep in touch, but also a means by which they make contact with the spirit world, the domain the aborigines call "dream time." The texture of tremolo strings in association with an image of intimidating power, the sense of a force larger than life, is a combination just as much to be reckoned with in the classical world of Bach, Mozart, and Beethoven. In Bach's music, for example, we perceive an ongoing fascination with complex mechanical processes; in the Mozart of the finale of the "Jupiter" symphony (and other Presto movements of the *Sturm und Drang* era) powerful, noisy, and unstable processes are set in motion in the cellos and basses, and move rapidly up and down the scale in tremolo textures. The storm scene of Beethoven's "Pastoral" symphony is a perfect precursor to Stockhausen's helicopters: an image of nature in turmoil as full, noisy, and tremolando in texture, rising to a dissonant peak, then descending and fading away. Finally one has to mention the turbulent X-moments in Stockhausen's *Carré*, which burst into life and whirl around the four orchestras like turbines.

A helicopter besides being an instrument of flight is also a machine that produces a certain kind of sound. In "Helikopter-Streichquartett" the musical action in its simplest form consists of four helicopters with individual string players on board taking off, hovering, and landing again, in the course of which rotors are set in motion, starting off as a rhythm and rising to a pitch, stabilizing on the hovering pitch, then descending to the ground, parking, and shutting off allowing the rotors to descend in pitch, slow to a rhythm once again, then to a stop. What the audience experiences in essence is the transformation of a regular beating or pulsing sensation into a tone of variable pitch and back again, in association with the idea and (via television monitors) the imagery of flying, like a tourist excursion. To the mechanical sounds each member of the string quartet adds a modulated and tuned vibration. Some of the time the rise and fall of the string tremolo coincides with shifts in pitch of the helicopter; at other times it sounds like a phase shift within the sound (an effect of relative movement in space).

Why choose a string quartet? The work was commissioned for the Arditti Quartet, so that part of the instrumentation is a given. Why helicopters? That is the interesting question. Not "what do I write for string quartet" but "how can the sound of a string quartet be incorporated into the sound and gesture vocabulary of *LICHT* and in particular *Mittwoch aus LICHT*?" And the answers that come back specify up-and-down movement in real space, real sounds in the extended bass, and real string textures in succession to the simulated synthesizer textures of *Freitag aus LICHT*, which as has been noted, are already an improvement on *Dienstag*. It means that we should perceive the piece as a sudden and dramatic irruption into the world of real sounds, of processes latent in the electronic domain. The function of string quartet and helicopters as real sound sources is identical to that of the real instruments in *Kontakte*, and the genius of the work lies in the improbable logic of the coupling, a mimesis further explored in the miniaturized sound-world of "Orchester-Finalisten."

"Helikopter-Streichquartett" is a work of exceptional strength and vitality, of stunning simplicity and absolute integrity. It is as hard as nails—or as stone. Like an ammonite it is an aesthetically beautiful image of a process that is both natural and universal, the sound of the four helicopters providing a mechanical-impulsive shell as it were, and the fricative motions of the four string players a softer living acoustic tissue that in the long run adds its own nacreous interior gleam to the hard outer carapace.

At the same time, let's not be squeamish either. Stockhausen has no particular love for the violin family. Here he takes an almost perverse delight in creating conditions that are the opposite of what a string quartet relies on to make harmonious music. First, he separates the four players so they can neither see nor hear one another. Second, he limits the tonal range of these aristocrats of emotional expression to strident and abrasive tremolandi. Third, he has them strapped awkwardly into the passenger seats of hovering aircraft that are not only unstable platforms but potentially dangerous considering the value of the instruments and their owners. It would be interesting to learn if the Arditti Quartet chose to perform on their "best" instruments—and if they did, how would we know?—and who covered the insurance. But the views of the players are not of interest, and not reported.

The composer declares that the work came to him in a dream. It is not the first time. A dream can be a way of avoiding discussion. The work comes fully-formed as if in a vision. By definition there is nothing more to say. However, when Stockhausen says "dream" he is making a coded allusion to the tradition of dream in artistic creation, and in particular to the surrealists and other persecuted "degenerate artists" he is making it his mission to rehabilitate. We look therefore to the literature of twentieth-century art for some basis or rationale for a music of helicopters in action, the most striking being Luigi (LU-IGI sounds like a relative of LU-DON or LU-ZIFER, but that will have to wait)—Russolo's Futurist Manifesto, in which, speaking of a new music based on the sounds of machines, he refers specifically to "noises produced by rotary motion [in] a complete ascending and descending chromatic scale," and of an instrumental music "to fix the pitch of noises . . . [and] give definite gradation of pitch to the stronger and more predominant of these vibrations."

A number of issues arise from the use of helicopter imagery. Flight is one, the image of rotation is another, and Stockhausen's history of employing pulsating sounds, especially in relation to acceleration in time, yet another. A rich tapestry of musical and theoretical associations begins to emerge.

Stockhausen was inquiring about the possibility of having musicians fly through the air as long ago as 1953, when

I discussed at length with my studio technicians whether it would be wise to put musicians in chairs and swing them around, for example, and many said they might object. So then we thought it would perhaps be preferable to let them play into microphones and connect the microphones to speakers and then swing the speakers around, and then they would not object, but they objected to that too. They said, oh no, you can't do that with me, I'm here, and the sound has to come from here.[12]

Later in 1959 he experimented with rotating sounds for four orchestras (the inserts in *Carré*) and devised the "rotation table" for the manual rotation of independent layers of taped sound in *Kontakte*. An improved rotating potentiometer or "sound mill," again manually operated, was employed at the 1970 Osaka Expo to make sounds spiral upwards and downwards, while for *Sirius* the composer had a motorized rotation turbine capable of very high speed revolutions specially built to simulate the sound of a quartet of arriving and departing flying saucers. Again in 1982–1983, the electronic music composed at IRCAM for "Kathinkas Gesang als Luzifers Requiem" is supposed to whirl round the solo flutist like a tornado. In every case the audience is surrounded by the rotation, and the rotation process itself is associated with the idea of being transported to another world, a world of make-believe. "Helikopter-Streichquartett" is one more quartet in a long line of such foursomes: four helicopters, four flying saucers in *Sirius*, four channels in *Kontakte*, four orchestras in *Carré*.

Helicopters are a genial idea for a host of reasons. They come ready-made, like objects chosen by Marcel Duchamp. They are real transportation. A musician can actually ride in such a machine. They embody another of the composer's fantasies, this time for "a cockpit . . . with lots of buttons."[13] They produce sounds more powerful than any synthesizer, with a truly deep bass into the infrasound. And they actually fly.

Rotation is one thing, the texture of helicopter sound is another. What is important in this case is a source of vibration that demonstrates an unequivocal continuum between pulsating rhythm and pulsatile tone and pitch. A helicopter produces a sound of such wide range as to manifest both rhythm and pitch simultaneously, the engine generating the pitch component, the rotors the rhythmic component, and both locked together so that they rise and fall synchronously. A similar relationship obtains in *Kontakte* where electronic sounds created by acceleration of patterns recorded on a loop of tape are then subjected to spatial (in this case nonsynchronous) rotation by means of the rotation turntable. A distinctive feature of the rotating sounds in *Kontakte* is the audible "flap" as the sound passes from one speaker to the next, which by sheer coincidence sounds very much like the beat of a helicopter rotor.

Impulse generated sounds are not limited to mechanical devices such as sirens or rotors. The reason a siren wails like a human voice is because the mechanism of a human voice resembles a siren: compressed air interacting with the valve process of the vocal folds to produce a train of impulses that can be varied in frequency to vary the pitch and thereby the expression of the voice. Other examples of pulsatile sound in Stockhausen include the clapping "Klatsch-Moment" in *Momente*, the "running offstage to find the clipping shears" scene in *Musik im Bauch*, the "applause" temptation in *Der Jahreslauf* (which makes the connection between the sound of running clogs and that of hands clapping), and the scene "Luzifers Abschied" from *Samstag aus LICHT* where the sound of multiple running clogs is combined with rotational motion above the heads of the audience.

In the case of *Kontakte* the flap effect from speaker to speaker is at least consistent with the impulse generated tone material. An impulse generator is a square-wave signal generator, with controls for the repetition rate (periodicity) and duration of impulse, that can be used not only as a source of sound in its own right but also to control the outflow of a continuous signal from a secondary source (in exactly the same ways as the holes in a siren modulate the flow of air to produce a sound). Stockhausen's own colleagues at the Cologne Radio electronic studio were frankly embarrassed by sounds produced by mechanical rotation. In a modest lexicon part-authored by Herbert Eimert the influence of sirens on the theory of electronic tone synthesis is traced back to:

> F. W. Opelt's siren researches and his theory of music "founded on the rhythm of pulsed sound waves" (1852), [since when] theorists have frequently sought to clarify the relationship between quantifiable impulses and unquantifiable impulse-generated tones. . . . Serial technique in its ongoing development and tendency toward free form has opted to put this whole problem to one side in favor of a more or less independent juxtaposition of the two parameters pitch and duration. Whether duration is a moment in time, or time a product of duration may be a matter of fertile discussion for psychologists or philosophers but does not resolve the question over the potential for integration of the two parameters.[14]

We are now in a position to put together the formal process represented by the four helicopters and the expressive dimension represented by the four string players.

The note material on which the string quartet material is based is a "given" in the sense of being already prefigured in the composer's master plan or formula. In his usual fashion Stockhausen conceives the role of the performer as imitating or coloring preexisting mechanical sound. The violin family are a product of the new humanism of the Italian Renaissance, designed by the Cremonese as instruments for imitating the human voice with unprecedented naturalism. In assigning the glissando element of his *LICHT* formula to the string quartet the composer is making a connection between gliding tones, string sound, and feminine emotion,—that is, with instability, weeping and wailing. It follows that the combination of imagery of departure (the helicopters ascending heavenward) together with weeping and wailing (tremulous glissandi sliding up and down) suggests a ceremony of valediction.

In 1976 I noted a curious resemblance between a passage in *Kontakte* and a similar passage in the final movement of Bartók's Second Violin

Concerto, a presumption for which I was roundly scolded at the time. This occurs as we recall at Structure XI at 21' 30" in the published score, the "Splitting of the Sound," where a stream of impulses centred around f above middle c gives rise to a series of layers that peel off and move away in different directions in a wavy motion. I was reminded of the Bartók concerto third movement, at "Risoluto" two measures before 167, where a tremolando solo violin starting at about the same pitch begins to undulate up and down in much the same manner and within the same intervals of superimposed fourths. (The entire last movement of the Bartók, by the way, is a fascinating exercise in glissando movements and textures.) Here we have not just one, but a series of resemblances: a violin, tremolando, glissandoing up and down, and sounding like impulse-generated electronic sound. Electronic sound that also rotates round the audience and sounds like a helicopter. To me that is more than a random coincidence.

The most talked about segment in *Kontakte*, Structure X at 17' 0,5", begins with a machine-like descending undulation accompanied by a lighter decelerating process that eventually settles on e below middle c. I hear those decelerating tones in the cello's acceleration at the beginning of "Helikopter-Streichquartett," and if I am not mistaken, their abrasive tone is quickly smoothed away to nothing by the composer at his digital editing console. In *Kontakte*, Structure X continues with a series of sustained low pulsating notes, broken occasionally by rasping and metallic textures. These are the most powerful tones in the entire piece, and directly comparable with the rasping sounds of the helicopter rotor winding to a stop.

Frictional tremolando sounds come to the foreground only occasionally in *Kontakte*, although all the continuous electronic tone material in the earlier work arises from tremolo or rotational (tape-loop) processes. Where the suggestion of string tone is more marked, as at the peeling-off of layers of sound at XI, the relationship of the layers is analogous to multiple sources coming together and moving apart against a constant drone of impulses, and compares to the ascent and descent of the four helicopters in real life. Most striking of all however is the final sequence in *Kontakte*, at Structure XIV, from 31' 0,5" to the end. Although focused high in the treble, and accelerated in pitch, the texture of sound and interaction of partial sounds seems exactly to parallel the effect Stockhausen is striving for in "Helikopter-Streichquartett." The entire segment is frictional and rotational in character and also ventures into new territory of continuous glissandi up and down, in a way both echoing Bartók and prefiguring the new work. In contradiction to the Zen-like principle of moment-form, that the music has no beginning or end, but implicitly goes on forever, this final section of *Kontakte* has a clear sense of direction, an air of finality: there is a palpable emotion to the music, a sense of brooding melancholy, of loss, of weeping.

In his notes the composer mentions that after hearing the work, he extended the final descent by a few minutes. "After the world premiere, I added a circa 3-minute, synchronous formation to the end of the work before descent and landing." This "Schluss-Choral" segment (as I call it) begins at around 26' 52". It is the best segment in the entire recording, a controlled

deceleration in which the four voices come together in what sounds suspiciously like a textbook harmonization of a descending chromatic scale. It is
an unexpected and very emotional moment, lasting to the end of the
recording at 30' 40". Like the ending moment of *Kontakte* it is music that
one is convinced has been specially composed and inserted to impart a sense
of closure.

Scene IV: Michaelion (Michaelion)

1997: No. 70 (Stockhausen-Verlag)
For choir, bass with shortwave receiver, flute, basset-horn, trumpet, trombone, synthesizer player, 8-track tape, 2 dancers, sound projectionist; 19 microphones, 8 transmitting microphones, 8-track tape recorder, 19 loudspeakers, 4 monitor loudspeakers; 7
video cameras, 7 video monitors, additional small loudspeakers.
Duration: 53'.

Bassetsu-Trio (Bassetsu-Trio)

1997: ex No. 70 (Stockhausen-Verlag; cd SV-55)
For basset-horn, trumpet and trombone.
Duration: 26'.

Until the world is ready to produce a DVD edition of "Michaelion" as the
composer intends it,—and it may take the resources of a Hollywood studio
to do so,—the actions remain an enigma. While the dancing three-layered
electronic music of "Mittwochs-Gruss" circles round the audience in low-
level quadraphony, a series of actions for choir in togas unfolds on stage. We
are accustomed to large-scale pop music events taking place on stage with
camera operators sharing the platform and producing live action visuals
from all sides. What "Michaelion" demands is an apron stage, eventually
dominated in the center by a podium with impressive looking equipment
including a shortwave radio and talk-back loudspeakers. Around this piece
of staging, which the occasion demands should look impressively high-tech
and futuristic ("lots of buttons") the choir members and a trio of instruments
rotate, like planets around a dark star. Spatial movement and constantly-
changing perspectives are the essence of the live action and music, as of the
electronic background music quietly circulating in the auditorium (a duality
comparable with that of "Michaels Reise" in *Donnerstag*). From a video
recording, one judges the work's premiere, at Munich on 26 July 1998, as a
"quasi-concertante" performance on a conventional stage. The performers
are the very best: Rupert Huber directing the Munich Radio Choir, Stockhausen in charge of sound distribution, and his personally trained collaborators on solo instruments (including new faces Marco Blaauw on trumpet
and Andrew Digby on trombone). And yet, as a stage spectacle, on a regular
stage, it makes almost no sense. It is an object lesson, if one is needed, on
the perils of "quasi-concertante" performances of a music so critically
dependent on acoustic subtleties.

Not only is this music conceived in the round, and ideally experienced
in the round (preferably in a baroque church of moderate size), it needs to be

produced and stylized musically in such a way as to realize the composer's musical choreography. For the singers, all of whom are holding microphones, a thin, clear, microphone style of singing, without the least vibrato, is not only logical but absolutely necessary: for locating individual voices, and for perceiving changes of direction (one wants the effects of individual megaphones, but without the metallic timbre of a megaphone). As for the solo instruments, it is one set of challenges to imagine them as oscillating circuits producing quasi-electronic waveforms that can be picked up by semi-contact microphone and mixed at a console, and quite another challenge to employ them as moving sources of sound in real space. In real space, particularly a space surrounded by hard reflecting flat planes at fixed angles,—in this case, a regular platform with side screens,—the precise location and movement of a sound is not easy to follow by a member of the audience. (It would be a different matter if the audience were listening from the flies directly above, or if the movements of performers were relayed from microphones suspended above the stage to speakers above the audience.)

No matter how elegantly a performer may move, a change of position will only begin to make a difference at a certain speed and within a certain band of frequencies. This first point was made by Brant in the same article on spatial effects that Stockhausen consulted for *Samstag*. As Gabrieli, Tallis, Schütz, and many other polychoral composers from the sixteenth century were well aware from practical experience, in order to create a poetry of directional effects, you need distance; and with distance comes delay, and with delay difficulties of coordination. Because sound is emitted via the finger holes as well as through the open end, flute and basset-horn patterns of directed sound are multilobed and vary continuously with pitch. Trumpet and trombone emit sound from the bell, but even so the spread of radiation varies considerably with pitch, and in the mid-frequency range (600–850 hertz) is nearly omnidirectional. Only at extremely high frequencies is the sound projection more focused, like a torch-beam: for the flute, above 8 kilohertz, directed *sideways*; for the basset-horn, above 5 kilohertz, *upwards*; for the trumpet, 4–15 kilohertz, *straight ahead*; and for the trombone, from 2–10 kilohertz, *angled downwards*.[15] Since none of these instruments is pointing in a similar direction in the frequency region that matters, the reflected sound is uncontrollable. In order to hear an effect of movement the ideal arrangement would be for the performance to take place on an apron stage, preferably a carpeted stage. An apron stage is a practical possibility, but a carpeted apron stage would deprive instrumentalists and singers alike of a vital reflecting surface. However since every player already has a microphone, this may turn out to be a good thing.

As a studio production, in the round, and without the absorbency of an audience to contend with, the *Bassetsu-Trio* recording is better able to exploit spatial and directional effects. As one might expect, these work reasonably well in stereo as modulations of amplitude and changes of direction audible in the notated mid-range; but the more sensitive issues of individual rotation and face-to-face interaction, notated with exquisite precision in the music, are once again limited in effect for the reasons previously mentioned.

In the absence of effective staging, a quasi-concertante or even a fully staged performance is bound to be seriously diminished; the only effective long-term solution being a production combining real and virtual surround sound, and recorded as a computer game. Given that the action takes place in a space station on the outer fringe of the universe, one can imagine it as a hologram performance occupying the same space as the audience, but transparent to it, with beings floating like plankton in a faintly phosphorescent atmosphere. It would be a mistake to base a judgement of "Michaelion" on its points of resemblance to conventional opera. When performed as such, it sounds conventional but looks foolish. The large-scale action is rudimentary: in "Präsidium" people in light blue togas come in from the wings, form groups, change places, disperse, and leave. (If they were wearing masks, on the other hand, their individual voices would resonate and be directed forward; and if the masks were equipped with little LED headlights for eyes (in different colors, of course), an audience would at least be able to understand and follow their changes of acoustic direction.) The action, such as it is, is interrupted by the arrival of "Luzikamel," a nonspeaking circus horse in a brown camel suit (resembling a digital cartoon character out of *Toy Story*)—a new emanation of Luzipolyp as régisseur, the name a composite of Luzifer, Ka(rlkeinz), and Mel(odie),—whose chief function is to disgrace itself on stage, evacuating more colored spheres of the kind presented to Michael in *Donnerstag* and for just the same reason, as Jovial tokens of achievement. These are reverently gathered up as if one were promenading a valuable pet in a public park, and ceremoniously removed. And that is that.

"Operator" has a great deal more comic potential, due in large measure to a virtuoso performance by Michael Vetter, seated at a virtual console, tuning a shortwave receiver at random, and vocally interpreting the results in different languages. The role may be a reference to Roland Barthes' characterization of the modern (1950s) critical reader as "operator" of the text, though now operating out of a floating and desolate astral body in a remote corner of the universe. Musically speaking, there is certainly a suggestion of a multidimensional perspective, with shortwaves issuing from a virtual black hole, the Operator as interpreter in real space, and the choir, confined to the edges, as reflecting surfaces. It is a sign of the times that a radio receiver now seems so antique a device, and a little bit sad, given the personal and emotional resonances the instrument used to convey.

Mittwochs-Abschied (Wednesday Farewell)

1996: No. 71 (Stockhausen-Verlag; cd SV-55)
Electronic and concrete music; 8-track tape recorder, 8 × 2 loudspeakers, mixing console.
Duration: 44'.

This is the tape music for "Orchester-Finalisten" remixed and slightly shortened to serve as closing music for the opera. In his own words, Stockhausen has used the opportunity further to enhance or exaggerate the spatial illusion of his 8-track tapes. "It is essential to *fly along* in this transreal world (which cannot exist in "concrete" human life), and in the free flight of fantasy as a bodiless spirit *to hear* the Earth as music within and around oneself."[16] It is a music assembled from prerecorded materials and projected onto the interior faces of a virtual cube as if they were images on multiple screens. After the pastoral atmosphere of Scene II, where the interaction between live instruments and tape has a certain innocence and charm, the treatment of this same material is powerfully disturbing, willfully distorted, smeared, unbalanced, and destroyed. Something very strange is going on, as if Luzifer, or some other of the composer's demons, has sneaked into the room at dead of night and covered the walls with graffiti. It may well be that the composer is seeking to explore an acoustic space "beyond the cube" in the manner of computer representations of eleven-dimensional space, or the later paintings of Salvador Dalí (e.g., the *Hallucinogeneous Bullfighter* of 1983–1984). After the reflective tranquility of the earlier presentation, however, this is not a journey to be undertaken lightly.

Notes

1. George Antheil, *Ballet Mécanique.* Revised 1952. New York Percussion Group cond. Carlos Surinach. Columbia CML 4956-PXLP 31166.

2. George Antheil, *Ballet pour Instruments Mécanique [sic] et Percussion.* Original version 1925. "Digital Re-Creation of the Carnegie Hall Concert of 1927." New Palais Royale Orchestra & Percussion Ensemble cond. Maurice Peress. Musical Heritage Society 513891L.

3. George Wickes, *Americans in Paris.* Reprinted with a new Foreword by Virgil Thomson (New York: Da Capo Press, 1980), 39.

4. Standish D. Lawder, *Cubist Cinema* (New York: New York University Press, 1975), 152.

5. Up to the entry of high-octane percussion, track 4 of *FSOL: We have Explosive* (ASW 6196) inhabits the same emotional landscape as "Mittwochs-Gruss," reaching beyond it to the heavily abraded imagery of Varèse's *Poème Électronique,* composed forty years before.

6. MEV: acronym of Musica Elettronica Viva, a group formed in 1966 by American composers Alan Bryant, Alvin Curran, Frederic Rzewski, and Richard Teitelbaum.

7. *SoM*, 32.

8. *SoM*, 145.

9. Stockhausen Composition Courses 1998, course booklet (Kürten: Stockhausen-Verlag, 1998), 17.

10. "Contingencies." Igor Stravinsky and Robert Craft, *Themes and Episodes* (New York: Knopf, 1966), 19n.

11. Luigi Russolo, "The Art of Noises: Futurist Manifesto" tr. Stephen Somervell. 642–48 in Nicolas Slonimsky, *Music Since 1900* (Third rev. enl. edition. New York: Coleman-Ross, 1949).

12. *SoM*, 101.

13. *SoM*, 132–34.

14. Herbert Eimert and Hans Ulrich Humpert, *Lexikon der elektronischen Musik*. Regensburg: Bosse, 1973, 143–44.
15. Jürgen Meyer, *Acoustics and the Performance of Music* tr. John Bowsher and Sibylle Westphal. Frankfurt/Main: Verlag Das Musikinstrument, 1978, 157–70.
16. Booklet of compact disc SV-55, 31.

CHAPTER TWENTY-NINE

Sonntag

At sixty-five a new and sustained inspiration had set him off writing poems in emulation of the fourteenth-century Persian lyricist Hafiz. . . . Reflection and evocation sometimes have an almost mystical intensity, as past insight and experience are concentrated in fresh perceptions of beauty. The poet can see the woman he loves in every shape and stimulus of the sensible world. . . . In loving her, he loves the world and whatever god is immanent in it; none of these loves is merely a derivate of any other, they compose a single embracing reverence. . . . He also discovers a sense of unity across historical time. . . . Life resolves into archetypes. Even so, the freshness and value of each new occasion stays intact. Archetype, occurrence, myth—the perspective they offer never blurs or attenuates the single instance.[1]

The writer is speaking of Goethe, but the sentiment is equally appropriate to Stockhausen, whose *Sonntag aus LICHT*, nearing completion in 2003, brings the composer's monumental cycle of seven operas to a close after a quarter-century with a lyric celebration of marriage incorporating love poems in Hindi, English, Swahili, Chinese,—and in particular from the odes of Hafiz.

For a work representing the culmination of a seven-day cycle, *Sonntag aus LICHT* is a serene and restrained affair. Neither with the bang of a "Hallelujah Chorus,"—which of course is all about imperial might,—nor with a whimper, and certainly not going out in a blaze of glory, the music reaches back to the religious temperament of Byzantine ritual and its solemn processions, droning organ points, incense burning, and elevated admonitions of belief that to audiences of an oral culture were encrypted statements of the obvious as well as markers of a spiritual journey that is ultimately not about words.

LICHT is an idea the realization of which has been at least partly determined by fate. Its progression from the grandiose forces of *Donnerstag* and *Samstag* to the signally more modest resources of *Sonntag* may be read in different ways: as a waning of personal charisma, or as a deliberate and progressive shedding of superfluous apparatus,—including the conventional keyboard, orchestra, and auditorium acoustics as we know it,—to reveal an illuminated core, most purely expressed in the modulated cadences of the human voice.

One can only speculate about what might have been had the composer's vision taken hold of a wider musical constituency, and attracted more generous funding and support. One is also reminded of the older Schoenberg, focusing his vision on works for choir a cappella, unable to complete *Die Jakobsleiter*, believing the technical challenges (multiple orchestras, quasi-electronic "distancing" of voices, etc.) to be unrealizable. Schoenberg was also unable to resolve the drama of *Moses und Aron*, though in the latter case the dilemma is more philosophical in nature, of what to do about Aron, the Luziferian eternal populist and self-styled interlocutor whose mission of persuasion is fatally corrupted by vanity and a desire for public adulation. It is perhaps inevitable that parallels of such a kind should be drawn, given that both Schoenberg and Stockhausen's careers bear witness to the same crippling cultural legacy of intellectual and political populism, propaganda, institutional indifference, and academic disbelief that came to a head in the terrorism of Nazi Germany and the final solution of the atomic bomb.

Sonntag aus LICHT (Sunday from LIGHT)

1998–2003: No. 75–80 (Stockhausen-Verlag)

Opera in six scenes and a farewell. For 10 solo voices (high soprano, 2 sopranos, contralto, high tenor, 3 tenors, baritone, bass), boy's voice, four instrumentalists: flute (alto flute, also ring-modulated), basset-horn, trumpet (ring-modulated), synthesizer; 2 choirs (1. a cappella), 2 orchestras (solistic), electronic music, sound projectionist. Duration: 4 hours 38'.

For his culminating sermon of *LICHT* Stockhausen is withdrawing it seems to a timeless zone, more a Romantic than a medieval heaven, of a cappella choirs, his philosophical message easier to follow but still largely reduced to acoustic subtitles and symbolic gestures. To what Promised Land, one wonders, or to what elevated state of illumination, was *LICHT* ever destined to lead? From a generation of composers that includes Boulez, Berio, Pousseur, and Nono, a generation tried and tested by war, motivated by an evangelical passion to reform Western society, the message of *Sonntag aus LICHT* seems more reactionary than revolutionary (a revolution by definition being fated to return to an earlier starting-point).

Over the quarter-century gestation of *LICHT*, popular awareness of the intellectual range and quality of historic Western music (and also ethnic music) has been greatly enhanced through the nonpartisan cooperation of historians, performers, instrument makers and record producers in the

search for authentic performance practices,—or at least, a plausible synthesis of appropriate music, performance, instruments, and acoustic conditions.
Credit is due to the avant-garde of Stockhausen's generation for raising
awareness of the nature and behavior of sound, the design and disposition of
instruments, and the correlation of music and the acoustic environment.
But that same message it seems has been lost on the very composers whose
endeavors set the process in motion: the avant-garde aspiration toward a
common goal of a functioning and truly interactive new musical language, a
goal prefigured in the aleatory and mobile forms of the *die Reihe* era, has
virtually ceased—even as research and development in the profane fields of
voice recognition by computer, motion capture (in the visual domain), and
interactive games,—to name but three,—continues to thrive.

It is a sign of our musical times that in a new century and culture of
interactive data management, the trend toward open form notably endorsed
by Stockhausen in *Momente*, and by Boulez in the original scheme of . . .
explosante-fixe . . . , seems to have been abandoned at the very time the
public has embraced the technology and discovered the inclination to pursue
it. That these two great survivors of the avant-garde era continue publicly to
isolate themselves in doctrinaire fashion from a tradition of Western classical music (medieval, renaissance, baroque) mistakenly assumed to have
nothing to offer them, is almost as striking as their inability to agree on
where to go next, a loss of motivation thrown into even sharper relief by the
relaxation of political tensions and ending of the cold war initiated by
another MI-KA-EL, former Soviet president Mikhail Gorbachev.

Stockhausen's extraterrestrial sphere of reference allows him to interpret the religious beliefs and practices of humanity as imperfect models of a
higher order mythology that, as for Lévi-Strauss and other visionaries, has
its basis in abstract scale relationships. That Stockhausen's music itself is
necessarily anthropomorphic (patterned to human measures and perceptions) is not entirely a contradiction of the ultimate goals of transhuman
serialism; but that the composer himself has not delved more extensively in
recent years into time- and pitch-scales beyond human hearing, given the
technologies available to him, is surely disappointing: no groundbreaking
discoveries, for example in the field of high frequency modulation of instrumental sounds, nor any further manifestations,—other than the rotors of
Sirius and the "Helikopter-Streichquartett,"—of the perilous but promising
realm of infrasound, which can have strange effects on the body's physical
systems.

For an avowed mythologist, as even for the hieroglyphists of ancient
Egypt whose sacred inscriptions were likewise addressed to civilizations
several thousand years in the future, there is surely more content to myth
and to language than is suggested by Stockhausen's ineffably redundant
libretti. For so adept and prolific a writer and speaker to have said so little
of intellectual substance in these seven operas, is almost the action of one
who, imagining himself a prisoner of war, after giving his name, rank, and
serial number, has nothing more to say. After seven operas it is beginning to
sound as though the hermetic and fractured language of Stockhausen's

rituals is actually how the composer conceives religion to be, as formal recitations in an alien tongue that to the laity is no more than an abstract pattern of vowels and consonants, of no local or practical relevance. His verses certainly convey little of the emotional resonance of a Beckett, the hallucinatory vividness of a William Burroughs, or the tactile quality of a Heissenbüttel.

Scene 1: Lichter-Wasser (Lights-Waters)

1998–1999: No. 75 (Stockhausen-Verlag; cd SV-58)
For soprano, tenor, and orchestra (solistic) with synthesizer; 2 transmitting microphones, 29 microphones, 4 × 2 loudspeakers, mixing console.
Orchestra: 2 flutes, oboe, English horn, e flat clarinet, clarinet, bass clarinet, 2 bassoons, baritone saxophone, 2 horns; 2 trumpets, 2 trombones, tenor horn, euphonium, tuba; 5 violins, 5 violas.
Alternative title: "Sonntags-Gruss" (Sunday Greeting)
Duration: 51'.

This is no foyer greeting. It is *Ylem* with voices: a moment in the history of the Big Bang where the expansion of the local universe has reached its maximum and the musical configuration of the instruments has stabilized to a point where intergalactic communication is possible. The setting, a rectangular space in which the seating has been arranged to form a pattern of rectilinear and diagonal shapes resembling the British Union flag. Within this space and among the audience, tenor and soprano solo voices engage in an echo of medieval courtship dance in which the movement of king and queen, male and female, sun and moon, act out the mutually dependent orbits and obeisances of a celestial harmony. The music's polarities of high and low, and at times the harmonic language as well, resemble *Formel*, but in this universe the metallic tempered keyboards of glockenspiel, vibraphone, and celesta no longer occupy pivotal roles. In their place are the two voices representing Michael and Eva, and it is they who move while the instruments of the orchestra, in more cooperative mode than in "Orchester-Finalisten," stand quietly in their allocated positions among the audience, or looking on from galleries above, circulating messages in *klangfarbenmelodie* from one to another at the behest, so to speak, of the singing intelligences moving among them. Of his 1966 composition *Terretektorh*, in which the musicians of a large orchestra, each armed *Momente*-style with a simple percussion instrument, are distributed among the audience, Xenakis said

> [It is] a radically new kinetic conception of music which no modern electro-acoustical means could match. . . . The musical composition will thereby be entirely enriched throughout the hall both in spatial dimension and in movement. The speeds and accelerations of the movement of the sounds will be realized, and new and powerful functions will be [possible], such as logarithmic or Archimedean spirals, . . . [and] ordered or disordered masses, rolling one against the other like waves. . . . The listener will find himself . . . in a universe dotted about with little stars of sound, moving in compact nebulae or isolated.[2]

Stockhausen's instrumental forces are fewer, twenty-nine to Xenakis's eighty-eight, and his mood is more subdued, but the imagery of planetary systems, and of waves of music following and interacting like waves of light is common to both: "12 MICHAEL-waves and 12 EVE-waves begin synchronously, separate polyphonically, and meet at 7 further synchronous beginnings, connected by 6 bridges," as he puts it.[3]

It is almost as though Stockhausen has taken the implicit spatial counterpoints and rotations of "Michaelion" (implicit in their dependence on electronic transference from the platform to auditorium loudspeakers), and realized them in somewhat simplified form in real time and space. The three-dimensional distribution of instruments and voices is real and the audience is actually in the midst of the acoustic field. The mood is calm and relatively serene, the aesthetic a combination of Jugendstil and the chrome and travertine of Mies van der Rohe's Barcelona Pavilion. The two voices, singing texts more lucid and connected than usual, meet and intertwine in a form of palindromic counterpoint that is also medieval in origin and of a kind previously encountered in *In Freundschaft*. Stockhausen's distribution of instruments also reproduces in "real space" the virtual (i.e., electronically assisted) matrix of relationships only subliminally audible in "Michaels Reise," suggesting that the vocal and instrumental roles in "Lichter-Wasser" can both be understood in the *Kontakte* sense as physical incarnations of previously immanent relationships.

The combination of male and female voices in this idyllic instrumental setting is both a distillation of the composer's lifelong experience in spatial relationships, and a return to a sense of spiritual purity, or to the primal innocence of a Garden of Eden in which the spatiality of Brant and the lyricism of Webern are reconciled. What the title actually signifies is light of knowledge and water of life, but in the plural "lights" is also (tone-) colors: the fact that conventional orchestral instruments appear only in an accompanying, hence subordinate role in *Sonntag*, underscores a message that "in the beginning was the word" (of command, of intelligence, of revelation), and that all other instruments are simply colors, or wordless derivations, of the singing voice.

If so, it is a remarkable return to the Church's doctrinal position in the age of Gabrieli, which asserted that the only proper function of instruments was to double and support the voice, and that the sole purpose of the singing voice was to praise God. In the layout of "Lichter-Wasser" one is inevitably reminded of the galleried musicians of the Elizabethan age, the heavenly choirs of Thomas Tallis, or of Heinrich Schütz,—and indeed the polychoral motets for voices and instruments of the Venetian school,—except that Gabrieli, Monteverdi, and their contemporaries were taking exactly the opposite view from what Stockhausen now appears to be saying. Gabrieli's celebrated *Sonata pian' e forte* and other works like it were intended to usher in a new era of mobility of instrumental and tonal expression, a freedom from the restrictions of vocal range and of service to a sacred text.[4]

Of all the scenes of *LICHT*, the music of "Lichter-Wasser" is among the most perfectly composed, in every sense. Restraint and refinement are keys to an unexpected depth of allusion, and iridescent color, gratefully assisted in the recordings by voices of a crystalline purity of tone and precision of delivery that the operas of *LICHT* have always asked for but not always received.

From the opening introit for the two voices and synthesizer (the latter sounding more than ever like a small church organ), a listener is aware of undisguised tonality, literally a music of chromatic harmonies. As the music unfolds, the old polarities of the Goeyvaerts era reemerge: one recognizes not only the mirror-imagery of high and low from *Formel*, but also references to the relationship of voice and electronic music from *Gesang der Jünglinge*, now restated as between voices and orchestral instruments; also the relationship of the two melody instruments of *Kreuzspiel* (oboe and bass clarinet) that condense in the the middle register out of a cloud of points of piano and percussion converging from extremes of pitch. What is missing is the fractured texture arising from serial dynamics, an entire parameter now restrained to a degree allowing the ensemble balance (and a listener's sense of space and directional play) to be more sensitively managed.

In his handling of multiple-voice glissandi from the time of *Montag aus LICHT*, the composer has allowed brief and transitional accidents of tonal harmony to come to the surface. Now for the first time the tonal implications of these same polyphonic processes are positively emphasized in a music of decorated cadences that seems finally to resolve the dramatic and philosophical contradictions of movement and cadence, of starting and stopping (it is surely no coincidence that Stockhausen produced a revision of the 1965 composition *Stop*, retitled *Stop und Start*, in 2001). Some of these cadential movements are plainly self-referential: at measure 318, and again at 530, chord "compressions" in the style of *Dr. K.–Sextett*; elsewhere, hints of the final chorale of *Trans* at 559, of *Inori* (not to mention a touch of Stravinsky's *Symphony of Psalms*) at 692, even a muted echo of *Freitag's* Bells of Monsalvat in the measures leading up to the closing cadence in g at 728. The perceived effect of cadential movement gives the instrumental music here a welcome lightness and joviality, even under the admonitory direction of the two voices. The music is infused with a sense of discretion and tact, expressed especially clearly in the neo-Webernian line of melody passing from one intrument to another, the same line that is heard to so lyrical a purpose in the London Sinfonietta recording of *Kontra-Punkte*, with whose amiable elegance of gesture the new work has so much in common.

The composer's good humor extends to a spontaneous repeat of the grand tutti at the Fourth bridge, measure 461, an *Inori* moment of palpable elation introduced by a soprano high d flat to the synthesizer timbre of a glockenspiel (or musical box), and ending in a well-deserved (even if it is scripted) burst of applause. The repeat that ensues ("after such applause, wouldn't we want to repeat the Fourth bridge for one more time,—and for the same money?" urges the soprano, clearly in exultant mood) leads her to climax on an even higher e flat, transcending into a new dimension to the accompaniment of a Messiaen-like coda of distinctly sugary harmonies sounding like outtakes from the *Poèmes pour Mi.*

Scene 2: Engel-Prozessionen (Angel Processions)
2000: No. 76 (Stockhausen-Verlag; cd SV-67)
For choir a cappella.
Duration: 40'.

At first glance, the idea of a conception as grand as *LICHT* concluding to a hymn of praise, in which groups of voices assume a succession of spatial configurations like movable letters in a toy acrostic on their way to spelling out an ultimate message of goodwill, seems a long way removed from the discarnate visions of a Scriabin or a Kandinsky that the composer may initially have entertained. Though in every sense an ecstatic ritual, this does not seem at all like a music aspiring to the Artaudian delirium of a Boulez, the hallucinatory orchestrations of late Feldman or Scelsi, the resonant emptiness of late Cage,—or even the alien music conjured up by Louis and Bebe Barron to represent the vanished and disembodied superior intelligences of Altair 4 in the 1957 movie *Forbidden Planet*. Nevertheless, on the composer's own terms, which after all have been shaped by a lifetime of involvement, through the atomization and reconstruction of language, with information science, the linguistics of de Saussure, the structuralism of Piaget, and the legacy of linguistics in structural anthropology, the new work has to be regarded as a vocal tour de force of quite breathtaking genius.

When composing for instrumental forces, Stockhausen has always seemed to prefer the broken consort. *Zeitmasse* is not to be considered in terms of a uniform quintet of instruments of the same family; the "characteristic ensembles" of *Stop* are collections of deliberately (and to some ears, perversely) variegated timbres; and even the string quartet of "Helikopter-Streichquartett" is split asunder into unit soloists performing in separate enclosures to the timekeeping of click tracks transmitted from ground control. But while his inclinations instrumentally tend toward diversity, in composing for voices Stockhausen has always seemed to recognize their potential for timbral as well as harmonic unity. *Stimmung* is perhaps the most notable example of a composition for an ensemble of voices treated in effect not just as the delivery system for a text of generalized praise, but as the ultimate living synthesizer. Over the years, this music in turn has attracted the attention of increasing numbers of specialized vocal ensembles, many of them identifying with the intellectually demanding polyphony of medieval, renaissance, and baroque eras, a European history in which (as we can now discern) music is understood as occupying a borderland between text and tone. Such ensembles identify with earlier conventions of harmonic and timbral unity associated with instrumental consorts of lutes, viols, recorders, and with the organ, and have evolved a tone of voice that is as well-adapted to Stockhausen as to Pérotin, Machaut, Dufay, Willaert, and other composers of highly wrought polyphony.

In their different ways, Webern's development of a linear melody of tone colors, and Messiaen's exploration, most notably in his organ music, of the vertical dimension of colored resonances of unconventional mixture stops, can be reconciled as x and y coordinates of this third zone, between melody and harmony, in which timbre itself becomes an expressive variable for music and not just the random byproduct of speech. Since at least 1980, as we have noted, that same awareness of timbre as a variable has dominated musical researches at IRCAM as well as the instrumental choices and orchestrations of Messiaen and Boulez.

In fact the remarkable sense of genuine elation communicated in "Engel-Prozessionen" could be interpreted as a triumphant conclusion that may also be read as a sardonic and knowing criticism of the lack of progress achieved by IRCAM's combined efforts of information science and computer technology in recent years. It is the message of *Hymnen* all over again: a demonstration of Stockhausen's intellectual and musical pre-eminence in the face of the best and most advanced developments science and technology have to offer. In 1966–1967 the challenge was Max Mathews and the calculation of melodic probabilities; in 2000 the challenge is voice modulation and the simulation of coherent movement in a three-dimensional space. In the new as in the earlier work, Stockhausen faces his opponents with a handcrafted musical artifact more advanced and more perfectly realized, both in a musical and in a technical sense, than anything they are capable of achieving. For *Hymnen* the composer created an image of an artificial intelligence creating hybrid melodies out of national anthems; here in "Engel-Prozessionen" he conjures up an acoustic experience, in real time and real life, of continuous linguistic and spatial modulation that all of the intellectual and computing power of IRCAM and MIT combined would dearly love to emulate, but could never hope to attain, at least for now.

All of which is demonstrated, needless to say, under a cloak of the most brazenly unctuous and self-righteous religious sentiment that only a Stockhausen could get away with. Remember, too, that for all its richness of effect, this is still a simulation of a process identified by the composer as one that has yet to be achieved, in the technical domain, even by himself. To transform an admission of technical failure into an expression of masterful superiority involves the same logical inversion as *Gesang der Jünglinge,* another work of genius that is also a disguised technical failure (in voice synthesis). Attaching a higher value by default to works aspiring to some sacred purpose, over the more modest but practical results of patient scientific research, is oddly reminiscent of the policy aims, say, for German architecture under Albert Speer, which were to create sacred artifacts: tombs, or monuments, or tombs in the style of monuments, in preference to structures for actual use.[5]

Given the composer's impatience with the twelve-tone "variations" or "suite" form practiced by Schoenberg, Berg, and Webern,—even by Boulez, in the case of *Le marteau sans maître*—there may also be quiet satisfaction in some quarters to note that "Engel-Prozessionen" is yet another instance of the composer's attachment to the sevenfold suite. The recording is distinguished by superbly disciplined singing; the music,—which for all of its complexity is singularly grateful to listen to,—by a number of genial inventions. The general temperament reaches back to the high spirits of

Carré and *Momente*, but one wonders at the same time if the technical virtuosity of the vocal writing would have been conceivable without the composer's more recent trials of vocoder modulated soprano and bass voices. Although the choir groups are not mechanically modulated, Stockhausen's harmonic idiom has certainly developed stylistically in ways freely based on the effects of the vocoder and harmonizer in *Freitag aus LICHT*. These new techniques, which include forms of heterophony also familiar in ethnic music, are deployed with a wonderful looseness that accompanies bountiful self-confidence.

Discretion and care in the placing and movement of musical sources within the horizontal plane are further welcome signs of a benign, and indeed, quietly radiant composure that no longer needs to make rhetorical demands on a performers' skills or an audience's patience. The animated and virtually continuous flow of text is literally colored by the distinctive textures of seven different languages into which Stockhausen's versicles of praise are translated. We are used to hearing Stockhausen in French, German, English, and (from time to time) the metalanguage of Afro-American jazz, but the imaginative leap to embrace Persian, Hindi, Chinese, and Spanish is not only welcome from a diplomatic and musical point of view, but also as a paradigm shift to real languages from the fractured syllables of earlier operas in the cycle that have proved such an obstacle to comprehension for singers and audiences alike. The musical settings of Chinese are truly wonderful: the inflection characteristics of the language proving especially congenial to Stockhausen's angular melody formations, and introducing a number of authentic and enchanting new and appropriate timbres, gliding inflections, and trills. A shorter verse in Swahili, associated with *Samstag*, is repeatedly delivered with a Jovial and quite un-Luciferian joie de vivre, and at various times sounds more like the "Ur-Sonate" of Kurt Schwitters than Schwitters himself.

Of equal acoustic significance is the spatial opposition of moving choirs within the auditorium (along rectilinear aisles in conventional St. Michael's cross formation), against a background of pianissimo "wall-sounds". This is an effect that would be understood and admired by the Venetian school. Once again, Stockhausen's lengthy period of reflection on conceptually necessary but dramatically challenging pedal points has resulted in a genial breakthrough, this time the invention of a choral resonance that as well as producing harmonic effects of great beauty and subtlety, actually serves to enhance a listener's impression of spatial depth and presence. (It is in fact a choric version of Meyer-Eppler's "aleatoric modulation.") Even as recently as "Lichter-Wasser" the use of sustained synthesizer harmonies to provide discreet coloration could not entirely allay suspicion that the instrument's other function is, well, to fill the gaps. Here, however, the "wall-sounds," more than *Fresco* ever did, create a perfectly imagined and serene imagery of acoustic enclosure.

Nothing is exaggerated. Everything works. The music ends with a "Schluss-Chorale" of unbelievable richness. The overriding impression is, quite simply, glorious.

Scene 3: Licht-Bilder (Light-Pictures)

2002: No. 77 (Stockhausen-Verlag)

For basset-horn, flute with ring-modulation, tenor, trumpet with ring-modulation, synthesizer, sound projectionist.

Duration: 40'.

The designer Johannes Conen, whose ingenious costumes for the meta-morphic couples brought a much-needed sense of Bosch-like fantasy and lightness of touch to *Freitag aus LICHT*, is welcome collaborator in this work to be premiered at the Donaueschingen Musiktage in October 2004. It is the final and only appearance in *Sonntag aus LICHT* of the instrumental trio representing the personae of Michael as trumpeter, Eva as basset-horn, and Ave as flute. The work combines video sculptures by Conen, moving in four temporal layers (revisiting the time-runners of *Der Jahreslauf*, but in the electronic domain), and spatial movement by the performers. With trumpet and flute also ring-modulated, it is clear that once again the com-poser is playing a looking-glass game of counterpointed virtual (electronic) and real-time images of musical processes. It will be interesting to find out if this announced description means that the square-wave basset-horn is to be ring-modulated alternately with the ramp-wave trumpet and the sine-wave flute, a union of waveform personae in keeping with *Sonntag*'s theme of consummation. The fact that the basset-horn is the one instrument not to be ring-modulated does not rule out the possibility of its low-register square wave being employed not only as a carrier, but also potentially as a gate function, for the two other instruments. Such a use of the three instruments would represent a long anticipated extension of Stockhausen's two-part harmonic idiom into the domain of a cleaner and more versatile *Mantra*. To achieve an optimum quality of modulation and a minimum of sideband distortion, the amplitudes of all three instruments would have to be very carefully controlled.

Scene 4: Düfte-Zeichen (Scents-Signs)

2002: No. 78 (Stockhausen-Verlag; cd SV-69)

For high soprano, soprano, contralto, high tenor, tenor, baritone, bass; boy's voice (treble), synthesizer; 8 transmitting microphones, cd player, 7 loudspeakers, 4 monitor loudspeakers, mixing console.

Duration: 58'.

What comes vividly to mind is a memory of sharp smells, stale air, singing heads all around, and the curious timelessness of a caffeine-induced waking dream that comes over a listener at four in the morning after an early evening of recording has seamlessly passed into a night shift of adjusting levels. On the surface "Düfte-Zeichen" is just another public ceremony in the cycle of ceremonies of *Sonntag aus LICHT*, this time a rite of incense-burning and naming that might easily be read as a trip back to the never-never land of campfires and joss sticks. "The seven soloists sing about the 7 scents and 7 signs of the days of the week. They burn the scents and explain the scents and signs," the composer explains.[6] Below the surface, however, the combination of perfumes and disembodied voices evokes an anti-world of studio life in which the central character sits isolated behind a desk in a control room in the dead of night, playing back the same multiple tracks over and over, adjusting their relative positions,—here a little to the left, there a little to the right,—and the levels, up and down, searching for the ultimate balance. During this time the secondary voices continue to be heard in the background, rehearsing their lines as it were, waiting their time, signaling their presence and ready for attention. Through the control room glass you could see the vocalists, eyes firmly closed, a single headphone pressed against one ear, striving for the perfect inflection. Only by now the studio is empty, its lighting dimmed; the musicians long since departed, climbing out of a cab on the other side of town, tired and dingy, heading for bed. All that is left beyond the glass is a detritus of unattended microphones and discarded headphones, empty water bottles, unfinished cartons of egg fu yong, and half-eaten hamburgers in paper napkins stained with ketchup and fat. Through speakers surrounding the mixing desk, the singers' disembodied voices continue effortlessly to sound, over and over, interrupted only by the lighting of another cigarette and the reech of rewinding tape.

The poetic of radio drama is as old as radio, and this is a portrait in music of an idealized radio drama, birthplace of electronic music, and a largely alien world to many listeners. Here is the young playwright Tyrone Guthrie, writing in 1929:

> There is no narration; scene and interlude follow one another without a break. After the end of each episode there should be a stroke of the bell, then the scream of a syren [sic], suggesting a rush through time and space. The "scenes" should be played very intimately in a rather low key; in contrast to the "interludes," which are to be bold and reverberating.[7]

Lance Sieveking, a contemporary of Guthrie and pioneer BBC radio dramatist and producer, described the new art of voices as a music to be orchestrated, in terms startlingly foreshadowing Stockhausen. Of his dialogue *Intimate Snapshots*, also from 1929, we read that in it he "so to speak, *slow-motioned* small pieces of speech in several places, sometimes in order to emphasise the meaning of the words as *words*, and sometimes in order to give them special significance as sound forms."[8]

> He admits that this may sound high-falutin, but says that he had in mind that moment of mental contact when people suddenly understand each other not only emotionally but intellectually. Sieveking might have added that he was here trying to present a radio equivalent of the exchanges of gestures and looks which can be witnessed at such moments on the stage. But, like Guthrie, he was seeking by such orchestration of speech to extend the dramatic range of expression which had become stereotyped. It must have seemed to [Val] Gielgud that these portrayals of social archetypes attended by choric interludes and slow-motion speech were aiming at some purely abstract form.[9]

"Düfte-Zeichen" evokes an aural world of scents and disembodied voices moving in and out of conversation like a celestial diplomatic cocktail party (and even extending to traditional "moi-moi" greetings of symbolic affection). In ancient times a dialogue of unseen spirits would be perceived as the voices of the gods; today the prevailing caricature is of a Frankenstein laboratory reeking of chemicals, containing an array of severed heads or brains floating in jars of saline solution, barely alive, longing for extinction, their endlessly circulating thoughts still connected to the world of the living by electrodes and threadlike wires. A way of saying, to readers of a Romantic disposition, that images of eternity have their darker side, and that a composer of Stockhausen's acute sensibilities is both aware of the shadow and determined to acknowledge that a voice preserved is also a voice doomed to wander forever in a timeless limbo: "auch Engeln sind ewig unterwegs," as the choir sang in *Donnerstag*. It also goes some way to explaining the absence of content of the composer's libretti.

There are two principal actions. The one is Luzifer's return, snarling and honking like a disdainful Lord Haw-haw. The other is the presentation of a new Michael, picked out of the audience like a plant in a celebrity chat show. Both are reminders that there is, after all, life after *LICHT*, and that the dramatic tensions of the opera cycle are the ongoing consequences of human life on earth. Since it is crucial to Stockhausen's message to bring home the reality of Michael, the Eva-persona (now a contralto), and Luzifer as living reincarnations and not voices from the past, it would make sense I think to present the alternate voices in a more disembodied way, in masks, or as celestial teleconferencing faces on separate monitors, perhaps (the lips moving not quite in synch, like satellite interviews on television). The seven signs of the days are already proudly on display; to superimpose the seven singers' faces on the seven banners would not be entirely out of character.

The work is scored for synthesizer (once again sounding like a modest church organ with limited, but very elegant glissando effects) and the same seven-voice ensemble, consisting of beautifully matched high soprano, soprano, alto, high tenor, tenor, baritone, and bass, that previously played a leading role in "Engel-Prozessionen." (It is not hard to understand why the composer is now recommending that a performance of *Sonntag aus LICHT* be spread over three days, whatever havoc this is likely to create for future planners of a festival of the entire week.) Toward the end of "Engel-Prozessionen" one hears a number of hints of the musical idiom of "Düfte-Zeichen": they include tight voice trills—a wonderful discovery, by the way, —a clustered imitation of buzzing bees, a return of the multivoice water sounds of "Invisible Choirs," and metallic voice harmonics delicately drawn from a slow articulation of the diphthongs of [Tiusday], [Freitag], [Montag], etc. The musical language of "Düfte-Zeichen" brings together elements of "Orchester-Finalisten" (for example, animal impressions), with the new free-floating heterophony and polyphony that has emerged out of the composer's long engagement with "rounds" (since *"Atmen gibt das Leben . . ."*), and more recently with the vocoder and harmonizer. The composer's handling of tempi and vocal textures, and his notation of them, is deceptively simple, but the gestural and harmonic vocabulary of *Sonntag aus LICHT*, here and else-where, is wonderfully subtle and refined.

The music is sectioned into groups corresponding to the seven banners and scents, followed by a coda and "Annunciation" (probably the appropriate term) of a new Michael-incarnation. The seven cardinal divisions are further divided into segments treating the scent, the sign, and the essential char-acter of the day in various voice combinations related to the spiritual status of the personae involved. In the setting of the composer's texts (mostly in German and English), the prevailing style resembles a baroque cantata, alternating recitatives, strictly harmonized chorales, and choruses of freer counterpoint. The supporting role of the synthesizer in all of this is remi-niscent on the one hand of the chiming punctuations of *Refrain*, and on the other hand, of a Bach organ or harpsichord accompaniment. Even after so many years, Stockhausen's ear for new harmonies has not deserted him; a new feature (also relating to *Refrain*, and perhaps also *Adieu*) is the frag-mented undulation and dispersal by voices of the notes of a synthesizer chord, in the manner of ripples on a pond.

Luzifer's reemergence into the light,—he is very much alive and a force to be reckoned with,—is a little like Frankenstein returning to the labo-ratory for a recharge. In a music that inverts the earlier and almost tragic "Luzifers Traum" evocation of a spirit fading away, he bounces back in full snoring voice to deliver a stuttering "Samstag-Solo" in which, among other expletives, the syllable "Rot" (red) mutates via a succession of hiccups (Rut, Blut, shoot, toot, etc.) to *ud*, Saturday's scent of the Indian eaglewood tree, to end finally (yes, you guessed it), on the formerly magic syllable "Hu!"

Viewed for the first time in full array, Stockhausen's banner signs of the week, combining elements of the heraldic and the erotic, begin to resem-ble a Stravinskian deck of cards. What each actually signifies, as if that were not already obvious, is willy-nilly laid out in song, in verses of a blush-ing and overripe symbolism from the era of Aubrey Beardsley. They amount in sum to a declaration that the range of gender preferences and combi-nations represented among the characters of *LICHT* is now, and ever shall be fully compliant with the totality of modern-day relationship practices, —though personally I fail to see Michael and Luzifer in any other than a stand-off relationship.

In productions from the late nineties the name of Kathinka Pasveer has appeared not only as a performing artist, but as an assistant in the recording process itself. There is nothing unusual about that: somebody has to take on the task of carrying the composer's aesthetic forward, and a sec-ond pair of ears is always a help. All the same, the recording of "Düfte-Zeichen" shows a few inconsistencies. While the bulk of the recording is very dry, the chorale-like tutti that follows immediately after "Sonntags-Duett" is suddenly reverberating like an empty gymnasium. Added to which there is an obvious and nasty edit affecting harmony and reverberation at the entry point of the synthesizer immediately following, leading into the alto reci-tative (another glimpse of Bach, this time of the *St. Matthew Passion*) that forms a bridge between nocturnal limbo and the real world of Michael, the chosen one sitting amongst the audience.

Scene 5: Hoch-Zeiten (High-Times)

2001–2002: No. 79 (Stockhausen-Verlag; cd SV-73)

For choir and orchestra in separate locations (2 performances); 33 microphones (choir), 41 microphones (orchestra), 2 × 5 loudspeakers, 2 mixing consoles, 2 sound projectionists.

Choir in five groups: I First sopranos, 3 + 3 (or 4), II Second sopranos, 3 + 3 (or 4), III Altos, 4 + 4, IV Tenors, 4 + 4, V Basses, 4 + 4.

Orchestra in five groups (each with a subconductor): I 3 flutes, 3 violins; II 3 oboes, 3 trumpets; III 3 clarinets, 3 violas; IV 3 horns, 3 bassoons; V 3 trombones, 3 violoncellos.

Percussion instruments for timekeeping are played by subconductors of the instrumental groups and also by leaders of the choir groups, the same instrument(s) for each group: I antique cymbal, II 4 rin (Japanese temple bells), III 4 bronze gong plates, IV 4 domed Thai gongs, V 4 duraluminium bell plates.

The conductor, seated in the audience of the orchestra-performance, also plays a synthesizer in the final trio.

Duration: 2 × 35'.

In 1967 Stockhausen made sketches for a work of around 25 minutes in duration entitled *Projektion für Orchester*, for large orchestra divided into nine mixed groups of 8–10 players. From the few pages that were fully orchestrated before the project was abandoned, one can discover echoes of the final 1966 revision of *Punkte 1952/1962*, as well as anticipations of the layered structure and parallel harmonies of *Trans*. It had been Stockhausen's idea to have the piece performed in front of a film projection of the same orchestra playing the same work, the latter also performing against a filmed back projection of the same orchestra playing the same piece, making a polyphony of one layer of "present tense" and two layers of "past tense." The musical material was designed, after the manner of the temporal layers of *Solo*, to allow the filtering out of different layers of music at different times, and also for performances at different tempi.

Stockhausen's fascination with mirror-relationships, and in particular the implications of a live performance interacting with a complementary music that is prerecorded, or at least issuing out of a loudspeaker, shortwave radio, or ring-modulation circuit, is oddly reminiscent of the character Zelig from the movie by Woody Allen, a blank-faced Everyman with an uncanny compulsion to insert himself into the context of historic newsreel footage. This same interplay of the living with recorded history is revived in "Hoch-Zeiten," with the difference that this time the real face and the face in the mirror get to change places, a twist in the tale that could also be read as a paradigm shift that puts eternity on an equal footing with a continuous present,—at least to the extent of allowing an ongoing dialogue between the "NOW" and the forever. Perhaps Sunday for Stockhausen is the day in which, as Carl von Weizsäcker predicted, time ceases to exist, and "intensity of experience will replace extensity." As well as meaning "marriage," the title "high-times" suggests not only the timeless moment of ecstasy (or "perpetual high," as they say), but also the *coincidence* of all such moments across time. That very sentiment of unity of experience is also in harmony with the scene's manifest subtext of sexual union (which on this occasion is celebrated in verse rather than gesture), and equally with the composer's profession of spiritual identity with artists and composers of former times whose ideas have come to be realized in his compositions.

There is a residual irony, nevertheless, in the notion of a marriage that obliges the two parties to live in separate locations and communicate by radio. Stockhausen had previously floated the idea of a music performed simultaneously on different continents and communicating by satellite, but we know from live telecasts from the other side of the world, that for a world even as small as our own the speed of light is still not fast enough to ensure the synchronization of ensembles in widely-separated locations. That might not have been an issue for a modern Gabrieli writing in a canonic idiom designed to cope with freely variable time-delays, but it is certainly an issue for Stockhausen, whose layered structure of five different tempi demands a degree of synchronicity available only among ensembles within the same time zone.

This marriage is strictly between man and woman, and West and East, so the composer's notes tell us; it is also between the temporal and the eternal, and between voices and instruments, who we are invited to consider as complementary aspects of vocal communication, singing being uniquely able to convey a text. Given that the pitch content available for the scene is extremely limited, Stockhausen has devised alternative ways of enriching his basic material. For voices, a collection of texts, some of them recycled from "Engel-Prozessionen," some newly invented, but also incorporating verses extracted from the Persian poet Hafiz (from Odes I, III, VI, VII, and IX, in the translation by John Nott), from the Indian *Bilavamangala Stava,* from a Chinese love poem, and other sources. For the sake of thematic consistency the composer has grafted the name Michael, or Micha, or Michael-trumpeter, onto these original verses, and while these additions tend to look incongruous in print, even in the International Phonetic Alphabet, and do nothing for the poetry, they blend well enough into the polyglot texture of the music.

From a beautifully-imagined beginning, a musical sigh of pleasure that works wonderfully in both the instrumental version (with choral insertions) and the choral version that comes later (with instrumental insertions), the celebration quickly expands in complexity until both sides begin to resemble a Boulezian brainstorm, or indeed a Cageian circus. The temptation to go with multiplicity and density of effect rather than restraint is understandable, but given the potential for subtlety of movement in differing tempi, and bearing in mind the work's structural affinity with the five-part cadenzas of *Zeitmasse,* for example, it seems a mite disappointing.

Though based on a very limited repertoire of precise tonal centers, the verse-setting itself, on the other hand, is inventively realized in a form of decorated *sprechstimme* in which the central tone or *accent* (in Messiaen's terminology) corresponds to the formula pitch, while the *anacrouse* and *désinence* are modeled after typical inflections of the chosen language.

Stockhausen is clearly enamored of the sounds and rhythms of Chinese and Swahili, which he employs with an infectious enthusiasm. The graphic notation is not difficult in itself; what is a challenge is the timing of the temporal layers, which are controlled from click-tracks via earpieces. In performance the superimposition of layers is often so dense, and the underlying pitch material so inert, as to give the illusion of a much simpler common tempo. The composer's tempo-schema is essentially a tempered scale in which the frequency interval between successive steps is in the ratio roughly of 4 : 3 (MM 30, 40, 53.4, 71.2, 95.6, 134, 180). Not quite, I think, the classic tempo-scale from the time of *Kontra-Punkte*, as the composer's notes appear to claim, but rather an ascending scale in approximate fourths, as in *Studie II*, *Kontakte*, or *Mantra*.

The five groups each of singers and instrumentalists are arranged in corresponding arc formations on their respective platforms, Groups I, of treble instruments and singers, to the right, graduated through to Groups V, of bass instruments and singers, to the left. This is not according to recent convention of associating the higher-pitched with heaven on the left, and the lower-pitched with hell on the right, but a return to Stockhausen's baroque keyboard arrangement of *Kreuzspiel* and *Spiel*. Suspended above the front of each platform, *Trans* fashion, are five loudspeakers that relay the music from the corresponding unseen group in the other place. There is a deliberate symmetry between the instrumental and the choral ensembles, and they perform from the same tonal material, embroidering it in different characteristic ways, so that when the sound of one group breaks through, as it were, into the other performance space, the music is essentially the same to a point where the listener is able to hear transitions from inarticulate inflections into articulate speech, or from singing voices into disembodied instrumental tones,—literally depending on where the audience and music are coming from.

It is good to report that this work is also a collaboration, hence also a reconciliation, with Cologne Radio. It is also a pleasure to hear Stockhausen writing with such evident goodwill and high spirits for a coherent body of conventional instruments, organized in multiples of the same instrument. A layout of timbre-clusters facing one another suggests rich possibilities of dynamic intermodulation, and the nature of the heterophonic material itself offers scope for the same delicate transient effects previously encountered in *Adieu*, and at least hinted at in the two-voice *Indianerlieder*. Any composed interference effects, vocal or instrumental, tend to disappear, however, in the turbulence of the moment. Of the action it might be observed, not for the first time, that it seems to pass directly from a magical onset to an extended fade without delivering much by way of a mission statement in between, but the elusiveness of the content is a large part of the music's implication and charm, and the high spirits are certainly palpable.

The recording on compact disc is close-set and rather lacking in the antiphonal distance suggested both by the physical separation of the two ensembles, and by the dramatic conception of worlds at once conjoined and apart. It seems that Stockhausen has opted, as in some others of his more recent recordings, to create as exact a superimposition as possible, relying on the degrees of tonal presence of the absent ensemble in each case to convey the mystery of union in separation. A by-product of arranging the two groups of performers by pitch across the stage is that the center of activity, in terms of frequency, seems displaced toward the right side, a tendency not altogether helped by equalization of some of the lower-pitched instruments to darken the tone, making the cellos sound at times like double-basses. The entire instrumentation, to be sure, reverts to the triples of the *Formel* era, a decision perhaps making aesthetic sense for the end of a cycle that is both personal and global, but one that also raises the old specter of an inherently unbalanced totality.

Sonntags-Abschied (Sunday Farewell)
2001–2003: No. 80 (Stockhausen-Verlag)
Electronic music for 5 synthesizers.
Duration: 35'.

Strahlen (Rays)
2002: No 80½ (Stockhausen-Verlag)
For a percussionist and 10-track tape; 3 microphones, 10-track tape recorder, 5 loudspeakers, mixing console.
Duration: 35'.

"Strahlen," Stockhausen's title for the derivative composition, indicates straight away that this is a work destined to convey the impression of an overwhelming radiance that, at the time of its initial conception all those years ago, might also have hinted at the possibility of global destruction by radiation (out of which *LICHT* would have been intended to survive as an encrypted legacy of twentieth-century Western culture). Since the immediate danger of such an eventuality has receded, in spite of Chernobyl, and despite even more recent events (among which the Berliner Festspiele's scheduling of the official German premiere on the third anniversary of 9/11 could conceivably be misinterpreted), the tone, if in keeping with earlier scenes, should be more benign than confrontational.

A composition for synthesizers based on the number five inevitably calls to mind the five channels of *Gesang der Jünglinge*, the five instruments of *Zeitmasse*, and the 25th root of 5 tuning of *Elektronische Studie II*. At the very least, this ultimate expression of Josef Matthias Hauer's "modern orchestra" provides a rich resource for timbral counterpoint and manually controlled lateral (and even vertical) movements of sound in space. Stockhausen's collaboration with Antonio Pérez Abellán has enlarged and refined the range of tone colors and textures available to the synthesizer, though the instrument still cannot match the physical presence of electronic sounds from the early tape era. Its great drawback remains a lack of real substance, a consequence of design principles that have never taken proper account of the physical nature of musical instruments as signal generators and cavity resonators. It would not be too much perhaps to hope that the new work might attempt to create virtual sonic images moving in a three-dimensional space through the mutual interference of otherwise inaudible frequencies. A more realistic expectation, given the indications of Piano Pieces XVI and XVII, suggests a work in the original spirit of *Carré* and *Kontakte*, perhaps even *Kurzwellen*, in which a principal solo keyboard interacts with four ancillary synthesizers to create a dynamic polyphony in which gestural and timbral imitation, supplemented by a degree of inspired intuition, are the defining features.

Notes

1. T. J. Reed, *Goethe* (Oxford: Oxford University Press, 1984), 88–89.
2. Mario Bois, "Iannis Xenakis: the Man and his Music. A conversation with the composer and a description of his works." Catalogue essay (London: Boosey & Hawkes, 1967), 34–35.
3. "Lichter-Wasser" compact disc notebook, cd SV-58, 22–23.
4. Robin Maconie, *Second Sense: Language, Music, and Hearing* (Lanham, Md: Scarecrow Press, 2002), 111–13.
5. Berthold Hinz, *Art in the Third Reich* tr. Robert Kimber and Rita Kimber (Oxford: Basil Blackwell, 1979), 189–204.
6. "Düfte-Zeichen" compact disc booklet, SV-69, 65.
7. Tyrone Guthrie, cited in Ian Rodger, *Radio Drama* (London: Macmillan, 1982), 17.
8. Lance Sieveking, cited in Ian Rodger, *Radio Drama*, 20.
9. Ian Rodger, *Radio Drama*, 20.

BIBLIOGRAPHY

Adorno, Theodor W. *Philosophy of Modern Music* tr. Anne G. Mitchell and Wesley V. Blomster. New York: Continuum, 1973.

Anderson, Alan Ross ed. *Minds and Machines*. Englewood Cliffs: Prentice-Hall, 1964.

Armitage, Merle ed. *Schoenberg: Articles*. New York: Schirmer, 1937. Reprint, Westport, Conn.: Greenwood Press, 1977.

Astrov, Margot ed., *The Winged Serpent: American Indian Prose and Poetry*. Reprint, Boston: Beacon Press, 1992.

Ayer, A. J. *Philosophy in the Twentieth Century*. London: Unwin, 1984.

Babbitt, Milton. "Twelve-tone Rhythmic Structure and the Electronic Medium." *Perspectives of New Music* I/1 (1962), 49–79.

Barker, Ernest. "International Broadcasting: Its Problems and Possibilities." *BBC Annual 1935*. London: British Broadcasting Corporation, 1935, 145–63.

Barrault, Jean-Louis. *Memories for Tomorrow* tr. Jonathan Griffin. London: Thames and Hudson, 1974.

Barrow, John D. *Artful Universe: The Cosmic Source of Human Creativity*. Boston: Little, Brown, 1995.

Barthes, Roland. *Image–Music–Text* tr. Stephen Heath. London: Fontana, 1977.

Beck, R. T. "Austrian Serialism." 135–91 in *Music in the Modern Age* ed. F.W. Sternfeld. London: Weidenfeld & Nicholson, 1973.

Beckett, Samuel. *Ping. Encounter* Vol. 28 No. 2 (1967), 25–26.

Beckwith, John, and Udo Kasemets ed., *The Modern Composer and His World*. Proceedings of the International Conference of Composers, Stratford, Ontario, 1960. Toronto: University of Toronto Press, 1961.

Berio, Luciano. "Aspetti di artigianato formale." *Incontri Musicali* 1 (1956), 55–69.

———. "Form" 140–45 in *The Modern Composer and His World*. Proceedings of the International Conference of Composers, Stratford, Ontario, 1960, ed. John Beckwith and Udo Kasemets. Toronto: University of Toronto Press, 1961.

———. *Luciano Berio: Two Interviews*. With Rossana Dalmonte and Bálint András Varga. Tr. ed. David Osmond-Smith. New York: Marion Boyars, 1985.

Blum, Bruce I. *Beyond Programming: To a New Era of Design.* New York: Oxford University Press, 1996.

Boulez, Pierre. "At the Ends of Fruitful Land . . ." 19–29 in *die Reihe 1: Electronic Music* tr. Alexander Goehr. Bryn Mawr: Theodor Presser, 1958.

———. "Éventuellement . . ." 117–48 in *L'Œuvre du XXe Siècle, La Revue Musicale* numéro spéciale 212 ed. Nicolas Nabokov (April 1952).

———. "Incidences actuelles de Berg." 104–8 in "Le Rythme Musical." *Polyphonie* 2e cahier ed. Albert Richard. Paris: Richard-Masse, 1948.

———. "Music and Invention: Pierre Boulez interviewed by Misha Donat." *Listener* Vol. 83 No. 2125 (22 January 1970).

———. *Orientations: Collected Writings* ed. Jean-Jacques Nattiez, tr. Martin Cooper. London: Faber and Faber, 1986.

———. "Perspective-Prospective." 23–33 in Brigitte Marger and Simone Benmussa, ed., *La Musique en Projet: Le Premier Livre de l'I.R.C.A.M., Direction Pierre Boulez.* Paris: Gallimard, 1975.

———. "Propositions." 65–72 in "Le Rythme Musical." *Polyphonie* 2e cahier ed. Albert Richard. Paris: Richard-Masse, 1948.

———. *Rélévés d'Apprenti.* Paris: du Seuil, 1966.

———. "Son et Verbe." 57–61 in *Rélévés d'apprenti.* Paris: du Seuil, 1966.

———. "Strawinsky demeure." 151–224 in *Musique Russe I.* ed. Pierre Souvtchinsky. Paris: Presses Universitaires de France, 1953.

Boulez, Pierre, and Célestin Deliège. *Conversations with Célestin Deliège* tr. Robert Wangermée. London: Eulenberg, 1976.

Bouquet, Mary. *Reclaiming English Kinship: Portuguese Refractions of British Kinship Theory.* Manchester: Manchester University Press, 1993.

Brady, Philip. "Helmut Heissenbüttel," obituary. *Independent,* London (25 September 1996).

Brant, Henry. "Space as an Essential Aspect of Musical Composition." 223–42 in *Contemporary Composers on Contemporary Music* ed. Elliott Schwartz and Barney Childs. New York: Holt, Rinehart and Winston, 1967.

———. "Uses of Antiphonal Distribution and Polyphony of Tempi in Composing." *American Composers' Alliance Bulletin* IV/3 (1955), 13–15.

British Broadcasting Corporation. *BBC Annual 1935.* London: British Broadcasting Corporation, 1935.

———. *BBC Handbook 1940.* London: British Broadcasting Corporation, 1940.

———. *BBC Year-Book 1934.* London: British Broadcasting Corporation, 1934.

Bruch, Walter. *Erinnerung an Funkausstellungen.* Berlin: Presse- und Informationsamt des Landes Berlin, 1979.

Budd, Malcolm. *Music and the Emotions: The Philosophical Theories.* London: Routledge, 1992.

Burbank, Richard, ed. *Twentieth-century Music: A Chronology.* London: Thames and Hudson, 1984.

Burrows, A. R. *Story of Broadcasting.* London: Cassell, 1924.

Cage, John. *I–VI.* Cambridge, Mass: Harvard University Press, 1990.

———. "Lecture on Indeterminacy." 260–73 in *Silence.* Cambridge, Mass.: M.I.T. Press, 1966.

———. *Silence.* Cambridge, Mass.: M.I.T. Press, 1961.

Calder-Marshall, Arthur. *Innocent Eye: The Life of Robert J. Flaherty.* New York: Harcourt, Brace & World, 1963.

Cardew, Cornelius. "Report on Stockhausen's *Carré.*" *Musical Times* 102–3 (1961),

169–22; 698–700.

———. *Stockhausen serves Imperialism*. London: Latimer New Dimensions, 1974.

Carter, Elliott. *Writings of Elliott Carter* comp. ed. Else Stone and Kurt Stone. Bloomington: University of Indiana Press, 1977.

Chomsky, Noam. *Modular Approaches to the Study of the Mind*. San Diego: San Diego State University Press, 1984.

———. *Syntactic Structures*. The Hague: Mouton, 1957.

Cocteau, Jean. *Cocteau on the Film, a Conversation recorded with André Fraigneau*, tr. Vera Traill. London: Dennis Dobson, 1954.

Cott, Jonathan. *Stockhausen: Conversations with the Composer*. London: Robson Books, 1974.

Culhane, John. *Walt Disney's* Fantasia. Reprint, New York: Abrams, 1999.

Cunningham, Merce. *Danseur et la Danse: Entretiens avec Jacqueline Lesschaeve*. Paris: Belfond, 1980.

Debussy, Claude. *Debussy on Music* ed. François Lesure, tr. Richard Langham Smith. London: Secker & Warburg, 1977.

Decroupet, Pascal, and Elena Ungeheuer. "Through the Sensory Looking-Glass: the Aesthetic and Serial Foundations of *Gesang der Jünglinge*." 97–142 in "A Seventieth-Birthday Festschrift for Karlheinz Stockhausen, Part One" ed. Jerome Kohl. *Perspectives of New Music* 36/1 (1998).

Demuth, Norman comp. ed., *Anthology of Musical Criticism*. London: Eyre & Spottiswoode, 1947.

De Saussure, Ferdinand. *Course in General Linguistics* ed. Charles Bally and Albert Sechehaye in collaboration with Albert Reidlinger; tr. Wade Baskin. Glasgow: Collins, 1974.

Descartes, René. *Philosophical Works* tr. E. Haldane and G. R. T. Ross. *Discourse on Method*, Vol. I. Reprint, Cambridge: Cambridge University Press, 1967.

Douglas, Alfred. *Oracle of Change: How to Consult the I Ching*. Harmondsworth: Penguin Books, 1972.

Eaglefield-Hull, A. *Dictionary of Modern Music and Musicians*. London: J. M. Dent, 1924.

Ebbinghaus, Hermann. *Memory: A Contribution to Experimental Psychology* tr. Henry A. Ruger and Clara E. Bussenius. Reprint. New York: Dover Publications, 1964.

Eimert, Herbert. "How Electronic Music Began." *Musical Times* (1973), 347–49.

Eimert, Herbert, and Hans Ulrich Humpert. *Lexikon der elektronischen Musik*. Regensburg: Bosse, 1973.

Eimert, Herbert, and Karlheinz Stockhausen, ed. *die Reihe: Information über serielle Musik. 1: Elektronische Musik*. Vienna: Universal Edition, 1955.

———. *die Reihe 2: Anton Webern*. Vienna: Universal Edition, 1955.

———. *die Reihe 3: Musikalisches Handwerk*. Vienna: Universal Edition, 1958.

———. *die Reihe 4: Junge Komponisten*. Vienna: Universal Edition, 1958.

———. *die Reihe 5: Berichte—Analyse*. Vienna: Universal Edition, 1959.

———. *die Reihe 6: Musik und Sprache*. Vienna: Universal Edition, 1960.

———. *die Reihe 7: Form—Raum*. Vienna: Universal Edition, 1960.

———. *die Reihe 8: Rückblick*. Vienna: Universal Edition, 1962.

———. *die Reihe: A Periodical Devoted to Developments in Contemporary Music* (English edition). *1: Electronic Music* tr. Alexander Goehr. Bryn Mawr: Theodor Presser, 1958.

———. *die Reihe 2: Anton Webern* tr. Leo Black and Eric Smith. Bryn Mawr: Theodor Presser, 1958.

——. *die Reihe 3: Musical Craftsmanship* tr. Leo Black and Cornelius Cardew. Bryn Mawr: Theodor Presser, 1959.

——. *die Reihe 4: Young Composers* tr. Leo Black. Bryn Mawr: Theodor Presser, 1960.

——. *die Reihe 5: Reports—Analyses* tr. Leo Black and Ruth Koenig. Bryn Mawr: Theodor Presser, 1961.

——. *die Reihe 6: Music and Language* tr. Ruth Koenig and Margaret Shenfield. Bryn Mawr: Theodor Presser, 1964.

——. *die Reihe 7: Form—Space* tr. Cornelius Cardew. Bryn Mawr: Theodor Presser, 1965.

——. *die Reihe 8: Retrospective* tr. Cornelius Cardew and Ruth Koenig. Bryn Mawr: Theodor Presser, 1968.

Eisenstein, Sergei. *Film Sense* tr. Jay Leyda. London: Faber and Faber, 1948.

Eliot, T. S. *Collected Poems 1909–1962*. London: Faber and Faber, 1974.

——. *Selected Prose* ed. John Hayward. Reprint. Harmondsworth: Peregrine Books, 1963.

Eller-Rüter, Ulrike-Maria. *Kandinsky: Bühnenkomposition und Dichtung als Realisation seines Synthese-Konzepts*. Hildesheim: Georg Olms, 1990.

Empson, William. *Seven Types of Ambiguity*. Reprint. Harmondsworth: Penguin Books, 1961.

Forsyth, Michael. *Buildings for Music: The Architect, the Musician, and the Listener from the Seventeenth Century to the Present Day*. Cambridge: Cambridge University Press, 1985.

Fox, Edward. "Light fantastic." *Independent Magazine*, 7 August 1993.

Friedländer, Walter. "Experiment oder Manier?" *Frankfurter Allgemeine Zeitung* (25 July, 1952).

Frisius, Rudolf. *Karlheinz Stockhausen. 1: Einführung in das Gesamtwerk, Gespräche mit Karlheinz Stockhausen*. Mainz: Schott, 1996.

Froebel, Friedrich. *Education of Man* tr. W. N. Hailmann. London: Appleton, 1906.

Fuller Maitland, J. A. ed. *Grove Dictionary of Music and Musicians*. London: Macmillan, 1911.

Gardner, Martin. *The Night is Large: Collected Essays 1938–1995*. New York: St. Martin's Griffin, 1996.

——. "White, Brown, and Fractal Music." *Scientific American* Vol. 238 No. 4 (1978). Reprinted with additions in *The Night is Large: Collected Essays 1938–1995*. New York: St. Martin's Griffin, 1996, 375–91.

Gay, Peter. *Enlightenment: An Interpretation; The Science of Freedom*. Reprint. New York: Norton, 1977.

Gehlhaar, Rolf. "Zur Komposition 'Ensemble.'" *Darmstädter Beiträge für Neue Musik XI*. Mainz: Schott, 1968.

Gielgud, Val. *British Radio Drama 1922–1956: A Survey*. London: Harrap, 1957.

Goethe, Johann Wolfgang von. *Zur Farbenlehre* (Goethe's Color Theory). New York: Van Nostrand Reinhold, 1971.

Goléa, Antoine. *Rencontres avec Olivier Messiaen*. Paris: Julliard, 1961.

——. *Rencontres avec Pierre Boulez*. Paris: Julliard, 1958.

Grant, M. J. *Serial Music, Serial Aesthetics: Compositional Theory in Post-War Europe*. Cambridge: Cambridge University Press, 2001.

Gunderson, Keith. *Mentality and Machines: A Survey of the Artificial Intelligence Debate*. Second edition. London: Croom Helm, 1985.

Hale, Julian. *Radio Power: Propaganda and International Broadcasting*. London: Paul Elek, 1975.

Harding, E. A. "Listening Post 1939." 84–87 in *BBC Handbook 1940*. London: British Broadcasting Corporation, 1940.

Harrington, Anne. *Reenchanted science: Holism in German Culture from Wilhelm II to Hitler*. Princeton: Princeton University Press, 1996.

Hartley, Anthony ed. *Mallarmé*. Harmondsworth: Penguin Books, 1965.

Harvey, Jonathan. *The Music of Stockhausen: an Introduction*. London: Faber and Faber, 1975.

Heikinheimo, Seppo. "Electronic Music of Karlheinz Stockhausen: Studies on the Esthetical and Formal Problems of its First Phase" tr. Brad Absetz. *Acta Musicologica Fennica* 6. Helsinki: Musicological Society of Finland, 1972.

Heisenberg, Werner. *Der Teil und das Ganze*. New edition, Munich: Piper, 2001.

Heissenbüttel, Helmut. *Einfache Grammatische Meditationen*. Freiburg: Walter-Verlag, 1955.

———. "Simple Grammatical Meditations." *Texts* tr. Michael Hamburger. London: Marion Boyars, 1977, 30–31.

Helmholtz, Hermann. *On the Sensations of Tone as a Physiological Basis for the Theory of Music*. Second rev. edn. tr. Alexander J. Ellis. Reprint, New York: Dover Publications, 1954.

Helmore, Frederick. *Speakers, Singers, and Stammerers*. London: Joseph Masters, 1874.

Henck, Herbert. "Karlheinz Stockhausens Klavierstück IX: Eine analytische Betrachtung." Reprint from *Musik und Zahl: Interdiziplinäre Beiträge zum Grenzbereich zwischen Musik und Mathematik* ed. Günther Schnitzler. Bonn–Bad Godesberg: Verlag für Systematische Musikwissenschaft, 1978.

Henderson, Linda Dalrymple. *Fourth Dimension and Non-Euclidean Geometry in Modern Art*. Princeton: Princeton University Press, 1983.

Hendrickson, Janis. *Roy Lichtenstein*. Cologne: Taschen, 1994.

Herzfeld, Friedrich. *Musica Nova*. Berlin: Ullstein, 1954.

Hesse, Hermann. *Glass Bead Game* tr. Richard Winston and Clara Winston. Harmondsworth: Penguin Books, 1972.

Heyworth, Peter. "Spiritual Dimensions." *Music and Musicians* (May 1971): 32–39.

Hiller, Lejaren A. and Leonard M. Isaacson. *Experimental Music*. New York: McGraw-Hill, 1959.

Hillier, Bevis. *Austerity/Binge: The Decorative Arts of the Forties and Fifties*. London: Studio Vista, 1975.

Hinz, Berthold. *Art in the Third Reich* rev. tr. Robert Kimber and Rita Kimber. Oxford: Basil Blackwell, 1979.

Hodeir, André. *Musique depuis Debussy*. Paris: Presses Universitaires de France, 1961.

Holland, James. *Percussion*. London: Macdonald and James, 1978.

J. O., "Poème électronique." *Radio et T.V.* No. 5 (May, 1958), 349–55.

Jakobson, Roman, and Morris Halle. *Fundamentals of Language*. Second edition. Berlin and New York: de Gruyter, 1971.

Jean, George. *Writing: The Story of Alphabets and Scripts* tr. Jenny Oates. New York: Abrams, 1992.

Jones, Daniel. *Pronunciation of English*. Cambridge: Cambridge University Press, 1956.

Julesz, Bela. "Experiments in the Visual Perception of Texture." 34–43 in *Scientific American*, 232 (1975).

Kandinsky, Wassily, *Concerning the Spiritual in Art* tr. M. T. H. Sadler. New York: Dover Publications, 1977.

———. *Point and Line to Plane* tr. Howard Dearstyle and Hilla Rebay. Reprint. New York: Dover Publications, 1979.

Khan, Hazrat Inayat. *Sufi Message of Hazrat Inayat Khan.* Vol. II. Reprint. Alameda, Calif.: Hunter House, 2001.

Kirby, Michael, and Richard Schechner. "An Interview with John Cage." 50–72 in *Tulane Drama Review* 10/2 (Winter 1965).

Kirchmeyer, Helmut. *Zur Entstehungs- und Problemgeschichte der 'Kontakte' von Karlheinz Stockhausen.* Essay enclosed with Wergo lp recording Wergo WER 60009, 1963.

Klee, Paul. *Notebooks Volume I: The Thinking Eye* ed. Jürg Spiller, tr. Ralph Manheim. London: Lund Humphries, 1961.

———. *Notebooks Volume II: The Nature of Nature* ed. Jürg Spiller, tr. Heinz Norden. London: Lund Humphries, 1973.

Koestler A., and J. R. Smythies ed., *Beyond Reductionism: New Perspectives in the life sciences. Proceedings of the Alpback Symposium 1968.* London: Hutchinson, 1969.

Kohl, Jerome, ed. "Guest Editor's Introduction." 59–64 in "A Seventieth-Birthday Festschrift for Karlheinz Stockhausen, Part One" ed. Jerome Kohl. *Perspectives of New Music* 36/1 (1998).

———. "A Seventieth-Birthday Festschrift for Karlheinz Stockhausen, Part One." *Perspectives of New Music* 36/1 (1998).

Köhler, Wolfgang. *Gestalt Psychology: An Introduction to New Concepts in Modern Psychology.* New York: Mentor Books, 1959.

———. *The Place of Value in a World of Facts.* New York: Mentor Books, 1966.

Kostelanetz, Richard ed. *John Cage.* London: Allen Lane, 1974.

Krishna, Gopi. *Die biologische Basis der religiösen Erfahrung.* With an Introduction by C. F. von Weizsäcker. Munich: Wilhelm Heyne, 1968.

———. *Biological Basis of Religion and Genius.* New York: Harper and Row, 1972.

Kultermann, Udo. *Art-Events and Happenings* tr. John William Gabriel. London: Mathews Millar Dunbar, 1971.

Kunzig, Robert. "Falling forward: Why humans move like an imperfect pendulum." *Discover* (July 2001), 24–25.

Kurtz, Michael. *Stockhausen: Eine Biografie.* Kassel: Bärenreiter, 1988.

———. *Stockhausen: A Biography* rev. tr. Richard Toop. London: Faber and Faber, 1992.

La Musique et ses Problèmes Contemporains 1953–1963. Paris: Julliard, 1963.

Lawder, Standish D. *Cubist Cinema.* New York: New York University Press, 1975.

Leach, Edmund. *Lévi-Strauss.* Fourth edition rev. James Laidlaw. London: Fontana, 1970.

Le Corbusier (Charles-Édouard Jeanneret). *Le Modulor: A Harmonious Measure to the Human Scale Universally Applicable to Architecture and Mechanics* tr. Peter de Francia and Anna Bostock. London: Faber and Faber, 1961.

Lendvai, Ernö. "Einführung in die Formen- und Harmonienwelt Bartóks." 105–49 in *Béla Bartók: Weg und Werk* ed. Bence Szabolcsi. Kassel: Bärenreiter, 1972.

Levinson, Stephen E. and Mark Y. Liberman. "Speech Recognition by Computer." *Scientific American* 244/4 (1981).

Lévi-Strauss, Claude. *Raw and the Cooked: Introduction to a Science of Mythology.* Reprint. London: Pimlico, 1994.

———. *Structural Anthropology* tr. Claire Jacobson and Brooke Grundfest Schoepf. New York: Basic Books, 1963.

Lewis, Cecil A. *Broadcasting from Within.* London: Newnes, 1924.

Lindlar, Heinrich, ed. *Musik in der Zeit Heft 3.* Bonn: Boosey & Hawkes, 1953.

Lodge, David. *Art of Fiction.* Harmondsworth: Penguin Books, 1992.

———. "Some *Ping* Understood." *Encounter* Vol. 30 No. 2 (1968), 85–89.

Macdonald, Hugh. "Alexander Scriabin—Towards the *Mysterium.*" Booklet to cd *Scriabin: Preparation for the Final Mystery.* Decca 289 466 329-2.

Maconie, Robin. *Concept of Music.* Oxford: Clarendon Press, 1990.

———. "French Connection: Motor Phonetics and Modern Music. Serialism, Gertrude Stein and Messiaen's 'Mode de valeurs.'" http://www.jimstonebraker.com/maconie_lingtherory.html. Accessed 1/23/2004.

———. "Opera Aperta." 3–8 in *Canzona* (1991).

———. *Science of Music.* Oxford: Clarendon Press, 1997.

———. *Second Sense: Language, Music, and Hearing.* Lanham, Md.: Scarecrow Press, 2002.

———. *Works of Karlheinz Stockhausen.* Oxford: Oxford University Press, 1976.

———. *Works of Karlheinz Stockhausen.* Second edition. Oxford: Clarendon Press, 1990.

Maconie, Robin, and Chris Cunningham. "Computers Unveil the Shape of Melody." *New Scientist* Vol. 94 No. 1302 (1982), 206–9.

Mandelbrot, Benoît B. *Fractals: Form, Chance, and Dimension.* San Francisco: W. H. Freeman, 1977.

Manion, Michael, Barry Sullivan, and Fritz Weiland ed., *Stockhausen in Den Haag.* Documentation of the Karlheinz Stockhausen Project. English edition, The Hague: Koninklijk Conservatorium, 1982.

Manning, Peter. *Electronic and Computer Music.* Oxford: Oxford University Press, 1985.

Marger, Brigitte, and Simone Benmussa, ed. *La Musique en Projet: Le Premier Livre de l'I.R.C.A.M., Direction Pierre Boulez.* Paris: Gallimard, 1975.

Martin, Frank. "La responsabilité du compositeur." 85–88 in "Le Rythme Musical." *Polyphonie* 2e cahier ed. Albert Richard. Paris: Richard-Masse, 1948.

Martin, Steven M. *Theremin: An Electronic Odyssey.* VHS videotape; MGM Orion Classics, 1993.

Mathews, M. V., and L. Rosler. "Graphical Language for the Scores of Computer-generated Sounds." 84–114 in Heinz von Foerster and James W. Beauchamp ed., *Music by Computers.* New York: Wiley, 1969.

McLuhan, (Herbert) Marshall. *Gutenberg Galaxy: The Making of Typographic Man.* London: Routledge & Kegan Paul, 1962.

———. *Letters of Marshall McLuhan* ed. Matie Molinaro, Corinne McLuhan, and William Toye. Toronto: Oxford University Press, 1987.

McLuhan, Marshall, and Quentin Fiore. *The Medium is the Massage: An Inventory of Effects.* Harmondsworth: Penguin Books, 1967.

Medawar, Peter. *Limits of Science.* Oxford: Oxford University Press, 1984.

Mersmann, Hans. "Der Spätstil Bartóks." In *Musik in der Zeit* Heft 3 ed. Heinrich Lindlar. Bonn: Boosey and Hawkes, 1953.

Métraux, G. S., ed. *Cultures I / 1: Music and Society.* Paris: Unesco et La Baconnière, 1973.

Meyer, Jürgen. *Acoustics and the Performance of Music* tr. John Bowsher and Sibylle Westphal. Frankfurt/Main: Verlag Das Musikinstrument, 1978.

Meyer-Eppler, Werner. "Die elektrischen Instrumente und neue Tendenzen der elektroakustischen Klanggestaltung." 88–93 in *Musik: Raumgestaltung: Elektroakustik* ed. Wolfgang Meyer-Eppler. Mainz: Ars Viva, 1955.

———. "Statistic and Psychological Problems of Sound." 55–61 in *die Reihe 1: Electronic Music* ed. Herbert Eimert and Karlheinz Stockhausen, tr. Alexander Goehr. Bryn Mawr: Theodor Presser, 1958.

Meyer-Eppler, Werner, ed. *Musik: Raumgestaltung: Elektroakustik.* Mainz: Ars Viva, 1955.

Milhaud, Darius. *Notes Without Music* tr. Donald Evans. London: Calder and Boyars, 1952.

Miller, Dayton C. *Science of Musical Sounds*. New York: Macmillan, 1916.

Moles, Abraham A. *Informationstheorie und ästhetische Wahrnehmung* tr. Hans Ronge in collaboration with Barbara and Peter Ronge. Cologne, Germany: M. DuMont Schauberg, 1971.

Moorer, James. "Synthesizers I Have Known and Loved." 589–97 in *Music Machine: Selected Readings from* Computer Music Journal ed. Curtis Roads, Cambridge, Mass.: MIT Press, 1989.

Mooser, R.-Aloys. *Panorama de la Musique Contemporaine*. Geneva: René Kister, 1955.

Morawska-Bungeler, Maria. *Klingende Elektronen: Eine Dokumentation über das Studio für Elektronische Musik des Westdeutschen Rundfunks in Köln 1951–1986*. Köln-Rodenkirchen: P. J. Tonger, 1988.

Münsterberg, Hugo. *Film: A Psychological Study*. Reprint. New York: Dover Publications, 1970.

Myers, Rollo, ed. *Music Today*. London: Dennis Dobson, 1949.

Nabokov, Nicolas. "Introduction à L'Œuvre du XXe Siècle." 5–8 in *L'Œuvre du XXe Siècle, La Revue Musicale* numéro spéciale 212 ed. Nicolas Nabokov (April 1952).

———. *Old Friends and New Music*. Boston: Little, Brown, 1951.

Nabokov, Nicolas, ed. *L'Œuvre du XXe Siècle, La Revue Musicale* numéro spéciale 212 (April 1952).

Nattiez, Jean-Jacques, ed. *Boulez-Cage Correspondence* tr. ed. Robert Samuels. Cambridge: Cambridge University Press, 1993.

Newman, Ernest. *Testament of Music: Essays and Papers* ed. Herbert Van Thal. London: Putnam, 1962.

Nyman, Michael. *Experimental Music: Cage and Beyond*. London: Studio Vista, 1974.

Olson, Harry F. *Music, Physics, and Engineering*. Second edition. New York: Dover Publications, 1967.

Ouellette, Fernand. *Edgar Varèse: A Musical Biography* tr. Derek Coltman. London: Calder & Boyars, 1973.

Partch, Harry. *Genesis of a Music*. Second edition. Reprint, New York: Da Capo Press, 1975.

Petzold, Charles. *Code: The Hidden Language of Computer Hardware*. Redmond, Wash.: Microsoft Press, 2000.

Peyser, Joan. *Boulez: Composer, Conductor, Enigma*. London: Cassell, 1977.

Photophone Handbook for Projectionists. Second edition. Camden, N.J.: RCA Manufacturing Company, 1941.

Piaget, Jean. *Structuralism* tr. ed. Chaninah Maschler. London: Routledge and Kegan Paul, 1971.

Pierce, John R. *Science of Musical Sound*. New York: W. H. Freeman, 1983.

Popper, Karl R. *Logic of Scientific Discovery*. Revised edition. London: Hutchinson, 1988.

———. *Quantum Theory and the Schism in Physics*, ed. W. W. Bartley, III. Reprint. London: Routledge, 1992.

Porter, Andrew. *Musical Events. A Chronicle: 1980–1983*. London: Grafton Books, 1988.

Potter, Ralph K., George A. Kopp, and Harriet Green Kopp. *Visible Speech*. New edition. New York: Dover Publications, 1966.

Poullin, Jacques. "Von der musikalischen Transmutation zur Klangprojektion aufgenommener Schallvorgänge." 97–102 in *Musik, Raumgestaltung, Elektroakustik* ed. Werner Meyer-Eppler. Mainz: Ars Viva, 1955.

Prieberg, Fred K. *Musica ex Machina*. Berlin: Ullstein, 1960.

Pritchett, James. *Music of John Cage.* Cambridge: Cambridge University Press, 1993.

Queneau, Raymond. *Exercices de Style.* Paris: Gallimard, 1947.

Read, Herbert. *Philosophy of Modern Art.* Reprint. New York: Meridian Books, 1955.

Reed, T. J. *Goethe.* Oxford: Oxford University Press, 1984.

Regardie, Israel. *Golden Dawn: A Complete Course in Practical Ceremonial Magic.* Sixth edition, St. Paul, Minn.: Llewellyn, 1995.

Rhode, Eric. *History of the Cinema from its Origins to 1970.* Harmondsworth: Penguin Books, 1978.

Richard, Albert, ed. "Le Rythme Musical." Special edition of *Polyphonie* 2e cahier. Paris: Richard-Masse, 1948.

Richter, Hans. *Dada: Art and Anti-Art* tr. David Britt. Revised, London: Thames and Hudson, 1997.

Ribe, Neil, and Friedrich Steinle, "Exploratory Experimentation: Goethe, Land, and Color Theory." *Physics Today* Vol. 55 No. 7 (July 2002).

Ritzel, Fred. "Musik für ein Haus." *Darmstädter Beiträge zur Neuen Musik.* Mainz: Schott, 1970.

Roads, Curtis, ed. *Music Machine: Selected Readings from* Computer Music Journal. Cambridge, Mass.: MIT Press, 1989.

Rognoni, Luigi. *Second Vienna School: Expressionism and Dodecaphony* tr. Robert W. Mann. London: John Calder, 1977.

Ronan, Colin A. *Cambridge History of the World's Science.* Reprint. London: Book Club Associates, 1983.

Rudlin, John. *Jacques Copeau.* Cambridge: Cambridge University Press, 1986.

Ruppel, K. H. "Neodadisten." *Suddeutsche Zeitung,* 3 November 1961.

Russolo, Luigi. "The Art of Noises: Futurist Manifesto" tr. Stephen Somervell. 642–48 in Nicolas Slonimsky, *Music Since 1900.* Third rev. enl. edition. New York: Coleman-Ross, 1949.

Sabbe, Hermann. *Karlheinz Stockhausen: . . . wie die Zeit verging . . .* Munich: texte + kritik, 1981.

Sagan, Carl. *Dragons of Eden: Speculations on the Evolution of Human Intelligence.* London: Coronet, 1978.

Salazar, Adolfo. *Music in Our Time: Trends in Music since the Romantic Era* tr. Isabel Pope. London: Bodley Head, 1948.

Schaeffer, Pierre. "L'Objet Musical." 65–76 in *L'Œuvre du XXe Siècle, La Revue Musicale* numéro spéciale 212 ed. Nicolas Nabokov (April 1952).

―――. "Sound and Communication." 53–80 in *Cultures I / 1: Music and Society* ed. G. S. Métraux. Paris: Unesco et La Baconnière, 1973.

Scharf, Aaron. *Art and Photography.* Harmondsworth: Penguin Books, 1968.

Schatz, Ingeborg, ed. *Heinrich Strobel: "Verehrter Meister, lieber Freund:" Begegnungen mit Komponisten unserer Zeit.* Stuttgart: Belser, 1977.

Schillinger, Joseph. *Schillinger System of Musical Composition.* Two volumes. New York: Carl Fischer, 1946.

Schneede, Uwe M. *Essential Max Ernst* tr. R. W. Last. London: Thames and Hudson, 1972.

Schoenberg, Arnold. *Letters* ed. Erwin Stein, tr. Eithne Wilkins and Ernst Kaiser. London: Faber and Faber, 1964.

Schuller, Gunther. "American Performance and New Music." *Perspectives of New Music* I/2 (1963).

Searle, J. R. *Minds, Brains, and Science.* London: British Broadcasting Corporation, 1984.

Shahn, Ben. *Love and Joy about Letters*. London: Cory, Adams & Mackay, 1964.

Sherlaw Johnson, Robert. *Messiaen*. Berkeley and Los Angeles: University of California Press, 1988.

Singh, Simon. *Code Book: The Science of Secrecy from Ancient Egypt to Quantum Cryptography*. New York: Anchor Books, 1999.

Slonimsky, Nicolas ed. *Music Since 1900*. Third rev. enl. edition. New York: Coleman-Ross, 1949.

Smalley, Roger. "Novelty and variety." *Musical Times* (1968), 1046–48.

Sontag, Susan and others, *Dancers on a Plane: Cage, Cunningham, Johns*. London: Thames and Hudson, 1990.

Souvtchinsky, Pierre, ed. *Musique Russe I*. Paris: Presses Universitaires de France, 1953.

Springer, A. M. "Ein akustischer Zeitregler." *Gravesaner Blätter* 1 (1955), 32–37.

Stefan, Paul. "Josef Mattheus Hauer." 225–26 in *Dictionary of Modern Music and Musicians* ed. A. Eaglefield-Hull. London: J. M. Dent, 1924.

———. *Neue Musik: Versuch einer Kritischen Einführung*. Göttingen: Vandenhoeck und Ruprecht, 1958.

Stein, Gertrude. *Gertrude Stein: Writings and Lectures* ed. Patricia Meyerowitz. London: Peter Owen, 1967.

Sternfeld, F. W. ed. *Music in the Modern Age*. London: Weidenfeld & Nicholson, 1973.

Stetson, R. H. *R. H. Stetson's Motor Phonetics: A Retrospective Edition* ed. J. A. S. Kelso and K. G. Munhall. Boston: College-Hill Press, 1988.

Stockhausen, Karlheinz. *Ein Schlüssel für 'Momente.'* Kassel: Edition Boczkowski, 1971; from 1981 published by Stockhausen-Verlag.

———. "Electroacoustic Performance Practice." 74–105 in *Perspectives of New Music* 34/1, 1996.

———. Interview in "The Talk of the Town," *New Yorker* (18 January, 1964).

———. "On the Evolution of Music." *Finnish Music Quarterly* No. 3 (1989), 8–13.

———. "Orchester-Finalisten: Sketches for the orchestra soli." Stockhausen Composition Courses 1998, course booklet. Kürten: Stockhausen-Verlag, 1998, 17.

———. *Texte zur elektronischen und instrumentalen Musik. Band 1: Aufsätze 1952–1962 zur Theorie des Komponierens* ed. Dieter Schnebel. Cologne: M. DuMont Schauberg, 1963.

———. *Texte: zu eigenen Werken, zur Kunst Anderer, Aktuelles. Band 2: Aufsätze 1952–1963 zur musikalischen Praxis* ed. Dieter Schnebel. Cologne: M. DuMont Schauberg, 1964.

———. *Texte zur Musik 1963–1970. Band 3: Einführungen und Projekte, Kurse, Sendungen, Standpunkte, Nebennoten* ed. Dieter Schnebel. Cologne: M. DuMont Schauberg, 1971.

———. *Texte zur Musik 1970–1977. Band 4: Werk-Einführungen, Elektronische Musik, Weltmusik, Vorschläge und Standpunkte, Zum Werk Anderer* ed. Christoph von Blumröder. Cologne: DuMont, 1978.

———. *Texte zur Musik 1977–1984. Band 5: Komposition* ed. Christoph von Blumröder. Cologne: DuMont, 1989.

———. *Texte zur Musik 1977–1984. Band 6: Interpretation* ed. Christoph von Blumröder. Cologne: DuMont, 1989.

———. *Texte zur Musik 1984–1991. Band 7: Neues zu Werken vor LICHT, Zu LICHT bis Montag, Montag aus LICHT* ed. Christoph von Blumröder. Kürten: Stockhausen-Verlag, 1998.

———. *Texte zur Musik 1984–1991. Band 8: DIENSTAG aus LICHT, Elektronische Musik* ed. Christoph von Blumröder. Kürten: Stockhausen-Verlag, 1998.

———. *Texte zur Musik 1984–1991. Band 9: Über LICHT, Komponist und Interpret, Zeitwende* ed. Christoph von Blumröder. Kürten: Stockhausen-Verlag, 1998.

———. *Texte zur Musik 1984–1991. Band 10: Astronische Musik, Echos von Echos* ed. Christoph von Blumröder. Kürten: Stockhausen-Verlag, 1998.

———. "Une Expérience Électronique." 91–105 in *La Musique et ses Problèmes Contemporains 1953–1963.* Paris: Julliard, 1963.

Stockhausen, Karlheinz, and Robin Maconie. *Stockhausen on Music: Lectures and Interviews* comp. ed. Robin Maconie. London: Marion Boyars Publishers, 1989.

Stokowski, Leopold. *Music for All of Us.* New York: Simon & Schuster, 1943.

Stravinsky, Igor. "On 'Oedipus Rex.'" *Encounter* Vol. XVIII No. 6 (1962), 29–35.

———. *Themes and Conclusions.* London: Faber and Faber, 1972.

Stravinsky, Igor, and Robert Craft. *Conversations with Igor Stravinsky.* London: Faber and Faber, 1959.

———. *Dialogues.* Reissue. London: Faber and Faber, 1982.

———. *Memories and Commentaries.* London: Faber and Faber, 1960.

———. *Themes and Episodes.* New York: Knopf, 1966.

Stuckenschmidt, Hans Heinz. *Arnold Schoenberg: His Life, World and Work* tr. Humphrey Searle. London: John Calder, 1977.

———. "Strawinsky und Sankt Markus." Berlin *Tagesspiegel* (18 September 1956).

Szabolcsi, Bence, ed. *Béla Bartók: Weg und Werk.* Kassel: Bärenreiter, 1972.

Tannenbaum, Mya. *Conversations with Stockhausen* tr. David Butchart. Oxford: Clarendon Press, 1987.

Taylor, Charles. *Sounds of Music.* London: British Broadcasting Corporation, 1976.

Toop, Richard. "On Writing about Stockhausen." *Contact* 20 (1979), 25.

———. "Stockhausen's *Konkrete Etüde.*" 295–300 in *Music Review* 37/4 (1976).

———. "Stockhausen's other piano pieces." 348–52 in *Musical Times* (April, 1983).

Tootell, George. *How to play the Cinema Organ: A Practical Book by a Practical Player.* London: Paxton, 1928, 89–92.

Truelove, Stephen. "Translation of Rhythm into Pitch in Stockhausen's *Klavierstück XI.*" 190–220 in "A Seventieth-Birthday Festschrift for Karlheinz Stockhausen, Part One" ed. Jerome Kohl. *Perspectives of New Music* 36/1 (1998).

Turing, Alan M. "Computing Machinery and Intelligence." *Mind* Vol. LIX No. 236 (1950). 4–30 in *Minds and Machines* ed. Alan Ross Anderson. Englewood Cliffs: Prentice-Hall, 1964.

———. "On Computable Numbers, with an Application to the Entscheidungsproblem." *Proceedings of the London Mathematical Society* 42, (1937), 230–65.

Valéry, Paul. "Remarks on Poetry" (1927). 48–50 in *Symbolism: an Anthology* tr. ed. T. G. West. London: Methuen, 1980.

Vallas, Léon. *Theories of Claude Debussy, musicien français* tr. Maire O'Brien. London: Oxford University Press, 1929.

Viertel, Berthold. "Schoenberg's *Die Jakobsleiter.*" 165–81 in Merle Armitage, ed., *Schoenberg: Articles.* New York: Schirmer, 1937. Reprint. Westport, Conn.: Greenwood Press, 1977.

Vinton, John, ed. *Dictionary of Twentieth-Century Music.* London: Thames and Hudson, 1974.

von Foerster, Heinz, and James W. Beauchamp ed., *Music by Computers.* New York: Wiley, 1969.

von Meiss, Pierre. *Elements of Architecture: From Form to Place.* London: E & FN Spon, 1990.

von Weizsäcker, Carl F. *Relevance of Science: Creation and Cosmogony*. London: Collins, 1964.

von Weizsäcker, Viktor. *Gestalt und Zeit*. Göttingen: Vandenhoeck und Ruprecht, 1960.

Walker, D. P. *Studies in Musical Science in the Late Renaissance*. London: Warburg Institute, University of London, 1978.

Wardle, Irving. "Exclusive lines under the desert stars." *Times*, September 12, 1972.

West, T. G. tr. ed. *Symbolism: an Anthology*. London: Methuen, 1980.

Wickes, George. *Americans in Paris*. Reprinted with a new Foreword by Virgil Thomson. New York: Da Capo Press, 1980.

Wieser, Wolfgang. *Organismen, Strukturen, Maschinen*. Berlin: Fischer, 1959.

Willett, John. *New Sobriety: Art and Politics in the Weimar Period 1917–1933*. London: Thames and Hudson, 1978.

Williams, John R. *Goethe's Faust*. London: Allen & Unwin, 1987.

Williams, Raymond. *Culture and Society 1780–1950*. Harmondsworth: Penguin Books, 1961.

Winckel, Fritz. *Music, Sound and Sensation: a Modern Exposition* tr. Thomas Binkley. New York: Dover Publications, 1967.

Wise, David. "Spook Art: Was the CIA really behind the rise of Abstract Expressionism?" *ARTnews* Vol. 99 No. 8 (September 2000), 160–64.

Wittgenstein, Ludwig. *Tractatus Logico-Philosophicus* tr. C. K. Ogden and F. P. Ramsey. London: Routledge and Kegan Paul, 1922.

Wittkower, Rudolf. *Architectural Principles in the Age of Humanism*. Fourth edition. London: Academy Editions, 1988.

Wolff, Christian. "New and Electronic Music." *Audience* V: 3 (1958), 122–31.

Wörner, Karl H. *Karlheinz Stockhausen: Werk + Wollen 1952–1962*. Rodenkirchen: P. J. Tonger, 1963.

———. *Neue Musik in der Entscheidung*. Mainz: Schott, 1954.

———. *Stockhausen: Life and Work* rev. edn. tr. ed. Bill Hopkins. London: Faber and Faber, 1973.

Würffel, Stefan Bodo. *Das Deutsche Hörspiel*. Stuttgart: Metzler, 1978.

Young, J. Z. *Doubt and Certainty in Science*. New York: Galaxy Books, 1960.

Young, LaMonte. "Lecture 1960." *Tulane Drama Review* 10/2 (1965), 73–83.

Zwanzig Jahre Musik im Westdeutschen Rundfunk: Eine Dokumentation der Hauptabteilung Musik. Cologne: Westdeutsche Rundfunk, n.d.

INDEX

1914–1918 war 5, 13, 44, 99, 237, 254, 415, 441, 469, 478
1939–1945 war 4, 13, 76, 97, 161, 237, 365, 415, 441, 478, 484
4X synthesizer 384, 432, 445–46, 449, 450, 486

Abellán, Antonio Pérez 510, 543
abstraction 43, 44, 228, 309, 378, 478, 492
absurdist drama 378
Adams, John 78
Adorno, Theodor Weisengrund 1, 38, 40, 42, 60, 174, 196, 469
—*Philosophy of Modern Music* 40, 60
Adrion 24, 177, 193
advertising 74, 307
AEG Telefunken 129
aetherophone. *See* terpistone
African music 87, 434, 496
Aimard, Pierre Laurent 469
airplane sound. *See* propellor sound
aleatoric modulation 213, 215
aleatory 74, 132, 160, 216, 234, 487, 498, 529
alienation 20
all-interval series 202
Allen, Woody 512, 540
—*What's up, Tiger Lily?* 512
—*Zelig* 540
Ambrosian chant 301
amplification 351, 444, 447, 464
anacrouse–accent–désinence 76, 78, 81, 251, 283, 293, 448, 541–42
anacrusis 76, 394
anamorphism 98, 279, 381, 512

Andreae, Doris 20, 46, 47. *See* Stockhausen, Doris
anechoic chamber 89, 214, 266
animation 164
Antheil, George 507
—*Ballet mécanique* 507
anthropology 188, 254, 413, 428, 495, 513, 533
anthropomorphism 529
Antonioni, Michelangelo 20, 280
—*L'Avventura* 20, 280
—*Blow-Up* 280
—*La Notte* 20
Apollinaire, Guillaume 405, 412, 469
Arditti Quartet 516–17
Aristotle 348, 412
armonica, glass 66, 126, 490
Arnold, Malcolm 223, 485
—*United Nations* 223, 485
Arp, Hans 13, 280
ars nova 50, 403
art criticism, 7–8, 9, 31, 199
Artaud, Antonin 99, 100, 223, 378, 533
artificial intelligence 161, 174, 286
artificial syllables 111
Astrov, Margot 343
atonality 49, 53, 175, 250
attacks 84, 90, 187, 189, 266
augmentation 80, 103, 164, 251
Aurobindo, Sri 48n, 239, 308, 316, 323, 410
—*Synthesis of Yoga* 323
automata, musical 126
avant-garde music 43, 50, 528
Avery, Tex 35

Ayer, A. J. 65

Babbitt, Milton 203
Babylonian calendar 407
babytalk 405
Bach, J. S. 110, 153, 194, 195, 240, 277, 314,
    362, 380, 403, 425, 430, 452, 454, 516, 539
—*Art of Fugue* 362, 380, 403
—*St. Matthew Passion* 403, 539
—*Well-tempered Klavier* 430
Backus, John 3–4
Bacon, Francis 338
Baker, Josephine 405, 430
Balanchine, George 96
ball and stick aesthetic 46
Ball, Hugo 219
Balla, Giacomo 229
barbershop singing 33
Barbier, Charles 55
Barcelona Pavilion (Mies van der Rohe) 127,
    531
baroque style 115, 194, 218, 250, 380, 452,
    472, 539
Barraqué, Jean 80
Barrault, Jean-Louis 99, 162, 359
Barron, Louis and Bebe, 103, 533
—*Forbidden Planet* 533
Barthes, Roland 59–60, 523
Bartók, Béla 21, 24, 28, 47, 63, 70, 87, 91,
    142, 194, 207, 216, 217, 268, 380, 388, 433,
    454, 519–20
—*Concerto for orchestra* 268
—*Music for strings, percussion, and celesta*
    87
—*Out of doors suite* 142
—*Second Violin concerto* 207, 519–20
—*Sonata for two pianos and percussion* 24,
    27, 91, 194, 217
Battier, Marc 449
Baudelaire, Charles 35, 36, 422
Bauermeister, Mary 188, 218, 219, 221, 223,
    233, 236, 238, 253, 254, 308, 416, 435
Bauhaus 4, 37, 127
Bayle, François 187, 222
—*Oiseau-chanteur* 222
—*Points critiques* 187
Bayreuth 346
Bayreuth bells. *See* Montsalvat bells
Beardsley, Aubrey 539
beat 76, 206
Beatles 322
—*Sergeant Pepper* 322
Beckett, Samuel 214, 240, 261, 308, 343, 359,
    422–24, 429, 481, 530
—*Innommable* 308
—*Krapp's Last Tape* 343
Beethoven, Ludwig van 2, 19, 50, 59–60, 122,
    126, 128, 145, 195, 218, 229, 280, 283, 301,

305, 306, 319, 370, 479, 516
—*"Coriolan" overture* 229
—*Heiligenstadt Testament* 305
—*"Pastoral" Symphony No. 6* 516
—*"Prometheus" overture* 228
—*Variations on "God save the King"* 280
—*Wellingtons Sieg* 126
Beethovenhalle, Bonn 321–23, 345
Bell, Alexander Graham 77
Bell Laboratories 77, 85, 126, 128, 182–83,
    277–78, 314, 460, 499, 502
Benjamin, Walter 38, 60
—*Ursprung des deutschen Trauerspiels* 60
Benny, Jack 126, 498
Berberian, Cathy 222
Berg, Alban 1, 7, 49, 51, 74, 80, 81, 96, 153,
    180, 196, 233, 234, 262, 276, 334, 353, 407,
    430, 474
—*Kammerkonzert* 234, 334
—*Lulu* 276
—*Lyric Suite* 81, 153
—*Three pieces for orchestra* 153, 233
—*Violin concerto* 153
—*Wozzeck* 80, 96, 153, 353, 430
Bergisch-Gladbach Gymnasium 20
Bergman, Ingmar 493
—*Smiles of a Summer Night* 493
Berio, Luciano 63, 89, 170, 214–15, 238, 240,
    243–44, 274, 277, 308, 339, 350, 379, 428,
    495, 528
—*Allelujah I* 350
—*Allelujah II* 350
—*Circles* 238, 243–44, 308
—*Différences* 89, 214
—*Sequenza V* 428
—*Sinfonia* 277, 308, 339, 495
—*Thema: Omaggio a Joyce* 170, 240
—*Visage* 240
Berlin Wall, fall of 478
Berlioz, Hector 85, 440
—*Grande Messe des Morts* 440
Bernstein, Leonard 281
Beyer, Robert 37, 128
bias tone 18
Biber, Heinrich 330
Bilavamangala Stava 541
Bill, Max 188
binary code 413
Bingen, Hildegard von. *See* Hildegard von
    Bingen
biorhythms 342–44
Birdland 177–78, 185, 223, 434
birdsong 382, 472, 511, 514
Birtwistle, Harrison 429
—*Yan Tan Tethera* 429
bitonality 53
biwa 433
Blaauw, Marco 521

Blacher, Boris 405–6
—*Abstrakte Oper Nr. 1* 405–6
Blair, Henry 126
Blake, William 253, 416
Blume, Friedrich 387–88, 398
Blumlein, Alan 93
Böhm, Karl 96
Bohr, Niels 228, 413
bokusho 266, 267
Bonn University 132, 173, 211, 212
Bornemann, Fritz 313
Bosch, Hieronymus 468, 536
Boulanger, Nadia 49, 152
Boulez, Pierre 5, 8, 42, 43, 49, 50–51, 52, 53, 55, 60, 72, 73, 78, 80, 81, 89, 94, 96, 98, 99, 101–2, 104, 106, 111, 113, 116, 121, 122, 123, 131, 134, 137n, 144, 151, 153, 156n, 157, 158, 160, 162, 165, 166, 169, 174, 180, 184, 185–86, 189, 190, 193, 196, 197, 212, 214, 216, 222, 234, 238, 239, 240, 244, 260, 262, 276, 291, 308, 331, 332, 334, 338, 368, 384, 391, 393–94, 404, 415, 418n, 432, 441, 445–48, 452, 473, 487, 490, 514, 528, 529, 533, 534, 541
—*Anthèmes 2* 89
—*cummings ist der Dichter . . .* 473
—*Dialogue de l'ombre double* 446
—*Domaines* 308
—". . . éventuellement . . ." 95, 101–2
—*. . . explosante-fixe . . .* 213, 334, 447, 529
—*Improvisations sur Mallarmé* 189, 216, 394
—*Livre* 185–86, 308
—*Marteau sans maître* 165, 169, 185–86, 239, 368, 534
—*Messagesquisse* 5, 334
—*Penser la musique aujourd'hui* 234
—*Pli selon pli* 184, 238, 240, 244
—*Polyphonie X* 80, 113, 116
—*Répons* 89, 180, 193, 432, 446–47, 514
—*Rituel* 393, 452
—*Second Piano Sonata* 490
—*Soleil des Eaux* 42
—*Structures* 78, 80, 104, 113, 121, 144, 162, 331
—*Sur Incises* 89, 332, 445
—*Troisième sonate* 121, 144, 160, 165
—tape étude 99, 103, 134
Boullée, Étienne-Louis 329
Boyé, Harald 304
Bradley, Scott 35
Brahms, Johannes 51, 195
braille 54–55, 59
Braille, Louis 54
Brant, Henry 152, 176, 180, 190n, 296, 320, 379, 440, 443, 447, 451, 454–55, 509, 522, 531
—*Galaxy 2* 176
—*Grand Universal Circus* 190n

—*Orbits* 443
—*Signs and Alarms* 176
—"Space as an Essential Aspect" 296
—"Uses of Antiphonal Distribution" 296
—*Voyage Four* 296
Braque, Georges 99, 229, 279, 301, 434
Braun, Alfred 365
breathing 5, 100, 357, 360–62
Brecht, Bertolt 20, 197, 405, 430, 474
Breton, André 13, 97, 99, 410, 412, 417, 508
—*Nadja Étoilée* 97
British Broadcasting Company 94, 273
British Broadcasting Corporation 2, 16, 17, 18, 54, 96–97, 305–6, 334, 372, 465, 475n, 537
—drama suite 96–97
—international broadcasting 16
—Reith Lectures 465
British Empire 416
Britten, Benjamin 433
Brown, Carolyn 221
Brown, Earle 120–21, 147, 182, 201
Brubeck, Dave 63
Bruckner, Anton 280
Bruegel, Pieter the Elder 261
Brussels 1958 World Fair 46, 182, 314, 502
Buchla synthesizer 351
Büchner, Georg 221
—*Dantons Tod* 221
Budd, Malcolm 59
Buffalo State University 176
bull-roarer 383, 516
Buñuel, Luis 229, 469
—*Chien andalou* 469
Bunyan, John 74
Burroughs, William 161, 529
Burrows, A. R. 94
Burzum 480–81
—*Dunkelheit* 481
Buson 361
Bussotti, Sylvano 218
Butor, Michel 276
Byrd Hoffman School 423

cabbalistic ternary 100
cadential form 34, 267–68, 514, 532
Cage, John 7, 8, 22, 48n, 78, 82, 102, 103, 111, 112, 121, 123, 139, 140, 142, 143, 145, 147, 148, 151, 152, 153, 157, 158, 160, 162, 177, 182, 188, 189, 194, 201, 213, 221–22, 224, 234, 236, 238, 239, 241, 250, 261, 266, 274, 277, 305, 308, 309, 321–22, 359, 368, 404, 418n, 422, 429, 441, 444, 464, 541
—*4' 33"* 78, 308
—*Atlas eclipticalis* 241
—*Concerto for prepared piano and orchestra* 111
—*Fontana Mix* 188, 221

—*Imaginary Landscape No. 4* 305
—"Lecture on Indeterminacy" 234
—*Music of Changes* 111, 121, 123, 140, 142, 143, 144, 160, 162, 189
—*Music Walk* 188, 221
—*Sounds of Venice* 221
—*Theatre Piece* 221, 250
—*TV Köln* 188, 221
—*Variations IV* 322, 464
—*Variations V* 322
—*Water Walk* 221
—*Where are we going?* 221
—*Williams Mix* 103
—*Wonderful Widow of Eighteen Springs* 444
Calder, Alexander 240, 243, 368
calligraphy 57, 397
canon 194, 324
Cardew, Cornelius 181, 218, 234, 252
cardinal wave forms 113, 114, 435, 445
caricature 164, 261, 442, 451–52
Carlyle, Thomas 199
Carmeli, Boris 381
Carné, Marcel 99
—*Enfants du Paradis* 99, 359
Carrillo, Julián 197, 462
Carroll, Lewis 223, 275, 373, 387, 412
—*Alice in Wonderland* 223–24
—*Through the Looking Glass* 275, 509, 514
Carter, Elliott 87, 151–52, 391
—*Partita* 87
—"Rhythmic basis of American music" 151–52
—*String Quartet I* 152
cartoon music 35
Caskel, Christoph 185, 219
Catholic ritual 240
cavity resonance 200
cellule rythmique 56, 72–73, 101, 103, 111, 112, 250, 292
cell modification 103
Central Intelligence Agency 96, 107n
Chagrin, Francis 223, 485
Champollion, Jean-François 5, 53–54, 58, 59, 77, 417
chance operations 221
Chaplin, Charlie 20, 165, 239, 489
—*Gold Rush* 20
—*Great Dictator* 239
—*Modern Times* 489
Char, René 240
Chaucer, Geoffrey 302, 403
Chernobyl 543
Chevreul, Michel 229
Chipmunks 473
Chladni figures 342, 343
Chomsky, Noam 111, 182, 287, 465
—*Syntactic Structures* 287
Chopin, Frédéric 122, 218

choreography 338, 362, 365
cipher 5, 94, 161, 409
Clair, René 79, 508
—*Entr'acte* 508
—*Paris qui dort* 79, 508
Clarke, Arthur C. 309–10
Claudel, Paul 71, 99
click track 337, 394, 533, 542
Clouzot, Henri-George 264
Club d'Essai 99, 366
clusters 217, 338–39
cluster-glissandi 217
coarticulation 244
cocktail party effect 71, 345, 464, 538
Cocteau, Jean 70, 89, 98, 161, 229, 271, 378, 399, 471, 489, 512
—*Orphée* 70, 89, 161, 271, 378, 399, 489, 512
code 70, 94, 161, 254, 378, 478
Coeur de Basset 470
cold war 127, 173, 274, 414, 478, 529
Colette, Sidonie Gabrielle 492
collective composition 312
Cologne Cathedral 327–28
"Cologne manifesto" 236
Cologne New Music Courses 251, 262, 290
Cologne Radio electronic studio 25, 26–27, 105, 114, 126, 129, 139, 201, 211, 274, 351, 366, 382, 445, 499
Cologne Staatliche Hochschule für Musik, 20
Cologne University, 228, 479
color fringe effects 416
Columbia University 176
Columbus, Christopher 376
comb filter effect 344
comics art 224, 425
communication theory 128, 197, 236, 287, 413
communism 416
complex note 163, 194
complexity 94, 482, 541
Composer 3
compound rhythms 123
computer music 161, 277, 286, 287
computer science 94, 161
Conan Doyle, Arthur 360
Conen, Johannes 492, 536
Congrès pour la Liberté de la Culture 96
Conservatoire, Paris 4, 47, 49, 362
Constable, John 417
constellations. *See* star music
constructivism 45
Cooke, Deryck 53
—*Language of Music* 53
Copeau, Jacques 97, 100
Copland, Aaron 376
copy head (tape) 204
Corno di Bassetto, pseud. G. B. Shaw 475n
Cortez, Ferdinand 376
Cott, Jonathan 133, 359, 378, 423, 489

Count Basie 177–78, 223
counterculture 227, 405, 416
counterpoint 194
counting tic 424, 427, 429, 444, 474, 489
Couperin, Louis 81, 189
Cowell, Henry 152
Craft, Robert 334
critical theory 214
crystal goblet 83
cubism, 228, 406
cummings, e e 214, 238, 243–34
cunieform script 54, 77
Cunningham, Merce 221, 359, 362
—Canfield 359
—Suite 359
cyclical formations 76, 298, 378, 380, 494
Czerny, Carl 297, 374

d'Anglebert, Jean-Henri 189
dada 13, 23, 220, 221
Dada-Messe, Erste Internationale 1920 220
daguerrotype 52
Dalí, Salvador 98, 223, 279, 410, 468, 469,
    523
—Evocation of Lenin 469
—Hallucinogenic Bullfighter 523
—Necrophilic Spring 469
Dallapiccola, Luigi 214
Danhauser, Josef 225n
—Liszt am Klavier 225n
Dante Alighieri 311, 403
Darmstadt International Summer Courses
    35, 37–38, 40, 66, 128, 166, 212, 236, 239,
    251, 305, 311, 312, 313, 334, 351, 353
Darwin, Charles 5, 58, 199
Davies, Hugh 4
da Vinci, Leonardo 75, 393, 452
Davis, Miles 434
Debussy, Claude 49, 64, 72, 75, 76, 79, 80, 85,
    87, 102, 123, 136, 216, 233, 338, 355, 474
—Feu d'Artifice 216
—Jeux 233, 355
—La Mer 474
—Martyre de Saint-Sébastien 136
—Prélude à l'Après-midi d'un Faune 64
—Voiles 216
Decroupet, Pascal 166
degenerate art 31, 230
de Gourmont, Remy 288n
—Litanies de la Rose 288n
Delacroix, Eugène 97
—Odalisque 97
Delaunay, Robert 229
Delphi, temple of 412
Depression years 97
de Saussure, Ferdinand 57–59, 65, 76, 81, 88,
    91n, 158, 197, 231, 238, 244, 290, 405,
    415–16, 432, 460, 533

Descartes, René 371
Desmond, Paul 63
Désormière, Roger 42
detective fiction 74, 110, 158
Detmold Music Academy 128
Deutsche Grammophon 477–78
Deutsch, Max 49
de Vos, Martin 468
di Chirico, Giorgio 131, 272
—Uncertainty of the Poet 272
Dietrich, Marlene 15, 472
Digby, Andrew 521
di Guigno, Giuseppe 384, 445–46, 449
diminution 80, 164
directional effects 522
disc jockey 96
Disney studio 182, 183, 223, 314, 430, 471,
    502
—Alice in Wonderland 223
—Bambi 430
—Fantasia (1940) 183, 314, 502
—Snow White 470
dissonance 50, 494
distinctive features theory 244
distortion 510, 523
divinity in art 200
documentary 20, 75, 367, 417, 425
Dom. See Cologne Cathedral
dome acoustics 327–28, 330
Donaueschingen Festival 47, 146
Donen, Stanley 404
Donizetti, Gaetano 65
—Lucia di Lammermoor 65
Doppler effect 205, 206
doubt, existential 227
Doxology 428
dramatic control panel, 96
dramatic form, 61
dreams, significance of 59, 253
Duchamp, Marcel 224, 229, 508, 518
Dudley, Homer 128
Dufay, Guillaume 533
Dullea, Keir 310
duration scale 79, 117, 198
Dürer, Albrecht 477
Durkheim, Émile 58, 197, 287
Dutilleux, Henri 49
Dutschke, Rudi 416
dynamic melody 101, 352
dynamics 85, 86, 117, 197, 198, 353, 357, 542

early music 330, 472, 528, 533
Ebbinghaus, Hermann 111
echo chamber 96, 502
echolalia 427
Eckhart, Meister 361
écriture 56, 93, 102, 151
Edison, Thomas Alva 71

educational theory 4, 28, 46, 110, 253,
    343–44, 421–22, 436
Egk, Werner 405
eigentone 344
Eimert, Herbert 3, 23, 25, 26–27, 35, 37, 84,
    104, 127, 128–29, 140, 170, 201, 202, 257,
    260, 264, 274, 366, 449, 498, 519
—Atonale Musiklehre 23, 25, 35
—Einführung in die elektronischen Musik
    127
—Epitaph für Aikichi Kuboyama 170, 260
—Zu Ehren von Igor Stravinsky 134, 449
Einmaleins 422
Einschub 195–96, 244–45. See Stockhausen,
    Karlheinz, inserts
Einstein, Albert 14, 28, 29n, 44, 227, 228,
    416, 433, 494
Eisenstein, Sergei 75, 278
—Film Sense 278
electrical instruments 113, 128, 174
electronic music, 2, 126, 127, 128, 174, 198,
    250, 478, 491, 505
electrostatic field 356–57
elementary propositions. See sachverhalten
Eliot, T. S. 43, 240, 422
Ellis, Alexander J. 94
EMI 93
empiricism 417
Empson, William 9, 275
—Seven Types of Ambiguity 275
EMS 114, 127, 351, 500
encryption 93, 478
Enlightenment era 38, 229, 414
entartete Kunst. See degenerate art
epic poetry 411, 414, 417
Epstein, Jacob 465
equal temperament 126, 150, 297, 430, 494
Ernst, Max 13, 111, 223, 229, 279, 413, 417,
    466, 468, 488
—Pietà 488
—Semaine de Bonté 468
estarrt (transfixed) pose 19, 372, 466
ethnic music 73, 84, 104
evolution 58, 199, 316, 343, 344, 409
exploratory experimentation 415, 501

Fano, Michel 80
Fantasound 183, 314, 431
Faraday, Michael 134
feedback 284
Feldman, Morton 140, 157, 201, 259, 533
Fellini, Federico 245
Ferrari, Luc- 222
Fibonacci series 26, 27, 28, 187, 216, 262, 265,
    268
Fichte, Johann Gottlieb 28
filtered noise 132, 255–56
finalism 513

Fink, Wolfgang 89
Fires of London 319
Flaherty, Robert 158
flugelhorn 487, 489
foley art 313
folk music 21, 153, 266, 388
Ford, John 280
form, development of 6, 44, 162, 218
formants 153, 298
formula composition 65, 330, 353, 362, 369,
    380, 388, 392, 395, 403, 430, 448, 459, 471
Fortner, Wolfgang 37
found object 195, 403, 504, 518
Fourier, Jean-Baptiste 134
Fox, Edward 418n
fractal mathematics 195, 331
Frankenstein 134, 278, 380, 538, 539
Franklin, Benjamin 65, 490
free association 222
free jazz 293, 312
freedom, symbolism of 38, 96, 478, 491
Freier, Reicha 432
Freud, Sigmund 3, 52, 59, 103, 229, 254, 469
Friedländer, Walter 66
Frisius, Rudolf 105, 466
Fritsch, Johannes G. 513
Froebel, Friedrich 4, 10, 28, 45, 252–53, 292,
    314, 409, 421–22, 436
—Law of Connection of Contrasts 10, 252–53,
    292, 409, 421–22
Frontberichte 17, 365–66
fugue 110, 194
Fuller-Maitland, J. A. 439
Future Sounds of London 510, 524n
futurism 228, 507, 515
Futurist Manifesto 515, 517

Gabo, Naum 45, 337
Gabrieli, Giovanni 181, 290, 328, 335, 480,
    522, 531, 541
—Sonata pian' e forte 532
gagaku 266, 338, 391, 396–400, 433, 512
Galileo Galilei 290, 430
Galilei, Vincenzo 150
Galvani, Luigi 236
gamelan 433
Gamow, George 348
Gandhi, Mahatma 239
Ganzheitslehre (holism) 44, 316
Garbo, Greta 359
Gavin, Barrie 2
Gay, John 405
—Beggar's Opera 405
Gay, Peter 416
gegliederte sprache 91n
Gehlhaar, Rolf 296, 304
géophone 98
Gerron, Kurt 15

Gershwin, George 355, 462
—*Rhapsody in Blue* 462
gestalt 63, 100, 104, 194, 197, 277, 290–92
Gestalt psychology 100, 103, 237, 291
Ghedini, Giorgio 214
Giacometti, Alberti 492
Gide, André 99
Gielgud, Val 96, 107n, 537
Gillespie, Dizzy 178
Giotto di Bordone 7
Givelet organ 128
Glass Bead Game 19, 32, 42, 46, 60, 140, 251,
  324, 395, 407, 413, 441
Glass, Philip 78, 152, 298, 424
globes, colored 436, 523
Globokar, Vinko 311, 428, 448, 466
Glock, William 223
glossolalia 428
Goebbels, (Paul) Josef 15, 129
Goethe, Johann Wolfgang von 5, 23, 100, 128,
  229, 387, 397–98, 403, 407, 411–12, 414–17,
  422, 432, 435, 436, 480, 492, 493, 497, 527
—*Farbenlehre* (Theory of color) 23, 228, 407,
  414–15, 416, 432, 436, 492, 497
—*Faust* 229, 414, 417, 422
—*Trilogie der Leidenschaft* 417
—*Wahlverwandschaften* 417, 493
Goeyvaerts, Karel 40, 41, 42, 44, 47n–48n, 51,
  62, 65, 79, 84, 105, 106, 130, 131, 132, 140,
  145, 175, 441, 532
—*Nr. 1 for two pianos* 41, 42
—*Nr. 2 for thirteen instruments* 41
—*Nr. 3 for bowed and struck sounds* 41
—*Nr. 5 for sine tones* 41, 140
golden mean 26, 86
Goléa, Antoine 42, 146
Golyscheff, Jefim 23
Goon Show 372
Gorbachev, Mihkail 529
Gould, Glenn 430
Goya, Francisco 261
grace-notes 142–44
Grainger, Percy 142
grammar, generative 111, 182
grams 96
graphic notation 120–21, 187, 188–89, 201,
  259
Gravesano Review 213
Gray, Jerry
—*String of Pearls* 18, 19
Gredinger, Paul 140
Greek drama 20, 485
Gregorian chant 72, 76, 79, 301
Grierson, John 225
Grimaux, Yvette 80
Gris, Juan 229, 407, 414
Grock 428

Gropius, Walter 4, 127
Grosz, Georg 15, 34, 474
group composition 117, 118, 121, 145, 146,
  154, 162–63, 335–36, 441
Group Stockhausen 304, 305, 513
Gsell, Paul 231, 246n
Gutenberg, Johann 330
Guthrie, Tyrone 537

Habá, Alois 197, 472
Hadamovsky, Eugen 15
Hafiz, Shams al-Din Muhammad 527, 541
Hailmann, W. N., 12n
Hair 381
Halle, Maurice 244
Hammond organ 128, 433, 459, 499
Handel, Georg Frideric 334, 425, 480
—*Royal Fireworks music* 334
—*Water music* 334
happening 221, 224, 424
harmonizer 535, 539
Harrington, Ann 46
Harrison, Lou 176
—*Four strict songs* 176
Harvard University 176, 237, 309
Harvey, Jonathan 460
—*Mortuous plango, vivos voco* 460
Haubenstock-Ramati, Roman 187
—*Liaisons* 187
—*Mobile for Shakespeare* 187
Hauer, Josef Matthias 1, 23–24, 37, 56, 119,
  407, 424, 543
Haussmann, Raoul 468
Haw-Haw, Lord 539
Hawking, Stephen 93, 445
Haydn, Joseph 115, 126, 370, 436, 470
—"*Farewell*" symphony 115
—*Trumpet concerto in e flat* 461
hearing 85, 132, 145, 330, 473
Heartfield, John 7
Hegel, Georg Wilhelm Friedrich 22, 28, 38,
  59, 412
—*Vorlesungen* 412
Heidegger, Martin 240, 371
Heike, Georg 173, 212
Heinlein, Robert A. 382
Heisenberg, Werner 44, 45, 227, 228, 230–31,
  232, 416, 494
—uncertainty principle 230–31, 494
Heiss, Hermann 23, 37, 407
Heissenbüttel, Helmut 261, 429, 465, 530
—*Einfache grammatische Meditationen* 261
Heister, Hans 365
helicopter sound 516
Helm, Everett 37, 47n
Helms, Hans G 219, 221
—*Fa:m' Ahniesgwow* 221
Helmholtz, Hermann 94, 135, 151, 197,

297–98, 485
—*Sensations of Tone* 94
Henck, Herbert 215
Henry, Pierre 94, 98, 255
—*Tam Tam IV* 255
Hertz, Heinrich 231
Hesse, Hermann 19, 22, 24, 32, 42, 46, 60,
    140, 251, 324, 407, 409
—*Glasperlenspiel* 19, 22, 324, 407. See also
    Glass Bead Game
—*Magister ludi* (English) 407, 409
heterophony 375, 434, 535, 542
hichiriki 433
hieroglyphs 5, 53, 182, 417
Hildegard von Bingen 460
Hiller, Lejaren A. 161, 277
Hillier, Bevis 46
—*Austerity/Binge* 46
Hindemith, Paul 21, 37, 52, 94, 114, 403
—*Harmonie der Welt* 403
—*Hin und Zuruck* 405
—*Konzertstück für Trautonium* 114
—*Neues vom Tage* 405
—*Violin sonata* 37
Hitler, Adolf 15, 51, 237–38, 468
Hodeir, André 160
Hoffmann, Heinrich 372
—*Struwwelpeter* (Shock-headed Peter) 372
Hoffnung Festivals 223, 485
Hoffnung, Gerard 223, 399, 401n, 485
Hogan, Paul 383, 516
—*Crocodile Dundee II* 383, 516
Holbein, Hans 512
—*Money-Changers* 512
holism 44, 46, 48n, 73, 100, 174, 253, 316,
    377, 410, 414, 492
Hollaender, Friedrich 15
—*Jonny, wenn du Geburtstag hast* 15
Holland, James 210n
Holliday, Billie 33
Holmes, Sherlock 360
Homer, 403
Honegger, Arthur 49, 272
—*Pacific 231* 272
Hopkins, Bill 220
Hörfilm 365
Hörspiel 365
Horst Wessel-Lied 279, 417
"Hu!" syllable 254, 349, 351, 353–54, 357,
    430, 497, 539
Huber, Rupert 521
Hübner, Herbert 60
Huelsenbeck, Richard 412, 468
Humayun novella (Stockhausen) 32
Hunt, William Holman 34
—*Scapegoat* 34
Huxley, Aldous 48n, 253, 470
—*Brave New World* 470

I Ching 22, 140, 155n
Illiac Suite 161
imitation 16, 61, 114, 193–94, 199, 301, 307,
    412, 513–15
imitation game 287, 472
Imperial Gagaku Ensemble 399
impressionism 339
improvisation 74, 193, 219, 293, 317
impulse generator 519
impulse shower 146, 181, 205
indeterminacy 140, 185–86, 228, 234, 238
inflection 53, 76, 460
information science 43, 160, 173, 182, 235,
    414, 417, 460
infrasound 342, 487, 516, 518, 529
intelligence 93, 478
interference 343, 542
interior monologue 274
International Exposition of the Arts 1952 96
International Phonetic Alphabet 181–82, 444,
    541
international style 127
Internationale 279
internationalism 38
internet 55, 376, 498
interpolation 460
interval series 133
interversion 62, 64, 79, 283, 427
intonation 53, 93, 182, 472
intuitive music 170, 263, 312
invention, method of 110
Ionesco, Eugene 223, 406
Ipcress File 18
IRCAM 379, 382–84, 445, 449, 460, 480, 486,
    505, 534
irrational values 122
Irwin, Lady 480
Isaacson, Leonard 161, 277
ISCM (International Society for
    Contemporary Music) 7, 118, 218, 223
isorhythms 79, 382
Issa 361
Ives, Charles 152, 233, 278
—*Fourth Symphony* 152, 233

Jaja, Bruno Heinz (Humphrey Searle) 223,
    485
—*Barber of Darmstadt* 223, 485
—*Punkt Kontrapunkt* 223, 485
Jakobson, Roman 244, 251
James, Henry 78
James, William 78, 152
Japan tea ceremony 397
Japanese National Theater 397
Japanese theater 20, 73, 481
Jarry, Alfred 223, 406
jaw harp 300, 343

jazz 15, 18, 19, 35, 36, 153, 185, 193, 201, 338, 399, 405, 413, 452, 495
Jeanneret, Albert 315
Jeita caves, Lebanon 335
Jeune France 49
John, Elton 489
Johns, Jasper 279
Johnson, Philip 127
Johnson, Robert Sherlaw 81
Johnson, Samuel 253
Jolivet, André 49
Jolson, Al 15, 405, 430, 495
—Jazz Singer 15, 405, 495
—Singing Fool 15, 430, 495
Jones, Daniel 181–82, 337
Jones, Spike 467, 472, 490
—Baby Buggy Boogie 467
—Der Führer's Face 467
Joyce, James 170, 214, 221, 240, 243, 277, 403
—Finnegans Wake 221
Jugendstil 530
Juilliard School 176, 222
Julesz, Bela 502
Jung, Carl 229, 253
jungle music 87, 434
Jupiter 408

Kagel, Mauricio 201, 215, 234, 334
—Anagramma 334
—Sur Scène 234
—Transición II 201
Kandinsky, Wassily 73, 83, 118, 219, 228, 315, 404, 415, 427–28, 533
—Der gelbe Klang 315, 404, 427–28
—On the Spiritual in Art 315
Kaprow, Allen 221, 224
Karg-Elert, Sigfrid
—Sieben Idyllen für Harmonium 427
Keaton, Buster 157, 165, 452
Keiser, Reinhardt 50, 66n
keisu 266, 267
Kelly, Gene 404
—Singin' in the Rain 404
Khan, Hazrat Inayat 358, 360, 410
Kido, Toshiro 397
King, Martin Luther 239
kinship relations 254, 413, 495
Kirchmeyer, Helmut 208
klangfarbenmelodie 117, 169, 530, 534
Klebe, Giselher 134
Klee, Paul 4, 79, 179, 187, 387, 434, 443, 447, 474
Klein, Yves 309
Klemperer, Otto 38
Klingon language 152
Klopstock, Friedrich Gottleib 411, 414
—Der Messias 411

Kloth, Franz-Josef 16, 20
Knecht, Joseph 22–23
knowledge, theory of 58
Kodály, Zoltán 376, 442
Koenig, Gottfried Michael 205, 212, 218
Koenig, Rudolf 343
Kohl, Jerome 146
Köhler, Wolfgang 100, 237
Kokoschka, Oskar 51
Kolisch, Rudolf 1
Konservatorium der Stadt Köln 251
Kontarsky, Alfons 260
Kontarsky, Aloys 218, 304, 311, 351
koto 433
Kraftwerk 480
Kraus, Karl 406
Krauss, Else C. 23
Krenek, Ernst 134, 200, 405, 430
—Jonny spielt auf 405, 430
—Spiritus Intelligentiae Sanctus 200
Kreuder, Peter 15
Krishna, Gopi 45, 316
—Biological Basis of Religion and Genius 45, 316
Kroeber, A. L. 413
Kubrick, Stanley 272, 309–10, 315, 418, 466
—2001: A Space Odyssey 272, 309–10, 315, 418, 466
Kuhn, Thomas 230
Kundt tube 342
Kunzig, Robert 246n
Kurtz, Michael 35, 211
Kurzweil synthesizer 480
kymograph 77

labyrinth 243
Lang, Fritz 19, 61, 452
—Metropolis 19, 61, 452
Langdon, Harry 452
language game 46
language, philosophy of 52, 57–58, 69, 77, 94, 110, 128, 182, 231, 289, 307
language, rules of association 111, 291, 380
langue 56, 65, 81, 158, 405
Laurel, Stan 452
Lautgedichte 429
Leach, Edmund 196, 254
Lear, Edward 412
Leary, Timothy 310
Leavis, F. R. 9, 416
Le Corbusier (Charles-Édouard Jeanneret) 26, 41, 56, 106, 127, 133, 195, 216, 265, 314–15, 387, 406
lecture 59, 74, 76
Ledoux, Claude Nicholas 328
Leibowitz, René 37, 49
—Introduction à la musique de douze sons 49
Leipzig Opera 492

leitmotiv 283
Lenya, Lotte 472
Leonard, Lawrence 223
—*Mobile for seven orchestras* 223
Leonardo da Vinci. *See* da Vinci, Leonardo
letter forms 307
lettrism 73, 78, 103, 167
Lévi-Strauss, Claude 196, 240, 251, 254–55, 302, 370, 409, 413, 417, 418, 432, 436, 495–96, 529
Lewis, Cecil A. 273, 404
—*Broadcasting from Within* 273
Lewis, John 177
Liberace, Wladziu Valentino 469
Lichtenstein, Roy 224, 425
Ligeti, György 56, 66, 184, 201, 215, 222–23, 234, 309–10, 315, 347, 351, 373, 491
—*Artikulation* 201, 222–23, 234, 309–10, 315
—*Atmosphères* 56, 66, 184, 309–10, 315, 347
—*Grand Macabre* 491
—*Lux Aeterna* 309
—*Poème symphonique* 347
light as metaphor 406
likeness 3–4
Lindisfarne 376
Lindvai, Ernö 26
linear amplitude modulation 265
linguistics 54, 56, 111, 286, 413, 533
Linnaeus, Carolus 5, 295
Liszt, Franz 81, 87, 122, 222, 225n, 388
—*Mazeppa* 87
live electronic music 255
Livingstone, David 193
Lodge, David 308
London Sinfonietta 349–50
Looney Tunes 374
loop (tape). *See* tape medium
Lorber, Jakob 379, 410
Loriod, Yvonne 80
low frequency sound 487–88
Lowrey organ 128, 459
Lucier, Alvin 152, 263
Lucifer 22, 407
Luening, Otto 212
—*Fantasy in space* 212
Luther, Martin 240, 253
lyric poetry 414

Macdonald, Hugh 418n
MacDonald, Ramsay 97
Mach, Ernst 231
Machaut, Guillaume de 249, 533
machine intelligence 286
MAD magazine 224
Maderna, Bruno 139, 213, 214, 393–94
—*Musica su due dimensioni* 213
Maeght, Fondation 312
Maelzel, Johann 126

Mager, Jörg 174
magic names (*Stimmung*) 79, 299
magic syllables (*Harawi*) 79
Mahler, Gustav 180, 280, 329
Malevich, Kasimir 228, 308
Malinowski, Bronislaw 254, 255, 371, 409
—*Sexual Life of Savages* 254
Mallarmé, Stéphane 157–58, 162, 238, 239, 243–44
—*Livre* 158, 244
—*Un coup de dés* 157, 162
mandala 448
Mann, Thomas 40, 42
—*Doktor Faustus* 40, 42
manometric capsule 343, 447
marching music 18, 451
Marconi-Stille tape recorder 365
Marey, Louis 164, 231
Marinetti, Filippo 412, 429
Markoff series 160, 286
Mars 408, 477
Marschner, Wolfgang 37
Marseillaise 275, 467
Martenot, Maurice 485
Martin, Frank 24, 407
Martinu, Bohuslav 405
—*Revue de cuisine* 405
Marx, Harpo 359
Marx, Karl 59, 109
Masonic ritual 470
Massachusetts Institute of Technology 176, 534
Mathews, Max 277–78, 285–86, 380, 504, 505, 534
Matter, Herbert 368
McEnroe, John 8
McLuhan, (Herbert) Marshall 74, 82, 110, 272, 404
McPhee, Colin 433
meditation 179, 188, 296, 307, 312
medium 194
Meistersinger tradition 412, 414
Meliès, Georges 228, 279, 463
melochord 129
Melos 7, 21, 26, 387
memory 75, 179, 180, 232, 278, 301
Mersmann, Hans 21, 26
Merzbild (Schwitters) 72, 224, 360
mesostics 429
Messiaen, Olivier 4, 23, 40, 41, 42, 47, 49, 52, 53, 54, 55, 62, 65, 71–73, 75–76, 79, 80–81, 83, 87, 91, 98, 102, 103, 111, 125–26, 129, 140, 157, 159, 163, 174, 197, 208, 249, 250, 283, 286, 291, 318, 339–40, 355, 362, 380, 382, 383, 415, 427, 428, 429, 435, 441, 452, 489, 511, 514, 532, 534, 541
—*Cantéyodjayâ* 79, 429
—*Catalogue d'Oiseaux* 78

—*Chronochromie* 382
—*Des Canyons aux Étoiles* 98
—*Harawi* 79
—*Île de Feu 1* 42, 72, 73
—*Île de Feu 2* 72
—*Livre d'Orgue* 76, 79, 133, 163, 283, 427
—*Messe de la Pentecôte* 126
—*Mode de valeurs et d'intensités* 23, 42, 80–81, 83, 111, 163, 198, 286, 441
—*Neumes rythmiques* 72, 76
—*Oiseaux exotiques* 208
—*Poèmes pour Mi* 532
—*Quatre Études de Rythme* 42
—*Quartet for the end of time* 75, 452
—*Sept Hai-Kai* 339
—*Technique de mon langage musical* 40, 53, 72, 76, 157
—*Timbres–durées* 129
—*Turangalîla-Symphonie* 65, 83, 87, 91, 355, 452
method acting 219, 222, 310
metronome 122, 347, 373, 512
Metzger, Heinz 236, 239
MEV (Musica Elettronica Viva) 512
Meyer-Eppler, Werner 37, 84, 94, 104, 128, 129, 131, 132, 137, 142, 149, 151, 153, 160, 161, 166, 168, 173, 181, 184, 197, 201, 211, 212–13, 216, 222, 234, 253, 257, 286, 293, 417, 460, 464, 474n, 498
—*Elektrische Klangerzeugung* 128, 131
—"Statistic and Psychologic Problems of Sound" 132
MGM lion 207, 255, 433
Michelangelo Buonarotti 409, 452
microphone skills 97
microstructure 106, 112, 154, 187, 195, 198, 199, 201–2, 504
microtones 197, 268, 336, 375, 459, 462, 472
midi interface 446, 480
Milhaud, Darius 47n, 70–71, 72, 74, 78, 99, 404
—*Christoph Colombe* 99, 404
—*Cinq études* 70
—*L'Homme et son désir* 71
—*Notes sans musique* 70
Miller, Glenn 18, 19, 62
Miller, Henry 374
Milton, John 403
minimalism 78, 152, 463, 494
Minnelli, Vincente 280
Miró, Joán 46
Miron figure (*Tierkreis*) 370–73
mirror imagery 89, 285, 304, 324, 396, 471, 532
miscegenation 381, 434, 495
Mitchell, Donald 53
—*Language of Modern Music* 53
Mizelle, John 323

modern architecture 127
modern art 38, 173
Modern Jazz Quartet 177
modern orchestra 24, 260, 543
Moderna Museet, Stockholm 475n
modes 72
Modigliani, Amedeo 434
Modul 69A 497
Modul 69B 305, 331, 497
modular form 157
modulation 164, 181, 194, 250, 267, 305, 331–32, 494, 499, 502, 529
Modulor (Le Corbusier) 26, 195, 406
mogukyo 266, 267
Moles, Abraham 104, 161, 197
Molière (Jean-Baptiste Poquelin) 69
Moloch 19, 452
moment-form 219, 242, 259
Monday Evening Concerts 176
Mondrian, Piet 44, 267, 308, 387, 433
monism 65
montage 75, 98, 110, 158, 240, 380
Montessori, Maria 28
Monteverdi, Claudio 117, 193, 328, 347, 350, 474, 494, 531
—*Vespers* 117, 193
Montreal Exposition 1967 313–14
Monsalvat bells 107n, 440, 444, 449, 498, 506, 510, 532
Monty Python 436
Moog, Robert 351, 356
Moog synthesizer 351
Moore, Henry 280, 428
Moorer, James 450
Mooser, R.-A. 87
Moquereau, Dom 72
moral relativism 415, 494
Morawska-Bungeler, Marietta 212–13
Morgenstern, Christian 387
Morgenstern, Otto 413
morphing, 274
morse code 54, 59, 71, 81, 510
morse rhythm 27, 54, 217
Morse, Samuel 54
Morton, Lawrence 176
Motherwell, Robert 280
motion capture 163, 231, 529
motor phonetics 77–78, 81, 94, 100, 167
mousike 411
moving pictures 52, 75, 163, 231–32, 255, 398
Mozart, Wolfgang Amadeus 50, 79, 118, 126, 218, 228, 370, 403, 430, 496, 516
—*Clarinet concerto KV 622* 461
—*Flute concerto KV 313* 461
—*"Jupiter" Symphony KV 551* 516
—*Magic Flute* 403, 430, 496
multiplexing 71
Munchausen 19

Munich Radio 521
Münsterberg, Hugo 78, 232
Murnau, F. W. 19
—Nosferatu 19
music and language 53, 56, 93, 228
music industry 93
musical box 126, 369–73, 448
musicality 16
musique concrète 37, 47, 96, 99, 103, 111,
    132, 140, 162, 166, 194, 211, 222, 255, 266,
    274, 282, 366, 394, 478, 504, 509
Mussorgsky, Modest 355
—Boris Gudonov 355
mutes 449
Muybridge, Eadweard 164, 231–32, 246n
mythology 2, 23, 44, 110, 193, 302, 370–71,
    409, 410, 412, 413, 432, 473, 495, 529

Nabokov, Nicolas 38, 96
Nancarrow, Conlon 152, 197, 431
Napoleon Buonaparte 414
narrative form 74–75, 158, 371, 378
National Socialism 4, 27, 220, 237, 239, 279,
    405, 416, 425
nationalism, German 411, 413, 416
natural selection, 199
Nazi regime 4, 38, 44, 51, 230, 410, 528
—accession to power 14
—broadcasting policy 15
—people's radio 15
—propaganda 17, 27, 410
Nebuchadnezzar 165, 470
neoclassicism 49, 51
Neue Sachlichkeit, die 15
neumata 76, 362
New York Philharmonic 281, 433
Newman, Barnett 308
Newman, Ernest 405
Newton, Isaac 70, 329, 414, 416, 417, 480
NHK Radio Tokyo 265–67, 499
Niemecz, Pastor 126
Nietzsche, Frederick 316, 377, 439
nihilism 8, 234
Noguchi, Isamo 280
Noh drama 267, 337, 447
noise 98, 132, 515
nonlinear narrative 74
Nono, Luigi 40, 166, 202, 528
—Il Canto sospeso 166
—Incontri 202
nonsense 405, 412
notation 70, 76, 92, 94, 118, 140, 142, 149,
    187, 205–6, 249, 256, 282, 290, 293, 294,
    296, 310, 317, 324, 460, 541
Novalis (von Hardenberg) 22, 377
—Heinrich von Ofterdingen 22
number symbolism 79, 413
NWDR. See Cologne Radio

objet musical 95, 99, 100, 250, 277, 282
octophonic sound 484
Olson, Harry F. 127, 174
Omizutori (water consecration) ritual 410,
    455
ondes martenot 65, 128
onset–steady state–decline. See anacrouse-
    accent–désinence
Opelt, F. W. 519
open form 243, 276, 293, 302
opera aperta 243
operator (Barthes) 59–60, 523
optical sound recording 97
oral traditions 302, 366
organ 73, 76, 112, 125, 132, 340, 534, 539
origin of species, 58
origin of water myth 302, 495
Orpheus 272, 274, 512
Orwell, George 60, 283
Osaka World Exposition 1970 313, 324,
    329–30, 335, 481, 518
Ouellette, Fernand 314
owl, symbolism of 359, 497, 499

Pachelbel, Wilhelm 472
Paik, Nam June 218, 219
—Hommage à John Cage 218
pain, existence of 465
panharmonicon 126
pan-rotation 181, 209, 383, 447, 510
parameter 198
park music 296, 335
Parmenides 65
parole 56, 65, 76, 158, 405
Partch, Harry 53, 65, 94, 151
particle physics 45, 60, 231, 361, 362, 367,
    398, 400, 409, 497, 505
Pascal, Blaise 387
Pastor-Löhr Gymnasium 17
Pasveer, Kathinka 430, 446, 461, 472, 510,
    514, 539
Pathé Frères 158
pattern recognition 161
Penderecki, Krzystof 184, 233
—Threnody 184
perambulator scene (Montag aus LICHT) 20,
    467
percussion 84, 105, 185, 212
Pérotin 249, 533
personnages rythmiques 79, 427
perspective 164, 206, 228, 329–30, 338, 354
Perspectives of New Music 3, 122, 146
Pestalozzi, Johann-Heinrich 28
Petronius 411
Peyser, Joan 153
phase coincidence 134
Pheloung, Barrington 54

Philadelphia Academy of Music 183
Philadelphia Orchestra 183
Philips Electrical Industries 183, 314, 502
philosophy of music 44, 73, 210
phonautograph 56
phonogène 99, 267
phonograph 52, 77
phonology 76
Piaget, Jean 103–4, 162–63, 250, 533
piano as fetichistic object 469
piano of pain 343
piano tone-color 77
pianola 430, 507. *See also* player piano
Picabia, Francis 508
Picasso, Pablo 36, 46, 99, 224, 229, 264, 279,
    434
—*Blue Guitar* 36
pictogram 5, 53, 254, 474
Pied Piper 461, 472
Pioneer spacecraft 418
Piscator, Erwin 152, 219
Piston, Walter 47n
Pitt-Rivers, A. H. 254
plainchant 72, 76, 117, 182, 362
Planck, Max 227
planetary motion 407, 494
Plato 2, 11, 12n, 289, 290, 371, 413
player piano 126. *See also* pianola
plus-minus notation 9, 101, 164, 170, 250–55,
    283–87, 292, 307, 323, 409, 412, 495
Poe, Edgar Allan 74, 194
pointillism 42, 43, 47, 48n, 66, 88, 111, 132,
    133, 154, 241, 281, 334, 348–49, 395,
    434–35, 441–42
Pollock, Jackson 280
polytonality 71, 74, 79
pop art 224, 425, 492
Pope, Alexander 415
Popol Vuh 479
Popper, Karl 230–31
popular music 15, 430, 480
Porter, Andrew 218, 223
Poulenc, Francis 72, 405, 433, 469
—*Mamelles de Tirésias* 405, 469
Poullin, Jacques 99, 267
Poulsen, Valdemar 343
Pousseur, Henri 140, 214, 240, 276, 277, 313,
    485–86, 528
—*Électre*
—*Rimes* 214
—*Tarot d'Henri* 277
—*Trois Visages de Liège* 277, 313
—*Votre Faust* 276
prayer gestures 353
pregnant boy myth 496
prepared piano 82, 102, 112, 140, 145, 252
Prieberg, Fred K. 328, 356
Princeton-Columbia synthesizer 127, 174

Priuli, Giovanni 330
process composition 99, 110, 250
propaganda 20, 96, 194, 417
Propaganda Ministry, Nazi 7, 15, 19, 20, 27,
    129
—*Frontberichte* 17
—*Sondermeldung* 17
propellor sound 180, 205, 279, 484, 507–8
Protestantism 240
Proust, Marcel 243
psycho-acoustics 213
psychoanalysis 5, 103
psychology 69, 71
pulse-code modulation 203
pun 3, 254, 497
punktuelle Musik 42. *See also* pointillism
Purce, Jill 428
Pushkin, Aleksandr 16, 75
Pythagoras, 329, 413

quantum theory 232
quasi-concertante performance 521–22
Queneau, Raymond 161, 261
—*Exercices de style* 161

racial supremacy 48n
radio 4, 14, 94, 97, 139, 174, 193, 194, 240,
    282, 301, 365, 377, 464, 466, 470, 541
radio drama 96, 97, 240, 261, 272–74, 365–66,
    404, 429, 457, 464, 468, 537
raga 80
Rameau, Jean-Philippe 283, 406
random dot stereogram 502
random walk 163
randomization 140, 160, 161
Rank, J. Arthur 207, 255
Rauschenberg, Robert 279, 359, 428
Ravel, Maurice 13, 64, 72, 80, 83, 338, 353,
    492
—*Bolero* 13, 64, 83, 353
—*Enfant et les Sortilèges* 592
Ray, Man 508
RCA (Radio Corporation of America) 182–83,
    314, 502
Read, Herbert 45
realism 97
rebus 5, 9, 222, 473–74
recognition (re-cognition) 9–11
Red Baron 477
red, symbolism of 408, 416
refrain 189
register form 41, 46, 62, 82, 84, 85, 374, 390
Reich, Steve 152, 362
Reihe, die 3, 4, 122, 176, 188, 197, 328, 529
Reinhardt, Ad 309
Renaud, Madeleine 99
repetition 216, 217
representation 53, 59, 231

reproducing piano 94, 445
resonance 89, 298
revelation, music as 10
reverberation, 89, 96, 135, 180, 216, 256, 296, 391, 465
reverse induction 74, 110, 309, 404
Reynolds, H. Robert 451
rhythm of variable velocities 147
rhythmic cell. See *cellule rythmique*
Ribe, Neil 418n
riddles 215
Riefenstahl, Leni 435
Riley, Terry 152, 263
—*In C* 263
Rilke, Rainer Maria 34
Rimbaud, Arthur 415
rin 266, 267, 323
ring modulation 129, 170, 257–60, 265–66, 274, 331, 381, 448, 481, 487, 498, 536
ripple effect. See wave motion
Risset, Jean-Claude 280
Ritzel, Fred 311
Rockmore, Clara 356–57
Rodet, Xavier 384
Rodin, Auguste 231–32, 246n
—*St. John the Baptist* 231–32
Rolling Stones logo 453
Romanticism 199, 253, 388, 414, 415–16, 417, 441
Rosbaud, Hans 87, 96
Rosetta Stone 5, 53, 58, 417, 435
Rosler, L. 277–78, 285–86
rotary motion 187, 315, 355, 362, 374–75, 378, 383, 389, 487, 510, 515, 516, 517, 518, 521, 529
rotation turbine 374, 378, 383–84, 385n, 393, 485, 516, 518
rotation turntable 182, 209, 517
Rotha, Paul 425
Rothko, Mark 308
Rousseau, Jean-Jacques 28
Rousselot, Abbé 78, 81, 149, 244
Rowlandson, Thomas 261
Royal Society 415
Ruggles, Charles 152
Ruppel, Karl Heinz 220
Ruskin, John 199
Russolo, Luigi 515, 517
Ruyer, Raymond 6
—*Genèse des formes vivantes* 6
Rzewski, Frederick 252

St. Francis of Assisi 72, 454
St. Mark basilica, Venice 328
St. Paul 8
St. Paul de Vence, 335
St. Thomas gospel 361
Sabbe, Hermann 47n

Sacher, Paul 334
sachverhalten 46, 307
Sade, Marquis de 493
Sagan, Carl 376
Saint-Exupéry, Antoine de 272
—*Night flight* 272
Sainte-Phalle, Niki de 465, 475n
—*Hon* ("She") 475n
Sala, Oskar 113
Salazar, Adolfo 47n–48n
sampling 498
sarrusophone 115
Sartre, Jean-Paul 51, 215
Satie, Erik 98, 301, 324, 404, 441, 470, 508
—*Parade* 98, 99, 301, 404, 470
—*Relâche* 508
saturation, auditory 480–81
Saussure, Ferdinand de. See de Saussure, Ferdinand
Sayer, Dorothy L. 74
Scala Opera, Milan 477
scale transformation 165, 194, 195, 197, 514, 529
scat singing 405, 412
Scelsi, Giacinto 66, 234, 533
—*Konx-Om-Pax* 66
Schaeffer, Pierre 37, 47, 81, 89, 94, 96, 97, 98, 100, 112, 113, 121, 128, 129, 161, 163, 174, 250, 267, 272, 277, 282, 504, 515
—*Étude aux chemins de fer* 98, 272, 515
—"Objet musical" 95, 101
Scharf, Aaron 231, 246n
Scherchen, Hermann 118, 213
Schieri, Fritz 35
Schiller, Johann Christoph von 411–12, 480
—*Ode to Joy* 480
—*Über epische und dramatische Dichtung* 412
Schillinger, Joseph 147, 151
—*System of Musical Composition* 147
Schlegel, Friedrich von 414, 417
—*Prosaische Jugendschriften* 417
Schmidt-Neuhaus, Hans-Otto 20
Schoenberg, Arnold 1, 4, 7, 13, 23, 29n, 31, 33, 36, 37, 49, 50, 51, 52, 53, 66n, 71, 74, 75, 79, 81, 94, 96, 102, 145, 149, 174, 175, 196, 197, 243, 299, 315, 334, 355–56, 380, 387, 403, 404, 405, 429, 441, 454, 474, 505
—*Drei Klavierstücke* 23, 331
—*Erwartung* 96
—*Five Orchestral Pieces* 299, 334
—*Glückliche Hand* 176, 404
—*Harmonielehre* 175
—*Herzgewächse* 21, 175
—*Jakobsleiter* 175, 315, 255, 403, 528
—*Kammersinfonie I* 105
—*Klavierstück Op. 33a* 23
—*Kleine Klavierstücke* 23

—*Moses und Aron* 51, 175, 403, 474, 528
—*Pelleas und Melisande* 505
—piano music 23, 175
—*Pierrot Lunaire* 81, 175, 190, 243
—*Suite* 71
—*Survivor from Warsaw* 36, 190, 429
—*Third string quartet* 1
—*Variations for Orchestra* 13
—*Von Heute auf Morgen* 405
Schöffer, Nicolas 313
Schopenhauer, Arthur 38, 59
Schroeder, Hermann, 21, 35, 36, 42, 361, 411
—*Der römische Brunnen* 21
Schuller, Gunther 122
Schumann, Robert 5, 283, 388
—*ABEGG Variations* 5
Schütz, Heinz 129, 264, 330, 449, 498, 522, 531
Schwitters, Kurt 72, 219, 224, 225n, 279, 360, 412, 429, 535
—*Ur-Sonate* 535
scians 69
science, public mistrust of 28, 44, 237, 416, 494
Scott, Léon 56
Scriabin, Alexander 72, 75, 404, 415, 533
—*Mysterium* 404
—*Prométhée* 72
Searle, Humphrey 223, 485
Searle, John 465, 475n
semaphore 54
semeiology 460
semiotics 52, 69, 76, 81, 94, 103, 158, 161
sequence 164, 194
sequencer 315, 382, 391
serialism 41, 50, 51, 52, 55, 69, 81, 85, 93, 94, 110, 113, 121, 148, 168, 196, 197, 239, 276, 330, 381, 388, 403, 411, 478, 492, 519, 529
shadow play 437
Shadwell, Thomas 69
—*Virtuoso* 69
Shahn, Ben 56, 57, 307
Shakespeare, William 3, 221, 275, 308, 411, 423, 429, 453, 493–94, 496
—*Hamlet* 308, 338, 429, 453
—*Julius Caesar* 221
—*Macbeth* 423, 453
—*Midsummer Night's Dream* 493–94, 496
—*Othello* 497
shamanistic succession myth 495
Shannon, Claude E. 236, 286, 413
—*Mathematical Theory of Communication* 236, 286, 413
Sharngadeva 72
Shaw, George Bernard 97–98, 475n
Shelley, Mary 134
Shepard paradox 280
Shiki 361

Shinohara, Makoto 290
Shiraz Festival 423–24
shô 339, 433
shortwave radio 16, 76, 193, 251, 262, 266, 267–68, 301–5, 308, 323, 338, 350, 473, 513, 523
Sieveking, Lance 537
—*Intimate Snapshots* 537
silent movies 165, 278, 404
sillon fermé 98
similarity 290
simultaneous lectures 380
sine tone generation 104, 129
siren 94, 135, 206, 462, 485, 519
Sirius (star) 7
Slotover, Robert 2
Small Faces 510
Smalley, Roger 218
Snow, C. P. 416
socialist realism 290
sociology 58, 69, 234
Socrates 361, 411
sonagram 114, 153
sondermeldung 17, 467
sound effects 96, 99, 313, 381, 466–67, 468, 470, 472, 486, 500
Soviet realism 51
space-time notation 121, 182
spatialization of music 180, 295, 330, 389, 454–55, 482, 486, 510, 516
speech analyzer 126
speech, dynamics of 56, 76, 77–78, 81, 123, 160, 167, 257, 460, 478, 537
speech sounds 61, 77, 78, 85, 168–69, 182, 197, 205, 261, 293, 361, 429, 460, 534, 538
Speer, Albert 534
sphärophon 113, 128
sphere, symbolism of 328–29, 523
Spek, Jaap 201, 218, 256
Spielberg, Steven 376, 442
—*Close Encounters* 376, 442
spindizzy 374, 383
spiral sign 317, 324
sprechgesang 176
sprechstimme 190, 514, 541
springboard 355
Springer-machine 267, 473
Stanislavsky, Konstantin 219
Stanley, Henry Morton 193
star music 42, 311, 334–37
Star Trek 272
stasis 78, 88
statistical form 228
stave notation 249
Stefan, Rudolf 118
Stein, Erwin 29n
Stein, Gertrude 78, 96, 152, 232, 238, 250, 412, 424, 508

Stein, Leonard 122, 176
Steinberg, Saul 206, 280
Steinecke, Wolfgang 37, 236
Steinle, Friedrich 418n
Stephens, Suzanne 373, 395, 461, 470
stereophony 93, 273
Sterne, Laurence 74
—*Tristram Shandy* 74
Stetson, R. Harold 77, 78, 81, 94–95, 100,
    101, 149, 152, 232, 244, 263, 293
—*Motor Phonetics* 77
—motor theory of rhythm 78
—piano tone-color 94–95
Stewart, Rod 510
Still, Clyfford 309
stock market collapse 1931 14
Stockhausen, Christel 220
Stockhausen, Doris 20, 46, 47, 131, 361, 389
Stockhausen, Gerd (half-brother) 17, 21
Stockhausen, Gertrud (mother) 13, 14, 17, 19,
    194, 422, 425, 430
Stockhausen, Karlheinz
—Adam 400, 497
—*Adieu* 262, 267–68, 282, 348, 514, 539, 542
—*Alphabet für Liège* 341–45, 499
—"Am Himmel wandre Ich . . ." (*Alphabet*).
    See Stockhausen, Karlheinz, *Indianerlieder*
—*Amour* 388–90
—"Aries" (*Sirius*) 66, 375, 383
—*"Atmen gibt das Leben . . . "* 6, 33, 338, 344,
    360–62, 367, 370, 400, 409, 433, 497
—*Aus den sieben Tagen* 79, 209, 308, 310–12,
    318, 334, 335, 358, 367
—Ave 471
—"Ave" (*Montag*) 34, 358, 471–72
—aversion to pain 465
—"Baby Buggy Boogie." *See* Jones, Spike
—Bartók analysis 24, 26–27, 47, 194
—*Bassetsu-Trio* 521–23
—*Burleska* 25, 218
—cadenzas for Haydn and Mozart 461
—Caino 495, 497
—"Cancer" (*Sirius*) 383
—"Capricorn" (*Sirius*) 55, 383
—*Carré* 178–84, 187, 203, 207, 209, 218, 233,
    241, 350, 357, 362, 375, 409, 510, 516, 535,
    543
—Catholic faith 14, 16, 19, 60, 109, 238, 529,
    534
—"'Chances' de la musique électronique" 234
—childhood 4, 13ff, 421–22
—*Choral* 21, 24, 36–37
—"Chor-Spirale" (*Freitag*) 501
—*Chöre für Doris* 32–34, 471
—*Chöre nach Verlaine. See* Stockhausen,
    Karlheinz, *Chöre für Doris*
—"Concept of unity in electronic music" 206
—conducts Haydn and Mozart 461

—deafness 16, 330, 483
—*Dienstag aus LICHT* 87, 408, 477–90, 491,
    511, 512, 516
—"Dienstags-Gruss"(*Dienstag*) 479–81
—doctorate studies 211, 212
—*Donnerstag aus LICHT* 14, 79, 212, 379,
    381, 408, 411, 421–37, 474
—"Donnerstags-Abschied" (*Donnerstag*) 435,
    514
—"Donnerstags-Gruss" (*Donnerstag*) 426
—"Drachenkampf" (*Donnerstag*) 429
—*Drei Chöre* 24 (Chöre für Doris)
—*Drei Lieder* 15, 24, 34–36, 37, 196, 222,
    239, 429
—*Dr. K.–Sextett* 319–20, 333, 532
—"Düfte-Zeichen" (*Sonntag*) 34, 536–40
—"Duo" (*Pole für 2*) 316, 323
—dynamics 85, 86, 130, 198
—"Electronic and instrumental music" 174
—*Elektronische Studie I. See* Stockhausen,
    Karlheinz, *Studie I*
—*Elektronische Studie II. See* Stockhausen,
    Karlheinz, *Studie II*
—"Engel-Prozessionen" (*Sonntag*) 533–35,
    541
—*Ensemble* 293–96, 321
—"Erfindung und Entdeckung" 236
—*Europa-Gruss* 508–9
—Eva 409, 411, 427, 459, 495, 497, 520, 536
—Eva sign 432
—Eva statue (*Montag*) 465, 469
—"Evas Erstgeburt" (*Montag*) 463–68
—"Evas Zauber" (*Montag*) 471–74, 486
—"Evas Zweitgeburt" (*Montag*) 468–71, 482
—"Examen" (*Donnerstag*) 212, 430, 431, 512
—*Expo für 3* 316, 323, 324
—family members in *LICHT* 20
—*Formel* 19, 47, 56, 63–66, 83, 84, 118, 123,
    130, 148, 233, 369, 390, 433, 530, 543
—"Four criteria of electronic music" 206, 329
—*Freitag aus LICHT* 209, 261, 491–506, 511,
    516, 535
—"Freitag-Versuchung" 493
—"Freitags-Abschied" (*Freitag*) 503–6
—"Freitags-Gruss" (*Freitag*) 503–6
—*Fresco* 296, 321–23, 335, 338, 463, 486
—*Für kommende Zeiten* 209, 319, 333–34,
    423
—*Gesang der Jünglinge* 61, 105, 120, 146,
    149, 153, 166–71, 180, 181, 195, 199, 200,
    201, 205, 208, 211, 214, 239, 240, 274, 357,
    377, 412, 427, 429, 469, 486, 500, 532, 534,
    543
—*Gruppen* 65, 66, 145, 146, 148–55, 158,
    159, 170, 179, 180, 208, 217, 234, 375, 486,
    504
—hammer 13–14, 367, 443, 469
—*Harlekin* 338, 358, 373–75, 389, 447, 486

—"Helikopter-Streichquartett" (*Mittwoch*) 206, 207, 378, 462, 505, 507, 513, 514, 515–21, 529, 533

—*Herbstmusik* 98, 366–69, 371

—*Hinab–Hinauf* 313–16, 343, 422, 433

—"Hoch-Zeiten" (*Sonntag*) 350, 509, 540–43

—home page, 7

—". . . how time passes . . ." 94, 144, 149, 152

—*Humayun* novella 32

—humor, sense of 222, 261, 324, 333, 503, 532

—*Hymnen* 6, 193, 265, 272, 273–82, 285, 301, 308, 309, 322, 368, 376, 380, 381, 409, 423, 436, 470, 472, 486, 487, 498, 506, 510, 511, 515, 534

—*In Freundschaft* 338, 343, 358, 389, 395–96, 447, 461, 531

—*Indianerlieder* 341–45, 349, 502, 542

—*Inori* 66, 83, 234, 254, 338, 344, 351–60, 375, 431, 481, 495, 502, 532

—inserts (*Einschube*) 15, 181, 183, 195, 196, 209, 244–45, 251, 260, 261, 355, 396, 400

—instrumentation 34, 61, 84, 186, 350

—"Intuitive Music" 312

—"Invasion—Explosion mit Abschied" (*Dienstag*) 483–90

—"Invisible Choirs." *See* Stockhausen, Karlheinz, "Unsichtbare Chöre"

—*Jahreslauf* 19, 36, 73, 98, 272, 355 , 396–400, 409, 433, 486, 509, 512, 519, 536

—*Jahreslauf vom Dienstag* 190, 272, 400, 481–83, 509

—jazz pianist 19, 31, 177, 193

—"Jenseits" (*Dienstag*) 489

—"Jenseits" (*Trans*) 338

—*Jubiläum* 346, 390–94

—"Kathinkas Gesang als Luzifers Requiem" (*Samstag*) 212, 375, 382, 446–51, 461, 486–87, 506, 518

—"Der Kinderfänger" (*Montag*) 472

—*Klavierstücke I–IV* 75, 105, 118–23, 136, 148, 441

—*Klavierstücke V–VIII* 121, 141–44, 145, 146, 148, 158, 164, 18, 189, 206, 215, 445, 469

—*Klavierstück IX* 141, 187, 215–16, 217, 228, 469

—*Klavierstück X* 141, 143, 215, 216–18, 228, 445, 469, 507

—*Klavierstück XI* 141, 157–65, 170, 185, 228

—*Klavierstück XII* 430–31, 444

—*Klavierstück XIII* 42, 443–46, 449, 464, 465, 484, 509, 539

—*Klavierstück XIV* 468–71, 503

—*Klavierstück XV* 482, 489–90

—*Klavierstück XVI* 503–4, 543

—*Klavierstück XVII* 498, 543

—*Kleine Harlekin* 373–75

—*Konkrete Etüde* 82, 84, 104–6, 115, 120, 121, 133, 135, 168, 194, 198, 285

—*Kontakte* 8, 79, 89, 94, 105, 114, 143, 182, 184, 185, 188, 189, 193, 195, 200, 201–10, 214, 215, 217, 218, 219, 234, 236, 240, 241, 250, 256, 259, 274, 282, 294, 301, 350, 374, 376, 380, 381, 412, 449, 472, 487, 494, 498, 516, 517, 519–20, 531, 542, 543

—*Kontakte* realization score 201–2, 212

—*Kontra-Punkte* 63, 79, 112, 113, 115–18, 121, 141, 146, 150, 233, 442, 532, 542

—*Kreuzspiel* 19, 23, 41, 47, 56, 61–63, 79, 83, 84, 90, 112, 354, 429, 532, 542

—*Kurzwellen* 16, 89, 101, 193, 209, 217, 262, 266, 301–5, 473, 513

—*Kurzwellen mit Beethoven* (*Opus 1970*) 16, 262, 301, 304–5, 448, 497, 499

—"Laub und Regen" (*Herbstmusik*) 366, 368

—layout of orchestra 83

—"Libra" 370, 376

—librettist 20, 382, 421, 464, 529, 538

—*LICHT* 20, 62, 65, 100, 141, 211, 239, 261, 344, 354, 362, 371, 396, 400, 403–18

—"Licht-Bilder" (*Sonntag*) 536

—*LICHT-Ruf* 508–9

—"Lichter-Wasser" (*Sonntag*) 296, 530–32

—"Liebe tönt in deine Stimme" (*Mittwoch*) 512

—"liking is remembering" 2, 9–11

—listens to jazz in secret 18, 338

—Ludon 495, 497, 517

—Luzifer 400, 408, 409, 411, 417, 427, 434, 440, 454, 459, 466, 492, 517, 536, 539

—Luzifer sign 432

—"Luzifers Abschied" (*Samstag*) 346, 453–57, 463, 475

—"Luzifers Tanz" (*Samstag*) 339, 450–53, 482, 487, 513

—"Luzifers Traum." *See* Stockhausen, Karlheinz, *Klavierstück XIII*

—"Luzifers Zorn" (*Montag*) 467–68

—"Luzikamel" (*Mittwoch*) 523

—*Mantra* 27, 36, 54, 65, 66, 82, 89, 193, 217, 259, 305, 330–32, 337, 342, 344, 351, 353–54, 362, 369, 371, 376, 381, 403, 410, 423, 448, 473, 497, 499, 501, 502, 536, 542

—Michael 212, 409, 411, 422, 427, 430, 434, 449, 459, 514, 530, 536, 539

—"Michael Angel" pseudonym for Paul Sperry (*Donnerstag* III Akt.) 475n

—Michael sign 432

—"Michaels-Gruss." *See* Stockhausen, Karlheinz, "Donnerstags-Gruss"

—"Michaels Heimkehr" (*Donnerstag*) 435–37

—"Michaels Jugend" (*Donnerstag*) 426–31

—"Michaels Reise" (*Donnerstag*) 276, 426, 431–35, 448, 453, 472, 521, 531

—"Michaelion" (*Mittwoch*) 60, 509, 521–23,

530
— "Microphony" 207
— *Mikrophonie I* 90, 114, 217, 255–57, 260, 264, 269n, 282, 290, 294, 295, 298, 300, 324, 330, 444, 485, 501, 513
— *Mikrophonie II* 245, 260–61, 262, 274, 296, 331, 351, 481, 499, 502
— *Mittwoch aus LICHT* 60, 508–24
— "Mittwochs-Abschied" (*Mittwoch*) 190, 590, 523–24
— "Mittwochs-Gruss" (*Mittwoch*) 509, 510, 520
— *Mixtur* 89, 258–60, 262, 266, 274, 276, 290, 315, 331, 341, 446, 448, 481, 498, 502
— *Momente* 66, 114, 149, 215, 217, 219, 221, 239–45, 250, 254, 256, 261, 308, 338, 355, 357, 367, 376, 377, 400, 409, 416, 436, 459, 466, 467, 468, 495, 513, 519, 529, 530–31, 535
— Mondeva 430, 434
— "Mondeva" (*Donnerstag*) 470
— *Monophonie* sketch 234
— *Montag aus LICHT* 180, 200, 380, 405, 459–74, 501, 503, 515, 532
— "Montags-Abschied" (*Montag*) 200, 471–74
— "Montags-Gruss" (*Montag*) 462–63
— movie preferences 20
— "Music in space" 188, 328
— musicology studies 21, 212
— *Musik für die Beethovenhalle* 296, 321–23
— *Musik für ein Haus* 296, 312–13, 321, 342
— *Musik im Bauch* 19, 338, 393, 429, 481, 519
— name as letter code 5
— name as note code 6
— "Oben und unten" (*Sieben Tagen*) 79
— "Oberlippentanz" (*Samstag*) 453
— opera repetiteur 20
— "Orchester-Finalisten" (*Mittwoch*) 127, 214, 280, 509, 511, 512–15, 517, 523–24, 530
— "Orientierung" 406
— *Originale* 218–21, 340–41, 456–57
— "Origins of electronic music" 115
— Paris studies 70ff
— parodied in Hoffnung Festivals 223
— piano lessons 16
— Piano Piece *see* Klavierstück
— "Pietà" (*Dienstag*) 484, 487
— *Plus-Minus* 80, 187, 221, 250–55, 282, 292, 295
— poetry 17, 300, 411
— *Pole für 2* 316, 323–24
— *Präludium* 37
— *Projektion für Orchester* 540
— *Prozession* 101, 209, 282–87, 292, 300, 301, 317, 336
— *Punkte 1952* 41, 63, 112–15, 116, 151, 154, 233, 281
— *Punkte 1952/62* 215, 217, 228, 232–35,

322, 442, 540
— radio talks 25–27, 139, 166, 255–56, 354, 391
— recording problems 344–45, 351, 375, 426, 447, 467, 482, 501–3, 539, 543
— recycling of music 509
— *Refrain* 120, 131, 137, 182, 184, 188–90, 201, 205, 216, 539
— *Refrain 2000* 189–90
— research 211, 212
— "Rouge, rouge" (*Hymnen*) 277
— *Samstag aus LICHT* 19, 379, 430, 433, 434, 436, 440–57, 459, 509, 513
— "Samstags-Gruss" 442–43, 462
— *Schlagquartett (–trio)* 27, 41, 60, 63, 88–91, 395
— schooling 16ff, 421–33, 425, 427–28, 430
— *Sirius* 66, 190, 272, 338, 371, 375–84, 399, 407, 467, 470, 485, 487, 491, 518, 529
— *Solo* 262–65, 284, 317, 540
— *Sonatine* 23, 24, 35, 37–38, 71
— *Sonntag aus LICHT* 215, 527–44
— "Sonntags-Abschied" (*Sonntag*) 543–44
— *Spiel* 63, 82–87, 104, 112, 130, 151, 154, 198, 233, 281, 348, 354, 433, 542
— *Spiral* 16, 101, 316–19, 324, 335, 391
— star sign 337
— *Sternklang* 16, 334–37, 342, 344–45, 349, 352, 358, 369, 436, 442
— *Stimmung* 79, 106, 217, 268, 296–301, 332, 335, 343, 344, 344, 357, 358, 408, 410, 432, 454
— *Stop* 193, 217, 262, 294, 322, 350, 532, 533
— *Stop und Start* 532
— *Strahlen* 543
— stretcher-bearer 19. *See also* Stockhausen, Karlheinz, *Dienstag aus LICHT*
— *Studie I* 105, 106, 129–31, 136, 140, 146, 148, 149, 153, 171, 194, 199, 403, 415
— *Studie II* 105, 131–37, 140, 148, 153, 159, 168, 171, 185, 194, 198, 199, 202, 266, 317, 391, 415, 502, 542, 543
— "Study on one sound" 105
— superformula of *LICHT* 414
— "Susani" (*Montag*) 471
— "Synthi-Fou" (*Dienstag*). *See* Stockhausen, Karlheinz, *Klavierstück XV*
— *Telemusik* 73, 142, 195, 262, 265–67, 268, 296, 323, 337, 349, 377, 432, 472, 502, 511
— "Third Region of *Hymnen* with Orchestra" 280–81, 285, 348, 433
— *Tierkreis* 66, 369–73, 379, 382
— "Tonszenen aus *Freitag*" (*Freitag*) 498–503
— tour of United States 1958 174–78, 508
— *Trans* 19, 147, 193, 262, 315, 337–40, 355, 380, 391, 392, 400, 429, 454, 532, 540
— "Trio" (*Expo für 3*) 316, 323
— triplet relationships 29, 257, 430, 460, 494

—truth 1, 3, 6, 7, 8, 199, 228, 377
— *Tunnel-Spiral* 265, 323
— university studies 228
— "Unsichtbare Chöre" (*Donnerstag*) 280, 426–27, 430, 432, 456, 514, 538
— "Verliebte Lyriker" (*Herlekin*) 374
— "Vieldeutige Form" 236, 238–39
— "Vortrag über HU" 351, 357–60
— "Welt-Parlament" (*Mittwoch*) 511–12
— "Wochenkreis" (*Montag*) 470
— word-setting 33, 34, 36, 428–29
— *Xi* 358, 462–63
— *Ylem* 254, 320, 338, 344, 348–51, 352, 358, 362, 373, 530
— *Ypsilon* 471–74
— *Zeitmasse* 105, 144–47, 148, 164, 239, 391, 533, 541
— "Zungenspitzentanz" (*Samstag*) 453
— *Zyklus* 79, 137, 143, 182, 184–88, 201, 217, 219, 243, 251, 324
Stockhausen (Nell), Luzia (stepmother) 17, 21
Stockhausen, Majella 430, 443, 444
Stockhausen, Markus 220, 434, 461, 488, 509
Stockhausen, Simon (father) 13, 15, 17, 19, 31, 239, 422, 425, 430, 434
Stockhausen, Simon (son) 10, 480, 489–90
Stockhausen, Suja 131
Stockhausen-Verlag 478
Stockhausen, Waltraud (half-sister) 17, 21
Stokowski, Leopold 183–84
Stonebraker, James 7
Strasberg, Lee 219
Strauss, Richard 340, 439, 485
— *Also sprach Zarathustra* 439
— *Salome* 439
— *Schlagobers* 404
— *Till Eulenspiegel* 340, 359
— *Tod und Verklärung* 439
Stravinsky, Igor 3, 12n, 13, 21, 31, 35, 38, 43, 54, 56, 65, 75, 79, 96, 101, 102, 115, 134, 137n, 145, 149, 157, 160, 181, 195, 234, 264, 276, 283, 289, 291, 324, 334, 341, 355, 360, 389, 430, 440, 452, 539
— *Apollo* 13
— *Canon* 264
— *Concerto for two pianos* 331
— *Fairy's Kiss* 13
— *Firebird* 264, 283
— *Flood* 393
— *Histoire du Soldat* 404, 440
— *Jeu de cartes* 276
— *Movements* 115, 146
— *Noces* 89
— *Oedipus Rex* 96, 360
— *Petrushka* 35, 334
— *Requiem Canticles* 264
— *Sacre du Printemps* 55, 75, 103, 154, 283, 452

— *Symphonic Variations* 54
— *Symphonies of wind instruments* 341
— *Symphony of Psalms* 532
— *Three Pieces for Clarinet* 389
— *Three Pieces for String Quartet* 283
— *Threni* 115
— *Zvezdoliki* 72, 355
stream of consciousness 97
Strobel, Heinrich 146, 155n, 239
structuralism, 103–4, 162, 250, 417, 495, 533
Stuckenschmidt, Hans Heinz 29n, 134, 137n
Studio di fonologia musicale 214
stumble 355, 359
Sturm und Drang 516
subject-object dualism 3
sub-woofer 487
sum and difference stereo 502
Sumerian language 77, 82
sumo wrestling 397
superego 470
Superman 377
suprematism 308, 315
surrealism 5, 13, 43, 97, 99, 103, 110, 111, 173, 222, 223, 228, 404, 405, 410, 416, 464, 501, 508
Surréalisme, Exposition du 1938 220
surround sound 432
Suzuki, Daisetsu 125
swing, 74
syllabic unit 81, 100, 283
symbolic logic 292–93
symbolist poetry 110, 158, 464
synaesthesia 72, 415
syncopation 33, 123
synthesizer 24, 125, 200, 351, 459, 480, 486–87, 532, 539, 543
Synthi 100 114, 280, 351, 357, 361, 369, 374, 379–84, 389, 391, 400n, 445, 470, 485, 491, 499, 501, 502
systems theory 413

taboo language 412
taku 266
tala 80
Tallis, Thomas 181, 531
— *Spem in alium* 181
tam-tam 207, 255–57, 349
tape editing 103, 130, 135, 365–66, 494
tape medium 18, 126, 145, 147, 185, 194, 263, 351, 365–66, 370, 391, 485, 494, 505, 518
Tartini, Giuseppe 433
Tati, Jacques 127
— *Mon Oncle* 127
Taubman, Howard 314
Tchaikovsky, Peter Ilyich, 6, 184, 334
— *1812 Overture* 334
— *Slavonic march* 6
Telemann, Georg Philipp 50

television, 5, 377
temperament 297
Tempo 334
tempo scale 117, 150, 151, 152, 202, 370, 390–94, 542
Termin, Leon 356
terpistone 356
Tesla, Nikola 393
text messaging 55
texture composition 233, 234, 322
theater of revolution 99
Théâtre Marigny 99
thematicism 74
theremin, 356
Thomson, Virgil 96
—*Four Saints in Three Acts* 96
Thor 408
throat music 300, 343, 456
Thureau-Dangin, François 77
Tibetan ritual music 300, 453, 456
Tillmann, Hans Gunther 173
timbre, serial 112, 113, 115, 199
time dilation 98, 145, 200, 494, 504
time-layers 65, 220, 536, 541
timelessness 74, 76, 117, 181, 194, 463, 528, 540
timpani 90
Tolkien, J. R. R. 480–81
Tolstoy, Nikolai 75, 403
tonality 53, 512, 532
tone analysis 110, 205
tone generation 94, 101, 200
tone mixtures 133
tongues, speaking in 411
Toop, Richard 41, 131, 141–42, 400n
transformation 103, 112, 162, 163–64, 169, 194, 213, 249, 250, 251, 257, 261, 277, 278, 282, 301, 368, 380, 388–89
transparencies 188
trautonium 113, 114, 128
Trautwein, Friedrich 113, 485
trinity, educational doctrine of 28, 409
triplet formations 79, 101, 257, 283, 291, 351, 403, 409, 411, 453, 460, 471, 494
triptych 407
trombone tones (flute) 449, 487
Truelove, Stephen 159
Tudor, David 123, 140, 145, 177, 189, 201, 218, 219, 221, 241
Turing, Alan R. 22, 29n, 287, 472
Turner, J. M. W. 393, 479
twelve-note (-tone) method 1, 23, 38, 49, 50, 51, 53, 174, 175, 196, 414, 454
Tzara, Tristan 111, 162, 458n
—*Le coeur à gaz* 458n

Uccello, Paolo 477
uncertainty, 230, 234

Ungeheuer, Elena 166
Union flag (Great Britain) 530
unities (French theater) 78
Universal Edition 319, 478
University of Michigan symphony band 451
unmeasured prelude 74, 81, 189, 205
Urantia Book 489
Usher, Bishop James 5

Valéry, Paul 34, 464
van der Rohe, Mies 127, 531
Varèse, Edgar 37, 52, 53, 83, 87, 94, 109, 139, 152, 170, 176, 180, 182, 258, 280, 283, 314–15, 356, 378, 433, 462, 479, 485, 498, 502, 510, 515
—*Astronome* 378
—*Déserts* 139, 152, 170, 180, 258, 280, 498
—*Ecuatorial* 356, 479
—*Espace* 378
—*Hyperprism* 462
—*Intégrales* 283, 479
—*Poème électronique* 180, 182, 314–15, 502, 515
variable tempi 147
vari-speed 97, 98, 99, 143, 205, 362, 504, 505
VE 301 "people's radio" 14–15, 29n
Verdi, Giuseppe 51, 474
Verlaine, Paul 32, 34
Vetter, Michael 523
vibraphone, 65
video sculpture 536
Vietnam 274, 417
Vieux Colombier theater 100
Vigo, Jean 79
—*Zéro de conduite* 79
Vikernes, Varg 480–81
violin tone 103, 200, 505, 517
Virgil 403
visible speech 132, 153, 180
Vivaldi, Antonio 180
vocoder 85, 126, 127, 128, 167, 170, 257, 264, 381, 444, 449, 460, 494, 497–98, 499, 500, 501, 502, 505, 535, 539
voice recognition 93, 153, 166–67, 478
Volta, Alessandro 236
voltage control 351
von Bülow, Hans 354
von der Vring, Georg 32
von Neumann, John 277, 413
von Sternberg, Josef 474
von Weizsäcker, Carl Friedrich 45, 230, 236, 241, 253, 316, 416, 540
von Weizsäcker, Viktor 44, 45, 73, 97
—*Gestalt und Zeit* 45
Voss, Richard 331
Voyager space probes 376

Wagner, Richard 18, 50, 74, 283, 359, 403,

409, 412, 427, 440, 449, 496
—*Parsifal* 440, 444, 449
—*Rheingold* 427
wall sounds 321–23, 337–40, 451, 535
Walton, William 404
—*Façade* 404
Warner Brothers 405
waveform 113, 114, 159, 185, 198, 200, 370, 374
wave motion 319, 389, 394, 530–31, 539
WDR Westdeutscher Rundfunk. *See* Cologne Radio
Weaver, Warren 236, 286, 413
Weber, Max 44
Webern, Anton 1, 7, 13, 40, 42, 43, 47, 49, 51, 64, 70, 74, 79, 83, 102, 111, 117, 118, 146, 174, 196, 228, 234, 291, 311, 334, 361, 380, 387, 474, 531, 532, 533
—*Concerto* 27, 64
—*String quartet* 142, 228
—*Symphony* 40, 215
—*Trio* 13, 40
—*Variations for piano* 40, 42, 43, 361
Weill, Kurt 13, 15, 194, 405, 430
—*Dreigroschenoper* 13, 15, 197, 405
—*Mahagonny* 405, 430, 470
Wellesz, Egon, 29n
Wells, H. G. 484, 503
—*Things to Come* 484
Wen-Chung, Chou 176
white space 307, 309
Whitehead, Alfred North 110
—*Science and the Modern World* 110
Whiteman, Paul 462
Wiener, Norbert 44, 413
Wieser, Wolfgang 165
Wilde, Oscar 194
Willaert Adrian 533
Williams, Raymond 9
Wilson, Robert 423–24, 436
—*Deafman's Glance* 423

—*Einstein on the Beach* 424
—*Ka Mountain and Guardenia Terrace* 423–24 , 436
wind machine 485
Windsor and Newton 408, 416
Winterhilfe 15, 425
Wittgenstein, Ludwig 41, 46, 58, 230–31, 238, 307
—*Tractatus Logico-Philosophicus* 46, 307
Wizard of Oz 393, 449
Wolff, Christian 140, 144, 157
wordplay 3, 4, 5, 95, 170, 250, 254, 334, 387, 397, 416, 422, 475
Wordsworth, William 5
Worner, Karl 208, 328
Wyndham Lewis, D. B 404

Xanten, LBA (*Lehrbildungsanstalt*) 17, 18
Xenakis, Iannis 233, 243, 314, 530
—*Polytope de Montréal* 314
—*Terretektorh* 530

Yamaha synthesizer 480, 487
Yeats, W. B. 98
ylem 348
"Yo-Ho!" cry 267, 337
Young, J. Z. 59, 289, 465
Young, LaMonte 177, 307, 309
Young, Thomas 53–54, 58, 77

Zarlino, Gioseffo 150
Zeitverzogerung 265
Zemlinsky, Alexander von 71, 505
Zeno of Elea 230
ziffer 409, 448
Zinovieff, Peter 351, 382, 501
zodiac melodies *see* Stockhausen: *Tierkreis*
Zoroaster 497
Zwolftondauerkomplexen (Golyscheff) 23
Zwolftonspiel (Hauer) 23, 56, 119
Zyklus complex 203–4

ABOUT THE AUTHOR

Born in New Zealand, Robin Maconie studied piano with Christina Geel and read English literature and music at Victoria University of Wellington under Frederick Page and Roger Savage. A government bursary enabled him to study under Olivier Messiaen at the Paris Conservatoire 1963–1964; the following year a grant from the Deutscher Akademischer Austausch-dienst took him to Cologne to study composition, electronic music and interpretation under Karlheinz Stockhausen, Herbert Eimert, Bernd-Alois Zimmermann, Henri Pousseur, Georg Heike, Aloys Kontarsky, and others. He has held teaching appointments at the universities of Auckland, Sussex, Surrey, Oxford, the City University in London, and the Savannah College of Art and Design. While working as a free-lance music correspondent for the London *Daily Telegraph* and *Times Educational Supplement*, he completed *The Works of Karlheinz Stockhausen*, for many years the most readable and complete assessment in English of one of the most difficult and controversial composers of the twentieth century. He devised and coauthored *Tuning In*, a television documentary on the composer produced by Barrie Gavin in 1980 for the BBC, and in 1989 edited and co-authored *Stockhausen on Music*, a collection of lectures and interviews that remains in print.

In these and subsequent titles *The Concept of Music* (1990), *The Science of Music* (1997), and *The Second Sense: Language, Music, and Hearing* (published by the Scarecrow Press in 2002), his aim has been to restore simplicity, a sense of humor, and intelligent conversation to the study of modern and classical music. His writing has been noted for its conceptual boldness, clarity of exposition, and freedom from jargon. Robin Maconie returned to New Zealand in 2002 and lives in Dannevirke in the North Island. He has been married twice and has a daughter of whom he is very proud.